PASSIONATE COMMITMENTS

PASSIONATE COMMITMENTS

The Lives of Anna Rochester
and Grace Hutchins

JULIA M. ALLEN

STATE UNIVERSITY OF NEW YORK PRESS

STATE UNIVERSITY OF NEW YORK PRESS, ALBANY

For information, contact
State University of New York Press, Albany, NY
www.sunypress.edu

Production, Laurie D. Searl
Marketing, Fran Keneston

Library of Congress Cataloging-in-Publication Data

Allen, Julia M., 1947–
    Passionate commitments : the lives of Anna Rochester and Grace Hutchins / Julia M. Allen.
        p. cm.
    Includes bibliographical references and index.
    ISBN 978-1-4384-4687-5 (hardcover : alk. paper)
    ISBN 978-1-4384-4688-2 (pbk. : alk. paper)
    1. Rochester, Anna. 2. Hutchins, Grace, 1885–   3. Women social reformers—United States—
Biography.   4. Women labor leaders—United States—Biography.   5. Women communists—United States—
Biography.   I. Title.

HQ1412.A45 2013
303.48'4082—dc23   2012025921

10 9 8 7 6 5 4 3 2 1

To Cedar

for the title and for all her love and patience

Contents

Illustrations

Foreword

Passionate Commitments recovers two life stories that, as told here, emphasize intersections between histories that are not often treated together—the history of the American Left, women's histories, and queer histories. Grace Hutchins and Anna Rochester, born into wealthy nineteenth-century East Coast families, spent the first half of the twentieth century in love with one another and at work agitating for social and economic justice. They researched and wrote for labor unions, donated hours and money in support of a free press, raised bail for friends and comrades, ran for public office, and always insisted on women's independence. They left behind a rich archive of letters, books, and essays that chronicled public lives, deep private commitments, and constant personal reinvention as they moved ideologically away from institutional Christianity and women-centered service organizations, which were the sites of careers for many middle-class women of their era, toward mixed-gender organizations and labor activism. This dual biography describes, with affection and meticulous scholarship, Hutchins's and Rochester's love for one another and their many accomplishments. It describes, as well, the principle by which they lived and transformed themselves, their "rhetoric of the whole person," in which every part of their lives—from their writing and their partnership to their living arrangements and financial choices, even including their choices in clothing—contributed, without contradiction, to their revolutionary aims.

The central mystery of Allen's book is an utterance by Hutchins that seems to stand out as a shocking exception to her diligent efforts to live through a coherent social justice rhetoric. In 1949, she accused Whittaker Chambers, who was acting as an informant for anticommunist federal agents, of being a "homosexual pervert." This utterance defies easy explanation. It is not easily explained away as evidence that Hutchins and Rochester had an asexual partnership, as Allen shows. Nor is it understandable as naïveté: by the time Hutchins made this comment, Freud and the sexologists had popularized the notion of same-sex partnerships, such as that of Hutchins and Rochester, as sexual (if often pathologically so). Nor can the utterance be understood in terms of scapegoating; Hutchins was not trying to draw attention away from her own homosexuality by accusing someone else, as did many in the era about which Allen writes. This utterance, moreover, reveals a broader ideological mystery: but for the important example of their lives together, which was openly acknowledged by many who knew them, Hutchins and Rochester did not directly advocate for freedom for those who, like themselves, chose same-sex partners. Given their rigorous attention to a rhetoric of the whole person, how do we understand this failure to incorporate the class newly being identified as homosexuals into their social justice platform? Neither naïveté nor self-defense serves as an adequate explanation here. Moreover, the choice to attribute Chambers's anticommunist lies to his homosexuality, combined with Hutchins's silence about her own partnership with Rochester, made it more difficult for Hutchins to intervene to defend herself or others against the simultaneously antihomosexual and anticommunist government attacks that increased in intensity during the 1950s. This silence, in turn, Allen argues, substantially delayed the inclusion of rights for homosexuals into the Left platform for change.

So how do we understand this—the biggest rhetorical mistake of Hutchins's life, as Allen describes it? How did Hutchins and Rochester understand themselves, and how did their partnership inform those identities? In her search for answers, Allen links the development of Hutchins and Rochester's identities to the writing of the sexologist Edward Carpenter. Allen thus writes her subjects into an often-told history of the development of contemporary gay and lesbian identities. As Michel Foucault enables us to tell this history, contemporary gay and lesbian identities are products of sexological writing of the late nineteenth and early twentieth centuries, in which same-sex sexual behavior accrued meaning-making power. One of the effects of sexological writing was an increase in explicit legal and social disapprobation of homosexuality, such as that experienced by Hutchins, Rochester, and Chambers; another effect was the emergence of a homosexual minority that could recognize itself and thus advocate for civil rights based on a shared identity.

Carpenter's writing about the relationship between sexuality and identity, however, is more multidimensional than this version of sexology, which has become part of queer history. Carpenter was a Christian socialist who argued for the existence of a sexual minority—a third sex—defined not only by same-sex erotic choice but also by a heightened commitment to social justice and to alliance, in the name of social justice, across difference. Carpenter's delineation of a third sex asserts that homoerotics and heightened ethical sensibilities are mutually constitutive. Following Carpenter, Hutchins and Rochester saw their work in social justice as a more significant meaning-making characteristic of their lives than their sexuality. This is not the same thing as saying that sexuality did not matter to them or isn't important for those who tell their stories; rather, in the absence of labor toward social justice across gender, class, race, and nation, sexual behavior is not meaning-making.

In the early twenty-first century, when the face of civil rights is often the gay man or lesbian who would like to marry and whose claim to the right to do so is made based on his or her choice of a same-sex partner, the stories of Hutchins and Rochester told here provide a reminder about the pitfalls of single-issue politics. *Passionate Commitments* traces intellectual descent lines from Carpenter's version of sexology through contemporary queer social justice work in which alliance building across difference is an essential meaning-making activity. Contemporary queer activists will rightly reject a tactic that seeks to demonize political foes by calling them perverted or that turns on an association between lies and homosexual acts. We are also likely to dismiss, with a chuckle, the idea of a super-ethical third sex. We can, however, with the help of this biography, see alliance making across difference as constitutive of queer identities rather than as pragmatic politics, subject to being forgotten, provisionally sidelined, or otherwise neglected.

Robin Hackett
Associate Professor of English
University of New Hampshire

Acknowledgments

One of the particular gifts of this project has been the friendships I have made in the course of the research. Anna Rochester and Grace Hutchins have led me into circles of especially kind and interesting people. To all of the people whom I have met during this process: you have enriched my life immeasurably, and I am most grateful.

Research support for this book has been provided by the Episcopal Women's History Project and by Sonoma State University; the California State University Emeritus and Retired Faculty Association has granted funding to assist in production and promotion. I am thankful to Congresswoman Lynn Woolsey and her staff for assistance in obtaining the FBI files of Grace Hutchins and Anna Rochester through the Freedom of Information Act. I owe a great debt to the interlibrary loan staff at Sonoma State University, who made heroic efforts to locate and borrow rare books, pamphlets, and articles for me. I am also grateful to numerous other libraries and archival collections for their provision of pertinent materials: Special Collections and University Archives of the University of Oregon Libraries; State Historical Society of Wisconsin Special Collections; Archives of the Episcopal Church; Tamiment Library at New York University; Columbia University Rare Books and Manuscripts Collection; Diocese of New York Archives; Union Theological Seminary Manuscripts Room; Sophia Smith Collection at Smith College; University of Vermont Special Collections; Friends Historical Collection at Swarthmore College; Swarthmore College Peace Collection; Archives of the Society of the Companions of the Holy Cross; Lesbian Herstory Archives; Jean and Charles Schulz Library at Sonoma State University; Southern California Library for Social Studies and Research; Syracuse University Library; Schlesinger Library at Radcliffe College; Libraries of the University of California, Berkeley; Langson Library at the University of California, Irvine; Bryn Mawr College Library; Multnomah County Library; Portland State University Library; Dorset Historical Society; Reed College Library; Aubrey R. Watzek Library at Lewis and Clark College; Cline-Tunnell Library of Western Conservative Baptist Seminary; Claremont School of Theology; Knight Library of the University of Oregon; Sacramento State University Library; Niebyl-Proctor Marxist Library; Hoover Institution Library; Perry-Casteneda Library of the University of Texas at Austin; Yale Divinity School Library; Library of the State Historical Society of Wisconsin; University of Wisconsin Library; Labadie Collection at University of Michigan; Harvard Law School Library; Elmer Holmes Bobst Library of New York University; New York Public Library; Butler Library at Columbia University; and the Reference Center for Marxist Studies. I appreciate the responsiveness of Joseph Roby III, Betty Smith of International Publishers, Teresa Albano of *People's World*, Dr. Lorene Potter and Susan Butler of the Society of the Companions of the Holy Cross, Nora Bonosky, Marc Geltmann, Judith M. Whiting of the Community Service Society, and Ethan Vesely-Flad of the Fellowship of Reconciliation as I sought permission to quote from unpublished materials.

The list of those who have given of their time and memories to help construct this narrative is long. It includes, but is not limited to, the following generous individuals: Margaret P. Aldrich, former archivist of the Society of the Companions of the Holy Cross, who pointed me toward key resources, then read the entire manuscript and offered valuable editorial suggestions; Nancy Porter, Robin Hackett, and my mother, Betty Helen Braden, all of whom also read the entire manuscript and helped me to shape the narrative more successfully; Warder and Judy Cadbury, who offered me the hospitality of their home, took me to see Back Log Camp, and gave me detailed recollections of Hutchins and Rochester; the Reverend Jeanne Knepper, who gave me all of her dissertation research materials on Winifred Chappell; Bettina Aptheker, Herbert Aptheker, Philip Bonosky, Thomas Shipley Brown, Stephen G. Cary, Cara Lee Davis, Si Gerson, Sophie Gerson, Mary Hansen, Lement Harris, Harry Hay, Mary Louise Henson, Ruth Kahn, Jan Kleinbord, Mary Licht, Andrew Marber, Betty Millard, Annette Rubinstein, William B. Spofford, and Dorothy Wick, who all shared their knowledge of Hutchins and Rochester or their contemporaries with me; Aaron Cohen, Jane Hodes, Edith Laub, and Bob Patenaude, who made available to me all the resources of the Niebyl-Proctor Library; Lottie Gordon, Esther Moroze, and Michael McBrearty, who welcomed me to the Reference Center for Marxist Studies; Rosalyn Baxandall, Joanne Benton, Kathy Charmaz, Jocelyn Cohen, Pele deLappe, Pat Gallagher, Victor Garlin, Robin Hackett, Jerry Harris, Amy Kesselman, Sadie Krieger, Deborah LeSueur, Charlotte Marzani, Patti Palen, Mary Sicilia, Clarice Stasz, and members of the Eastside Women's Research Group, who gave me insights and directed me to new sources of information; Toni McNaron, who read the entire manuscript and gave me her enthusiastic support; an anonymous reviewer for SUNY Press, whose comments helped me improve the narrative substantially; Robert Coleman-Senghor and Sonja Franetta, who translated key passages for me; and Vicki Carpenter, Rose Gubele, and Pam Judd, who provided exceptionally fine research and technical assistance.

Errors of fact or interpretation are entirely my responsibility.

Introduction

Your stuff is grand. I am, however, still working on a couple of pages of background. Really hopeful, however, of cleaning the subject up by Friday. You won't mind if I use chunks out of your memo, but not many whole pages as such. . . . Oh, so very glad, that you are coming back so soon. Very eager to hear all the news you will have to tell. . . . Thou knowest that I love thee.

Anna.

—Anna Rochester to Grace Hutchins, July 26, 1939

Wish we'd had time for you to tell me more about your work on "The Nature of Capitalism" and how much you found was involved in expanding some parts of it. You'll tell me about it tomorrow night. . . . "Since we parted two hours ago" you are ten times dearer, 10 times sweeter, and all the rest of the song which I don't quite remember but echo heartily. Never did anyone have such a grand and wonderful partner as you. . . .

With *all* my love
from
Grace.

—Grace Hutchins to Anna Rochester, October 8, 1945

In 1995, I came upon the papers of Anna Rochester (1880–1966) and Grace Hutchins (1885–1969) in the Special Collections at the University of Oregon. Filed among copious materials on the structures of capitalism and women in the labor force were eloquent expressions of devotion—letters, poems, notes—offering a glimpse of the forty-five year partnership of Rochester and Hutchins. I wanted to know more about these women, whose love for each other so clearly fueled their work to create a more egalitarian world.

Archives are never able to deliver fully the individuals whose lives produced the welter of paper housed in a few boxes. Yet, at the same time, archives offer a different, perhaps more useful range of prospects, lying, as Penny Russell has argued, "at a point of interface between the subject and her world—a power-laden domain of imagination and experience, ideology and discourse, negotiation and agency."[1] It is this point of interface, or, rather, the many points of interface between Hutchins and Rochester and their worlds, that I sought to explore.

Grace Hutchins and Anna Rochester came of age during the early twentieth century in well-connected East Coast families, both active suffragists and both eligible for membership in the Daughters of the American Revolution. Rochester, tall, reserved, a talented pianist, spoke and wrote in several languages and proved adept at theory and statistics. Hutchins, also tall, a basketball and field hockey player in her college years, exuded warmth, building families among those near her, shaping her feminism around women's traditional and potential strengths and insisting upon women's economic independence as the key to liberation.

1

Hutchins and Rochester both matriculated at Bryn Mawr, joining other young women from upper middle class homes who were attending the new women's colleges. These colleges offered women hitherto unexplored opportunities for love and work. At the time, fully 50 percent of Bryn Mawr graduates did not marry; many formed partnerships among themselves,[2] and success was measured by the public contributions students made after leaving the college. Hutchins was able to stay the full four years and graduate, later spending time in China as a missionary. Rochester left Bryn Mawr after her sophomore year in 1899 to care for her mother after her father's sudden death.

In 1904, however, Anna Rochester met Wellesley English professor Vida Dutton Scudder and her partner Florence Converse, who, recognizing her intellect and independence, began to mentor her and introduced her to the Society of the Companions of the Holy Cross (SCHC), an Episcopal laywomen's organization, offering her another opportunity to experience a community of thoughtful, committed women.[3] At the Companions' annual retreat in 1919, Rochester found Grace Hutchins, who by then was living in New York and teaching the New Testament at the New York Training School for Deaconesses. They would spend the rest of their lives together, determined to have an effect upon the world.

Rochester and Hutchins were two among many women crafting new identities in the late nineteenth and early twentieth centuries, women who first separated from their families and then, independent of traditional expectations, lived in partnerships with each other. In her groundbreaking study *Spinsters and Lesbians*, Trisha Franzen notes that "in attempting an analysis or even a description of these women's lifelong relationships, it is important to find the reasons they came together. If there is one cause, a common thread, among this diverse group it is the waged and political work that was shared between the two."[4] Although they were not unique, Hutchins and Rochester exemplified the women who created same-sex partnered lives for themselves during the early part of the twentieth century,[5] eager to make contributions in social, political, scientific, and educational fields. Their lives were informed by what I will call *a rhetoric of the whole person*.[6] They consciously structured their writing, their partnership, their living arrangements, and their financial choices to cohere as a whole, exclusive (inasmuch as possible) of contradictions.

What distinguished Hutchins and Rochester was the fact that they aimed for revolution rather than reform. During their lives, they moved from one organization to another, searching for a site where their work was valued, where they could press for the rights of all women to choose marriage or independence, and where they could have the greatest effect on the greatest number. Franzen points out that by the beginning of the 1930s, "very few people still held a political analysis of women as oppressed by a system of male dominance." Yet Hutchins and Rochester were among those "very few people," and Hutchins especially worked to keep feminism alive in the United States during the 1930s through the 1950s.

A Rhetoric of the Whole Person

The SCHC offered Rochester and Hutchins a site where women could explore the links between social and theological issues and could evaluate new ways of engaging with the world. Reading lists for the annual retreats included work by Christian Socialists Walter Rauschenbusch and Edward Carpenter. Carpenter, a British socialist and former Anglican priest, sharply criticized bourgeois cultures of accumulation and leisure.[7] He argued for women's rights, and he talked about sexuality, linking same-sex love and social improvement. Significantly, Carpenter did not emphasize physicality, noting that he used "the word

Uranians to indicate simply those whose lives and activities are inspired by a genuine friendship or love for their own sex, without venturing to specify their individual and particular habits or relations towards those whom they love (which relations in most cases we have no means of knowing)."[8] Vida Scudder favored Plato's *Phaedrus*, an extended argument coupling same-sex love and ethical persuasive speech, as a life template, as well as the work of Marx and Engels. Both she and Florence Converse translated the men's theories into semifictionalized narratives of action by women.[9] And although Hutchins and Rochester undoubtedly read both Plato and Carpenter—and Rochester pored over Marx's *Capital*—they, like many of the Companions, found direction in the narratives by Scudder and Converse. These narratives featured characters located not within homes, identified by husbands and children, but out in the world, their lives defined by love for other women and work for social justice.

Although the SCHC provided a community in which new identities could flourish, the social conditions that fostered these new identities changed over time, and Hutchins and Rochester changed, too. Leaving the SCHC and moving from religious to pacifist to political organizations, Hutchins and Rochester changed discourse communities several times, pushing each one to its logical conclusion and then moving on, sometimes by choice, sometimes not.[10]

Secular Conversions

As the economic situation worsened during the 1920s, more people began to move out of traditional political organizations, increasing the groundswell of opposition to capitalism. After the revolution that created the Soviet Union, possibilities for human arrangements seemed to open, and methods of persuasion and questions of genre were the subjects of lively debates in community forums and in the pages of commercial and radical publications. Hutchins and Rochester brought with them a range of discursive styles, left over from college, missionary training, and social work, yet as they addressed new audiences, they too considered new methods and made every effort to adapt their methods to different situations.

Although most of the debates have gone unrecorded or can be found only in the pages of ephemeral periodicals, the published work of American rhetorical philosopher Kenneth Burke, himself affected by the movements for social and economic justice and an active participant in the debates, synthesizes and comments upon some of the issues that preoccupied writers of the period. This is not to say that his work should be read as a neutral recording or as the last word on any given question, but it does provide a lens that focuses our attention on the ways in which writers such as Hutchins and Rochester responded to the exigencies of the era.[11] Burke's 1935 collection *Permanence and Change*, as well as his 1937 volume *Attitudes toward History*, present explanations of the mechanisms by which Hutchins and Rochester reshaped themselves during their lives and how they sought to persuade others.

In *Permanence and Change*, Burke offered a dialectical schema of rhetorical moves, roughly equivalent to a thesis-antithesis-synthesis pattern, merging Marxist and psychoanalytic efforts to explain how people change. He called the changes he had in mind "secular conversions." "Midway between an old weighting and a new weighting," he said, "is the realm we have called 'perspective by incongruity' (a term that designates one way of transcending a given order of weightedness)."[12] Each "weighting" he termed an "orientation," "a bundle of judgments as to how things were, how they are, and how they may be."[13] As members of a group having a particular orientation, we have "interests" that focus our attention; we "identify" with a given leader, group, or idea; we may engage in "faulty means-selecting" (placing blame where it does not belong); and we are usually afflicted by "occupational psychoses," basing the ways we interpret the world on our experiences. Regarding "identification," a key concept in his rhetorical universe, Burke maintained that one's identity is not "something private, peculiar to himself"; rather, we identify ourselves with "all sorts of manifestations" beyond ourselves. This is normal, he said, and "the psychoanalyst 'cures' his patient of a faulty identification only insofar as he smuggles in *an alternative identification*."[14] The same process would apply to anyone seeking to shift the identifications of others.

Any one or all of these functions may help to determine our "orientation." An orientation, Burke argued, "is largely a self-perpetuating system, in which each part tends to corroborate the other parts." Likewise, any orientation has "pieties," the sense of what properly goes with what in any given situation. Nevertheless, every orientation "contains the germs of its dissolution."[15]

How is the rhetorician to take advantage of this "germ of dissolution," or contradiction? By means of "a planned incongruity." Perspective by incongruity, which Burke defined as "a method for gauging situations by verbal 'atom cracking,'" involves shifting pieties. "That is," he said, "a word belongs by custom to a certain category—and by rational planning you wrench it loose and metaphorically apply it to a different category."[16] Putting two things together impiously may call one or the other of them into question, a method both Hutchins and Rochester used on more than one occasion to challenge received gender and class verities.

As an audience takes in such a planned incongruity, members become more likely to respond with a "secular conversion," locating interests in a new orientation, with new weightings. "A new fixed way of reading the signs" is then called for, Burke said. In order to release the grip of an orientation, a secular conversion often functions as "conversion downward," away from that over which an audience has no control to something more manageable. Moreover, an audience rarely shifts dramatically from one orientation to another but rather moves slowly via gradual steps, a principle Burke referred to as *lex continui*, or the law of continuity.[17]

It should be noted that although Burke emphasized the process of changing orientations by means of *planned* incongruities (the realm of the rhetorician hoping to provoke action), *situational* incongruities, or contradictions, may have a similar effect. During the course of their lives, Hutchins and Rochester responded to both planned and situational incongruities; they also produced innumerable planned incongruities themselves, seeking to intervene at moments of intense social struggle.

New Orientations

Hutchins and Rochester went through several "secular conversions," moving gradually from religious to political orientations. After leaving the New York Training School for Deaconesses, Hutchins attended the New York School of Social Work. Rochester spent years working for the National Child Labor Committee and the US Children's Bureau. During the 1920s, both were active in the Fellowship of Reconciliation. Early members of the Socialist Party, they shifted their memberships to the Communist Party USA (CPUSA) in 1927 after a trip to the Soviet Union, joining former Socialist Party comrades to organize the Labor Research Association. Prolific writers and researchers, they produced books, pamphlets, and articles on labor and economic issues. Equally important, they used their inherited wealth to fund multiple progressive publication venues, from books to magazines to newspapers to radio.

As Rochester and Hutchins worked in each group they joined, they continued to read and talk with others about the issues that concerned them. Rochester was most likely to respond to economic arguments, often those propounded by her friend Scott Nearing; Hutchins would brook no disparities between an organization's desire to appeal to women and that organization's actual policies and behavior toward women. In this way, they moved from one group to another, refining their requirements and seeking a place that would welcome their rhetorical efforts.

During their years of activity, the organizations in which they took part, including the Student Volunteer Movement for Foreign Missions, the Episcopal Church, the US Children's Bureau, the Fellowship of Reconciliation, the League for Industrial Democracy, and the CPUSA, all held frequent meetings and congresses on questions of rhetorical efficacy—how to address audiences with the purpose of moving them to adopt the principles of a given group. Articles on the same topics appeared frequently in publications produced by these organizations. Indeed, during the 1930s, the CPUSA published an entire journal, *The Party Organizer*, devoted to discussions of organizing methods. Grace Hutchins and Anna Rochester attended and participated in these discussions, and their writings often reflect the rhetorical consensus within each group at any given time. Their work also reflects the fact that their partnership and joint interests and decisions served as their foundation.

Material Rhetorics

A rhetoric of the whole person, then, requires an awareness of the rhetoric of the material as well as of the process of reorientation. In his introduction to *Rhetorical Bodies*, a collection of articles on "the material situatedness of rhetorical acts," Jack Selzer maintains that "language and rhetoric have a persistent material aspect that demands acknowledgment, and material realities often (if not always) contain a rhetorical dimension that deserves attention: for language is not the only medium or material that speaks."[18] This insistence on the rhetorical dimension of bodies and other materials constitutes a significant aspect of Anna Rochester and Grace Hutchins's rhetoric of the whole person.

Selzer identifies two aspects of the material that function rhetorically. First, there are physical bodies and the ways that they shape and are shaped by "literate practices."[19] Not only was Hutchins and Rochester's partnership foundational to their work, but their choices of dress, living accommodations, and even vacation sites all had rhetorical significance, aiming to disrupt conventional profit-making systems. They elected, for instance, to wear only black, except for the occasional seersucker dress in the summer, in order both to save time and money and to refrain from participating in the antifeminist fashion industry. Indeed, almost every action they took carried rhetorical nuances and was part of their own system of planned incongruities challenging class and gender assumptions.

Second, Selzer cites the ways in which literate practices should be examined in "light of the material circumstances that sustain or sustained them."[20] Over the course of their lives, Rochester and Hutchins came to understand that under capitalism, rhetoric means, first of all, a struggle for access to audiences; that freedom of speech means having the *economic* freedom to speak; and that, in short, rhetoric far exceeds the margins of documents and extends to the basis of the entire social structure. Stopping short of a dialectical rhetoric, however, Selzer asks, "If 'materialism' now takes us to bodies and to tangible physicality instead of to Marx, what happens to Marxist categories?"[21]

In his review of *Rhetorical Bodies*, Bruce McComiskey answers Selzer's question briefly, pointing to a dialectical rhetoric and citing Engels, who argued that "the ultimate determining element in history is the production and reproduction of real life. . . . The economic situation is the basis, but the various elements of the superstructure . . . also exercise their influence upon the course of the historical struggles and in many cases preponderate in determining their form." McComiskey then leads us back to Marx's contention that mere criticism is inadequate and concludes by asserting that "critical knowledge is 'good' only insofar as it is 'useful,' and it is useful only insofar as it leads to positive rhetorical interventions into the material and discursive processes of oppressive political formations."[22]

Dana Cloud, in "Change Happens," elaborates on the same issue and in doing so, provides a framework for understanding the dynamic logic behind Rochester and Hutchins's material rhetoric. She points out that "the dialectical interrelationships among contending classes and between their experience and its contradictory ideological rendering pose opportunities for rhetorical, political intervention."[23] Like Kenneth Burke, Cloud argues that "tension between opposites yields the possibility of the emergence of something new." Wage labor and capital form the classic contradiction in Marxism, but "another totality," Cloud continues, "is the opposition between how people live and the ideas they hold in their heads—in other words, the contradiction between experience and ideology."[24]

Living their rhetorics, Hutchins and Rochester aimed to cancel that contradiction in their partnership. They lived simply, in cooperative housing, and although they had inherited wealth, they justified their incomes by working at least forty hours a week for no remuneration. They understood that, as Cloud says, "there is a difference between a class as an objective entity and *class consciousness*, which is a rhetorically produced understanding of one's class position."[25] Thus, as two of the three primary staff members of the Labor Research Association from 1928 until their deaths in the 1960s, Rochester and Hutchins strove to build class consciousness—positive rhetorical interventions—among working people and middle class allies.

Moreover, as Cloud points out, "Sectors within the working class are oppressed differently and to different degrees on the basis of identity categories." Like most Marxist theorists, Cloud sees that "challenging divisions . . . among ordinary people is necessary to th[e] project" of organizing working people around their shared "interest in overcoming exploitation."[26] While Rochester provided detailed economic analyses, charting interlocking directorates and exposing the foundations of capitalism, Hutchins directed her efforts toward working women of all races, aiming to heal artificial divisions that could divide an organization, stretching the framework of economic analysis to disrupt rigid gender ideologies. Like other independent women of her generation, Hutchins worked through an established organization to address the chief source of women's oppression: economic dependence, both on men and on a system that not only devalued women's labor but pitted men against women to bring down men's wages as well. At the same time, she took the opportunity to address such features of the sex/gender economic system as the sexual objectification of women, which encouraged women to trade intellectual power for an evanescent sexual power.

What's more, both Rochester and Hutchins knew that only with a program of institution building and the calculated shifting of ownership of the means of publication into working class hands would Americans come to understand the economic system under which they labored and the possibilities for collective action to change that system in the workplace and in the voting booth. Thus, making use of their independent wealth and their publishing expertise, they set about to establish a knowledge production and distribution system that would give working class people, across racial and gender boundaries, freedom of speech and access to audiences.

Germs of Dissolution

And yet, as hard as they worked to maintain a rhetoric of the whole person through one conversion after another, contradictions not of their own making shadowed the lives of women such as Rochester and Hutchins; one in particular: the new taxonomies that reduced individuals to their sexuality, "the packaging of sexual and gender norms as homogenized standards of individual mental/psychic health," as Franzen declares.[27] Although public representations—medical and psychological—of same-sex relationships between women were growing exponentially during the early twentieth century, these representations, often by professionals seeking to advance careers on new disease categories, offer little insight into the Progressive Era communities of women who abjured conventional gender roles in favor of same-sex partnerships and work for social improvement, whether reformist or revolutionary.[28]

The era of change that offered so many opportunities to women such as Rochester and Hutchins wound down with the passage of the suffrage bill. Rosemary Hennessy points to the role of profit motives in the restructuring of twentieth-century gender and sexual identities: "As sexuality was being wrenched free from reproduction and everyone was potentially being sexualized, the threatening possibility of a genderless sexual desire was contained by a new paradigm of sexual identity that articulated it in a heterogendered frame." This move she attributes to capitalists' desires to maintain a profitable gendered division of labor.[29] Within this new paradigm, Hennessy argues, identities—heterosexual, homosexual, bisexual, transgender, to name a few—became narrow and reified, not allowing for movement or complexity.[30]

Carroll Smith-Rosenberg specifies the sexologists and suggests that Havelock Ellis in particular may bear considerable responsibility for pathologizing the committed partnerships that helped to make possible many of the social transformations of the early 1900s. "Feminism, lesbianism, equality for women, all emerge in Ellis's writings as alarming phenomena. All were unnatural, related in disturbing and unclear ways to increased female criminality, insanity, and 'hereditary neurosis,'" Smith-Rosenberg says.[31] Jennifer Terry concurs, saying that Ellis emphasized the "mannishness" of women who sought independence, "while criticizing their feminist beliefs as pathological."[32] Like Smith-Rosenberg, Lillian Faderman traces the public shift in attitude toward women's intimate partnerships from acceptance to condemnation, pointing to "the work of the sexologists, which was disseminated slowly to the layman but finally became part of popular wisdom after World War I."[33]

However, in addition to the matter of assigning responsibility, there is the question of who to include in the category of sexologists. Jo-Ann Wallace, in her discussions of Edith Ellis, the wife of Havelock Ellis, makes a distinction between the sexologists (in which category she includes both Carpenter and Ellis) and the psychoanalysts, placing the blame for pathologizing same-sex relationships squarely with the latter. At the same time, however, she credits Carpenter, not Ellis, with the development of a system of "homogenic and sapphic idealism" that influenced a generation of women, including Ellis's wife, Edith, who later separated from her husband, fearing that he might have her incarcerated in an asylum.[34] Havelock Ellis, on the other hand, offered simply a classificatory approach to sexuality, "characterising inversion as a matter of what he call[ed] 'organic personality.'" Thus, "if inversion is not a matter of personal agency or moral responsibility, it should not be a matter for legal prohibition or moral censure."[35] Despite this liberal argument for tolerance, the communities—and the social activism—that Carpenter's work enabled women to develop were very different from those that located identity in a narrow emphasis on sexuality, and, for women, Carpenter's arguments necessitated a strong feminism that Ellis considered pathological.

Although Faderman suggests that the new categories of sexual identity propounded by Ellis made it possible for some women to locate themselves and thus find a measure of freedom, the new language did not serve women such as Rochester and Hutchins well. Both Hutchins and Rochester exhibited a combination of emotions similar to that found by Wallace in her reading of Edith Ellis: a celebration of their love for each other, a view of their partnership as the foundation from which they would help to create a new world, plus a quietude that grew over time, as multifarious relationships were reduced to a single phenomenon and labeled perverse.[36] What's more, women's relationships were merged with men's under one single term: homosexuality. There remained few positive or even neutral ways to speak of relationships such as that between Rochester and Hutchins.[37]

Franzen has documented the problems these discourses created for women like Rochester and Hutchins, commenting on their silence on the subject and noting that "until now [ca. late 1920s] it had been unnecessary to define their attractions and lifestyles. . . . To have admitted to lesbianism *as it had been defined by the sexologists* would have made them immoral and negated their positions as respectable females" (emphasis mine).[38] Organizations such as churches and political parties debated persuasive methods, but there were few, if any, meetings or congresses of women hashing out terminological problems of same-sex relationships or debating the linkages between a same-sex partnership and women's equality in the larger world. Whatever conversations took place, few extant publications resulted.

Because they offered little organized resistance to these representations, women, including Scudder, Converse, Hutchins, and Rochester, ceded the power of naming to the professionals. Apart from the semiautobiographical novels of Vida Scudder and Florence Converse published at the time, the partnerships of women such as Rochester and Hutchins remained relatively untouched by analysis on the parts of those who participated. Despite Faderman's suggestion that some women welcomed the new medicalized names, which they felt gave them a roadmap where they had had none before, it is likely that most women felt powerless to address the new taxonomies. Indeed, Vida Scudder, whose narratives thirty years earlier had helped to shape a movement, commented acerbically in the draft of her 1935 memoir: "[The emphasis on sex in modern biographies] is all the fault of Mr. Freud, and I do think he has a good deal to answer for."[39] Even Eleanor Roosevelt and Lorena Hickok, as Dana Cloud suggests, may have struggled to "find language for their desires,"[40] leading some biographers to discount or even erase their relationship. "This group [Progressive era independent women] left evidence," Franzen reports, "both public and personal, that they felt under siege, judged and labeled both as single women and as women who loved other women."[41]

Although Hutchins and Rochester themselves imported and advanced a set of core feminist values emphasizing women's economic independence in every organization they joined, they maintained their relationship by means of the rhetoric that had birthed the partnership in the Companions. After their trip to the Soviet Union, they briefly updated their rhetoric by writing messages of love and affection to each other in Russian, then reverted to their original rhetoric after a few years.

Moreover, despite the fact that their work was indivisible from their partnership, the specific dialectical system in which they had immersed themselves after 1927, the CPUSA, provided no new ways of talking about same-sex partnerships between women, relying instead upon silence and the sexological categories promoted by medical and scientific establishments and, in the process, creating a ready-made gap just waiting to be exploited to destabilize the movement.[42]

In what I sense was a gesture to counteract this concealment, Hutchins endeavored to make sure that the otherwise invisible work and sacrifices of women (usually women like herself and Rochester) were recognized and acknowledged. But rather than attempting to elaborate and articulate their identities or, indeed, make any direct mention of women who sought independence or a partnership with another woman, Rochester and Hutchins simply lived their lives structured by their original axiological framework and grew more and more quiet about themselves and others like themselves as they developed and published more trenchant arguments against capitalist inequities.

Over time, they lived in two increasingly separate discursive worlds, a world of published arguments for social change and a private world of letters and notes to each other and to old friends.[43] This bifurcated system undoubtedly offered some benefits. It kept the spotlight off of them and away from their class background. It may also have protected some of their old friends from any undue scrutiny. However, this failure to recognize the political dimensions of divisions based on same-sex desire would have serious consequences for them in later years and for the movement they championed.

Within the CPUSA, Rochester and Hutchins were not alone in their strategy. Looking back from a distance of fifty-plus years, gay rights pioneer Harry Hay (in his trademark deeply ironic tone) described women such as Hutchins and Rochester whom he had known in his work in the CPUSA:

> Well, it was not *THAT UNUSUAL* to see two women known to be fond of one another being affectionate with one another. After All! One doesn't have to imagine unmentionable things simply because two old friends, who have worked together as writing partners (or whatever it is that they do together) for just years and years, occasionally getting—well—perhaps a little *TOO* affectionately carried away with each other. It's not like they don't turn out just splendid work with one another—because everyone knows that they DO![44]

This attitude of benign neglect enabled the party, for a while, at least, to include and make working space for women whose partnerships were based on their efforts to create a more just world. Women worked for the movement, and no questions were asked.

Like the women Harry Hay described, Hutchins and Rochester, in particular, were remembered as "extremely well-respected," according to Annette Rubinstein, although "distanced," giving an impression of "austerity." Dressing "respectably," they were always "rather formal, even "straitlaced."[45] Lem Harris noted that both Hutchins and Rochester "worked unobtrusively," and "kept to themselves," although they were "invited to attend conventions and plenums because their knowledge was wanted." "They had their own attitude about life," but Harris had never "heard unpleasant talk about them."[46] Si Gerson found Hutchins "gracious and cheerful." She and Rochester, he commented, "were inseparable."[47] These generally positive descriptions suggest that few people really knew them.

And the restrained etiquette of acceptance could easily shift. According to Sophie Gerson, although Rochester and Hutchins were completely trusted and respected for their knowledge and contributions, their presence led to speculation and occasionally crude humor. Some CPUSA members assumed, patronizingly, that Rochester and Hutchins had joined the party because they felt unwelcome elsewhere.[48] Another CPUSA activist and writer commented somewhat acidly that because of their wealth they could afford to be partners. This comment reflects thinking not uncommon among some party members—that same-sex love and desire are degenerate bourgeois conditions that will somehow wither along with the state.[49]

At the same time, Hutchins and Rochester's strategy of living openly but quietly together allowed others to remain unaware of their partnership—and to continue to entertain beliefs about the degenerate nature of same-sex desire. Annette Rubinstein mentioned that her friend Myra Page "would have been startled to think that Anna Rochester and Grace Hutchins were anything more than friends."[50]

More unfortunately, younger women whose confusion might have been allayed were unable to seek them out as mentors. During my first encounter with Betty Millard, then 87, one of Hutchins and Rochester's friends who had spent her entire life trying to free others from economic servitude, she suddenly became tearful. It wasn't until the following day that she could tell me what was wrong. "I couldn't sleep last night," she said. "I didn't understand why I was weeping." Finally, she said, she realized that, for as long as she had known Hutchins and Rochester, they had never once said a word to her about their love for each other. She, too, hid her love for other women, spending 15 years in psychoanalysis in an unsuccessful effort to change her feelings. Only within the past five years had she been able to share that part of herself openly. Silence and rumors of suicide still surround the memories of other women whom Hutchins and Rochester knew.

In the case of Rochester and Hutchins, the sexological siege was considerably more complicated that it was for some women and had implications far beyond themselves. In 1949, soured Party activist Whittaker Chambers took advantage of popular linkages of same-sex desire and death, publicly claiming that Hutchins had delivered a death threat against him some ten years earlier. Hutchins, slipping from her usual sophisticated and thoughtful rhetorical stance, offered up a slur of her own, outing him to the FBI. In early 1952, about three years after Chambers had launched his original attack, he took his revenge in his alleged autobiography, *Witness*, which began appearing in serialized form in *The Saturday Evening Post*; shortly thereafter it appeared in a hardcover edition published by Random House and was a fixture on the *New York Times* bestseller list for several months in 1952.[51] The book, purporting to tell the story of Chambers's work as a Soviet spy, mentions Hutchins and Rochester several times and is shaped by references to gay cultural phenomena. But if any readers noticed these references at the time, they said nothing publicly about them.[52] Sheltering himself in an invincible cloak of heterosexuality, Chambers had set a sophisticated trap for Hutchins and Rochester. If they decoded the references, they linked themselves to a "degenerate" subculture—and any number of others along with them. If they remained silent, they risked the possibility that the validity of Chambers's story would not be questioned. Although many readers did scoff at Chambers's allegations, his book, with the help of major publishers, captured the national imagination, helping to fuel the anticommunist fervor of the 1950s with its associated job losses, deportations, and imprisonments.

Legacy

Whittaker Chambers's attacks were devastating, but they did not completely foreclose Hutchins and Rochester's work. Because of their solidarity with other women like themselves—their mentors, friends, and comrades, as well as women they would never know—Anna Rochester and Grace Hutchins not only kept alive but strengthened and developed the feminist efforts of their generation.[53] Estelle Freedman could have been writing about them when she said, "when feminism survived, it did so largely where the traditions of separate women's organizations and women's intimate friendships survived."[54] Their intimate partnership formed a foundation for critical work that allowed new ideas to take hold and old ideas to stay alive. During her lifetime, Rochester parlayed her systematic thinking and feminist sensibilities into positions within the League for Industrial Democracy, the Fellowship of Reconciliation, and finally the predominantly male committees of the CPUSA, challenging gender prerogatives. Together, Rochester and Hutchins pushed the CPUSA to live up to its theoretical claims by including women and addressing women's issues. Championing women's overlooked strengths and contributions, Hutchins also did much of the kinship work of the CPUSA, insistently publicizing the antifascist efforts of women such as Maud Malone, Helen Bryan, and Betty Millard, whose own allegiances were primarily to women.

In each instance, Rochester and Hutchins dedicated their lives to shaping and promoting languages, stretching religious discourse to address economic and gender inequities, pushing Marxism-Leninism to address women, challenging the commodification of women in the capitalist press. Even more significantly, both Hutchins and Rochester, realizing that freedom of speech means having the *economic* freedom to speak, endeavored to create access to audiences, funding progressive publishers and even paying the mortgage on a building housing a major left-wing press and bookshop.

This study charts the lives of Grace Hutchins and Anna Rochester as they traversed several twentieth-century social movements, examining their rhetorical allegiances and strategies in light of their own origins and partnership. Hutchins and Rochester's ongoing challenges to the requirements of gender and insistence on recognizing the economic components of gender assumptions have come down to us through later feminist writers and activists. Tracing Hutchins and Rochester's lives and the shifting social languages they negotiated offers us a way to understand some of the passionate commitments of the previous century and to uncover an edge of the discursive foundation supporting more recent feminist and gay rights movements.[55]

I have divided the narrative into three parts. The first describes Hutchins and Rochester's meeting in 1919, their early years with their families, and their trajectory through several social movements up through the 1920s. The second part discusses their work in the Labor Research Association and the CPUSA during the 1930s, including their writing for publications such as *New Masses*, the *Daily Worker*, and *Labor Defender*, as well as their book-length studies published by International Publishers. The third part documents the effect on Hutchins and Rochester of the changing discourses of sexuality and the rise of government-sponsored anticommunist repression from the post–World War II period until their deaths.

Part One

Beginnings

Chapter One

1919

<hr>

"They shall walk in white for they are worthy."

—Revelation 3:4 (quoted in Emily Malbone Morgan's *Adelyn's Story*, p. 12)

I take wings through the night and pass through all the wildernesses of the worlds, and the old dark holds of tears and death—and return with laughter, laughter, laughter:

Sailing through the starlit spaces on outspread wings, we two—O laughter! laughter! laughter!

—Edward Carpenter (*Towards Democracy*, p. 14)

Grace Hutchins and Anna Rochester first met in August 1919 at the annual conference of the Society of the Companions of the Holy Cross (SCHC).[1] An Episcopal laywomen's organization, the SCHC gave Rochester and Hutchins two indivisible freedoms: the freedom to form a committed partnership with each other and the freedom, indeed, the necessity, to devote themselves to creating a more just society.

The conference was held, as always, at the retreat site of the Companions, north of Boston, and this year's theme was "Internationalism: A Consideration of the Social and Religious Forces that Make for It." Discussions were heated, as the Companions, none of whom was even yet recognized as a voter in the US Constitution, debated the advisability of establishing a League of Nations.

Both Hutchins and Rochester were raised devout Episcopalians. As young adults, both had joined the Socialist Party and with the onset of World War I had become pacifists. When they met in 1919, they found themselves on the same side of the SCHC debates and discovered that they both supported Paul Jones, the bishop of Utah, who had been censured by the Episcopal House of Bishops for speaking out against the United States' entry into the war. They also found a shared interest in the newly formed Church League for Industrial Democracy (CLID).

Anna Rochester's mother had died in January 1919, after many years of ill health, leaving her only child financially comfortable but adrift. In June, Rochester left her position as editor with the US Children's Bureau, giving the retreat site as her forwarding address: Adelynrood, South Byfield, Massachusetts.[2] On August 18, a day before her thirty-fourth birthday, Grace Hutchins came in from New York, where she was teaching the New Testament at the New York Training School for Deaconesses. Although first Rochester, and

Figure 1.1. Anna Rochester and Grace Hutchins at Adelynrood, ca. 1921

then Hutchins, would leave the Companions a decade later, as if shedding an ill-fitting coat, their lives and work remained profoundly shaped by the strengths and visions of this small group of women.

"To Develop the Companionship Life"

Hutchins and Rochester both came to develop the Companionship life,[3] a life that fostered consecrated work and unrestricted love designed to bring about a new social order. The Society of the Companions of the Holy Cross was (and still is) devoted to intercessory prayer, thanksgiving, and simplicity of life. The *Manual of the Society of the Companions of the Holy Cross* reminds members that "Companions shall seek to practice and to encourage systematic intercession for the coming of God's Kingdom on earth."[4] From the beginning, the Companionship was far more than just a social organization. The organization's founder, Emily Morgan, enjoined the Companions to "realize that we are organized for companionship as well as intercession, but for companionship on a higher plane, and with a higher bond of union than the mere ordinary social relationships of the world."[5]

Although the names of most early Companions will not be familiar to readers today, some members are still recognized for their brilliance as catalysts of social change: they included Vida Dutton Scudder, a Wellesley English professor who worked to establish the first College Settlement for Women on Rivington Street in Manhattan's lower east side; Scudder's life partner, Florence Converse, a radical novelist, poet, and assistant editor at

The Atlantic Monthly; Ellen Gates Starr, a founder of Hull House and activist in the strikes of women textile workers in Chicago; Helena Stuart Dudley, head of Denison House in Boston; and Mary Simkhovitch, director of Greenwich House in Manhattan.[6]

Rochester had met Vida Scudder and Florence Converse at a summer resort in Shelburne, New Hampshire, in 1904. Scudder had made every effort then to convince Rochester of the importance of labor unions. It took four years, but finally, in 1908, Rochester signaled her agreement and accepted an invitation to join the Companions, where Scudder was in charge of probationers. For more than fifteen years, Rochester's ideas and activities paralleled those of Vida Scudder, and even later the two women remained connected, despite political differences.

At the time the Society was organized, women were encouraged to serve as missionaries, deaconesses, and members of the Women's Auxiliaries,[7] but they were not allowed leadership roles in the governance structures of the Episcopal Church. The small group grew quickly as women recognized that here was a place where they might actively engage their Christian principles in a community of like-minded women. Because the SCHC was not formally affiliated with the church, members were free to engage in discussions of theology and its relation to social practices—as well as to organize, design, and construct their own retreat center—without having to submit to the church hierarchy. By 1919, there were 406 members and probationers in the spiritual community.

As Companion in charge of probationers, Vida Scudder shaped much of the Companions' thinking through lists of recommended reading. Among the books on Scudder's lists were Edward Carpenter's *England's Ideal* and *Civilization: Its Cause and Cure*.[8] These volumes, along with Carpenter's other writings, offer us one of the most direct avenues to the meanings of Hutchins and Rochester's lives.[9] Speaking to members of the middle class, Carpenter argued for simplifying one's life, enjoining them to divest themselves of

Figure 1.2. Main room, Adelynrood, early twentieth century

the material conventions produced by industrialism in order to avoid living off the labor of others. "It cannot be too often remembered," he said, "that every additional object in a house requires additional dusting, cleaning, repairing, and lucky are you if its requirements stop there."[10] What's more, Carpenter pointed out, much of the household labor is done by women: "Woman is a slave, and *must remain so* as long as ever our present domestic system is maintained. I say that our average mode of life, as conceived under the bourgeois ideal of society, cannot be kept up without perpetuating the slavery of woman."[11]

Carpenter's point that ownership of things tends to enslave people—either oneself or someone else—became a key element in the Companions' concern for a "reconciliation of classes." How could the classes be reconciled if Companions themselves perpetuated the class system by hiring servants? Although a few workers were hired to maintain Adelynrood, members did much of the housework and gardening themselves, taking pleasure in their self-reliance.

The Companions were, thus, a new form of social organization, devised by women, one that fostered the independence of members, independence especially from the traditional family structure in which women were wards of men, first of their fathers and then of their husbands—and where a daughter's lack of a husband by a certain age was sure to constitute a family crisis. Although married women were welcome, the SCHC was founded and run, at least for the first twenty to thirty years, primarily by single women like Grace Hutchins and Anna Rochester. The unmarried members, moreover, were those most likely to be out in the world as deaconesses, missionaries, and settlement workers.[12] They were the ones working with the labor unions and writing articles and books explaining the problems of industry. They were the active committee members, passing around petitions, seeking a new trial for labor leader Tom Mooney[13] or organizing conferences to promote church unity. They had, in short, translated their lives from the isolation of traditional families to the active construction of the Kingdom of God but within the supportive context of a community of women. This active construction meant puzzling out new ways of being in the world.

The Kingdom of God on Earth

During 1919, one of the most serious issues before the membership was the Pittsburgh-based steel strike. Union members had voted in August to strike on September 22. At the heart of public discussions of the strike was the question of reform versus revolution. Local papers had been stirring up antipathy toward the strikers by claiming that they were revolutionaries and wanted nothing less than the ownership of the mills by the workers. Central to the strikers, however, was the question of the closed shop and the eight-hour day. The union was not asking for a closed shop; the mill owners, however, *were*, in the sense that they not only maintained a so-called open shop but also reserved the right to discharge any union members, thus, in essence, creating a shop closed to unionists. Hours for steel workers ranged from miserable to inhuman; blast furnace employees, for instance, were required to work seven-day weeks and twelve-hour days. Yet the strikers knew that they were up against the "interlocking machinery of mill, town, county and state."[14]

It was conditions such as this colliding with a theology seeking to establish the Kingdom of God on earth that had prompted Vida Scudder and others to form the Church League for Industrial Democracy in May 1919. Scudder made a practice of organizing and affiliating herself with Episcopal organizations such as the CLID and the SCHC that were free from the control of the more conservative church hierarchy. Three Companions,

Ellen Starr, Mary Simkhovitch, and Vida Scudder, were among those signing the original call to organize the CLID. Anna Rochester added her name shortly thereafter and began organizing a chapter in New York.

If the Kingdom of God on earth was understood to be constructed of love, it was not meant to be simply a two-way street between God and individual humans but a multidirectional network, extending throughout humanity, creating the foundation for new forms of social organization. In the years to come, Hutchins and Rochester would build their partnership upon this foundation.

"A Love that Purifieth the Soul and Exalteth Desire"

The implications of this new understanding of love were profound and far-reaching. By 1919, the Companions had a long history of shaping their lives with this new understanding and expanding upon it in their writing. In her 1903 historical novel of medieval life, *Long Will*, Florence Converse developed Will Langland, the author of *Piers Plowman*, into the novel's protagonist. Will said to his daughter, who was briefly smitten by the attentions of a knight:

> But hark, Calote: this love of knights and damosels is not the one only love. Read thy Reason in the Romaunt,—and she shall tell thee of a love 'twixt man and man, woman and woman, that purifieth the soul and exalteth desire; nay, more: Reason shall tell thee of a love for all thy fellows that haply passeth in joy the love for one. The King's Son of Heaven,—He knew this love.[15]

Converse echoed here Edward Carpenter's words in *Towards Democracy*, published in 1883. First condemning the effects of capitalism, Carpenter said, "Wealth is slowly and visibly putrefying and putrefying the old order of things."[16] He called out: "Lovers of all handicrafts and of labor in the open air, confessed passionate lovers of your own sex, Arise!"[17] And in a gesture pointing to a transformative same-sex love as the source of social renewal, he exclaimed: "I who desired one give myself to all. I who would be the companion of one become the companion of all companions."[18]

Six years earlier, in 1897, Converse had described such a love that "purifieth the soul and exalteth desire" in *Diana Victrix*, a semicloaked version of her commitment to Vida Scudder.[19] Scudder's autobiographical[20] novel, *A Listener in Babel*, is also about love, beauty, and persuasion, and it resonates with the language and ideas found in both Plato's *Phaedrus*[21] and Edward Carpenter's *Towards Democracy*.[22] In the novel, published in the same year as Converse's *Long Will*, Scudder expounded on the "quest for Reality" that was to define her life.[23] Like Converse and Carpenter, Scudder argued for love that reaches beyond the limits of one man and one woman. Scudder ended *A Listener in Babel* with a type of same-sex alliance as well, although it was closer to Carpenter's vision than to Plato's: the main character, Hilda, decided to live with two young working class women and work in factories, learning skills which she aimed to use to establish a cooperative.

In the work of both Scudder and Carpenter as well as in the lives of Hutchins and Rochester, we find attempts to fuse a Platonic *eros*, or desiring love, with New Testament *agape*, or sacrificing love. This meant both a recognition and a celebration of same-sex desire and a channeling of that desire away from personal gratification and into the work of creating of a society based upon love and collectivity rather than individualism and greed.

Figure 1.3. Florence Converse, ca. 1910

Carpenter's larger vision, drawn from Plato, Walt Whitman, and H. M. Hyndman, author of *England for All*, was of a socialist society to include clearly, in his words, "homogenic love." Carpenter explained what he meant by "homogenic love" in his 1912 book *The Intermediate Sex*, a book that undoubtedly would have been read by Anna Rochester, Vida Scudder, and Florence Converse, among others. In it, Carpenter offered an extended argument in favor of same-sex devotion. Above all, Carpenter emphasized the naturalness of this love (which he, following some Continental sexologists, frequently called Uranianism) and, indeed, the benefits to society offered by those who were engaging in work motivated by love. "I think myself," he said, "that the best philanthropic work—just because it is the most personal, the most loving, and the least merely formal and self-righteous—has a strong fibre of the Uranian heart running through it."[24]

Carpenter's categories were based upon emotional engagement rather than sexual activity. "It would be a great mistake," he insisted, "to suppose that their attachments are necessarily sexual or connected with sexual acts. . . . and to confuse Uranians (as is so often done) with libertines having no law but curiosity in self-indulgence is to do them a great wrong."[25] Most important, Carpenter believed that "the Uranian people may be destined to form the advance guard of that great movement which will one day transform the common life by substituting the bond of personal affection and compassion for the monetary, legal and other external ties which now control and confine society."[26]

However many Companions may have privately identified themselves as "Uranian" or as belonging to the "intermediate sex," we have no way of knowing. It is unlikely that many spent time making such distinctions. Most were more interested in their work and in maintaining the cohesion of the group. Carpenter's construction of same-sex love describes for us a culture that flourished at the turn of the century, a culture that celebrated the social value of same-sex love and reversed the social condemnation traditionally accorded "spinsters."

Certainly Florence Converse's message that the Kingdom of God will not be constructed on the exclusive love of one man for one woman reflected the social organization of the Companions. Companions instead drew from their religious heritage to describe the emotional closeness they experienced. Emily Morgan said to the membership in one of her annual letters: "To me, the greatest features of our annual conferences have been the strong, even spiritual friendships which have grown out of our association together"[27] "Spiritual friendships" denotes friendships based upon a belief in a divine source of love and dedicated to celebrating that love and to the spiritual growth of both parties.[28]

The close friendships and partnerships between members were affirmed within the Companions just as they were recognized in other liberal women's organizations at the time.[29] When Companion Ethelwyn Upton died in November 1920, the New York Chapter expressed "its sympathy with especially Miss Gaylord" as well as with Miss Upton's relatives.[30] As the writings of Florence Converse, Vida Scudder, and Edward Carpenter indicate, these partnerships were rarely attempts to emulate heterosexual marriage. They were expansive, open to including others in communities of like-minded souls. Vida Scudder and Florence Converse, for instance, brought Helena Stuart Dudley into their home after she retired from her position at Denison House. Likewise, Anna Rochester and Grace Hutchins made a place for Lucie Myer in their Greenwich Village apartment. Companions' partnerships, Hutchins and Rochester's chief among them, were outward looking, supportive of each person's independence, and built on a need for work and companionship in the larger world. Nonetheless, it had not yet occurred to them that their freedom to establish such partnerships came from their independent incomes. Nor did they foresee the ways in which the partnerships built in the context of the SCHC would be diminished, erased, or misread by a society preoccupied with categories and pathologies.[31]

"Intercession and Labor"

In January 1919, Anna Rochester asked in the SCHC Intercession Letter that members give thanks with her "for a long, rich companionship with her mother; for the blessing of friendship and affection; for the beauty and consolation of the Eucharist; for the crumbling of the old social order in European countries." She also sought prayers "for all who disagree with accepted teaching, and especially for Anna, Companion, humility, sincerity, courage, imagination, loving kindness."[32] Already, Rochester was pushing at the limits of the Episcopal Church.

At the conference that summer, Rochester chaired a panel on "The Aim of Revolutionary Labor," with Ellen Gates Starr, Mary Emily Bruce, Margaret Shearman, and Helena Stuart Dudley explaining their positions on the Industrial Workers of the World (IWW), Marxism, the English Labor Movement, the Lawrence strike, and the Bolshevik

Revolution in Russia. Closing the panel, Rochester asked the Companions to consider that "the very charges that are brought against the revolutionists, the revolutionist is bringing against the present order,—Violence. He points to the millions of lives lost in the war. Cruelty? He can tell of cruelties in our industrial system. The revolutionist asserts that the evils of his movement are incidental to the struggle towards an order based on justice and brotherhood, while in the present rule, those evils are inherent and permanent."[33] This calculus informed her work for the rest of her life.

After spending the summer of 1919 at Adelynrood, Rochester returned to the empty family home in Englewood, New Jersey, from which she began to attend classes at the socialist Rand School and worked to organize the New York chapter of the CLID. The purpose of the latter organization was to bring together "for intercession and labor" Episcopalians who were committed to making "justice and love" the prevailing motives for social change.[34] The group grew quickly, because people were feeling a sense of urgency. The Bolshevik revolution had taken place only two years before, and Russia was still struggling against counter-revolutionary forces. World War I was just ending as well, and a red scare loomed in the United States. One of Rochester's first recruits was Grace Hutchins. Hutchins and Rochester were now working together in both the SCHC and the CLID.

Still teaching at the New York Training School for Deaconesses, Hutchins, too, was straining against Episcopal limits. Specifically, with respect to deaconesses, the question was one of authority. Whereas the vow of obedience to the bishop is the last vow in the rites of ordination for clergy, it was the first for deaconesses.[35] Although societal pressure was building for women's suffrage, women's rights within the church lagged. In 1916, a committee on constitutional amendments had tabled a motion to grant women the right to serve as deputies to the General Convention, calling the motion "inexpedient."[36] The next General Convention was scheduled for October 1919, and Rochester and Hutchins were hoping that the Episcopal Church, along with the rest of the country, would offer women the opportunity to serve alongside men.

Until such time, they poured their energy into the SCHC. At the Companion Conference of 1919, the New York Chapter of the SCHC agreed to take charge of the following summer's conference, and Rochester volunteered to be a member of the planning committee, along with Mary Simkhovitch, Adelaide Case, and others. The theme was to be "Sacrifice: A Creative Force." It was no accident that this theme emerged from the conference discussions on internationalism. Some Companions had protested that the topic had been too worldly, too concerned with material conditions and not central to the mission of a religious society. The fact that a conference on "Sacrifice" followed one on "Internationalism" exemplifies the dialectical thinking that Vida Scudder and others practiced. Sacrifice was not simply a private practice engaged in by religious zealots, Scudder said, but would be the linchpin of the new social order, as "the individual joyously surrenders all claim to special privilege, and finds in subordination his true liberty."[37] By this, she did not mean an institutionalized inequality, but rather its opposite, insisting that "the ethics of inequality have proved on inspection always unsatisfactory, progressively rotten."[38] Although Scudder did not dwell at length on questions of personal relationships in her explication of Christian socialism, *Socialism and Character*, she advocated strongly for love as a "discipline, the fiercest and most compelling in the law of self-subordination and the subjugation of desire that life affords." Nonetheless, she signaled her own choice by placing a dedicatory letter "To Florence Converse, Comrade and Companion," at the beginning of the book, thereby demonstrating in her own partnership the synthesis of the two disparate movements—socialism ("comrade") and Christianity ("Companion")—that she sought to unite.

Both Hutchins and Rochester spent the next several months working together on the conference program, drawing closer to each other, continuing to define for themselves and others what it meant for women to live sacrificial lives without reproducing women's traditional roles. Neither one had been raised in a household that "joyously surrender[ed] all claim to special privilege." Quite the contrary. Yet while this year, 1919, brought them onto the same path of intercession and labor, each had begun the journey years before.

Chapter Two

Anna Rochester

Now let us all arise and sing
The Coming Kingdom of our King,
The time when all shall brothers be,
Each loving each, all loving Thee.

—Emily Greene Balch (*The Adelynrood Hymnal*)

Anna Rochester was born on March 30, 1880, in New York City, into a family tracing itself back to the founding of Rochester, New York.[1] Anna's father, Roswell Hart Rochester, went to work for the Western Union Telegraph Company in 1865. Six years later, at age 32, he was appointed treasurer of the company. He was, according to a historian of the telegraph industry, "a man of marked character, direct, outspoken, brusque. . . . No officer [was] more thoroughly relied upon and trusted."[2] The description could have been written about Anna Rochester herself, so much was daughter like father. For Anna Rochester's mother, Louise Agatha Bamman, and her family, little information is available, although evidence suggests that she was a teacher in the New York Public Schools before her marriage.[3] Anna was the only child, born when her father was 41 years old and her mother was 38 years old.

Anna grew up from age two in Englewood, New Jersey, a fashionable suburb of New York City, and spent her childhood visiting relatives, traveling, studying music, and attending the private Dwight School for Girls. Louise Rochester recorded Anna's activities from 1880 until 1918. This record of Anna's early life provides a clear map to the qualities, events, and family and cultural dynamics that contributed to her later life, arguing against the written and unwritten rules of class and gender.

Anna's language ability developed quickly. By the age of one year, she was creating sentences of five or six words, and at age three, "she [would] invent and romance and chatter without intermission . . . , daily excit[ing] surprise by revealing knowledge of facts and acquaintance with stories which she was supposed ignorant of."[4]

By April 1883, when the family moved into "Chestnut Cottage" in Englewood, Anna had lost all interest in being indoors and wanted only to be outside helping Thomas, the gardener and stablehand.[5] When she did have to stay inside, her mother wrote, she "[took] great pleasure in assisting in house work and wishe[d] to be called 'Waiter girl' or 'Chambermaid' and to be suitably attired according to her occupation."[6] Along with household labor, she continued to teach herself language skills. In December 1883, she demonstrated that she could recite by heart the entire poem, "The Night Before Christmas."[7]

Figure 2.1. Anna Rochester, 1897

That same Christmas, when she was allowed to open her presents, she exhibited an awareness of others unusual for her age. Although "she proceeded to investigate her new wealth with great deliberateness and seriousness . . . she exclaimed, . . . 'Santa Claus was such a good fellow to bring something to everybody.' "[8]

By the time Anna was four years old, in 1884, her mother had begun to experience physical debilities, the symptoms of which suggest trigeminal neuralgia. At first, the problem was headaches, seemingly related to one or both eyes. During 1884 and 1885, Louise Rochester had "surgical treatment of her eyes." In August 1885, she had her left eye removed. Although she continued to document Anna's development, she was increasingly preoccupied with her own physical condition.

Like most affluent families, the Rochesters hired a nurse, Nellie Clancy, to care for their child. In December 1884, Louise Rochester arrived at a plan, perhaps a remnant of her public school teaching days, both to "improve" Clancy's linguistic skills and to ensure that Anna spoke using accepted grammatical constructions: she had the four-year-old and the nurse correct each other's grammar and usage. Anna wisely chose not to pursue this exercise too enthusiastically; when Clancy was heard to say "bring" instead of "take," Anna was asked if she had corrected her. She replied: "No, it was only a wash rag. I don't correct Nellie in little things. Nellie hasn't a corrected mind."[9]

Louise Rochester's pride in Anna's early literacy soon turned to concern that she was spending too much time reading and writing. Still, when Anna retold the story of Lot and Sodom at the dinner table, the family was rightly enough astonished, although also apparently pleased with the performance.[10] Then, however, they began to worry about her exceptional skill with numbers. She had become so interested "in figures that she [was] in danger of becoming a mathematical prodigy."[11] At the same time, she was developing physical capabilities that were unusually advanced, and by the summer of her sixth year she was driving the horses skillfully.[12] What she wasn't developing were the traditionally feminine occupations. Her mother worried that she "[was] not constant in her devotion to her doll."[13]

Over the next few years, as Anna's mother's health remained poor, the family hired a companion for her, Miss Hull, who also served as Anna's private tutor. Seeking cures, Louise Rochester traveled frequently to sanatoriums, accompanied by Anna or Miss Hull or both. When they went into New York City for any reason, Anna took charge, as her mother's left-side blindness made her fearful of crowds.[14] This early dependence probably encouraged a certain inflexibility on Anna's part.

When Anna reached the age of fourteen, her mother remarked, "At this period her character in developing shows great persistence in trying to carry her own point, but, with all her faults, there is firm adherence to principle." This practice, however, caused her to suffer some losses. Her mother reported that she preferred the company of adults and had become quite critical of those her age. Predictably, she had no close friends.[15]

Just before her fifteenth birthday, Anna was confirmed in St. Paul's Episcopal Church in Englewood. For the first time, her mother noted her developing religious fervor, again ascribing to her a maturity beyond her years: she "seems to realize in an unusual degree, for so young a girl, the reality of the sacrifice of the Savior and struggles very hard to overcome her faults."[16] She was rewarded by the gift of a baby grand piano from her father for her fifteenth birthday, a gift that she would use for years, studying music performance and theory in Germany and later at Columbia University.[17]

Around this time, Anna's mother noted that she had a "handsome face and fine carriage, but is apparently devoid of vanity as to her personal appearance."[18] This, along with her failure to attend to her doll and her conversational infelicities, provided more cause for concern. Then, during her last year at the Dwight School, Anna finally developed some friends, including Alice Dillingham, later to become a New York City lawyer, who was to remain her closest friend throughout her life, apart from Grace Hutchins.

That spring, Anna's exemplary performance on the entrance examinations for Bryn Mawr College earned her the "'First Matriculation Scholarship' or Prize of $300 in the New York and New Jersey Division."[19] With this acknowledgment of her abilities, Anna entered Bryn Mawr, a liberal Quaker school for women presided over by M. Carey Thomas, who devoted herself to creating the finest possible education for women. For the first time, she was free of responsibility for her mother.

This idyllic life ended abruptly, however, when Anna returned home for Thanksgiving Day. At 9:45 that evening, her father died, at age 58, from a heart attack.[20] Although she spent three weeks out of school following her father's death, she passed the exams in all her courses, some with high credit or merit.[21] Louise Rochester had been struggling before this event; now her health became even more compromised. Anna returned for the second semester of her freshman year, but she came home to her mother before the postyear social events began.[22]

Likewise, although her sophomore year at Bryn Mawr went well, Anna dashed home on May 3, fearful that her mother's condition was worsening. In fact, Louise Rochester had written in her diary rather oddly, referring to herself as usual in the third person, that she "had the misfortune (?) to show unmistakable signs of nervous collapse about April 1st. She struggled hard to resist and finally resorted to the comforting presence of Miss M. K. Browne—a trained nurse . . . to receive massage and other helpful treatments."[23] It was after this trip home that Anna made the decision to leave college permanently in order to care for her mother. She wrote her a long, effusive letter, explaining why she had come to this decision.[24] The strange placement of the parenthetical question mark next to "misfortune" may have been Louise Rochester's way of indicating that if her "signs of nervous collapse" had the effect of bringing her daughter home, perhaps they were not such a "misfortune."

It didn't take much to convince Louise Rochester to accept this plan, and she decided that they would spend the next fifteen months in Europe. Still, she wrote: "May God who directs our paths, grant that the noble sacrifice made by the dear child may so enrich her character that the loss of the two subsequent years of college life may be as nothing compared with the joy of the sacrifice."[25] Whether Anna benefited from the "joy" of this particular "sacrifice" is questionable; she clearly struggled with her mother's invalidism.

Then in the summer of 1904, Anna and Louise Rochester made a choice that would change everything in Anna's life. They elected to go to a new summer resort site, Philbrook Farm at Shelburne, New Hampshire, where Vida Dutton Scudder and Florence Converse had been vacationing for years. As Rochester reported twenty-two years later, "I . . . became involved one day in an argument with a certain well-known and brilliant woman. She had defended labor unions, and I had used all the familiar commonplaces about the iniquities of plumbers."[26] This argument did not precipitate an immediate epiphany, however, even in the young woman who as a child had so happily worked alongside the family's gardener and had refused to correct her nurse's grammar. Still, her class-based assumptions had been challenged in an atmosphere of mature love and commitment between women that Rochester had never experienced before.

It is easy when reading Louise Rochester's comments to see where Anna absorbed her class biases. During the summer of 1907, Anna, her mother, and her mother's current companion, Anne Selleck, sailed for Europe. They traveled to France and Switzerland, spending most of their time at a spa near Geneva. On the return voyage, Louise Rochester reported that although the boat was steady and their large room was comfortable, "the class of people in general was not encouraging and the limited supply of the right kind of food have not left the pleasantest impression on the mind."[27]

Upon their return, Anna Rochester had her first, and apparently only, male suitor. The clergyman " 'announced his intentions' in a very rapid and earnest manner." No other comment about this occasion exists except Louise Rochester's cryptic "but that is now over."[28] Apparently neither Anna nor her mother welcomed this suit, no doubt for different reasons. Instead, Anna buried herself in Bible study, ostensibly preparing herself for her weekly Sunday School lessons but also anticipating another visit with Vida Scudder and Florence Converse.

During the summer of 1908, Anna and her mother returned to Philbrook Farm. By now Anna was allowing the influence of Vida Scudder and Florence Converse to affect her, as Louise Rochester observed that "Anna's interest in sociology gathered great impetus from associating with Miss Vida Scudder and Miss Florence Converse." To which she added approvingly: "both notably Godly women and highly intellectual."[29] But for Anna Rochester, it was the combination of Vida Scudder and Florence Converse's mentorship and her discovery of Walter Rauschenbusch's *Christianity and the Social Crisis* on the local library's shelf of new books that caused the epiphanic moment that was to change her life—her first conversion.

Figure 2.2. Vida Scudder and Florence Converse, ca. 1925

A Baptist theologian, Walter Rauschenbusch taught New Testament interpretation at Rochester Theological Seminary. His Social Gospel theology, however, was born during his first pastorate, at Second German Baptist church in New York City, located right outside Hell's Kitchen. There he saw firsthand the effects of capitalism on workers, lamenting especially the funerals he had to conduct for children whose deaths were directly attributable to poverty.[30] Soon he was arguing that Christianity was not just a personal religion, designed to save individuals; it was, rather, a religion that emphasized the Kingdom of God—the immanence of God in social relations and, thus, the responsibility to live in concert with others. The "essential purpose of Christianity," he argued, is "to transform human society into the kingdom of God by regenerating all human relations and reconstituting them in accordance with the will of God."[31]

By 1907, when Rauschenbusch wrote *Christianity and the Social Crisis*, his system was well developed. He began with the topic that first drew Anna to the book, looking for information for her Sunday School students: the Hebrew prophets. The prophets, he pointed out, as few were acknowledging at that time, "insisted on a right life as the true worship of God," whereas Christianity now, he said, was mostly ritual, and religious ardor was spent on acts of ceremony rather than acts with a social purpose.[32] Moreover, the prophets were the "heralds of the fundamental truth that religion and ethics are inseparable and that ethical conduct is the supreme and sufficient religious act."[33] The morality that Rauschenbusch called for took responsibility for community and even national life.

Rauschenbusch aimed to update Christianity for twentieth-century conditions. Jesus, he argued, was not a modern reformer; he was a man of his times who spoke from the conditions of which he was a part: his words should not be enshrined as "timeless . . . generalities."[34] Nonetheless, there were lessons to be learned from Jesus' teachings; he "bore within him the germs of a new social and political order."[35] The basis of this order was both a vitiation of the individual and a commitment to the social. Morality itself, as Jesus taught, is profoundly social, Rauschenbusch argued; to be antisocial (or to place too much emphasis on the individual) is to be immoral.[36] This new perspective, calling into question capitalist individualism by viewing all social relations through the lens of Christian ethics, was exactly the "perspective by incongruity" that Anna needed to disrupt the attitudes she had inherited—and that were not serving her well.

Rauschenbusch also critiqued the Bible as it has come down to us, pointing to Revelation 13 as an element of early Christianity that expresses revolutionary hopes and discounting the New Testament emphasis on Paul, whom he called a theological radical but social conservative.[37] After a thoroughgoing analysis of biblical support for revolutionary ideas—and ecclesiastical hesitance to carry out these ideas—Rauschenbusch turned to current conditions in America and across the world, excoriating the Church (by which he meant all of organized Christendom) for its lack of mindfulness regarding child labor, sweatshops, and the wage system in general: "We cannot join economic inequality and political equality."[38] In order to support this system, the Church, he charged, had allowed the historical material in the Bible to be "numbed by allegorical interpretation." This "neutralized the social contents of the Bible by spiritualizing everything."[39]

Rauschenbusch, however, was not a radical when it came to family relations. In fact, he wanted to see the organization of the traditional family supplant that of the current political order. Moreover, he asserted, "attraction between men and women is just as fundamental . . . as physics,"[40] and he supported Paul's condemnation of "sexual indulgence" and "unnatural vice." He did, nonetheless, make a space for those who were not part of traditional families. Sounding not unlike Edward Carpenter, he said, "Childless people should adopt the whole coming generation of children and fight to make the world more habitable for them as for their own brood. The unmarried and the childless should enlist in the new apostolate and march on the forlorn hopes with Jesus Christ."[41]

That is exactly what Anna Rochester did. Seeking a "new apostolate" in which to enlist, she accepted Vida Scudder and Florence Converse's invitation to become a probationer in the SCHC. Late in that summer of 1908, Rochester accompanied Vida Scudder and Florence Converse to Byfield, Massachusetts, for the annual retreat of the Companions—her first of many.

As a probationer, Rochester took the society's commitment to simplicity to heart, living an increasingly ascetic life. The question of how to interpret—and live out honorably—the Companions' ideal of simplicity apparently was a problem not only for Rochester, as Emily Morgan made it a point to address this question in her annual letter to the Companionship, calling it "a ghost that haunted Adelynrood last summer." More important than personal asceticism, Morgan said, was a response to the contrasts between the appalling luxury available to some and the abject poverty in which others must live. This response should not be monetary but rather a public outcry, in which each individual opinion was important. "Knowledge of conditions," she said, "is what produces righteous opinion and actually forces an ideal of simplicity of life on all those who *know*."[42]

Although in her circumstances Anna Rochester could not effect a complete change in her life, and she continued to practice a certain amount of self-denial, she did commit herself to a practice of *knowing*—reading and studying the Charles Kerr edition of Marx's *Das Kapital* as well as Vida Scudder's *Social Ideals in English Literature*. Understanding that *knowing* without acting was insufficient, that fall, in the November presidential election, Rochester supported the presidential candidacy of Eugene Debs, and she made plans to spend time in the spring at Denison House, the Boston settlement house directed by Helena Stuart Dudley, one of her SCHC sponsors.

Thus, it was not to European capitals or elegant East Coast guesthouses that Anna Rochester traveled in June 1909 but to Denison House, a center of fellowship and service. The girl who had delighted in being "waiter girl" and "chambermaid" finally had some work beyond running a household for her mother and herself. For her work at Denison House, she had prepared herself by spending one afternoon each week in "parish visiting," calling on parishioners of St. Paul's "whose material blessings and social position have differed from her own."[43] During the six weeks she worked at Denison House, she visited families, made picnics, took babies to the hospital, and did clerical work, all the while absorbing the culture of the settlement movement, a culture to which she was drawn but which she found personally difficult. That same summer, seeking to join the house in heart as well as mind and body, she asked for the intercessions of the Companions: "that A.R., probationer, may be more faithful in prayer, and that her nature may grow warmer and more loving."[44]

At her second Companion Conference, in August 1909, this time addressing "The Church and Social Justice," Rochester became a participant as well as an observer, reporting to the assembled on Walter Rauschenbusch's *Christianity and the Social Crisis*. Having been immersed in arguments about social justice for ten days, Rochester returned home in the fall of 1909 more convinced than ever of the logic of—and desperate need for—socialism.[45] Yet, she remained as isolated at home with her mother as she had been for the past ten years; the only clues to her turmoil are requests to the Companions for intercessions.

Later that year, Rochester put much of her energy into preparing a paper on "Modernism" for the next Companions' summer conference; finally, she was able to return to the scholarship she had given up when she left college after her sophomore year. The subject of the 1910 conference was "The Reunion of Christendom." Although no copy of her paper on Modernism is extant, a consideration of this topic would have included both the current discussions of modern science and historical criticism of the Bible. In brief, modernist theologians argued that Darwinism was "a friend in disguise to Christian theology" because it made "the deistic idea of a purely transcendent God no longer tenable" and had "forced Christian thought to recover the forgotten truth of divine immanence."[46] In other words, God is present (immanent) in all of nature. This argument, of course, created problems for the notion of Original Sin; however, those problems were variously solved by compartmentalizing nature and spirit or by restricting science to phenomena and keeping "ultimate questions" in the realm of religion. Episcopalians sought answers in the Incarnation, the corporal embodiment of divinity in the person of Jesus, whose sacrifice was the ultimate challenge to evil and signaled the way that Christians were to approach the world.

At the same time, the "Higher Criticism," a method of literary and historical analysis, was applied to the Bible, revealing the unreliability of some of its narratives and thus undermining traditional beliefs in its infallibility as the Word of God. Using the Higher Criticism, theologians determined that Jesus' thought had its bases in the Jewish apocalypses—"the expectation of the approach of the end of the age."[47] One of the key tenets of Modernism was the notion of the possibility of achieving the Kingdom of God on earth. In order to reach this goal, however, the various Christian denominations would have to be reunited; thus, Modernists actively sought the "reunion of Christendom."[48]

Rochester read her paper on Tuesday, August 23, 1910. Her ability, as revealed in her well-researched paper, as well as her demonstrated commitment to the Companionship, convinced members that, despite the fact that she was a relatively new member, they wanted her to chair the conference committee for the next summer, 1911. After consultation with some of the older members, she accepted the job, joining a committee whose members included Euphemia Macintosh, Helena Stuart Dudley, Sophie Brown (longtime partner of Marion Rollins), and Margaret Lawrance. Thus, in the context of a laywomen's organization, Rochester developed the intellectual skills traditionally reserved for men. And, following Walter Rauschenbusch's directives, she began to use them outside of the SCHC.

On December 6, 1910, Rochester wrote a letter to the editor of the socialist New York *Call* in response to an opinion piece penned by one W. E. P. French.[49] In the article, Comrade French had argued that churches should be taxed. The Protestant Episcopal Church, he pointed out, owned $45,000,000 worth of property in the borough of Manhattan alone, and the main church was located, he noted trenchantly, at the head of Wall Street. Moreover, he charged, the land owned by the church was also host to tenements, in which the trustees had declined to install running water. Returning to his main point, Comrade French claimed that the failure to exact taxes from churches was tantamount to an indirect subsidy of religion by the government.[50]

Rochester's letter demonstrates the fact-based logic as well as the forthright criticism that would characterize her work from that point on. It also illustrates the ways in which she constructed a Christian Socialist perspective on the economic position of the churches. She began her letter first by acknowledging the logic of Comrade French's argument about taxation. Then she quickly moved to discount the rest of his argument, charging him with confusing the issue by making "bitter statements about the present character of the Church." In a series of caustic questions, she wondered whether he really thought that distributing the Church's property would make any broad necessary social differences. And what, she asked, was the connection between the Church's exemption from taxation and its failure to practice Christian charity? She then set out her main argument in two parts. In the first part, she maintained that the Church's concern was with spiritual rather than material matters. It was discouraging, of course, that those who went to church and those who represented the church sometimes did not act on the spiritual truths conveyed by the Church's teachings; however, the Church itself should not be held responsible for these lapses.

Furthermore, Rochester argued in the second part of her letter, Jesus did not teach economics. Rather, he taught "social principles, justice, cooperation, and brotherly love." He worked with individuals in order to bring about individual renewal and through them to bring about social renewal. The Church still offered these teachings, she said. In a ringing peroration, she proclaimed, "When the Church awakens to the full implications of all that she is teaching, she will in many things do differently and her denunciations of capitalism will be more searching and terrible than any Socialist's tirade." In the meantime, she said, summing up, please don't be so hard on the Church, which was only made up of people struggling within a "vicious" system.[51] This particular incongruity would continue to haunt her, but her arguments here reflect the state of her thinking in 1910.

Rochester apparently wrote to her mentor, Vida Scudder, telling her of the conversation in the pages of *The Call* and looking for her approval, as the argument closely mirrored Scudder's thinking. Scudder wrote back on December 20, 1910, to "My Dearest Anna," saying, "I am *wild* to see your discussion with 'Comrade French' but I am not now taking *The Call*, & I had not seen it at all. Can't you, won't you, get me copies?"[52]

Rochester had found an intellectual home, a "new apostolate," and she was beginning to speak. Still, she felt responsible for her mother's care. In June, they traveled to England for the summer, arriving during a massive transportation strike. This close association with a basic industrial struggle brought home to her even more urgently the need for a change in the economic system, an awareness that was strengthened later that summer when she returned to the United States to lead the 1911 Companion Conference at Adelynrood. There, amid discussions about the Episcopal Church and its worship, activities, and ideals, Rochester listened to Companions reporting on their work in settlements and labor organizations. Ellen Gates Starr, a Hull-House resident and member of the Women's Trade Union League, gave the conference-goers a "thrilling account of recent shirt waist strikers in Chicago in which Miss Coman and she played prominent parts in the work of arbitration." Margaret Shearman's appeal for help for the Westmoreland coal strikers generated a "sympathetic discussion."[53] These reports of activism affected other Companions enough so that when members of the New York chapter met during the conference, they talked about their need for a meeting place where they might discuss things in order to be able to do more than act just by intercession, a move in which Rochester's leadership is evident.[54]

Through all this, Louise Rochester reported that her daughter was spending as much time as ever in reading about and attempting to practice socialism but that she had refined her arguments in order to avoid startling or alienating her audiences,[55] a sign of her growing rhetorical sophistication. Rochester began to develop her arguments about the Church's responsibility for social change into a book to be used in Sunday Schools, outlining the New Testament basis for socialism. Apparently the work she did to adapt her arguments to her audience was at least briefly successful, because she was appointed to serve on the Board of Education of the Episcopal Diocese of New Jersey. However, there is only one mention of the Board of Education, and in October 1911, she asked the Companions to join her in thanksgiving for "the humiliations that deepen the penitence of Anna, Companion, and bring her nearer to the Cross"; she continued, in a section of the Intercession Paper reserved "for spiritual and temporal blessings," asking "that Anna, Companion, may see more clearly what she ought to do, and may have grace to persevere."[56] Apparently the church hierarchy outside of the Companions did not share Rochester's enthusiasms, particularly for socialism, her rhetorical skills notwithstanding. Although she would not leave the Church for many years, this event marked the first in a series of disappointments that would lead to a final break.

Yet Anna Rochester did persevere. At the same time that she was working to change the church from within, she was, following the practice of many SCHC members, moving out from the church into secular organizations devoted to social transformation. The first such organization that she joined was the Consumers League of New Jersey. By 1911, she had been appointed to the Consumers League's Board of Foremen. In 1912, she accepted the volunteer position of chair of the publicity committee campaigning for a law requiring employers to limit women's labor to ten hours per day.

While chairing the Consumers League publicity committee, Rochester also joined the New Jersey Child Labor Committee, beginning "work to make the world more habitable."[57] Clearly, the focus of her life was shifting during this crucial period, a period which had begun in 1904 when she had first encountered Vida Scudder and Florence Converse.

Rochester's skillful handling of the ten-hour law campaign led to an invitation from the National Child Labor Committee in New York asking her to do publicity work part time on a six-week trial basis during May and June of 1912. The invitation may have come at the behest of Florence Kelley, a former Hull-House resident and friend of Ellen Gates Starr, then living at the Henry Street Settlement in New York City and serving as executive secretary of the National Consumers League. Rochester's six-week trial at the National Child Labor Committee was successful, and she returned in September to work for the committee four to five hours per day, remaining for the next three years.[58]

Before returning to the new position in New York, Anna Rochester attended the seventeenth annual conference of the SCHC in the summer of 1912. Although the subject of this conference was "The Mystical Element in Religion," the reports indicate that mysticism was broadly interpreted, as "Miss Dudley, Miss Scudder, and Mrs. O'Sullivan thrilled us with a description of the Lawrence Strike, and made us feel the wonder of the great sense of brotherhood inspired in those 25,000 workers of twenty nationalities who for weeks were held together in a spiritual bond of suffering and of hope."[59]

The IWW-led strike of the mostly immigrant woolen-mill workers in Lawrence, Massachusetts, just a few miles from Adelynrood, had taken place from January through March of 1912. The state legislature, responding to pressure from the American Federation of Labor, limited the number of working hours to 54 per week. Mill owners reacted by lowering wages to compensate themselves for the fact that laborers would be working fewer hours. Conditions in Lawrence were appalling to begin with—the death rate was the highest in the country—and workers had little to lose by striking. The strike was a magnet for progressives such as Vida Scudder, who saw in it the struggle between capital and labor writ large and, as indicated by the conference report, a representative instance of the power of community. Rochester later reflected on her own growing awareness during that moment in a 1926 letter to Elizabeth Gurley Flynn, saying, "I remember when I was living in Englewood, a newly converted young bourgeois uncertain what to *do* about my Socialist ideas, hearing of you at the Paterson strike; also Boston friends [probably Vida Scudder, Florence Converse, and Helena Stuart Dudley] told me about you at Lawrence."[60]

The position with the National Child Labor Committee gave Rochester something to do about her Socialist ideas, something beyond *knowing*, a task that would engage the persuasive skills she had been developing since infancy. Her first title was "Special Agent"; later she was designated "Publication Secretary." Her actual job was publicity, working especially with the newspapers.

From 1912 through 1915, the committee campaigned against child labor in cotton mills, mines, glassmaking factories, canneries, and street trades. Although Anna Rochester undoubtedly produced many written documents during her first year at the National Child Labor Committee (she even attended the committee's national conference in Florida in March 1913) her first byline appeared in the *Survey* of April 19, 1913. "The Battle Lines of Child Labor Legislation" traced the state-by-state progress of the "uniform child labor law" that the committee was attempting to put into place. In this article, published under the heading of "Editorial Grist," Rochester first demonstrated her ability to pull together a large amount of information and use that information as the basis for a logical appeal. At the same time, her mordant wit is evident: she noted that the Pennsylvania House was reading the uniform law—with several changes, including a reduction of the mini-mum age for street traders from 12 to 10—for the third time, and "if its friends can still protect it from the mutilations desired by the glass interests, the telegraph companies, the textile manufacturers and other opponents," she said, "Pennsylvania will be in a fair way to protect the 29,170 children employed in manufactories in that state."[61] She went on to discuss the fact that several states were considering special street trading laws, but "their outcome is doubtful because the average legislator seems to be blind to the bad results of street trading, and cheerfully reflects the popular view that these 'sturdy, little merchants' are all supporting widowed mothers and headed straight for the White House."[62] Around the same time, she wrote a letter to the editor of *Life* magazine countering an argument in Massachusetts against the passage of the child labor law and exhibiting even more caustic irony:

> I suppose a real Puritan would reason that children need the discipline of a ten hour day in the mills; and this may explain why the Pilgrims' state has never accorded the riotous leisure of an eight-hour day to its child workers, but reserved that dangerous limitation for the strong men employed on public works.[63]

While engaged in this new work, acting on her Socialist ideas, Rochester remained in the bourgeois world of her mother, who had spent the summer of 1912 in the resort village of Dorset, Vermont, still attempting, unsuccessfully, to overcome facial neuralgia. Still, Louise Rochester felt that the time in Dorset had been so pleasant that in September 1912, she bought a lot in Dorset, with the idea that this was to be Anna's and that she would build a summer cottage on it. Anna Rochester immediately set about supervising the plans and the building of the "cottage" (which would appear to most of us today as a good-sized two-story house). In November 1912, she traveled to Dorset to check on the building of the house and was assured that the construction was progressing well.

We can only imagine how Anna Rochester was struggling to hold the parts of her life together at this point—attending to her mother's chronic illness, yet trying to protect herself from being overwhelmed by her mother's needs. She worked four hours per day for the National Child Labor Committee, and her mother wrote: "Alas—the four hours are very long her mother thinks—." Louise Rochester's persistent facial neuralgia required a visit to a specialist in Chicago, and during November 1912, Anna accompanied her mother on that trip. However, she managed to make the trip a viable experience for herself by arranging to meet Jane Addams at Hull-House.[64] She also met Maria Yarros and her husband Gregory. Maria Yarros (née Sukloff) had been arrested for "terrorism" in prerevolutionary Russia, had been sent to Siberia, and had fled through China to the United States.[65] This first contact with Russian revolutionaries made a profound impression on Rochester. Still, the construction of a vacation home remained her primary accomplishment. The incongruity could not have escaped her.

The house in Dorset was ready for occupation in June 1913 and was christened "Anadyddit" (Anna did it). Anna, accompanied by two maids, Margaret and Mary Carroll, traveled to Dorset for a ten-day stay to set up housekeeping. Here she made lifelong close friends: poet and teacher Sarah N. Cleghorn and writers Dorothy Canfield Fisher and Zephine Humphrey Fahnestock.[66] The press of other obligations allowed her only a four-week visit that summer, although her mother stayed longer.

As dedicated as her mother was to rest cures, Anna could not rest with the understandings she now had. Even while supposedly vacationing in Dorset during the summer of 1913, she spoke to the Dorset Missionary Society on child labor, seeking to bring members into the number of those holding "righteous opinions" and then moving from that point into action. "The working children should have a special appeal to a missionary society," she said, "for if there was ever in the world an offense to God's little ones that deserved the mill stone penalty that offense is child labor. Of course," she conceded, "it is only a part of our un-Christian order of society, but it is a part which could be abolished tomorrow if people willed that it should, and its continuance is a glaring indictment of the sincerity of our ideals."[67] After describing child labor in detail, she asked members of the missionary society to write their senators and representatives endorsing a child labor bill and to write the National Child Labor Committee, offering support. What marks this effort is Anna's implicit redefinition of "mission." Using a social organization already in place and available to her—the Dorset Missionary Society—she asked members not to contribute to classic missionary work (converting the heathen) but rather to engage in action to change the very economic order from which these members were probably benefiting. She hoped to accomplish this by appealing to both their Christian principles and their sympathies for children. We have no way of knowing how successful she was, but we can see here the beginning of her ability to take an existing structure and reframe it to address a problem not usually within its purview.

After the summer in Dorset, Rochester returned to her job at the National Child Labor Committee, turning out an article on the eight-hour day for child workers for the *Child Labor Bulletin* of February 1914. Congress was considering the Palmer Federal Child Labor Bill, and although she pointed out the absurdity of arguing for an eight-hour day for children when adults had been lobbying for—and achieving—such conditions for themselves for years, she also laid out all the reasons that the bill should be passed, providing mostly counterarguments to the arguments against the bill already launched into wide circulation by employers. She informed readers that at the time she was writing, approximately a hundred thousand children under the age of 16 were working more than eight hours a day in factories and mills. Seeking to convert readers accustomed to comfort, she laced her fact-based arguments with irony—a form of incongruity which requires a knowing reader who understands that she is saying what is not true in order to emphasize what is true. In this case, she said: "The complaint that workers as a class are apathetic, stupid, incompetent, and generally inefficient, is repeated so often by certain employers that one might fancy the entire race was degenerating." Then she added, pointedly, and without irony: "But wouldn't you be apathetic if you were chronically tired?"[68]

Clearly, Rochester felt that her work did not compare with that of child laborers and did not qualify her for the prolonged rest that her mother thought she needed. During her remaining year and a half as a special agent at the National Child Labor Committee, she wrote several articles in addition to editing the *Child Labor Bulletin*. One of the most significant was "Newspapers and Child Labor," published in May 1914, in which she argued that readers must take responsibility for reshaping the material that newspapers publish. Implicit within her argument is the claim that it is through written—and widely distributed—texts that social compacts are drawn up and reinforced and that social change takes place. This insistence on written argument as a critical element in social reorganization informed her work for the rest of her life.

In one of her last items for the National Child Labor Committee, Rochester wrote about the work being done to develop a Children's Charter. This article, distributed widely through the Survey Press Bureau, explained that a national committee made up of experts such as Roger N. Baldwin of St. Louis, a former probation officer of the juvenile court[69]; Edward N. Clopper, the National Child Labor Committee's secretary for the northern states; C. C. Carstens of the Boston Society for the Prevention of Cruelty to Children; and Julia Lathrop of the US Children's Bureau had been working to develop a charter that would guarantee the rights of children in much the same way that the Magna Carta had established the rights of the people of England seven hundred years earlier. Such a charter would enable all those working with children—school attendance officers, juvenile court officers, factory inspectors—to cooperate with each other more easily than was the case at the time.[70]

Within a week or two of the article's publication, on June 22, 1915, Rochester received a letter from Julia Lathrop asking her if she would be willing to come to Washington to work at the US Children's Bureau—as Julia Lathrop's personal secretary. Lathrop had successfully lobbied, against much opposition, for increased funding for the Children's Bureau. Lillian Wald wrote to Jane Addams, explaining that the Appropriations Committee had budgeted $25,000 for the Children's Bureau and at the same time provided $165,000 for free seeds and $400,000 for hog cholera. "J. L. [Julia Lathrop] is taking the stand that she approves of $400,000 for hog cholera, as tending to higher standards of living, but it makes the $25,000 for children impressive."[71] This argument was effective, and Lathrop received her increased budget, expanding the bureau from fifteen to seventy-six workers.

In making a list of Rochester's achievements some thirty years later, Grace Hutchins suggested that it was Rochester's articles in *The Survey* and other publications that had attracted Lathrop's attention—in other words, her rhetorical skills placed in the service of children. What's more, Lathrop was a close friend, from Hull-House days, of both Ellen Gates Starr and Florence Kelley.

The letter of offer from Julia Lathrop arrived while Rochester was in New York and her mother was in Dorset with Edith Klein.[72] Rochester dashed up to Dorset to consult with her mother about whether she should take the position; they both agreed that even though it would mean that they would move to Washington, DC, this could even prove beneficial, as they would live in smaller quarters and thus save money and work for the housekeeper. After a trip to Washington to discuss the position with Julia Lathrop, Rochester was hired at a salary of $1500 per year.[73] The position would include publicity work similar to that which she had been doing previously. She was to begin work in Washington, DC, on September 16, 1915. Louise Rochester reported that "some friends" told Anna that "to be associated with a woman of Miss Lathrop's calibre [would] be 'a liberal education in itself.'"[74] These "friends" were probably Vida Scudder, Florence Converse, and Helena Stuart Dudley, who would have known how much Anna had sacrificed by leaving Bryn Mawr.

Julia Lathrop then joined Vida Scudder as one of Anna Rochester's mentors, the women who provided for her a way out of the isolated invalidism charted by her mother.

Lathrop, born in 1858 in Rockford, Illinois, had become a close friend of Jane Addams during their freshman year together at Rockford College. After Lathrop transferred to Vassar, she kept in touch with Addams, and in 1890 she joined Addams at Hull-House in Chicago. She had been active in the settlement from its opening in 1889, however, leading the Plato Club, during which neighborhood residents read together and discussed Jowett's translations of Plato. Addams describes Lathrop as marked by "disinterested virtue," which she defined as an "unfailing sense of moral obligation and unforced sympathy." This sense included " 'the refusal to nurse a private destiny' "[75]; in other words, a rejection of what we might now call "careerism."

During the early years at Hull-House, Addams, Lathrop, Ellen Gates Starr, Florence Kelley, and the other residents had realized that local work was insufficient; they began to extend their efforts beyond the neighborhood to the city and the nation. Lathrop worked primarily to establish more humane systems of corrections and facilities for the mentally ill, serving as a member of the Illinois State Board of Charities and Correction, the first woman to do so.[76] She understood that " 'grinding poverty . . . [is] the basis of our social problem.' "[77] Her method of attacking that poverty included both public information, specifically the popularizing of government-provided statistical reports, and statesmanship, the ability to bring the people and their government together for the common good. Edith Abbott, former Hull-House resident and professor of economics at Wellesley, acknowledged Julia Lathrop's contributions to the field of social reform, saying: "To Miss Lathrop we owe our staunch belief in the importance of social research as a sound means of social reform."[78] Although Lathrop had early on said to Jane Addams, "If Hull-House does not have its roots in human kindness, it is no good at all,"[79] she was not content to work from sentiment. Neither was she a propagandist. Rather, she was a pragmatist, in the sense that she was " 'determined to stand for getting the facts and to limit the application to the place where solid work [could] be done.' "[80]

Anna Rochester admired and absorbed these qualities as she worked with Lathrop. Not only did she learn new skills, but she began to appreciate a different approach to the world than that advocated by Vida Scudder. Lathrop was not religious. Although deeply ethical, she did not find in organized religion the answers to the questions posed by the worlds with which she came in contact. Instead, she sought to intervene where she could. Although she was obviously well versed in Platonism, she did not, as did Scudder, attempt to apply a Platonic dialectic to bring the church and the world into an idealist merger. Neither was she a Marxist, as was Scudder.

Nonetheless, Anna Rochester continued to be deeply engaged in the SCHC—in December 1915 she sponsored her friend Zephine Humphrey Fahnestock of Dorset as a probationer—yet she could not have failed to appreciate Lathrop's more active, fact-based approach to social change. Having, by this time, read Marx, she understood the need to intervene rhetorically when and where the opportunity arose. She thus continued to hone her ability to turn government-provided numbers into material the public could use, and she watched as Lathrop built the US Children's Bureau on the belief "that data collection and scientific analysis would lead to reform."[81]

Anna Rochester's last publication for the National Child Labor Committee appeared during the fall of 1915, a pamphlet entitled "What State Laws and the Federal Census Say About Child Labor." Thereafter, the focus of her writing shifted to the issues Lathrop felt that the Children's Bureau could reasonably hope to address without risking its funding or continuance. The question of child labor was much too volatile for a publicly funded agency, so Lathrop elected to work on infant mortality and other quality of life issues for which she could count on wide support, especially from the women's clubs.

Thus, Rochester's first project, in 1916, was a report entitled *Facilities for Children's Play in the District of Columbia*. Since at least 1908, The General Federation of Women's Clubs had been working with the National Playground Association to establish places for children to play in localities across the country; the Children's Bureau built on this foundation. In *Facilities for Children's Play*, Rochester was able to make a strong argument, laced with irony, as she challenged the class-bound naïveté of her audience. The point she wished to make was that many children in Washington, DC, had few recreational opportunities. This information, she assumed, would be difficult for her audience to accept, based on their superficial knowledge of the Washington neighborhoods. Thus, she said:

> Persons who go through Rock Creek Park, around the Speedway, or out Sixteenth Street to the reservoir and then eastward to the Soldiers' Home hardly think of Washington as a congested city. And where these people go no congestion exists. However, if any of these pleasure seekers should turn off the Speedway and strike into the section known as "South Washington," or should drive east from Sixteenth Street through the district south of Florida Avenue, they would find neighborhoods not only badly congested but almost totally unprovided with recreation facilities.[82]

Rochester's sarcastic use of the term "pleasure seekers" to describe those who apparently are her primary audience is a signature move on her part, dropping an element of satire into an otherwise sober and direct government report—and is probably one of the reasons she was considered "one of the young radicals" in the Children's Bureau. The term "pleasure seekers" echoes her friend Sarah N. Cleghorn's 1913 quatrain "The Golf Links,"[83] and both contain echoes of Thorstein Veblen's 1899 study, *The Theory of the Leisure Class*. Unlike Julia Lathrop, who excelled in diplomacy, Rochester still had little patience with those who could not see beyond their own privilege, and she aimed to enhance their vision.

Rochester went on to point out the fact that not only did the law prohibit street play, but because the streets were defined from building to building, even the sidewalks had been eliminated as available play spaces. Of course, with no playgrounds nearby, the children played in the streets and on the sidewalks anyway, unwittingly becoming juvenile lawbreakers. Although Washington was clearly segregated, Rochester took special care to note the variances between conditions for white children and those for children of color.[84] She made it a point to consider not only the play facilities available but the availability of children for play in the first place, noting that a significant number of the children were, in fact, working. Of the white children surveyed, 31.8 percent reported that they were working on Saturdays, and of the children of color surveyed, 65.5 percent reported working on Saturdays.[85]

Following this report, Rochester worked on two publications: "Summary of Report on Mental Defectives" and "Governmental Provisions in the U.S. and Foreign Countries for Members of the Military Forces and Their Dependents," both contributing to larger efforts the Children's Bureau was making to address issues of concern to the public, thus bringing government unthreateningly into matters of the home and family, previously considered private. She passed the Civil Service Exam in January 1916, and on July 1, after almost a year as Julia Lathrop's private secretary, Rochester was promoted to the position of clerk (actually an editorial position). She continued to work with the press and began to take more responsibility for directing the efforts of others, providing outlines for research and shaping the material they produced.

Shortly thereafter, Rochester left to attend the annual conference of the SCHC; the theme this year was "Social Justice." Conference Chair Helena Stuart Dudley had invited Walter Rauschenbusch, who pushed the Companions to consider the injustices of capitalism: "The capitalistic system demands two groups," he said: those who owned land and machinery and those who had only their physical bodies with which to work. "Can these two groups be merged into one?" he asked of those who were naïvely still calling for a "reconciliation of classes." "Only if land and machinery is owned by workers."[86] Not a radical in the sense of wanting to see absolute equality, Rauschenbusch saw nothing wrong with differences in income, if those differences were earned. What he objected to was the use of income to gain power over the lives of others. "Property extorted by power is expended in excess and luxury, with no sense of sin." Yet, this power over others is thoroughly sinful, he insisted, framing the issues in terms his audience understood.

Rauschenbusch's plan for reform included the "Single Tax"[87]; public ownership of utilities, such as the water supply, mines, gas, transportation, and communications; and control over the food supply to ensure that no one should suffer want while others were enjoying excess. He spoke in favor of child labor laws, unemployment and disability insurance, legal recognition of trade unions, free legal representation, and public recreation facilities. "In short, get rid of the exploiters!" he beseeched his listeners.[88]

After several arguments for the spiritual necessity of organized social action, Companions took the unusual step of a "corporate stand" (a statement supported by all members of the organization), and a committee including Vida Scudder, Margaret Lawrance, and Margaret Shearman drew up a resolution to present to the General Convention of the Episcopal Church. They resolved "that the service of the community and the welfare of the workers rather than private profits should be the aim of every industry, and the test of its value; and that the Church should seek to keep this aim and this test constantly before the mind of the public."[89] Anna Rochester undoubtedly argued strongly for this move, the most radical ever undertaken by the SCHC. Coached by Vida Scudder and Julia Lathrop, she had grown accustomed to challenging men in positions of power on their own terms.

Following a number of other publications, Rochester wrote a press release dated July 4, 1917, entitled "Babies Dying in Poor Homes," a precursor to her largest study, published several years later, *Infant Mortality in Baltimore*. It was clear to her by now that infant mortality was not a question of morality or even primarily of education. Instead, it was linked most closely to the economic resources available to families, defined at that time as the father's income.

Probably because of this most important work, Anna Rochester did not attend the annual conference of the SCHC in 1917—and she missed meeting Grace Hutchins, attending for the first time. They would have to wait another two years before finding each other.

Rochester was taking on more and more responsibility at the Children's Bureau, now planning and supervising research and writing on the study of foreign child welfare and subtly scripting a pacifist message for readers. In February 1918, she wrote a lengthy article, published in the *Child Labor Bulletin*, entitled "Child Labor in Warring Countries." Although children in war zones were obviously deeply affected by the war, Rochester argued, children behind the lines were also paying a heavy price, as the conditions which might not have been good to start with had only deteriorated. She noted that the war time "falls into three fairly definite periods:" first, the chaos of the autumn of 1914, with the shift from peacetime production to war mobilization; then a reordering of societies, as the unemployed were drawn into wartime production; and finally, the conditions of 1917–1918, when the heavy pressure and increased hours were threatening to wear out workers, causing renewed calls for a return to protective legislation, which had been subject to exemptions in the quest for military victories.

Rochester focused specifically on the effect of these exemptions on women and girls, noting that "in Austria night work by girls was to be allowed more readily than night work by boys since the welfare of *boys* was essential to the defense of the nation"[90] (emphasis in the original). Moreover, she pointed out, when women were exploited, that exploitation was also visited upon their children, as "their homes are destroyed as truly as if the walls had been shattered in a bombardment."[91]

The study led to the conclusion that public opinion in the countries studied had swung around to the belief that childhood must be protected. The public had begun to realize that it was not mere sentimentality, Rochester alleged, but practical considerations that dictated laws protecting child workers. Worn-out or undereducated workers were simply less productive. And in countries devastated by war, she argued, the people were realizing that winning the war was not enough; the young people of those countries must have sufficient education, health, and vigor to rebuild the countries. Rochester ended the article by pointing out that as America entered the war, she should not have to relearn

Figure 2.3. Anna Rochester, 1918

the lessons already learned by the European nations; instead, America should take steps to pass laws protecting children against exploitive labor conditions and to ensure that school attendance laws were enforced. Despite Rochester's acknowledgment that the protection of childhood is an economically sound practice, she concluded by saying: "Our response to the needs of children in the present stress will be a measure of the spiritual level which we, as a people, have attained."[92]

This linking of the economic and spiritual is evidence of the continuing influence of the SCHC, and Vida Scudder in particular, on Rochester's thinking. Despite the fact that she had been unable to attend the 1917 annual conference, SCHC events and activities continued to be the focus of her life outside of work—and the two overlapped considerably. In April 1918, Rochester sought intercessory prayers from the Companions: "For Anna, Companion, more tenderness, more perseverance, less self."[93] And in May, it was probably she who requested that Companions pray "For the growth of the Children's Bureau into a national power for good."[94]

Although, like Julia Lathrop, Anna Rochester had little interest in personal success and sought only to be an effective agent for children, she felt pleased that her abilities were being recognized within the bureau. On September 16, 1918, her annual salary was raised to $2120, and in December 1918 she was made Director of the Publications Division of the Children's Bureau.[95] She continued working on her largest project to date, the study of infant mortality in Baltimore. Her mother, however, was quite ill.

In the January Intercessions Paper of the SCHC, Rochester asked the Companions to join her in Thanksgiving: "Anna, Companion, gives thanks for a long, rich companionship with her mother; for the blessing of friendship and affection; for the beauty and consolation of the Eucharist; for the crumbling of the old social order in European countries" (a reference to the October 1917 revolution in the Soviet Union). She also asked for their prayers for herself, in the category entitled Deepening of the Spiritual Life: "For all who disagree with accepted teaching, and especially for Anna, Companion, humility, sincerity, courage, imagination, loving kindness." The request was another signal of her coming rupture with the church.

Louise Rochester died on January 14, 1919. Although Anna had given thanks for a full life with her mother, she was clearly feeling bereft and alone during the spring. In the April 1919 News Leaflet of the SCHC, her poem "Lament" appeared, unsigned, an expression of disgust with what she felt was her preoccupation with self:

> I've seen the love that kindles till it leaps
> Beyond the self, consuming judgment,
> Transmitting life to pure and selfless flame
> But still I cherish self.
> Must I be poor and cold forever?[96]

Clearly, she was ready for a new life.

Still, Rochester continued to work on the study of infant mortality in Baltimore, a study which, by the time it was published in 1923, ran to several hundreds of pages of text, with 227 tables, twenty-two charts, and a map. In her Letter of Transmittal prefacing *Infant Mortality: Results of a Field Study in Baltimore, MD. Based on Births in One Year*, Grace Abbott, who succeeded Julia Lathrop in 1922 as head of the US Children's Bureau, said that this study "is the eighth and in many respects the most important of the unique and valuable series of infant mortality studies which the Children's Bureau made while

Julia Lathrop was its chief. Because Baltimore is the largest city studied by the bureau, the number of births is larger, and a more detailed comparison has been possible than in other studies."[97]

In fact, the detail is remarkable. Rochester considered all possible correlations provided by the material collected. And, although there are some anomalous findings, the study points unmistakably to the connection between low family income and high infant mortality. Moreover, the study makes an undeniable statement about racism, demonstrating that African American families have the lowest incomes and the highest rates of infant mortality. This high rate of infant mortality occurred in spite of the fact that African American mothers actually had better access to prenatal care than did mothers in some other categories, leading to the conclusion that prenatal care alone is insufficient to prevent infant disease and death. Moreover, because of low wages paid to African American men, African American women had the highest rates of working during pregnancy and working outside the home after the births of their children. These two factors correlated with higher infant mortality rates, and, although she did not need to include this information, Rochester made it a point to say that African American women were almost uniformly engaged in laundry and domestic work, heavier labor than that usually performed by white women. In another move that may have gone largely unnoticed at the time, Rochester revealed that African American families were having to pay much higher rents for their (often substandard) housing than were members of other ethnic groups. Thus a much larger percentage of their incomes was going to rent, leaving even less money available to provide the conditions that would be conducive to infant health and safety. When discussing child welfare, an acceptable topic for a woman, Rochester pushed the argument well into male economic and political territory, subtly indicting the capitalist system that fed racial and gender injustice.

Anna Rochester resigned from the Children's Bureau on June 30, 1919, several months after her mother's death, in time to move directly to Adelynrood for the summer.[98] In her final secretary's report of what had been, for a while, the multimember Washington "chapter" of the SCHC, she had a little fun with the language, noting that the Washington "Verse" had now been reduced to "two words" (that is, only two members remained).[99] Rochester, however, was moving into a new life, bringing her commitment to social justice and her growing concern over the frozen traditions in the Church into the newly formed Church League for Industrial Democracy as well as the Social Justice Committee of the SCHC, the Fellowship of Reconciliation (FOR), and the secular League for Industrial Democracy (LID). She was also on the verge of meeting the woman who would become her life's partner, Grace Hutchins, finally finding the "love that kindles till it leaps beyond the self."

Chapter Three

Grace Hutchins

The Evangelization of the World in this Generation

—motto of the Student Volunteer
Movement for Foreign Missions

Although Susan Hutchins was as devoted to her children as Anna Rochester's mother was to Anna, she did not leave us a narrative of Grace's early life. Instead, she chronicled the deaths of Grace's two older sisters, ages six and three, from diphtheria, just before and after the Christmas of 1887. Grace, two years old, survived, and she continued to commemorate these dates decades later, sending her mother flowers each year. This pattern of death and commemoration and, most important, survival, set early in her life was probably as important to Grace's development as Anna's single childhood with an invalid mother was to Anna's development. And, like Anna, Grace spent her young adulthood unlearning years of acculturation into the expected behavior of a woman of the upper middle class and developing a commitment to persuasion as a means to feminist ends.

Grace entered this world on August 19, 1885, the daughter of Edward Webster Hutchins, born 1856, and Susan Barnes Hurd Hutchins, born 1860. Edward Hutchins was a partner in the law firm of Hutchins and Wheeler and served as director of the Second National Bank of Boston and of the Boston Safe Deposit and Trust Company. Two children joined Grace after the deaths of her sisters: brother Henry, born January 19, 1889, and brother Ned, born August 10, 1890. During most of Grace's early childhood, the family lived at 113 Marlborough, moving in 1897 to a four-story brick house at the somewhat more prestigious Back Bay address of 166 Beacon Street, Boston. Both residences were well supplied with servants.

Like Anna Rochester, Grace Hutchins could trace her ancestry back to early colonists and was eligible for membership in the Daughters of the American Revolution. Her ancestors had fought in both the American Revolution and the Civil War (on the Union side). Susan Hutchins, in fact, was a Colonial Dame; she gave her time to the boards of the Home for Aged Women and the Boston School for Crippled Children, often opening her home to meetings.[1] Unlike Louise Rochester, she led an active life, engaging in charitable work and establishing a model for Grace to follow.

Harvard graduate Edward Hutchins served on boards of directors of banks and was a vestryman at Trinity Episcopal Church. Although respected and trusted by his peers, Edward Hutchins was socially and politically conservative, testifying against the nomination of Louis Brandeis to the Supreme Court[2] and either actively working for the prosecution

Figure 3.1. Grace Hutchins, 1900

on the Sacco-Vanzetti case or at least being friendly with those who did.[3] Grace absorbed her parents' social skills and deep sense of integrity, but as she entered adulthood, she began to interpret that integrity differently, clashing with her parents over political issues.

Grace was privately educated; she attended Miss Folsom's School in Boston. In 1898, when she was thirteen years old, the family traveled around the world, leaving in early September and returning in early April 1899. During the trip, the first of several she took during her lifetime, Grace sent back letters to her Aunt Grace, who collected and bound them for her. This record provides a glimpse of her incipient feminism as well as the class and race assumptions she would later discard.

The family rode the train from Montreal across Canada and embarked on the RMS Empress of China from Vancouver, British Columbia. When the ship arrived in Victoria, taking on more passengers, Grace displayed the racism typical of her class, describing Chinese workers traveling steerage: "There are three hundred and fifty of them, the most hideous, monkey-like looking things you ever saw. Their sleeping quarters are small, and they are packed in like sardines in a box." Still at the beginning of the journey, she had not yet taken account of her own position vis à vis others, commenting that "they are terribly dirty too, but rather interesting to watch. They eat their dinner where we can look down and see them, and it is very funny to see how skillfully they use their chopsticks."[4]

After disembarking in Yokohama for a ten-week stay in Japan, the family traveled by rickshaw to the Grand Hotel. Grace reported that "the young girls are some of them very pretty, and all are clean and neat, but the old women are ugly hags with blackened teeth and shaven eye-brows. It used to be the custom for all married women to do so but that barbarous law is not in force now. The small children are nearly naked, and filthy beyond measure."[5] In contrast, the Mikado's palace and a Shogun's castle in Kyoto impressed Grace with their elegance—the silken curtains, beautifully polished floors, ceilings lined with gold paper.[6] Grace and her mother spent hours shopping, "revel[ing] once more in the silk shop to satisfy mamma."[7]

Writing from the Kanaya Hotel in Nikko, Japan, Grace reported on an excursion the family took over the mountains from Ikao to Lake Haruna. Each family member selected a different method of conveyance, her mother choosing a chair carried by four men, her father electing to walk, and Grace wanting very much to ride horseback. Alas, she said, "It seemed fated that I should not get a horse-back ride, for there was no side-saddle in the town, and papa did not want me to ride a gentleman's saddle."[8] Finally, when she was able to have her horseback ride, she reported: "The guide and I went on horse back, and papa and mamma in rikishas! The pony I had had never had a ladies' saddle on before, and did not at all approve of it. As my legs were on the left he must necessarily keep to the left hand side of the road, and there was no getting him to the right."[9] Upon returning to the hotel, she enthused: "About six o'clock I alighted at the Lakeside Hotel so lame and stiff that I could hardly walk. A whole day of horse-backing is a good deal when you were never on a horse before, but I enjoyed it immensely and intend to learn to ride."[10]

After just having reveled in her new physical freedoms and mobility, Grace was alarmed at seeing the bound feet of the Chinese women she encountered in the next port, Shanghai, articulating in a few sentences her sudden understanding of embodied rhetorics. The fusion of pain, immobility, and beauty for women in Chinese culture left Grace wondering what the women would think of her feet. "We drove through the town and saw quantities of Chinese women with little bits of feet scarcely three inches long. For when they are born their toes are bent back and strapped. It is considered a mark of grace and beauty to have tiny feet, (I wonder what they say to mine)! but the poor women can hardly walk."[11] The sidesaddle had been a minor insult compared with this evidence of women's subjection. Consciousness was beginning to dawn for Grace, in the form of incongruity between her own struggle for physical freedom and the bound feet of Chinese women. China would later draw her back in her first attempt to remake the world for women.

This consciousness continued to develop as the Hutchins family traveled to Hong Kong, where Grace noted the ubiquitous presence of English soldiers in the streets, and thence by ship to Singapore, Penang, and Ceylon. In Ceylon, Grace made her first factory visit, seeing the process of tea manufacture. Women, she noted, were paid eight cents a day to pick tea, and in the "busy months must pick twenty pounds."[12] After describing in detail the process of drying, fermenting, grading, and packing tea, she observed: "I really think the rebellious Americans in the beginning of the Revolutionary war would not have thrown so many casks of tea over-board if they had known what a trouble it was to make it."[13] Grace's initial conversion, an understanding of class and gender in a colonial context, suddenly took a giant leap, opening pathways of thinking that she would follow for the rest of her life.

Leaving Ceylon, Edward Hutchins made the decision not to go to India, as they had planned, as travel there was said to be uncomfortable, and many people were afflicted with plague at the time. Instead, they set sail for Egypt on board the S.S. Australia, where Grace found that there was an English noblewoman, Lady Clarke, and her family, including a fifteen-year-old girl. "I don't dare make the young girl's acquaintance," she said, easily aware of her lower class position here, "for fear she should look down on a 'free born American.'" Typically, this reserve didn't last, and one day later she was reporting that the young girl was "exceedingly nice."[14] The "exceedingly nice" young English girl notwithstanding, when Grace saw an American cruiser, probably bound for Manila, she was ecstatic: "Hurrah! Hurrah! for 'America.' There is nothing like it in the whole world over!!!!!!!!" she exclaimed, having wearied of the English presence in all the places they had visited to this point.[15] It had not yet occurred to her to question the American presence in those places. Responding to a comment that her young cousins thought the US president should receive more homage, she said that she was glad that she was "a Republican, when the Japanese Emperor rode abroad, and the people for miles around him had to take off their hats and go down upon their knees. And he was just as ungracious in return as he could be."[16] Already Grace was developing her keen disapprobation for unwarranted hierarchies.

In the spring of 1899, Grace returned to her America, a comfortable source of pleasures and opportunities, temporarily putting aside the memories of the bound feet of the Chinese women and the labor required to produce the tea she consumed. In addition to their Beacon Street residence, the Hutchins family owned a large summer home, Fir Cone, in Brooksville, on Cape Rosier, near Castine, a town located on a peninsula in the East Penobscot Bay Region of Maine. The summer people in this area were known, rather ironically, as "rusticators"; in fact, the summer houses were far from "rustic," often being much grander than those occupied year-round by most people. They arrived each summer by train, and it was here that Grace made the acquaintance of Polly Porter, who was to become one of her closest, life-long friends. (Polly Porter was, from 1911, the partner of Molly Dewson, who later became a Democratic Party activist during the New Deal.) Polly Porter and Grace Hutchins spent idyllic days in their youth playing tennis and canoeing.

Life in Boston offered its share of diversions, as well. Memorial Day weekend (ca. 1900) included visits to several family members in a hired victoria (an elegant, high, four-wheeled open carriage with driver) pulled by two horses, as well as a dinner at Young's Hotel (considered to have one of the city's finest restaurants) consisting of what might appear to us now a rather astonishing menu: raw oysters, cold consommé, soft-shell crabs and tartar sauce, pluvvers, potato chips, asparagus with hollandaise sauce, and coffee and ice cream for dessert.[17]

Unlike Anna, Grace received early training in the social arts—and she learned that service was both a social and a religious responsibility. Confirmed in the church during Lent in 1901, she began to teach Sunday School at Trinity Church, Boston. After graduating from Miss Folsom's School and passing the exams for entrance to Bryn Mawr College, Grace did not, unlike Anna, leave immediately for college. Instead, she took a year off in order to "come out" in Boston society. During that year, although she attended the necessary social events, she also taught once a week at the Bennet Street Settlement in Boston and "visited" at Trinity Church Home for the Aged and at Children's Hospital, where her mother volunteered.[18]

Having been thus schooled to her social position, Grace began her studies at Bryn Mawr in September 1903, majoring in English and philosophy. Although she was a reasonably good student, her interests were not primarily academic. Devotion to outdoor pursuits and sports was a hallmark of the turn of the century "New Woman," who proudly displayed her muscles and tan line. Grace was the quintessential New Woman, serving as captain of the basketball and baseball teams and as halfback on the field hockey team, as well as placing second in the shot put competitions.[19,20,21] Another hallmark of the New Woman was her ability to form close friendships with other women. Grace's two closest college friends were Ellen Thayer and Margaret Reeve; she maintained the friendship with Margaret Reeve (later Cary) throughout her life and actively participated in the Bryn Mawr Alumnae Association.

In addition to excelling in athletics and creating strong sports teams, Grace devoted the better part of her intellectual energy to extracurricular religious studies, an attempt to fuse familial values with the attractive new opportunities for women. When she arrived at Bryn Mawr, she joined the Bible study class and was a member and officer of the Bryn Mawr Christian Union, a precursor of the Young Women's Christian Association. However, despite these activities, during her freshman and sophomore years she weathered a crisis of faith in which, she says, she "seemed to lose all faith and doubted the fundamental Christian truths."[22] What precisely caused her to renew her faith Grace did not say, but when she attended a student conference at the YMCA Silver Bay conference site in June 1905 at the end of her sophomore year, she "worked out a course on The Life of our Lord to teach in a Bible Class, and found faith in the Incarnation."[23]

Thus reinvigorated, Grace returned to Bryn Mawr in the fall of 1905 and threw herself into religious activities with renewed fervor, teaching the freshman Bible class and serving on the Christian Union board, first as secretary, then as treasurer, and finally, in 1906, as president. In March 1906, she experienced a moment of illumination while attending a national conference of the Student Volunteer Movement for Foreign Missions (SVM) in Nashville, Tennessee. "At the Nashville Convention in 1906," she said, "I began to see that Christianity was essentially missionary, and that the non-Christian peoples needed its message."[24] By rhetorically reframing the community in which she had been raised, Grace opened a space for herself to move actively into the world. What's more, the SVM not only welcomed but encouraged women to become missionaries.

The SVM, founded in 1886 at a student conference in Mount Hermon, Massachusetts, and organized by the immensely popular revivalist Dwight Moody, was an outgrowth of the Young Men's Christian Association. Within five years there were missionary bands on 350 campuses in the United States and Canada. The movement grew exponentially: in 1890, there had been only 934 American Protestant missionaries in the field; by 1915, there were 9,000.[25]

The watchword of the movement, "The Evangelization of the World in This Generation," expressed both a sense of urgency and a belief in the centrality of persuasion. In other words, as Grace realized, if one is to identify as a Christian, one, by definition, *must* engage in persuasion. One of the speeches Grace heard during the Nashville conference was an address by Rev. Hunter Corbett, entitled "Permanent Factors which Make China a Most Inviting Field." Among other things, Rev. Corbett said: "The very essence of the Christian religion is missionary." And, he pointed out,

> A question of overwhelming importance is, What are Western nations going to do with the millions of the Chinese? Or perhaps the question may be asked, What are the Chinese going to do with the people of the West in coming centuries? To evangelize China and treat her justly was never so urgent as now. It is not simple duty, it is true wisdom, it is wise warfare.[26]

Corbett was not the only one to speak in military metaphors. The evangelization of China—and other countries—was seen as part and parcel of an otherwise unspoken

American imperialism. Grace had no interest in—or understanding of—China's strategic importance or Chinese markets or raw materials, the subtext of some missionary efforts. Instead, she sought to change the lives of Chinese women—and change her own life as well, removing herself from the social obligations impressed upon her during her precollege year.

The persuasive presentation of Jesus as Christ had two distinct elements. There were, of course, the efforts to convert the nonbelievers, but equally important were the attempts to persuade parishioners back home to support the missionaries and their schools, hospitals, and churches. Speaking of the need to educate those in the church about missionary endeavors, Rev. John Bancroft Devins outlined the requirements for articles in religious magazines. These articles, he said, must be brief, attractive, and informing. They must, above all, be truthful and have present-day interest. And they must picture real life. Invoking a romantic ideal, he claimed that the writers of such articles are most often born, not made, but he supposed that with some effort and a good editor anyone might produce an effective article.[27]

Conference-goers also heard in great detail about other religions, not to appreciate or understand them but to fix Christianity in their minds as the "only absolute religion." The Right Reverend Thomas F. Gailor, Bishop of Tennessee, addressed himself to this point, arguing that "it is a paradox but true that even an educated heathen, an educated unbeliever, has to defend his error in Christian language and from a Christian point of view. Last year, when a defense of Chinese civilization was attempted in the book 'Letters of a Chinese Official,' it had to be written by an Englishman at a Christian university."[28] It was Christianity's "moral qualities" that had made science—and presumably colonialism—possible, he averred.

In addition to persuading the students that Christianity was the only true religion and that they must become persuaders themselves, conference organizers and speakers planned a special set of meetings just for women. Una Saunders of Somerville College, Oxford (and a member of the SCHC), spoke on "The Missionary Possibilities of the Women Students of the World," telling women conference participants that they had a special reason for entering the mission field: "the great mass of the women in the non-Christian countries can only be reached by the women of the Christian countries."[29] She called upon the women students to advance the Kingdom of God by going wherever they might be of use, mentioning China as the place of greatest need, as did many other speakers during the conference. Indeed, SVM organizer Sherwood Eddy commented, years later, that " 'China was the goal, the lodestar, the great magnet that drew us all in those days.' "[30]

Perhaps the greatest influence on Grace came from her friend Margaret Reeve. After the conference, Grace began to attend meetings of the Bryn Mawr SVM Band, initially to hear Reeve speak on Africa. The band decided to hold extra weekly meetings for all those who had decided to be missionaries but who had not yet signed the declaration cards. Grace did not come to any more meetings that year, but her friend Mary James, with whom she would subsequently work in China, did start attending, as did Louise Pettibone Smith, who would go on to become professor of biblical history at Wellesley and would figure again much later in Grace's life as the co-chairman of the American Committee for the Protection of Foreign Born during the 1950s.

According to Grace's own account, it was in June 1906, just before she left for the Student Conference at Silver Bay at the end of her junior year in college, that she determined she would become a missionary. She signed the declaration card on June 19, 1906. When she filled out the detailed application form three weeks later, she described herself as "very strong physically."[31] Although she had spent a year being presented to Boston society, a prelude to marriage, her decision now would propel her into a life of service in communities of women. This move can be read as Grace's first articulation of her rhetoric of the whole person. Although she had no interest in a life as a Boston society matron, her decision to apply to the mission field was not just an escape route. Her experiences and understandings to date—the bound feet of the Chinese girls and women, the laboring of Chinese women in the tea factory—had made it clear to her that, as important as written and spoken persuasion were, systemic social change required more than discourse. Indeed, her own comment about her physical strength acknowledged the fact that she intended—and wanted—to place herself entirely in the situation to which she was applying.

As exciting and filled with promise as the mission field was, immediate departure was out of the question; not only was her family unwilling to allow her to leave directly after college, but the policy of mission boards was to accept only those who had passed their twenty-fifth birthdays, to ensure clarity of decision and maturity in their volunteers. After college, Grace Hutchins returned home, shocking her parents with her belief in equal suffrage yet acquiescing to their desire that she remain in the family home. She spent the next five years working in the church and preparing herself for service as a missionary. She did not have many options: there were few employment opportunities for women, and she depended upon an allowance from her father for support. Still, she continued to attend meetings designed to recruit new missionaries. At a conference in New York City, she met Bishop Logan Roots and his wife Eliza Roots for the first time. After meeting the Rootses, Hutchins was determined to work with them in the Hankow district of China. She said, "Each day has deepened my appreciation of the present unparalleled opportunity for advance of the Kingdom all over the world, especially in China."[32]

In 1909, as Anna Rochester was becoming involved in the SCHC, Grace Hutchins sent in her application to the SVM and then continued to do so every year while developing her teaching skills by leading a Bible class in Trinity Sunday School. She was also a member of the New England Territorial Committee of the YWCA and served as president of the Massachusetts Junior Auxiliary, the young women's division of the Women's Auxiliary of the Board of Missions of the Episcopal Church.[33]

Grace Hutchins's church-related activities during these years enabled her to forge new friendships with other young women who were active in the church, chief among them Lucy Sturgis and Grace Lindley. In 1910, when, at age twenty-five, Hutchins sent her application to the Episcopal Board of Missions, she asked Grace Lindley to write one of her recommendations. Lindley's response was overwhelmingly positive. In her final summary, she said: "It is difficult for me to say just what I want to for I am aware of the danger of over praise, but I do not know of any young woman more fitted for missionary service than Miss Hutchins. One of her friends [probably Lucy Sturgis] summed it up by saying 'I think she is so wonderful that I can't talk about her!'"[34]

Lucy Sturgis could not locate or invent adequate language to express her feelings for Hutchins, but Sturgis and Hutchins had no lack of racist and colonialist discourse to call upon (unwittingly) for their article for "The Churchman's Supplement" to "The Upward Path." The article, later turned into a pamphlet entitled *Pickaninnies' Progress*, was intended for Episcopal Sunday School students at the junior (ages approximately 9–12) level. It follows the enslavement of a West African girl and her transport to the United States, her work for a white family, her conversion to Christianity, her marriage and the births of her children, the Civil War, and the allegedly improved lives of African Americans in the South after the war, with special attention paid to an Episcopal school for African American children in South Carolina. Sturgis and Hutchins provided study questions in order to help teachers direct discussions of the material and suggested appropriate biblical passages for reading with each chapter. The argument of the booklet reinscribes the paternalism and cultural and religious imperialism that characterized the missionary movement in general.[35]

Despite claiming to be unable to talk about Hutchins, Lucy Sturgis pulled herself together and wrote an acceptable, if bland, recommendation, saying that she had found her to be "earnest, tactful, a good organizer, & faithful" as a leader and "level-headed and zealous" as a group member.[36] Both Lucy Sturgis and Grace Lindley knew Hutchins well, and they show us an early picture of Hutchins and the qualities that defined her.

When Grace Hutchins herself filled out the application form for the Board of Missions, she answered the questions clearly and confidently, with even perhaps a suggestion of humor. When asked if she could cook, she replied "a little." And when asked if she could cut, fit, and make clothing, she said: "Could, if I had to." The third question asked if she could keep accounts; to this question, she answered definitely: "Yes."[37] In fact, most of her work had been with the Church in the women's organizations, teaching and raising money for missions.

Why, then, did Hutchins not sail for China in 1910, as she wished? She was twenty-five years old and in excellent health, and she wanted more than anything to go. The answer can be found on line 9 of her application: "Are your parents living, and are they in sympathy with your purpose?" She responded: "They are living. One of them is in sympathy with my purpose, and the other only partially." Hutchins's father supported her desire to serve in the mission field; her mother was less enthusiastic. A month later, she wrote to John Wood at the Board of Missions, telling him that a visit from Bishop Roots had helped to sway her mother toward allowing her to go, but, she said, "I am convinced that her health is not yet such as warrants my leaving. If I wait now I am very sure, as are my father, mother, and the Bishop, that I may before long have my mother's full sympathy in the matter."[38] It seems probable that Susan Hutchins was perimenopausal at the time; this would explain Hutchins's confidence that time would solve the problem of her mother's health.

The decision about whether Hutchins should go to China was not confined to the Hutchins household, however; a significant element of the church and civic hierarchy was invoked in order to forestall Hutchins's application, should she have insisted upon pursuing her dream. On August 21, Rev. Alexander Mann, rector of Trinity Church in Boston, wrote to Mr. Wood at the Board of Missions, saying: "I have reason to believe that her going to Hankow would be not only *strongly* opposed by her Mother who is a good deal of an invalid, but would also have a very serious effect upon her health (her mother's health, I mean)."[39] In a postscript to the letter, he added: "I may add that I understand that in two years the danger to her mother's health (and possibly reason) would be over."[40] A few days later, John Wood received letters, from the bishop of Massachusetts, William Lawrence, and from Judge Gudger, arguing that "her present duty is at home."[41]

So for two years, Hutchins remained in the family, hoping that her mother and the hierarchy of male authorities would agree to send her at some time in the not-too-distant future. In a stubborn challenge to the invalidism of her mother and a celebration of her own physical health, Hutchins enrolled in the Sargent School for Physical Education (now part of Boston University), a private academy devoted to the education of women in the field of physical training. Established in 1881 by Dudley Allen Sargent, the school emphasized several principles: "the physical superiority of civilized peoples, the connections between muscles and morals, the need for educators to embrace physical culture, a moderate view on intercollegiate athletics, and concern for the health of females."[42] Students were measured and tested when they matriculated at the school and activities were designed to address each woman's weaknesses and to build on her strengths.

Although more forward looking than most, Dudley Allen Sargent was not completely free from the prejudices of his age. In 1913, he said, "It is a physiological fact that women are nearer the infantile stage than men—they have the thin, highpitched voice, the smooth, soft skin, and the rounded limbs of a young child. There can be no physiological condition without a corresponding mental condition, and in many ways women are children."[43] Nonetheless, he believed that at least some of women's debilities were the result of centuries of conditioning and that "female bodies 'had been held in arrears and were pining for freedom of movement and exercise.' "[44] If Hutchins did not complete the entire course of study, Sargent's antifeminist attitude might explain why.

Hutchins finally sailed for China on March 19, 1912. She had been appointed to China at the request of Bishop Roots. On April 13, she arrived in Shanghai and proceeded on April 15 up the Yangtse River to Hankow, arriving in Wuchang on April 19, 1912. Wuchang, a city of approximately five hundred thousand at the time, is across the river from Hankow; both are six hundred miles from Shanghai. This area had been the center of the revolution during the previous few months; yet, as Bishop Roots commented in his annual report, the military forces were particularly careful not to harm the missions or missionaries. He argued that this was the case because people realized that "the ideas behind the Revolution came in no small measure from the foreign strangers within their gates."[45] Perhaps this information helped Hutchins's parents to acquiesce and approve her plan to go to Wuchang; it no doubt became part of Hutchins's personal commitment to the possibilities of revolution.

The Episcopal mission journal *Spirit of Missions* reported Hutchins's arrival in December 1912, saying, "In sending Miss Grace Hutchins to the work in China, Trinity Church, Boston, is giving of its best. She is the only daughter of one of its vestrymen, and has been for some years an active worker and a leader in mission study classes."[46] This assessment of Hutchins, which defined her as the daughter of a vestryman, seems to have been taken almost verbatim from the recommendation form of Alexander Mann, the rector of Trinity Church. Despite this official definition, Hutchins herself went to China specifically to teach at St. Hilda's School for Girls in Wuchang. She joined Katherine Scott, who had arrived during the previous September. One of the features of the revolution was the increased permission and desire for women's education. Mission schools made this possible, and the government encouraged them.

Women made up some 60 percent of the North American missionaries in China[47]; many had been recruited by the SVM.[48] What was the attraction? The mission field provided opportunities for achievement and adventure in the company of other women that were rarely available to single women in traditional American life; in fact, in many respects it offered a continuation of the camaraderie and challenge of the recently formed women's colleges. Indeed, "explicit in many of the SVM recruitment addresses to women was the argument that as missionaries they would be able to pursue career goals that would be denied them in America."[49] Moreover, the SVM promoted a sense of "generational solidarity" that contrasted with the previous generation's expectations for women.[50] This solidarity encouraged women to volunteer for the mission field, but once they arrived, they often shifted their loyalty to the intergenerational communities of women who worked together at the mission stations. Although some women married men they met during the

Figure 3.2. Grace Hutchins, ca. 1916

course of their service, many women who chose to be missionaries did so precisely in order to escape the intense pressures of conventional expectations of courtship and marriage.

As Edward Carpenter argued at the time and Blanche Weisen Cook has reiterated more recently, women (and men) whose primary attachments are to those of their same sex must not be assumed to be heterosexual.[51] The mission fields provided splendid opportunities for women to live lives of "homogenic love," in Carpenter's words, whether those lives took the form of singular, long-term attachments (of which there were many) or a more diffuse devotion to a community of women. Thus, Hutchins's aspiration to serve as a missionary in China—specifically in a girl's school where she would live and work with other women—can be seen as an expression of her desire to continue a life that was woman centered as well as a gesture of independence from traditional family and social expectations. And an independent, woman-centered life at that time meant, perforce, a life that was socially, politically, and intellectually active.

Hutchins established more long-term friendships during this time. On October 1, 1913, Deaconess Julia Clark arrived at the Hankow mission station; following that, on January 28, 1914, Dr. Mary Latimer James, one of Hutchins's Bryn Mawr classmates, arrived to take charge of the women's ward of the mission hospital. And on March 28,

1914, Helen Hendricks, a musician from Chicago, came to St. Hilda's. All were to remain Grace Hutchins's friends throughout her life.

Meanwhile, Hutchins threw herself into the development of the school, which had been reduced to nine students before she came, a result of the upheaval attendant upon the revolution. Because financial support from the United States determined much of the success of the missions, Hutchins wrote her first fund-raising article since *Pickaninnies' Progress* during the summer of 1913.

In 1910, the Woman's Auxiliary to the Board of Missions had dedicated $10,000, raised through the United Offering,[52] to construct a new building for St. Hilda's. Realizing the importance of keeping donors informed of the progress made on projects they were supporting, Hutchins described the development of the new building for St. Hilda's in "Outside the Little East Gate" for the July 1913 *Spirit of Missions*, following the rhetorical advice of Rev. Devins of the SVM. Establishing time, place, and characters involved in purchasing the land, Hutchins narrated the conflicts that had to be resolved, pointing out that "our affairs were concerned with the international questions of the loan to China and the recognition of the Republic, because the railroad plans depended so largely upon those questions."[53] With this statement, she demonstrated a dawning awareness of the indivisibility of missionary work and the larger governmental aims of the countries from which those missionaries had come. However, as a fundraiser, she maintained her focus on feminist goals, using the medium of the missionary magazine to advance these goals. She ended with the message that now fewer girls would have to be turned away from the education they desired, a message sure to appeal to her audience of largely middle class, native-born women in the United States. At this point, in the summer of 1913, both Anna Rochester and Grace Hutchins had begun their practice of working at the edges of existing organizations, pushing them into areas that were beyond their traditional scope.

Recognizing in Hutchins an intellectual and social progressivism that he found congenial, Bishop Roots wrote to her on September 22, 1913,[54] advising her about an article he had just re-read in the July issue of the *International Review of Missions*. According to Bishop Roots, Mary M. P. Hogg argued in "The Place of the Foreign Missionary" that "'the place of the foreign missionary is to be the comrade instead of the superintendent and organizer, and that the noblest fruits are won through personal intimacy.'"[55] He asked Hutchins to read the article and let him know what she thought about it. He feared, he said, that many of the mission staff would not agree with it. But what troubled him even more than this was the fact that he did not know how to change behavior once one admitted the truth of Hogg's claim. He noted barriers of race and environment, but said that he thought barriers of money were the most difficult to overcome. Although he asked that she discuss the matter with Katherine Scott and "even the Deaconess," he doubted that she would get much help from them. Still, he said, "If we could, within the next five years, see our way more clearly on this point, I think we could count it a proof that God is guiding and helping us."[56] He ended by thanking first her—and then God—for the "steadfastness and devotion and kindness you bring to all your tasks." Clearly Hutchins had matured since the publication of *Pickaninnies' Progress* and now shared with Bishop Roots a social vision that others—adhering to a more imperialistic approach to missions—did not understand or accept.

Before leaving for a trip home to the United States, Hutchins wrote another fund-raising article for the *Spirit of Missions*. Some fifteen years after she first began to comprehend embodied rhetorics in the bound feet of Chinese women, Hutchins crafted a material way to respond. Appearing in the August 1914 issue, the article "St. Hilda's

Outside the Wall" continues narrating for readers the story of the new building they had financed for St. Hilda's School. Hutchins appealed to her readers as women who wanted to protect other women, this time adapting biblical language to deliver a feminist message. She repeated the sermon of a "Bible-woman," a woman trained by the mission to preach to other women. This woman told the story of the raising of Lazarus and said that although people might not think that today people were raised from the dead, she had herself witnessed such a miracle. A girl had been brought to the mission nearly dead from violent mistreatment by her husband. Although everyone prayed for her, they were not sure she would survive. But she did, and now she was at St. Hilda's, helping with the younger children. " 'She is strong and useful. It is as if she had been raised from the dead.' "[57]

During the summer of 1914, Hutchins's father paid for her to come home for a visit. When Hutchins left to return to China, Lucy Sturgis wrote a heartfelt letter describing her feelings on having seen Hutchins again and having to endure another parting. She had decided not to see Hutchins off at the train station but to allow Hutchins's brother Ned that privilege. With Hutchins safely on board the train bound for the West Coast and for China, Lucy Sturgis finally cobbled together some language with which to express herself: "You are literally the only person I know upon whom I dare lean my whole weight, so to speak, without any fear of being a burden. It is partly, I think, because you lean, too, and we prop one another up. Whatever it is, you are the biggest kind of a comfort, and if you were a man, I would marry you tomorrow."[58] Sturgis never did marry a man, but Hutchins maintained the friendship throughout her life, not only through personal commitment but as part of her larger project of feminist political solidarity.

As soon as Hutchins returned to Wuchang from the United States on September 17, the school moved into its new facilities; within a few weeks, a new teacher, Dorothy Mills, arrived, bringing the total of American teachers to five. In his report for 1914–1915, Bishop Roots reported that although tension was high between China and Japan and there had even been some fighting on Chinese soil, the district itself had been peaceful.

Bishop Roots's report was not exceptionally reassuring, and Hutchins's parents continued to worry about the dangers in Wuchang. By November 1915 they asked her to come home at the end of the school year. There were active struggles taking place in and around Wuchang beginning in the summer of 1915 between forces of the president of the Chinese Republic, Yuan Shih-kai, who had aspirations to become emperor, and those resisting this monarchical movement.[59] Hutchins had written to Bishop Roots after receiving her parents' letter, asking permission to leave her position and sail for the United States on July 1, 1916, a request the bishop undoubtedly found disheartening.

Hutchins's close relationship with Bishop Roots was underscored in a letter she received from his wife, Eliza Roots, two days after Christmas 1915. Thanking her for the gift of a vase, Eliza Roots exclaimed "Your heart is as big as the world, I think!" She went on to say that Hutchins's faith and patience would surely be rewarded someday—and, in the meantime, she should know what a comfort and help she was to Bishop Roots, as well as an inspiration to everyone else.

What accounted for this effusive praise was not only Hutchins's growing understanding of political and economic forces but her application of that understanding to her work at St. Hilda's. She had been responsible for humanizing the place, moving it away from a practice heavy on "discipline." She would replicate this practice over and over throughout her life, in one organization after another, with greater and lesser degrees of success.

The warm friendship with Bishop Roots would grow chillier as time passed, however, in a way that illustrates the larger divisions that would come to affect Hutchins and

Figure 3.3. Fund-raising brochure from St. Hilda's School for Girls

Rochester. As Grace Hutchins sailed for the United States, a man by the name of Frank Buchman was preparing to sail in the other direction, heading for China in an attempt to evangelize that country in a way that had not been done before: by aiming for the highest echelons of Chinese power brokers. Not all missionaries were enthusiastic about Buchman's approach, a highly emotional, individualized emphasis on sin, but Buchman managed to gain control of the semiannual missionary conference held in Kuling. At the conference, he raised what would turn out to be one of his primary emphases henceforward, charging that "'absorbing friendships'" or "'crushes'" between missionaries were "unhealthful." According to Buchman's biography, "the reaction was explosive." Bishop Roots, chair of the committee organizing the conference, was "inundated with protests," and he conveyed his displeasure to Buchman, who remained unmoved. Shortly thereafter, for a variety of reasons, Bishop Roots directed that Frank Buchman should leave China. However, Buchman had undoubtedly realized the power of the charges that he had leveled, and he would come to focus on same-sex attraction as chief among sins.[60] Buchman's campaign both fueled and fed on the pathologizing of same-sex relationships. For reasons that remain unclear, Bishop Roots, over the years, drew closer and closer to Buchman's organization, later named Moral Re-Armament, and farther and farther from the progressive approach that he had shared with Grace Hutchins. In later years, although not addressing Buchman's "sexual sins" campaign directly, Hutchins would make clear her disdain for Buchman and Moral Re-Armament.

Before she left, Hutchins had recommended to Bishop Roots that Katherine Scott take over the principalship of St. Hilda's, and she had assured him that she intended to be "an agent of the Mission stationed in Massachusetts." True to her word, Hutchins worked to raise funds to construct a new women's wing for the Church General Hospital in Wuchang, where Dr. Mary James and Elise Dexter, who had arrived in January 1915, were stationed. Although she had only arrived in the United States on August 3, by August 30 Hutchins had written to Bishop Lloyd seeking the appointment of another nurse to the Woman's Department of the hospital in Wuchang. Quoting from a letter she had received from Elise Dexter describing the miserable conditions under which they were working and their resultant depression and feeling of abandonment, Hutchins suggested that an advertisement be placed in *Spirit of Missions* requesting nursing applicants. Bishop Lloyd demurred, fearing that such a move would only draw out those who were not well suited. Instead, he recommended prayer and said, "I know the people are waiting just because the need is so acute. The trouble is to find them."[61] Thus began Hutchins's struggle with the denominational hierarchy. Officials were happy to have her work in China and raise funds but less enthusiastic about allowing her to control the direction of the work.

Nonetheless, within another month, Hutchins was thoroughly involved in the fundraising effort. One of her first activities was a trip to St. Louis in October 1916 to attend meetings of the Board of Missions preceding the triennial General Convention of the Episcopal Church. The Executive Committee and the Board of Missions of the Domestic and Foreign Missionary Society of the Protestant Episcopal Church passed two resolutions during these meetings. The first, passed by the Executive Committee, expressed regret at Hutchins's resignation and commended her for her work at St. Hilda's, and the second, passed by the Board of Missions, approved the fund-raising effort for the Church General Hospital requested by Bishop Roots. With that approval, the Women's Committee of the Church General Hospital in Wuchang, China, was formed, with Hutchins as the chairman. The *St. Louis Star*, for its part, featured Hutchins and other missionaries on the Daily Pictorial Page of Friday, October 13, 1916, headlining the page "Women Who Are Carrying Religion to the Heathen."[62] Although she kept the article, Hutchins was no doubt annoyed by the headline, which bore so little resemblance to her experience. It would not be the last time that public media would reshape her work to fit agendas other than hers.

Having been given a new task, Hutchins began speaking to women's groups about the need to build a new Church General Hospital and, specifically, to finance the women's wing. Along with Bishop Roots, Eliza Roots, and Dr. Mary James, she wrote a pamphlet entitled "Our Plan for the Church General Hospital, Wuchang: A Statement of the Most Urgent Need in the District of Hankow." Hutchins's article "A Day at the Woman's Department of the Church General Hospital" describes a typical day at in the Woman's

Department, with the leg of a patient's bed falling through the rotten floor and Dr. James and Elise Dexter each having had only two hours of sleep because of overwork. Quoting from a letter written by Elise Dexter—as she had in her letter to Bishop Lloyd—Hutchins ended her short article pleading for another nurse to go to Wuchang.[63] She had succeeded in her desire to advertise the position, stretching the male-controlled discourse to place at the center those issues that were of concern to the hospital's independent women. We may wonder whether the description of such miserable conditions would have inspired anyone to answer the call, but perhaps the spirit of adventure and sacrifice would have been strong enough in some to make the position seem appealing.

On the last page of the pamphlet, the names of the members of the Woman's Committee are listed; beneath the list is the message: "It is hoped that a men's committee may soon be formed and that some interested and influential layman may be found who will be willing to give his time and energy to the cause and take the chairmanship." This question of the gendered division of effort would prove to be more than footnote material; in fact, it can be seen as a harbinger of a serious power struggle that would arise within the church.

When the "men's committee" was finally formed, it was called the "National Committee for the Church General Hospital," and it was charged with raising funds within the church as a whole; the Women's Committee was raising funds within only the women's auxiliaries and the Sunday Schools. The women, however, had generated sufficient funds for the women's wing of the hospital by February 1917, before the National Committee had even been formed. Predictably, this disparity in commitment caused problems. In February 1917, Hutchins wrote to Janet Waring, the treasurer of the Women's Committee, in a letter accompanying more checks from women's auxiliaries, "When the main committee of *men* gets organized here in Boston with Mr. Ludlow as field secretary, we may expect a much more widespread campaign."[64] A few days later, she wrote again, with more checks: "There is another meeting here tomorrow of the 'National Committee' to make plans for getting men. But Dr. Wood agrees with us that the Woman's Committee is still very necessary 'if only as a Godly irritant to the men.'!"[65]

Although Hutchins remained humble for quite some time and encouraged the development of the National Committee, her patience was clearly being tested by April 1917, when the men of the National Committee asked her to serve as "publicity secretary" in order to take care of their publications needs, and the Board of Missions' representative chastised her for not channeling all the publicity requests through him. "I don't in the least mind giving up the 'publicity' job which belongs to a man anyway," she remarked pointedly to John Wood, foreign secretary of the Board of Missions. She then mentioned that she had forwarded Mr. Wood's letter regarding publications to Mr. Mason, who had turned over to her the publicity work that Mr. Wood had asked of him, adding, "It doesn't matter who does it so long as it is done quickly and thoroughly."[66]

The situation did not improve when Hutchins discovered that the pamphlet being prepared by the Board of Missions staff failed to mention the Women's Committee at all, listing only the members of the National Committee despite the fact that all the money raised to date had come from the Women's Committee. She wrote to John Wood again: "It seems strange to have a leaflet in use with the names of a committee who can do so little in comparison with what Miss Littell, Miss Waring, Miss Tiffany, Miss Ely, and Mrs. Ames have done." The men of the National Committee now were able to meet alone, she said, but did not feel that they were responsible for raising money, only for forming local committees—"which they have not yet succeeded in doing." She continued, warming to her subject: "You requested the Boston New China Fund Committee to organize the

National Committee largely in order to interest laymen. Let us hope that interest is coming. When you sent that request to Boston and overlooked the existence of a Women's
Committee, we were humble enough to be glad and to hope that men were going to take
it all up in a larger way. But months have gone by. . . . Now I think the time has come,"
she said, "for you to recognize that there *is* a Women's committee. Fortunately for your
peace of mind, Miss Littell is an anti-suffragist and has restrained me when I would have
hammered you! I am ashamed to have my own name appear on that National Committee when the others of the Women's Committee are ignored. . . . The receipts," she said,
"seemed to come mysteriously from somewhere without anyone's efforts!"[67]

Hutchins had been exerting a great deal of effort, however. To raise the funds for
the Women's Committee, she spoke to Episcopal women's groups across the northeast,
telling stories of her work in China, especially of the terrible conditions for women—girls
and women bought and sold, the practice of having multiple wives, wife beating, child
enslavement, and child prostitution—creating a rhetoric of embodiment that her audience
could counter materially with their donations. She stressed the unity among the protestant
missions and the fact that the Chinese people had little use for the doctrinal debates that
absorbed Americans: "Mrs. Li [who had been in the Church General Hospital, having had
a complete hysterectomy] talked with me saying there was really no fundamental difference between the Wesleyan Mission and ours. I quite agreed. Her friend in the next bed
chimed in. 'And I am a Mohammedan. That also is just the same thing.' "[68] Hutchins was
becoming increasingly aware of the dichotomy between the pronouncements of churchmen
and the realities of women's lives.

Telling stories, connecting the work of the mission hospital to the political realities of
China, and demonstrating the centrality of women to political and social intervention and
change, Hutchins persuaded her listeners to send money to support the desperate hospital
staff and to provide them with an adequate space in which to treat patients. Hutchins
made sure to follow up her stories with specific needs and the costs to fill those needs.
She always came away with money, both small and large amounts.

Yet despite the financial success of Hutchins's persuasion, the question of control
over publications continued, and Hutchins finally simply moved on, taking her fund-raising
ability with her. In the summer of 1917, Dr. William Gardner asked if she would be willing to work part-time teaching the New Testament at the New York Training School for
Deaconesses, and she accepted the position, which was to begin with the fall semester
of 1917. Hutchins also had been invited to join the SCHC on February 15, 1917. Soon
she was devoting herself to the Companions with the same fervor that she had previously
given to the Women's Committee of the Church General Hospital. In the fall of 1917,
Hutchins began work at the New York Training School for Deaconesses. What was offered
as a part-time position had become full-time, and Hutchins moved into St. Faith's House,
a large building with space for classrooms and a dormitory next to the Cathedral Church
of St. John the Divine in New York City. At the first meeting of faculty, on September
26, Hutchins began anew her efforts to democratize an organization, offering to serve as
advisor to the student government. She also noted that a large room was available for
students to engage in indoor exercise.

Classes began on October 3, with Hutchins offering a course in the New Testament,
emphasizing the idea of the Kingdom of God[69] and posing questions specific to conditions
in 1917: Can we make a defense of war based on the New Testament?[70] Although she
posed this as a question for her students, Hutchins's clear answer would have been, "No."
This position did not always endear her to her colleagues or to her superiors.

Adding to her duties at the school, Hutchins enrolled in courses nearby at Union Theological Seminary, studying the New Testament in Greek during the first semester in order to improve her reading and interpretive abilities. Here she did often find support for her ideas and in fact made more lasting connections. Her life at St. Faith's was not unlike her life in China: she lived her work, her own embodied rhetoric, from the moment she arose until she retired at night. At the end of the first month, she reported on her activities, adding: "N. B. First month, have wasted much time in talking! G. H."[71] One wonders whether the time was really wasted, though, as Hutchins's daily presence in the lives of her students and her willingness to share her ideas with them was probably as important as the formal training she offered. In fact, some of the students became her close friends, absorbing from her a vision that was not always congruent with that officially offered by the Training School.

It was during this initial month that the first clash of ideas took place on an administrative level at the school: a West Indian student "with a strain of Negro blood" applied for admission. Apparently some of the teachers were unsure whether the school should accept her, because of her racial background. Although the minutes of the faculty meetings do not record the tone of the conversation, they do indicate that Hutchins argued for the student's acceptance and said that she would like to have her in her class. However, in a turn of events the irony of which we may hope was not lost on the recalcitrant faculty members, a few days after this conversation took place, the student notified the school that she would be enrolling in a PhD program instead.[72]

The next serious confrontation between Hutchins and the school administration took place that fall. As she told it later, Hutchins was threatened with dismissal from her position for the crime of posting on the wall of her room cartoons from the radical magazine *The Masses*. It is likely that the cartoon in question, a masterpiece of planned incongruity, was one by George Bellows, published in July 1917 on page 4, which showed Jesus in a striped prison uniform, chained hands and feet, and with the suggestion of a crown of thorns accompanied by the text: "This man subjected himself to imprisonment and probably to being shot or hanged. The prisoner used language tending to discourage men from enlisting in the United States Army. It is proven and indeed admitted that among his incendiary statements were—THOU shalt not kill and BLESSED are the peacemakers."[73] Hutchins's view of Jesus as a radical social activist attempting to establish the Kingdom of God on earth was in place by this time. Although she apparently reached some sort of agreement with those who objected to her wall décor and thus avoided dismissal from her position, the event did not dull her radical edge. She maintained her identity of returned missionary but had by this time located herself well outside the theological mainstream.

Hutchins hoped to establish a culture of democratic governance among students at the New York Training School for Deaconesses because she saw the Kingdom of God on earth as egalitarian, a place that women were responsible for building as well as men. By May 15, 1918, the constitution and bylaws of the student government were completed. The plan called for officers, to include a president, vice president, secretary and treasurer, who together would form an executive board. The bylaws outlined an honor system for the students as well as a series of house rules designed to make the living situation comfortable for everyone. They also designated two standing committees, one to develop the social life of the school and one to promote athletic activities. Faculty retained control of all academic matters, health, household committees and housekeeping, and overnight absences. The student association had charge of lights, quiet hours, conduct in examinations, and evening-out registration. During the following year, the students voted on such matters as whether to tax themselves in order to pay for new baskets for basketball and whether students would give one hour per week to Red Cross work (the outcome in the latter case was yes). Yet even this relatively minor assignment of responsibility to students was called into question within the next two years.

During a Monday morning talk shortly after the fall term began, Hutchins spoke to her students on "our corporate life as a life of intercession,"[74] another iteration of her concept of a rhetoric of the whole person. What Hutchins seems to be suggesting by this statement is the idea that a life lived with others means a life of connection with God through concern for those with whom one lives as well as for others outside that corporate life. She developed this statement a month later, proposing in a faculty meeting that each individual had a responsibility as a member of the household for the community life of the house.[75] This vision of individual wholeness through responsibility for the community became Hutchins's most cherished principle, a conviction that offered a serious challenge to the American creed of rugged individualism that benefited some and left many others impoverished. She lived in accordance with this principle and dedicated herself to persuading others to adopt it.

Hutchins had found a community in the SCHC in addition to that of St. Faith's, and she was increasingly taking responsibility not only for the corporate life of the SCHC but for the community's efforts to reach out to others. In January 1919, Hutchins chaired a second conference on church unity held at the YWCA National Training School in New York, with her faculty colleague Adelaide Case assisting her as secretary. Methodist deaconess Winifred Chappell joined the committee—and moved into Hutchins's circle of friends. Although she had been a full member for only a little more than a year, Hutchins was actively recruiting new Companions by the spring of 1919. She sponsored Ruth Kent of the American Church Mission at Hankow, China, as well as Lucie Myer, her student and advisee at the New York Training School for Deaconesses. Hutchins's decision to invite Lucie Myer, who came from a home offering her no independent income, served to confront the class structure of the Companions. As she often did, Hutchins made her statement by means of a material action rather than relying only on a written or spoken argument. On an individual level, Hutchins was making every effort to dissolve barriers of race and class and to reconstruct gender to allow for women's independence.

Hutchins continued to seek and find support for her work at Union Theological Seminary, this time in a course on religious education with George Albert Coe, author of a key 1917 text in the field: *A Social Theory of Religious Education*. The book, and presumably Coe's class, attempted to answer the question: "What consequences for religious education follow from the now widely accepted social interpretation of the Christian message?" Coe's answer to this question articulated the same ideas that Hutchins had been expressing: It is not enough simply to add a new duty to our present lives. "We are required to organize the whole of life upon a different level."[76] Coe made it clear that he envisioned a "divine-human industrial democracy," and thus religious education as he saw it was not merely the process of repeating the standards of the past but was a dynamic process engaged in continual revision of those standards. Crediting John Dewey with providing the concepts upon which he built his method, Coe dedicated the book to Methodist minister and Union Theological Seminary faculty member Harry F. Ward, "who sees and makes others see." Ward would prove to be another significant person in Hutchins's life, from the early 1920s through the 1960s.

Life at St. Faith's became more difficult for Hutchins, however, after the spring term of 1919. Deaconesses Jane Gillespie and Romola Dahlgren were placed in charge. Hutchins wrote to them, thanking them for allowing her to continue teaching at St. Faith's and enthusing over their appointment: "The more I think of it, the happier I am about St. Faith's. All will be well, with the school. The coming year will be the very best it has ever known in all its history."[77] However, there are no extant minutes of faculty meetings after Gillespie and Dahlgren arrived, suggesting that the democratic governance system had been replaced by a more autocratic method—exactly the type of educational leadership that Hutchins had struggled to remove at St. Hilda's in Wuchang. Moreover, by December 1919, the student government was questioning its viability and, after a lengthy debate, entertained a motion to dissolve: " 'Believing in the principles of student government but realizing that under present conditions it is unwise to continue it at St. Faith's House, I move that we withdraw from our agreement.' "[78] Although the motion was defeated, a second motion, that the constitution and bylaws be revised, was seconded and carried. There are no student government minutes after this meeting, pointing to the fact that, in practice, the first motion might as well have carried. Hutchins remained at St. Faith's for the 1919–1920 academic year, but she was either forced or chose to resign after the General Convention vote in September disallowing deaconesses any leadership functions in the church and reorganizing women's work. *The Alumnae Bulletin* of June 1920 says rather obliquely: "The change in organization of Women's Work in the Church has taken from us another whose personality and teaching have been vital influences in the life of the school for the past three years—Miss Grace Hutchins."[79]

Rebuffed once again by the church hierarchy, Hutchins maintained her connections to the missionary community[80] but turned specifically to the SCHC, which offered her a place where her work was valued and a community wherein individuals took responsibility not only for the corporate life but for life outside the community. At the 1919 Companion Conference, the New York Chapter was selected to plan the 1920 conference, and both Hutchins and Anna Rochester were appointed to the committee on the conference program.[81] Hutchins and Rochester thus began to spend more time together, collaborating on the program, the theme of which was "Sacrifice: A Creative Force." On January 11, 1920, the New York Chapter held a day of devotion at St. Faith's and the Cathedral Church of St. John the Divine. Along with Rochester, Ann Mundelein and Josephine Starr, Ellen Gates Starr's niece, were present. All would come to be close friends during the next few years.

Hutchins provided a meditation on the subject of sacrifice. Following the example set by Jesus, she said, we must live, not die, in sacrifice. We must become pure, she argued, "honest consecration down to the bottom of our souls," and provide reasonable service, using our minds to the utmost. Following Hutchins, in the afternoon, Professor Dickinson Miller spoke on sacrifice in relation to social welfare. Democracy, he said, calls for the most difficult of sacrifices because democracy is governed by the exchange of ideas. "We induce people by persuasion. We govern by discussion. We must, therefore, sacrifice our feeling. We must cultivate the open mind."[82]

By the end of this year, Hutchins had moved out of St. Faith's and was beginning a new life, cultivating an open mind and committed to government by discussion and persuasion, outside the rigid and gender-biased constraints of a church institution. She continued to look for ways to consecrate herself and to take responsibility for the life in the larger community, finding her efforts welcomed in the SCHC, the CLID, the FOR, and the New York School of Social Work. Most important, her life with Anna Rochester was about to begin.

Chapter Four

Community Consciousness

They tell us the chief characteristic of women is the instinct of nurture. The whole trend of thought is leading us to apply this instinct to all suffering and neglected people. But by nothing so much as work, is our pity cleansed of sentimentality. We learn to discriminate between the good and the bad in the present social order. We realize, as we never could from the narrower world of home, how the coming of justice depends on an interweaving of the social and the individual, of external structure and of character.

—Anna Rochester (SCHC, *A Church Yearbook of Social Justice*, 339)

Grace Hutchins and Anna Rochester found each other in the Society of the Companions of the Holy Cross, but it was the combined influence of the SCHC and the activist Church League for Industrial Democracy that drew them together in a common purpose—and ultimately a partnership—giving their lives a meaning each had been seeking. One December evening in 1920, Hutchins, then 35, and Rochester, 40, had dinner with Horace Fort, a 1919 graduate of the Yale Divinity School and the treasurer of the CLID. According to records kept by Sally Cleghorn, Horace Fort,

> in the course of conversation about how to live more usefully and beautifully, in the present world, expanded the idea of a Community of men who might follow [with modifications and variations] Mr. Simpson's propertyless plan of life.
>
> After some time spent in this discussion, Grace Hutchins said, "Why not a community of women?" This thought had been in her mind for some time; for four years, indeed.
>
> "I'm game," said Anna Rochester, who had not been thinking of it so long.[1]

Following their conversation, Horace Fort did not create a men's community, but Grace Hutchins and Anna Rochester immediately set about establishing a women's collective household in the Chelsea-Lowell district of New York City. Although Hutchins had lived as a missionary in China for four years and had lived at St. Faith's while teaching at the New York Training School for Deaconesses, this household would be another step toward crafting her own wholistic feminist rhetoric. Taking seriously the Companions' ethos, Hutchins and Rochester were moving into a world of Christian radicals, among whom was William Simpson, a Franciscan friar, who argued that property is antithetical to love.[2] Linking Simpson's principles to Edward Carpenter's and Vida Scudder's calls for simplicity and same-sex engagement in social renewal, Hutchins and Rochester's vision for the household asked that members engage in productive labor and that each member live on no more than the wages of the average working woman: $18 per week. The household began operations on February 15, 1921. It was an experiment that would teach Hutchins and Rochester much about the processes of capitalism that they had not learned as daughters of privilege and that would challenge them to take their rhetorical feminist principles and their partnership beyond the limits of women-only space.

At the Companion Conference the previous summer on "Sacrifice: A Creative Force," both Hutchins and Rochester had contributed energetically to the discussions, attempting to push the group toward more radical conclusions. During an extended discussion of the Sacrifice of Exclusiveness, a study of the person of Paul, Hutchins had pointed out to the group that Paul had "sacrificed many of the privileges of his citizenship, his conservatism, his wealth."[3] On the following day, Helena Stuart Dudley had explained Jesus' sacrifice, pointing specifically to the difficulties that stand in the way of fellowship, especially wealth, self-love, egotism, desire for popularity, and fear of life. "Get away from loneliness," she said, "making it your purpose to be a giver of life." To this, Rochester, who had struggled so long with loneliness, added:

> We sacrifice in order to reach a point of good outside of self. We stand as two groups, looking at things, back to back, all looking for the Kingdom on earth. One Group looking for the Kingdom on earth too eagerly, seeing externals; the other dwelling too much on the interior life, contemplative. Can we not turn about, and see the world with each other in the foreground?[4]

Rochester's reference to "two groups" points to the crisis that was developing in the SCHC. Father Huntington had stressed to the Companions before the 1920 conference that the society was an organization devoted to prayer rather than to activism, reminding them that there were plenty of organizations outside the Companions to which members could turn in order to accomplish work in the world.[5] Yet much had taken place outside the society to which Companions were responding. The Episcopal Church had voted against allowing women to assume leadership positions in the church. The overthrow of the czar and establishment of the new Soviet Union was cause for celebration among some Companions and alarm among others. The mood of the country was clearly conservative, as war protesters continued to be held in prison, and Emma Goldman and other lesser known noncitizens were deported in massive shipments. Using Vida Scudder's Platonic methodology, Rochester tried to effect a religious merger of the two opposing camps, those advocating prayer alone and those pressing for action.

In her meditation ending the conference, Hutchins also addressed the tectonic shifts taking place. "We are a society for prayer," she said, echoing Father Huntington, "not for corporate action, but the individual *must* act as moved by the Spirit. Let us rejoice in it. Some people fear a great bloody revolution," she went on. "There is no such thing in sight. The 'revolution' desired by many is here. . . . Some of us," she said pointedly, "must become more articulate, more willing to drop our so-called 'noble reserve.'"[6]

Indeed, both Hutchins and Rochester had been struggling with the question of how to drop their "noble reserve," as the church offered fewer and fewer opportunities. After leaving the New York Training School for Deaconesses and with it her studies at Union Theological Seminary, Hutchins had enrolled in the New York School of Social Work, later to be incorporated into Columbia University but at this time an independent institution.

Figure 4.1. Helena Stuart Dudley

The course of instruction was two years and emphasized the case study method.[7] Students did field work during each of the school year's three terms.[8]

In the fall of 1920, while living at 94 Macdougal Street[9] in Greenwich Village, Hutchins was placed at the State Public Employment Bureau for her first field work assignment. Her second assignment required that she engage in labor typical of that available to working class women, so, from December 8–20, she rolled cigars full-time for Seidenberg & Company.

Those two weeks in the cigar factory made a profound impression on Hutchins, providing the case study for her 1932 pamphlet on "the double burden" for working women:

> Working for a time in the cigar-rolling department of a large tobacco factory owned by the American Tobacco Co., the writer found that practically every one

of the 200 women in the department had home responsibilities before and after the day's work, which began at 7:15 a.m. and ended at 5:45 p.m. It was winter, dark when we went into the factory in the morning and dark when we came out at night. The sun might as well never have shone for all we saw of it through the small dirty windows of the plant.

Yet many a woman worker had already done at least an hour's work, preparing the breakfast, getting the children up and ready for school or day nursery, and the beds made before she came to the factory. When she washed up, ready to leave the plant at night, the woman was planning what she would buy on the way home to cook for supper, and it would be 7 p.m. before she could have the food ready. If she had children it was late in the evening before she had finished the house-work.[10]

Conditions such as these compelled Hutchins to seek a place where she could "*act as moved by the Spirit,*" yet she wasn't convinced that professional social work held the answer. Rochester, likewise, continued to edit her work on infant mortality, but was otherwise at loose ends. Horace Fort's innocent suggestion on that December night provided just the necessary catalyst to draw Hutchins and Rochester together in a setting that would simultaneously allow them to develop a committed partnership and enable them to explore new methods of Christian Socialist engagement.

By January 10, 1921, they had located a large house in the Chelsea-Lowell district of New York, 352 West 27th Street. Hutchins, Rochester, Josephine Starr (Ellen Gates Starr's niece), and Edith Klein went to look at it, and they agreed to rent it for $150 per month. This sum seems ridiculously low to us now, but if we recall that they had agreed to live on the wages of the average working woman—$18 per week, or $78 per month—then we can begin to understand the scope of the venture they had undertaken. Several residents would be required in order to make the rental payments and do the housework under the system they had created.

Their first task was to renovate the place, which was in a state of serious disrepair. It was a big house, described in the house annals by Sally Cleghorn as having a three-room basement, supplied with a coal range, a gas range, and a sink, opening onto a small yard; a main floor consisting of two living rooms with marble fireplaces and two bedrooms; a second floor with a room for the oratory,[11] a double bedroom, another living room, and two single bedrooms, plus a bathroom; and a third floor with two bedrooms, a bathroom, and a trunk room. Cleghorn also exclaimed over the copious closets and cupboards ("nineteen in all!"), clearly a source of amazement to her in that era when many houses came furnished with none at all.[12]

Sally Cleghorn narrated the moving-in process, slyly acknowledging the project's affront to class and gender imperatives: "Grace amazonianly brought the chairs by hand and foot into the house. To bring some later furnishings she borrowed a baby-carriage." Rochester apparently provided an endless stream of puns—her method of disrupting language codes—as they scrubbed and cleaned, until "their faith and elbows conquered, and it subsided into a clean and sightly order." This was not the old "clean and sightly order," however, but a new one that had been in the making for several decades. Vida Scudder, undoubtedly recalling her own 1902 novel *A Listener in Babel*, wrote to Ellen Gates Starr, saying: "You give your prayers I know to the great Plan of Anna and Grace and our darling Josephine. If I were twenty years younger, and alone, I should be of their sweet company. God bless them!"[13]

Scudder had been struggling with the postwar tensions that were developing within the Episcopal Church and specifically within the Companions. A year before this, Ellen Gates Starr had decided that, having been hurt by events that took place at the 1919 General Convention, she would convert to Roman Catholicism. Her "defection" devastated Vida Scudder. Rochester and Hutchins's later move would be equally painful, but for now she was excited by their prospects.

Sometime after the move-in date of February 15, household members realized that they were unwittingly sharing the house with large numbers of cockroaches. They decided to save the cost of a professional exterminator and spray the place themselves, recording their efforts in two cartoons which simultaneously poked fun at their own piety and celebrated their conquest over the roaches—masterpieces of planned incongruity offering an early suggestion of their conversions away from the institutional church. They maintained a chapel upstairs but also brought ecclesiastical images and language downstairs to demonstrate their distance from lives unbothered by cockroaches and other earthly matters.

Continuing to operate in a liminal social space, household members discussed the question of a name for the house, suggesting "Saint Eugene's" to honor Eugene Debs, or "Unsettlement House," a successor to the settlement house movement aimed at unsettling the current order. Finally, they decided upon "Community House," a combined reference to the community houses of the religious sisterhoods and brotherhoods, the wish to let go of the noxious individualism fostered by American society, and the desire by the residents to be truly members of the neighborhood community in which they were living. The name also contained echoes of Edward Carpenter's arguments for developing communi-

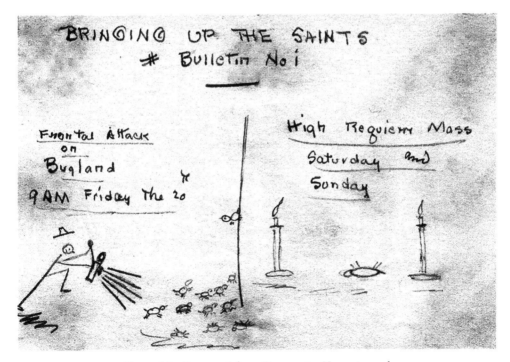

Figure 4.2. Cartoon 1 from Community House journal

Figure 4.3. Cartoon 2 from Community House journal

ties from the isolation of individual lives, especially the lives of those who loved others of their same sex. Having named the house, the group devised a name for themselves as well, drawing on Hutchins's experience in China: tong-wu-li, Chinese for "housemate."[14] They also called each other "sister," following the practice of the Episcopal sisterhoods.

Soon the household was attracting more new members. Helen Hendricks, who had worked with Hutchins at St. Hilda's, moved in, but within a few weeks she left to return to her home in Chicago—a foreshadowing of the household's continuing instability and eventual demise. Despite its volatility, the household meant much to those who spent time there. When she left, Helen Hendricks wrote to the household, telling them, "I may not be a radical, but to live in an atmosphere of unselfish striving toward ideals that express heights and depths of nobleness and service, is to probe a little deeper into one's own motives and push a little higher one's own ideals toward a goal of unselfishness."[15] Hutchins and Rochester struggled to shed their "noble reserve," but Hendricks's message suggests that it nonetheless permeated the household. It would take a couple of whacks from the "invisible hand of the market" to push them into even more radical efforts.[16]

This was an uneasy time for radicals and progressives. The Socialist Party had been decimated by the inability of its members to agree on support or nonsupport for US entry into the war, and new struggles had emerged around the question of support for the Soviet Union. In 1912, the party had had 108,000 members; by 1920, only 26,766 remained. Attorney General A. Mitchell Palmer was enthusiastically raiding the offices of just about any organization suspected of promoting progressive thought, including the offices of the party.[17] Many party leaders either languished in prison, having been convicted on sedition charges during the war, or had been deported. Lives of working people were difficult; unemployment never fell below 10 percent during the 1920s, and working conditions for those who were employed were harsh, often featuring long hours and physical dangers.

Meanwhile, the conversation, if it can be called such, continued among the Companions of the Holy Cross about the nature and means of creating the Kingdom of God. Shortly after the household's launch, Emily Morgan wrote at length in her annual letter about the need for Companions to respect and understand each other. More conservative Companions worried about the positions taken by members such as Rochester and Hutchins, whereas radicals in the group were afraid the others "were missing the great vision of a world released from economic bondage."[18] Morgan went on to make a distinction between the rights of Companions as individuals and as members of the society, a distinction that some Companions, most notably Rochester and Hutchins, may have found wanting.

Emily Morgan's admonishment came from her heart, and it was designed to keep the society together. She freely admitted that her thoughts were not theoretically based, saying that because she kept being asked to pray both for and against the Bolsheviki, she thought she should find out what the Bolsheviki were all about and so purchased some books by Lenin and Trotsky. But when some people in Boston were arrested, she said, she hid the books under her summer clothes.

So, in short, she asked the Companions to adopt "two household pets" at Adelynrood. "They are two bears, but not of the fierce variety. One is plain 'Bear,' the other is 'Forbear.' If we constantly pet them, they will respond to our caresses and become a real asset not only in the leading of our corporate life but during any meetings we may have together during the year. In fact, all Companions might adopt them as household pets."[19] This comment was probably difficult for Rochester to appreciate, as she had struggled for years to let go of self-involvement and class bias—she *was* reading Lenin and Trotsky—and now undoubtedly felt that others were too easily being confirmed in their prejudices, rather than being asked to "see the world" in a new way, "with each other in the foreground."

Hutchins and Rochester joined other Companions in the Fellowship of Reconciliation, where members were raising some of the hard questions. On April 9, when the council of the FOR met in New York, Margaret Shearman, a Companion of long standing and also a member of the fellowship, raised the question of what to do with unearned income.[20] The problem of investments had long bothered some of the Companions, and now Margaret Shearman was raising it in another venue. The fellowship responded by appointing a committee to deal with the matter. The same question had come up at a meeting of the CLID, where Roger Babson, a Christian capitalist, had been a featured speaker, arguing for "The Christian Approach to Investments."[21] Babson's 1920 *Report*, according to Richard Roberts, who also wrote for the FOR-related magazine *The World Tomorrow*, said: " 'The value of our investments depends not upon the strength of our banks as upon the strength of our churches. . . . The religion of the community is the bulwark of our investments,' " on which Roberts commented sharply: "It is a novel and startling doctrine that religion, the life of the soul, should be encouraged because it secures investments." More to the point, he said, "The business of religion is . . . to secure the man himself, and if necessary to secure him against his investments."[22]

At the same time, Emily Morgan was reminding the Companions of their vow of simplicity. Yet she recast the vow not in matters of labor or finance but in terms of personal organization and punctuality as means to simplify life. Were the Companions, along with some other religious progressives, shifting gradually away from the revolution that Ellen Gates Starr and Vida Scudder had prayed for toward an easier, more personal religion? Perhaps the answer is that although some Companions had developed their radicalism within the context of the Companions, the group as a whole, led by Emily Malbone Morgan, wished to retain its original shape, emphasizing thanksgiving, simplicity, and intercession.

Rochester and Hutchins were finding more affinity with Richard Roberts now than with many of the Companions. Still, their household, living simply and collectively, retained the spirit and shape of Adelynrood. Living simply was foundational, but Hutchins and Rochester felt the need to speak out about, as well as live, their principles; a rhetoric of the whole person required both. To this end, Rochester and Hutchins agreed to coauthor a book applying the principles of Jesus to the present-day world, to be used in study groups. In June, they left 352 and went up to Hutchins's family's summer home in Maine in order to have an uninterrupted span of several weeks in which to work. It was during this time that their love and partnership solidified, grounded in common work.

Although the popular magazines were now dispensing sexology to the masses and some women were beginning to identify with the categories dreamt up by such sexologists as Havelock Ellis and Richard Krafft-Ebing,[23] Hutchins and Rochester belonged to an earlier generation and class of women who had found liberation in same-sex educational and religious institutions. Whatever the "experts" might say, they remained invested in the culture of college and of the Companions who celebrated partnerships between women devoted to creating a better world. Indeed, they were well acquainted with many pairs of women who were committed to each other and to their work in the world.

Their work at that moment was creating an argument that would sway their religious colleagues toward a more radical interpretation of Christianity. Rochester and Hutchins drew from several sources they had each explored during the previous decade in order to construct the book—to be titled *Jesus Christ and the World Today*—using as a foundation the Synoptic Gospels and adopting interpretations found in *The New Social Order* by Harry F. Ward and *The Untried Door* by Richard Roberts. Suggested reading included these materials plus work by Shailer Matthews, a well-known modernist theologian, and Ernest Findlay Scott, with whom Hutchins had studied at Union Theological Seminary, as well as William Z. Foster's book on the 1919 steel strike. They also consulted John R. Mott's *Intercessors: The Primary Need*, the little booklet that Bishop Roots had sent to Hutchins in 1915, and Kirby Page's 1921 book *The Sword or the Cross*.[24] These sources served their purpose at the time, but it would not be long before both Rochester and Hutchins would find them inadequate to address conditions in the world.

For now, following the principles of the CLID and the FOR, Hutchins and Rochester attempted to bring religious discourse to bear on secular conditions. Although their ideas were not entirely original, they were pushing the conversation into new territories—and, perhaps more alarming, they were women publicly engaging in theological, economic, and political arguments. They were still talking to themselves, however, or at least to people with backgrounds and resources very much like theirs, asking them to consider: "What is the relation of individual conduct to the root evils of the industrial world and to the social revolution? What can we learn now from the decisions and experience of Jesus in relation to the social and economic problems of his day?" Hutchins and Rochester continued to frame issues for their readership with appeals to morality, a method that they would later have to rethink. Comparing the social conditions in Palestine during the time of Jesus with those in the United States in 1921, they asked readers: "What visible witness are Christians bearing today to the way of Christ in the apparently impersonal but actually powerful relationships that make the web of our industrial and national fabric?"[25]

They directed the financially comfortable reader's attention to a question that pre-occupied the Companions—where to locate the line between luxury and simplicity. The answer to this question, they suggested, is to live in such a way that one is not divided from the life of the multitude, a key element in Hutchins's rhetorical scheme. This argument against separateness led directly into a chapter on Jesus' work in the community. "Why are people drawn to Jesus?" they asked. "Why should a group of IWW, casual laborers, despised by American citizens, pause before supper, raise tin mugs of coffee and drink to 'Comrade Jesus'?"[26] Because Jesus shows us the meaning of life, they answered, and the meaning of life is to be found in community with others. Why is this so difficult? One of the most significant barriers to understanding and action is the press, they asserted, which "is deliberately committed to the satisfactoriness of the present order." A Christian can-not count on the opinions with which he is surrounded. "The newspaper he reads, and pamphlets and books fed out to the public by the possessing class do not encourage him to go deeper than the results of war, the disorganization of credits, and the unreasonable demands of labor"[27]

Jesus, they pointed out, defined the issues: covetousness, desire for domination, and race prejudice. Setting an example for others to follow, he let his name be associated with that of John the Baptist—an outsider—and chose a life of conflict over a life of security. "There is no such thing as neutrality," they asserted in a pointed comment to Companions such as Emily Malbone Morgan who sought to maintain group cohesion by minimizing discussion of controversial topics. Unless people will seek information behind that given by the newspapers and commit to "any sacrifice that the solution may involve," it must be assumed that they are "on the side of those who are comfortable and who think that all is right with the world."[28] At the end of the chapter entitled "The Conflict," they provided a scenario for nonviolent revolution, asking: "What if a hundred thousand men, in the spirit of goodwill, should take over the control of some one great industry? With a declaration that they would produce goods not for private profit, but for the benefit of the community, they could assume the responsibility for that industry."[29] The study ques-tions they provided asked readers to consider whether they would join a union—and, if so, which union: the United Textile Workers, affiliated with the AFL, or the Amalgamated Textile Workers, a union aiming for control of the textile industry. After considering the conflict the chapter addressed, readers were asked to decide under what conditions laws should be broken in order to uphold what is morally right.

In the penultimate chapter, Hutchins and Rochester asked a question that is central to all rhetorical efforts. Seeing Jesus as the consummate rhetorician and organizer, they asked: Was Jesus successful? And they equivocated in answering this question. In fact, those who attempted to follow Jesus were still persecuted. At the same time, they saw hope in the fact that those who had devoted themselves to unpopular causes—including Karl Marx, Mary Lyon,[30] and Susan B. Anthony—were beginning to be recognized. It was not enough, however, that *individuals* sacrifice. If we must depend upon the sacrifices of individuals, progress will be painfully slow, they argued. Rather, they said, in a plea for collective action, "when a group, acting with common purpose, will lay down its life for the sake of others, the world will see the hastening of the Kingdom of righteousness."[31] Preparing for the final chapter, Hutchins and Rochester called for a conference, asking readers to meet for the confession of sins and adoption of a code of organic ethics. This, they said, might mean the end of the Church as we know it—the end of comfort, of beautiful buildings, of ceremonies. But the Church in her death, they insisted, would find new life.

Returning to their earlier question about Jesus' success, Hutchins and Rochester closed the book assuring readers that Jesus' resurrection meant success and not defeat. What's more, "the day is not yet when our conflict can be a merely interior matter, an imaginative sharing of the sufferings of Christ."[32] They followed this admonition with hard questions for the 1920s reader of means: Are we earning with work and not with investments? How are we to arrive at the facts of current international situations, such as the recognition of the Russian Republic or the US military occupation of Haiti and Santo Domingo?[33] The Christian will never be a lawbreaker for his own advantage, they pointed out, and where the laws are unjust, the Christian will work openly and fairly to change them.[34] The claim that a Christian would never break the law for his own advantage unfortunately suggested that Christians should disregard their own oppression, an interpretation of sacrifice that might help to explain Rochester and Hutchins's later choice not to address their own erasure in linkages between same-sex desire and various forms of illness and corruption.

Reviews and dust-jacket blurbs attest to the fact that, once published, Hutchins and Rochester's message attracted a loyal cadre of readers, those willing to entertain the expansion of Christian discourse beyond church walls. But it took several months for the book to find a publisher and to be seen on bookstore shelves. Originally, the Church Service League of the Episcopal Church sponsored the book; then, for reasons at which we may guess, the League withdrew that sponsorship.[35] After several other similar rejections, Hutchins and Rochester approached George H. Doran, who agreed to publish it, but only if they would shoulder some of the costs of publication. The book appeared, published by Doran, on May 23, 1922, one of many publications underwritten by Rochester and Hutchins. This practice of supporting the media that carried their messages became a crucial element in Hutchins and Rochester's material, wholistic rhetoric, as they realized that established publishers did not welcome their arguments.

In the meantime, the household was changing, and Hutchins and Rochester were becoming more involved in the activities of the FOR and the CLID, offering their services to the speakers bureau of the FOR, although they continued their membership in the SCHC. Rochester, with Vida Scudder, also belonged to the Intercollegiate Socialist Society, an organization separate from but related to the Socialist Party, founded by Florence Kelley and others to attract young intellectuals to socialism. During the summer of 1921, Josephine Starr left, telling the housemates with regret in a long letter that she couldn't handle both her paid job and housework responsibilities. That same month, Rochester wrote to Lucie Myer, Hutchins's former Deaconess Training School student, welcoming her to the household, telling her that "hearing of you constantly from Grace I feel that you are already one of the Community." She continued, as if her words could construct the collective: "And our life at 352 is real, and not playing at simplicity. . . . The possibility of such a Community seems to me so very great, but much depends on our sense of belonging together and taking counsel on all our plans."[36] More, however, would depend on economic realities, as they would all soon learn.

Before returning to the house and meeting Myer, Hutchins and Rochester attended the annual conference of the SCHC at Adelynrood. The subject that summer of 1921 was Joy, appropriate for the happiness they both felt at having found each other, having completed the manuscript of their book, and looking forward to returning to the household. Yet Rochester did not hesitate to remind SCHC members that joy was not a personal or private matter. Leading an intercession service, she recapitulated the message of the book: that it is the responsibility of the Church to create a just world. Even in seeking to encourage thankfulness within the Companionship, Rochester articulated topics that others might have wished to leave unsaid, asking that God help them

> to discern the true causes of thankfulness that lie deep in our confusion and
>   suffering today,
> In the nation's political life
> industrial life
> In our relations with Negroes
> In our own church
> In the relation of our Church and other Churches
> In our own communities
> In the Companionship.[37]

Figure 4.4. Adelynrood chapel

After the conference, Hutchins and Rochester continued their efforts to build the New York City household on SCHC principles, holding a meeting to determine the direc- tion of the collective for the coming year. In another attempt to create permanence, members planned to have rings made signifying their commitments to each other, to the community, and to a life of service. That fall, the household functioned reasonably well, and residents Rochester, Hutchins, Lucie Myer, Ann Mundelein, and Mary Ellen Daniels took pleasure in the most mundane of household tasks, following a detailed and whimsical housework chart of Rochester's design. Still, changes were afoot. Sally Cleghorn arrived in November 1921, having been eased out of her position as a teacher at Brookwood Academy when A. J. Muste, Dutch Reformed minister and pacifist turned trade union activist, took over the site for a labor training school.[38]

The Brookwood transition had not been an easy one, in part because it meant that Cleghorn could no longer work with William (Bill) Fincke, who, with his wife, Helen, founded and ran the school for children based on the principles of the FOR. Other faculty included Bill Simpson and Spencer Miller, Jr. Cleghorn was, very privately, in love with Bill Fincke, a fact she dared to share with only a few close women friends because he was, obviously, already married to Helen.

Arriving in New York, Sally Cleghorn threw herself into household chores at Com- munity House, exchanging her past struggles for new ones. "I'd thought myself a pretty fair cook," she related, "but Grace and Anna, with a quarter my experience, proved infi- nitely better. They turned their fine minds to their cooking, and served delicious meals." Hutchins and Rochester may have had "fine minds," but they also had had the benefit of newer cooking technologies, having been accustomed to "the hot intensity of gas," while Cleghorn "baked according to the milder warmth of coal." One day, Rochester invited Julia Lathrop to dinner at Community House, and Cleghorn confessed a decade and a half later in her autobiography that "I baked my scalloped oysters so solid and dry that Anna suffered, I know, real distress at serving them to her beloved guest; but she said nothing, and I was too mortified myself even to thank her for the eloquent kindness of her silence."[39]

Cleghorn was not the only one struggling with the material conditions. Ann Mun- delein documented her experience, this time finding in Hutchins the source of warmth: "The mornings are cold and dark and sleepy on the third floor these December days, and it is oh—so hard to get up—there seems to be no joy at all in life—when suddenly out of the darkness comes the sound of the coal shovel, and saintly Community Consciousness and the dragon Sleepiness have a struggle, and Com. consciousness finds itself coming downstairs." Encountering Hutchins fueling the coal-burning stove, she said, "makes half awake Com. Consciousness have a very warm, comfy feeling inside. And if she isn't too sleepy to appreciate, the Fireman makes quite a charming picture—a genre as it were, in her blue apron and pig tails kneeling in front of the glowing coals."[40]

Mundelein was clearly celebrating the healing power of laughter, but she was also quietly referencing Edward Carpenter's notion of the three-stage struggle of the self toward consciousness—a concept he contrasted with conviction—of the oneness of all life. What this meant politically, according to Carpenter, was that the struggle for democracy in a society would be mirrored in a similar struggle within the individual.[41] Thus, when Munde- lein described the struggle to wake up in the morning, she was referring to a larger struggle to "wake up" as well. Still, Edward Carpenter notwithstanding, it would take more than consciousness for the household to survive.

The cold and darkness were not only physical, and the household warmth came from sources in addition to the glowing coals. Rochester began working as associate editor of

Figure 4.5. Grace Hutchins tending coal stove

The World Tomorrow in January 1922—although she worked without pay—and Hutchins had a generous allowance from her father on which she survived without worry.[42] Yet Lucie Myer could ill afford to live without an income, not having a parental allowance as Hutchins did or investments as did Rochester, so Hutchins and Rochester invented a job for her, working with the neighborhood children. Nor could Cleghorn find work during the recession that accompanied the end of World War I, so a position was devised for her as well. Sally Cleghorn recalled how the offer of work was made: "They represented with all their kind eloquence how valuable I should be in these capacities—work they'd both felt the need of somebody to do—work I could do to the queen's taste. I needn't think they'd thought this up to help me out—oh, dear no—I should be filling real vacancies."[43]

She, too, would be working with the neighborhood children, plus serving as a contributing editor for *The World Tomorrow*.

Thus, several household members were working, primarily as writers, for the pacifist FOR, an as-yet small organization with approximately twenty-five hundred American members.[44] *The World Tomorrow* was not an organ of the fellowship, but it was one means by which fellowship members sought to promote fellowship principles. Few received wages from the FOR or *The World Tomorrow*, however. There was plenty of work to be done to change the world, but little money to pay for its accomplishment.

As financial constraints threatened their home, Rochester began writing on the economic causes of war, reviewing G. F. Nicolai's *The Biology of War* and John Bakeless's *The Economic Causes of Modern War* and placing Bakeless's claim in her first sentence: "Mr. John Bakeless has done a great service in assembling under the respectable aegis of the Department of Political Science of Williams College an array of evidence that modern wars are primarily economic in their origin." Nicolai, too, offered an economic motive for war, she said, maintaining that humans are not biologically predisposed toward war; in fact, he claimed, "humanity is organically one; all individuals are physically united, genuinely parts of a single whole." Moreover, he argued, she said, that "the habit of war within the species developed only with the sense of property."[45] It was no accident that Rochester chose to review these books—and to highlight these statements. Although she was not particularly enamored of the biological argument, she felt strongly that economic motives were the source of wars. This position defined her work on *The World Tomorrow* and ultimately, some years later, led to her removal from the editorship of the magazine. For now, however, she had established herself fully within the largely male discourse system, seeking to redirect it. She was not talking about economics in terms of children but rather in terms of war.

The personal axis of the attempt to merge an understanding of economic causation with a Christian belief system, including questions of "how to live more usefully and beautifully, in the present world," continued to press on Rochester and Hutchins, with mixed results. For the February issue, Rochester wrote a poem that gives evidence of her deep distrust of a language-based solution to economically caused conditions, despite her own commitment to persuasion as a means of change:

New York, 1922

The sunset calls us home to firelight;
We gather, well content, to dine.
But they—its glory mocks their homelessness;
Hungry they wait in long despair.

* * *

And I am merry
Having turned a verse
About their sorrow.[46]

Rochester's belief in the feasibility of moral solutions was fading by the day as her sense of the inevitability of class struggle in a capitalist economy grew. How to locate herself within this system continued to puzzle her, however. She was not alone in her confusion. About this time, despite her own economic instability, Sally Cleghorn tried to do something for the homeless people she met on the streets, asking Community House members whether she could invite six of them into the house once a week for something hot to drink: "Do you suppose we could?" she asked. "One hour, or two of comfort and graciousness would be a real help, I believe, even though we can't keep them all night." She acknowledged that the idea might not work, deferring to the reason of others: "I'm very featherheaded, I know, and I've only just thought of this—by morning I may remember reasons myself against it."[47]

This request more than likely precipitated one of Rochester's lectures on the nature of class struggle, which Cleghorn later documented in her autobiography: "Anna, bending upon me her unflinching gray eyes, threw a bucket of cold water in my face. 'We don't want anybody in the [Socialist] party who isn't convinced of the reality of the class struggle,' she exclaimed. 'It isn't something we're trying to bring about! We're trying to get away from it. It's ten feet deep all over us.'"[48] Cleghorn, however, would spend her life offering hot drinks to the homeless while Rochester tried to persuade anyone who would read her work just exactly how they were mired in the class struggle.

In February 1922, Rochester offered a glimpse into that bog with a review of five books on the labor movement, her first discussion of labor per se and more evidence of the direction in which she was moving. She was clearly happiest with the most radical of the five books, the one written by a worker who "punctures the reader's faith in the past sincerity and the future possibilities of any government in a capitalist country." Yet she ended the review with what appears now to be almost an afterthought—an observation that none of the books considered religion at all, much less Christianity. This silence she interpreted as an indication of "how far we Christians have withdrawn from the living issues of the present."[49]

Hutchins, meanwhile, tried to bring Christianity back into the conversation, offering a list of discussion questions and bibliographic resources for readers wishing to "test the conditions under which men and women do their work by three principles of Jesus, the value of personality, the necessity of brotherhood, and the law of service." We find here some of the basic questions that Hutchins had been asking—and continued to ask for the rest of her life: "Tested by the law of brotherhood, is it right that security should be based on compulsory insurance for some and on investments for others?" "Is competition for private gain the motive universally accepted as the basis for the work of human society?"[50]

For now, Hutchins and Rochester continued their attempt to carve out a space— Community House—in capitalist society where competition for private gain did not define work. This was far from easy. Other Community House members documented their struggles with heating and cooking systems, but Rochester and Hutchins never uttered a word about the material conditions. Nonetheless, Vida Scudder wrote to Ellen Gates Starr, saying: "Grace and Anna, I understand, have been going about with their arms in slings because cleaning floors was too much for them. I hear that Anna looks badly. But they won't give up, and claim to be very happy. . . . And I wonder whether Grace and Anna are really best used in that way. Well they must follow their star."[51]

Certainly Rochester and Hutchins were following their star, and that star was gradually slipping from Vida Scudder's constellation. Although she continued to be active in the CLID as well as the secular League for Industrial Democracy, Scudder was undergoing a degree of retrenchment during the 1920s, seeking meaning in her research into the Franciscan movement rather than in "modern reforms," as she put it. Rochester and Hutchins initially had more energy for the CLID, believing in the efficacy of its mission. Yet both Rochester and Hutchins, who served as educational secretary, began to feel dissatisfied with the direction of the organization. They wrote to the Reverend Mr. Hogue, the orga-

Figure 4.6. Community House resident

nization's general secretary, to express their feelings—most particularly their concern that the organization was putting work with college students ahead of efforts to create change within the Church.[52] By May 1922, Rochester had withdrawn from active participation, choosing to focus her efforts on *The World Tomorrow*.

Having left the School of Social Work after her last internship in the Lowell district offices of the Charity Organization Society, where her work included taking children for visits to the doctor, Hutchins began looking for a broader and more challenging assignment. Her opportunity came on March 21, 1922, when the FOR Executive Committee appointed her to the position of associate secretary specializing in study groups, returned missionaries, and "the general spreading of the message."[53] She and Rochester had taken a trip by themselves to Saddle River, New Jersey, on March 20, absenting themselves so as not to have to appear at the Fellowship's Executive Committee meeting, where Hutchins's position was to be discussed. Rochester wrote a gleeful letter back from Saddle River to the house members, parodying the letters of Paul, much as she had parodied the arguments of capitalists in her writings for the National Child Labor Committee—an indication of her incipient skepticism about the viability of traditional Christian doctrine:

> To sister Sarah, custodian of the archives, we commend unto you the epistle from our beloved Anna, to be kept for all the saints who may follow us in the Lord. . . . From Grace and Anna, . . . to them that are called to be saints, . . . Greetings. . . .
>
> Sistern, it is meet that Stella should seek relief from the burden of sickness and find refreshment of spirit and body as we also ourselves have set you an example above reproach—and not I, but the Grace that is with me. To Lucie and Mary Ellen we would counsel a more abundant diet for their stomachs' sake, even though meat maketh sister Sarah to offend.
>
> Let not the gas boiler burn out. Remember us in your prayers.[54]

Rochester still considered prayers paramount, but they served primarily as glue holding the group together. The needs of the gas boiler were equally compelling—and, finally, more so.

Having received her appointment, Hutchins began work on April 15, 1922, and at the executive committee meeting on April 27, her proposal (the first of her efforts in "the general spreading of the message") that the "thought of the year be centered upon the application of Fellowship principles in all economic and industrial applications" was approved.[55] Along with Rochester, Hutchins was having a strong effect on fellowship policy and activities, although that effect would not be acknowledged in later fellowship histories.

Rochester, meanwhile, having resigned from much of her active work in the SCHC and the CLID, had been working hard on the Property issue of *The World Tomorrow* scheduled for April. She wrote two substantial articles for the issue, the most significant of which was an opinion piece entitled "What Property Does to the Individual." In this article, Rochester pointed out that property in itself is neither entirely good nor entirely bad; what matters is the deep disparity between luxury and poverty. Those who are trying to live according to the ethics of Jesus, she said, continue to be troubled by this disparity and, she maintained (harking back to many discussions with the Companions and still addressing those with sufficient resources to find this a compelling topic), can find no clear definition of simplicity by which to be guided. One of the contributing factors is the taboo against talking about one's income, which she called a "poisoned secrecy." Listing other barriers, she cited the "whole code of culture and manners." "Can we," she asked, "ever rise to a human kindliness so genuine and perceptive that it expels from our minds that semi-conscious checking off of others' superficial differences?" Challenging her readers to let go of their sense of entitlement, she pointed out that however much individuals may want to change, large-scale shifts were needed: "We must find the way toward group changes and a new economic order in which our rudimentary good will may find expression and growth."[56]

On May 23, 1922, the household celebrated the publication of *Jesus Christ and the World Today*, although by now both Rochester and Hutchins were seeking a wider audience than those for whom they had been writing a year earlier. Nonetheless, as reviews extolling the book began to appear in periodicals such as *The World Tomorrow*, *The Nation*, and *The Literary Review*, Hutchins and Rochester watched them carefully. Some were written by friends, others by acquaintances or strangers. Many who knew Hutchins and Rochester commented that their decision to live simply in a working class neighborhood gave them the authority to ask readers to consider hard questions. Both Norman Thomas and Adelaide Case wrote cover blurbs, Adelaide Case noting that the book "is profoundly disquieting—as it should be" and Norman Thomas calling it "frank, thoroughgoing, and suggestive."

Rochester and Hutchins clipped and filed many of the reviews as they appeared, but throughout the summer, Rochester kept looking for a response from Vida Scudder. When none had arrived after the book had been in print for more than two months, she wrote to Scudder, asking if perhaps a letter from her had been lost in the mail. Scudder replied quickly, saying that no letter had been lost; instead, she had simply been lazy and had not yet written. But she continued in her typically effusive way, offering love and appreciation in addition to a few points of disagreement—both testimony to her careful reading and foreshadowing of the nascent rift between Rochester and Scudder. "I do rejoice in the book," she said. "It seems to me that you have knit the modern economic thought not artificially but organically into the spiritual thought and the exposition of Scripture."[57] She had feared, she said, that Hutchins and Rochester would have given "a handle to our enemies by far-fetched inferences or debatable assertions" but was pleased to discover that they had not done so.

One of the key points on which Scudder disagreed, however—and she didn't go into this point in detail because, she said, they had already discussed it quite thoroughly—was their statement that to receive interest on investments is contrary to the will of Jesus. It was her opinion that the capitalist *system* was outdated and needed to be replaced, but if an individual was living under that system, receiving interest income was not wrong. She didn't press the issue, however, offering the possibility that her thinking was "muddle-headed" in order to avoid any semblance of contentiousness. Hutchins and Rochester felt that Scudder's approach was not "muddle-headed" at all but rather an excuse. On the other hand, they realized that as individuals, giving up their incomes would be of no consequence in the larger scheme of things. Also, they had no intention of taking paying jobs when so many others really needed those jobs. Instead, they located positions with impecunious progressive organizations in which they could work to advance the development of a more egalitarian social and economic system. In this way, they "earned" the incomes that came from their investments and tried to hasten the end of the system that divided people by class, race, and gender.

The message that may have pleased Rochester and Hutchins most in this letter comes on the fourth page, as Scudder pondered the question of which of them might have written which sections: "You work together most harmoniously, and it is a big joy to me that you have found each other. Anna dear, I think your mother would have loved Grace, and rejoiced in this good friendship."[58] Scudder placed this endorsement on the same page on which she told of her visit with her elderly aunt, Dr. Julia M. Dutton, her "last charge from the older generation," who was suffering from the recent loss of "her great friend," thus nudging Rochester and Hutchins toward a community of women extending over time.[59] She closed by telling them that she would be attending the annual conference of the SCHC but not the conference of the FOR, perhaps a gentle reminder to them of which organization supported and fostered relationships such as theirs.

But Hutchins and Rochester were reading Edward Carpenter's "community consciousness" differently, seeing the necessity of love and work in the world, and so, just as they had begun to limit their activities in the CLID, they decided not to attend the annual conference of the SCHC. Although they still maintained their committee memberships in the SCHC, Rochester and Hutchins went instead to the FOR conference at the George School, a Quaker institution in Pennsylvania, where Rochester, along with Scott Nearing and Helena Stuart Dudley, was elected to a two-year term on the Fellowship Council and where Nearing was charged with drafting a concrete program for the organization for the next year—1923. Ideologically, Hutchins and Rochester were now moving in tandem with Scott Nearing—and away from Vida Scudder. This shift, an attempt to live without hypocrisy, would mean relinquishing a language of love and commitment and separating from the community of women in which it flourished. At the same time, however, it was that very language and community that had propelled them down this road and into the work they were doing. Both Hutchins and Rochester would craft imperfect solutions to the disparity between the old language upon which they had built their lives together and new languages of economic justice that threatened to erase them—or worse.

The struggle with Scudder became obvious in the June 1922 issue of *The World Tomorrow*. In that issue, along with an article entitled "What Is Luxury?" by Vida Scudder, Rochester published "What Eleven Families Spend: The Cost of Comfort that Is Not Luxury." Scudder's article attempted to answer the question posed in its title, dividing the matter into right and wrong, quoting from Plato, addressing the question of asceticism, and dwelling at length on the Franciscans. She ended by pulling back from the question, claiming that luxury was relative to historical place and time. "What is luxury today will be necessity tomorrow. The time approaches perhaps when the individual bathroom will be as common and as little luxurious as the individual towel."[60] Still, she advised that four principles may be followed: "Any object or privilege is luxury which (1) can not be used sacramentally, (2) is not needed by the world, (3) involves injury to the producer, (4) can not be widely shared."[61]

Spurning Scudder's Platonist definitions, Rochester collected and presented quantifiable facts: the budgets of eleven families. Having provided columns of figures and paragraphs of explanatory text, she asked: "Has this analysis brought us any nearer to a definition of simplicity? Do we know more exactly what it costs to be comfortable without luxury?"[62] Even the most basic of the budgets analyzed, she pointed out, was higher than the minimum suggested by the Bureau of Labor Statistics—and that was above the "average actually available for families in the United States. It is far above the earnings of the coal miners who are now resisting a cut in their wages."[63] Calling for a move away from definitions of terms such as "comfort" and "luxury" toward "something far more fundamental," she advocated raising wages, improving public education, and socializing medicine. Still, by the end of the article, Rochester herself was without concrete directives. "And meanwhile," she asked, "what are we individually to do? We who can afford a simple comfort which is beyond the reach of the majority weigh our health, physical and mental, and our hunger for quiet and beauty, against the intangible separateness and class grouping that are almost inevitable. There is much to be said both ways. I, for one, have no ready answer."[64]

Having no ready answer was not where Rochester wanted to be, and she continued to take advantage of her position with *The World Tomorrow* to read and review current books and pamphlets, to interview leading thinkers and activists, and to engage in dialogue with other writers and editors in an attempt to put together a more satisfactory answer to the question of individual responsibility in a capitalist society.

Such responsibility meant, among other things, not allowing the organizations to which one belonged to persist in nonegalitarian work arrangements. In late 1922, Rochester had protested her rank as associate editor of *The World Tomorrow* to Managing Editor Devere Allen, seeing in the title an implied hierarchy and a gender-related lack of respect, given that she was doing an equal amount of work (if not more). Devere Allen had conveyed her feelings to Editor-in-Chief John Nevin Sayre, telling him that he understood from Hutchins that "her feeling is not so much actuated by her sturdy feminism as by a real belief in the value of a co-operative, equal basis of work, and a reaction against the way some folks have unconsciously spoken of and to her as a subordinate."[65] Nevin Sayre then apparently approved the change, although his residual antifeminism would resurface later.

Individual responsibility also meant addressing issues others in positions of leadership preferred to leave undisturbed—or, worse, about which they exhibited their ignorance. In the January 1923 issue, Rochester published a review of two books on "the Jewish question," not mincing words in her condemnation of Socialist Party stalwart John Spargo's suggestion that Bolshevism was a Jewish conspiracy. Her assessment of Walter Hurt's *Truth about the Jews, Told by a Gentile* was less harsh, especially as she found his primary thesis—that "the root of racial antagonism is economic competition"—accurate and useful.[66]

Still, the question of how to replace economic competition remained. In the next issue, Rochester ventured to address that question with a review of Scott Nearing's *The Next Step*, which she called a "challenging blueprint for a reorganized world." The foundation of this reorganized world, Nearing said, is "an international society controlled not by owners but by producers." Rochester admonished readers who might find the book utopian or who might cavil about certain points that they should bear with his "overemphasis on the supreme rights of the producer" and "catch something of the genuine internationalism which no one has yet stated in so challenging a way."[67] Within the next four years, Rochester came to agree more and more with Nearing—and later probably regretted her use of the word "overemphasis" to describe the rights of the producer.

Along with Nearing and other fellowship members advocating an international society controlled by producers, Rochester and Hutchins were challenged by world events. On January 9, 1923, Germany defaulted on the payments required by the Treaty of Versailles; within two days, the French, who were owed much of the reparations, had invaded and occupied the Ruhr region of Germany, where 80 percent of that country's steel and 71 percent of its coal were produced. The official German response was passive resistance, although large demonstrations took place across Germany. Inflation yielded to hyperinflation, which benefited the wealthy but starved members of the middle and working classes.

Witnessing the devastation wrought by the Versailles Treaty, Hutchins and Rochester continued to press within the FOR for a more radical economic approach to world events. At the five-day February 1923 meeting of the Fellowship Council, all present made plans to test new methods of "propagating the Fellowship idea." This need for new methods led members to consider whether the theme for the September national conference should be "developing the technique of propagating our message in such a way that it would grip people and transform them into individuals fired with an enthusiasm for that way of life which eliminates all bitterness and conflict," a theme probably proposed by Hutchins. Council members also spent time discussing "a new type of evangelism which would result in a person's giving his whole self to the whole community." Although the records do not indicate who started this conversation, the details offer a precise description of the lives Hutchins and Rochester were attempting to live.[68] Whether they initiated or simply adopted the idea, Hutchins and Rochester had committed themselves to giving their whole lives to the whole community; they had only to ascertain how to do that effectively.

Although Rochester had been writing articles seeking to determine the role of the individual in creating social change, and Hutchins was writing discussion materials asking readers to consider whether a follower of Jesus should live on the income from investments, it was no secret that both had private incomes. Hutchins received a monthly allowance from her family, and Rochester had inherited the considerable wealth accumulated by her father in his role as treasurer of Western Union. Rochester did not accept a salary for her work on *The World Tomorrow*, and Hutchins declined the $100 per month to which she was entitled as associate secretary of the fellowship—although the executive committee insisted on paying her anyway. This arrangement was the most honorable they could devise in a less-than-perfect world. Perhaps it did not occur to Rochester and Hutchins at this point that the new methods of "propagating the Fellowship idea" that they sought to initiate could be engaged in only by those for whom steady, well-paid work was not an issue, although it should have been dawning on them by now, as they were supporting at least two unemployed members of Community House, an arrangement that threatened the household's future.

Chapter Five

Into the World

A new type of evangelism which would result in a person's giving his whole self to the whole community.

—discussed at the meeting of the Council of the
Fellowship of Reconciliation (February 9–13, 1923)

Community House allowed Hutchins and Rochester to cement their partnership as they moved away from charitable work and into the world. Yet Community House could not last. There would be no rings, no lasting commitments to a community of women. Economically, the household was not viable. What's more, the Episcopal Church, at the core of the community, had proved resistant to the changes that had inspired the household's formation in the first place. The situational incongruities were inescapable, sending the household into a crisis. Most household members left because they had to find paid work, but Hutchins and Rochester, with independent incomes, were able to shift their affiliations to a religious organization that offered them both the promise of more specific action and a platform from which to speak. They traded their ironic cartoons and parodies for more direct attempts to persuade readers to address the causes of inequality and war. Although this foray out of same-sex institutions would end in another economic debacle, it increased Hutchins and Rochester's understandings of the difficulties inherent in challenging gender and class systems. And it didn't stop them.

Sally Cleghorn left the household in June 1922; she had found a teaching job again with Bill and Helen Fincke at Manumit Farm in Dutchess County, New York. Some housemates had left before Cleghorn; others would follow. After leaving, Cleghorn wrote to Hutchins, offering her assessment of the house and its mission, an assessment that served, following the *lex continui*, to propel Hutchins farther from the comfortable world she had inhabited, confronting directly and painfully the privileges and assumptions of her class.

Apparently Hutchins had written to Cleghorn questioning her use of the word "monastic" in a conversation with Lucie Myer. "Monastic" would have alarmed Hutchins, as it was this word that had been seeping into conversations among the Companions. Vida Scudder, in particular, had been seeking to push the SCHC in a direction more defined by historical religious communities, perhaps attempting to preserve from the culture of the 1920s the community of women that had meant so much to her. But the word "monastic" represented the antithesis of all that Hutchins had envisioned. Hutchins did want a community of women, but she did not want a community that separated itself from the common life of the neighborhood. Responding to this letter from Hutchins, Cleghorn wrote that she remembered using the word *monastic* in conversation with Lucie Myer. "By it," she said, "I meant two totally different things; one was the exclusively feminine character of the family, and the other was the sense of dedication."[1]

Cleghorn went on to explain. While she liked living with women, she also missed men, especially "big boys" such as those she used to teach. What she would prefer, she said, was a community consisting of both sexes and all ages. Or perhaps, she mused, if there were class differences among the women, that would take care of the feeling of exclusivity. The "sense of dedication," she said, means that the "common lazy (moral) self can't find a footing. And then," she continued, "one finds oneself laboring under a faint sense of not quite hypocrisy, but at least of having a far far less attractive personality hidden away about one somewhere which under less dedicated conditions would issue, to be most appallingly apparent." Perhaps, she ventured, it's not really a "monastic tinge in the house" but rather an "atmosphere of very great though unconscious refinement."[2]

Despite all this, Cleghorn said, she loved the house and the "wildness" that it allowed, "its lovely comradeship, its burning warmth, its reality of meaning, its truly humble sisterliness." "Humor," she said, "keeps it fresh, respect for differing opinion keeps it sane, vital reverence for life itself prevents it from growing stiff or suspicious of change."[3] What exactly Cleghorn meant by "wildness" we can only guess, but the household was groundbreaking in creating a space in which women could live together without the oversight of husbands or fathers—or institutions of some sort—and residents thoroughly enjoyed their freedom. Although the household was crumbling under its own contradictions, it was an important first step toward full social and civic liberation, especially for Rochester and Hutchins.

Like Vida Scudder, Hutchins found it hard to give up the community of women which had been her dream and in which she had flourished. However, Hutchins finally began to shift her allegiance to the FOR. And when she was selected to represent the American chapter on the International Council, which would mean that she must travel to the international conference of the FOR that summer in Denmark, she found the courage to leave behind the collapsing household in order to investigate, firsthand, conditions in Europe.

Anna Rochester, too, was struggling with her own "noble reserve" issues. It was not easy for a small group of people on a low budget to put out a high-quality magazine exploring the sources of human aggression without differences of opinion and work style becoming chronic stressors, if left unaddressed. In the spring of 1923, differences between Rochester and her friend Alice Beal Parsons, the publicity director, began to create tension in the organization.[4] Writing to Parsons on May 26, 1923, Rochester acknowledged the parts of herself that Parsons might find difficult:

> I do come bursting out with a sudden idea, or a sudden annoyance, and I speak my mind without sufficiently considering the other fellow. I know that when I foresee a hopeless, emotional argument I try to ward it off with a chilly dignity which is the only self-protection I seem to have been able to develop but which must seem like an air of top-lofty superiority.[5]

Apparently, Rochester's honesty and directness in this case did not lead to a permanent resolution between the two of them, as the situation continued for the next year. The traits Rochester lists, though, are those she continued to exhibit for the rest of her life—and that led to other misunderstandings later on, although none were as threatening to an organization as this one. Fortunately, on this occasion, she and Hutchins were soon to set sail for an extended stay in Europe.

Rochester's last article before they set sail, an attempt at the ready answer she hadn't had a year earlier, outlined her vision for the world they all were seeking to create. In the February 4, 1923, issue of *The Call*, Scott Nearing had argued that a radical has three distinct tasks: The first is to demonstrate why the present order is unworkable. The second is to offer the possibility of a better system. And the third is to show how that system may be attained.[6] The third task of the radical, according to Nearing, is to be accomplished through education, which would include journalism; the arts, such as literature, painting, and drama; and political action. "'For the time being, and for a long time to come, the job of the radical will be an educational one,'" he insisted.[7] In her previous article, Rochester had accomplished the first of Nearing's tasks; in this article, she achieved the second.

The new world, Rochester said, recalling her analysis of the year before in "What Eleven Families Spend," will be healthy, will have a culture "grounded in truth and in respect for personality," and will have an economic organization that is a "happy blend of craftsmanship, science, and the satisfaction of human wants." Health care, she said, will focus on the maintenance of health rather than the curing of disease, and culture will cease to make arbitrary divisions between people based on skin color or national origin; moreover, it will abolish prisons in favor of a more humane approach to crime. Work will improve, she forecast, as labor unions grow in strength.[8]

Having offered this possibility of a better system, Hutchins and Rochester left New York on June 26, 1923, in high spirits, despite the fact that Lucie Myer had had to return to Baltimore to be with her father, who was suffering from a terminal illness. Writing to Lucie Myer from aboard their ship, the *Majestic*, on the day they departed, they wished that they could know "just how things are with you this minute as we write and that other minute when you will read," as they were planning to write "frivolously—and chiefly about food."[9]

Write about food they did—enumerating and describing all the packages of comestibles sent to them by well-wishers. In the spirit of Community House, they were traveling third class, and their friends and family apparently had decided that third class fare would be inadequate, so they sent baskets containing everything from chocolates to cornflakes and cream. "The whole episode," Rochester wrote, "is a . . . dramatic revelation of the way we expect to eat and our friends expect us to eat—and never imagine we should be content with proletarian fare."[10] Hutchins and Rochester shared the food with their tablemates and with other travelers on deck—drawing the line, however, when a Belgian-Albanian family gave a stuffed date to their one-year-old. "Quite corrupting," Rochester opined.[11]

Despite their friends' preoccupation with their diet, the European trip was actually a succession of meetings with people. After reaching Denmark, Rochester commented in a letter to friends that they felt "a quite arrogant superiority to the tourist who sight-sees. We have not entered a museum or a picture gallery. One should not boast—we know they are interesting and valuable, but who would sacrifice a chance to talk with live Danes in order to see pictures and relics of dead ones?"[12]

The trip, much like their lives in the Chelsea neighborhood of 352 W. 27th Street, was an education in class consciousness, offering more incongruous realities for them to manage. They had become intensely aware of the lives of workers on the continent in part through reading the work of Martin Andersen Nexo, author of the *Pelle* and *Ditte* books, series featuring young Danish working class protagonists. Of the two series, although *Pelle* brought fame to Nexo, Rochester and Hutchins were most absorbed by *Ditte*, whose life is chronicled from her illegitimate birth through her near-rape and delivery of an illegitimate child to her work as a wet nurse and servant and, finally, to her death at 25 from overwork. *Pelle* is a happier tale, ending with the protagonist working with the Social Democrats, a move that the author himself later criticized as inadequate[13]; *Ditte*, written later, shows the interconnectedness of gender and class and makes no attempt to protect readers' sensibilities. Arriving in Denmark, Hutchins and Rochester told their correspondents, all of whom had read the books, that they were on AA Boulevard, where Ditte "got her first place as a servant."[14]

Rochester had written to Martin Nexo asking if she and Hutchins could meet with him to discuss *The World Tomorrow*. He not only said yes to their request, but he and his wife entertained them well, making a strong impression on Rochester. The Nexos's two maids were "the only really happy looking working people" they saw in Denmark,[15] and Nexo himself she described as having "a radiant, simple, human kind of way—and spirit—that is quite rare." He is a "real bolshevik," she said, but then puzzled over what she saw as a mismatch between his spirit and his philosophy. "He deplores humanistic effort (much more broadly interpreted than social work)," she said, "as a diversion from the main job of changing the economic order. But actually his analysis of the human spirit in individuals is far more generous and warm than his mass-action rather cynical philosophy."[16]

The question of mass action, as announced by the establishment of the Third International in 1919, had been debated at length within FOR circles. By "cynical," Rochester was referring to the lack of any moral component in Nexo's system. The place of morality in the revolution, however, was a highly contested point, with John Reed having argued that it didn't matter that Socialism was *right*, because the capitalists were not going to give up their privileges in response to a moral argument.[17]

Despite this apparent difference of opinion with the left wing, represented at that time by the Workers' (Communist) Party, Hutchins and Rochester were, by now, firm advocates of revolutionary change to establish an industrial democracy.[18] The highlight of the conference for Rochester and Hutchins was Hutchins's speech, delivered on Saturday evening, July 21. Drawing together her past training in individual solutions in the SCHC as well as her developing awareness of the need for large-scale economic change, Hutchins issued an appeal both for simplicity and for "an outspoken stand by the international FOR for radical economic change."[19] This speech offers evidence of significant conversions on Hutchins's part. Whereas in early 1920, serving as a member of the executive committee of the SVM, she had delivered a speech to some 2,000 women celebrating "The Joy of Being a Missionary," now, in mid-1923, she was advocating radical economic alterations on an international scale to an audience of both women and men.[20] Her elegantly simple speech was followed by the "very great oratory" of M. Revoyre, a Frenchman who, Rochester took care to note, was both a Christian and a Communist, having been first a Catholic priest, then a Protestant minister, and finally, at the time of his speech, a proletarian worker. Hutchins's call for radical economic change and the shifts in M. Revoyre's affiliations were reflected in the conference as a whole, with some conference-goers feeling that there was less dependence upon religion here than there had been at previous conferences. Rochester and Hutchins were not alone in redirecting their analysis.

From Denmark, Hutchins and Rochester traveled to Hellerau, Germany, near Dresden, for a conference of the "German Youth Movement." More than likely, this conference was held under the auspices of the Verband der Sozialistische Arbeiterjugend Deutschlands, which Peter D. Stachura describes as the one featuring the most opposition to militarism and support for pacifism and internationalism.[21] This organization struggled with more radical youth associated with the Communist Party, the *Kommunistische Partei Deutschlands* (KPD), sometimes considering a merger and other times holding out for a separate identity, at the cost of allegations by the Communists that they were hopelessly bourgeois. Hutchins and Rochester were most impressed by the *Freie Proletarische Jugend*, a small, non–party affiliated group.[22]

The struggle between radical and reformist orientations was coming to represent much of Rochester and Hutchins's experience on the trip. After the German Youth Movement conference, they traveled to the Ruhr to document conditions for the *World Tomorrow*. What they undoubtedly witnessed were Communist attempts to demonstrate to French workers that it was not in their best interests to support the Versailles Treaty: such support would only put more money into the pockets of industrialists.

Before heading to the Ruhr, Hutchins, venturing into uncharted territory in response to Sally Cleghorn's criticisms, had invited Kurt Klaeber (later to be known as the beloved children's book writer Kurt Held) to come to the United States to speak to the youth groups that the FOR was organizing.[23] Klaeber accepted Hutchins's invitation, and a month later, he arrived at Ellis Island, giving Hutchins's name as his sponsor and the FOR office address as his destination. Ann Mundelein had sailed for China in August, while Rochester and Hutchins were gone, having signed on as a missionary. Thus, Community House as a women's household was now defunct; it had lasted for two and a half years and had never been stable for more than a few weeks at a time.[24] So Kurt Klaeber moved in. And he lived at 352—his soon-to-be wife Lisa Tetzner joining him some time later—for four months, through January 1924. It is likely that he influenced Hutchins and Rochester as much as they influenced him, reminding them of the conditions they had witnessed in the Ruhr and arguing that neither reform nor prayer would suffice to change those conditions.

Nonetheless, Hutchins and Rochester's shifting loyalties continued to be theologically informed. That fall, Hutchins returned to Union Theological Seminary, enrolling in a course taught by Professor of Christian Ethics Harry F. Ward, author of the 1919 book on social change *The New Social Order*.[25] Ward approached ethics through texts representing diverse communities and classes, asking students to read the work of James Weldon Johnson, Willa Cather, Claude McKay, Walter White, Countee Cullen, Ruth Suckow, and Steven Vincent Benét, among others, hoping that the diversity of experiences represented would challenge students' self-interested ethical systems. Through these and other similar texts, Hutchins came to a deeper understanding of lives beyond her own.

On October 2, Hutchins revisited the question of methods of persuasion that she had raised in the spring. She called a meeting of those in the fellowship who had been to Europe during the summer so that they could discuss "ways of making their presentation of the situation most effective and far-reaching,"[26] a question that would continue to preoccupy her. The discussion of methods of persuasion extended throughout the FOR committee structure, as the executive committee and the council also strove to find language that would deliver the fellowship's message to a wider audience.

Meeting at Community House in November 1923, the council heard a report from the committee chaired by A. J. Muste concerning the FOR mission statement, a committee of which Rochester had been a member. Muste reported that the committee felt that three groups, especially, should be targeted for the FOR message: members of Christian churches or, if not members, at least those having Christian backgrounds; workers, both of the United States and of the world; and individuals not of these two groups, yet who were "of one spirit with us," such as internationalists, revolutionaries, or humanitarians.[27] According to the committee, the problem with the current statement was that some people "are definitely repelled by the language." Others, labor activists in particular, might not be repelled but might simply not understand the language, as it did not speak to them. Thus, the committee decided, no one statement was likely to appeal to everyone, and the solution might lie in offering one general statement with supplementary materials designed to interpret the basic message "in language natural to various groups," an awkward solution at best.[28]

As the FOR tried to craft appeals for diverse audiences, Hutchins struggled to locate herself as a speaker in this new community. Although she had addressed the international FOR successfully, she was still mourning the demise of her dream of a women's community. Writing one of her longest articles for *The World Tomorrow*, "Our Inferiority Complex," she articulated the position of (mostly middle class, educated) women seeking entry into wider society, pointing out that women who wanted to contribute to society had, in the recent past, done so by forming women-only groups. She herself, she averred, had been "a big frog" in such a "little pool." But ultimately, she argued, "I can see it is no permanent solution that the women frogs should go off and have a pool by themselves." Single-sex organizations keep women away from the larger and more significant decisions affecting society as a whole, she said, signaling her realization that Community House was not the answer she had hoped it would be—and neither was the Women's Auxiliary of the Board of Missions or St. Faith's or the Society of the Companions of the Holy Cross. Now, Hutchins said, she was a little frog in a big pool—but she suffered from an "inferiority complex."[29]

Women, Hutchins alleged, herself included, have internalized the sense that they must not speak or assume positions of leadership. The only way to change the pattern is for women to transform themselves—to start speaking. "Yes," she said, "it is mainly we women who must get over this inferiority business." Although it might have appeared that she was personalizing and individualizing a social issue, she continued her argument, insisting that men must change, too. Of course, she said, they must begin to *expect* women to take an equal part in any given situation. The combined efforts of both women and men would be required in order to establish the new democracy, she argued; without these endeavors, no true democracy could occur.[30] Adopting the new language of psychology, Hutchins did not realize that this language, although apparently useful in the moment, would not prove to be her friend. Yet she was making every effort to act in accordance with her analysis, devoting her "whole self to the whole community" and beginning to understand the economic substrate of the "new evangelism."

Rochester, meanwhile, sought to promote the new evangelism by writing a fundraising pamphlet for the FOR. Her efforts to reach the membership show little evidence of the appeals crafted for diverse audiences, another reminder of the relative uniformity of the FOR membership. The question she suggested that the pamphlet's readers ask themselves was: "Am I doing my share?" She then proceeded to ask the next logical question: "But what *is* my share?" The answer, she said, could not be given for anyone, but neither could anyone answer it for himself until he knew all that the fellowship was doing—and then she enumerated the activities of the fellowship, starting with the most primary: that each member was endeavoring to "make one's own life an immediate expression of goodwill," a modified version of the "new evangelism" that FOR Council members had discussed, but still retaining the shape of a "whole person" rhetoric, now grounded in the specifically material imperative of funds for the continuation of the collective project. There were thirty-five hundred members in the United States, she said. Reiterating her belief in the efficacy of people working together for a common purpose, she said that these thirty-five hundred people were not "scattered and isolated individuals, united by an invisible 'spiritual' bond." Instead, "we have certain very definite common responsibilities."[31]

Building on this foundation of belief in common responsibilities, but extending it beyond personal and national borders, Scott Nearing suggested at the February 7 meeting of the executive committee that the topic for the next annual conference—to be held in September 1924—should be "Imperialism and Fellowship."[32] Using British economist J. A. Hobson's analysis in his 1902 book *Imperialism: A Study*, Nearing determined that the United States had become an imperialist nation, abandoning its democratic roots and allowing corporations to create the structure of empire.[33] (Nearing, however, followed Lenin rather than Hobson in seeing imperialism as a result of capitalism.) The executive committee and the fellowship council, of which Rochester and Hutchins were key members, agreed, and Hutchins joined Nearing and others on the conference committee.

At the same time, Hutchins still held on to a vision of democratic governance less informed by class consciousness. In "Prophets and the People," published in the June 1924 issue of *The World Tomorrow*, she argued that it was not in the schools that democracy had been conveyed, as many people thought, but rather people absorbed their sense of democracy from the spirit of Jesus. "Yes," she said, "it is from Jesus, whether through some branch of the church or in spite of the church, that many of us have learned the best of what we know about democracy." What's more, she explained, similar doctrines could be found in the teachings of Confucius and of Mahatma Gandhi.

Perhaps due to differing visions of the road to democratic governance, a degree of discord continued to unsettle *The World Tomorrow* offices. Whatever the cause, John Nevin Sayre resigned his position as editor on May 15, 1924, saying that he never really felt that editing a magazine was his true calling and that he believed he would be of greater use working in the larger fellowship efforts.[34] This meant that Rochester and Devere Allen were to share the editorship as coeditors. Hutchins, meanwhile, was feeling restless in her position as secretary of the FOR, because, although ostensibly she shared the position as an equal with Paul Jones, in reality, he was looked upon as the administrator and she as his assistant. What's more, she understood the central role of publication in social change—and the need for money to support that publication. She asked Rochester whether she might move into the position of business manager at *The World Tomorrow*, should the current business manager, Alice Parsons, leave.[35]

Rochester wrote to Devere Allen broaching this topic. It is clear from the letter that Rochester understood Hutchins—her impulsiveness and her fluctuating interest in her work, evident in less-than-regular work habits. She also understood the fact that Hutchins taking the position might give the appearance of a sort of nepotism on Rochester's part; she referred to Hutchins as her "partner" in the letter, as a statement of fact that was clearly recognized by everyone in the fellowship. Rochester also said directly that Hutchins realized "that the situation is delicate because of our intimacy."[36] However difficult it had been for Hutchins to move into the "big pool," at least this part of the pool acknowledged her close relationship with Rochester. How other staff members felt in private about this we can't know, although the increased use of the language of psychology during this period couldn't have been helpful.

Finally, Hutchins was given a month's leave of absence from the fellowship to work in the business office of *The World Tomorrow* raising money, her specialty. The magazine needed $10,000 by the end of the year for operating expenses. Moreover, because John Nevin Sayre, who was independently wealthy and volunteered his time (as did Rochester and Hutchins), had resigned from the magazine, they faced the possibility that an additional $2,000 might have to be raised in order to hire another editor to work with Rochester and Devere Allen.[37] Hutchins's earlier fundraising had been to support her friend

Mary James at the Church General Hospital in Wuchang; now she was supporting her partner, Anna Rochester, and the emotional stakes were that much higher.

Once again, Hutchins collided with an official in upper management—this time, John Nevin Sayre. And this time, rather than withdrawing into other work, as she had before, she exploded. Apparently Sayre had resigned but continued to come around, making use of the resources that she was working so hard to fund and offering criticisms of the ongoing work.[38] Although she was personally offended, the real cause of Hutchins's anger was the criticism directed at Rochester, which she would not tolerate. Sayre retreated temporarily, but the related questions of money and control of editorial policy remained.

Although gender issues preoccupied her and Christian theology still framed her thinking, Hutchins, by now, was beginning to pay more attention to arguments about class. In July 1924, she published her first article exploring the successes of the 1917 revolution in Russia, reviewing Iury Libedinsky's A Week, the narrative of a week during a White Russian–led peasant revolt against the Bolsheviks in the spring of 1921. As always, she was most affected by the human suffering portrayed, the "terrible realism of the death first of one living man or woman and then of another and another and another," which she saw, at that point, in pacifist terms: "the result of hatred begetting hatred, force begetting force." Nonetheless, she contrasted this narrative with "our academic discussions of Russia, our queries as to whether the Soviet government is a democracy or an oligarchy, our debates on pacifism and the revolution," all of which she found "thin and unreal"[39] beside Libedinsky's story. She would maintain this emphasis on narrative as the most direct route to an audience even as her analyses of political situations grew more defined and complex.

Rochester found more to explore in the "academic discussions" of revolutionary Russia, publishing several interviews with prominent economic and social analysts such as George W. Norris, Sanford Griffith, and Bertrand Russell. Most notably, in June 1924, she published an article by Robert W. Dunn, one of her colleagues in the LID, entitled "Democracy and the Russian Revolution." In this article, Dunn, who had recently returned from working with the American Friends Service Committee in the Soviet Union, culled from Trotsky's writings to present a mock interview, the gist of which was that democracy no longer exists in the United States in any viable form. Dunn argued, in Trotsky's voice: "The apparatus of your democracy, no matter how you construct it, obeys the will of your Morgans who control your lands, workshops, banks, newspapers, universities, Teapot Domes, bipartisan political machines and if necessary even your third parties." Thus, according to Trotsky, although democracy has been a force for progress, it has outlived its usefulness and simply cannot function in the present world. "The path divides into two, my friends, either the dictatorship of the imperialist clique or the dictatorship of the proletariat."[40] Rochester then understood the choice before her—Hutchins would come to this understanding in time—and this early connection with Dunn would deepen into the closest friendship of Rochester and Hutchins's lives.

The next month, demonstrating the shift in her thinking that had taken place since the previous summer, when she had written the vaguely utopian and reformist "The Future in the Present," Rochester launched arguments presaging her work and thought during at least the next two decades. In "The Pacifist's 'Preparedness,'" Rochester attempted to fulfill the third task Scott Nearing had called for a year earlier: outlining how to attain a better system. One way not to get there, she argued, was to be lured by psychology away from "the main road toward revolutionary change."[41] This statement would get her into no end of difficulties later with John Nevin Sayre.

Posing the questions "Can we in the United States accomplish without violence the transition from private capitalism to a socialized industrial order, before new generations of workers have been sacrificed? And what can we pacifists do about it?" Rochester reminded her readers that "most revolutionary radicals expect violence in the course of the struggle but they do not propose to fight until after violence has been used against them."[42]

Her answer to the questions now clearly echoed Scott Nearing rather than Vida Scudder. What was needed was information, she said: "The one great encouragement is the public's increasing demand for facts and more facts, and its decreasing interest in statements which are merely expressions of uninformed opinion. But, back of the facts, the radical movement needs, it seems to me, more fearless and persistent study of the phenomena which we desire to change." Attempting to bring together pacifists and working class activists, Rochester insisted that pacifists must not use the excuse that workers are violence prone in order to avoid engaging in the fundamental struggle to change conditions in the United States. Rather, pacifists must "plunge into the struggle and share the lot of the workers . . . for words alone will not demonstrate the victorious power of truth and non-violent courage."[43]

Still determined that their lives must reflect their vision of the new social order, in April 1924 Rochester joined another experiment in community consciousness, purchasing 585 shares, at $5.00 apiece, in the Consumer's Co-operative Housing Association, an early cooperative apartment house in New York, established by members of the Socialist Party.[44] Rochester's 585 shares did not buy her an apartment; rather, they entitled her to lease an apartment from the association, which she did at a cost of $92.68 per month. The shares also entitled her to participate in cooperative buying with the other members—appliances and food were purchased in bulk and resold to members at cost. On July 31, 1924, Rochester and Hutchins moved from the house at 352 West 27th Street to a third-floor apartment at 85 Bedford Street in Greenwich Village, where they would live for the rest of their lives.[45]

Although they joined the Socialists economically, within the privacy of their home, Hutchins and Rochester created yet another version of Adelynrood, each claiming a small "cell-like" room for her own.[46] Knowing that Lucie Myer lacked sufficient funds to rent an apartment, they invited her to join them, creating another room by shortening their already-small living room. Lucie Myer lived with them on and off for the rest of her life, as well.

Hutchins and Rochester also returned to Adelynrood, their first visit in several years, this time for the second Social Justice Conference, held during early August 1924.[47] Rochester had been asked to give a paper at the conference on the topic of "Christian Social Journalism." She used the occasion to reiterate her commitment to the importance of living with and for a community of others—the new evangelism as Hutchins had helped to articulate it. Quotations from her paper—exhibiting her mordant wit—occupy three pages of the brief conference report, an indication of the effect the paper had on participants. She began by criticizing a speaker (unnamed) who had addressed the Companions during the previous winter, "'bemoaning the fact that there was no longer a safe magazine left in the United States except *The Ladies Home Journal* and *The Saturday Evening Post*. Even *The Atlantic* had an article by that terrible James Harvey Robinson,[48] and chapters from the Autobiography of James H. Maurer, a socialist.'" She then praised Florence Converse for her contributions to the "danger that this woman scented in *The Atlantic*." But, she said, none of the commercially successful magazines "really jolts from their comfort those who have the benefits of the world as it is today." From this springboard, Rochester launched into her main point: "Christianity, as I see it, must for ages to come,—yes, until our human life on this earth is completely transformed to express in every relationship the Christlike ideal, be essentially a prodding and disturbing force rather than a sedative and refuge for the individual soul." Thus, she argued, "a Christian Journal should, of necessity, be also a social journal, and the deeper it cuts into the question of human relationship, including the impersonal relationships which we mask under such phrases as 'economic forces,' 'political principles,' 'social tendencies,' the more truly it is carrying out a Christian purpose. For," she insisted, "the Christian cannot be isolated. Our lives really have no meaning apart from our share in the common life."[49]

But, for the very reasons Rochester listed, the common life that Rochester and Hutchins were sharing could no longer be centered in the SCHC. The community house of Adelynrood had shrunk to their Greenwich Village socialist co-op apartment, and they were now devoting themselves full-time to the FOR and, in Rochester's case, to the LID. Although they maintained their memberships for several more years, this was the last major contribution made by either Rochester or Hutchins to the Society of the Companions of the Holy Cross. Henceforth, although nourished by a partnership born in the women-only space of the SCHC, Rochester and Hutchins sought to extend their freedoms to others in the world at large.

October 1924 brought Hutchins's first participation in a labor action, the Paterson silk strike, and her introduction to working conditions for American silk workers, a subject about which she would later write *Labor and Silk*, the first in the Labor and Industry series of International Publishers. The strike, by thirteen thousand broad-silk workers, members of the Associated Silk Workers' Union, had begun on August 12; members of the United Textile Workers (ribbon weavers) did not cross the picket lines and soon joined in the effort to support the Associated Silk Workers. Police had been "overactive," arresting picketers and beating those who attended meetings in support of the strikers.[50] On the night of October 14, Hutchins, probably invited by Harry F. Ward, attended a meeting organized by the American Civil Liberties Union.[51] The meeting was designed to test free speech, and for once the police held back, not attacking those at the meeting.[52] Although the calls for an end to speed-ups and an introduction of the eight-hour day were not entirely met, workers learned from their mistakes in strategy, Hutchins later argued.[53]

Hutchins's primary commitment at this point, however, was to raising funds to support Rochester's work on *The World Tomorrow*, and she left New York shortly thereafter on a two-month fund-raising trip across the country. Writing to Devere Allen from a train in Utah, she mused about the difficulties and successes she was having raising money for the magazine. Despite criticisms from potential donors and, undoubtedly, recalling Rochester's arguments to the SCHC, Hutchins insisted that "our kind of journalism is needed more than ever," and she anticipated returning to the East with "a gold bag on [her] knee."[54]

She may or may not have been able to bring back the putative "gold bag." However, during her absence, Alice Beal Parsons, *World Tomorrow* business manager, submitted her resignation, and the conversation turned again to the possibility of Hutchins taking over the position. On Christmas Day, between family functions in Boston, Hutchins wrote to Devere Allen, outlining the possibilities and problems associated with her assumption of the position, as she saw them. One of the difficulties, she said, was her "relationship to Anna, which would make the work too much of a close corporation" if she were to take on much more responsibility.[55] She also feared that the young women in the office, Esther Shemitz and Grace Lumpkin, would miss Parsons, who contributed a "kind of 'spice'" to the office that she felt she did not have. And she worried about the fact that Devere

Allen and the others perceived her as an inconsistent worker. The most significant of these problems, she said, was her relationship with Rochester. Nonetheless, she said, she would like to offer her services, and, she thought, as long as she and Rochester kept to their own areas of responsibility, their partnership would not prove to be a problem.[56]

Although she had reassured Allen throughout the letter that her feelings would not be hurt if he thought this plan would not work, Hutchins was invited to take on the position of business manager for *The World Tomorrow* beginning in January 1925. With her assumption of the position—the title for which she never claimed, preferring to be called simply "secretary"—she set about to reorganize the office in a more egalitarian manner, much as she had done at St. Hilda's and at St. Faith's. According to the office workers, "the whole work of *The World Tomorrow* became a cooperative enterprise, with each person a responsible worker, sharing definite responsibility for the collective task of the whole organization."[57] The new collectivity, however, remained an island in a sea of capitalism, not unlike Community House, and was thus open to a similar fate.

As Hutchins tried to create a model collective, Rochester was making every effort to educate her readership to support fundamental economic change. In January, she published an article entitled "Need We Fear Class-Consciousness?" No, in short, was the answer. Rather, she argued for reshaping "our notions of property so that we recognize as lying entirely outside of the individual's domain, whether he be banker or wage-earner, such kinds of property as involve power over the tools and resources needed by the people." Thus, what was needed was a class-conscious labor party—but, Rochester insisted, "not class-consciousness in the Communist sense, for, at least in the United States, war tactics and dictatorship of the proletariat which the Communists have bound up with the idea of class consciousness are not the way to successful economic change."[58] Most of her readers, however, would not have appreciated this fine point, a point which would only become more nuanced in the years to come.

Although she did not yet understand the logic of the dictatorship of the proletariat, Rochester had by now spurned the language of Anglo-Catholicism. Recounting her religious trajectory—a secular conversion in every sense of the term—at the request of the editors of *Religious Education*, she described Vida Scudder introducing her to Anglo-Catholicism, which taught that Holy Communion was the "very Bread of Life . . . the channel of [Jesus'] response to our common dependence upon him." Rochester saw herself during this time as "one of the chosen few who were helping him to re-order human society." And, at times, she experienced "an intense consciousness, indescribable but unforgettable, as of a mysterious Power to which one yields, passively, joyously, with a sense that one may go out from the silence strengthened by a Gift peculiar to one's own soul." This happy situation—which she admitted was quite individualistic in its orientation—was shattered by the war, when the Socialist Party was hopelessly divided into two camps: those supporting the war and those opposing it. As Rochester told the story, she herself "was one of those socialists who escaped being fooled by slogans and propaganda," which is to say, she did not support the war. But "when men and women nourished by the Holy Communion shouted and slew with the worst, the glory faded from the Sacrament." Since that time, she said, she had found it difficult to accept all the language of the service, as so much of it "offend[ed] [her] sense of truth."[59]

One of the most significant changes in her belief system at this point was that she had become much more inclusive. Gandhi, Rochester said, was "the greatest religious leader since Jesus." And she saw in the devotion and sacrifice of conscientious objectors a contribution to the Kingdom of God, although accompanied by "a complete theological agnosticism." What's more, the IWWs, also irreligious, dedicated themselves to "the release of the workers from bondage." And the quest for beauty and sincerity found in the German Youth Movement was "a stirring of a spirit akin to Jesus," although no church could comprehend it. In these actions, she saw prayer, just as others might find it in the sacraments of the church.

In her own life, Rochester said, referring to her old requests to the Companions for intercessions, "the self-centered petitions against selfishness are crowded out." Sally Cleghorn, she said (without naming her), had been able to retain "the mystic sense of the loving presence of God" as she had made the transition to a new understanding of the sacramental importance of social action. "For others," Rochester conceded, including herself, "the way is colder." What, she questioned, is the source of evil? Perhaps we must acknowledge that we will not know why, "if Love *is* the central quality of the universe," suffering is requisite to growth. Nonetheless, "the Power of Love seems clearly to function as a cosmic force," she asserted, leaving love open and undefined, the space available for her love for Hutchins, as well as for other permutations. This carving out of space was the first of many written by Hutchins and Rochester, their way of marking the location for themselves and others like them. The tactic joined irony and parody in their arsenal, strategies to use when standard persuasive techniques were inadequate. Rochester concluded in a prophetic—and vague—mode: "When humanity has genuinely appropriated this truth, demonstrating it not only in the exceptional individual but in the common experience, then the way may open for further discoveries about the mystery which is life."[60]

What would it take for humanity to appropriate this truth? This question absorbed Rochester, Hutchins, and Scott Nearing, among others. Nearing's thinking and observations led him to resign that month from the executive committee of the FOR. According to Roger Baldwin, Nearing "felt that [the fellowship's] supporters were too largely coupon-clipping Protestants to whom pacifism had become mere dogma."[61] Moreover, he was preparing to travel to the Soviet Union in order to study the education system there; he was also beginning to accept the likelihood that the working class would need to respond with violence in order to achieve a "social order not based on struggle and domination."[62]

Rochester and Hutchins remained in the fellowship for another year, still trying to craft a method of argument that would carry the message of love as a cosmic force to everyone. This effort to speak to everyone—with a minimally capitalized operation—was depleting both Rochester and Devere Allen. In March 1925, Rochester succumbed to an unnamed illness that doctors at first thought could be cured by a week's rest but that later required surgery, keeping her away from the office for almost a month. She returned to work largely because Devere Allen, her coeditor, fell ill himself, although apparently most people undergoing her operation would have required a six-month period of recuperation. Allen was away from the office from April until August 1925. The magazine continued to pay his salary, and Rochester and Nevin Sayre covered his medical bills.[63]

Rochester and Hutchins understood that support for the magazine meant supporting the people producing the magazine, so Rochester also loaned Devere Allen the money to purchase a piece of land with a house in Wilton, Connecticut, although their financial agreement called for him to make interest-only payments to her. The land was relatively uncultivated, and Hutchins, now forty years old but without Rochester's financial resources, wrote to Devere Allen offering to come up to work on the land:

> Will you let me come up some Sunday, with a box lunch under my arm and do
> a half-day's work for you, either on caterpillars or chopping away dead branches

(or trees) or clearing underbrush, or anything you may direct? I really am as good as a man at that sort of thing, did it every summer for 5 months over a period of 10 years, and can wield an axe over quite a sizeable tree (if it has to come down,) but am especially good at clearing up underbrush.[64]

Apparently Hutchins's offer was not accepted. For outdoor activity, she had to wait until August.

Because Rochester and Hutchins no longer found meaning at Adelynrood, they chose to spend two of their three weeks of vacation in 1925—and for many years to come—at a family-run, Quaker primitive camp in the Adirondacks: Back Log Camp. The camp, mostly wood-floored tents (plus a modest lodge added in 1929) on the shore of Indian Lake near Sabael, New York, attracted primarily Philadelphia Quakers and other pacifists in the beginning; as word traveled, others began to sign up as well. The camp was especially attractive to single women and women couples, as there were few other places where they could go comfortably during the early part of the century. Hutchins and Rochester were clear, too, that they did not wish to go on a vacation just by themselves; they wanted community—and they found that, year after year, at Back Log Camp.

Thomas Kite Brown, an avid outdoorsman and mathematics teacher at the Westtown School, a private Quaker boarding school twenty-five miles outside of Philadelphia, started the camp. In 1896, "former students who had become wealthy Philadelphia entrepreneurs suggested that he set up a summer camp in the Adirondacks for them and their families." He established campsites on state land until, daunted by the increasing number of luxury hotels and private estates in the area, he purchased "a lumbered lot surrounded by state land fronting on Indian Lake" in 1910. By 1930, camp attendance had reached 100 guests, although it slowly declined after that until finally closing in the 1960s.[65]

Figure 5.1. Back Log Camp logo

Hutchins and Rochester attended in the years during which the camp flourished, from their first visit in 1925 until the early 1950s, dressing in knickers and work shirts and becoming known as "regulars." They always came during the last two weeks of August, celebrating Hutchins's birthday. Although many campers participated in canoe trips and hiking ventures, Rochester and Hutchins usually stayed closer to camp, especially in later years, spending their time reading and writing.

The conversation, especially over meals in the open-air dining tent, among camp-ers and staff (Thomas Kite Brown's six grown children and their spouses had taken over the running of the camp), was lively, as the campers included educators, businesspeople, and a wide range of professionals from government and private agencies. In the evenings, campers gathered at the Focus, a semicircular, canvas-covered area facing a campfire, for entertainment supplied by the campers themselves, often lectures on hobbies or interests or, on Sunday evenings, hymn singing led by Henry Cadbury, the eminent New Testament scholar and early member of the FOR.[66]

In 1925, returning refreshed from their first year at Back Log Camp, Hutchins and Rochester faced the perennial budget shortfall on *The World Tomorrow*. This time, they hoped that the American Fund for Public Service, also known as the Garland Fund for its founding benefactor, Charles Garland,[67] would make up the difference between what the magazine had and what it needed, a matter of some $5,000. The fund had already contributed $2,000 to the magazine in March and had provided a loan of $3,000 in May. Hutchins wrote to Elizabeth Gurley Flynn, then the administrator of the fund, explaining *The World Tomorrow*'s plight as well as its attempts to raise funds from its readership and its attempts to reach out to the labor movement. She had never had this kind of difficulty raising money before.

As Hutchins attempted to secure the necessary funds to maintain the magazine, Rochester wrote another article that was to have serious consequences for Hutchins's efforts and, ultimately, for Rochester's editorship. In "Sowing the Wind," published in the November 1925 issue, Rochester stated quite forthrightly that "three conflicts, world-wide and inextricably bound up one with another, lie before us on the road down which the white peoples are leading the human race." In her most direct attempt thus far to intervene rhetorically at the point of struggle, she explained, "Whether the storm breaks first as a war between capital and labor or a war between colored peoples and white, the class struggle and the race struggle will reenforce one another. And," she continued, "if by the maneuvering of power and propaganda these explosions are postponed while the cultivation of 'undeveloped' areas continues, a clash of empires will be ready to set the world aflame. . . . We are sowing the wind. We are preparing to reap the whirlwind." She then went on to argue: "The fact that modern wars have had their roots in economic conflicts is becoming since the Great War more generally recognized. . . . Imperialism has also come to be generally understood for what it is: the expansion of political power for the protection of expanding financial interests." In fact, she said, "The separateness of the political world from the economic is increasingly fictitious."[68]

This revelation, however, did not encourage donations from the well-to-do, which the magazine desperately needed at that point. Few moneyed individuals shared Rochester's belief in living contrary to one's own economic interests. In fact, on December 28, a let-ter came in from a Mrs. Elmhirst, informing them that her regular contribution of $3,000 per year was being withdrawn, ostensibly because she was moving overseas.[69] The fiscal difficulties were compounded by the fact that the FOR was seeking funds largely from the same people that the magazine was courting. At the November meeting of the fellowship council, which neither Hutchins nor Rochester attended, John Nevin Sayre urged that the emphasis of the fellowship be "upon war mainly, and among the causes to specialize on the psychological causes."[70] Rochester was undoubtedly distressed by this rightward turn on Sayre's part and probably did not refrain from saying so.

For the time being, despite Sayre's proposal, the organization continued to address industrial conflict, such as the strike in progress at the time at the American Thread Company mills in Willimantic, Connecticut. FOR leaders also agreed that their position was one of "left-wing pacifism," a phrase they left undefined, although they did advocate working "for a revision of the ideas of patriotism and nationalism in order to eliminate their militaristic flavor."[71]

Perhaps as a palliative, on December 17, the executive committee elected Rochester and Hutchins as their official representatives to the Women's Industrial Conference, to be held in Washington, DC, January 18–21, 1926.[72] The cost of this trip, plus the contributions she was making to the magazine and the fellowship, caused Hutchins some financial problems of her own. She sought relief from her father, who increased her allowance from $1,800 per year to $2,400 per year, saying: "You should remember that the principal object for which one has a father is to call upon him for assistance in times of distress, and I am very glad indeed to be able to help you in this way."[73] The question of sources of income—which had preoccupied the Companions—continued to be a situational incongruity, or contradiction, in the lives of Hutchins and Rochester; their solution was not to refuse the money, but simply to use the funds to disrupt and change the systems that provided them. This was the last time Hutchins asked her father for anything beyond the monthly sum he provided, her feminist sensibilities no doubt stung by his kindly but patronizing message.

Hutchins's increased income, however, did not solve the larger problems of the magazine, the fellowship, or the movement. Devere Allen remained unwell, and Hutchins spent part of her time raising money to support him while he rested. At the same time, she tried to find someone to take over his work so that Rochester did not have to do the work of two people. On March 3, during a brief hospital stay of her own, Hutchins pledged herself to another year of fund-raising and proposed that E. Merrill Root, a young English professor at Earlham College, be asked to serve as coeditor of *The World Tomorrow*.[74] This proposal may have come in part from her awareness that Devere Allen was not alone in experiencing what we now call "burn-out." She must have known that Rochester was in danger of collapse as well. On top of this, on March 28, the American Fund had turned them down, saying "that *The World Tomorrow* 'should be supported by liberal, religious and pacifist elements or else if such contributions are not forthcoming, it should more directly ally itself with the labor movement.' "[75] This development precipitated a more severe financial crisis for the magazine. Almost simultaneously, Rochester fell ill again.

Nevin Sayre, taking advantage of the fact that both the financial and editorial situations at *The World Tomorrow* were precarious, had come up with another plan, in line with his previous contention that the fellowship should emphasize the psychological causes of war. After consultation with Harold Hatch, a major contributor, he suggested that the editorship of the magazine be turned over to Kirby Page, then serving as chairman of the Fellowship for a Christian Social Order. Page was a close collaborator with Sherwood Eddy; the two had just finished coauthoring *Makers of Freedom*, "a series of biographical sketches in social progress." Page and Eddy were distinguished by both their insistence on a thoroughly Christian focus for their activities and their suspicion of the new social order in the Soviet Union. Rochester had argued strongly against this course of action, indicating that she would not find it agreeable to work with Kirby Page. During her illness, however, on April 9, she was removed as editor, and the magazine was turned over to Page. What made the package acceptable to the board of directors was the solution of the question of the $7,000 deficit. The "present management" would "turn things over to [them] substantially free from debt," and then, with the help of Kirby Page, Nevin Sayre said, "enough financial support could be secured."[76] This suggests that Rochester and Nevin Sayre would be responsible for supplying the $7,000, or perhaps Sayre shouldered it alone or with Harold Hatch.

On April 17, Kirby Page sent out a mass mailing advising people of his assumption of the editorship of *The World Tomorrow*. Devere Allen would remain as executive and literary editor, and he hoped that Rochester would continue as a contributing editor. The infusion of cash—from his own resources or from those of Nevin Sayre or Sherwood Eddy—that came with his assumption of the editorship was evident in his promise to pay "liberal honorariums" in order to attract "the ablest writers in this country and abroad."[77]

Rochester, trying to recuperate from another round of surgery, was devastated by the loss of her work and the change in direction of the magazine she had constructed. Although she realized that she could still write, she felt most intensely the loss of a group engaged in a common purpose, of which she could be a part[78]; what's more, she had failed not only at her paramount task of persuasion but in her attempt to work as an equal in an organization run primarily by men, a blow to her self-definition and to her efforts to make space for other women. In sum, the editorial position had been for Rochester not simply a job but a commitment to a community, and that community had unceremoniously turned her out. Although the most immediate cause of Hutchins and Rochester's removal from their positions was the magazine's unbalanced budget, their gender and partnership may have been additional factors. It undoubtedly did not escape their notice that the new administration was composed entirely of men.

Hutchins also was stricken by the loss, and she and Rochester sought refuge in Valeria Home, a sanitarium or convalescent center in Oscawana (near Peekskill), New York, where they carried on a correspondence with Devere Allen that ranged from warm and affectionate to bristling, depending on the topic.

Because Devere Allen retained his position on the magazine, there was a sense that he was more closely connected with the new administration and should share information more completely than he did. Moreover, he apparently told both Kirby Page and Nevin Sayre that he did not want either Rochester or Hutchins to participate in the reorganized magazine; nor did he want Esther Shemitz. (One hopes that she was not singled out because she was Jewish.) Finally, Hutchins, attempting to take care of Rochester, wrote to Devere Allen asking him to write a friendly letter to Rochester (with no mention of Hutchins's suggestion) about their work together during the past few years. He responded well to this suggestion, writing a letter that probably helped to cement a friendship that continued over the next several decades, although in attenuated form.

Hutchins, too, was coming to terms with the fact that it was her inability to raise the necessary money that had led to the financial crisis and ultimately to the "sale" (in her words) of the magazine to another administration. This was her first failure in fundraising, a humbling experience that brought home to her the contradictions inherent in soliciting substantial contributions to argue against capitalism.

Seeking to comfort Rochester, Hutchins came up with a plan for their lives: they would travel around the world, still giving themselves wholly to the whole community, studying and reporting on education and labor issues in eastern and central Asia, the Soviet

Union, and Europe—especially Germany. Immediately, they set about making arrangements. Rochester was fluent in French and German, and Hutchins could speak and read
Chinese, but neither of them knew a Slavic language, so in May they began studying
Russian. Hutchins also wrote to her old missionary colleagues, including Grace Lindley
and Bishop Roots, asking them for advice about places to stay. And both Rochester and
Hutchins sought letters of introduction to leaders in the places they planned to visit. They
would represent *The World Tomorrow* in addition to other publications.

Grace Lindley responded quickly with names and descriptions of people they should
visit and a letter of introduction to General Wood, American administrator of the Philippines. They should also talk with Mrs. Wood, she advised. Lindley herself had traveled
extensively in India, and she recommended mission houses—places that took in travelers
at a modest charge—in all the major cities.[79] FOR colleagues supplied several letters of
introduction to Mahatma Gandhi. Anticipating a stay in the Soviet Union, they sought
letters of introduction to various Soviet officials from Scott Nearing. Harry F. Ward provided them with a letter of introduction to Anatoly Lunacharsky, people's commissar of
education. Other former colleagues provided letters of introduction to people throughout
Japan, China, Singapore, the Philippines, India, and the Soviet Union so they would be
well supplied with contacts to interview during their travels. Their aim was to send back
articles on the information they uncovered—information not likely to have been printed
in the mainstream capitalist press.

In early June, at a meeting at the home of Norman Thomas, Rochester submitted her
letter of resignation from the board of directors of the LID. On a motion of Paul Jones,
the resignation was accepted with regret.[80] At its June meeting, the fellowship council
asked Hutchins and Rochester to represent the fellowship during their year abroad.[81] And
Bishop Roots cabled Hutchins in mid-June, welcoming them to Wuchang and asking if
they would like to teach at St. Hilda's for a year, or even half a year, an invitation they
politely declined.[82] They asked Grace Lumpkin, who had left *The World Tomorrow* along
with her friend Esther Shemitz, if she would process their mail during their absence, to
which she agreed. They sublet their apartment and wrote to all of their friends, advising
them of their plans.

Before they left, Rochester wrote one last item—a letter to the editor of *The Nation*
seeking funds to help the widows and children of Bulgarian writers and journalists who
had been killed on account of their political writings.[83] After all, she had only lost her
editorial position, not her life.

Finally, Rochester and Hutchins departed by train for the West Coast, where they
would board the S.S. *Empress of Russia* in Vancouver, British Columbia, on August 13,
bound for Japan. In the space of five and a half years, they had wrung dry the promise
of same-sex organizations and were close to abandoning the Episcopal church, the FOR,
and the LID. Their only stop en route was Chicago, where they visited Carl Haessler of
the Federated Press, the labor press service cofounded five years earlier by Scott Nearing. Telling Haessler of their plan to study labor and education issues in Asia, the Soviet
Union, and Germany, they offered to send back news items. This offer marked their first
full step into the labor movement.

Part Two

Love and Work

Chapter Six

Love Requires a New Form

Love will always be love . . . , but it requires a new form. Everything will come through and attain new forms, and then we shall know how to forge new links.

—Fyodor Vasilievich Gladkov (*Cement*)

The trip would provide the most significant conversion of Rochester's and Hutchins's lives, although both had experienced several reorientations before this. Their 1927 conversion was not an epiphany, nor was it the result of a planned incongruity; rather, it was dialectical change on fast forward, new insights occurring on an almost daily basis.

As they were shifting their commitments to the labor movement and adopting new methods of persuasion, Hutchins and Rochester maintained close ties to the communities of women that had nurtured their partnership. During the next few years, as their reorientation solidified, some of these ties would be challenged in ways from which they would never entirely recover. Now, however, when they arrived on the ship in late August 1926, they were greeted by almost a hundred letters from friends, among which was a long letter from Vida Scudder, who told Rochester that her letter had "seemed to bring you right back into our little circle here, quite as in the old days. . . . I do so like to think of you and that dear Grace starting on your travels." Offering Rochester mentorly advice as usual, she went on: "I observe that all travellers find precisely what they look for and are colorblind otherwise." Then, turning to herself and Florence, she said: "Florence and I, for the first time in our long friendship, have been enjoying what, to be frank, we always craved—a solitude a deux. . . . Delicious!" In the lower right hand corner, Rochester wrote—and underlined—"*Do not destroy*," savoring the love, understanding, and optimism from Scudder.[1]

The degree to which she heard and understood what Scudder was saying to her is evident in the first of several round-robin letters Rochester wrote to friends—mostly women—during the trip. Writing from on board ship, on August 27, she said: "Miss Scudder reminds me that most travelers get from their travels only what they expect to see." She went on to say that she had had an "interesting discussion" with Carl Haessler "on the usefulness of the open mind." An open mind, however, was not to be confused with a lack of commitment: "he was hot against those who hold their opinions in such free solution that they never crystallize." She might have added that crystallization by itself was not enough, finding the missionaries on board ship especially difficult: one physician returning from furlough declared that he found the theory of evolution entirely "inconsistent with his religious faith." Rochester, however, was determined to uncover facts. "I have grown or drifted during these *World Tomorrow* years," she said, "to believe that the facts and the facts back of the facts, and only then an attempt at analysis of trends, cannot be overemphasized."[2]

Having issued this challenge to her readers, Rochester reached out to them with her trademark humor, drawing her friends back close to her again in a private community. "Tonight there is a costume ball!" she announced. "We intend to blossom out in our evening gowns specially acquired for this trip, the first in ten years for either of us. We shall not attend the ball but the daily radio press urges every one to come to dinner in costume. (How will they know that for us an evening gown *is* [a costume]?)"[3]

How would they know, indeed? Rochester left the question unanswered, and it hung in the air, an in-joke by which she recreated the bond with her private world of friends. The unspoken answer, of course, was that they wouldn't; Hutchins and Rochester's embodied rhetoric would not be read correctly by anyone apart from themselves. At the same time, casting the observation as a question suggested Rochester's desire to be known, a preference for a world free of fixed gender requirements. Being misread was the price they paid for moving out of the comfortable niche of same-sex activities in which they had found each other; the price would only become steeper as time passed.

In June 1926, however, while Rochester and Hutchins dismissed gendered costuming with private irony for a closed group, they reserved their public outrage for the increasing repression they witnessed in Kyoto, especially as conditions affected women. Several students, they learned, had been imprisoned for a number of months without charges and without access to counsel after their papers and books had been searched. Later, in Tokyo, they discovered that another thirty-seven university students had just been indicted, after being held for nine months without bail, for violation of the "Peace Preservation Law and the Press Law." In an article that apparently went unpublished, Rochester wrote: "The present government is determined to suppress all revolutionary propaganda, whether in the labor movement or in the universities. Even any explicit recognition of the class struggle apparently is banned as a 'dangerous thought.'" However, she anticipated—wrongly, as it obviously turned out—that the present reactionary trends would not be able to continue; there were too many Japanese, she claimed, who did not find the level of repression acceptable and who were beginning to speak out. "That they will permit a continuance of extreme reaction is scarcely conceivable."[4]

Much of Rochester's journalism followed the form she had learned while working with Julia Lathrop at the US Children's Bureau, drawing social and political conclusions from economic data, the "facts behind the facts." Rochester reported that "even the highest paid Japanese factory workers earn less than unskilled workers in the United States." Yet, she said, prices are as high as they are in the United States.[5] The largest employers were cotton and textile manufacturers, and most of their employees were women, many girls under 16 recruited from the countryside and housed in factory-owned dormitories. In 1924, the latest date for which figures were available, women weavers were reported to be earning 45 cents per day. In contrast, the semiannual dividend for the first half of 1926 for Japanese cotton manufacturers, she said, was 15.3 percent.[6]

Although Hutchins accompanied Rochester on her visits to cotton mills and her interviews with labor leaders, she herself crafted personal narratives designed to inspire action, after the manner she had learned at the Student Volunteer Movement conference in 1906. In her first article, written for *Christian Century*, she explained the role of Rev. Toyochiko Kagawa as one of the organizers of the new Labor Farmer Party. She began the article in her trademark way, with an intensely emotional description of his eyes—afflicted with late-stage trachoma[7]—and told her readers that within a few months he would be blind. This condition, contracted while he lived with the poor in the slums of Kobe, she contrasted throughout the article with his devotion to the Japanese working class and his determination to work against government policies. Finally, Hutchins noticed what others overlooked—that Kagawa's chosen life had perhaps been hardest on his wife, who "was often in danger from the men of violence in the slums" and who had not had any help running the household. Still the charity fundraiser, she closed by advising readers where they could send contributions to help Rev. Kagawa.[8]

From Japan, Rochester and Hutchins traveled to Peking, where they stayed at the Peking Language School, founded in 1916 to furnish education in Chinese language and customs for businessmen, diplomats, and missionaries.[9] It also provided comfortable accommodations for Western travelers. From this station, Hutchins and Rochester wrote their next round-robin letter—noting in the first lines their anxiety at hearing that their friend and former *World Tomorrow* colleague Esther Shemitz had been assaulted and arrested on the picket line in Passaic.[10] Alice Dillingham, Rochester's old high school friend, now a lawyer, had apparently represented Esther (a defense undoubtedly paid for by Rochester), and had written indicating that her injuries were not severe.

Once established at the Language School, Hutchins and Rochester set about the task of determining conditions in China—a process that involved learning not only about the history of China per se but also about the colonial policies of such countries as England, France, Portugal, Japan, and the United States. These policies entailed *settlements*, or legation quarters, Chinese land under the control of resident foreign consuls, and *concessions*, de jure colonies leased by foreign nations. Additionally problematic was the practice of *extraterritoriality*, whereby the citizens of treaty nations were subject not to the laws of China but to the laws of the nation in which they held citizenship.[11] These policies, they were to learn, provided the impetus for Chinese Nationalist (Kuomintang) organizing.[12]

More than anything, Rochester wanted to convey to her readers the conditions in China. They had gone with the aim of investigating and reporting on education and labor conditions in the various Asian countries, but their questions kept eliciting commentary on the political situation, and soon they began to realize—thanks to Rochester's desire to understand the "facts back of the facts"—that they could not ignore the question of armed force, nor could they overlook the various centers of power and the ideas fueling those centers of power. Peking at that time was still under the control of foreign-supported generals and their armies; the Kuomintang had just liberated Wuchang. After listing a panoply of outrages involving blatant theft and assaults, Rochester focused on what she found to be the most worrisome aspect of the "reign of terror": "Since last spring, thirty newspaper editors in North China have been executed." The only remaining newspaper in Peking that was supporting the Kuomintang was the English-language newspaper the *Peking Leader*, then being published out of the home of two Americans, Mr. and Mrs. Grover Clark, liberals of the Dewey school, according to another American, Rayna (Raphaelson) Prohme.[13]

Rayna Raphaelson Prohme, daughter of the vice president of the Chicago Board of Trade, was a slight red/brown/gold-haired woman with an engaging laugh and a commitment to social justice that grew from her feeling of "genuine relationship to all forms of human life."[14] A close friend of Dorothy Day (founder of the Catholic Worker movement), Anna Louise Strong, and Mme. Sun Yat-Sen, Rayna Prohme was devoted to the Chinese revolution. What was most important for Americans to understand, Prohme insisted, was that the Canton government was *not* Communist. The Canton government, she said, "could stabilize China, but foreign capital is labelling it 'red.'"[15]

The newspaper situation, Rochester and Hutchins discovered, was on the verge of worsening. Mr. and Mrs. Clark were planning to return to the United States for an extended stay, leaving the *Peking Leader* in the hands of a Mr. Abend, a Trinidadian and former employee of the *Los Angeles Times*, whose attitude toward the British and their considerable abuses was quite uncritical. In her letter home, Rochester described Abend's probable assumption of the *Peking Leader* as "a minor tragedy," saying that he "obviously has no possibility of sympathetic understanding with the Kuomintang or the labor movement."[16]

Of all their nearly forty interviews with both Chinese and foreigners alike in the Northern Chinese cities of Peking and Tientsin (now Tianjin), Hutchins and Rochester found their talk on September 27 with P. C. Chang, former dean of Tsing Hua College, the most enlightening. The mission schools, Chang said, have "tended to de-nationalize," providing too little Chinese culture and too much Western culture.[17] Historically, Chinese students went to Japan for education in the early twentieth century; then they began to realize that they were receiving only a superficial education, obtained at second hand from Europe. So after 1911, students (most of whom graduated from mission schools during 1909–1915) turned to the United States; it was these US-educated students, he said, who were now running China's educational institutions, but they were "on the wane." They paid too much attention, he said, to religious instruction—a humbling point for Hutchins.

Professor Chang's challenge to Americans to understand China more thoroughly provided a temptation to Rochester and Hutchins, who gave momentary thought to cancelling the rest of their trip to remain in Peking studying for a year at the Language School with Arthur Hummel, Dr. Lucius Porter, and other instructors. When she talked with Dr. Porter, Hutchins's rhetoric of the whole person enabled her to understand the situation as he explained it, translating the issues into terms upon which she could begin to act. Dr. Porter asserted that "interracial relations [are] the great problem in the world today." "We are ourselves a problem," Hutchins wrote in her notebook during her conversation with him. "We are the units of contact."

Hummel explained to them that the Chinese have power over the Americans because they understand both cultures, whereas Americans know only their own. But what about the anti-Christian movement? they queried, still fixed in their American orientation. It is an attempt to "dig us out of our finalities," he responded, challenging Hutchins, especially, to rethink her missionary years. And then, answering their questions about peace, Hummel went on to explain that although the young Chinese thought that force provided the way, "militarism cannot prevail as in the West." Why? Because the desire to compromise and to negotiate and be reasonable were at the heart of Chinese life. The problem was that China had tried to approach the West reasonably and failed, so it seemed as though the West understood only force. The May 30 incident, he said, illustrated this.[18]

Showing evidence that she was quickly repositioning herself, Hutchins wrote an explanation of the Nationalist efforts. Although the Kuomintang leaders were all in hiding, through one of their contacts, most likely Rayna Prohme, Rochester and Hutchins were taken to two prominent Nationalists. With this article and several others written during their stay in China, Rochester and Hutchins tried to join a larger conversation going on in the Western press—both the mainstream dailies and the missionary monthlies—attempting to provide information not found in these publications. The capitalist press, Hutchins said, was calling the armies of the South "Reds," saying that they were accepting support from Russia. The Nationalist leaders, however, insisted that they had only purchased arms from Russia; no direct aid had been provided. The Soviet Union *had*, however, been the only country to voluntarily give up "extraterritorial rights and privileges," she said, a key issue in the battle.[19]

Already, Hutchins and Rochester's quick dismissal of Communists was yielding to a more nuanced analysis, based on their observations. Yet, it would take many more interviews and experiences before their views had shifted completely and they began to occupy the spaces opened to press for economic freedoms for both women and men. In early October 1926, they were still in Peking, listening to as many people as they could find, learning that 70 percent of a workingman's budget went for food. And although the wages of carpenters were set by the guilds, those of unskilled laborers were not. They "*cannot* earn a living," Hutchins wrote to herself.[20] Apparently these questions had not occurred to her during her years at St. Hilda's.

Although there were ongoing international conversations, however misleading, about Chinese politics, Hutchins was one of only a few trying to enlarge those conversations to include women, yet her questions often elicited nothing more than elaborate justifications for maintaining traditional systems. Nancy Lee Swann,[21] using the China-centric argument, told them that women students were looking too much to the West for inspiration and models. Chinese women were still economically bound, she said, but the spirit of younger women was for a career rather than for marriage. There had been a generation of women educated in mission schools, with Western teachings, since 1905. "Yet consider," she said, "what a bound-footed woman does. [She] has had complete control of the family purse."[22]

Unimpressed with Swann's reasoning, Rochester and Hutchins faced more challenges as they investigated labor conditions. In silk factories, Hutchins learned, "workers for days together do not leave the filatures, but work and sleep in the same building."[23] Responding to conditions such as these, a Peasants', Workers', Soldiers', and Students' Alliance in Canton had agreed "'to work for the overthrow of imperialism and militarism.'" And all those involved, they learned, were opposed to the principles of the Kuomintang, seeing a Nationalist solution as inadequate.

With this disturbing introduction to the situation in China, an introduction that was beginning to convince them that they might have been asking the wrong questions, Hutchins and Rochester left on October 12 for Wuchang to revisit the mission where Hutchins had lived for four years. There, they found that Francis Wei, dean of Boone College and acting president of the Central China University, who had been politically neutral before, now felt that the Kuomintang "was the hope of China." Bishop Roots, likewise, said that he thought the coming into power of the Nationalists "would be the completion of the 1911 Revolution."[24]

Yet missionaries were hardly of one mind about the events and changes in China. Not surprisingly, a significant number were resisting the changes. In March 1926, the Episcopal *Spirit of Missions* published "An Attempt to Analyze the Situation in China," signed only "An American Observer in China." This writer declared that in the Kuomintang "there are two factions, known as the right and left wings; the right is the more moderate and the left the more extreme. The left adds to the political program a social and economic one and is eager to spread the communistic principles of Russian bolshevism in China."[25]

This story was repeated frequently by John W. Wood, the head of the Board of Domestic and Foreign Missions of the American Episcopal Church. In November 1926, he wrote that the fighting in the Wuchang area "may be described as a contest between the radical and reactionary elements in China. The Southerners, with Canton as their capital, are the aggressors. Canton, for several years the stronghold of the late Sun Yat Sen, has been a fertile field for Soviet propaganda."[26] In January 1927, he wrote: "Corruption is rife. The hand of Soviet Russia becomes steadily more apparent, especially in the anti-British propaganda."[27]

Yet John Wood's analysis differed markedly from that of Edward H. Littell, who wrote in September from Nanchang:

> Everybody in Nanchang, foreign and Chinese, longs for the return of Southern control, and there is certainly not the least comparison between the Southern and Northern troops. The morning after the South came in the police were told to stay on duty and all business went on peacefully. Since the North came back there is murder and robbing everywhere and the dead are carried through the streets like pigs. Every southern soldier in the Methodist Hospital can read and write, whereas the Northerners are chiefly coolies. The Cantonese are all fighting for a cause that they have at heart, and during the battles their wounded could not be kept at the hospital. "We're needed" they would say, and limp off.[28]

Within this maelstrom, Bishop Roots was the one member of the mission community with whom Hutchins and Rochester seemed to feel the most affinity. He mentioned to them the fact that those in command now were scholars. In the past, he said, scholars studied alone; they were very conservative, and "the mind of China was held in bondage by their great past." Now, however, the scholars were the very ones who were studying widely. And Russia, he pointed out, "treats them better than any other nation."[29]

Leaving Hankow, Rochester and Hutchins traveled back down the Yangtse to Nanking, where they met with Hutchins's former student Phoebe Hoh, who emphasized to them again the need for missionaries to come out publicly for a change in the treaties. Phoebe Hoh was teaching Chinese and serving as general counselor to students at Ginling College, a school for women in Nanking. "Our people are awakening now," she said. "The treaties were arranged when China was sleeping." But what about Bolshevism? they asked, as usual. Bolshevism could not be put down, she answered, while the causes of it were still there. The missionaries, she pointed out, were not helping China to develop industries.[30]

By November 18, Rochester and Hutchins had moved on to Canton, seeking out representatives of labor as well as Fanny Borodin, the wife of the Russian advisor. Fanny Borodin spoke with Rochester and Hutchins shortly before fleeing China for Moscow with Rayna Prohme and Madame Sun Yat-Sen, anticipating the Kuomintang's rightward turn. If Rochester and Hutchins's minds had not been opened by all their contacts thus far, Fanny Borodin completed the job, telling them that it had been her experience that foreigners in China ignored what was happening around them, like the little boy with his eyes closed in the middle of a room who declares, "I am not here." Perhaps she was prodding Hutchins and Rochester to understand the significance of what they were seeing; Vincent Sheean later claimed that the fall of Hankow to Chiang Kai-shek was to determine the conduct of the Comintern for years afterwards, that it "turn[ed] the mind of the Russian Soviet government away from the militant internationalism of Trotsky to the national socialism of Stalin."[31]

Writing from Canton for the *Survey* on November 23, 1926, Hutchins summed up their experiences, countering the fear-mongering stories of the capitalist press with clear explanations of labor organizing and social research gleaned from their interviews. "But of revolutionary Communism, in principle or in practice, either in this or in any other part of China, there is not enough to alarm even a Daughter of the American Revolution," she reassured her readers, neglecting to mention the Peasants', Workers', Soldiers', and Students' Alliance in Canton. "A leading Communist in China gave us letters of introduction to his fellow Communists in different centers, but when we came to talk with them we found they were only Nationalists after all."[32]

Nonetheless, Hutchins pointed out, China had *invited* Russian advisors, and, in fact, any nation might enjoy the same friendly relations with China that Russia had, if only it would take the same path: relinquish privileges such as extraterritoriality and concessions. Americans seemed to insist on behaving in a manner guaranteed to offend the Chinese. There were fifty-two American gunboats in Chinese waters, she said, a situation that the Chinese did not find endearing. Not only that, but "Americans offend in smaller matters also. The American Club in Shanghai, as all the others excepting the Union Club, has closed its doors to Chinese guests. The general secretary of the YMCA, David Yui, was to meet a well-known American architect at the club, but could not get in until a servant led him around by way of the kitchen."[33] What America needed to do, she insisted, was to remove itself from joint operations with other countries, especially Britain, and act independently in a manner that was respectful and recognized the Nationalist government of China.

Rochester spent what little time she had in Canton writing news items on labor issues, reporting on conditions and events in both Shanghai and Canton. In Shanghai, she said, the Commercial Press, a Chinese-owned concern, had built recreational facilities for the workers but still maintained low wages and long hours; the workers organized and struck successfully, but the company fired two hundred organizers. The workers walked off the job again, troops were called in, and forty strikers were injured, after which management decided to meet the strikers' demands. Workers, she noted, would not be bought off with a few luxuries if wages remained low and hours long.[34]

Leaving China for the Philippines, Rochester wrote on December 10 to their friends, predicting that

> within five years at the very outside, and probably very much sooner, the Kuomintang will split into two and more likely three component parts—for the present alliance against foreign domination holds together capitalists and labor sympathizers who will fly apart when the emergency situation is passed. . . . The capitalist who believes in domination by the few who own will hardly stay in the same political group with the communist who wants the few to dominate for a revolutionary change toward communism. And, reluctantly, one must admit that the avoidance of some sort of dictatorship while the majority are still illiterate—or reading without understanding as in the U.S.A.—is a Utopian dream.[35]

She said that it would be interesting to see what would happen—providing the Communist minority was still in the Kuomintang—when the Nationalists took the Yangtse Valley, including Shanghai. She pronounced Rayna Raphaelson and her husband, William Prohme, the "most interesting" of the foreigners they met in Canton. For Rochester and Hutchins, Rayna Raphaelson Prohme would have presented a clear contrast to the "very trying anti-labor diatribes" to which they were subjected by their Canton Christian College hosts, and she would have encouraged them to appreciate the Communist influence in the Kuomintang, an appreciation that would grow for them with time and added exposure to colonial outrages.

After they arrived in the Philippines, Hutchins and Rochester confronted any number of these outrages. A short distance from their hotel, they discovered two American-run gold mines, one employing twenty-five hundred Filipino laborers and utilizing roads built with Filipino money and labor. During four days in Manila, their interviews focused on the topic of whether the United States should withdraw from the Philippines: "With Bishop Mosher at one extreme and Speaker Roxas at the other and about a dozen Filipinos and

Americans in between we certainly did not get only *one* view."[36] After hearing from Filipino FOR friends that Filipinos found it difficult to go to the Luneta Hotel, they moved from the Luneta to the Plaza Hotel—although they admitted that they would probably stay at the Manila Hotel, a more upscale place, when they returned to Manila, after having seen "the size of the cockroach that crawled under the bureau and the size of the bat" that dropped into their room at dawn.[37]

From Manila, Hutchins and Rochester traveled to Baguio, the summer capital of the Philippines, a small Westernized city up in the mountains, always less hot and humid than Manila, and even chilly in December, when Rochester and Hutchins arrived. Unlike the rest of the Philippines, Baguio had asphalt roads in 1926, and in the center of the city, a lake was surrounded by multicolored electric light bulbs that shone in the night. "Europeans of affluence, Americans with big businesses in the islands, and rich Filipinos lived in Baguio. Their beautiful white houses dotted the hills."[38] Hutchins and Rochester were staying in this rarefied environment with the Bartters, an American-English missionary couple; Mrs. Bartter, they told their readers, would be familiar to those who had been to Adelynrood. Despite the apparently racial motivation behind the hotel difficulties, Rochester reported to her friends that she was realizing "how much more the economic and political domination matter than any racial differences." This confirmed for her, she said, her "conviction that our race conflict in the United States is secondary also to our still-continued economic exploitation of the Negroes."[39] Whether Hutchins agreed with this analysis, given her comments after talking with Dr. Lucius Porter, we don't know. Nonetheless, they were still profoundly embarrassed to observe the condescension with which one of their missionary friends in Baguio treated the Igorot people with whom she was working.[40] In contrast, however, they visited with Congregational missionaries Frank and Effa Laubach, who within a few years would develop the "Each One Teach One" literacy education system, and both of whom heartily supported Philippine independence, the only missionaries they encountered who did so.[41]

In Baguio, they used their letter of introduction to General Wood, which had been provided by Grace Lindley. "We were stirred to great respect for the dispassionate, impersonal way in which [General Wood] analyzed his view of the situation," Rochester commented. "The Governor's attitude was in marked contrast to the rather emotional diatribes against the Filipinos to which certain American acquaintances in Manila had treated us." Nonetheless, she followed with criticisms of his authoritarian regime, pointing out how he had given offense, and concluded: "The whole tangle . . . will be settled only when we as a people, recognizing the real issues involved, so reorganize our economic life and purify our national ideas that encroachments on the liberty of other nations and people shall become unnecessary and intolerable."[42]

Returning to Manila, they rededicated themselves to this goal before leaving the Philippines, locating the nascent labor movement. Rochester reported to the Federated Press that the thirty-thousand–member cigar makers' union had struck successfully against their Filipino employers in order to push back a wage cut. The cigar makers, she pointed out, were one of three unions not affiliated with the Federation of Labor. This union and a more radical printers' union, she said, repeating her previous analysis, held that "while political freedom for the islands is desirable the real conflict for Filipino labor will come with the increase of highly organized industrial capital."[43] They had found only one person during their stay in the Philippines—the editor of *El Debate*, an independent newspaper— who agreed that the conflict was founded in the struggle between labor and corporations; everyone else viewed it in political terms, leaving out the economic elements.

On Christmas Day 1926, having left the Philippines, Hutchins and Rochester were at sea, on a ship of the Dollar line, which, they noted, provided a Bible in every cabin and only novels and the memoirs of founder Robert Dollar in the library—no encyclopedia to which they could turn to look up information on the rubber industry they planned to investigate in Singapore. So once they were in Singapore, they did not have "the facts and the facts back of the facts" without which they found analysis of their observations and experiences difficult. Nevertheless, they toured rubber plantations, declining to debate with their Sinhalese guide, who quoted ancient Sanskrit verses expounding man's unquenchable thirst for more acquisitions, because "he would not have brooked argument from two women." Rochester did not have to explain to her readers her complicated position vis à vis the Sinhalese guide as an Anglo woman clearly possessed of sufficient funds for travel. She and Hutchins did understand and appreciate his comment on the opulent residence of the British governor of Singapore: " 'Supported by *our* money.' " And after describing the new naval base, conveniently located across from a large British-owned rubber plantation, Rochester said: "I can't quite convey the vivid impression of complete control." Again, after writing another few paragraphs to her friends about rubber and tin, Rochester reasserted, "The completeness of imperialism comes over one with fresh impact."[44] That completeness included a petrified gender hierarchy that served the colonizers well.

The impact of imperialism would only grow as Rochester and Hutchins made their way to India, where they spent the month of January. Having been let down by many of the Americans they had met to date, they were cheered when, on board the ship, they encountered two men traveling together, one of whom was reading, Rochester observed, a book by G. Lowes Dickinson: *The International Anarchy, 1904–1914*, an analysis of the causes of World War I. A close friend of E. M. Forster, Lowes Dickinson was a Cambridge history don, who, like Vida Scudder, found in Plato, especially in the *Phaedrus*, support for same-sex love; he also was a pacifist who had coined the name "League of Nations." Rochester mentioned this incident to the readers of her round-robin letter, who would have included Scudder, Florence Converse, and a host of others who subscribed to the Anglophile Platonist tradition. "But it turned out," she said, clearly disappointed, "that his traveling companion, a retired Boston physician, was as imperialistic as they make them."[45] Thus, without directly pointing out the contradictions of those, such as Scudder, who simultaneously held both Platonist and Socialist ideas, she let her readers know that the system that had nurtured her to this point was proving inadequate to address the larger international issues she was encountering—and, apart from her personal life with Hutchins, the influence of Edward Carpenter was on the wane. Carpenter's attempt to mend the split between the personal and the political was coming undone. Hutchins and Rochester were searching for a replacement.

Having landed in India, Hutchins and Rochester combined their research with some "tourist" activities, notably a visit to the Taj Mahal. They moved from Agra to Delhi, where they stayed at the YWCA, "surrounded by a half-dozen female imperialists." Rochester reported that they had "combined with the mildest two of the F. I.'s for an all day car to see the really impressive array of ruined cities extending for some miles south of Delhi." It was here, she said, that she "got a lovely kodak of Grace 'en touriste,' studying ceiling carvings by the archway of the oldest tomb in north India."[46] The reference to the reactionary "female imperialists" would serve to remind her readers that feminism is about liberatory ideas—not biology. With the photo of Hutchins, however, Rochester drew her reader's eyes back to the two of them and without flatly declaring her love for Hutchins, unnecessary with this audience, let her readers experience that love through the camera lens.

Rochester and Hutchins's primary activity in India, however, was a visit with Mahatma Gandhi, to whom they had been given several letters of introduction. One of their chief difficulties in locating him was, after they arrived in the vicinity of his next appearance, to find the proper conveyance. They hoped for a "one-horse tonga," but after walking a half-mile in the heat, settled for a two-horse, two-man phaeton.[47] Rochester's commentary on this vehicle exhibits her capacity for self-criticism couched in ironic use of the language of imperialism, as well as her understanding that, in the eyes of the local population, there was no difference between her and the "female imperialists" with whom she felt no ties, another iteration of Hutchins's ownership of an embodied rhetoric and insight that "we are ourselves the problem": "The second man does not add quite as much elegance as one might fancy, as his chief duty is getting out the hay from the back of the carriage and feeding the horses whenever the mem-sahibs choose to stop."[48] When they arrived at the large open area where the meeting was to be held, they were ushered to two chairs in an enclosure near the platform and then quizzed by an Indian policeman about their motives. Having passed this test, they waited and watched some more. Rochester said, "We found ourselves thinking of the feeding of the five thousand," although by this time the crowd had grown to more than ten thousand.

Shortly after four o'clock, the FOR letters of introduction did their work, and Hutchins and Rochester were taken to see Mahatma Gandhi in "a little stonewalled, stone-floored room, two thirds of it raised two steps above the rest." They wanted to talk with his wife, who was preparing food, but were told to go to the upper level of the room and wait there. "We had just sat down on the floor when he came—lively, radiantly smiling, as unlike the sombre ascetic of his pictures as one could well imagine. The face is thin, even bony, and the loss of some front teeth is conspicuous, but this you only realize afterwards." The conversation focused on the question of nonviolence, with Gandhi explaining the concept of *ahimsa*, or civil resistance in the tradition of Thoreau, to Hutchins and Rochester; when Hutchins mentioned that the Passaic strikers had engaged in nonviolent resistance, calling it "Hindu resistance," he objected, saying, "But that exalts my religion above others. The principle is universal."[49] It meant more than simply "a resolution not to use violence in action," he told them. "Of the five vows taken by his disciples at the Satyagrah As'ram, the vow of *ahimsa* means, 'It is forbidden to harbor an uncharitable thought about anyone who may regard himself as an enemy. The person so dedicated must not resent injury, or desire that harm should come to an enemy, or use any violence even to guard the honor of those who are in his charge.'"[50] From them, Gandhi wanted to know about pacifism in the United States—and about Eugene Debs, of whom he had only recently learned.

Rochester commented to the readers of her round-robin letter that they had tried to discern from him whether he believed that the method of nonviolence would be sufficient to ward off class wars, but he declined to engage in such prophesizing. And she added: "We could have had a glorious argument on the hand-spinning idea but naturally in one short talk this could not be." She also felt that his analysis of caste was inadequate, although that was not a topic of conversation. "In everything else," she exulted, "he carried my mind with him."[51] A few years later, after having studied the inner workings of capital and moved into a community committed to class struggle, Rochester would remember the conversation less warmly.

After their meeting, Rochester and Hutchins were returned to the gathering of the ten thousand by a Muslim follower driving an American car. Rochester had called the group "the real rank and file of India," and Hutchins took special note that they were the only women there. This, combined with the inaccessibility of Gandhi's wife, suggested a movement that, although impressive, remained deficient in significant ways. They sat on the ground this time, up in the front, and listened while Gandhi addressed the multitude on the topics of "spinning, and untouchables, and goodwill between Hindus and Moham-medans in spite of the recent murder of a Hindu leader by a Mohammedan."[52]

When he had finished speaking, Gandhi drew them up onto the platform with him, so that they would not be crushed by the throngs of people; he bid them farewell and departed, and they returned to their travelers' bungalow to begin preparations for leaving India. "I for one am not sorry to leave India," Rochester wrote. "I found the superlordly British quite unbearable—one only marvels that there has been only one armed revolt in all these years." And she added: "it sends one home with renewed determination to work for the new order in the U.S.A."[53] Of course, Hutchins and Rochester had been and were continuing, via their articles and letters, to work for "the new order," if the precise shape and method remained unclear.

Before leaving India, Hutchins and Rochester stopped in Calcutta, where they "had a chance to see [Rabindranath] Tagore under the spotlight—just where he likes to be." Apparently a performance of his latest play was being presented in the courtyard of his home—which Rochester termed "palatial"—by girls from Santinikstan. The audience, she said, was "well-fed and comfortable," in deep contrast to those who had come to see Gan-dhi.[54] Her comments about Tagore were calculated to reach many of the Companions, who admired his work but were not familiar with the circumstances in which it was produced. Yet, although both Rochester and Hutchins were now members of the Social Justice Com-mittee of the Society of the Companions of the Holy Cross, and Rochester was still on the Chapel Music Committee, they were, in fact, Companions in name only. Rochester had decided that upon her return to the United States, she would devote three hours per day to the Labor Research Department of the Rand School, joining Scott Nearing, Alexander Trachtenberg, Solon De Leon, and other friends from the LID.[55] They would not return to Adelynrood.

Rochester and Hutchins spent most of February 1927 at sea, traveling from Colombo, Ceylon, to Genoa, Italy, preparing for their visit to the Soviet Union. Rochester continued to wrestle with her feelings about the ten-year-old Russian revolution; she now acknowledged that "against the record of Russian history (as set forth by a good Russian patriot) even the methods of the communists mark a tremendous advance." Arriving in Genoa on February 21, Rochester and Hutchins left immediately for Geneva, Switzerland, where they investi-gated some of the forty-odd international organizations housed there, such as the Society of Friends, the Permanent Mandates Commission,[56] and the International Labor Office.[57]

They quizzed dignitaries at the Permanent Mandates Commission during the day, and in the evening they wrote letters seeking to persuade the Companions to define simplic-ity in more global terms. At the same time, when they met up with other "independent" women who were not "female imperialists," they sought to introduce them to the political work they were doing, which they still saw in the pages of The World Tomorrow, despite the magazine's rightward turn. Rochester wrote to Devere Allen, advising him of a poten-tial donor whom they had met on the boat from Colombo—a "talkative lady doctor from [San Francisco,] California" named Dr. Adelaide Brown.[58] She suggested that he send Dr. Brown some issues of The World Tomorrow, including one with an article by "Miriam Van Waters, whom she knows."[59] Thus, they continued to bridge worlds, addressing women in person and intervening in organizations run by men, seeking to draw women out of their traditional conservatism and making space for them in progressive circles.

Arriving in Berlin on March 3, 1927, having been invited to stay with Kurt Klaeber and Lisa Tetzner, Rochester and Hutchins began trying to obtain a visa for the Soviet Union. As they waited, they continued to study Russian, read widely, and write to friends and former associates. One problem in the *World Tomorrow* offices so distressed Hutchins that she wrote to Devere Allen seeking to intervene. Apparently Grace Lumpkin had written to her, telling her that Wallace Thurman, who had been hired to manage the subscriptions, was on the verge of being fired. Thurman was a young African American writer who had come to New York from Los Angeles seeking to join the cultural activism now known as the Harlem Renaissance. Hutchins worried that if he were to be let go, he would find it nearly impossible to locate work elsewhere[60]; furthermore, she argued, understanding the importance of precedents, it would be just that much harder for another African American to find work in largely white-owned enterprises. What else she knew or sensed remains unstated, although she would have found Thurman's behavior—heavy drinking, sexual adventuring—difficult to appreciate.[61] Nonetheless, she sought to protect him, as she had protected and would continue to protect many others, including both Lumpkin and Shemitz. (The degree to which her protection was welcomed was another matter.)

Devere Allen wrote back to Hutchins, telling her in detail what had led to Thurman's dismissal—for, by this time, he had been fired. The problem was that he was spending more time on the new magazine he was editing, *Fire!!*, than he was on *The World Tomorrow* subscriptions. Staff and friends of *The World Tomorrow* provided the money for *Fire!!*; one woman, a staff member, took out a loan to fund the magazine. When Allen explained to Hutchins the lengths to which the staff and friends of the magazine had gone in order to make Thurman's job there manageable and then explained to her that Thurman had used some of the money to host a lavish party, she backed down, apologizing for assuming that Allen had not thought out the situation thoroughly before acting. We can only guess at Thurman's motives.[62] Hutchins, for her part, could not countenance what she saw as self-serving behavior that hurt others, especially women.[63] She was disheartened, just as Rochester had been disappointed by the imperialist physician on board the ship.

Kurt Klaeber was, for them, a contrast to Thurman. "[He] has a completely devoted and idealistic spirit," wrote Rochester. "Still—as we always felt—a very rare person." Rochester reminded her readers that Klaeber had stayed with them on West 27th Street for four months and had married Lisa Tetzner immediately after his return to Germany in January 1924. Now he was working as a writer, preparing articles for newspapers and magazines in addition to writing fiction and verse, and his work, she wrote, was in great demand, even more by the radical social democratic press than by the Communist press, although he was frequently sought after for party work. He had, at that point, published one volume with the Communist press, one with the syndicalist-anarchist press, and one with a social-democratic press. In late March, Rochester wrote, "a non-political radical-in-literature review, *Die Neuer Bucher Schau*, had a special number on Marcel Proust, as the leading writer of the decadents, and Kurt as the leading writer of the young proletariat."[64] Already new lines were being drawn that placed those articulating same-sex desires (such as Proust) on the wrong side of the revolution. As these lines became more rigid, Rochester's and Hutchins's positions would become increasingly difficult.

The German Youth Movement, of which Kurt Klaeber and Lisa Tetzner had been a part, had collapsed, with the various parties each maintaining their own youth group. "The free, thrilling, idealistic searching of the youth themselves is mostly past," Rochester reported sadly. Although Hutchins and Rochester did attend a meeting of the Freie Proletarische Jugend, the group that had most impressed them at Hellerau in 1923, they were disappointed to find that the meeting consisted of "three dogmatic political speeches from three viewpoints and a largely unresponsive listening by the audience."[65]

This hardening of positions in Germany was obvious to them in other ways as well. Hutchins sent a dispatch to the Federated Press about their experience of the International Women's Week celebration in Berlin. At the last minute, the government had decreed that all the districts could not join together for a parade; they also sent large numbers of police to surround the festivities, so what Hutchins and Rochester saw was "300 women, red bandannas on their heads" following a band of worker musicians, accompanied by five trucks of police, "each truck . . . filled with armed cops, every one carrying a rifle, a pistol and a hand grenade." In addition, "Young Pioneers in white jackets sang, 'Brothers march on to the sunlight of freedom' and a company of Worker Red Cross marched with the women. Workers in Germany," she added, "have learned from long experience that their own Red Cross is needed when police are present at a worker gathering."[66]

The International Women's Week "celebration" was not an isolated incident. Rochester wrote to their friends on April 3, 1927, relating an attack on a Communist marching band that had been written up not just in the Communist newspaper but in the *Tageblatt* as well.[67] "On the suburban train coming back to Berlin they were set upon by several hundred 'steel-helmet' men. . . . The steel-helmets rioted around like a mob in a southern lynching, and after they had damaged the communists sufficiently they marched on through the city, hitting over the head any passers by who looked like Jews!" In short, Rochester wrote, despite the fact that they had been rather quiet for the past couple of years, the Communists "are getting constant persecution at present in Germany." The government, she said, is the most reactionary since the war, "and the social democrats do not seem to be standing up against reaction."[68]

What most concerned Rochester and Hutchins was not only the brutal repression exhibited by the police and often upheld or, at best, ignored by the courts but the serious efforts to shut down Communist publishers and distributors. "Writers are not interfered with," Rochester said, "and so the principle of free speech set forth in the constitution of the German Republic is respected, but the sale or publishing of certain books is being prosecuted as sedition." One of Kurt Klaeber's books, *Barrikaden auf der Ruhr* (Barricades on the Ruhr), had been banned, she wrote, and the publisher sentenced to a fine plus nine months in prison. On the other hand, she pointed out, Communist theoretical tracts were easy to come by. "Rightly," she said, "the authorities realize that fiction can be more effective than economic or political dissertations."[69]

Political tensions notwithstanding, Rochester and Hutchins appreciated the many instances of Russian culture in Berlin, although even there they encountered censorship. The theaters, they noted, always offered several Russian films, although *Potemkin*, about the 1905 revolution, had been censored as dangerous propaganda, so they were unable to see it. They did see Gorky's *The Mother*, which, they commented, "has up to the minute significance with its industrial struggle." They also saw "a most gory film on Ivan the Terrible," which they said was "safely historical and remote, but full of parables in the legends."[70] The German repression—combined with "the feverishdash" and with what they called "showiness," a combination of advertising and shows—was enough to convince them that Europe was declining. By this time, neither Rochester nor Hutchins was indulging in the facile anticommunist commentaries that had marked earlier letters, instead saying, "the new life must come from the East."[71]

Perhaps Vida Scudder was correct when she advised Rochester at the beginning of their trip "that most travelers get from their travels only what they expect to see." Or perhaps the contrast between life in the Soviet Union in 1927 and life in Germany—or in India, China, Singapore, the Philippines, or Japan—in 1927 was enough to convince them. Certainly they loved Kurt Klaeber and Lisa Tetzner, so communism now looked very different. Whatever the cause, with their study of Russian and their letters of introduction to Soviet officials, Rochester and Hutchins were prepared to be happy in Moscow—and they were. Reporting to friends, they commented that the lack of "commercial display advertising" was "a relief to eye and spirit." But it was in the faces of the people that they found the most telling evidence of the success of the Revolution: "more solid, intelligent, purposeful-looking people I have never seen anywhere than on the Moscow streets and in the theatres," wrote Rochester about a week and a half after their arrival. "And I would hazard the guess," she said, "that there are more book shops and book buyers here than in all the New England states—in spite of Boston."[72]

Hutchins and Rochester intended to study only labor conditions, leaving aside for now the study of education, because Scott Nearing had done such a fine job already on that subject.[73] As it happened, they arrived in Russia just at the beginning of the Russian Orthodox Easter and discovered that everything—shops, government offices, Communist bookstores—was closed for several days. A week later, everything closed again for May Day. In between, however, they took their letter of introduction from Scott Nearing to Boris Reinstein, a former member of Daniel De Leon's Socialist Labor Party in Buffalo, New York, who had gone to Russia in February 1917, shortly before the revolution. He had served as secretary to Lenin and was, when Hutchins and Rochester saw him, heading up the Bureau of International Revolutionary Propaganda, responsible for publishing and distributing foreign-language newspapers and pamphlets. Hutchins and Rochester met with Reinstein several times during their six weeks in the Soviet Union and reported to their friends that he "always . . . gave us something to ponder over in the spirit of the communist who does not seek his own individual glory but who submits his personal life to the interests of communism."[74] This spirit they could understand, as it replicated neatly Hutchins's rhetoric of the whole person. Although the language differed slightly, the concept also varied little from the final lines of Harry F. Ward's *The New Social Order*: "Whether the new order desired by multitudes will now appear, depends finally upon whether those multitudes have sufficient capacity for sacrifice to send new life coursing through the exhausted veins of humanity."[75]

With their new openness, Hutchins and Rochester appreciated the May Day celebration in Red Square. They had tickets that allowed them a place to stand (everyone stood except, as Rochester noted ironically, the cavalrymen) near the north end of the square. There they stood for four hours, watching as the Red Army paraded through the square, stopping to take the annual oath of allegiance. At this point, another American standing nearby, a Miss Eddy[76] of California, turned to them and murmured, to their amusement, "They don't give the Red Army any nonsense about joining the Marines to see the world!" Most thrilling to Rochester and Hutchins were the "rivers of workers," singing and carrying banners and accompanied by marching bands, that "began to flow into the Square," from the streets radiating out in all directions, a marked contrast to what they had witnessed in Germany.[77]

Although the May Day celebration was the most spectacular, Rochester and Hutchins made it a point to attend as many other events as possible, seeking in this way to understand the revolution through its cultural manifestations. In fact, they wrote home twice about one play in particular: *Constantin Teryokhin*, which they saw during their first week in Russia at the Trade Union Theatre. Its subject matter was life in the Komsomol, the international Communist youth organization, focusing on the question, as Rochester put it in her first letter, written on May 2, of "how much the party should bother anyway about members' individual way of living."[78] This analysis of the play suggests that she was not convinced that the party had any business concerning itself with the private lives of members. When Hutchins and Rochester wrote again on June 11, 1927, however, their description of the play had changed—or perhaps Hutchins wrote this second statement. Now they said: "In [the play], the conflict in the Komsomol (the Communist Youth Organization) between the serious and the frivolous and the whole question as to how much personal conduct should be the concern of the organization were resolved by the vindication of the earnest and the expulsion from the Komsomol of the ring leader of the frivolous."[79] In any event, the fact that they chose this play, out of several that they saw, to discuss in detail indicates that the question was important to them—and their final statement on the play indicates that they had decided that frivolous personal behavior (whatever that happened to be) was counterproductive to the extent that it deserved sanction by the organization (although not, it should be noted, by the state). It was not the last time that the question would come up for them.

After the holidays, and as they had in Japan, China, the Philippines, India, and Switzerland, Hutchins and Rochester sought out people whom they could interview about labor conditions and about the new country in general, visiting several times with Albert Rhys Williams, an American noncommunist who had been in the Soviet Union for almost ten years, writing about conditions there. Williams knew more, they said, about the new country than any other one American. Harry F. Ward had given them a letter of introduction to Lunacharsky, the People's Commissar of Education, whose task it had become to serve as a "kind of liaison officer between the dictatorship of the proletariat and the bourgeois intellectuals whose services were needed for the new State."[80] They may well have discussed *Constantin Peryokhin* with Lunacharsky, a deeply humane man whose special concern was "the morals of the revolution and the morality of the future society."[81]

From Robert Dunn, whom Rochester had met in the LID, Hutchins and Rochester had received a letter of introduction to Melnachansky, the president of the Textile Union and a member of the Presidium of the Central Executive Committee of the Soviet Union. Dunn, a Yale graduate and friend of Alexander Trachtenberg, had recently returned from a trip to the Soviet Union with the American Trade Union Delegation.[82] Melnachansky, Rochester and Hutchins wrote, "was so friendly and so easy with his American-English that we were especially grateful for the talk with him and also for the magic letter he gave us to open doors along our way."[83]

One of the doors Melnachansky opened was that of the large government-run cotton mill in Moscow, where Hutchins and Rochester were impressed by conditions that were so humane compared with those they had seen in colonial Asia. The director had been elected to his position by the workers early in the revolution, they noted, and when the Supreme Economic Council took over the appointments of directors, he was retained in his position. Workers' benefits, they said, included free medical care, temporary and permanent disability insurance, and insurance for unemployment, old age, and funeral expenses. Women were allowed two months' leave of absence before and after giving birth, with more time available if necessary. Once a child was born, working mothers could make use of the day nursery. When they visited the nursery associated with the cotton mill, Rochester and Hutchins "had to leave coats, hats, and hand bags and wear enveloping white aprons in order to see this children's home."[84]

Provisions were also made for families if the primary wage earner should die. Each worker was guaranteed two weeks' vacation per year, with those in dangerous occupations and those under eighteen receiving one month. Union members received 50 percent off on theater tickets, and clubs for workers, often located in mansions previously occupied by the wealthy, were jointly funded by the industry and the union. Employers supplied the funds for these benefits. Hours of work did not exceed eight per day; those in dangerous occupations worked less, as did most office workers.[85] Those in extremely hazardous jobs, such as those involving contact with lead, worked as few as three hours per day.

Describing a workers' club, Hutchins and Rochester told their friends what they had seen: "the library, rooms for games, a big hall with a stage for theatrical entertainments, the women's club room, class rooms for educational circles, the Red Corner . . . and then a big exhibit on the production of that factory making it possible for every worker to understand the relation of his job to the increase of production in the whole concern."[86] Although wages did not match those paid in the United States, they conceded, the benefits more than made up for the difference. Moreover, retail prices had been reduced 10 percent between January 1 and June 1, 1927, by order of the government, thus increasing the buying power of workers. What made the greatest difference, though, Hutchins said, was the fact that the Russian workers were proud of the fact that the industries belonged to them and to their fellow workers. That fact meant that Russian workers had a greater sense of security than did their American counterparts, she added.[87]

What did all this mean for productivity? The director of the cotton mill showed Rochester and Hutchins charts on his wall indicating that production was then at 107 percent of the prewar level. The net profit of that plant for the last year had been $1,500,000 in American dollars. Americans were helping to increase the productivity as well, especially at the Russian-American Farm Colony in Prikumskaya, where Harold Ware,[88] Jessica Smith,[89] and Karl Borders, along with several other Americans, were running four estates in the middle of one of Russia's wheat regions south of Moscow. Touring the estates, Hutchins and Rochester reported that "the young American electrical engineer has installed a small dynamo for the needs of the house and outbuildings, and is cooperating with the government in preparatory work for a power plant which will use the water power of the river and give current for the entire village."[90]

From Prikumskaya, Hutchins and Rochester took a day trip with Hal Ware, Karl Borders, and Jessica Smith to another village where twenty families were working the land in common. While Ware and Borders attempted to solve tractor problems on the farm, Jessica Smith talked with the women, learning about their efforts to gain equal pay, because at this point only factory workers were legally required to be paid equal wages regardless of gender. The peasant leader, a man, announced cheerfully to the assembled women that, no, wages would not be increased, because " 'women are cheaper.' " Jessica Smith advised the women that the "women workers at Prikumskaya had challenged the men and had demonstrated in three contests that they did more than the men in a given time. As a result the local union had agreed that women should have equal pay for equal work." The handling of traditional misogyny in the USSR contrasted sharply with the colonial uses of indigenous misogyny Rochester and Hutchins had encountered earlier. Rochester's comment on this exchange was: "We fancy . . . that [the peasant leader] has not heard the last word of his women on that subject!"[91] Although the issue was handled in a relatively lighthearted manner, Rochester could not have been more serious. American women might have the vote, but the revolution for women was being completed in the Soviet Union.

In Rostov-on-Don, Hutchins and Rochester met a young English woman who had been orphaned six years earlier in the Soviet Union and had been cared for there by the women's division of the local federation of labor unions; now she was supporting herself as a tobacco worker, and although she was not a Communist, she was a union member and spoke enthusiastically about working conditions in Rostov. She told Hutchins and Rochester about a meeting she had recently attended of the three thousand workers in her factory, at which speakers had talked to the workers about the English raid on the Russian trade headquarters in London and the subsequent severing of relations between the two countries. The workers were asked whether they thought they ought to fight—and they voted overwhelmingly in the negative. Rochester and Hutchins told their friends: "Perhaps this illustrates the skill with which the communist party builds up public opinion, perhaps it was spontaneous expression from the rank and file. Either way it testified to the intentions of Russia to keep out of war."[92] What they did not have to point out explicitly to feminist friends: a young working class woman was engaged in the political process.

Clearly, Rochester and Hutchins did not accept everything they saw at face value— and they did not ignore the obvious problems in the ten-year-old country, saying that they had seen beggars and street peddlers and "every now and then a ragged vagabond child"; acknowledging, in short, that "Russia is in no sense a finished paradise."[93] Indeed, they had to leave Russia earlier than they had wished because Rochester came down with a bronchial infection and felt that a return to Germany, where the benefits of bourgeois medicine were available, was the best course.

But if the country was not yet a "finished paradise," it was a very different place from 1920s America, where a veneer of wealth covered extremes of poverty, racism, and exploitation, and, Rochester and Hutchins posited, "Dictatorship is scarcely the word for a rule in which the two great groups—peasants and industrial workers—enjoy a sense of freedom." The term "dictatorship of the proletariat" had never been an easy one for Americans. Less than a year—but many miles—had passed since Rochester had dismissed Japanese Communists as "left-wing radicals . . . who believe in dictatorship."[94] Now, having seen the revolution, she acknowledged: "They are led, it is true, by the communist minority, approximately one million workers and teachers and technical specialists and administrators. But the non-communist peasants and workers do find a genuine self-expression in the labor unions, the consumers' cooperatives, and the political soviets."[95]

Moreover, the new economic relationships and shifting power relations were offering the promise of new interpersonal relationships, opening spaces that Hutchins and Rochester had dreamed of and had tried to create in protected enclaves at St. Hilda's, St. Faith's, Adelynrood, and 352. While in Berlin, Rochester had found and read *Cement*, a recently published novel by Fyodor Gladkov, newly translated into German, which explored the changes that were taking place in women as a result of their economic equality with men, the changes that men were reluctantly making in return, and the new emotions that were being celebrated, especially love. Dasha, the main woman character, said to her husband at the close of the novel: "Love will always be love, Gleb, but it requires a new form. Everything will come through and attain new forms, and then we shall know how to forge new links."[96] This novel differs in almost every way from Martin Nexo's *Ditte*, the novel that had informed their previous journey. Perhaps there really would be room for them in this new movement.

Eager to share their experiences, Rochester wrote to Sally Cleghorn from Berlin after they left Moscow to console her on the death of Bill Fincke and the resultant loss of Manumit School. Above all, she wished that Cleghorn, with whom she had argued so often about class consciousness and the need for revolution, could share in their transformative experience of the Soviet Union: "Sally," she said, "I wish you could once have the thrill of the living sense of human solidarity that reached us many times in Russia. It has quite slipped through and escaped expression in the printed letter we shall be mailing from here shortly. But it lifts one out of one's self—as mystically real as any vision," and she signed herself: "Your devoted and always-meaning-to-be-loving friend, Anna."[97]

Hutchins and Rochester's love for each other had deepened and reshaped itself during the trip, finding its ground in a larger freedom, equality, and solidarity than they had ever known before. In her letter to Cleghorn, Rochester wrote: "Together we have in this year quite rebuilt our little world so that the stormy feelings over the W. T. seem remote and foolish. But they were real and difficult at the time."[98]

By the time they left the Soviet Union, Rochester and Hutchins had announced their commitment to the revolution. Speaking to a reporter for *The Hammer*, a newspaper published in Rostov-on-Don, they said: "Our political views have gradually moved to the left and now we stand on the platform of the Communist Party." The chief problem they identified in the United States was the propaganda pumped out by the conservative newspapers. "American conservative newspapers write so many lies about the USSR, to the point of absurdity," they said. What's more, they said, "Conservative newspapers use all their means to try to hold back the development of trade relations with the USSR, they try to intimidate with the idea that the USSR will not fulfill the obligations it assumes."[99]

They closed the interview by sending—and signing—a personal statement to all Russian journalists:

> We salute the worker-journalists here in Soviet Russia, who are working so intensively and firmly on the soil of socialism, growing stronger. We know how much work lies ahead of us in America, in order to raise the workers' level of class consciousness. We will devote all of our energy and all our work efforts so that American workers will walk hand in hand with the other proletariat of the world in the class struggle.[100]

Chapter Seven

Worker Journalists

Now listen to me, workers, listen to what I tell.
Remember the textile workers, in their dirty cell.
Now we must stand together, and to the boss reply,
"We will never, no, we'll never, let our leaders die."

—Ella May Wiggins (textile worker and singer,
murdered by vigilantes outside Gastonia in 1929)

"Purtiest singin' I ever heard," said one woman, who stood throughout a meeting at
which Ella May sang.

—Jessie Lloyd O'Connor, Harvey O'Connor, and Susan M. Bowler
(*Harvey and Jessie: A Couple of Radicals*)

We will devote all of our energy and all our work efforts so that American workers
will walk hand in hand with the other proletariat of the world in the class struggle.

—Anna Rochester and Grace Hutchins
(*The Hammer*, Rostov-on-Don, May 22, 1927)

Hutchins and Rochester set sail for the United States from Southampton on the Cunard
line R.M.S. *Carmania* on July 9, 1927, "restless for home." "It's high time we were back
at work," Rochester wrote to Sally Cleghorn.[1] Although they had never stopped working, sending back articles and dispatches from many points of the globe, what Rochester
and Hutchins longed for now was a new organizational home, a new community. But
not just any community: they had moved beyond the Companions, the FOR, and the
LID, dissatisfied with what they felt were half measures in every organization, although
they could not dismiss friends in these groups as easily. They were seeking a community
whose members not only addressed the economic roots of inequality without compromise
but whose practices would allow Rochester to challenge the gendered division of labor,
researching, writing, and speaking alongside the men and whose policies would allow
Hutchins to work to enlarge the discursive space for other women. They sought a community, in short, in which they would be welcomed as they were and could advocate
greater liberties for others as well. Within two months, they would apply for membership
in the Workers (Communist) Party.

During the ensuing two months, Rochester and Hutchins brought their new vision to
old relationships, sparking new conflicts and reigniting old ones, a portent of the direction

their lives were taking. Harry F. Ward had said, "Whatever form the new order may take, its vital breath is the sacrificial spirit."[2] Although they were not sacrificing their identities or their partnership, they were pioneering into a space that few people from their past understood, and that meant that they sustained losses.

When Hutchins made arrangements to visit her family at their summer home in Castine, Maine, she told her mother that she had begun the "change of life" more than a year earlier and that it was making her more "nervous" than usual. Anna, she said, had been "the most perfectly understanding comrade," a sly joke to herself. But given her "nervousness," she said, she did not want to discuss or be reproached for having cut her hair or for her opinions about Russia.[3] With that conveniently acceptable explanation in place, Hutchins took off for the north, writing to Rochester on her departure: "My Dearest, I . . . have read three Boston papers to see what they are doing about Sacco and Vanzetti. All three report amiably a meeting of protest held here yesterday by the Workers' Party, with Earl Browder speaking. But the Herald states that the S. V. Defense Committee disclaimed all connection with the W. P. meeting." Hutchins and Rochester knew then, if they hadn't known already, that they would be signing on with the party of least approbation but, they hoped, with the most promise. In a manner that would become typical, Hutchins followed this political commentary with a counterweight, a tender expression of affection: "I have pulled up my slip in the back and am looking tolerably respectable, but I miss my partner to brush my shoulders! Dear, dear Partner, how lucky we are to have our pleasant apartment and to be getting it settled so well. . . . I love you more and more and more."[4]

Apparently Hutchins's parents agreed to the conditions she had outlined for her visit, because Hutchins later reported to Rochester that the stay had gone well: "Beloved," she wrote, "all is well! Father pronounces my hair 'not so bad.' . . . Mother says nothing but seems to survive."[5] There was evidently no discussion of Russia. Nonetheless, Hutchins cut the visit short, staying only two nights, because what she really wanted to do at that moment was to return to Rochester in the apartment at 85 Bedford Street in New York City and begin her work.

During her stay in Castine, Hutchins had taken the opportunity to write to Devere Allen and Nevin Sayre, thanking them for welcoming her back but telling them that she was resigning her position as secretary of *The World Tomorrow*. She had asked, she said, that her name be retained on the masthead during their trip to facilitate meetings with people abroad; however, now that she was becoming active in labor organizing, public association with the magazine was counterproductive.[6]

In fact, Hutchins was about to begin working with the Paper Box Workers' Union, the approximately twenty-five hundred members of which had engaged in a bitter strike from October 1926 to February 1927, seeking improved pay and hours and, above all, recognition of the union. The strike had been supported by a broad coalition, including Hutchins and Rochester's old friends Rev. Harry F. Ward, Mary Simkhovitch, Mary Van Kleeck, Florence Kelley, and Rev. William Spofford of the CLID. Yet the strike had been called off by the members on February 8 due to an inability on the part of the union to provide adequate strike funds and "the uncanny cooperation of the Police Department with the bosses." The union agreed, however, "to maintain their organization and keep up their struggle for better conditions." Commenting on the disheartening end of the strike, the union manager, Fred Caiola, said, "In closing, we wish to call your attention to this sad observation, namely: A mountain of moral force did not have the immediate material effect which a cross look would have from a guerilla's eye."[7] Although they had not resolved for themselves the question of moral force, this was the struggle into which Hutchins and Rochester had moved.

Some of Rochester and Hutchins's old friends and colleagues had not moved far during their year abroad. Shortly after she returned to New York, Hutchins received a letter from Nevin Sayre accepting her resignation and indicating that he was looking forward to hearing her report of her travels at the upcoming annual conference of the FOR.[8] What Hutchins did not know, although she probably could have guessed, was the attitude displayed by Nevin Sayre in an informal note he wrote at the same time to Devere Allen, commenting on her resignation: "Dear Devere, The enclosed letter from Grace is self-explanatory. The wimmin, Oh the wimmin! Yours affectionately, Nevin."[9]

The Society of the Companions of the Holy Cross, a haven from the misogyny of such as Sayre—and the scene of Rochester and Hutchins's first encounter—nonetheless seemed hopelessly remote. When Rochester and Hutchins had returned to the United States in mid-July 1927, a letter from Scudder had reached them soon after. In it, she seemed to share their enthusiasm for the USSR, saying, "Florence thinks the Russian communist party may be antiChrist. That is her imagination. Don't worry, she is quite gentle about it! But my own stubborn instincts of enthusiastic sympathy refuse to be daunted, and you justify them."[10] Still, Scudder herself remained focused on the past. Trying to draw Rochester back to her, she said, "Please read my *Brother John* and talk to me about it! The request is modest! and mean! But it is the book of my heart and some things you will understand especially well, I think, and others you may dislike, and you may not think it was worth writing anyway."[11]

Brother John was Scudder's 1926 novel depicting the Franciscan movement in the years immediately following the death of Francis in 1226. Without knowing exactly what Scudder had in mind when she told Rochester that there were "some things you will understand especially well . . . and others you may dislike," we may guess that one part was the central struggle between the Franciscan factions over the question of whether to create bodies of knowledge and construct churches or to follow the propertyless way of Francis. This struggle, as represented in Scudder's novel, can be taken as a symbolic reference to the struggle over approaches to social justice within the SCHC. Brother John, the character with whom Scudder seems to identify most closely, claims that factual evidence is insufficient. "His mind works on too high a level,"[12] says John of Pope Gregory, explaining why he is discarding letters based upon logical appeals, having persuaded Gregory to take action by "forgetting" his memorized arguments and speaking extempore from his heart. This fictionalized event demonstrates Scudder's commitment to a rhetoric that not only set up a vertical scale of knowledge but insisted, following the precepts of Augustine, that the persuasiveness of a discourse comes from the wisdom, conviction, and righteousness of the speaker rather than from learned methods of eloquence alone.[13]

Another element in the book that Scudder might have felt Rochester would "understand especially well" is the pivotal romantic relationship between Brother John and Pierre. After Pierre dies, John's task is to learn to live without him and without concern for the material, especially the body, just as Scudder herself had had to learn to live after her great love, Clara French, died shortly after they finished college. This transcendence of desire Scudder called "the secret of Naughting." Following in a general sense the outline of Plato's *Phaedrus*, *Brother John* moves from a realization of the limited but spiritually enriching nature of earthly (same-sex) love to an exposition of spiritually informed persuasion based on that same love, transformed to Love. The novel is a reworking of Scudder's 1902 *A Listener in Babel* and is another clear articulation of same-sex love, especially as the source of energy for social transformation. Here, however, writing in 1926, Scudder had concealed the love affair with heavy curtains of medievalism.

Although Rochester certainly understood Scudder's cri de coeur, she could not return to the old life or to the old arguments. Rochester and Hutchins had fallen in love in the context of a religious community that no longer sufficed, yet they still had each other. Their love fueled by a passion for social transformation, they felt encompassed now not by the "lonely spaces of eternity" but by the revolutionary society from which they had just returned and toward which they hoped to build in the United States. The gulf between Vida Scudder (and Florence Converse) and Anna Rochester (and Grace Hutchins) had deepened and widened to a nearly impassable degree. And although Hutchins's family had not protested too loudly at the symbolism of her bobbed hair, the next intervention at the point of struggle that she and Rochester made was not only not shared by Vida Scudder but provoked a torrent of outrage from Hutchins's family.

As the execution date for Angelo Sacco and Bartolomeo Vanzetti[14] drew near, demonstrations and other methods of protest increased. Hutchins began working with the Citizens' National Committee for Sacco and Vanzetti. According to the New York Times, she had, as one of the members of this committee, signed a telegram to President Coolidge, asking him to intervene.[15] He didn't. In mid-August, Rochester and Hutchins traveled to Boston to participate in a large demonstration where Hutchins was arrested, joining John Dos Passos, Dorothy Parker, and Rose Pesotta, among others. In an event predating the widespread use of tear gas and pepper spray on protestors, the police grabbed the men by their collars and "held on to the arms of women and girl prisoners with muscular grips," despite assurances that no one intended to leave. Hutchins was charged with "sauntering and loitering." Later a charge of "obstruction of traffic" was added.[16] The newspapers loved it, and both the Herald-Globe-Post and the Transcript published pictures of Hutchins, giving as her address her parents' home at 166 Beacon Street and identifying her as the daughter of Edward W. Hutchins, of the law firm of Hutchins and Wheeler. The law firm may have been involved in the case—on the prosecution side—so this connection with the protests was met with dismay bordering on panic by Hutchins's mother and father. Despite this antagonism, Hutchins's brother Ned offered to arrange her release from prison, but she declined the offer, waiting instead for the International Labor Defense (ILD) to raise the bail money for all those arrested.[17] According to Ella Reeve Bloor's account, "The police began arresting people right and left and toward evening, we had 160 arrests on our hands, among them, that of Grace Hutchins, the first Bostonian to be hauled in. We sent people around to collect money and for $25 each we bailed them out."[18]

Susan Hutchins wrote to her daughter, saying that it was of no use to attempt to tell her of their feelings, as she would not understand. But she did describe the events in the household when the newspapers arrived: "As Father can not read to himself the fine print of the paper, I was obliged to read to him: 'Grace Hutchins of 166 Beacon Street daughter of Edward W. Hutchins of the law firm of Hutchins & Wheeler' etc. I guessed the result would be serious and had the nitroglycerin tablets ready which I gave. Father lowered his head and said the one word 'disgrace,' which sums it all up."[19]

This reaction was mild compared to that of Hutchins's uncle, Harold Hurd, an attorney in Roswell, New Mexico, who went on for two typed single-spaced pages, reaching a paroxysm of patriotism and saying that "those who are against our Courts, our Laws and our Institutions and who by their acts or writing or conversations seek to upset or destroy those elements should be removed to an Island Colony and there remain for the balance of time."[20] He also advised that the family cut off her income. Hutchins's response was decisive and eloquent: "My dear Father and Mother," she wrote on August 21, "My arrest, which you call a disgrace, is to me one of the few real honors which have ever come to your family."[21] She went on to say that she would no longer accept money from her father, from whom she now realized she differed "so fundamentally," and, enclosing a check for $50, she said that she would return the balance of his last check as soon as possible. She had applied for a job that would provide for her expenses, she said, and if she were in any difficulty, she would "accept help from Anna who has more than she needs," thus obliquely cementing her partnership with finances, the fundamental American adhesive of marriage.

Hutchins and Rochester were both distressed by the unfairness of the trial of Sacco and Vanzetti and especially by the selective use of evidence. On August 23, they wired the Citizens National Committee at its headquarters in the Hotel Bellevue in Boston, saying: "Earnestly hope before you separate you will arrange for writing of book by Frankfurter or other genuinely interested attorney supplementing Frankfurter's book with review of unused evidence and recent history."[22] As they saw it, publication—writing—was a necessary antidote for social inequities. Although mass demonstrations were critical in the moment, published work would be available as a corrective to the historical record.

By August 26, 1927, Hutchins had been hired by the New York Department of Labor in a temporary position as an investigator for the Bureau of Women in Industry, to begin work on September 1 at a salary of $2000 per year plus retirement insurance. The position would become permanent after she passed the civil service examination. The fact that she had friends in the bureau undoubtedly facilitated her hiring, but she acquitted herself well in the job, which, perhaps not coincidentally, included a special study of the Paper Box workers in New York City. In late September, she took the four-hour written civil service examination and began the five-month wait to hear whether she would be offered a permanent position. When she wrote to tell her mother about the exam, apparently the tension of the previous month had subsided to a manageable level. She included news of her brother Henry and his wife Marian, saying, "Marian always wins my heart because she appreciates Anna, sends her love to her, and includes her in invitations," another signal of her partnership, this one far less concealed than Vida Scudder's medieval tract.

Rochester, meanwhile, had started working three hours per day at the Labor Research Department of the Rand School, as she had promised months before, assisting Director Solon De Leon by writing chapters for the 1928 Labor Year Book. She also had been asked to write an article for *Labor Age*, to be entitled "Wages and Prosperity." Both the Rand School and *Labor Age* had strong connections to the Socialist Party. At the same time, however, Rochester was asked to write for *New Masses*, a magazine with close ties to the Workers (Communist) Party, and she produced a column for that magazine that she called "Class War Bulletins," collections of short articles similar to "Not in the Headlines," which she had compiled for several years for *The World Tomorrow*.

This was a time of transition for both Rochester and Hutchins. They had contacted their old friends and had even slipped back into some of the organizations they had left a year earlier. In fact, at the annual conference of the FOR, Rochester was elected to a two-year term on the FOR Council, and her name remained on the masthead of *The World Tomorrow*. Moreover, the outside world continued to package them together with their old cronies. In 1927, the Daughters of the American Revolution published their list of "Doubtful Speakers," identifying Rochester, Mary Simkhovitch, and Mary Van Kleeck as "radicals"; Vida Scudder, Grace Abbott, Dr. Alice Hamilton, and Julia Lathrop as "socialists"; and a variety of others as "communists," "revolutionary feminists," "internationalists," or "pacifists." (What exactly the DAR meant by these categories remains unclear.)

CLASS WAR BULLETINS
By ANNA ROCHESTER

Figure 7.1. "Class War Bulletins" headline

However, Rochester and Hutchins had meant what they said in Rostov-on-Don, and in September they sent their applications to the Workers (Communist) Party. Their applications were accepted, and they began to shift the focus of their work to publications and organizations closer to the Workers Party. Only 20 percent of the members were women, and membership stood at about nine thousand at best during that time. Many of the nine thousand belonged to foreign-language federations. Thus, in 1927, Rochester and Hutchins were among only a few native English–speaking women in the party.

Some former Socialists were making the same move, most notably their friends Scott Nearing and Alexander Trachtenberg; others moved closer to the program of the Workers Party without actually joining. In 1926, Scott Nearing had published a damning review of the annual conference of the LID, suggesting a disgust on the part of the more radical with the lack of militancy in the organization: conferees, he charged, were comfortable. Papers at the conference "merely described the different ways in which the ruling class of the United States was postponing class conflict by buying out the working class and by increasing its wealth and its capacity for exploitation."[23]

Nonetheless, when Norman Thomas of the LID wrote to Rochester in October 1927, commenting obliquely that he had heard that she had joined the Workers Party ("I suspect that various circumstances mean that I have no right to ask you about that $10 annual gift which you promised to this organization"), she responded with a check, saying that she was "delighted to send the $10 herewith."[24] In fact, Rochester was elected to the LID Board of Directors in 1928, along with Devere Allen, Solon DeLeon, Robert W. Dunn, Paul Jones, Norman Thomas, Robert Morss Lovett, Florence Kelley, and a considerable list of others. She also was elected to the board of directors of the American Civil Liberties Union (ACLU), an organization that had developed from early pacifist organizations during the World War I years[25] and was now, with Harry F. Ward as chairman and Roger Baldwin as president, working closely with labor unions to protect the rights of striking workers.[26] The lines between organizations were still fluid at this point, although the divergence that would become painfully clear in the 1930s had already begun.

By November 1927, Rochester came to realize that she no longer wished to be connected with *The World Tomorrow*, as she simply did not agree with much of the magazine's content. Writing to Devere Allen and Kirby Page, she asked that her name be removed from the list of contributing editors, saying bluntly, "I feel stultified by even nominal association with a paper that is boosting the League of Nations which to me is—and always has been—the alliance of capitalist-imperialist powers for the protection of the old order." Her primary criticism focused on the magazine's industrial number, in which, she felt, the editors had not analyzed "the basic industrial situations today and the problems of the immediate future in a way which lines up your intentions *with* the working class and not against it." She also objected to the fact that *The World Tomorrow* was the only paper she "had seen—conservative or liberal—whose November number completely ignores the anniversary of the Russian revolution."[27] She sent the letter to Devere Allen and Kirby Page separately, attaching a note to Devere Allen's saying that she would be happy to have lunch with him sometime soon, but "I do most emphatically *not* want to be tackled and persuaded and argued with."[28] She also sent a copy to Nevin Sayre, telling him that she was honored to have been appointed to the magazine's board of directors but that she must decline, for the reasons stated in her letter to Allen and Page. "I am sorry," she said. "You are all mighty nice folks. But this particular kind of commitment to a paper with which month by month I mostly do not agree is really unfair to all around."[29]

Rochester, along with Hutchins, had already contacted the person from her past with whom she felt more affinity now: Alexander Trachtenberg, head of International Publishers.[30] Rochester asked him where she might be put to use. And Trachtenberg— affectionately known as "Trachty"—outlined a plan that would create a key position for her in the developing movement. Although there was a substantial body of material from the international movement to be published, most significantly the writings of V. I. Lenin, few home-grown works were available. What's more, the Passaic strike had taught organizers that unions needed quick access to information. Thus, Passaic veterans sought to establish a bureau that "would function continuously in times of industrial peace as well as during a strike and act as a clearing house for the social and economic expression of the labor movement."[31]

Trachtenberg invited Rochester and Hutchins in late 1927 to join with several labor writers, including Scott Nearing, Solon De Leon, and Robert W. Dunn, author of *American Foreign Investments*, with whom he had worked since their days together at Yale, to establish the Labor Research Association (LRA). The organization would cooperate with, but not duplicate the services of, the Labor Bureau, the Rand School, and the Workers School. There is no evidence that Trachtenberg found Hutchins and Rochester's partnership problematic at all; as Elinor Ferry has commented, "[Same-sex partnerships were] not frowned on by the Party until the situation within the German party gave the party leaders concern."[32] That concern would not appear for another several years.

Rochester accepted the offer from Trachtenberg (as did Hutchins, although she was still working for the Bureau of Women in Industry), and at the November 2 meeting of the Political Committee of the Workers (Communist) Party, the formation of the LRA was announced.[33] In December 1927, the organization began operations, aiming "'to conduct research into economic, social, and political problems in the interest of the American labor movement and to publish its findings in articles, pamphlets and books.'"[34] The LRA would provide the basis for Rochester and Hutchins's work for the rest of their lives, and Dunn, born in 1895, would become like a brother to both Rochester and Hutchins.

While Hutchins was working for the Bureau of Women in Industry, Rochester spent her days in the New York Public Library, researching and writing her articles for *Labor Age* and *New Masses*. Her article for *Labor Age*, "Wages and Prosperity," which was reprinted as a pamphlet entitled *Wages in the United States*, outlined the disparity between the enormous wealth enjoyed by some in the United States (this was in late 1927 and early 1928) and the poverty-level wages paid to most workers, a perspective by incongruity that required only the provision of facts. The original article was subtitled "Poverty Remains Unconquered." Following the pattern she had learned in the US Children's Bureau and developed in her later work, Rochester built the article on statistical data regarding wages and hours worked in a range of industries, including rails, coal, hosiery manufacture, and clerical work. She then plotted the wage-depressing trends she foresaw, especially displacement of workers by machinery and the migration of large employers to the South.[35] Rochester had found a niche—a place where her contributions were valued and where she was not disparaged as one of "the wimmin."

Hutchins, however, was not doing well. By early February, she was in the hospital recovering from an operation. What sustained her during this time was her relationship with Rochester. On February 7, she wrote to Rochester from the hospital: "Beloved Partner, Can I ever, ever tell you what your loving care has meant to me? . . . I am afraid it is I, by being so trying, who have made you a saint! But oh, dearest, in this quiet here, I make good resolutions and hope I can keep them. Your buying that bed," she said, "is overwhelming, but I look forward to it with glee and thanksgiving to my Anna." Then she added: "If I had only the pen of a Wm. Ellery Leonard to tell you of my love and my *admiration* for you."[36] Hutchins could envision herself occupying the place of Leonard, who wrote passionate love poems to his wife, but she could not summon the language to write poems to Rochester. Instead, she followed Rochester into the labor movement, bringing the old homiletic form with her, focusing her emotions on conditions for women workers.

Realizing that she would not be able to return to work any time soon, Hutchins resigned with apologies from the Bureau of Women in Industry. This was an especially difficult period in Hutchins and Rochester's lives, yet they responded with love and commitment: "My *Beloved* Darling Partner," Hutchins wrote, "You've done everything in the world for me that I need. *Nothing* could have been more perfect in every way than the love and devotion you give me. I don't deserve it at all & I know it. But oh how I count upon it, & depend on it, & live for it—literally . . . I'd go through even a *4th* operation to live for you, my Partner." And she signed the message: "Your own Grace."[37]

After a lengthy recovery at home, Hutchins began working for the Federated Press, ignoring the fact that the Daughters of the American Revolution were pronouncing the press a dangerous organization,[38] and coauthoring her first article, "Organize South, Cry of Textile Conference," dated May 1, 1928, with Harvey O'Connor, then head of the press's Eastern Bureau.[39] Together they recounted the proceedings of a weekend conference, "The Remedy for the Textile Industry," hosted by the Philadelphia Labor College. Because, as was reported at the conference, 20 percent of textile workers in the Philadelphia area were unemployed, efforts needed to focus on organizing not only locally but in the South so that employers would not relocate jobs to a nonunionized area.

The Federated Press Eastern Bureau was located in the same building as the LRA: 799 Broadway, also numbered 80 East 11th, in Manhattan. The Federated Press, according to Harvey O'Connor, had two desks, typewriters, a mimeograph machine and one employee—himself; the organization was too poor to be able to send articles out by wire, having to rely instead on the US Postal Service. Even so, the press often scooped the wire services on labor stories, because those services didn't bother to attend labor events at all.

One of the distinguishing features of CPUSA work at that time was its emphasis upon educating workers at the point of struggle. Not only were party labor organizers going to places where no one else would go and organizing industries and populations previously thought unorganizable, but printed materials explaining the struggles in their larger contexts served as a key element in the organizing work. The LRA embarked upon the ambitious project of publishing a new series of books, the "Labor and Industry" series, each volume focusing on the labor conditions in a particular industry. Hutchins's book, already underway, on labor in the silk industry, became the first in the series. Rochester then began to work on a companion volume on conditions in coal.

As Hutchins collected material for *Labor and Silk*, she sent back reports on textile workers to the Federated Press. Her first report on conditions in the textile plants came from the New Bedford textile strike. It would take her some time to reorient herself to labor struggles; this article, unlike many that followed, adhered roughly to the form that she had established in her articles for *Spirit of Missions*, narrating the activities of the plucky (in this case) Portuguese strikers against the oppressive employers and ending with a plea for donations to the ILD to support the strike. The strike of twenty-six thousand cotton workers, begun in April in response to a 10 percent wage cut and speed-ups, lasted for six months and led to the formation later that year of a new industrial union, the National Textile Workers, associated with the Trade Union Educational League, as a counter to the conservative AFL craft union.[40]

Whatever its shortcomings, the form Hutchins chose allowed her to highlight the work of women in the strike, especially that of the song leader, Elizabeth Donnelly, saying that she was "tireless in mobilizing the singing brigades of children, grownups and young workers." She also described Ann Craton of the Workers International Relief "visit[ing] relief stations and hold[ing] the fort at headquarters."[41] Strike reports had rarely before mentioned the work of women, and now Hutchins was not only claiming space for women in a labor periodical but quietly demonstrating the ways in which these women were shifting gender boundaries, not just for themselves but in ways that served to create more space for others. A photo accompanying the article in the *Labor Defender* shows a group of women on the picket line; the caption reads: "Before the Shay Mill. 'Women's place' today is not only in the home but also on the picket line." This was a clumsy effort by one of the editors but an effort, nonetheless, to match Hutchins's observations.

Rochester, meanwhile, although not quite on the picket line, was close to it, having gone to Pittsburgh to cover the National Miners' Convention for the Federated Press. The convention aimed to build a new union, more militant than the United Mine Workers headed by John L. Lewis. After reading newspaper reports on the morning of September 10, Hutchins's feminist bravado momentarily dissolved. The *Daily Worker* headline read: "Over 100 Delegates Are Arrested After Miners Drive Back Army of 200 Gangsters and Detectives." Calling up the ACLU, the *Daily Worker* offices, and the ILD, she was unable to find word of Rochester. "Most Precious Anna," she wrote, "*What* an anxious hour and a half I had after reading the Times & the D. W. at the breakfast table until I could get word from you! . . . and was *that* relieved when your wire came. You blessed Darling, you got in for a lot!"[42] It was one thing to report on the efforts of others, but this was a new experience for two women who had recently changed hotels to avoid some outsized cockroaches.

Nonetheless, at an age when many women had settled in a comfortable pattern of beliefs, Hutchins, then 43 years old, was revising her staunch feminism. She was reading widely this year, from Lenin's *Imperialism, the Highest State of Capitalism*, to Virginia Woolf's *Mrs. Dalloway*, and she was charting a life in direct contrast to that of Woolf's character Clarissa Dalloway (defined in the novel's title by her husband's name), who recalls longingly her happiest moment kissing Sally Seton. Hutchins had not succumbed to a heterosexual imperative. Instead, gathering strength from her partnership, she was challenging the class framework that limited the possibilities for women who lacked her independent income. On July 9, 1928, Hutchins was initiated into a union herself for the first time, joining the Office Workers Union, of which she remained a member for the rest of her life. Then, a few weeks later, having attended a National Association of Manufacturers (NAM) meeting for the Federated Press, she described an embodied rhetoric that she had renounced, telling readers about "a parlorful of well dressed women, many wearing pearl necklaces," representatives of the National Woman's Party (NWP), most of them opposing any regulation of hours or working conditions for women. Suggesting that the NWP women were, wittingly or not, playing into the profit motives of the manufacturers, she quoted a representative of the NAM industrial relations department who wished to abolish all laws requiring that children be over 16 or have finished the seventh grade before going to work. Many children, he claimed, in his desire for cheap labor, were mentally incapable of finishing even the sixth grade.[43] Raised with the pearl necklace set herself, Hutchins nonetheless did not hesitate to expose the NWP's class interests in order to create a broader equality, a move that did not endear her to the DAR.

With her book *Labor and Silk*, published in February 1929, Hutchins launched a more detailed argument focusing on the experiences of textile workers, a large percentage of whom were women. The book was only the second published by International Publishers on the subject of women workers.[44] Although she emphasized the experiences of the workers, she did not limit the book to descriptions of the labor of silk production. On the contrary: Hutchins contextualized the workers' experiences, demonstrating why changes in the industry had taken place, taking the silk worker beyond his or her own sphere and exploring the causes behind the conditions. Just as any packaging of information is meant to move the reader toward one or another perspective and, often, toward a particular action, *Labor and Silk* offered a historically based argument for militant unionizing in the silk industry.

Hutchins traced the shifts in the silk industry, focusing closely on the introduction of rayon. Rayon can be manufactured on the same looms as silk, she pointed out, and is often added to silk in order to strengthen it but also to create a cheaper fabric. Between 1925 and 1927, she noted, the number of workers increased by 30 percent, but earnings fell. A key issue for workers, she said, is the fact that rayon plants are so easily converted to dynamite plants. Not only that, but the rayon cartel comes closer than any other to being an international trust, controlling 85 percent of production worldwide. What this trust—as any trust—aims to do is eliminate competition through, in this case, agreements on prices, specialization in marketing, and exchange of patents and technical improvements.

Having provided that background, Hutchins shifted back to the workers' experiences, explaining speed-ups—called variously "labor extensions" or "rationalization"—and unemployment as the result of improvements in machinery. She was careful to emphasize that these improvements should not be resisted; rather, the machinery should be under the complete control of the workers. Citing A. Losovsky[45] of the Red International of Labor Unions (RILU), she argued that demands should be made for shorter workdays, rest periods, wage increases, and improved safety measures. "A long view ahead sees machine development in a workers' republic giving all workers leisure enough to live and to create."[46] Setting a high standard for the new LRA series, Hutchins contracted with her *World Tomorrow* colleague and friend Esther Shemitz to provide original pen and ink illustrations for the book.

Using her cross-class advantages, Hutchins explained the lives of those who used the silk that was manufactured and who owned the mills that produced the silk. She described in detail the company towns and the fact that single workers, both men and women, had to live in boarding houses where they were "watched over." Although she was writing primarily for workers, she knew that a significant part of her audience would be middle class, or petit bourgeois, people who might be compelled to respond if they only knew the conditions under which their goods were produced, an argument Vida Scudder had used during the textile strike in Lawrence, Massachusetts. However, despite the fact that Rochester and Hutchins themselves had responded to such a moral argument, it was seeming less and less viable for large-scale change.

Still, it was precisely this moral element that Grace Lumpkin chose to highlight in her review of *Labor and Silk* for *The Office Worker*, emphasizing the facility with which the rayon machinery could be switched to dynamite production. (Later, Lumpkin would ride this moral continuum to the far right end of the line, causing significant problems for Hutchins.) Other reviews of *Labor and Silk* ranged from critical to laudatory, depending largely upon the affiliations and perspectives of the reviewers. Eleanor Lansing Dulles, a Bryn Mawr alumna ten years Hutchins's junior, wrote for the *Bryn Mawr Bulletin* that, although Hutchins's facts were irrefutable, her conclusions regarding the need for worker control of production were an "admitted bias" that did not allow for discussions of how to implement "slow progress."[47] A. J. Muste, who had known Hutchins well in the FOR, reviewed *Labor and Silk* in the *New Leader*, praising her solid presentation of facts about the silk industry but challenging her assertions about the ability of the National Textile Workers Union (NTWU) to sustain a mass union among silk workers in Paterson, New Jersey, saying that others before had tried to do the same thing, but they had been "missionary sects," undoubtedly a choice of terms aimed at Hutchins personally. She had not, Muste claimed, adequately supported her assertion that the NTWU would succeed where others had failed; it was, he said, in another metaphor aimed at Hutchins, "another case of generals without an army."[48] Hutchins clipped the review, disregarding the personal attacks but placing a small question mark next to his opening statement that the book "should be in the hands of all those who as organizers, worker educationalists, or socially-minded citizens are interested in the silk industry and the conditions of silk workers." Why, she seems to have been to be asking, should the book go to everyone *but* the workers themselves?

Reviews by Jessie Lloyd in *Labor's News* and Scott Nearing in *New Masses* were less combative. Jessie Lloyd, soon to be married to Harvey O'Connor, reproduced some of Hutchins's factual material and ended with her contrast between American and Russian silk workers, describing the building of a union "ignoring race, craft and sex lines and based on the need for militant struggle"[49]; Scott Nearing, reviewing *Labor and Silk* and Robert Dunn's *Labor and Automobiles* together, emphasized the huge profits gained by owners of the machines in both industries, profits swelled by speed-ups and stretch-outs. He concluded by pointing out clearly the reason for the books—to provide information to workers so that they could "build their struggle for economic and social emancipation."[50] Nearing correctly assessed the function of the materials produced by the LRA. Still, LRA writers attempted to respond to the shifts in rhetorical emphasis advised by party members who were trying to develop new strategies to keep pace with economic and political changes.

Rochester had by now begun her contribution to this series, *Labor and Coal*. After researching in the New York Public Library for several months, she had sent her first article on the subject to Karl Reeve, editor of *Labor Defender*, in January 1928. With revisions, "The Coal Miners and Injunctions" was finally published in the March 1929 issue, documenting the class interests of judges who issued injunctions forcing the end to strikes in the coal fields: "Of course a judge who owns thousands of acres of coal lands or shares of coal stock and whose job depends on the coal owners plays the game for the operators and against the miners."[51]

After this statement clearly identifying her position, Rochester continued to research quietly for the book. Meanwhile, Hutchins worked for the Federated Press, helping to establish the new publication *Labor's News*, a tabloid-style newspaper that would take the place of the newsletter-format *Federated Press Labor Letter*. Seeking comments from readers, Hutchins arranged for copies of the new publication to be sent to friends, including Harry F. Ward and Winifred Chappell at the Methodist Federation for Social Service and Ellen Hayes, former Wellesley mathematics professor, Socialist, feminist, and editor of *The Relay* in Wellesley, Massachusetts. Their enthusiastic responses were printed next to a subscription form in the next issues of *Labor's News*.

Hutchins also reported on the activities of the new textile union, the National Textile Workers Union, which, she emphasized, was *not* a spinoff of an AFL union but an entirely new union of formerly unorganized workers.[52] This fact did not prevent the AFL-affiliated United Textile Workers from attempting to organize in the same territory, especially in the South. Employers, of course, weren't keen on either one. Nor were local news media. One of the most violent episodes occurred in the spring of 1929 in Gastonia, North Carolina, when tension between striking textile workers and local police and vigilantes led first to the ambush and killing of song leader and local union member Ella Mae Wiggins and later, during a police raid on the strikers' tent colony, to the death of Chief of Police O. F. Aderholt. No one was ever arrested or charged in Ella Mae Wiggins's murder, but NTWU organizers were indicted for the death of Chief Aderholt. Although there was no evidence to connect union organizers with Aderholt's death—which may have been caused by a shot from one of his own officers—NTWU organizers were nonetheless charged with murder and assault with a deadly weapon with intent to kill. In this way, local officials tied up union time and resources and made sure that workers understood the danger of union involvement. The Gastonia *Gazette* helped out with "full-page ads allegedly 'paid for by citizens.' One was headed: RED RUSSIANISM LIFTS ITS GORY HANDS RIGHT HERE IN GASTONIA."[53] Apparently the best defense was a good offense.

Relating more of the employers' attempts to discredit the NTWU, Hutchins noted that the trade paper, *Textile World*, recommended "playing up racial antagonisms, since the left wing union includes in its platform the clause, 'abolition of the color line.' "[54] A few months later, Hutchins reported in *Labor Defender* on a police raid instigated by Charles Schwab's Bethlehem Steel Corporation on a May Day celebration of steel and textile workers. Eighteen-year-old silk weaver Anna Burlak was among those arrested, Hutchins wrote, documenting an early moment in Burlak's long life as an organizer and again locating women at the center, rather than the periphery, of the struggle.[55]

The summer of 1929 brought heart-wrenching changes for Hutchins, although these changes helped to strengthen her relationship with Rochester. On June 23, 1929, her father died at the family's summer home in Castine, Maine. Friends responded to the family's loss, but Rochester was Hutchins's primary source of support. Copying off part of a tribute written about her father, praising his dependability and loyalty as a friend, Hutchins wrote to Rochester, saying, "May you and I be able to say the same of each other 30–40 years from now! I know I could say it of you."[56]

By 1929, psychological treatises pathologizing relationships between women and setting them against a standard of "companionate" heterosexual relations were thoroughly inculcated into the popular imagination and were showing up in a wide spectrum of magazines and novels. As Christina Simmons has pointed out, "the new sexual ideology which achieved cultural hegemony by the 1930s . . . represented a morality more suited to the social needs of the corporate liberal state than its Victorian predecessor."[57] Hutchins and Rochester, no fans of the "corporate liberal state," remained unaffected up to this point. Their friends and families, too, disregarded the popular propaganda. Certainly, Hutchins's brother Henry recognized Rochester's importance to Hutchins: "You have Anna, Ned has

Emily, and I have Marian. But Mother has no work & must return to Cape Rosier, as she would want to, and to all those treasured associations. She has us and we must do our best to comfort her and cheer her."[58]

More than anyone who wrote to her, Kurt Klaeber seemed to understand Hutchins's feelings at the time: she was torn between her love for her father and her need to move into a new world with Rochester. Relating his own experience with his father, Klaeber said, "In my case something strange happened. When I was alone with the dead body I suddenly felt him dissolving in me as if only through his death his last energy and strength passed over to me. And he possessed both. Incidentally his determination crossed over as well even though it had no political direction. That's what I wanted to convey to you, Grace!" he said. "Death can make . . . the surviving person stronger."[59] Hutchins had always been a strong woman, but she seemed to take Kurt Klaeber's words to heart, absorbing her father's strength and his devotion to civic justice—if not the precise belief system which had guided his actions.

Although her father's death meant that Hutchins needed to be more attentive to her mother, it also meant that she had a somewhat larger income. In his will, written on September 6, 1928, Edward Hutchins left her the income from one-tenth of his estate (after bequests to institutions such as the church and to various household retainers), which he had placed in trust with his partner Henry Wheeler, Hutchins's brother Ned, and Walter Van Kleeck as trustees; each of her brothers received a similar bequest; and her mother received the income from the remaining seven-tenths of the estate. Thus Hutchins no longer needed to work for the Federated Press, although she could continue to send in articles as she wished. With a larger independent income, she could do work that needed to be done but for which no salary was available. She seized the opportunity to join Bob Dunn and her partner, Anna Rochester, in the LRA.

Her income thus assured, Hutchins was also able to involve herself more deeply in labor activities. In late August, while Rochester remained at Back Log Camp for their annual vacation, Hutchins left for the annual convention of the Trade Union Educational League (TUEL) in Cleveland. The New York delegates and guests, of whom she was one, met at midnight on the night of August 29 at the Workers' Center at 26–28 Union Square, fourth floor—the local offices of the Trade Union Educational League. After a short meeting, most of the delegates and guests boarded buses, to the cheers of hundreds of other workers, for an all-night trip through New Jersey, Pennsylvania, and New York to Buffalo, where they transferred to a boat that took them to Cleveland.[60] Hutchins, however, decided to take the train with a sleeper car, so as to be more alert during the convention. She was, in 1929, 44 years old, had recently recovered from surgery, and the prospect of an all-night bus and boat trip might have been more than she was prepared to endure voluntarily.[61]

The TUEL meetings focused on the fact that, at that time, in the United States, 1 percent of the population owned a third of the nation's wealth, and less than 25 percent of the population owned 90 percent of the wealth—and there was every indication that these trends would only continue in the same direction.[62] The program of the Trade Union Educational League, with the slogan "Class Against Class," emphasized the creation of new unions that would consist of semiskilled and unskilled workers. No lines were to be drawn on the bases of race, gender, age, or skill level, but the special interests of women and youth were to be recognized in the organization of special national and local sections for these populations.[63] During the convention, the Trade Union Educational League reconstituted itself as the Trade Union Unity League (TUUL), shifting its emphasis from working within the existing AFL unions to working to establish unions for the previously unorganized.[64]

Rochester wrote to Hutchins on August 30 as she prepared to leave for the convention, wondering whether "in the turmoil of the convention" Hutchins would "think it relevant to be informed of the little doings" at Back Log Camp. She wanted to write anyway, she said, if only to say: "This big tent is too big without you!" The "little doings" included hiking to Lewey Lake with Olga Halsey to swim. Olga Halsey, a 1912 graduate of Wellesley, where she had studied with Emily Green Balch and Vida Scudder, was one of Hutchins and Rochester's closest friends at camp, returning every year at the same time, as they did.[65] Other campers tried Rochester's patience. "Miss Weil" corralled Rochester at lunch, she reported, "wanting to know what kind of a conference you had gone to—Then as we left the table, she wanted to know more about it, because she is looking for a cause! I told her very briefly but I said, "I don't think it would appeal to you at all!" Whereupon, a long discourse about how she had been a Socialist, etc., etc. I touched a sensitive spot, evidently, for she burst forth just as she did the other day about housework."[66] Rochester's disdain for another woman whose theoretical sophistication did not rival hers reveals a flaw in her radicalism that would continue to dog her and weaken her efforts.

Moreover, although Rochester's understanding was comprehensive, she continued to couch her arguments in forms that were less than successful. Well-trained in Greek and Latin, she often shaped her articles following the classic argument form, documenting the increasing profits of the coal companies and the decreasing wages of the workers with a problem stated in the beginning ("Nearly one-half of the men employed in Montana coal mines in 1920 had been frozen out of the industry in 1928, according to figures just released by the U.S. Bureau of Mines"), followed by an analysis of the causes of the problem

Figure 7.2. Back Log Camp tents

("more of the coal is produced in big mines"), presentation of counterarguments ("The big operators boast of having stabilized employment"), concession of the validity of some of those counterarguments ("and it is true that in 1928 Pennsylvania mines averaged 218 days of operation against 180 days in 1924"), and refutation of the primary counterarguments ("But this partial stability has been achieved at the expense of thousands of miners [and their families] thrown permanently out of the industry. Also the operators have put over such drastic wage cuts that the miners who are still employed cannot make in 218 days as much as they earned in 180 days under the Jacksonville scale").[67] Neither Hutchins's missionary appeals nor Rochester's classical arguments were especially appropriate for the work at hand. What would be appropriate? That question remained unanswered for now, although not for lack of trying.

Rochester's work, as well as Hutchins', was part of a larger organizing effort within the CPUSA. The LRA, not an official CPUSA organization but run largely by CPUSA members, had been founded with education in mind, and there were constant reminders of the struggle to control channels of communication. Writing in *New Masses* in January 1928, Rochester had warned readers about a new law, the Native Affairs Act, imposed on South Africa by the white colonists. The law stated that " 'any person who utters any words or does any other act or thing whatever with intent to promote any feeling of hostility between natives and Europeans shall be guilty of an offense and liable to conviction to imprisonment for a period not exceeding one year or a fine of 100 pounds or both." Because the government was white controlled, the law, in effect, was aimed at the indigenous people. More recently, in the United States, the *Daily Worker*, describing the selection of jurors in Charlotte, North Carolina, to try the case of organizers and workers charged in the killing of Gastonia police chief Aderholt, reported that "reading the *Daily Worker* or the *Labor Defender* seems to disqualify a person for jury service, but reading the *Charlotte Observer*, the reactionary organ of the Duke Power interests and the mill owners, does not prejudice the prospective jurors, according to the state."[68]

In response to such situations, the new organizing effort emphasized publications as the key to improved communication and education that would bring in new members. During October 1929, the Central Committee of the CPUSA met and adopted a "Resolution on the *Daily Worker*," which was then published on December 10, 1929, in the *Daily Worker*. This resolution argued for the need to convert the *Daily Worker* into a mass organ and the twin need to recruit five thousand new members who would subscribe to the paper.[69]

Following that, in an editorial on January 1, 1930, Alexander Trachtenberg argued for more breadth in publishing and depth in recruiting, saying that the recruiting drive must not aim for mere numbers but should be a party-building campaign. Among the special groups he noted for inclusion were "working women, who, hardly organized and greatly exploited, represent a potential revolutionary force which must be harnessed for the Communist movement."[70] Although the campaign to organize women was a partywide effort, Hutchins and Rochester undoubtedly bore some of the responsibility for Trachtenberg's statement; Hutchins, especially, was eager to build women into the movement in ways that allowed them to define themselves, manage their own lives, and gain political influence.

In order to carry out this campaign successfully, literature distribution would be critical, Trachtenberg pointed out. "We should be on the spot with millions of leaflets and hundreds of thousands of pamphlets and shop papers explaining to the workers Hoover's fake prosperity, the Stock Exchange crash, the permanent unemployment."[71] Ten days later, Jack Stachel wrote an editorial celebrating the sixth anniversary of the *Daily Worker* and urging readers to help increase the paper from four to six pages, sell it at factories and meetings, and write in to the Workers Correspondence section.[72]

Offering one contribution to this publication drive, Rochester translated Lenin's "On Party Literature" from German for the *New Masses*. The essay begins with the ringing lines: "Literature must become party literature. In opposition to bourgeois standards, in opposition to the press of bourgeois business and trade, in opposition to bourgeois literary competition and individualism, to 'noble anarchy,' and to the hunt for profits, the class-conscious proletariat must set up the principle of party literature." Although acknowledging the need for personal initiative and imagination, Lenin argued that true freedom would come when writers were free from worry about the control of publishers and the fickle reading public: "Are you authors free in relation to your bourgeois publisher and your bourgeois public who demand from you a nicely presented and glossed over pornography, and want prostitution as the supplement to the 'sacred' drama?" he asked. In fact, he said, the process will be dialectical, as "a free literature . . . impregnates the achievements of revolutionary human thought with the experience and the living work of the class-conscious proletariat, creating a constant interplay between the experience of the past (with its development from primitive utopian forms of socialism to the scientific socialism of our movement) and the experience of today (in the present struggle of the comrade workers)."[73]

Already aware of the persuasive power of fiction from her experience in Germany, and as a first step in the dialectic, Rochester loaned money to her friend and former *World Tomorrow* associate Grace Lumpkin to support her while she wrote *To Make My Bread*, a novel about the Gastonia textile strike.[74] Literature was "free" in the United States only insofar as there was no government censorship; otherwise, working class literature was so far from free as to be almost nonexistent. Who had the time or material conditions to write? Working class literature by and about women was even more rare, for the same reasons.

Moving into this new dialectic, Rochester knew that the points on which she agreed with Vida Scudder were becoming fewer and fewer. *Brother John* did not come close to working class literature—and although it featured deep, same-sex love, it was exclusively about men. Apart from herself and Hutchins, Vida Scudder was probably the most radical of all the members of the Society of the Companions of the Holy Cross. It was time, Rochester realized, to let go of her membership in the society. Members were notified of her decision by a single line in the November 1929 issue of the Companions' Intercession Paper: "Withdrawn from the Society Anna Rochester."[75] Leaving the Companions meant leaving the people and the organization that had fostered her relationship with Hutchins. In 1929, there seemed no other path.

The FOR was next, but before leaving, Rochester made one last attempt to reach out to her former colleagues, explaining to them the shift in understanding that had begun for her during her years at *The World Tomorrow* and that had become cemented in place during her year of travel. In a final article published in the January 1930 issue of *The World Tomorrow*, Rochester clarified the Communist approach to social and economic change—an approach that included both cooperation with noncommunist movements expressing dissatisfaction with the capitalist status quo and educational efforts for workers that would counteract the biases of the capitalist press.

At the request of Kirby Page, and with some advice from Alexander Trachtenberg, Rochester revised the article for inclusion in Page's volume *A New Economic Order*, published later that year. Although she later laughed at this earliest attempt to explain communism—telling Trachtenberg in late 1934 that the article "resembled greatly the bleating of an over-grown calf"[76]—it was, especially in its revised form, a lucid articulation of the points most likely to be misunderstood by bourgeois readers. She was at her best when writing to an audience of her class peers, yet what was unusual in her presentation was her ability as a woman, only ten years after the passage of the suffrage amendment, to articulate the position of a theoretically complex and increasingly influential political party.

The first sentence of her chapter provided a definition: "Communism is the workers' international movement of revolutionary change from capitalism to Socialism." From there, Rochester moved through the class struggle as the "central point in Communist thinking and Communist tactics" to a refutation of the notion of easy transit out of the American working class. She explained the development of capitalism in a series of short phrases linked by semicolons, indicating the almost breathless rapidity with which the system can change, spiraling out of control.

Rochester went on to explain the manner in which capital is exported and finds a home in undeveloped countries, thus developing those countries and simultaneously ending the markets that industries in the home country had depended on for export of goods. "Only the workers in a workers' non-capitalist world," she insisted, "can transform the advance of industrial technique from a means of exploitation into a tool of human progress." In order to accomplish this transformation, the workers must engage in mass action. Unfortunately, not all mass organizations held the same interpretation: the Second International (the Socialist Party), along with many labor unions, Rochester argued, were simply trying to patch up the current capitalist system, trading short-term job maintenance (even at a cost of lower wages, in some cases) for long-term change.

After clarifying the history of the Third International—formed in March 1919—and the Red International of Labor Unions, Rochester explained the problem that she now had with the League of Nations and with nongovernmental pacifist organizations, such as the FOR. "The Communist," she said, leaving aside for the moment the dispassionate analysis that characterized the rest of the article, "regards the League of Nations as an alliance of imperialist governments, set off against the Soviet Union. . . . He believes that no capitalist League and no pacifist propaganda can prevent future wars between empires—to say nothing of military expeditions into colonial and other dependent territories."[77]

The shift from capitalism to socialism would not be accomplished without armed struggle, she pointed out, as the capitalists would resist with force any attempts on the parts of the workers to control industry. Moreover, the change would not take place uniformly across the world, because each country differed in its degree of capitalist development; the United States, she allowed, would be one of the last to change.

Referring readers to Lenin's *State and Revolution*, Rochester asserted that "the state is not and never has been an impartial force, representing society as a whole, but always the organ of the dominant economic class." What the revolution would accomplish would be the shift in power from the "veiled dictatorship of the capitalist class" to "an open and consistent dictatorship by the working class."

In the final section of the article, Rochester explained the Soviet Union to American readers—especially those readers with an interest in social change—addressing the major points of contention one by one. Harking back to the enthusiasm she expressed in her June 1927 letter to Sally Cleghorn, Rochester wrote: "Frank discussion of all problems, strong union organization, union representation on all state economic and industrial bodies, and the utter absence of a capitalist class exploiting the workers, give the Russian factories an atmosphere of freedom and intelligent participation and human liveliness which words cannot convey."[78]

If words could not convey the atmosphere in Russian factories, Rochester and Hutchins were convinced that words could move the revolution—a revolution that would build on the American revolution and benefit the majority of Americans; a revolution, indeed, which they could help to bring about—and they committed themselves to building the party press.

Chapter Eight

Love and Work

A Communist must understand what is happening about him in the world. He must understand the mechanism of the existing regime, must know the history of the growth of human society, the history of economic development, of the growth of property, the division of classes, the growth of state forms. He must clearly picture whither society is developing. Communism must appear to him not only a desirable regime but exactly that regime to which humanity is going, where the happiness of some will not be based on the slavery of others and where there will be no compulsion except strongly developed social instincts. And the communists must clear the road, as you clear a path in the wilderness to hasten its coming.

—Krupskaya (Lenin's wife) (copied by Hutchins into her personal notebook)

Building the party press, "clearing a path in the wilderness," meant more than simply setting up mechanisms for printing and distribution, although these mechanisms were vital—and expensive. Activists around the world debated larger rhetorical questions of language and format. Rochester and Hutchins had struggled with these questions during their years with the FOR and *The World Tomorrow*; now they confronted them again, offering their advice and taking the advice and direction of others. Although their methods differed, Hutchins and Rochester both understood persuasion. How to reach workers was another matter. Nor did the problems stop there. The new vision meant redefining the limits not only of class but of race and gender. Most importantly, intervening at the point of struggle now meant more than education; it meant moving readers to action.[1]

During the late summer of 1928, the Sixth Congress of the Communist International (Comintern) met in Moscow, analyzing the world situation and making decisions that would profoundly affect the movement—and Rochester and Hutchins's involvement in it.[2] For the first time, a complete program for the international Communist movement was outlined, partly in response to analyses made by the CPUSA's executive committee. The party's program included an analysis of the postwar era that divided it into three periods, the first of which was characterized by revolutions, the second by temporary stabilization, and the third, beginning in 1928, by increasing struggles between labor and capital. In response to this assessment, the congress recommended intensifying the opposition to arguments and actions that sought to blunt labor struggles.[3] The world congress also discussed questions of colonialism and, with strong participation by American delegates, arrived at an analysis of what was called the "Negro question," arguing that "the Negro people [were] an oppressed nation entitled to the right of self-determination."[4]

Hutchins seems to have ignored the specific question of nationhood, instead taking the new focus on African American workers and beginning her own campaign to inform readers about differential working conditions, attempting to erase racial distinctions between women workers through solidarity.

As Rochester was making her last attempt to convince her former colleagues in the FOR of the logic of the CPUSA's program, Hutchins started working closer to the front lines, in the ILD.[5] Here she became better acquainted with Juliet Stuart Poyntz.[6] Perhaps it was Poyntz who asked Hutchins to write an article for the *Daily Worker* outlining the work of the ILD in supporting women strikers and organizers. In any event, Hutchins had now established herself at the center of the movement, where she tried to clear two paths simultaneously: educating workers and pushing the party to recognize the struggles and accomplishments of women.

Among those Hutchins highlighted in the *Daily Worker* article were Anna Burlak and Mary Dalton, arrested in Atlanta, Georgia, for the crime of organizing black and white workers together in the National Textile Workers Union. (Five organizers, including Burlak and Dalton, had been arrested for "inciting Negroes to riot" and "inciting to insurrection." They were also charged with holding a mixed meeting.) "The prosecutor is demanding the death penalty and under a Georgia law passed in 1861 to kill leaders of Negro slave rebellions, they can be electrocuted if convicted," Hutchins explained.[7]

In a companion article written for *The Working Woman*, the party's newsmagazine for women, Hutchins described the abysmal working conditions many African American women had to endure. "Of all workers under capitalism," Hutchins wrote, "Negro women are the most exploited." They worked the longest hours for the lowest pay, she said, describing conditions in the industries employing the greatest numbers of African American women: domestic service, janitorial service, tobacco factories, textile factories, laundries, and the needle trades.[8] By now she had dropped her fund-raising closures, substituting instead a plea for solidarity, a critical first step toward action. However, a survey of her writing from this period suggests that she still was having difficulty distinguishing between what she wanted to tell the people she was accustomed to addressing and what her readership needed to hear. Certainly, it was not news to African American women that they were the most exploited workers.

Hutchins went on to produce articles for almost every party-related publication. Writing for *Labor Unity*, a magazine for all workers, she described the conditions forced upon young women working for Schrafft's, both the restaurant and the candy maker, and the profits the chain was making off their labor. Schrafft's workers receive $15 per week, she pointed out, even though the company declared a 200 percent stock dividend in August 1929 and announced a profit increase of 355 percent from 1923 to 1928. "Standing all day was bad, but not so bad as the intense driving speed under the overseer's whipping tongue," she said, shattering the linkage of enslavement to race and illustrating its direct correlation with surplus value. "Food Workers—Organize!" she urged, leading readers across ancient borders of race and gender and pointing to the Hotel, Restaurant and Cafeteria Workers' Union, affiliated with the Trade Union Unity League.[9]

Although she was now constructing arguments in favor of solidarity, Hutchins wisely offered her fund-raising services where they would be most useful: she served as treasurer of the ILD for several years, soliciting funds for wives of workers injured in labor actions, sending monthly checks to imprisoned workers, and providing bail money for those who had been arrested. She also made a public move that placed her in direct opposition to those for whom she had raised funds in the past, demonstrating her own willingness to

AUGUST, 1933   10c.

Figure 8.1. *Labor Unity* masthead

redefine limits; nothing, in fact, was sacred. During early 1930, she used her knowledge of financial practices to issue a report suggesting ties between churchmen's condemnations of the Soviet Union and the sources of ecclesiastical funds.[10] She began this article by citing a *Wall Street Journal* story on the assets of Trinity Church of New York, the "Church of Wall Street," whose former rector, now Bishop William T. Manning, had recently called upon "all religious bodies to join in a day of prayer as a protest against Soviet policy." Trinity Church, she reported, owned $15,000,000 in real estate and $16,923,956 in other assets. Listing the value of real estate owned by the six largest denominations (Roman Catholic, Methodist Episcopal, the Presbyterian Church in the United States of America, Protestant Episcopal, Northern Baptist, and Congregational), Hutchins pointed out that, although the amounts totaled in the billions, this amount was "a small fraction of that" owned by churches in the United States, including endowments of pension funds and trust funds of missionary societies. "The church pension fund of the Protestant Episcopal church," she said, "with J. P. Morgan as treasurer and chairman of its finance committee, now totals over $25,500,000. . . . The fund is invested in the leading railroad and industrial corporations in the United States," she said, listing several, "and most of them have broken strikes with gunmen, spies, and state and private police."[11]

Hutchins would have been even more keenly aware of the funding of religious organizations and individual churches from the recent revelations of her father's will, which dictated that $20,000 should go to Trinity Church in Boston and that, had all his heirs predeceased him, a sizable portion of his estate, some $500,000, would have gone to the church. There, in sum, was the capitalist patriarchy. Hutchins realized at this point that she, like Rochester, could no longer remain a Companion. The April 1930 Intercession Paper of the Society of the Companions of the Holy Cross lists under the heading Notes: "Withdrawn from the Society: Grace Hutchins."[12]

The Federated Press, ILD, and LRA, as well as the CPUSA itself, were now Rochester and Hutchins's organizational homes. Hutchins also served as a member of the National Advisory Council of the Workers' School.[13] It was within both the Federated Press and the ILD that Hutchins and Rochester became better acquainted with Jessie Lloyd, soon to become Jessie Lloyd O'Connor. Unlike Harvey O'Connor, Jessie Lloyd came from wealth. She also had a family history of radicalism from her grandfather Henry Demarest Lloyd and her aunt Caro Lloyd Strobell, who had been active in the LID. Thus Jessie Lloyd shared with Hutchins and Rochester the sense that having wealth did not relieve one of the duty to work—quite the contrary. Although never a member of the CPUSA, Jessie Lloyd was a fellow traveler whom Hutchins could count on to support the ILD and the LRA. Working salary free, she headed off to Gastonia in August 1929 with Federated Press credentials to report on the trial of the National Textile Workers' Union organizers charged with the murder of police chief Aderholt. Hutchins, meanwhile, stayed in New York, raising bail for the Gastonia workers and organizers who had been arrested.[14]

But as necessary as defense operations were, and as practiced as Hutchins was at raising funds, both Rochester and Hutchins wanted to be changing minds so that such defense work would not be necessary. Alexander Trachtenberg had been working on translating the need to address working class issues at the point of struggle into concrete activities. Beginning in early 1930, he had decided to create another publishing house in order to produce pamphlets. The idea was that the pamphlets would sell for a few pennies and would be pocket sized, so organizers could fill their pockets with them and workers could easily carry them to read in spare moments. He talked over the idea with Bob Dunn, Hutchins, Rochester, Solon De Leon, Jack Hardy, and others who were working at the LRA at the time. They agreed that cheap, easily read pamphlets, illustrated with drawings or photographs, would be a good educational and organizing tool. Rochester wrote to Hutchins at one point in late 1929: "Trachty is full of a new idea for smaller, cheaper more popular pamphlets. Ruth spoke up for it and Trachty, Bob, you and Ruth are a committee to take them up and make more concrete suggestions."[15] Thus was born International Pamphlets, housed also at 799 Broadway.

Hutchins underscored the threat of the pamphlets to those who profited from poverty, especially women's poverty, after visiting TUUL organizer Caroline Drew in the Women's Workhouse on "Welfare Island" in New York.[16] Drew told Hutchins about her companions in prison—an out-of-work Passaic woman who had stolen a dress for her child, another out-of-work woman who could not meet her mortgage payment and had stolen a pair of gloves for a Christmas present for her daughter, and several poor women who had been arrested for drunkenness. "Poor women who get drunk to forget for a few moments the haunting anxiety and misery of life are sentenced now to six months in jail," Hutchins reported. "'So much drunkenness,' put in the lady keeper, a massive woman who said she had a 'special aptitude' for her job of herding the poor into jail—and looked it. 'Yes, that is why we can't let the prisoners have any literature from outside, because of the drunkenness.'" Not surprisingly, Hutchins found this equation puzzling: "Just what drunkenness had to do with pamphlets by Labor Research Assn. and the volume, An Outline of Political Economy, which Caroline Drew wanted but was forbidden to receive, the lady keeper did not say." Then she answered the riddle at the end of her article with an architectural metaphor, saying: "But overshadowing the victims of poverty huddled in these gray buildings, are Chrysler's pretty bauble, resplendent steeple of the auto magnate, and Al Smith's Empire State, tallest building in the world, monument of Tammany, towering over this richest city."[17] Although she has a bit of morbid fun at the prison guard's expense, she also argues by virtue of scale that the prison guard, however foolish, is a creation of capitalism, gender this time gone awry as her outsized body reflects the surplus value in the massive structures around her, a message that altering gender roles alone will not serve to create fundamental change.

While Hutchins was visiting the imprisoned and raising funds for their bail and their families—and beginning her efforts to apply Marxism-Leninism to women—Rochester spent her days at the New York Public Library, researching the coal industry. At the same time, she was beginning to investigate the larger structures of capital in the United States in preparation for her second book, Rulers of America: A Study of Finance Capital, which would appear in 1936.[18] In an article coauthored with Harvey O'Connor, Rochester announced that 38 major corporations "each paid out in 1929 over $10,000,000 in cash dividends on common stock." She listed the dividends paid out by the top nineteen corporations, with General Motors heading the list at $155,000,000 paid in dividends during 1929 and Union Carbide bringing up the rear with only $20,606,859. She went on to say, with her trademark irony, "The other 19 companies [completing the total of thirty-eight] paying a paltry $10,000,000 to $20,000,000 in common dividends include Sears Roebuck, Sheel Union Oil [sic], Morgan's new Standard Brands, three other motor companies, Bethlehem Steel, United Fruit, and Westinghouse Electric."[19] Another article, "Rockefeller Dominates World's Largest Bank," dated March 21, 1930, and coauthored with both Hutchins and Harvey O'Connor, traced the interlocking directorates of the major US banks and noted that the center of world banking had now shifted from London to New York with the merger of Chase National Bank, Equitable Trust Co., and Interstate Trust Co. This merger, Rochester pointed out, was of no benefit to workers, and, in fact, it boded ill, because the antiunion policies of the merged companies would now only be strengthened. Moreover, directors of the new bank included representatives of all the major industries: "Strikes in the factories, mills and mines controlled by these directors have always been savagely broken as scabs, thugs, police, courts and churches have been lined up to break the workers' resistance."[20] Rochester had proven herself and had taken her place on the front lines of CPUSA discourse, attacking with fact-based prose the most powerful men in America.

Because Hutchins's efforts during this time were focused largely on women workers, documenting their working conditions and tracing the structures of capital that led to those conditions, she probably had a strong influence on the November report of the political committee. The report confessed to a feeling within the party that work among women was unimportant—that it could easily be referred to a "sub-committee" or could be handled by those who couldn't seem to manage anything else. But Earl Browder, then general secretary of the CPUSA, insisted, "Women are one of the largest groups of workers in this country. They have special oppressions, they have special grievances, special interests of their own."[21]

Certainly Hutchins had been making this point everywhere and often. Describing the advertising materials disseminated by the Dictaphone Corporation, which suggested that by using Dictaphones employers could increase office workers' productivity, Hutchins explained what this really meant: rather than having a variety of work activities, office workers would have to type nonstop for seven and a half hours a day, not pacing themselves, but forced to keep up with the voice coming out of the machine.[22] Meanwhile, Westinghouse, she reported, aiming her comments at those who would deny the importance of organizing women, was hiring women at two-thirds of men's pay to do the jobs that men had formerly done. Not only that, but "Negro workers are used on the worst jobs where the heat is fiercest and the danger of accidents is greatest."[23]

Then, pointing directly to an instance of intersecting interests between corporations and courts, Hutchins reported in November 1930 that African American organizers in the textile industry in the south had come to expect that lynchings would be used as a method to deter them. There had been five lynchings in two days recently in Georgia, she said. Yet the organizers insisted that they would not be deterred, nor would they stop advocating racial equality. She ended the article on lynching and the court system's collaboration in repression by allowing a representative of the court to explain. "The determination of the prosecution may be judged by the words of Asst. Atty. Gen. John H. Hudson who stated at the time of the indictment: 'As fast as these Communists come here and publicly preach their doctrine, we shall indict them and I shall demand the death penalty in every case.'"[24] As appalling as Hudson's pronouncement was, it was also, as intended, daunting to workers and organizers.

Figure 8.2. Cover of *Labor and Coal*

In the November–December issue of *The Communist*, Earl Browder insisted that "the next task of the Party is to find the way *how* to pass from the stage of agitation and propaganda to the stage of active struggle." How, indeed, with judicial death threats ringing in workers' ears? The Comintern had criticized the American party, alleging that its principal weakness was to be found in the fact that although it was good at disseminating information, it still was unable to mobilize masses "for struggle for their immediate demands and especially for their economic demands." Thus, without diminishing the propaganda efforts of the party, members needed to figure out how to make the propaganda serve people's most immediate needs. "We must pass from propaganda to action."[25]

And so, when Rochester's contribution to the LRA's Labor and Industry series, *Labor and Coal*, appeared in January 1931, it promised "not only graphic pictures of living and working conditions, but an interpretation of economic struggle and suggested programs of action to meet the offensives of the corporations,"[26] fulfilling the requirements laid out by Scott Nearing almost eight years earlier, as well as meeting current Party objectives.

Rochester assumed that the coal industry was unwell, and then, after documenting that ill health, she proceeded to analyze the causes from the perspective of the miners. She pointed out that despite the continuing loss of jobs and speed-ups in the industry, the coal companies had made substantial payments to their bondholders. To avoid paying dividends to stockholders, they created holding companies and manipulated their accounting practices in order to appear to have sustained losses, a practice implicitly condoned by the government, which protected information on companies.[27] Thus, although workers and small stockholders were suffering, the companies themselves and the financial institutions that were closely tied to them were doing well, through such measures as mechanization, layoffs, speed-ups, and questionable accounting practices. The problems, she said, stemmed from overproduction and lack of planning. In a cycle of overproduction and cost cutting, the net result would be that "every capitalist industry is headed toward mass unemployment and ultimately a condition of long drawn-out crisis when swollen capacity to produce and saturated markets reduce the profits of the capitalist class."[28]

In discussing the situations of the miners themselves, Rochester described conditions in the company towns built by the coal companies, asking, in a question reminiscent of Companions' debates: "But what is the real situation in this country that boasts of its bathtubs and plumbing?" The real situation, she said, was one of complete control over the miners' lives. Town services, such as police, preachers, and teachers, were hired by the company and paid for out of mandatory "dues." Moreover, the company lease was a "yellow-dog contract," dictating not only that the tenant forfeited his legal rights to join a union but that either striking or allowing a union organizer to stay in the house was grounds for eviction. Working conditions were unstable and equally designed to benefit the companies. Hours, she said, were the worst in the United States, followed by Europe. The best working conditions for miners were found in the USSR, she said, where workers spent no more than six hours per day underground and five hours at the face and were given four weeks paid vacation per year, as well as health and other social insurance. The poor working conditions in the United States led to dangerous situations, situations that had been increasing with speed-ups and mechanization; in the ten years ending December 31, 1929, 22,500 miners had been killed on the job, half of them in falls of coal or rock. However, she said, gesturing toward action, "the mines will never be as safe as modern technical knowledge can make them until the workers themselves compel the universal enforcement of the highest standards."[29]

Christian Century lobbed a verbal grenade at the book: "It is all communist propaganda, of course, and needs to be read with that in mind. It may even be subsidized from Moscow, and when one looks at these 250-page well printed books put on the market for a dollar apiece one believes that it must be." The reviewer did concede, however, that "there is much factual material here, well documented, which needs to be studied." *Book Review Digest* chose to begin its list of reviews with the dismissive "communist propaganda" excerpt,[30] a fact which must have only increased Hutchins's annoyance. She wrote to the editors of *Christian Century*, alerting them to the fact that they had been sent the wrong edition of the book by mistake—the $1.00 edition was reserved for bundle orders from labor unions; the publicly available edition cost $2.00. She also suggested that they might ask Winifred Chappell of the Methodist Federation for Social Service to write a more complete review, noting that Harry F. Ward had reviewed the book for *The World Tomorrow*.[31] This letter elicited a cool response from Paul Hutchinson, the managing editor, who declined to rectify any of the comments; quite possibly he was aware that Rochester's pattern of giving had shifted from Christian to Communist publishing and hoped, by the charge of "money from Moscow," to force her to reveal this.[32]

By contrast, Harry F. Ward praised the book, saying, "This volume is different from other books about coal. It is one of a series on American industry that have a human purpose. They are written to show by exact data in specific cases just what capitalism is doing to the workers, what they in turn are trying to do about it, and what the writers think they ought to be doing." Did this mean that the book could not be "intellectually respectable"? Absolutely not.

> Miss Rochester's book . . . makes the cult of pseudo-objectivity which often cloaks partisan work in behalf of the existing order look quite ridiculous. Here is painstaking and accurate research of the highest order. And its results are graphically alive in a picture of human values which makes clear to the reader that this business of getting the coal to run our mechanical world has become one of our major tragedies.

He went on to devote much of his review to a request for a more carefully outlined program for change, arguing that "phrases offer a convenient escape for all of us from the laborious job of program-building," an echo of the criticisms brought to the party's central committee by the political committee.[33]

Other friends to whom the book was sent wrote warm letters to Rochester, applauding her achievement. Rochester kept the letters from the women who had taught her so much earlier in her life. Julia Lathrop, now serving as an assessor for the Child Welfare Committee of the League of Nations, wrote to Rochester upon receiving an advance copy of the book, saying, "I want to tell you how glad I am that you have done this hard piece of writing. Labor needs your pen, steady, clear, convincing, modern in the best sense." Addressing Rochester more personally, she added, "I hope you are very happy. Somehow I believe you are. *Do be!* For *Labor* is a hard thing for the feelings."[34] Several months later, having read the book, and writing less than a year before her death in April 1932, Lathrop congratulated and encouraged Rochester, recalling their work together and saying, "Your mind is so vigorous and grasps detail with such noble patience that I hope you will keep on writing more and more. Sometimes it seems to me that the method of research is the one weapon that will gradually work out a decent measure of social justice." She then checked herself, probably noting the activist tone of the book—as well as her own experiences—and said, "At least it is a newly discovered essential."[35]

Helena Stuart Dudley, retired some years before from a lifetime of heading Denison House in Boston and now living with Vida Scudder and Florence Converse, told Rochester that the book was "a fine piece of work." "I love you and honor you for your work," she said, adding, "You and Grace are much needed leaven in our heavy complacent social group!"[36] That she still considered Rochester and Hutchins a part of the group was remarkable, given their resignations from the Companions. Vida Scudder was under no such illusion; she and

Virginia Huntington had come to visit Rochester and Hutchins in New York, a visit that marked the end of contact between Rochester and Scudder for some years.

Despite this painful rift in their private world, Rochester *was* very happy, her life with Hutchins and her love for Hutchins being intimately bound up with their work together. They were living out what Julia Lathrop had told her: "Never retire."[37] Writing to Hutchins, who was ill with bronchitis around this time and recuperating at a private home outside the city, giving her the details of an LRA meeting, Rochester closed: "Ever—wholly—thine—Anna,"[38] her choice of words recalling the genesis of their partnership. Although the radical edge of the Companions had dulled, and they had left the church entirely, Hutchins and Rochester retained the language for their private communications; the CPUSA had little to offer in that department, although Rochester would make an effort.

Hutchins, too, was happy, although she had her moments of despair, especially when she was ill, and at this moment she was suffering from the "inferiority complex" she had written about several years earlier, a result of her new location in a primarily male and working class organization with little support for the creative and complex ways in which she was intervening in both Marxist and bourgeois discourses. Rochester wrote to her, chastened at the thought that she had contributed to Hutchins's suffering by delivering more criticism than praise: "Precious, abused Pard [short for Partner], I'd like to say good-night again, but I mustn't risk waking you up this time." She went on, referring obliquely to their life-changing travels:

> Somehow I feel as if we were so close that you must *know* that I have a deep steady underlying respect for you—just as I really have for my own efforts!! But life doesn't work that way—and when it's only criticism that is expressed and the respect is mostly tacit—or brought out verbally for an emergency—it is difficult for you to realize that it is there. But it is, it is, it is—IT IS.
>
> And it is a cruel selfishness on my part that has accepted your imaginative help in getting on a fairly even plane of self-respect—perhaps really conceit—while pushing you back toward self-distrust. That is the truth![39]

As Hutchins recovered, Rochester wrote often, telling her, "I miss you, my dearest," now signing her letters using the familiar form of Russian: "I love you,"[40] a reminder of the new foundation of their partnership and Gladkov's announcement of the rebirth of love.

Although Hutchins and Rochester considered themselves partners, their love was far from insular. In addition to helping Lucie Myer, just as Vida Scudder and Florence Converse were including Helena Stuart Dudley in their household, they continued their practice of supporting younger women, especially those who were active in the party or in related organizations such as the ILD or the John Reed Club, helping them to remain independent and pursue their goals. Rochester had been supporting Esther Shemitz as she attended the Art Students' League, and, in that very difficult economic moment (1930), she had helped Shemitz find a job with Amtorg, the Soviet trade mission in the United States.

Recollections of Esther Shemitz reflect the gender rigidity of the time and help to explain why both Hutchins and Rochester felt especially protective of her. In interviews conducted by Elinor Ferry in the 1950s, Shemitz was characterized as being "masculine." Leon Herald found her appearance so off-putting that he did not want to speak with her;

she was, among other things, wearing pants, and her cropped hair stuck out "at all angles."[41] "Her language was sprinkled with 'four-letter words,' her clothing was plain, . . . her manner harsh and formidable. Make-up was shunned as 'bourgeois decadence.' She was never known to have had a boy friend."[42] A. B. Magil told Ferry that Esther Shemitz and Grace Lumpkin "*appeared* to be Lesbians. 'Esther was masculine in appearance and in her voice. Grace was the softer, more feminine type.' "[43]

We have no way of knowing anything more about either Shemitz or Lumpkin. Appearances are unreliable as are hostile reports years after the fact. Was Shemitz following Hutchins and Rochester in adopting an embodied rhetoric? Her comment that makeup was bourgeois decadence would suggest so. Moreover, having associated closely with Hutchins and Rochester for ten years, it is likely that Shemitz and Lumpkin, at the least, had absorbed their principled belief in women's independence. So, when Shemitz announced to them in 1931 that she intended to marry Whittaker Chambers, Hutchins and Rochester may have been more than a bit nonplussed. However, a generation younger than Hutchins and Rochester and lacking an independent income, Shemitz was less immune to the social pressures now requiring heterosexual marriage.[44]

Rochester and Hutchins knew Chambers only vaguely, but the stories that circulated about him did not serve to recommend him: Chambers was rumored to be unpredictable, both politically and sexually, given to seeking his own advantage and insensitive to the effects of his actions on others. He also did not have reliable sources of income. Most recently, he had been making money by translating French and German texts into English. Chambers is well known for having translated Felix Salten's *Bambi*; the other eighteen translations he did during 1928–1932 included Pierre Louys's *Songs of Bilitis* and Anna Weirauch's *The Scorpion*, two lesbian-themed texts. Were Hutchins and Rochester aware of these books? We don't know. If they had encountered the books, we can be fairly certain that they would have been less than enthusiastic, seeing in them a sort of libertine self-indulgence they would have found foreign. Although the taxonomies of sexologists had gained a cultural ascendancy during this period, packaging Rochester and Hutchins together with other same-sex couples with whom they had little in common, Rochester and Hutchins resolutely maintained their commitment to a life defined by work for social justice. Hutchins may have talked with Shemitz; if so, she probably delivered a feminist message to assure Shemitz that social pressure notwithstanding, she needn't marry if she didn't want to, and recalling the importance of the revolutionary work she had done and was continuing to do. She also may have hinted at Chambers' less than stellar personal reputation. The message, if delivered, wasn't enough to dissuade Shemitz, and the alleged conversation—as well as Chambers's translations—would come back to haunt Hutchins in later years.

Despite their misgivings, if Esther wanted to marry, Hutchins and Rochester would support her—so they were the sole witnesses at the ceremony, held on April 15, 1931, at New York's City Hall, the families of both Esther and Whittaker objecting, on the grounds that Esther was a Jew and Whittaker a non-Jew.[45]

Perhaps it was the realization that Esther could legally marry but they could not, or the reminder that their work could imperil them.[46] Whatever the cause, Rochester knew that if something were to happen to her, Hutchins would be left with very little. So, shortly before leaving for their annual vacation at Back Log Camp—from August 10 to September 5 this year—she wrote an informal will for Hutchins, articulating what she wished to have happen to the apartment, the furnishings, and her own personal belongings. "My precious Grace," she began, "I shall not try to make this letter a final word of friendship! For we look forward to many years still of common work and play. And we both know how each depends on the other. But," she said, referring back to the genesis of their partnership in a culture informed by Edward Carpenter, "the cause of the working class is bigger than our friendship, and it will give either one of us the stimulus and inspiration to go on alone after the other has died."

All her possessions, she said, including the co-op shares and other assets, should be Hutchins's, with the exception of a couple of family items—"Father's portrait" and "the inherited old spode cups," which she indicated should go to one of her cousins in the Roby family in Rochester. She wanted Edith Klein McGrath to have "the few bits of so-called jewelry in the black leather box." "But I want you to take yourself," she said, "the little round pin that we have passed back and forth." In closing, she added, "You have had my deepest affection."[47] Certainly the informal will was hardly a "final word of friendship," as Rochester and Hutchins spent another thirty-five years together, always with each other's "deepest affection."

That summer, however, Hutchins's self-esteem suffered another blow, this time in the mixed company of Back Log Camp. When she announced the title of her next project, *Women and Labor*, at the dinner table at Back Log Camp that summer, the assembled guests, after a moment, erupted in laughter, much to her puzzlement—until she realized that it sounded as though she were writing about pregnancy and delivery.[48] The incident helped to fix in people's minds an impression of Hutchins as hopelessly refined, despite the socially challenging content of her work.

This year, 1931, because they were away at camp, which received news only by short-wave radio, Hutchins and Rochester did not learn until they returned to New York

Figure 8.3. Dining tent at Back Log Camp

City that near Wuchang, the dike holding the Yangtse River had broken, flooding the surrounding area and killing many thousands of people. Although she rarely wrote about conditions outside of the United States, China had been Hutchins's home for four years, and she still knew many people there. She responded immediately, writing an article for *Solidarity* excoriating Chiang Kai-Shek and his policies: "Why? Why did the dikes burst? Why did the Yangtse River and the Grand Canal and the Hwai River turn suddenly into great lakes, drowning people by the thousands?" she asked. "Because," she answered, in one of her classic displays of anger at those who hurt the ones she loved, "General Chiang Kai-Shek, the human monster, had let the dikes fall into disrepair, had sold into private hands portions of the Grand Canal and had confiscated peasant lands in order to have more money to fight against the Communist Movement."[49] Although she was too far from China now—and her Chinese had lapsed from lack of use—to serve as an expert on Chinese affairs, she still knew the country and cared about the people and was able to turn her knowledge into articles informing at least some Americans of the conditions in which the people lived and worked.

In addition to researching the material for *Women Who Work* and responding to crises such as the flooding of the Yangtse, Hutchins was starting another new project, probably suggested by Alexander Trachtenberg, a *Labor Fact Book*, to be published by the LRA. It would be a compendium of facts similar to the *Labor Year Book* previously published by the Labor Research Department of the Rand School. Now that many of those who had published the *Labor Year Book* were working with the LRA, it was only reasonable that they should seek to publish a similar series under the new auspices.

Hutchins edited that volume—and all the others that followed, on a biennial basis, up into the 1960s. Commenting years later on LRA work, Philip Bonosky said there was "plenty of agitation," but "agitation alone was not enough," and the Labor Fact Books, "unassailable" and "authoritative," offered "hard facts to buttress the theories."[50] In the foreword, Hutchins articulated the rationale for the series: "The workers are forming militant organizations and fighting more vigorously the increasingly reactionary measures of the capitalist class. These militant movements must be in possession of facts, figures, and reliable information about a wide variety of economic, social, and political matters."[51] The book was meant to serve as a reference work for workers, students, writers, speakers, and any others needing "to know the prevailing conditions."[52]

In addition to committee work, books, and pamphlets, both Rochester and Hutchins continued to write and publish widely in the Federated Press, *Labor Defender*, *Daily Worker*, *Labor Unity*, *New Pioneer*, and *New Masses*. Rochester was serving as a contributing editor of *New Masses*, and Hutchins's name appeared on the mastheads of the *Daily Worker*, *Labor Defender*, and *New Pioneer*. Although when successful, Hutchins's writing cut through old limitations, there were times when her vision failed her. For *New Pioneer*, a magazine for children, Hutchins wrote two gloomy little tales featuring child laborers and evictions that were mitigated only by a cheerier story of the International Workers' Olympics, held at the same time as the regular Olympics but open to both black and white athletes, as well as to athletes from the Soviet Union, who had been barred from the regular meet. Her efforts for *New Pioneer* did not last long.

About that time, Rochester seems to have strengthened her grasp on the rhetorical needs of the moment. Reviewing five books on the Soviet Union for *New Masses*, among them one by her old adversary Sherwood Eddy, Rochester explained the understanding she had come to since her expression in 1923 of the need to establish "the facts and the facts back of the facts." She could not claim, she said, that "the latest crop of bourgeois

Figure 8.4. Cover of *New Pioneer*

books on the Soviet Union" were "ignorant slanders." However, this did not mean greater
friendliness. "Quite the reverse. The hostility is only more subtle, more insidious, for facts
accurate enough in themselves are only a small part of any story. Which facts are selected?
What standards are applied in interpreting them?" What characterized these books, she
noted, was that the author of each centered the universe in the bourgeois privileges to
which he was accustomed.[53]

The CPUSA had given Rochester a location from which she could address Eddy
and challenge his arguments as an equal. Although she had been remarkably successful in
finding a new center outside of self, Rochester had little patience for others of her class
who had not made similar attempts, especially if their work served to buttress a system
of inequality. Responding to Duke University professor Calvin Hoover, who claimed that

workers in capitalist countries had the same material and cultural advantages as did the workers in the Soviet Union, she queried pointedly: "What about textile workers and Negroes in North Carolina, professor?"[54]

In contrast to the self-serving dismissals of the USSR, Rochester found M. Ilin's *New Russia's Primer* "a treat." *New Russia's Primer* was written by a Russian engineer—in Russian—to introduce children to developments in the New Russia and enlist their aid in building the country. The book had been shared with a Teachers' College professor who recognized its value and translated it into English for publication in the United States, where its jaunty style and clear explanations served to counteract the grim descriptions produced by the capitalist press. "I pity the poor highbrow who scorns to glance at a 'primer.' He will miss the clearest and most interesting short account of the Five-Year Plan that has yet appeared," Rochester said in the first paragraph, encouraging readers of *New Masses* not to be put off by the book's title, because the message was far more profound than would be suggested by the word "primer." For instance, she said, Ilin's description of workers' struggles to build an electricity-yielding dam on the Dnieper contrasted vividly with a similar story of British colonial bridge builders battling a flood in India—Kipling's tale celebrated a "monument to the white imperialist"; Ilin's chronicled the victory of workers' collaboration: "as individuals they are barely mentioned."[55]

New Russia's Primer closed with a chapter entitled "New People," which gave descriptions of past living conditions and the changes being wrought by socialism, changes especially in attitudes toward work. "Men will cease to regard work as a punishment, a heavy obligation. They will labor easily and cheerfully," said Ilin. As for women—"Down with the kitchen! We will destroy this little penitentiary! We shall free millions of women from housekeeping. They want to work like the rest of us."[56]

Realizing that, regardless of the claims being made, an "us and them" approach to women verged on insulting, Hutchins used her own experiences to write "Away with that Little Penitentiary!" for *Labor Defender* in March 1932, telling the story of Margaret Dennis, the young Englishwoman whom they had met in Rostov-on-Don, quoting her on her feeling of security in the Soviet Union. Then Hutchins provided the details that would matter to many women: day nurseries, collective kitchens, and four months of paid maternity leave.[57]

After more than a year of attempting to move from education to action, in 1932, various international groups began to consider again the quality of party-related publications. The International Union of Revolutionary Writers (IURW) sent the editorial board of *New Masses* a "Resolution on the Work of *New Masses* for 1931."[58] The resolution evaluated the work of *New Masses* in terms of decisions made at the Kharkov International Conference of Revolutionary Writers in November 1930.[59] Praising *New Masses* for generally clearing the

Figure 8.5. *Labor Defender* masthead

correct path, the IURW predicted that if certain "defects" were eliminated, the magazine might develop from its current position as a publication for radical intellectuals into "a leading organ of the proletarian cultural movement in the U.S.A." The defects slated for elimination included, among others: paying insufficient attention to the achievements of the Soviet Union, failing to warn of the war danger and slighting the fight against fascism.

In the United States, fascism, in 1931, seemed remote compared with the economic depression. International writers, by contrast, could feel the storm moving in from the horizon. In addition, and more important, according to the IURW, *New Masses* was insufficiently political, in both literature and art. Specifically, the IURW charged, the magazine did not have "a sufficiently militant (in the Leninist sense of this term) line of its whole cultural and political activity." In short, the magazine must connect its work "with the day-to-day struggle of the American proletariat and its vanguard, the Communist Party of the U.S.A., by creating a wide worker-correspondents movement around the magazine [and] by drawing into the work of the magazine the maximum cadres of intellectual fellow-travellers."[60]

At the same time, *Labor Unity* published a similar critique, this one produced by the Red International of Labor Unions. The RILU said that the magazine was reasonably good and made better at times by its art and cartoons, but there was considerable room for improvement. It was, the RILU said, often "heavy and dull," the language too technical and sophisticated, lacking "a simple popular style" easily understood by the workers." Moreover, "the articles in the main deal generally and in a formal way with the work and tasks of the unions and leagues and not with sufficient concreteness." There was no worker correspondence, no reporting on international labor news, and the references to women and youth were vague. The mentions of the achievements of the Five Year Plan in the Soviet Union were minimal, and the imminent danger of war had not been sufficiently emphasized. To improve, the RILU said, the magazine should use simple, popular language, increase the number of cartoons and illustrations, and "focus attention on the methods of legal and semi-legal work in the factories." Certainly, the magazine should continue to point out the achievements of the Five Year Plan, agitate against war, and mount a "consistent struggle against white chauvinism."[61]

A bracing agenda—and the magazine did struggle valiantly in that direction, although it still focused largely on men. Neither Hutchins nor Rochester wrote for *Labor Unity* again. They did continue to write occasionally for *Labor Defender* and *New Masses*, magazines intended for a wider audience, one inclusive of middle-class readers. In addition to articles—many of them book reviews—Hutchins and Rochester devoted much of their time in 1932 to the publication of pamphlets. In July 1931, Mike Gold had published a statement in *New Masses*: "Toward an American Revolutionary Culture." Gold's argument was that capitalist propaganda surrounds us, although it is nearly invisible because we are so accustomed to it. "It is present in every short story, every piece of newspaper reporting, every advertisement, child's primer, popular jazz song. There are definite values, fixed attitudes toward love, money, friendship, war, industry. Break the unwritten laws of capitalist art, if you are a writer," he pointed out, "transgress any of the unformulated values, and you will soon find it impossible to be printed."[62] Although Gold called most directly for a workers' cultural movement, he was also underscoring the cultural control maintained by Hearst and Scripps, with an implicit argument for an untethered press.

In an effort to provide such a press, Hutchins wrote to a selected group of writers, seeking manuscripts for International Pamphlets. She herself, after a pamphlet on women and war, undertook to write "Women Who Work," a digest of her forthcoming book of the same title. Her primary argument was that capitalism uses divisions between people—divisions based on race, gender, age, and ethnicity or immigrant status—to create competition between workers that drives down wages: "Just as Negro workers are played off against white workers in the employers' wage-cutting drive; just as foreign-born workers are played off against native-born; so women workers are played off against men."[63] One of the primary demands, she insisted, should be for equal pay for equal work, thus blocking the employers' "divide and conquer" tactics. Historically, she said, women had been entering the job market in increasing numbers; thus, organizing women was of increasing importance.

Moreover, women's work sometimes looked different from that of men, as women occupied positions such as teacher, nurse, and secretary—working class jobs that might not give the appearance of wage labor. Even more important were the women who were not earning money for their work but who nonetheless were workers: the twenty-three million housewives who were wives of workers. "Their days are filled with a great burden of work for which they receive no wages at all," and they needed to be included in union auxiliaries, mass organizations, and special women's councils.[64] The demands of the unions, auxiliaries, and related organizations should focus not only on wages, hours, and working conditions but on social insurance, to include old age, maternity, health, and unemployment benefits.

It was here that Hutchins first introduced the notion of the "double burden," describing the lives of the women she had met when she was working in the cigar factory in 1920. Those women had to get the children off for school before putting in a ten and a half hour day at the factory, as well as planning, shopping for, and cooking dinner after the end of the shift. Although this analysis is familiar to us now, it was groundbreaking in 1932. Then, trying to move beyond analysis to a plan of action, Hutchins provided a detailed plan for organizing women workers called Women Delegate meetings, a system of "permanent organizations of elected representatives of groups of women in a particular factory" already in practice in several European countries.[65] Hutchins's plan for action did not catch on, but the concept of the double burden has become widely accepted in feminist critiques.

Building on Mike Gold's 1931 argument that capitalist propaganda in its ubiquity is nearly invisible to us, Rochester wrote two pamphlets that year—*Profits and Wages* and *Wall Street*—that were, more than anything else, debunking efforts rather than plans of action, attempting to show, by means of statistical data, that the information and explanations fed to workers about their lives were simply wrong. Debunking, however, as Kenneth Burke argued, was simply the "negation" of a "thesis."[66] It failed to move the reader or audience to the next step in a dialectic. Still, the data Rochester had uncovered in the process of writing about coal had given her a glimpse of the structure of capital in the United States; her work for the next several years was devoted to tracing in greater detail this structure and explaining its meaning to workers.

Profits and Wages, which came out early in 1932, demonstrated in excruciating detail the disparity between classes in the United States. It also indicated that although wages had fallen after 1929 and unemployment had risen, these trends had begun well before the stock market crash. To pin the Depression on the crash of 1929, therefore, was not entirely accurate. Rather, the Depression was simply the natural progression of capitalist forces, forces that aimed to extract wealth from the labor of workers without regard to the lives of those workers.[67]

Wall Street, Rochester's second pamphlet of 1932, explained the structure behind the income disparities she described in *Profits and Wages*. Working again to debunk commonly held assumptions, she noted that, for many people, Wall Street meant simply the sites where stocks and bonds were traded: the Stock Exchange and Curb Exchange. "But this is only part of the story," she said. "Always more important than the fortunes made and lost in Wall Street gambling are the wealth drawn directly from industry and banking and the resulting power which centers in the Wall Street area." Although technically separate, bankers and industrialists now worked together, and "Wall Street power is based on this fusion of banking and industry, which gives those who control a few closely interlocked big banks and corporations control over the economic life of the country."[68]

Figure 8.6. Cover of *Wall Street*

In the remainder of the pamphlet, Rochester outlined the interlocking directorates that produced this control, explained how capital controlled government, and spelled out the role of the media in maintaining the whole system. "Radio broadcasting, movies, schools, churches, newspapers are all engaged in putting over patterns of thought designed to prevent revolt against Wall Street domination," she said.[69]

In addition to the pamphlets, Rochester and Hutchins wrote frequently for *New Masses*, the periodical designed to appeal primarily to left-leaning professionals and members of the middle class, despite the RILU's critique. Pointing out the weaknesses of books that were probably being read and talked about by middle-class intellectuals was one of the chief jobs of reviewers. Irony, sarcasm, metaphor, and hyperbole all worked well in this situation, as the point was to disrupt readers' comfortable prejudices. These disruptions were presumed effective at the time; the movement was growing, attracting both middle class and working class members. However, as Kenneth Burke pointed out a couple of years later in his analysis of human motives aimed at producing viable programs of action, debunking as a method tends to see only utilitarian motives, becoming, in Burke's words, "a colossal enterprise in 'transcendence downwards,'" good only for "disintegrative purposes."[70] In contrast, "a supernatural scheme of motives," Burke alleged, offers only a "eulogistic covering" of utilitarian motives.[71] Thus, he suggested, only by means of "comic ambivalence" can debunking be rescued from purely cynical self-interest. In other words, as Ann George and Jack Selzer have pointed out, Burke admonished his comrades in the 1930s to modify their rhetoric so as to enable their audience to reflect upon themselves and their mistaken notions.[72] Caricatures, Burke added, don't help. They do "not equip us to understand the full complexities of sociality—hence they warp our programs of action."[73]

Burke undoubtedly included work by Rochester and Hutchins in the material from which he drew to construct his analysis. Rochester, continuing her arguments about mass media, engaged in a bit of caricature, drawing on her biting wit to explicate and attack the argument of Professor Duane McCracken of Duke University in his book *Strike Injunctions in the New South*, even going so far as to parody that classic of women's discourse, a recipe: "Take one lively subject," she said, "preferably a hot focal point in the class struggle; isolate it thoroughly from other elements in the class situation; soak it slowly in tepid comment, allowing an occasional rise in temperature by quoting "extremists" but cooling off immediately with generous dashes of "impartiality"; stuff with details; and serve with a garnish of footnotes."[74] Rochester's choice to use a feminine form to shape her parody was unusual. In most of her published writings, she did not identify herself as a woman, apart from her name. Here, however, her debunking ranged closer to "perspective by incongruity," as she linked the incongruous elements of strike injunctions and recipes, by this means suggesting that McCracken should take a look at his methods. Is his a cookbook approach? Perspective by incongruity assumes that the audience is simply mistaken rather than rationally committed to a given perspective. By introducing an incongruous element to disrupt that perspective, a writer might hope to disabuse the audience of its mistake.[75]

Like Rochester, Hutchins was using the platform of *New Masses* to calumniate liberal writers, pointing out the superficiality of their analyses in a bemused, ironic tone. Unfortunately, as Burke noted, this tone only met superficiality with more superficiality and did little to advance a movement. Reviewing *Only Yesterday*, a history of the 1920s by Frederick Lewis Allen, Hutchins pointed out that he only mentions a few strikes or labor actions, and when doing so, "he maintains the playful attitude which bourgeois society teaches its writer-servants to use. Nothing but trifles must be taken seriously. Laugh it off.

Remember that comfortable, well-fed America (the only America that has money to buy books) lives on its sense of humor. Be 'detached.' Above all, don't offend anyone in high places."[76] The line between a "comic ambivalence" or perspective by incongruity and a cynical "transcendence downwards" by caricature was not always easy to determine.

Indeed, Rochester and Hutchins's lives were spent writing, speaking, and organizing in ways guaranteed to offend people in high places, and although at times they seemed to understand the potential costs of their actions, at other times, especially in the decades that followed, they failed to grasp the ways in which they would no longer be protected by their inherited power, especially as powerful forces created new ways to subdivide the collectivities that Rochester and Hutchins sought to establish. In 1932, however, they both ran for office as presidential electors on the CPUSA ticket without incident. William Z. Foster was running for president and James W. Ford, an Alabama steelworker and CPUSA organizer, for vice president. The party platform sought, among other things, "unemployment and social insurance at the expense of the state and employers; opposition to Hoover's wage-cutting policy; emergency relief for the hard-pressed farmers without restrictions by the government and banks; exemption of impoverished farmers from taxes, and no forced collection of rents or debts; equal rights for Negroes."[77]

Although their primary contribution was their ability to do research and to write, Rochester and Hutchins were unwilling to limit their commitments to time spent in libraries and offices when others were putting their lives at risk on picket lines and in demonstrations. They traveled to Washington, DC, to take part with three thousand others in the December 5 Hunger March, organized by the Unemployed Councils, marching under the banner of the League of Professional Groups alongside both the John Reed Club and the American Civil Liberties Union. Hutchins's presence was noted by the FBI,[78] which was not surprising, considering the fact that "thousands of police and detectives had been mobilized from all over the country" and "troops at nearby forts were held in readiness."[79] People in high places were not only miffed by the marchers' band playing the *Internationale* on the capitol plaza but seriously frightened by the marchers' demands, which echoed much of the CPUSA's election platform: unemployment insurance, immediate cash and work relief, public work at union wages, food for school children, and racial equality.[80]

Yet while Hutchins and Rochester devoted themselves to a movement larger than themselves, they continued to celebrate their partnership and friendships. This year, 1932, Hutchins and Rochester considered their tenth anniversary, dating from the second year of Community House. Hutchins announced to her former Bryn Mawr classmates in the alumnae newsletter, *Turtle's Progress*: "Anna Rochester (Bryn Mawr 1901) and I have just celebrated the 10th anniversary of our partnership." About herself, she said: "From a pious missionary in China I became a 'Bolshevik,' active in the labor movement here in the United States. It was the War that turned the tide and made me a socialist."[81] Elinor Ferry has noted that the CPUSA at this time did not care about personal choices made by party members; however, with the rise of fascism in Germany, the international party and its national branches began to struggle with the politicization of sexuality. Hutchins's cheerful linkage of her partnership and her political affiliation was about to become problematic. Florence Tamagne has explained the situation: the German Socialist and Communist parties "adopted a two-faced approach to homosexual politics," she says. "On the one hand, they supported the homosexual movements and called for the abolition of 175 [the law proscribing gay male sexual activity], on the other, they took advantage of the homosexual scandals to tarnish the political bourgeoisie and their opponents, and did not hesitate to launch homophobic campaigns themselves."[82]

So, just about the time that Hutchins and Rochester were celebrating their tenth anniversary, the *Kommunistische Partei Deutschlands* (German Communist Party, or KPD), which had been championing a vigorous homosexual rights movement in Germany, ran headlong into the rising fascist movement. Providing some confusion were the widely published writings of Hans Bluher, whose work was an attempt "to establish an overall theory of the virile State."[83] This celebration of virility found adherents across the political spectrum. According to Tamagne, "Bluher wanted to found an elitist, aristocratic society, a cultural State joining together young men of valor, linked by the invisible bonds of their love. . . . Those who are not destined to govern must obey; such is the function of people as redefined according to an erotic and cultural hierarchy."[84] In tracing the effect of Bluher's work on Nazi ideology, Tamagne points out that "it provided the basis of the Nazis' ideology of power—they were supposed to embody the German elite, a political aristocracy called to dominate the inert masses."[85] Nonetheless, Tamagne insists, although "it is undeniable that Nazism was based partly on a homoerotic esthetics, . . . it should not be deduced that it was a pro-homosexual movement."[86] Indeed, Nazis tried to tar the Communists with the homosexual brush, alluding to the " 'vices of the East' . . . as if homosexuality, lesbian love and similar things had been invented by the Russians."[87] And although Bluher's work was attractive and undoubtedly led some men into the Nazi Party, most did not understand the linkages that were being created. As Klaus Mann later wrote, "In those days, certainly, in that era of political innocence and erotic exaltation, we had no idea of the dangerous potentials and aspects of our puerile mystique of sexuality."[88]

At the same time, the Nazi Party's paramilitary organization, the *Sturmabteilung* (SA), or brownshirts, was causing increased concern. The current chief of staff of the SA, Ernst Rohm, was openly homosexual, as were many of his lieutenants. The Communists and Socialists made sure that these facts were publicized, despite their support for gay rights organizations and individuals. According to Tamagne, "The campaign sought to reveal the hypocrisy of a party that was claiming it wanted to restore the virtue of the German people and which railed against homosexuality as a Jewish and Bolshevik plague."[89] Within a few years, Rohm and his confederates would be gone, but not forgotten.

The effects of these ideological confrontations would ripple outward, eventually arriving on American shores. Hutchins and Rochester would not be immune from their effects. However, as their identities had been forged in communities of women and informed by the work of Edward Carpenter, Hutchins and Rochester kept working to build solidarity among women and working people, ignoring the growing political hazards of their partnership.

Thus, however others might have been defining them, Hutchins and Rochester carried on as before. And although Hutchins and Rochester's lives now were dedicated to hastening the revolution, and their five-room apartment was a far cry from the elegant Beacon Street and Englewood houses they had known as children and young adults, they welcomed guests to their apartment and summer home as easily as if they were entertaining in the grand style. In November 1931, they purchased the land for a cabin at Harmon-on-Hudson, naming it, in the hope and anticipation of those years, "Little Acorn" and bringing out the old Community House guestbook for use at the new place.

Little Acorn was located on Mt. Airy Road, near houses inhabited a generation earlier by the old *Masses* crowd: Mabel Dodge, John Reed, Louise Bryant, Max Eastman, Floyd Dell, and Crystal Eastman. Robert Minor and his wife Lydia Gibson were still there, as were Boardman Robinson and his wife. Louise Bryant occupied a house with her husband, William C. Bullitt, the American ambassador to the Soviet Union.[90] Gradually, others followed Hutchins and Rochester: Robert and Slava Dunn, William Gropper,

and later, Victor and Ellen Perlo.[91] Harmon was annexed by Croton in 1932, and soon
the members of the little community on Mt. Airy Road were referring to themselves as
the "Croton Reds." Rochester and Hutchins lived in Croton from May until September
each year, commuting by rail into the city. Shortly after Rochester had the cottage built,
Hutchins began to construct a badminton court on the land for the use of the neighborhood children. Although the community offered them support and friendship, evidence
suggests that it was also somewhat insular—or at least that came to be the perception of
some residents of the town.

During this time, when Rochester and Hutchins were joining and helping to build
communities in New York City and Croton-on-Hudson, Hutchins's family was continuing to fragment. Her brother Henry and his wife Marian, who had been so accepting of
Rochester, were engaged in an acrimonious divorce. Henry was upset and even considered
resigning from his position at Yale, although Hutchins advised against that, and he took
her advice.[92] Still, as distressing as the divorce was, it shrank in significance compared to
the international struggles for power that were intensifying at a frightening rate at that
moment. Soon many personal joys and tribulations would be disregarded in the face of
the threat of fascism.

Hitler came to power in Germany on January 30, 1933. Terrorism by the SA, which
Rochester had documented in 1927, had not only continued but increased. Within the
next few weeks, there were almost daily extrajudicial murders, primarily of Communists,
although Social Democrats and Jews were also targets. Mass arrests began. Then the situation grew exponentially worse.

Around nine p.m. on February 27, 1933, the Reichstag was set on fire. A young
Dutch man named Marinus van der Lubbe was arrested on site; according to police, he
confessed to having set the fire. Beyond this, what exactly happened the night of February
27 probably never will be known. What is clear is that the Nazis claimed that van der
Lubbe was a member of the Dutch Communist Party. They promptly charged a member
of the German Communist Party and three Bulgarian Communists with the crime, claiming: "This act of incendiarism is the most monstrous act of terrorism so far carried out
by Bolshevism in Germany. Among the hundred centners [five thousand kilograms] of
material which the police discovered in the search of the Karl Liebknecht house, there
were instructions for carrying through of the communist terror on the Bolshevist model."[93]
The arrested Communist Party leaders were Ernst Torgler, Georgi Dimitrov, Blagoi Popov,
and Vassili Tanev; another four thousand German Communists were arrested as well. On
February 28, Hitler convinced President von Hindenburg to suspend the civil liberties provisions of the German constitution; within a month, the first concentration camp had been
established at Dachau, where Communists were the first to be imprisoned. Communists
countercharged that the Nazis themselves had set the fire in order to justify these arrests.
Because the regime was so new, the courts had not yet been populated with hand-picked
justices; the case was thus argued in an "old court," and it served to draw international
attention to the struggle between fascism and communism.

One particularly significant element in this international attention was a book published in September 1933, before the verdicts were rendered. *The Brown Book of the Hitler
Terror and the Burning of the Reichstag* was published in London by the World Committee
for the Victims of German Fascism, an organization presided over by Albert Einstein.
This 350-page book described, in excruciating detail, the rise of the National Socialists
and events taking place in Nazi Germany, beginning with the Reichstag fire and describing van der Lubbe as a "tool" of the Nazis. The writer narrated van der Lubbe's life in

Leyden, ending with a single-sentence paragraph: "Enquiries into his life in Leyden have definitely established the fact that he was homosexual. This is of great importance for his later history."[94] Were the writers of the *Brown Book* guessing at van der Lubbe's sexuality in order to establish a credible link between him and members of the Nazi party? According to the *Brown Book*'s narrative, van der Lubbe traveled in Germany during 1931; it was at this time that he made the acquaintance of SA Captain Rohm, through Dr. Bell, Rohm's foreign policy advisor. The *Brown Book* charged that Bell also was Rohm's procurer and kept a list, to be used against Rohm should any conflict develop. "Van der Lubbe's name was on this list."[95] In short, the *Brown Book* said, "Van der Lubbe's homosexual connections with National Socialist leaders and his material dependence on them made him obedient and willing to carry out the incendiary's part."[96] This would not be the last time that left and right, antifascists and fascists, would ground their arguments in charges and countercharges of homosexuality.

In a later chapter on the "campaign against culture," the *Brown Book* recounted the May 6, 1933, destruction of Magnus Hirschfeld's Sexual Science Institute and the offices of the Executive Committee of the World League for Sexual Reform. Among the books particularly sought by those carrying out the destruction were those by Edward Carpenter, Havelock Ellis, and Sigmund Freud. The writings of Oscar Wilde, Margaret Sanger, Andre Gide, and Marcel Proust also came under attack.[97] Despite the references to Carpenter and Sanger, neither Hutchins nor Rochester commented publicly on the destruction of the institute.

The court trying the Reichstag case adjourned on December 16 for a week's deliberations. Large demonstrations were held worldwide to support Dimitrov, Torgler, Popov, and Tanev, and a commission of inquiry held its second meeting in London, affirming that the charges against the four could not be supported. Regarding van der Lubbe, the commission held that a law making "high treason" a capital crime, which was passed by the Reichstag after the fire, should not be read as replacing the original Penal Code of Germany. However, although the court acquitted Dimitrov, Torgler, Popov, and Tanev, it sentenced van der Lubbe to death, ignoring the commission's statement.

Writing in March 1934, the World Committee for the Victims of German Fascism attempted to explain the reasoning behind their allegations about van der Lubbe's sexuality:

> This feature of van der Lubbe's character was nowhere raised idly, or with the desire to foment scandal; its importance lies in the fact that, in conjunction with the many statements made by van der Lubbe to his Dutch friends about the events of his travels in Germany, it furnishes strong indications of a connection existing before the Reichstag fire between van der Lubbe and certain leading national-Socialists, amongst them the notorious Roehm.[98]

It was significant, the committee felt, that the prosecution did not respond to these charges, instead simply commenting in closing arguments that they were an invention. "It would have been a simple matter," they said, "to call Rohm, together with his colleagues Goebbels and Goering, before the Court and to ask him for a complete denial of the suggestions. This course for some reason was not taken, although the Court made it its business to see that other, less vital, points in the Brown Book were 'contradicted' by witnesses summoned for the purpose."[99]

The World Committee professed its lack of interest in homosexuality as a moral question; rather, they saw it as simply evidence of connection between van der Lubbe and the National Socialists, although, given the May 6 state-organized destruction of Magnus Hirschfeld's Institute, it seems clear that they were also, as was their practice, indicating a significant breach between Nazi theory and practice. This evidence of connection would soon become a fixed argument linking fascism and homosexuality.[100] Hutchins may have been particularly susceptible to the argument because the linkage between fascism and homosexuality derived largely from Hans Bluher's assertions in favor of a masculinist state.[101]

At the same time, the committee claimed that van der Lubbe, at one time a member of the Dutch Communist Party, was now connected with a group having "'anarchistic tendencies'" and had, in fact, argued against the party's policies.[102] The presiding judge, however, conflated the organizations, saying, "'I am quite clear in my mind that you are a Communist.'"[103]

On December 17, 1933, one day after the court adjourned for deliberations, the Soviet Union passed Article 121, recriminalizing sex between men (women escaped notice for the time being). Because the entire prerevolutionary legal code had been abolished in 1917, the prohibitions against homosexuality had also been thrown out. Up until 1933, sexuality was a matter of little concern in the Soviet Union. Writing in the 1930 Great Soviet Encyclopedia, "the medical expert Sereisky" had said: "'Soviet legislation does not recognize so-called crimes against morality. Our laws proceed from the principle of protection of society and therefore countenance punishment only in those instances when juveniles and minors are the objects of homosexual interest'"[104] "While recognizing the incorrectness of homosexual development," he said, "our society combines prophylactic and other therapeutic measures with all the necessary conditions for making the conflicts that afflict homosexuals as painless as possible and for resolving their typical estrangement from society within the collective.'"[105]

By March 7 of the following year, however, Article 121 had been incorporated into the legal codes of all Russian republics. This shift was immediate and radical.[106] What's more, talk within and emanating from the Soviet Union politicized gay male sexuality, forging a link to fascism, the most famous line being that of Maxim Gorky, writing in May 1934, who said: "Wipe out homosexuality and Fascism will disappear."[107] In general, homosexuality was depicted in the Soviet Union as bourgeois decadence, a blight that would disappear in a true workers' state.

Not to be outdone, on June 29, 1934, later known as the Night of the Long Knives, Hitler ordered the SS to arrest Captain Rohm and some of the SA while they were vacationing. Some were murdered on the spot. Captain Rohm was killed two days later, after refusing to commit suicide. The arrests and murders extended beyond the SA to many who opposed Hitler for whatever reason. Although his motive seems to have been the elimination of a threat to his power, Goering, Goebbels, and Hitler publicly justified the murders on the basis of the homosexuality of Rohm and others. Hitler then used this event as justification for the larger Nazi program of extrajudicial murders, although such murders had been taking place on a small scale since January 1933, as documented by the *Brown Books*.

Although women's relationships were not subject to the same scrutiny as men's—and certainly the United States was not the USSR—cultural borders were porous, and Hutchins and Rochester must have felt pressure to screen their feelings for each other from public notice.[108] We cannot know exactly how they interpreted this moment or their place in it. They could not deny their bourgeois origins, and they would not deny their partnership. So they grew silent, a less toxic form of denial, perhaps. Hutchins's announcement to her

Bryn Mawr classmates in the summer of 1932 was her last public mention of her partnership with Rochester. Their partnership did not change; it did, however, like many others, go underground, as it were, a sacrifice to the larger struggles of the era. Although their silence ultimately would not protect them as much as they might have anticipated, for the time being their lives were not significantly affected, and they devoted themselves to building the party press, challenging the structures of capital that enabled fascist regimes, and advocating expanded freedoms for women.

Chapter Nine

Revolutionary Change

Photographer from the *New York Daily News* to Grace Hutchins:

"Why are you a Communist?"

Grace Hutchins:

"It is because the Communist Party alone is entirely devoted to the interests of the working class. The party leads day-by-day struggles for immediate needs and at the same time prepares for a revolutionary change from a profit system to a workers' and farmers' government."

—May 1934, CPUSA Headquarters, New York City

Hutchins and Rochester had, by now, established a rhythm of research, writing, and reviewing, with syncopation provided by demonstrations, meetings, and elections, all working against the swastika-draped silence. The LRA attracted volunteers, many from the Pen and Hammer Clubs, young men and women who brought their college-honed research and writing skills to bear on the deteriorating social and economic conditions.[1] Herbert Aptheker, for instance, began his long career of scholarship and activism at the LRA. Women of all ages felt especially welcomed to the LRA by Hutchins and often became part of Rochester and Hutchins's social network. One new friend who meant a great deal to them was Betty Millard, a Barnard graduate and volunteer at the LRA. Hutchins and Rochester were especially fond of Millard, adopting her in a sense, and frequently inviting her to dinner or to Croton-on-Hudson for outings. She was a promising young person who represented the younger generation of independent women to them, a generation that they hoped to nurture. They "saw something of themselves" in her, she felt. Yet only once, Millard said, did she hear a reference to their private life, when she had dinner at Hutchins and Rochester's along with a man associated with the LRA. After dinner, Rochester and the man went into the living room, while Hutchins and Millard remained at the table. Finally, Hutchins said, "Well, shall we join the gentlemen in the living room?" a clear message to Millard of Rochester's lesbian identity—and, by extension, Hutchins's.[2] Otherwise, conversations always focused on shared political work. Perhaps, after their experience with Esther Shemitz, Hutchins and Rochester felt less inclined to be open with younger women.

Between Rochester and Hutchins nothing had changed, however, as they continued to assure each other of their love. Preparing to leave on a train trip, Hutchins wrote to Rochester: "Dearest of all, I am sitting opposite you here but will mail this in the station, as I go through to the train, so you will have word from me in the morning to tell you that I love you."[3] Although she concluded the note with a message about when she would be back at work at the LRA, she closed, saying "Yours f'r ever 'n ever, Deepest love, Grace." This love fueled the research and writing that defined them to those outside what was becoming a private world for them.

Despite the increasingly straitened space for them, they understood the importance of being part of a movement larger than themselves. Thus, when the party, in an effort to reach wider audiences, refined its rhetorical approach, Hutchins and Rochester both reorganized their work as well. In doing so, they moved into venues where they could use their skills more effectively. The *Party Organizer* of November–December 1932 featured a translation and abridgment of a Soviet pamphlet, "Bolshevik Agitation Among the Masses," by Lev Perchik, that advised organizers to focus on local issues but not to dwell only on local issues; rather, organizers should work to *"raise the masses to general political and class conclusions"*[4] (italics in the original). Most important, according to Perchik, organizers must heed Lenin's statement in "On Slogans" that "'the art of every propagandist

Figure 9.1. Anna Rochester, ca. early 1930s

and every agitator consists in influencing the audience, in making for it a certain truth as convincing, intelligible and as easy of assimilation as possible.'"[5] In practice, this often meant continuing to focus on debunking, drawing attention to the inconsistencies and deceptions ladled out by the capitalist media, but at the same time, offering hope in the form of possible action. Thus a writer must negate the thesis but then move the reader or audience beyond that negation to a new synthesis. The agitator must, above all, be familiar with the audience, Perchik enjoined. Perchik's advice seems so obvious as to go without saying, but in fact there was often a deep divide between those doing the writing and those whom they sought to reach. Hutchins sought to bridge this divide.

In January 1931, Earl Browder had issued a strong statement regarding work with women, charging that it had been neglected because members felt it was unimportant. But, he argued, still using an unfortunate "us and them" construction, "anyone who has had experience will know that women are the best fighters when you once get them lined up in any kind of work connected with the labor movement."[6]

Two years later, *Working Woman*'s new format was introduced with the March 1933 issue, to coincide with International Women's Day, March 8. Leaving behind the tabloid newspaper format, *Working Woman* advertised itself as "A Magazine for Working Women, Farm Women, and Workingclass Housewives," the editors aiming "to reach the women masses, to act as a collective agitator and organizer, to win the women for struggles and for the final overthrowing of capitalism and the establishment of a workers' and farmers' government." Although she had little experience as a working class woman, Hutchins was at least a woman who was committed to feminist organizing, so she began writing almost exclusively for *Working Woman*, producing an article at least once every two months during 1933.

The magazine positioned itself in opposition both to bourgeois women's organizations, which, they said, "blur the class issues and bring forward the sex issue," and to pacifists, "who stand by helpless while American Marines kill South American workers and the American navy supports the Japanese assault on China." It also opposed bourgeois organizations that were trying to reach out to working class women and girls, such as the YWCA and the Girl Scouts, arguing that they "keep the working women safe for capitalism."[7] Hutchins had come a long way since her days at Bryn Mawr and her stint with the FOR.

According to the *Party Organizer* article, "*the whole agitation must be imbued, on one hand, with Bolshevist principle and purposefulness, and on the other, there must be connection with the masses, consideration of their needs, demands and interests*" (italics in original). Following Perchik's advice, Hutchins wrote a story (taken from the experience of a party member) for the March 1933 issue of *Working Woman* demonstrating the value of working class organizations. Unemployed mill worker Julia Martin, she wrote, lived with her mother and was active in the Unemployed Council; this activity worried her mother, who was afraid she would be blacklisted—never rehired at the mill. The action took place on a single morning, as Julia left to help put the furniture back in the home of a family who had been evicted. Over their meager breakfast of black coffee and bread, she and her mother argued, but Julia left anyway to help replace the furniture. Sure enough, the police attacked while members of the Unemployed Council were singing the *Internationale*, "Arise ye prisoners of starvation," and Julia was clubbed by a policeman and arrested. As she was being driven off in the patrol wagon with others from the Unemployed Council, she saw that her mother had replaced her on the line protecting the family and heard her singing "Solidarity Forever," her "thin soprano high above the others: 'For the Union makes us strong.'"[8] Solidarity between women, especially between mother and daughter, was not a topic often addressed in the press, capitalist or Communist. Yet Hutchins knew that women needed to join the movement—and especially older women, trained to compete with each other for the attention of men and easily cowed by employer threats.

As Hutchins aimed to add women to the party membership rolls, Rochester was working on a long article on the banking crisis for *The Communist*, the party's theoretical magazine. In her April 1933 article, Rochester explained to readers the credit structure of banks, demonstrating how this structure had been compromised and thus how some five thousand banks had failed during 1929, 1930, and 1931, including 522 during October 1931 alone. She assumed that her readership was generally literate, with some knowledge of Marx's *Capital* and Lenin's *Imperialism, the Highest Stage of Capitalism*, but without a thorough understanding of the banking system. For readers lacking the benefits of an advanced education—or childhood training in capitalist methods—she took complex concepts and rendered them accessible. In this way, she addressed directly the misinformation produced by the government and the capitalist press regarding the bank "holiday" of March 4, 1933.

A month later, Rochester followed up with a three-part series in the *Daily Worker* explaining "The Morgan Empire," J. P. Morgan's sphere of influence established by interlocking directorates among banks and corporations. At the time, she reported, more than $100 billion of capital investment was under the control of the Morgan Empire. Moreover, she said, "directorships are only one way of wielding power. Floating of securities and granting of loans to corporations is quite as important."[9] Although he controlled or influenced approximately one-third of the finance capital in the United States, Morgan was hardly a benevolent employer. On the contrary, "Morgan corporations have set the pace for aggressive hostility to workers who organize and strike."[10] By way of contrast, Rochester pointed out that Morgan banks had continued to pay dividends at the 1929 peak rate, concluding pointedly: "In other words, wage slashes have contributed toward maintaining the already fat pockets of the parasite banking class."[11] In the third and final article in the series, Rochester traced the development of the House of Morgan as a world financial power, demonstrating the ways in which the Morgans were using, and surpassing, British capital in establishing dominance.[12]

In addition to these analyses, Rochester prepared a two-cent pamphlet for mass distribution as an organizing tool. In *Your Dollar Under Roosevelt*, she began by asking readers, "How much will your dollar buy next month? Next year?" Answering the question, she argued that Roosevelt's policies were inflationary—but that capitalists *wanted* inflation now, in order to buy up commodities cheaply, hold them until prices rise, and sell them at a profit. In the process of explaining how workers fare under capitalist money schemes, she outlined the history of money in the United States, defining terms such as "gold standard." Government aid, she pointed out, went to corporations, not to workers, although it was the workers who financed that aid through taxes added to prices of items for sale. ("[Capitalists] have welcomed beer," Rochester explained, "as another excuse to tax the masses who drink it."[13])

In contrast, income taxes paid by the wealthy were low, she argued. Morgan, she revealed, paid $11 million in income taxes in 1929, less than $50,000 in 1930 and 1931, and none at all in 1932—writing off "capital losses" to avoid taxation but remaining "luxuriously rich."[14] As the government lacked income, austerity measures were introduced, causing income to drop even more. The Roosevelt administration was attempting to solve this problem, she argued, by going off the gold standard and printing money that "will represent no value except the promise of the government. Along with this there goes a tremendous increase in the government debt."[15] Usually, capitalists resisted inflation and debtor groups (often large farmers) pushed for it in order to lessen their debts. However, in this crisis, the lenders realized, she said, that they risked getting back nothing on their loans, so they, too, were pressing for inflation in order that farmers could pay their mort-gages. Would this solve the problem? No. Because capitalist industries produced far more than the workers could consume, imperialist war for control of overseas markets became the next solution. "Then there will be super-profits for the few on top, but for the masses slaughter and torture, speed-up of a new intensity, prices rising while wages will be held down with an iron hand that tries to crush out every least sign of revolt."[16]

Thus, after her explorations of capital-labor relations in *Labor and Coal*, Rochester was focusing her analyses on the structure of capital itself, uncovering the realities of the arrangement and disabusing readers—from workers to middle class and academic liber-als—of the notion that capitalism is a clean and upright system rewarding those who work hard.[17] Not mincing words, she said, "Of course capitalism breeds crooked dealing. Bright boys tutored from childhood in the art of living on wealth produced by the workers and appropriated by the capitalist class are bound to reconstruct the rules of the capitalist game to suit their own personal advantage." Yet reform is not the solution, she insisted. "Liberals crying out about 'irregularities' always refuse to recognize them as inherent in the capital-ist system."[18] Despite this hard-biting prose, Rochester was known as "shy" and "modest" in person. She interacted with others largely through her writing, and it was precisely through her writing that she was able to challenge the powerful, reducing them to "boys."

Hutchins, on the other hand, was socially adept, and she paired her persuasion with personal attention. In April 1934, she was sent a letter that was typical of many she received during her life. A comrade named Miriam (last name not given) wrote: "I often think of you and marvel. How could you stop so much and so long to talk with me—and the many other comrades who came in for knowledge, help, direction? It is very important to remain human. One can do so much more effective work."[19] Hutchins also took an active interest in the organizational elements of the party, giving of her time both formally through committee work and elective positions and informally through talking and listening to people, writing letters, visiting them in the hospital, arranging funerals. Although Rochester was more likely to express her support and caring for others by gifts or loans of money, reserving her time for research and writing, both she and Hutchins drove out in early October 1933 to New Jersey to visit Esther and Whittaker Chambers and bring them a gift for their first child, Ellen.[20] Chambers did not bother to mention the many kindnesses such as this when he publicly attacked Hutchins fifteen years later.

Although she used her social skills to draw women into labor activism, Hutchins did not hesitate to criticize women whom she felt were acting only in their own (upper) class interests. In an article for *Working Woman*, she castigated Eleanor Roosevelt and Frances Perkins for their enthusiasm over a scheme to create work camps for unemployed women. Not only did the camps—which, she pointed out, had only attracted seventeen women so far, out of 3.5 million who were unemployed—serve to draw women away from revolution-ary activities such as the Unemployed Councils, but they were ultimately demeaning as well. "It costs the Federal government only $5 a week for each of these girls who must perform all the 'regular camp chores' not only for themselves but also for the counselors or officers," she said. "In other words," she pointed out caustically, "they are doing domestic service work for nothing at all."[21] She did not need to add that putting women in camps was not a way to give them greater freedom.

By the end of 1933, Hutchins had completed the manuscript for *Women Who Work* and was looking for people to whom she could send it for prepublication critiques. She

chose, among others, Mary van Kleeck, director of the Russell Sage Foundation's Department of Industrial Studies, and David Saposs, a member of the faculty of Brookwood Labor
Institute, both of whom were deeply concerned with labor issues, although neither was a
member of the CPUSA. Van Kleeck shared with Hutchins her status as an "independent
woman," as well as membership in the CLID and the SCHC.[22] Unlike Hutchins, she had
not left these organizations. Van Kleeck and Saposs responded to the book with similar
criticisms, suggesting a fault line that ran through many of Hutchins and Rochester's
writings as well as the writings of others on the left. Saposs read the chapter "Women in
Strikes" and commented that in general he approved of it, although he felt that Hutchins
"features the 'left wing' unduly," slighting the contributions of unions that did not have
Communist affiliations and of noncommunist women organizers. He acknowledged that
he, too, was "very critical of the Amalgamated, ILGWU and the Hosiery Workers," but
at the same time could not support dual unionism—the CPUSA practice during the early
1930s of organizing workers into separate, more radical unions in a given industry.[23]

Mary van Kleeck, whose previous work had been in the areas of child labor and
women's labor conditions, wrote back, questioning Hutchins about her intended audience.
"If you are writing for women workers, I believe that at the very beginning you ought
to explain quite simply what is involved in your point of view. Otherwise the frequent
references to capitalism, "the ruling classes" and other phrases familiar to the initiated will
not carry their full meaning to working girls in America."[24]

When *Women Who Work* was published, in March 1934, the first chapter, "Women
Under Capitalism," offered just such an introduction. In it, Hutchins traced the history
of women's labor, recounting the analysis done by August Bebel in *Women Under Socialism* (English translation, 1904) although without attribution, adding references to Marx,
Engels, and Lenin and explaining the economic causes of worsening conditions for women
since 1929. "This slavery of women, in which sexual possessiveness and the exploitation
of the woman's labor power were always intermingled, is probably the oldest form of class
exploitation. Long after the changing forms of economic life had made it unprofitable—and
therefore unethical—for a man to keep several women, his sex domination over women
continued."[25] Here Hutchins suggested that a society's ethical system is founded on its
economic system, thus undoing any notions of reliance on "chivalry" to protect women.
She made a strong argument in this first chapter for capitalism's use of male dominance,
pointing to slavery in the South as the quintessential example, wherein African American
women were not only required to work at the master's behest but had to supply their bodies to him for his pleasure. Although that particular form of slavery had been abolished,
she said, the system continued, trying to ensure a steady supply of low-cost women's labor.
How was this accomplished? Again, Hutchins turned the concept of propaganda back on
American popular culture, stretching Marxism-Leninism to include no small amount of
radical feminism. "Take for example," she said, "a hundred advertisements in the press or
on the billboards and see what a high percentage of such 'ads' are addressed to women
as subordinate to men, simply as vehicles of sex charm, as if their sole end and aim in
life should be to attract and please the man."[26] Still, although she did not mince words
in her criticism of the capitalist expression of heterosexual ideology, she was not able to
question, except obliquely, the double subordination of women like herself who loved and
desired other women.

Hutchins did make it clear how class differences affect women, although she also
complicated the professionalism for women promoted by middle-class feminists. Whereas
10,750,000 women and girls were employed in the United States, she said, only 263,000

Figure 9.2. Cover of *Women Who Work*

of them were "business women." And, she explained, although bourgeois feminists point proudly to an increase in the numbers of women in the nursing and teaching professions, under capitalism, these were exploited positions as well.[27] Hutchins also pointed out that African American women had little access to the more highly paid jobs. Fully one-third of workers in domestic and personal service were African American women, she said, and most were in the South. In the tobacco industry, African American women were confined to working in the heavy dust and strong odors of the leaf and stripping departments.

Most significant about *Women Who Work* was the fact that it approached feminism using class as the primary frame for analysis. Hutchins understood that feminism was not a "one size fits all" movement and that those who needed it most were those for whom it had been least available. Women of the middle and upper classes had succeeded in gaining new opportunities for themselves—while hiring working class women to care for their children and clean their houses. But "a girl earning $12 a week or less in a mill or shop has about as much 'freedom' and 'opportunity' as a rosebush in a desert of sand," she commented acerbically.[28]

Feminism from a working class perspective was a very different conversation, according to Hutchins, focusing on wages, health, conditions of employment, family responsibilities, working conditions, and the availability of social insurance. Although she failed to address specifically such cross-class feminist issues as rape, incest, and abuse, Hutchins's analysis was prescient in its emphasis on the role of media in perpetuating women's oppression. She focused primarily on the economic basis of women's subjection, arguing that the capitalist class, in order to maximize profits, did whatever was necessary in order to "keep the masses of working women in a position of submission."[29]

The greater part of *Women Who Work* is devoted to descriptions of working conditions in a variety of settings, from home to farm to factory. Hutchins used both anecdotal and statistical evidence to support her claims, with emphasis on the anecdotal, which worked well for narrative effect. She devoted one chapter to comparing conditions for working women in the United States with conditions for women in the Soviet Union, taking note of social insurance, child care, meal services, and other advantages. At the same time, she was careful to qualify the seemingly Utopian description by adding that "the Soviet Union is no paradise. It is building Socialism, looking toward a Communist society."[30]

Following this comparison, Hutchins documented the courageous actions of women in American labor strikes, showing the benefits that had been won as a result, although she did comment that it would take an entire book to do the subject justice. Susan B. Anthony, Hutchins noted, thought that the ballot would solve the problems of working women: "She did not understand the economic basis of class divisions and did not see that the women of the capitalist class, no less than the men, would vote to continue and maintain the *status quo*."[31] Mother Jones, she said, was a strong leader who fought against John L. Lewis's collaborationist tactics, but she tended toward individualism, working freelance and failing to build permanent workers' organizations. Other women leaders were more effective, Hutchins said, including Lucy Parsons; Clara Lemlich, who led the "Uprising of the 20,000" shirtwaist makers in 1909; Rose Pastor Stokes; and Mother Bloor—"a general hell-raiser against capitalism extraordinary," she enthused, quoting Alexander Trachtenberg. Having established the exploitation and multiple oppressions of working class women in the United States—and having pointed out that such conditions were not necessary but were an effect of the economic system in place in the United States—Hutchins argued for continued organizing as the most effective tool to change conditions.

However, the process of organizing women was made more difficult by several factors, Hutchins explained. Women workers often aided in their own oppression by acting as if they were only working temporarily, she said, citing Theresa Wolfson's *The Woman Worker and the Trade Unions*, even though many eventually would discover that they needed to work all their lives. Male union members didn't help when they evinced an attitude of superiority toward women workers. Bourgeois women's organizations, which should have acted in solidarity with women workers, instead offered charity and let themselves be "used by the employing class to take the edge off the class struggle. . . . They cultivate also notions of individual 'culture' as attainable by the woman worker who can raise herself above her fellows and become a 'success' in the business or professional world." In this sense, they "repeat the ancient myth, still the theme of many a moving picture, of the poor working girl who marries the rich man's son!"[32] Throwing into relief once more the system of social indoctrination that she was challenging through the LRA, International Publishers, New Masses, and other periodicals, Hutchins said:

> Everything around us, the advertisements, the success stories in Liberty, The Saturday Evening Post, the Ladies Home Journal, the tabloids, all the papers that are read by millions in the United States; the daily propaganda that issues from comic strips—note the open anti-strike and other reactionary preaching in "Little Orphan Annie"—radio and the talkies; the teaching in a thousand schools and colleges; the sermons in a thousand churches; all accept the profit system as desirable and final, all urge the individual worker to forget her class and feather her own nest.[33]

Although, Hutchins noted, the Socialist Party and the American Federation of Labor had made some attempts to organize women and to counteract the social messages propagated by traditional institutions, these efforts had been inadequate. The CPUSA and the Trade Union Unity League, by contrast, she argued, offered the strength and resolve to create significant change for women.

Friends from her private world to whom Hutchins had sent copies of the book—Helen Hendricks; Adelaide Case, now on the faculty of Teachers' College of Columbia University; Dorothy W. Douglas of Smith College[34]; Mary Anderson, head of the Women's Bureau of the Department of Labor—began writing to her, expressing their admiration for her work. Molly Dewson enthused, "I think you were a brick to send us your new book. As I glanced through it I was much impressed."[35]

Olga Halsey, their friend from Back Log Camp, wrote to Rochester and Hutchins, praising the book and saying that Hutchins had "done an excellent job in writing easily and simply of what can be treated as a fairly technical subject and yet, in the simplified treatment, you do not give the impression of superficiality. That is an achievement."[36]

The range of responses to the book is indicative of its power to please or to irritate, with most reviewers in the capitalist press expressing little pleasure. The New York Times was perhaps most aggressive in its attack on the book, declaring, "She shows no understanding of the everlasting truth that the incompetency and low mental equipment of immense numbers of human beings are as much to blame for their sad plight as are economic conditions."[37]

It is true that those who agreed with Hutchins found the book exhilarating; it was, after all, the first feminist book on labor conditions to be written for an audience of working class women. "Dear Comrade Grace Hutchins," Lucy Parsons wrote, "The women whose lives that you so graphically depict are the mothers of future generations. It is terrible to contemplate. But such is life under capitalism."[38] Sasha Small in the Daily Worker commented: "It is not very often that a book so fully documented as Women Who Work, so inexhaustible a source of information, becomes at the same time a powerful indictment of the capitalist system and a call to struggle."[39] And Hutchins and Rochester's friend from the World Tomorrow, Grace Lumpkin, wrote in New Masses: "So much has been written from the point of view of the middle-class feminists who are making a sort of artificial heaven for themselves, with Miss Greta Palmer of the World-Telegram as the Gabriel who blows their horn, and Mrs. Roosevelt as the official spokesman, it is time a book written for working women and from their point of view should be published."[40]

Alice Hawkins, Hutchins's friend from Bryn Mawr days, said that she had passed the book on to Mildred Fairchild to review for the *Alumnae Bulletin*; Fairchild sent the review to the *Annals of the American Academy of Political and Social Science*. When this review appeared, Hutchins was not altogether pleased, although it was remarkable that the book had been reviewed in those quarters at all. Fairchild criticized Hutchins's methodology, applying academic standards and claiming that Hutchins had not supported her claims with sufficient data and had made "sweeping generalizations." She said, however, that the book's audience was women workers, not academicians, as if that should excuse the problem.[41]

Perhaps the review Hutchins found most startling was one written by Margaret Mooers Marshall of the *New York Evening Journal*. Marshall interviewed Hutchins before writing her very positive review. She quotes Hutchins at length on the National Recovery Administration (NRA) codes, building in a physical description of her: "bobbed gray hair, a young face and an attractive blend of force, feeling and intelligence in discussing the labor problems of women." "Horrors!" Hutchins wrote, on either side of this description.[42]

A Soviet reviewer, too, had several criticisms, each of which Hutchins answered in a long response. She agreed that there might have been more attention paid to women and militarism, although she noted that she had recently published a pamphlet on just that topic. She also conceded that, "in view of the coming International Women's Congress against War and Fascism, it would have added to the value of the book to include more material on the trends toward fascism in the United States." However, she pointed out, women were not playing any significant role in US fascist organizations. Nor were working women active in any of the bourgeois women's organizations, with the possible exception of the YWCA, which, she said, she did mention in the book. She disagreed most heartily with the reviewer's statement that women workers such as nurses, telephone operators, teachers, and office workers had "nothing in common but sex" with factory workers. "These workers," Hutchins protested, "have in common the low wages or salaries, described in the book, uncertainty of employment, dismissal on little if any notice, unemployment, speed-up, long hours of work, bad health conditions, exploitation at the hands of bankers and industrialists." Perhaps, she suggested, the problem lay partly in language. In English there was no distinction between "workers of hand and of brain, as there is in Russian."[43]

In addition to correcting Soviet misapprehensions of American workers, Hutchins continued to struggle against the sexism of some party members in the United States. The CPUSA was hardly a "finished paradise" for women, either. Early in 1934, Mike Gold published a column discussing the relations between men and women in the movement. Letters from women followed, arguing that "the proletarian husband has also a few things the matter with him." Gold acknowledged that they had a point: "There are so many old habits of mind to be fought and overcome, both on the side of men as well as women. The bourgeois system trains us to look down on women from the time we are small boys. You can't weed out such feelings overnight, but every real revolutionist must always try to make himself over into a new kind of human being."[44] Seizing the opportunity for publicity, Hutchins wrote in, commenting on the fact that some members of the Marine Workers Industrial Union had been teasing mineworkers' organizer Tony Minerich about an article he had written advocating that their wives and daughters organize as well. She explained the situation, and then said: "But, now, I ask you, Comrade Mike, how are we going to organize the wives and daughters and sisters of the men workers, if our own comrades take the attitude that it is something like a disgrace for a man to talk or write about organizing women?"[45] She noted that International Women's Day, March 8, was approaching, and that there was plenty of material for the men to distribute, including "Lenin's statements on the importance of organizing women, as told so vividly by comrade Clara Zetkin,"[46] pamphlets on women, and her own book, *Women Who Work*.

Hutchins was working several fronts at once, seeking to organize working class women, challenging working class men to include women, and challenging upper class women to consider the needs of working class women. She made the fight against international fascism central to her argument in a 1934 *New Masses* article, continuing to use her position to bridge classes in an effort to create a universal class-conscious feminism. Doris Stevens, president of the National Woman's Party (NWP), she said, had met with her and two other women to discuss their different viewpoints on questions of women's equality. Stevens insisted that "women should have complete equality before the law, always and everywhere. . . . All laws and regulations dealing with employment should be on a non-sex basis and thus insure equality of opportunity in the field of labor." Stevens conceded that women in the Soviet Union were closer to having equal status with men, but in practice women were still "kept in subordinate positions." Where, she asked, were the women "on the executive committee of the Communist International?"

Hutchins responded to the allegations, pointing out that Stevens's argument failed to take into account how far women had come during the seventeen years since the revolution. "Illiteracy has been practically wiped out—and it was especially high among peasant women." It took time to change old habits, she said, and time to train women for more advanced work. Responding to the charge that women were prohibited from taking some jobs in the USSR, Hutchins cited a statement made by the commissariat of labor to the effect that "if scientific study should determine that women, can, with safety to their health, dig and load coal underground, then women will soon be found digging and loading coal in the workers' state."

More important than what was going on in the USSR, however, Hutchins said, was what was taking place in the United States under the "New Deal": specifically, the marital status clause in the Economy Act of 1932, which called for married women to be discharged from their jobs. Although the NWP and the CPUSA both opposed this clause, Hutchins insisted that the CPUSA had been far more vocal in pressing the administration to rescind the law. Moreover, she said, the CPUSA had argued strenuously against the National Recovery Administration rules that codified lower wages for women than for men.

The Communist Party stood for equality for *all* workers, Hutchins asserted; it never wished to encourage conditions in which employers could play workers off against each other based on sex, age, or color. In contrast, fascist countries had developed the exploitation of women to its highest level. "No velvet gloves hide the brass knuckles of capitalists in control of the fascist state," she said, citing Nazi slogans: "'Mothers must exhaust themselves in order to give life to children.' 'Woman—her place is in the home, her duty the

Figure 9.3. *New Masses* masthead

recreation of the tired warrior.' Against the development of this fascist barbarism in the United States," she pleaded, "feminists and militant workers can unite on common ground." She asked members of the NWP to join with CPUSA members in picketing the embassies of fascist nations to gain the release of women political prisoners.[47] Hutchins closed her article with a ringing peroration: "We ask these members of the National Woman's Party to protest with us against the lynching of Negro workers in the United States. We ask them to use their abilities as speakers, writers, artists, teachers, or whatever they may be, not in attacking little pieces of labor legislation but in combating the increased exploitation of all workers in the fascist stage of capitalism."[48]

There was even more work to be done to combat fascism. As the repression of the left increased in Germany, Japan, and Italy, Communist parties in these countries sought the help of Americans not only to protest but also to transmit messages and maintain contacts between and within the parties. Hutchins and Rochester's acquaintances Whittaker Chambers and Juliet Stuart Poyntz were among those engaging in such work. Did Hutchins and Rochester help Chambers to obtain his job? We will never know, although it is certainly possible. The exact nature of their work remains unclear, but Chambers, who was fluent in German, may have been trying to aid German leftists by means of messages sent via sailors from German ships that docked in New York and Baltimore.[49] Juliet Stuart Poyntz apparently tried to recruit people, possibly students at Columbia University, to do Italian and German antifascist work.[50] In order to accomplish this work, Chambers and Poyntz ceased to be publicly aligned with the CPUSA. Apart from that, however, they remained members of their respective communities. Chambers's activities are unknown, but Poyntz spent much of her time doing research in the New York Public Library.[51]

Chambers had left the party in 1929, although he continued to work on *New Masses* during the early 1930s. At some point after he began his antifascist work, Chambers asked Hutchins for $50 to have his teeth fixed, one loan among several that she agreed to, just as she and Rochester had helped to support Esther in the past.[52] This event, too, would later become public knowledge and a source of speculation as reactionary forces sought to consolidate their power in the postwar decade. Although Hutchins would figure later in public conjecture about both antifascist workers, she appears to have had little contact with either one during this time, concentrating instead on her own domestic liberation efforts.

Indeed, Hutchins continued to work closely with both Mary Van Kleeck and Olga Halsey, pressuring the Roosevelt administration to develop a comprehensive plan of social insurance. Rochester, too, joined in this effort, explaining its importance to readers of the *Daily Worker*. On February 23, 1934, shortly before hearings were held in Washington on the Workers' Unemployment and Social Insurance Bill (H.R. 7598), the competitor to the Wagner-Lewis Bill, which would have provided only state-based unemployment insurance, Hutchins issued a public statement, saying: "It is the only inclusive bill that would provide true unemployment and social insurance, by federal law, and result in at least some measure of security under the present system."[53] The Wagner-Lewis Bill garnered the support of President Roosevelt but was allowed to die in committee—for the time being.

Opposition to H.R. 7598 was intense, especially on the part of the private insurance industry and the American Medical Association. Responding to the insurance industry's opposition, Rochester wrote an article for the *Daily Worker* in November pointing out to readers *why* the industry would be so desperate to defeat the bill. Before the advent of government-sponsored social insurance systems in the United States, workers often attempted to protect themselves by paying weekly premiums to private insurance companies such as John Hancock for an unemployment policy. If a worker lost his or her job before paying on the policy for at least three years, the policy was a total loss unless the premiums continued to be paid—an unlikely scenario. As a result, workers had forfeited more than $250 million during 1928–1933, Rochester revealed. "Even in the long run, including years of 'prosperity' and relatively steady work, the working class got back less than half the amount they paid to the insurance companies," she said. What happened to this money retained by the insurance companies? Directors of the insurance companies representing financial empires such as those of Morgan and Rockefeller manipulated the funds to "provide a market for bonds issued by the corporations in which they are interested." Moreover, insurance company executives drew high salaries, Rochester reported, challenging upper class men on the very foundation of their power. F. H. Ecker, president of the Metropolitan Life Insurance Company, she said, saw his annual salary increase from $175 thousand to $200 thousand in 1930.[54]

By December 1934, the CPUSA had grown to some 31 thousand dues-paying members,[55] and, with workers organizing and reading information such as Rochester provided in the *Daily Worker*, American capital was beginning to get nervous. The Hearst newspapers mounted a campaign of disinformation against the party, and the House of Representatives, under the guise of investigating fascism, began to harass party members. The *Party Organizer* of February 1935 published an article contending that the party had not mobilized sufficient opposition to these two forces. What to do? The party must "intensify the campaign of exposure in the whole Party press," the author argued, "which means not only in the *Daily Worker*, and the other daily and weekly papers, but in every shop and neighborhood paper issued by the Communist Party units, in all bulletins and in special leaflets." In fact, "the whole agitational apparatus of the Party must be utilized to counteract, with mass distribution of leaflets, the slanders of the Hearst press, to expose the methods of investigation of the McCormack-Dickstein Committee."[56]

In response, during 1935, Hutchins tried to increase readership among women, producing an article each month for *Working Woman*. Her articles included a brief biography of Mother Jones, an argument against the sales tax, and a strong statement in favor of birth control. Hutchins and Rochester also became members of the American League Against War and Fascism, an organization founded by their old friend Harry F. Ward to combat the increasing threats from Italy, Germany, and Japan—and from within the United States. The organization was designed to draw members from across classes. Ward began publishing a new periodical, *The Fight Against War and Fascism*, in 1934, for which Hutchins wrote "Who Makes the Guns?" Women, she said, made the war materiel, and according to *Fortune* magazine, the men who owned the factories collected huge profits. What she implied without saying overtly to this audience—which was much wider than the readership of most CPUSA publications—was that the women who were doing most of the work of production of war materiel should, above all, be made aware of their status and the meaning of their work.[57]

Within the pages of *Working Woman*, Hutchins was more blunt. In April 1934 she began publishing a regular column, entitled "You're Telling Me!" Her first two columns focused on the imminent war danger—and the profits that were being made off women workers in plants producing armaments, profits that went, in one case, to buy $10,000 worth of jewelry for the daughter of duPont and each of her friends. Hutchins continued to demonstrate the limits of a feminism that did not look beyond gender. Offering a contrast to the wealthy duPonts, Hutchins reported in October on the striking textile workers in North Carolina and Massachusetts, depicting their heroics—stopping a train for forty minutes, picking up tear gas bombs and throwing them back at the National Guard.

Expanding the article for the *Daily Worker* in celebration of the twenty-fifth anniversary of International Women's Day, she described women's actions on the picket line at the Gibson Mill in Concord, North Carolina, the previous September, quoting men who saw the action:

> "We've got women in this town with more guts than the men,' said one man striker. . . . "You ought to see them grabbin' those bombs and throwin' them back." . . . They caught the gas bombs in their hands and threw them back at the soldiers, "like the right smart ball players they were," as one man expressed it. One of the bombs landed back right in front of a machine gunner who promptly turned around and ran away, as if he had never really wanted to fight against fellow workers anyway.

Hutchins used this story as another opportunity to expand the space for women beyond traditional women's concerns and to articulate an explicitly feminist version of an embodied rhetoric.[58]

At the same time, Hutchins continued to pressure the federal government for unemployment and social insurance, as she was now serving on the National Sponsoring Committee of the National Congress for Unemployment and Social Insurance (NCUSI), held in Washington, DC January 5–7, 1935. The National Sponsoring Committee of the NCUSI was one of many organizations that exemplified the united front strategy against fascism adopted by the Communist International in the wake of Japan's annexation of Manchuria and the rise to power of Hitler in Germany. The organization worked for the passage of the Workers' Unemployment and Social Insurance bill, reintroduced in the 74th Congress in 1935 by Ernest Lundeen of the Farmer-Labor Party in Minnesota to compete with a rewritten Wagner-Lewis Bill. The Lundeen bill differed from the Wagner-Lewis bill in its insistence that the money for insurance should come from taxes on individual and corporate earnings over $5,000 plus a tax on gifts and inheritances rather than from contributions made by workers themselves. Although addressing a national issue rather than an international one, supporters of the Lundeen bill sought to empower workers—one way of countering the appeal of home-grown fascist demagogues such as Father Coughlin.[59]

In addition to her work for the organization, Hutchins wrote a small pamphlet in February 1935 specifically for women on the subject of social insurance, *What Every Working Woman Wants*. Hutchins's pamphlet argued forcefully for the Lundeen bill, emphasizing the maternity benefits included in its provisions. She began the pamphlet in her trademark fashion—with a representative anecdote designed to place the reader in the locus of the problem she was addressing.[60] She then reminded readers of what they already knew: that birth control was widely available to middle and upper class women who could pay to see a physician, but it was out of the reach of working class women. At that time, Section 211 of the federal Criminal Code classed the giving of contraceptive information with obscenity, pornography, and indecency, making it illegal to send information or supplies through the mail. Importation of birth control devices was also outlawed. Hutchins charged that "as a result of this cruel class legislation, working class women have no way of knowing the good from the bad methods of birth control." Women often resorted to the products of "bootleg" manufacturers, who used "such fancy names as "Feminine Hygiene," "Birconjel," and others."[61] With the one word "bootleg," Hutchins drew a subtle connection between the current sanctions against birth control and the failed Prohibition era, which had ended only a little over a year before. One of the chief arguments against Prohibition had been the illnesses and deaths (largely of men) caused by the consumption of bootleg liquor. Without saying as much, Hutchins implied that women's illnesses and deaths were not being comparably investigated or remedied and thus that women's bodies, especially the bodies of working class women, were seen as the dispensable property of the bourgeois men who made the laws.

Despite support from a broad range of working class individuals and organizations, including two thousand locals of the American Federation of Labor, the Lundeen bill failed. The Wagner-Lewis bill, its name changed in March 1935 from the "Economic Security Act" to the "Social Security Act," passed on June 19, 1935, becoming law on August 14, 1935. The United States had a social insurance system, finally, but the burden of old age insurance fell on workers and their employers, leaving the well-to-do exempt from responsibility. Nonetheless, although the Wagner-Lewis bill fell far short of the provisions made by the Lundeen bill, it was only because of the organizing and lobbying by Communists that any social insurance system at all had been constructed, and the party chose to build on that success.

Figure 9.4. Cover of *What Every Working Woman Wants*

As the need grew, plans for more and better publications—and more sophisticated rhetorical strategies—continued to develop within the party. In July 1935, the Seventh Congress of the Comintern began its month-long meetings. The main event of the Seventh Congress was a speech by Bulgarian Communist Georgi Dimitrov, then general secretary of the Comintern, pointing to the fascist danger and advocating a "people's united front against fascism," soon to be broadened to the "Popular Front." Although Rochester and Hutchins had not deliberately tried to alienate their friends during the revolutionary fervor of the early 1930s, some friendships, such as that with former *World Tomorrow* colleague Devere Allen, were more than strained. During 1935, they made a conscious effort to rebuild connections with old friends and colleagues.

Never having been enthusiastically sectarian, Hutchins drew notice for her efforts to reach out to a wider audience in *Women Who Work* and in her pamphlets, articles, and columns, and in the fall of 1935 the party placed her on the ballot, an unusual move only fifteen years after the approval of women's suffrage. She was selected to run for alderman of the Third District in Manhattan against incumbent Tammany politician Edward (Happy Warrior) Sullivan. An article contrasting Hutchins with the incumbent shows a photo of Hutchins under the headline "Red Candidate." She had been a New Yorker since 1917, leaving Boston, where her family had lived since 1639, said Roger Jackson, author of the article, adding that she "was active in the Paterson silk workers' strikes of 1924 and 1928, and was a leader in the defense of Sacco and Vanzetti," rather overstating the case. Her program, which she would explain often during the campaign, he said, called for "more schools and hospitals; slum clearance and building of low-cost, government-subsidized workers' apartment houses; playgrounds and athletic fields for the neighborhood; cash payment of the bonus[62]; abolition of the sales tax; huge increase in relief funds, with union wages on all projects; public utilities and a graduated income tax."[63] Hutchins's heritage—a family of "large, friendly, blue-eyed folk" with ancestors who had fought in the Revolutionary and Civil Wars—was now working in her favor as the party sought to shed its image of a largely foreign-born organization and appeal to the gentile, native-born population. But despite Hutchins's campaign promises, "Happy Warrior" Sullivan continued to represent Manhattan's Third District.

Probably not too startled by the loss, Hutchins continued to write for *Working Woman*, contrasting conditions for women in fascist countries such as Italy and Germany with conditions in the Soviet Union. She drew attention particularly to the arrests and torture of women in Germany. "In one month the sentences imposed increased by almost 40 per cent," she said. "A young woman worker, named Golla, 22 years old, from Silesia, was sentenced *to seven years of hard labor* by the Third Senate of the People's Court in Berlin, because she dared to speak against Hitler's war armament policy. . . . Helene Glatzer was tortured to death in jail and the police finally announced her death" (italics in the original).[64] Hutchins's reports of the imprisonment and deaths of women underscored both the women's strength and the need to identify and resist fascism wherever it arose.

At the same time, Hutchins was compiling the third volume of the *Labor Fact Book*, as well as helping Rochester complete *Rulers of America*. Rochester had worked for four years researching and writing *Rulers*, which appeared in print in January 1936.[65] "Taking up where Lenin left off," as Phillip Bonosky said, Rochester outlined the concentration of American industry.[66] Explaining the ways in which industry is controlled by finance capital, she aimed to break the rhetorical linkages between capitalism and democracy so thoroughly forged in the capitalist press. In 1931, Rochester had written that "facts accurate enough in themselves are only a small part of any story. Which facts are selected? What standards are applied in interpreting them?"[67] The standard she applied in interpreting the economic facts she had gathered in *Rulers*, she said, could be found in Lenin's *Imperialism, the Highest Stage of Capitalism*. The book "illustrates for this country" Lenin's basic argument, Rochester announced in the foreword, which was that imperialism meant the control of territories by finance capital rather than by armed force. Wealthy nations subjugated poorer nations not for raw materials to be shipped back home for industry but as sites for investment of capital. Thus work was accomplished abroad rather than at home. What this meant, of course, was a widening chasm at home between the working class and the owning class.[68] The book answered several questions, she said: "What is the essential pattern of control in the United States? What are the underlying trends from which it developed? What is the effect of this control in the life of the people? Will power pass from the financial rulers through their inner collapse?"[69]

Rochester began by explaining the development and structure of capitalism in the United States, paying particular attention to the men—the "inner oligarchs"—who created the structure. In the second half of the book, she analyzed capitalist control of key industries, such as steel, oil, chemicals, electricity, railroads, and aviation. Elsbeth Freudenthal, Rochester's former colleague in the LID (and another "independent woman," who shared her life with her partner, Jean), authored three of these chapters—chemicals, aviation, and steel.

Rochester acknowledged the difficulty in speaking within an advanced capitalist society, arguing that "every channel of social thought is deliberately used for the support of the existing order, including public schools, state universities, endowed colleges and universities, newspapers and magazines, movies and radios. . . . The substance of capitalist propaganda is of wide variety," she said, pointing to the Hearst press at one extreme and the "'liberal' studies and government reports" that fail to mention capitalism as a factor. In between, she said, are vast amounts of material intended to amuse the population, keeping "the workers and petty bourgeoisie from fruitful pondering on the causes of their sufferings and on the true significance of government policies."[70] Moreover, she said, although trade organizations, chambers of commerce, and related organizations issue specific propaganda materials, "the broader cultural apparatus is trying to guide the basic mind-set of the masses."[71]

To illustrate, Rochester revealed that on September 7, 1934, the American Newspaper Publishers Association sent out a memo telling members to restrict their use of particular words. Striking workers should not be called "workers" but rather "strikers." Scabs, on the other hand, should be referred to as "workers."[72] Likewise, she said, the *Wall Street Journal* praised the Warner film *Black Fury*, an inaccurate portrayal of mine workers, calling it "'a worthy and entertaining screen drama'" and suggesting that "'if trouble-makers can be scotched by the showing of such pictures as *Black Fury*, that is a worthy achievement in itself.'"[73]

Although she was interpreting the facts about the financial structure of the United States using Lenin's *Imperialism, the Highest Form of Capitalism*, Rochester added commentary on the facts through stylistic manipulation, as well. And it was probably this commentary—often taking the form of a caustic irony or parody—that created an opening for some reviewers to challenge her reading of the economic structure of America. Saying that "Rockefeller 'philanthropy' comes to its finest flower when the workers, in spite of spies and thugs, stand together and go out on strike," Rochester listed several murders committed by Rockefeller guards or government forces called in at Rockefeller's behest, including the Ludlow massacre. In doing so, she silently recalled Vida Scudder's near dismissal from Wellesley in 1899 for challenging a Rockefeller donation to the college.

Reviewers were largely split along the same lines as they had been when Hutchins's book was published two years earlier. For the most part, they did not dispute Rochester's facts, but they quailed at her interpretation. At least two reviewers, in thinly veiled misogynist attacks, accused her of emotionalism. Francis Brown, for instance, writing in the *New York Times*, said: "There is an emotional appeal based on the contrast of luxury to poverty, something that hardly seems to belong in a serious study."[74]

New Masses, however, said that *Rulers* "marks the highest point reached so far in American revolutionary research in this field. . . . [It] not only describes the rulers of America but illuminates the economic foundations on which the entire life of the American people rests."[75] Winifred Chappell, writing in *The Fight Against War and Fascism*, summarized the book's argument for readers, pointing out that Rochester credited capitalism with developments that could benefit humanity, "but it is incapable of using for human ends what it has created. Comes now the time . . . for the people who have been ruled to take a hand."[76]

At a dinner held by the LRA in March 1936 to celebrate the publication of *Rulers*, Rochester was characteristically modest, referring to *Rulers* as "our book" and crediting the staff and volunteers of the LRA, as well as Alexander Trachtenberg of International Publishers, for their assistance. Trachtenberg, she said, "is not only a very wise comrade, but he has the true gift of impersonal and penetrating criticism." She went on to list three points that she had learned in the process of writing the book: that "the rulers always and consistently deny their power," that "most of the financial rulers have been rather ignorant of economic facts," and that "the conflict between fascist trends and mass struggle for revolutionary change is rooted in the inner economic forces of capitalism." After these three points, she quickly shifted the attention from herself and her book to Earl Browder's new book, *What Is Communism*, saying that she did "most genuinely believe that the really important book of the month is Comrade Browder's *What Is Communism*."[77]

Although Rochester did not send a copy of *Rulers* to Vida Scudder, Scudder wrote to her on April 11, saying, "Anna Dear: I have bought it! I have read it! At least I have read a lot of it!" She did not mention Rochester's pointed remarks on Rockefeller or her own history with Rockefeller money, nor did she comment on the grounding of the book in Lenin's analysis, but she did exult: "And I must tell you of my admiration and my awe and my gratitude, that you have done this splendid and noble and immensely valuable thing." After this effusion, she slipped into their old common language, saying, "I am giving thanks for you."

Although Scudder admitted to stopping short of reading the entire book—perhaps an oblique commentary on her political differences with Rochester—she then announced that she was sending the book to the library established in memory of Helena Stuart Dudley to serve young people of Denison House and other Boston settlements. We cannot know how this emotional appeal affected Rochester, although we do know that she took care to preserve the letter. "Our love to you both,"[78] Scudder closed, speaking for herself and Florence Converse and thus reminding Rochester of the origin and continuing source of her political passion in a community of women linked by their love for each other and for the wider world. Notably, however, Scudder herself did not choose to review the book or to use it in any of her activities—or even to keep it.

Chapter Ten

Twentieth-Century Americanism

Life comes to us but once and it should be possible to live one's life in such a way that looking back one would feel no regret for years lived pointlessly; no shame for a petty worthless past—so that as one died one could say "*All my life and all my strength has been given to the most beautiful thing in the world—the struggle for the freedom of mankind.*"

> —Nicholas Ostrovski in *The Making of Hero* (quotation copied by Grace Hutchins into her personal notebook, ca. 1936–1937)

Rochester's affections had shifted irrevocably away from Vida Scudder and her efforts to create theological and political synthesis. Without abandoning Scudder entirely, Rochester, along with Hutchins, had become a devotee of labor activist and CPUSA organizer Mother Bloor, signing on as a sponsor for her forty-fifth anniversary banquet.[1] With Bloor, they honored the achievements of women labor activists and recommitted themselves to the fight against fascism. And as part of their response to the increasing fascist threat, they modified their rhetorical mode again, tempering their debunking with efforts to create a broad antifascist front. Indeed, the banquet can be seen as an attempt to draw in a wide range of celebrants.

Chaired by Heywood Broun and Roger Baldwin, the event celebrated Ella Reeve Bloor's forty-five years as a labor activist and organizer. Will Geer, Mother Bloor's son-in-law, performed alongside the International Workers Order Band, and a theater company offered a scene from Clifford Odets's "Waiting for Lefty." Hutchins, always more involved in social organizing than Rochester, was a member of the Celebration Committee and delivered a testimonial to Mother Bloor. Describing a visit Mother Bloor had paid to silk workers in Bethlehem, Pennsylvania, Hutchins withheld the identity of a special worker until the end: "Fired that night by Mother Bloor's enthusiasm, the girl threw herself into the labor movement and became a leader in organizing the textile workers. Her name is Ann Burlak."[2]

Hutchins knew the audience would recognize the name. If the rest of the program featured men, Hutchins would ensure that her testimonial placed women at the revolutionary center. What's more, by invoking the name of Ann Burlak, Hutchins chronicled a cross-generational tradition of women activists, a tradition usually taken for granted and unacknowledged in the larger movement but one with which Hutchins and Rochester were familiar because of their own experiences struggling to establish women's presence in the Episcopal Church and the FOR.

Despite having shifted their affiliations, Hutchins and Rochester continued to correspond with old friends and acquaintances. Sarah Cleghorn had just published her own memoirs, *Threescore*, writing in detail about Community House, about the job that Hutchins and Rochester had made for her, and about Hutchins and Rochester themselves, celebrating their partnership.

Seeing the review of *Threescore* in the *New York Times*, Hutchins had gone out immediately to buy it. "It just happened along at the time I am trying to recover from the grippe with that completely down-and-out limp, discouraged feeling which is, I suppose, characteristic of the trouble," Hutchins wrote to Cleghorn. "Feeling as if nothing could lift me out of the slough, I read what you wrote of Anna and me at 352. And presto, I felt better! If anybody could ever honestly think I had even one of those good qualities you describe, there must be some good in me. . . . Thank you for such a very generous and forgiving statement about me! It was certainly good for an inferiority complex," she added. "*Rulers of America* has not had such good luck in reviews as your book, but it is going well. It was the Book Union choice for February."[3]

Figure 10.1. Ella Reeve Bloor (Mother Bloor)

Rochester wrote a few days later, insisting that Cleghorn had been "too kind to *some* of your friends." Then, unable to resist the pull of the old argument, she lamented: "Some things I wish you had done differently—but that would be only if you saw some things differently! . . . But how *could* you fall for Mr. Roosevelt!" she exclaimed. "His whole administration is set to buttress a decaying capitalism. He is more suave than Hoover but his function is the same."[4]

Other old sparring partners reappeared around this time. In a somewhat less amicable continuation of another old debate, William Floyd, publisher of *The Arbitrator*, a humanist magazine, took the occasion to remind Rochester and Hutchins, rather gleefully, of their previous battles: "Do you remember the time when you and Miss Hutchins denounced the attacks upon religion contained in *The Arbitrator*? Now that you have become Communists, do you not agree that Christian doctrines are a part of ancient superstitions that should be discarded in favor of an evolutionary philosophy?"[5] Rochester responded to his most recent sortie, saying, "At least you will admit that we were consistent—when we were not yet liberated from religion."[6] Hoping that his "evolutionary philosophy" would grow to include the Soviet Union, she then suggested that he might read the recent work of Sidney and Beatrice Webb and Anna Louise Strong.

Rochester indeed continued to be an unwavering supporter of the Soviet Union. The degree to which she was aware of the increasing repression in the USSR is unclear. For instance, did she hear, in some roundabout manner, that in a March 1936 speech, People's Commissar of Justice N. V. Krylenko added "homosexuals to the list of class enemies, declassed elements, and criminal elements that had been the subject of urban social cleansing campaigns"?[7] If she did hear the pronouncement, she might not have been surprised, given Maxim Gorky's earlier pronouncement linking homosexuality and fascism. Certainly Rochester was wise enough not to have unreasonably high expectations of the socialist experiment. And, she might have interpreted this repressive measure and others, as some did, as part of a worldwide political contraction evidenced in varying ways across the globe.

In any event, if the question came up at all, it is likely that Rochester did not include herself or Hutchins, or any of the women in community with whom she had found Hutchins, in the category outlined by Krylenko. As Dan Healey has pointed out, Krylenko characterized homosexuals as pederasts, "frequently engaged in counterrevolutionary activity."[8] Rochester, of course, would have drawn the lines of identity differently, recalling Edward Carpenter's distinction between emotional commitment and sexual adventuring and continuing to value especially those women whose devotion to other women translated into efforts to remake society. She and Hutchins had little understanding of and little patience with men whom they felt were engaging in behavior that could threaten the movement.

If the Soviet Union was not a finished paradise for those transgressing borders of tradition in personal relationships, neither was the United States. Hutchins and Rochester understood that they were fortunate in being able to have a partnership—but as much as they worked to create better circumstances for other women, it is unclear how much they realized that their inattention to the public dimension of the partnership had consequences for others, especially younger women, who lacked their resources. After all, they *were* completely visible, for anyone who cared to look. But the rest of the world was becoming more inclined to define people in sexual terms alone—and, lacking any organized resistance, to use those definitions as a means of social and economic control. In their case, however, most people didn't look. Or pretended they didn't.

Hutchins was selected to run for election again, this time for New York State controller on the CPUSA ticket; she was also tapped to serve as treasurer of the National Election Campaign Committee headquartered at 799 Broadway, joining Alexander Trachtenberg, secretary, and William Z. Foster, chairman. The *Daily Worker* announced her position on the campaign committee on the front page: "Miss Hutchins, who is a descendant of an old Colonial family, is herself a candidate for Controller on the New York State Communist ticket. She has been associated for many years with the Labor Research Association and is the author of a number of books including 'Women at Work' [sic]."[9] It was Hutchins's most public moment thus far, and she threw herself into campaigning and fundraising with zeal. Bryn Mawr classmate "Tony" Cannon (Mary Antoinette Cannon, a medical social worker) told of

> walking along lower Sixth Avenue when she was startled to hear the name "Miss Grace Hutchins" shouted aloud as if some one were trying to page her. Tony looked behind her, and there she saw a truck slowly moving along near the curb, and from its vitals came through the medium of a gigantic loud speaker a passionate exhortation for the residents of New York to elect as State Comptroller the candidate for this office on the Communist ticket, who was none other than our own Hutchins. "Miss Grace Hutchins," the voice kept bellowing forth, "is the true descendant of her Revolutionary ancestors, and can be trusted to battle now for *your* liberties as her forefathers of old fought for *theirs!*"[10]

She lost the election but used the platform to call attention to women's strengths. Drawing on her "old Colonial family" heritage, Hutchins wrote an article on patriotism for *Woman Today* (the former *Working Woman*, renamed in order to gain wider appeal), pointing to the bravery of women during the American Revolution and distinguishing such patriotism from the fulminations of Hearst newspapers and the Liberty League. She spoke on street corners in Manhattan, "occasionally [having] to dodge a potato or tomato thrown by some Fascist opponent from across the street,"[11] a reference to her continuing commitment to an embodied rhetoric, and accepted an invitation to serve on the Central Committee of the New York State Communist Party.

In September 1936, the *Daily Worker* ran a several-column article about her, complete with photo, headlined "Grace Hutchins—Revolutionary," a masterpiece of euphemism and suggestive language and a testimony to the tortuous rhetorical efforts required to create a popular front while refusing to address the range of same sex-partnerships and desires. However, despite this refusal, Hutchins managed to stretch the fabric of Marxist-Leninist discourse to accommodate a feminist revolution. Hutchins told the writer, Sidney Streat, that had she not left Beacon Street in Boston to go to Bryn Mawr College and had she not "made certain early contacts in her life" (a veiled reference to Rochester and to the culture of same-sex love that drew them together), she "might today be married to a lawyer, settled down, bringing up children in atmosphere." In other words, Hutchins had avoided becoming "Mrs. Dalloway." "I'm very glad I didn't stay there," she said.[12] Articulating her life story as a series of choices rather than as the discovery of a fixed identity, Hutchins positioned herself both inside and outside traditional expectations, constructing herself to be read not as an antisocial pariah but as a rebel committed to the cause of greater freedom and equality. Noting that she had been active in the suffrage movement during college, she said that it was then that she "understood what Susan B. Anthony meant in devoting her life to a fight to free women." Hutchins left Anthony's "fight to free women" undefined;

Figure 10.2. Grace Hutchins speaking at Madison Square Garden

readers could choose to see it as a quaint reference to suffrage or a more radical reference to compulsory heterosexuality, as contained in the earlier allusion to marriage. Thus, by focusing on "the fight to free women," Hutchins simultaneously rescued herself from the perceived taint of a nonheterosexual partnership and invoked for all the world to see, if they would, her battle to make the world safe for women, especially women who do not meet standard gender expectations and whose primary commitments are to other women.

Regarding Hutchins's life-defining relationship with Rochester, Streat was predictably circumspect, saying only that "Grace Hutchins shares an apartment with Anna Rochester, whose very competent book, 'Rulers of America,' came out earlier this year. The apartment is at 85 Bedford Street where they have lived for 12 years." New York readers probably would have recognized the address as part of the socialist co-op; some readers, however, might have read more into the twelve years together at a Greenwich Village address. At this time, many American Communists were still willing to look beyond same-sex partnerships, especially those between women, but couldn't yet acknowledge them publicly. Among friends and colleagues, of course, Rochester and Hutchins's partnership was no secret. "They had their own attitudes about life," their friend and Rochester's Farm Commission colleague Lement Harris commented obliquely some sixty years later.[13] As it turned out, their discretion would not serve them well. At the time, however, with the threat of fascism increasing daily, it must have seemed the right course of action.

With people around her either oblivious or pretending not to notice her partnership with Hutchins, Rochester continued to defy them indirectly by occupying traditionally male spaces and arguing vehemently and publicly on the larger questions of capitalist control, aiming not for personal benefit or gain but for a more just civic polity. In April 1936, fearing that an angry middle class would find fascism attractive, she tried to agitate readers of *New Masses* on the decline of the middle class precipitated by the continued economic deterioration. Renouncing her earlier uses of caricature or irony, Rochester carefully explained the evolution of the middle class, locating its origins in small capitalist operations. But this middle class, she said, had been largely shut out because of pressure from large corporations. A new middle class had arisen "from the minor executives employed by corporations, from the increasing numbers of professional workers, from the army of subordinate white-collar workers, and from the inactive owners of small investments."[14] Although the middle class, now vulnerable to layoffs, had not completely vanished, she said, it was under considerable pressure and existed only in pockets, such as neighborhood trade, and even there it was threatened by the chain stores. "No broad revival with unlimited expansion of industry can be expected under capitalism," she cautioned, "apart from actual war production."[15]

Hutchins, too, tried to attract the middle class to the Popular Front, soberly reviewing Mary Van Kleeck's *Creative America: Its Resources for Social Security* in the July 1936 issue of *The Communist,* one of her gestures of solidarity in which she drew attention to the work of women like herself and Rochester. She introduced her review by saying, "Professionals have been organizing during the past five years as an important sector in the broad anti-fascist people's front that is developing in the United States." Echoing Rochester's article, she added, "As the economic crisis and depression deepened, salaried professional workers suffered unemployment, part-time work and salary cuts, while self-employed professionals found that increasing numbers of the population were unable to take advantage of professional services." Van Kleeck's book, she said, "is the first to present the viewpoint of professionals on their relationship with the labor movement." In it, Hutchins said, Van Kleeck counterposed creative forces—"America at work"—and possessive forces—ownership of resources and the means of production rather than ownership for personal use. Hutchins noted with approval Van Kleeck's advocacy of the Farmer-Labor Party as a means of achieving "dynamic security for the American people"; she urged that professionals find solidarity with the workers in order to prepare "'the masses for the present phase of the struggle to free America's creative forces from the bondage of possessive privilege.'"[16]

Concern for the middle class was only part of the antifascist effort. CPUSA writers also struggled to warn Americans about the fascist presence sprouting from America's Depression-fertilized soil. As part of this campaign, *The Communist* published Rochester's article "Finance Capital and Fascist Trends in the United States." In the article, Rochester explained the 1934 genesis of the Liberty League, a group of finance capitalists headed by the du Ponts, whose aim was to defeat Roosevelt in the 1936 elections. She argued that the Liberty League, along with related organizations such as the Crusaders, the Sentinels of the Republic, the Southern Committee to Uphold the Constitution, the Farmers Independent Council, and other smaller groups, aimed to create a home-grown fascism in the United States. "Basic to our analysis," she said, "is a correct understanding of fascism as a political form adopted by finance capital in its effort to meet the general crisis of capitalism."[17]

Rochester quoted the definition provided by the Executive Committee of the Communist International (ECCI) in the *Theses of the Thirteenth Plenum:* "'Fascism is the open terrorist dictatorship of the most reactionary, most chauvinist, and most imperialist elements of finance capital,'"[18] and she located the leaders of the named organizations within the hierarchy of American finance capitalism. The Sentinels, she noted, had been charged with anti-Semitism by the Black Committee, a Senate investigative committee, which meant that a proposed merger with the Liberty League had fallen through, "since the three du Pont brothers, Pierre, Irenee, and Lammot, had a Jewish grandmother, although they do not quite relish outside reminders of that fact."[19] Here Rochester allowed her own feminism to show: what sort of men, she seemed to be saying, would deny their own grandmother? And for profit!

The du Ponts and their compatriots were not working alone, Rochester asserted. The "most dangerous fascist demagogues in the country," she said, were William Hearst and Father Coughlin, both of whom reached the masses directly through media. Hearst owned many of the largest daily newspapers at that time, and he was investing in radio, creating a "small but growing radio chain." Father Coughlin had a national radio program and was creating his own organization, the National Union for Social Justice, which at the time of Rochester's writing claimed some six million adherents. Hearst, Rochester pointed out, was a finance capitalist himself, owning mines, ranches, and city real estate, as well as publishing ventures other than his newspapers. It was his newspapers, though, that she found most frightening. Of all the finance capitalists she enumerated in the pages of the article, he alone had been in closest touch with Nazi leaders, "and the power of his papers has been more sharply and persistently directed against the working class movement and the Soviet Union." Father Coughlin, although unceasingly anticommunist, had at times supported Roosevelt, she conceded. With the fascist danger growing from the right, Roosevelt was beginning to seem less noxious.[20]

Although the fascist movement in the United States was inextricably intertwined with finance capital, Rochester argued, the primary finance capitalists Morgan, Rockefeller, and Mellon were not themselves publicly associated with the fascist organizations—"their publicity men advise against it." But, Rochester said, those closely associated with them provided the organizations with sufficient funds to operate effectively. The way for workers to fight back against the "brigands who control the American highways of business" was to join a Farmer-Labor party, she advised, adding her voice to Mary Van Kleeck's, and build an antifascist consensus from the remnants of old progressive movements.[21]

With this consensus effort in mind, in mid-summer of 1936, Rochester returned to the summer community at Shelburne where 32 years before Vida Scudder had first accosted her with arguments about labor and capital, changing her life. Scudder had invited her to return, and, in the spirit of the Popular Front, Rochester had accepted. She read a paper to the group, probably on the subject of the Liberty League, the Hearst press, Father Coughlin, and their anticommunist attacks.[22] In mid-August, Scudder wrote to her, saying, "It meant a lot to have you come to us and give that fine paper; and I am sure the paper will do good work in enlarging many minds. It is time that all Christian people were released from the influence of the senseless anti-communist patter current in the religious press."[23]

Reiterating her lifelong desire for a dialectical unity, Scudder asked whether there were any church members in the party. Invoking the idea of the Popular Front, she said, "Fundamental divergence as to the philosophical basis of our thought should not preclude fellowship and common action among those who agree on the economic program and goal. You Communists on your side should not ignore or discredit the tremendous amount of dynamite present in the Gospels, and, yes, in the Church organizations, even if official Christianity does wrap that dynamite up in curl papers" (an interesting linkage of the church with traditional notions of femininity). Unable to help herself, she reached again for the elusive Platonic synthesis, saying,

You see my own conviction is that the struggle between Christianity and Communism is the best example of dialectical tension in the world of thought today, and that the synthesis already begins to appear. And what valuable contribution to that synthesis you might make, you and Grace, if only! * * *. Ah me! But I won't argue, I will only thank you for the service you rendered us, and tell you what you know anyway, that I love you both dearly, and steadily.

She closed by saying, "Now don't be cross if I say that I thank God for you, dear Anna," and signed her letter "Vida D. Scudder, S.C.H.C."

Yet however much Vida Scudder appeared to be attempting to create a dialectical unity with Rochester and Hutchins, she held fast to her own position, just as Rochester and Hutchins held fast to theirs. Writing to Virginia Huntington in September—probably in 1936 just following Rochester's visit—she said: "When the Enemy remarks 'Her financial assets are the foundation of the church,' or words to that effect, we know precisely where we are. Figliarola, I do love a fight!"[24]

The fight would not be resolved quickly or easily. Although Earl Browder was attempting to make common cause with religious groups, challenging demagogues such as Father Coughlin,[25] Rochester and Hutchins declined to be publicly identified as Christians, even for the sake of the Popular Front. When their old friend Bill Spofford asked if they would write an article for *The Witness* on "Why as a Christian I am Voting for Browder," they turned him down.[26] Still, Hutchins apparently could not refuse Lucy Sturgis when she asked if the Board of Missions of the Episcopal Church could reprint their 1912 pamphlet, *Pickaninnies' Progress*. The title was changed to *From Bantu Jungle to Church College*, but in most other respects it remained the same, surely an embarrassment for Hutchins.

Antifascism was Hutchins's first concern now. As part of her campaign, Hutchins reworked Rochester's article for *The Communist* on the Liberty League and related fascist organizations, calling it *The Truth about the Liberty League* and publishing it as a pamphlet with International Pamphlets.[27] This reworking ensured that an article otherwise buried in a rather esoteric publication was made available to the working class audience that the fascist organizations themselves were targeting. Not only that, but the material would be more likely to end up in the hands of women who would recognize Hutchins's name from her other writings, thus drawing women into the fight against fascism.

The fascist organizations were not alone in their efforts to sabotage the left. Using "legal" efforts not unlike those of the American Liberty League, Federal Bureau of Investigation (FBI) director J. Edgar Hoover was developing systems for monitoring "subversives" (and adding to that his own self-protective campaign against "sexual deviants"[28]). President Roosevelt, meeting with J. Edgar Hoover and Secretary of State Cordell Hull in August 1936, had asked that the Federal Bureau of Investigation begin monitoring the activities of Communists and fascists in the United States. Roosevelt's concern was that "'some [domestic] organizations would probably attempt to cripple our war effort [in an emergency] through sabotage.'"[29] Indeed, *The Brown Network*, a book written by the author of the two previous *Brown Books*, explained how the Nazis had infiltrated countries throughout the world, including the United States, organizing local groups to promote a fascist ideology, as Hutchins herself had noted in "The Black Night," an article published in *The Fight against War and Fascism*.[30] Roosevelt directed Hoover to inform Attorney General Cummings about the plan and asked Secretary of State Hull to confer with Cummings about the techniques to be used to gather information. Hoover took advantage of this directive to initiate a top-secret but wide-ranging investigation into left-wing activities. Hutchins

Figure 10.3. Vida Dutton Scudder at Adelynrood

and Rochester did not feel the effects of this investigation until several years later, and for the time being, they continued their work unaware of the increasing surveillance.

Having served as treasurer of the New York State Communist Party, the National Elections Committee, the LRA, and the Prisoners' Relief Fund, as well as having run for office on the CPUSA ticket, Hutchins had earned the party's trust and respect. Her financial acumen was clear, and she herself was beyond reproach. In September 1936, she, along with Bob Dunn and Julius Littinsky, a physician and the husband of Tillie Littinsky, a women's organizer and writer for *Working Woman*, was listed as a comortgagee of 50 East 13th in Manhattan, the building housing the *Daily Worker*, *Woman Today*, and the Workers' Bookshop.[31] The three would not have been paying the entire mortgage themselves but rather serving as a conduit for party-raised funds, especially funds from people who did not wish their names to appear in public.

This support for the *Daily Worker* marked one of Hutchins's first public efforts to build the party through the newspaper. Organizers were clear that the *Daily Worker* was the central organ of the party and emphasized its critical role in attracting and maintaining an informed membership. On February 22, the Special Conference of District Organizers adopted a statement outlining the tasks that they saw as crucial for party building. "The task of building the Party and that of increasing the *Daily Worker* and *Sunday Worker* are indissolubly bound up. One cannot be solved without the other. . . . *The building of the circulation of our press is a key task to both the solution of the inner problems of the Party and to the conversion of the most militant workers to Communism*" (emphasis in original).[32] They hoped to create a circulation of fifty thousand for the *Daily Worker* and 150 thousand for the *Sunday Worker* by June 1937, seeing the newspapers, as one organizer said, as "the most powerful educator of our Party."[33]

Although the *Daily Worker* was the most important periodical associated with the party, it was only one of many publications (including the magazines for which both Rochester and Hutchins wrote and the pamphlets they had written and that the LRA had sponsored) aiming to intervene at the point of struggle. Of the magazines, *New Masses* reached the widest cross-class audience. Both Rochester and Hutchins sent greetings to *New Masses* on its twenty-fifth anniversary. In the December 1 issue, Rochester occupied party discourse effortlessly, locating the magazine in the party's larger organizing efforts. "Today, more than ever before," she said, "the journalists and creative writers grouped about the *New Masses* have an urgent problem and a challenging opportunity. They are in a unique position for increasing and focusing the scattered little flames of revolutionary interest among the millions of middle-class Americans."[34] By contrast, Hutchins's message, which appeared in the December 29 issue, offered a glimpse of her more complicated position vis à vis the largely masculine *New Masses* discourse. In the message, she did not simply occupy the speaking position of a man but pushed the elastic edges of the discourse to create space for women: "As a Socialist during the World War," she said, claiming a twenty-year history in the movement, "I used to read the old *Masses* with appreciation. The vigorous cartoons stunned me somewhat at first, I must confess, and I nearly lost my job for having them in my room at the school where I taught." With this, she identified herself as a professional worker in a field dominated by women, one who almost lost her job because of her sympathies. She went on to establish solidarity with the women and children of the working class: "The *Masses*' account of the Paterson 1913 [silk workers'] strike is one of the most valuable records of that great struggle—preserved in the few libraries that have a file of the magazine. That was John Reed at his best, describing police terror in the city and conditions in the county jail." Then she made it clear that this attention to a labor action largely by women was what real masculine writing in the Communist tradition meant. "The *New Masses* today," she concluded, "is continuing that tradition of virile writing on present-day struggles—and we need all we can get. More power to its collective pen!"[35]

Having provided her bona fides with this greeting, Hutchins continued her efforts to splice feminism into the revolution. Suggesting that postsuffrage America was hardly a utopia for women, Hutchins pointed out in *The Woman Today* that "there remain upon the statute books of the various states and jurisdictions of the United States . . . over a thousand laws . . . that still mark the dependent position of women."[36] Then, describing the sculpture of Susan B. Anthony, Elizabeth Cady Stanton, and Lucretia Mott in the US capitol building for her far-flung readership, she celebrated the sculptor, Adelaide Johnson, and commented that Johnson had "shown the large, striking, sharply chiseled nose and strong chin of Susan Anthony, outstanding fighter of them all, who dared to challenge the 'God-ordained authority of men.'"[37] Reversing traditional description, she said that when Stanton and Mott went to the World's Anti-Slavery Convention in London in 1840, "the men stormed up and down the hall in a *shrieking* debate as to whether or not the women delegates should be seated" (emphasis mine). In a creative use of silence, she chose not to add that any retrograde efforts to exclude women now would surely be treated with the same disdain by future historians.

As if to underline the revolutionary centrality of conversations, even disagreements, between women, Hutchins engaged Vida Scudder in the pages of *New Masses* by publishing a not altogether positive review of *On Journey*, Scudder's autobiography. Rochester chose to remain publicly silent, although anyone familiar with the Companions or the CLID could not fail to hear echoes of old arguments in Hutchins's commentary. The headline was "A Socialist Reads Lenin." Making it clear to readers that Scudder was never a member of the Socialist Party leadership, Hutchins critiqued the autobiography but praised Scudder for her recent article on Lenin in *Christian Century*, saying that it was refreshing after the "mysticism of the closing chapters of her autobiography."[38] Shifting back and forth between praise and criticism, Hutchins noted Scudder's contact with the trade union movement through Denison House but quoted with disapproval Scudder's recollection of " 'laughing and weeping over the constant failure of communism.' "[39] In closing, Hutchins proffered her own version of a unified vision, saying that Scudder "concludes that Marxists, 'however one judges their ultimate theories'—which she rejects—have unprecedented understanding of the whole historic process. She is perhaps a little wistful about these Marxists. Is it because she does not accept what she realizes is an integrated and coherent conception of the universe?"[40]

Hutchins undoubtedly detected this wistfulness in the pages on which Scudder charted her sadness at the disintegration of a core group of Companions of the Holy Cross, including Ellen Gates Starr's move to the Roman Catholic Church. "Others, two in particular," Scudder said, "joined the Communist party, where they have since rendered noble service. The ranks of the forward-looking were broken and scattered."[41]

Vida Scudder had written to Virginia Huntington during December 1936 that she felt an "inward compulsion to write an article on Lenin, he thrills me so."[42] The resulting article, entitled "A Little Tour in the Mind of Lenin,"[43] noted with surprise that Lenin had a great mind. Clearly written for the middle class readership of *Christian Century*, the article enumerated those points in Lenin's writing likely to appeal to liberal readers—such as his call for working class people to read widely—and carefully ignored those points likely to cause distress, such as the notion of the dictatorship of the proletariat. Scudder did, however, end by asking the question: "How far can a Christian mind throw in its fortunes with communism?" And she responded to her own question by saying: "I will not close without stating my conviction that there is an impassable gulf."[44] This statement seems to contradict yet again her private plea to Rochester and Hutchins that they work with her to create a synthesis of Christianity and communism. Thus she struggled to knit together the ranks of the forward looking.

Yet neither Scudder nor Hutchins could begin to reveal the stitches that had served to unite so many women among their ranks. Although Hutchins seems to have been convinced that her silence, or coded language, at best, was imperative to the overthrow of fascism, Scudder edited references to same-sex love in her autobiography. Nan Bauer Maglin points to half a sentence Scudder excised from a discussion of women's friendships in her published autobiography (deletion italicized): "The women's colleges have helped develop these friendships which albeit beset by perils like all worthwhile human relationships, *and subject to undeniable abuses, on which prurient thought can dwell if it will*, can and do supply a great need."[45] In the margin of the manuscript, Maglin reports, Scudder wrote the single word *Sappho*, a reference to the Greek poet and teacher whose surviving, exquisitely beautiful fragments of poetry celebrate love between women. What mixture of emotions led to this multivalent exchange with herself, we can only guess. However, placing blame for the emphasis on sex in modern biographies, Scudder said pointedly: "It is all the fault of Mr. Freud, and I do think he has a good deal to answer for."[46] Hutchins, of course, had no access to this inner dialogue; the ranks of the forward looking were scattered in part by silence, but Hutchins would at least have added that the commodification of sex did little for women as it helped to fill capitalist coffers.

Working on the margins of their old liberal acquaintances, Rochester and Hutchins both continued to challenge Devere Allen in their semiannual correspondence. Hutchins sent Allen some pamphlets, probably those that she and Rochester had authored; Allen responded in his letter to Rochester, enclosing his check for the $26 interest payment on her loan to him and insisting that his support for the American Committee for the Defense of Leon Trotsky was not about Trotsky himself but rather about preserving the right of asylum. He promised to continue defending the USSR.[47]

Allen's mention of Trotsky was no coincidence. Rochester was becoming increasingly concerned about Trotsky and the trials in the Soviet Union. During August 1936, the first trial had been held; the second concluded during the last week of January 1937, only a few days before Rochester wrote to Allen. She later described the events of the trial in the LRA's *Arsenal of Facts*, saying that "17 other persons, charged with treason, sabotage, assassination and counter-revolution, were tried in Moscow. . . . Testimony of the defendants showed that the assassination of Kirov [December 1, 1934] was part of a wide-spread terrorist conspiracy. They confessed that under direction of Leon Trotsky, plans were also made to assassinate Stalin, Molotov, Voroshilov, and other Soviet government leaders."[48] She went on to argue that beginning in 1933, the Soviet Union, previously free from serious industrial disasters, began to experience "a considerable number of sudden unexplained . . . 'accidents,'" particularly in coal mining, railroads, and chemical industries. These acts of sabotage, she said, were revealed at the January 1937 trial to be connected to German and Japanese espionage agents.[49] Although since then the accuracy of these "revelations" has been seriously undermined, at that time, Rochester had no means of locating more precise information. And the international advance of fascism was undeniable. The fascists' trial run—the civil war in Spain—was intensifying.[50]

While deaths abroad accelerated, one death nearer home disrupted Hutchins and Rochester's life in May 1937. Hutchins's brother Ned, a partner in their father's law firm, Hutchins and Wheeler, was killed in an automobile accident with his friend and Harvard classmate Otis Russell as they returned to Boston from a fishing trip on May 16. Hutchins had not been close to Ned, especially after she had rejected his offer of legal assistance when she was arrested for demonstrating against the executions of Sacco and Vanzetti. She had other profound differences with him, as well. He had been a pilot during the World War, a war she had opposed and that led her to join the FOR and become an active pacifist. And he was a member of the board of managers of the trustees of donations to the Episcopal Church, a concentration of wealth against which Hutchins had argued vigorously. Nonetheless, he was her baby brother—and the third child that Susan Hutchins had lost, so Hutchins spent much of the year offering support to her mother.

Perhaps it was this preoccupation that prevented Hutchins from paying as much attention as she might have otherwise when her friend Juliet Stuart Poyntz disappeared on June 3 from her residential hotel, the American Woman's Association Clubhouse at 353 West 57th in Manhattan. Poyntz's disappearance has never been adequately explained, although many stories developed, especially during the 1950s, as the event became part of an arsenal of bizarre anticommunist propaganda. Certainly as someone involved in international antifascist activities, Poyntz was at considerable risk during the increasingly tense years prior to the war. Hutchins, however, knew only that she had vanished. When interviewed by reporters in 1944, she said, "I met her around 1927 when I returned from Russia. . . . People were talking of suicide and the police asked me if this was possible, but all I could say was that I had no idea. The entire case is such a mystery. I don't think she was 'spirited to Russia' as people said. I haven't any theory at all. She had a lot of friends and was a delightful person."[51] Hutchins kept the telephone number of the New York City Police Missing Persons Bureau in her address book for the rest of her life.

Evidence suggests that Poyntz was recruiting antifascist agents among the international student population in New York. Hutchins, meanwhile, tried to counter fascism by strengthening international labor accords, especially those serving women. Two days before Poyntz's disappearance, Hutchins submitted a report to Margaret Cowl, head of the Women's Division of the CPUSA, on the Women's Charter, an effort by (primarily middle class) women's organizations to press for equal pay, among other things. The charter had originated in discussions held by the International Labor Organization in Geneva; in the United States, the US Women's Bureau worked with various women's organizations to produce a positive report on the charter. The National Woman's Party opposed the charter, however, citing their support for the Equal Rights Amendment to the US Constitution.[52] The NWP objected to the charter's allowance for legislation that might have applied to women only.[53]

Because of this objection, Hutchins argued in her report, it was of paramount importance that the charter be discussed widely prior to a conference, called by individual sponsors, to be held on the topic in the fall. Moreover, what the charter—and the organizations supporting it—lacked, Hutchins noted, was any representation by African American women. "This was a serious omission," she said, "which must be constantly pointed out, until it is corrected."[54]

Despite all the grassroots work and even the support of Eleanor Roosevelt, the Women's Charter ultimately failed, because the National Woman's Party was able to gain the support of the National Federation of Business and Professional Women's Clubs for the Equal Rights Amendment, which, they felt, would preclude support for the Women's Charter. An inclusive feminist movement was foundering on questions of class.

Undaunted, Hutchins published an enthusiastic review of Child Workers in America, written by her friends Katharine Lumpkin (sister of Grace Lumpkin) and Dorothy Douglas, placing the review in New Masses to emphasize the fact that child labor was not just a women's issue. The review is another instance of Hutchins's quiet but insistent post-1933 practice of drawing attention to the progressive work of "independent women"—in this case, two women who not only coauthored the study but shared their lives as well, like Rochester and Hutchins. Calling the book "the most complete, the most logical, the most unanswerable argument for elimination of child labor that has ever been presented to the American public," Hutchins praised especially the chapters that provided clear refutations of the arguments of opponents of child labor laws. She also took the opportunity to castigate President Nicholas Murray Butler of Columbia University and President Emeritus A. Lawrence Lowell of Harvard for their opposition to child labor laws and noted that Lumpkin and Douglas "find that these lobbyists for child labor are of the privileged classes, constituting 'the vast bulk of the business class of the country,'" thus documenting another face-off between independent women and their upper class male adversaries and suggesting again that working class men were not well served by maintaining gender solidarity with men in positions of wealth and power. Despite these triumphs of the moneyed class,

Hutchins pointed out, Lumpkin and Douglas concluded with an optimistic vision of "an inclusive political party to be created by labor, to include large numbers of wage earners, farmers and the salaried middle classes."[55]

Coincidental with Hutchins's mention of labor as inclusive of farmers, Rochester began to shift the focus of her research and writing to agricultural issues, a shift that culminated in the 1940 publication of her book *Why Farmers Are Poor*. Serving as a member of the CPUSA's Farm Commission, Rochester spent most of the next three years working on the book. She may have met Ruth Erickson and Eleanor Stevenson during her days spent poring over volumes of statistical data in the New York Public Library. Both librarians, Eleanor Stevenson and Ruth Erickson were life partners and committed progressives. They joined the other "independent women" who made up Hutchins and Rochester's circle.

Erickson and Stevenson had met each other in January 1925 when Erickson was assigned to Stevenson's branch of the library. In a 1925 letter, Stevenson sent photos of herself to her brother and his wife, commenting on her appearance—an echo of Hutchins's confrontation with her parents over the same issue at about the same time: "Ted will hate the hair, and I think Glad will rather envy me while wondering how I *can* let myself look like that! Two of the Library girls one day, very interested, asked me if I didn't occasionally get tired of looking like a freak. Of making myself conspicuous with clothes and hair and such. Of 'being diff'rent.'" Apparently she did not get tired of being different.[56] Erickson, too, she described as conventionally unattractive, "except that certain expressions transform her face," expressions Stevenson was still trying to capture on film.

However, the Weimar 1920s of bobbed hair and increasing freedoms for women had become the economically depressed and fascist 1930s, and, like Hutchins and Rochester, Stevenson and Erickson had become increasingly circumspect. The dangers were hardly imaginary. Although most of the attention focused on men, women were not immune from suspicion. It was during the 1930s that the notion of the sexual psychopath was constructed, marking the shift from a discourse of behavior to one of identity. According to Estelle Freedman: "An older, hereditarian tradition merged with new psychiatric concepts to produce a crude model of the psychopath as oversexed, uninhibited, and compulsive. It was this image that found its way into the popular press and ultimately into the law."[57] The police responded by rounding up "perverts," usually male homosexuals. Because Freudian theory stated that homosexuality was the result of arrested development, the assumption was made that attacks on children were most likely initiated by homosexuals. This helped to solidify the notion of the homosexual as a specific—and pathological—identity.[58]

In a September 1937 article in the New York *Herald Tribune*, J. Edgar Hoover announced a "War on the Sex Criminal," capitalizing on newspapers' reporting of lurid sex crimes involving children.[59] Following close to two months' worth of almost weekly articles in the New York *Times*, the *New Masses* published an article on the topic in the October 26, 1937, issue. Asking "Are Sex Crimes Due to Sex?" Michael Brush took exception to the construction of the sex *criminal*, although not the sexual *deviant*. Brush argued that criminalization is the result of inadequate medical treatment of "mental defectives." Due to lack of funding for hospitalization, patients are put on waiting lists or are returned to the streets before they are cured. Brush also acknowledged that medical science does not yet know how to cure such problems. Brush left unexamined the construct of "sex perverts," reframing the conversation and claiming that, because of this lack of funding for hospitalization, "sex crimes are neither a sexual [medical] problem nor a legal problem; they cannot be removed by legal or medical instruments. They are a social problem."[60]

Shifting the frame more deliberately from medical to economic terms, Earl Browder, in a message to Catholics, assured readers that

> Contrary to much slander distributed by reactionary politicians in Catholic circles, the Communists are staunch upholders of the family. We consider sexual immorality, looseness and aberrations as the harmful product of bad social organization, and their increase in America today as largely products of the crisis of the capitalist system, of the demoralization among the upper classes which affects the masses by contagion, and we combat them as we combat all other harmful social manifestations.[61]

None of this spoke to Rochester and Hutchins's history or their commitment to principles outlined by Edward Carpenter. So, although Rochester and Hutchins did not go to extremes to hide their partnership, neither did they talk about it with anyone outside of a small circle of like-minded women. The circumspection worked in the short term, as Hutchins and Rochester were treated with respect in most party circles. They worked hard, and that was what mattered.

Yet beneath the surface, the struggle against fascism continued, and Hutchins would soon be drawn in more intimately—and ultimately more painfully—than she had imagined. On February 27, 1938, Whittaker Chambers advertised for sublease the house that he and Esther had been renting. He had been furloughed from a WPA position at the first of the month.[62] He also apparently abandoned the antifascist work he was doing. The exact date on which he left this job is unclear; however, evidence suggests that he had left his home in Baltimore on or about March 19. By May, around the time of the annual convention of the CPUSA, Chambers was clearly missing. Hutchins was sent to track him down, probably because she had at one time been close to Esther. She took Eleanor Stevenson with her; Chambers knew Stevenson, too, well enough, in fact to know that she was called Steve by friends, a fact that he would deliberately "forget" later. Was there some other design behind the fact that Hutchins and Stevenson were the ones who were delegated the task of locating Chambers? Given later events, it seems likely.

On May 19, 1938, a week before the party convention, Hutchins and Stevenson called at the law office of Reuben Shemitz, Esther Chambers's brother, leaving a note which read: "Dear Mr. Shemitz, There is a *very important* message for your sister: If she or her husband will call either Steve or me, we have some important news for them. Grace."[63] Neither Esther nor Whittaker Chambers saw fit to contact Hutchins or Stevenson. And, for Hutchins, the matter went dormant for more than a decade.

Part Three

Legacies

Chapter Eleven

War against Fascism

Money has everywhere become the ruling power. All the goods produced by the labour of man can be exchanged for money. Money can even buy men, that is to say, it can force a man who owns nothing to work for another who has money. In former times, under serfdom, land used to be the ruling power; whoever possessed land possessed power and authority. Now it is money, capital, that has become the ruling power.

—V. I. Lenin (*Selected Works*, vol. 2, pp. 253–4, quoted by Anna Rochester in *Lenin on the Agrarian Question*, p. 181)

Tension was building, with international and homegrown fascist aggression, the trials in Moscow, and unexplained disappearances. Although Hutchins and Rochester continued to write and publish new feminist and economic arguments in response to the varying exigencies of the times, they were increasingly buffeted by political storms arising from Europe and Asia, and their arguments grew less and less effective. What's more, their solution to the changing sexological taxonomies—to remain hidden in plain sight—discounted the growing politicization of same-sex love and desire. Although this politicizing move, like anti-Soviet publicity, was held in abeyance during World War II, it remained alive underground, waiting for the right postwar moment to emerge.

On March 23, 1938, Rochester had lunch with Marjorie White, a friend of Winifred Chappell. Although White was as strongly feminist as Rochester or Hutchins, she had difficulty understanding their choice of the CPUSA to frame and promote their feminism. White later wrote to Chappell telling her about the lunch and her resultant dissatisfaction. "I always have the feeling that I get nowhere when talking with her or Grace."[1] Rochester and White probably discussed the trials taking place in the Soviet Union and the problem of Trotsky. Certainly it was getting more and more difficult to comprehend or explain what was going on. Still, Rochester joined many of the men in signing a statement in *New Masses* on May 3, 1938, attempting to justify the trials.[2] Hutchins, however, did not sign. Within days, Congress established the House Un-American Activities Committee, known then as the Dies committee for its pugnacious chairman, Martin Dies, D-Texas. The committee would later come to investigate both Rochester and Hutchins, perturbed by their apparent class disloyalties.

Unfazed, Hutchins continued to focus on the issues that had drawn her into the movement in the first place—labor conditions and women's rights—reviewing Mary Heaton Vorse's new book *Labor's New Millions*, an account of the rise of the Committee for

Industrial Organization, later to become the Congress of Industrial Organizations (CIO). Rather than summarize the argument of the book, though, Hutchins showcased Vorse herself: her experience and the importance of her writing in the development of the labor movement. "Covering the steel strike of 1919," Hutchins wrote, "Mrs. Vorse did everything that a labor journalist could possibly do—and more—to help the strikers win. She saw that splendid struggle end in defeat, and she analyzed it in *Men and Steel*." Present at Passaic, Vorse had written a book about that strike and likewise about Gastonia. "But the past two years have seen something new in the labor movement, a force swift, mighty, and unbeatable. Not one major strike in a year, but a dozen or more and in basic industries at the very center of big business itself." Only a skilled labor journalist such as Vorse, Hutchins said, could possibly tell the story of this movement. The story required "what, for lack of a better name, is called *reportage*. It is that much discussed method of journalism that is more than mere reporting, something that includes interpretation, *feeling*, and the conveying of that feeling to others. Mary Vorse has that experience, that skill, and that power"[3] (emphases in the original). Hutchins followed this paean to Vorse with an explanation of the development of the CIO. In this way, Hutchins once again subtly placed a woman at the heart of the overwhelmingly male movement, demonstrating how Vorse had rhetorically intervened at the point of struggle over and over during the past few decades.

Meanwhile, international conditions worsened. Germany had invaded Czechoslovakia in September, gaining Sudetenland through a treaty signed with Britain and France. In November, a German diplomat was shot in Paris, and this incident served as the excuse for Kristallnacht, November 9, 1938.[4] Hutchins read about these events, remembering conversations she, Rochester, and Lucie Myer had had at Back Log Camp just a few months before, and sat down to write an article for *New Masses*, "It Comes on Cat's Feet" (invoking Carl Sandburg's 1916 poem "Fog"). Subtitled "Growth of the Fascist Menace in America," the article described a young camper, "a clever, attractive girl who had recently graduated with honors from a leading American college," who shared her experiences as a graduate student in Germany in an evening lecture. The young woman claimed that Hitler "was much misunderstood in the United States; in reality he had done wonders for the German people"; he had "practically wiped out unemployment, was working for peace in the world, and was preserving Christianity as Europe's bulwark against communism." The young woman had professed disagreement with Nazi principles, "but if the choice must lie, as she feared, between fascism and Communism, wasn't fascism preferable?"[5] Hutchins did not hesitate to criticize women who failed to see beyond their own self-interest. Neither biological womanhood nor advanced education, Hutchins seemed to say, was any guarantee of progressive thought. Even more disturbing, Hutchins explained, was the fact that in the discussion following the lecture, many of those present had agreed with the young woman, arguing that Americans were being unfair to Hitler and that, indeed, "how much less 'danger' (i.e., to comfortable men and women of property) there was in fascism than in Communism."[6] Only a Jewish instructor from Harvard and an English Quaker, both of whom had seen the concentration camps, expressed clear disagreement with the speaker.

Hutchins located the source of enthusiasm for fascism in big business, citing William S. Knudsen, president of General Motors Corp., who claimed that Germany was flourishing under Hitler and called the Reich "'the miracle of the twentieth century.'" In response to the blithe statement of Continental Can's Carle C. Conway that "'This organization in Italy has taken place without . . . the hampering of management or an undue extension of the prerogatives of labor,'" Hutchins added: "This is a model of understatement, since the entire trade-union movement and all its rights have been destroyed in both fascist Italy and Nazi Germany."[7]

Hutchins went on to list the industrialists, religious leaders, elected officials and public individuals who had been advocating fascism, including Henry Ford, Charles Lindbergh, and Angelo Rossi, the mayor of San Francisco. Most disturbing, she said, were those who actively argued against democracy, such as Professor Neil Carothers, dean of the College of Business Administration at Lehigh University, who "denounced the 'sweep of democracy . . . aggravated by depression.'" Roman Catholic priests, she said, routinely preached in favor of "General Franco's fascist war against the democratically elected government of Spain." And any number of protestant preachers joined in, such as the Reverend Samuel Shoemaker of Calvary Episcopal Church in New York City, who recently warned his parishioners against "'too much democracy.'" Shoemaker, she told readers, was a follower of Frank Buchman, founder of the Moral Re-Armament movement, who once stated publicly: "'I thank God for a man like Adolf Hitler.'"[8]

Hutchins had no use for either Frank Buchman or Samuel Shoemaker, who together were building an empire based on antilabor and anticommunist diatribes and a simplistic emotional fundamentalism fueled by group confessions of "sexual sins." In her article, Hutchins mentioned only the fascist sympathies, leaving readers to add to the equation the more publicized meetings featuring confessions of sexual "impurities" and thus create linkages between fascist sympathies and self-involved obsessions with sex devoid of personal commitments.[9]

How could this spread of fascism be checked? Hutchins asked. Middle class Americans had to be informed, so that they would not continue to "repeat the old clichés about Mussolini running trains on time and Hitler removing beggars from Berlin streets. Many of them can be won for the democratic front of all progressive forces by persistent, patient reasoning, based on a knowledge of facts,"[10] Hutchins insisted, alluding to the method to which she and Rochester were now devoting their lives, after a spate of debunking and action plans.

Such reasoning in favor of a democratic front drew Rochester away from her agriculture project briefly in early 1939. Joining with other writers from the seven-hundred-member League of American Writers, she wrote a statement for the league's publication *We Hold These Truths: Statements on Anti-Semitism by 54 Leading American Writers, Statesmen, Educators, Clergymen and Trade-Unionists*. Eight members of the league[11] started the project in November 1938 by contacting "prominent writers, public figures, and outstanding practitioners in certain of the arts and sciences," seeking their statements on anti-Semitism. Rochester took her place alongside such liberal and radical writers as Stephen Vincent Benét, Jerome Davis, Harry Emerson Fosdick, Granville Hicks, Langston Hughes, Harold Ickes, John Howard Lawson, Karl Menninger, Upton Sinclair, Rex Stout, Ida Tarbell, Dorothy Thompson, Mary Heaton Vorse, Mary E. Woolley, and Leane Zugsmith.

Rochester argued that anti-Semitism permeates American culture and requires a political analysis, "for people do not outgrow anti-Semitism merely by learning to like individual Jews, or being horrified by Hitler's brutality." What is necessary, she said, is to point out how Hitler's anti-Semitism is meant to divide, and thus maintain power over, the German people. "Hitler's latest outbursts reflect the economic weakness of his position. Jewish capital is seized to finance his desperately rapid preparations for aggressive war; Jewish workers and tradesmen are expelled to relieve the pressure on Germany's limited food supplies." It would not take much for similar events to take place in the United States, she cautioned. "As the conflict sharpens—and it will sharpen—anti-Semitism will be more definitely encouraged by the reactionaries as an indispensable weapon for separating the Jews from the non-Jews and splitting progressive forces."

Her solution? Like Hutchins, and like their old friend and mentor Scott Nearing—and Lenin before him—Rochester argued for a specific program of education. "Anti-Semitism can be checked and wiped out only by the widest possible program of education, to show, first, how it has been used politically by the worst tyrants of modern times, the Russian Czars and the fascist dictators; and second, how anti-Jewish feeling weakens the forces of democracy in the United States and helps to open the way to fascism in this country."[12] She argued, in short, that a logical political analysis would be stronger than even emotional ties—an assertion that still today could generate debate. In May 1939, Hutchins herself found such an analysis in Ida Tarbell's autobiography, *All in a Day's Work*, which she reviewed briefly for the *Book Union Bulletin*. Championing Tarbell as a feminist, Hutchins conceded that although Tarbell "has never opposed big business as such, she has come out to a clear-cut hatred of fascism, of the strong men who try to make a world to their liking and force us to live in it."[13]

Trying again to take a brief vacation from the world of the strong men, Hutchins and Rochester returned to Back Log Camp in August 1939, where Rochester wrote Hutchins a birthday poem, as she often did, this time on the back of a postcard picturing an edelweiss: "Noble white is Grace's hair/All her thoughts are true and fair/We bring her down from heights above/With daily thoughts of loving love."[14] If not the most elegant verse, it was written from the heart. Yet the moment of tenderness was soon interrupted. On August 28, the Soviet Union, unable to create a mutual defense pact with western Europe, had signed a nonaggression treaty with Germany. Given the intense antifascist work that Communists around the world—including Rochester and Hutchins—had been doing, this was a stunning move for many observers. And things only got worse in the next few days after Hutchins and Rochester returned to New York City. On September 3, British Prime Minister Neville Chamberlain broadcast that Germany must withdraw from Poland by eleven a.m. or face war with England. Germany did not withdraw, and at that point Germany and England were at war.

Unfortunately, the Nazi-Soviet agreement gave US congressmen more opportunities to investigate and disrupt the American left. On Wednesday, September 13, 1939, Alexander Trachtenberg, founder of International Publishers, was called to testify before the Dies committee on the subject of "Un-American Propaganda Activities in the United States." The committee plumbed the publishing activities of those associated with the party, and after some time, the questioning came around to the relationship between International Publishers and the LRA. Trachtenberg testified that the important persons in the LRA were Robert Dunn, Anna Rochester, and Grace Hutchins. Asked whether any of these people were Communists, Trachtenberg responded that Grace Hutchins was. After all, she had run for office for several years on the CPUSA ticket.

Chairman: What about the others?

Mr. Trachtenberg: Miss Rochester, I am not so sure.

Chairman: You would not be surprised, though?

Mr. Trachtenberg: No, I would not. She is quite a good student of communism, and a very good Marxist. She comes of a very good family.[15]

Figure 11.1. Grace Hutchins in the mid-1930s

The committee was not amused by Trachtenberg's linkage of Marxism and "good families," and the questioning continued until the members were convinced that Anna Rochester was not the head of the economics department at the New York Public Library, although she spent every day there studying, and that, actually, she was living on an independent income. This, however, was only the beginning of the government's concern with Hutchins and Rochester's politics and knowledge production activities.

As the Nazi and Soviet armies jockeyed for control of pieces of Poland during September and October 1939, Lydia Cadbury, known among friends and family for her direct and penetrating questions, wanted to continue the conversation from Rochester and Hutchins's previous summer's sojourn at Back Log Camp. On October 12, Rochester responded to a letter from Cadbury asking multiple questions about the CPUSA's position on the Nazi-Soviet pact. Writing three and a half single-spaced pages, Rochester tried to answer those questions, acknowledging their mutual commitment to fact-based persuasion as the foundation of democracy. "I am glad to hear from you and to know that you want to hear our side," she began. "And I am glad too to write you how things look to me, for if I could persuade you—and Henry—to see things just a bit differently I should consider it a great achievement."[16]

Rochester summarized, listing the historic attempts to undermine the Soviet Union and saying that what these events signified was that "*all* the chief powers of Europe, and also Japan, have been consistently eager to destroy the socialist country." Not only were all the European nations plus Japan attempting to undermine the USSR, but, had the "capitalist 'democratic' countries not prevented any legal sale of war materials to the duly constituted republican government" of Spain during the Spanish Civil War, fascist forces, including Germany and Italy, would have been defeated. In other words, Rochester suggested, the world would not be in its current condition had the capitalist countries come to the aid of Spain in a timely manner.

This brought Rochester specifically to the question of the Nazi-Soviet pact—which she assured Lydia Cadbury was not an alliance. British leadership, she argued, was trying hard to turn Hitler's aggression to the East. Although the Soviet Union had attempted, by joining the League of Nations, to promote collective security against fascism, the capitalist nations had little interest. All this became apparent during the negotiations to protect Poland from Hitler. Britain refused to allow the Soviets to assist in this effort, and "the Soviet Union turned to quite different tactics with the record speed that has upset some liberals' equilibrium." However, she pointed out, "what most people have failed to grasp is the fact that the new tactics did not and do not involve any basic change in underlying policy."

What mattered most in all of this, Rochester insisted, was the basic difference between the Soviet Union and fascism or Nazism, which

> lies in their inner constitutions, using that word in its broadest sense. All the European powers are capitalist powers, which means that the function of the state is primarily the protection of capitalist property rights. This is supremely true in nazi Germany, since the essential nature of fascism is to protect the privileges of the capitalist class when its economic structure is in crisis and the capitalists find that the apparatus of democratic government is being turned against their capitalist class interests.

Thus, friendship between Hitler and Stalin was impossible, she said.

"I do most deeply agree with you," Rochester concluded, "in hoping that the countries will make peace," although Britain and France would not want to replace the economic system in Germany, she thought, only the man in charge, with someone less brutal. "We Communists are not 'violent' as you imagine. Revolutionary changes might be speeded by a continuation of the war, but we realize quite as deeply as you do that wars bring vast misery to the poor people. And we know that economic forces will create new revolutionary crises without the aid of war." She hoped, she said finally, that Lydia Cadbury would share the letter with Henry. Rochester wanted to reach beyond private conversation into the halls of Harvard.

Hutchins, too, sought to mitigate the increased red-baiting that the pact had provoked. When *The Nation* writer Freda Kirchwey published such an article, Hutchins wrote back on October 15, 1939, lecturing the editors on the meaning of liberalism. "A true liberal," she cautioned, "attempts to understand the unpopular, minority viewpoint. He does not prejudge an issue before he has all the facts necessary from which to draw his conclusions." However, *The Nation* had now "forfeited its right to be called a liberal journal" because of the tone of articles recently published on the Nazi-Soviet pact. "The temper in which *Nation* editors have approached the subject is illustrated by Freda Kirchwey's article in the October 14th issue. The second half of her article purports to be a plea for tolerance—even for American Communists! But before the reader can arrive at this point, he is subjected to violent anti-red yelpings, indistinguishable from those of the Dies-Waldman hounds in pursuit of their prey."[17]

Hutchins and Rochester were feeling the proximity of the hounds and responded by becoming more careful in their personal correspondence. Whenever one left the other, even for a day, she wrote at least one letter, discussing work, giving thanks for favors conferred, and conveying love. On November 13, 1939, Rochester traveled to Washington to collect information for her next book. Once in Washington, having had a day of meetings with various consultants, she wrote to Hutchins, saying that she had "at last . . . had a real conference with our elusive friend," which she pronounced "very satisfactory," requiring "no major changes in the chapters already written." This person provided, she added, "constructive help in thinking out the closing chapter."[18] The fact that she did not name someone in a letter was a new development, an indication of the increasingly necessary secrecy as the FBI and the Dies Committee applied more pressure to American Communists.

Thanking Hutchins for seeing her off, Rochester confessed guiltily, "I never do that for you. Poor Grace. But very dear Grace." Continuing to fret about her behavior, Rochester referred to the satirical review in that day's *New York Times* of *Gentlemen Behave*, a 304-page tome by Charles Hanson Towne covering all manner of incorrect male behavior, including such offenses as gum-chewing in public and the wearing of one's hat on the back of one's head in warm weather. "I *hope* I'm never as bad as Towne is made out to be," she worried. "You have all the love I know how to give," she closed, losing her fear, for the moment, of uninvited third party readers.[19]

Indeed, Hutchins did think of the small and large personal expressions that served to hold people together. Undoubtedly it was she who prompted Mother Bloor to arrange a party in celebration of Rochester's sixtieth birthday on March 30, 1940, inviting a long list of Rochester's friends to her home, April Farm, near Coopersburg, Pennsylvania, for an "indoor picnic" with farm-raised pork and chicken. Writing to Rochester prior to the event, Bloor enthused: "Watch and Pray for a Sunny Day," then added drolly, "Lizzie says I've 'got religion.' She didn't mean it as a good acquisition, either. When you come we will vote on it," she said, a wry commentary on those accusing Communists of being antidemocratic.[20]

Rochester's party was one of the last happy times for many of those attending. On February 5, 1940, the American Civil Liberties Union passed a resolution "hold[ing] it inappropriate for any person to serve on the governing committees of the Union or on its staff, who is a member of any political organization which supports totalitarian dictatorship in any country, or who by his public declarations indicates his support of such a principle."[21] The majority of the ACLU board members were not placated by explanations of the Nazi-Soviet pact, such as the one Rochester had sent to Lydia Cadbury, and thus expanded their antagonism from the homegrown Nazi organizations to the CPUSA, a supporter of the Soviet Union.

One of the aims of the group promoting the resolution was to force the resignation of Rev. Harry F. Ward, then chairman of the ACLU, because of his historical association with Communists who had been welcomed in the American League for Peace and Democracy, formerly the American League Against War and Fascism. Although Harry F. Ward did resign from the ACLU, Elizabeth Gurley Flynn refused out of principle to vacate her seat on the board. A trial of Flynn, inspired by Norman Thomas,[22] was held on May 7, having been postponed due to the sudden illness and death of Flynn's only child in April. After a long and acrimonious discussion, Rev. John Haynes Holmes broke a nine-to-nine vote by siding with those who supported the resolution. Flynn, a member of the National Committee of the CPUSA, argued: "The demand for my resignation is an attempt to force a minority to conform to the political views of the majority or get out. I refuse to resign because I will not be a party to the saving of the face of this anti-civil liberties majority, nor to whitewashing their red-baiting."[23]

The board had claimed that Communists had never been elected or appointed to office within the ACLU; Flynn countered that charge, saying that not only had she been open about her CPUSA membership when she was elected to the board, but the board had, in the past, accepted without question "the reelection of Wm. Z. Foster, after his known membership in 1921 in the Communist Party" and "the election of Anna Rochester, known to be a Communist Party member."[24] This statement about Rochester did not escape the attention of the FBI, then expanding its exploration of the Left in the United States.

Rochester sprang to Flynn's defense, offering a statement that Flynn issued as a press release on May 13. Rochester insisted: "When I was elected to the Board about eleven years ago, the fact that I was a Communist was known to Roger Baldwin, Norman Thomas and other members of the Board. In fact, I was given to understand that one reason they wanted me on the Board was that I would represent the Communist viewpoint. I resigned of my own free will, long before they had turned into a red-baiting organization."[25] Four days later, Roger Baldwin, paid staff member of the ACLU and a vigorous supporter of the expulsion process, wrote to Rochester, thanking her for sending him a copy of Flynn's press release. He hadn't known that Rochester was a Communist, he said disingenuously, suggesting that perhaps she had "made up the memory to suit present circumstances."[26] Hutchins was incensed by this prevarication. She wrote back to Baldwin the next day, reminding him of exactly how he had known that Rochester was a CPUSA member before she was elected to the ACLU board.[27]

Among members of the National Committee, Vida Scudder, to her credit, voted against ratifying the expulsion. However, not surprisingly, Rochester and Hutchins's old colleagues John Nevin Sayre and A. J. Muste voted in favor, as did Sherwood Eddy. After the trial, a group of supporters, Robert Dunn, Nathan Greene, A. J. Isserman, Corliss Lamont, William B. Spofford, and Mary van Kleeck, published a pamphlet explaining the minority position. Dunn, Greene, Isserman, Lamont, and Spofford had all been present at the trial and had voted in Flynn's favor. They pointed out that "when the present wave of hysteria in America is over and calmer days have arrived, we are convinced that most of those who disagree with us now will realize that we stood firm for the basic principles of the Union and that the organization must return to those principles."[28] It would be a long time, and there would be more acrimony between former friends, before calmer days arrived and the ACLU regained its former stature as an upholder of free speech.

This troubling episode, reminiscent of the rifts that had sundered the Socialist Party some twenty years earlier, along with even more distressing international events—Germany's invasion of Holland, Luxembourg, and Belgium, among others—served to distract attention from the publication of Rochester's latest book, *Why Farmers Are Poor*. Nonetheless, the *Daily Worker* promoted the book, running an article on April 29 headlined "Rochester Papers, Please Copy!" The article, featuring a large picture of Anna Rochester and referring to her Rochester, New York, ancestry, began: "If the designation, 'Scholar of the Working Class,' existed in the United States, there is no doubt that it would be conferred by acclamation on Anna Rochester." Her new book, said Stephen Peabody, author of the article, was "the first book which makes a comprehensive study of agriculture from the Marxist view point by anybody writing in English." Explaining her cross-class alliances, he said: "Anna Rochester's alignment with the working class reemphasizes the fact that every declining ruling class produces persons who understand the historical processes amid which they live and because of that comprehension, join the new class which is arising to displace the reactionary rulers, and to release the great progressive forces in society." Moreover, he said, Rochester did not fit the stereotype of a tedious scholar. "She takes part in numerous progressive activities with an energetic spontaneity that would be exceptional in anyone half her years. . . . She is a magnificent example to all those in the labor movement, especially the youth, of how life-long activity in worthwhile causes enriches one's perspective and develops one's sense of participation in the historic struggle of mankind."[29]

Rochester's argument in *Why Farmers Are Poor* was that farm and nonfarm economies are inextricably related. In fact, she said, agriculture technically *is* industry, although it develops at a different pace than factory production. Throughout the nineteenth century, farmers produced a surplus, she pointed out. And

> while this surplus produce from American farms helped to make possible the rapid growth of industry and banking in this country, it held the farmers bound by a thousand threads to the movements of the entire capitalist world. It made them subject as a class to the traders and bankers in this country. It made their prosperity depend not on weather and diligence but on the ups and downs of employment and production and markets and prices in Liverpool and Hamburg and Buenos Aires and Bombay.[30]

The question of Rochester's Marxist-Leninist theoretical framework preoccupied reviewers, as it had before. Although she would have preferred that readers accept her arguments, at least her work was taken seriously and engaged on the same terms as that of any male writer. Addison T. Cutler, writing for *Science and Society*, said "Any working scholar tackling this job in earnest would need to utilize the best possible combination of theoretical and statistical instruments. This means Marxian theory at base." If anyone should think otherwise, he said, "try to imagine for one moment how such an analysis of American agriculture could possibly be made within the framework of neo-classical or 'marginal utility' economics. Or could it be done, perhaps with no theory at all—merely statistics guided by common sense?"[31]

T. W. Schultz of Iowa State College, writing for *The Journal of Political Economy*, seemed to beg the question. "Had Miss Rochester set aside her doctrine that surplus value is created only by labor," he insisted, "she would have seen that the evidence which she has so carefully and painstakingly marshaled demonstrates plainly and forcefully that farmers and their families are poor because in the main the only resource they have to offer is their own labor, which is essentially unskilled in character and commands a relatively low return." Nonetheless, he acknowledged, the book is valuable because of the "shrewd insights of the author which frequently open broad revealing avenues to the reader which those who are too close to the problems of agriculture are often prone not to see."[32]

Rupert B. Vance of the University of North Carolina offered a more generous appraisal, proclaiming the book "indispensable to agricultural economists." He solved the pesky problem of Marxist analysis by making Rochester's theoretical framework disappear altogether. Although "the author writes from a Marxist basis, . . . her pessimistic view of our agriculture is in an economic tradition that has already become orthodox," he said. "Except for occasional references to surplus value, finance capitalism, monopolistic pressures, and the desirability of farmer-labor cooperation, the particular bias of the Labor Research Association is not too evident."[33]

Rochester celebrated the publication of *Why Farmers Are Poor* in early June 1940 at a party thrown by International Publishers. That she was aware of international events and their likely influence on Americans is evident in her remarks to Alexander Trachtenberg afterwards. He wrote back to her, saying that she "needn't worry about not influencing our people with your ideas on the farm question." The book would be read and studied, he insisted. Indeed, it "would grow on people," he punned.[34] However, Rochester may have been correct in her analysis, as the world's attention was indeed being drawn away from domestic problems; on June 18, 1940, Churchill spoke before the House of Commons, anticipating the beginning of the Battle of Britain.

Thanking Rochester for allowing him to publish "two important works which greatly enrich our literature," Trachtenberg had advised her to "rest all summer." To all appearances, that is what she—and Hutchins—did, although Rochester couldn't keep from writing a couple of book reviews. Also, both Hutchins and Rochester probably were instrumental in arranging for the ownership of the *Daily Worker* to be taken over by their friends Susan Woodruff, Caro Lloyd Strobell, and Ferdinanda Reed in an attempt to protect the newspaper from governmental incursions and (probably) give it an infusion of cash. Significantly larger numbers of women were active in progressive political work than had been the case when Hutchins and Rochester joined the CPUSA, in part because of their work.

Rochester's book reviews were attempts to introduce women's issues into the otherwise largely male-dominated conversations about land use and agriculture; both endeavored to construct bridges between liberal- and Communist-inspired analyses by women documenting relationships between people and the land. In each case, she offered supportive commentary focusing on the strengths of the books, drawing women into conversation rather than arguing about the validity of a given theoretical framework. Writing about *Mothers of the South: Portraits of the White Tenant Farm Woman* by Margaret Jarman Hagood for the Sunday *Worker*, Rochester said, "Great vitality and strong human qualities have enabled the poor tenant farmers of the South to survive and develop in spite of exploitation, undernourishment and lack of medical care." The book, therefore, she said, is a strong rebuttal against "the fascist type of argument that southern rural poverty and illiteracy are due to feeble, degenerate racial stock." Because it focused on individuals, she asserted, the book provided a good supplement to Katharine Lumpkin's *The South in Progress*, "a broader and more penetrating analysis of social and political trends." The primary deficiency of the book, however, was the fact that it focused entirely on *white* tenant mothers; "a similar picture of Negro tenants [should] be drawn with equal care and respect," Rochester contended.[35]

Reviewing *My Country, 'Tis of Thee: The Use and Abuse of Natural Resources* by Lucy Sprague Mitchell, Eleanor Bowman, and Mary Phelps for *New Masses*, Rochester said, "Three clever women have given us a rare and tantalizing book about soil, coal, and oil. It is so well written that the conflict between waste and conservation lives against the background of American history and of geological development." Despite the detail with which the authors recounted the plundering of America's natural resources, however, they advocated only reformist solutions. Rochester referred the reader instead not to her own work, but to the work of another woman, *My Native Land*, by Anna Louise Strong, who pointed out that those who worked on the land were required to submit to the demands of government, although the upper classes made government work for their own purposes. "Shall it be a government controlled by the small moneyed class and primarily safeguarding its profits?" Rochester asked, hoping to move readers, as well as the authors, toward a more comprehensive analysis. "Or can we achieve a truly democratic government, controlled *by* the people [and] operating for their interests?"[36]

Unfortunately, this question was not of paramount interest to most people who were observing international events. The German forces were increasing their pressure on western Europe. On September 7, 1940, they bombed London at five p.m., just as workers were leaving their jobs. A week later, they bombed London again in the daylight; this attack signaled the beginning of seventy-six nights of bombing. Then, on September 27, Germany, Italy, and Japan signed the Tripartite Pact, establishing the Axis Powers and agreeing to a plan of cooperation for the next ten years.

Although alert to the continued incursions of Japanese, German, and Italian armed forces around the world, both Rochester and Hutchins continued to focus on the problems of American farmers and laborers. Hutchins published a review of *The American Labor Press: An Annotated Directory* in *New Masses* in October, noting that it was the first such compendium since Solon de Leon produced *The American Press Directory* in 1926. The book classified 676 labor papers according to their orientations (e.g., AFL, CIO, Socialist Party, CPUSA, farmer-labor), she said. The author, John R. Commons, told about finding the files of *The Workingman's Advocate* in the attic of a Kansas farmhouse—and Hutchins hoped, along with Commons, that future researchers would "treasure this directory of the labor press of 1940 as an aid in their efforts."[37] Perhaps. It wasn't wildly popular at the time.

The year 1940 saw not only an increase in lighted factories and a decreasing interest in labor issues but also the loss of one of the last of the older generation of radicals. Shortly after they returned to New York, Hutchins and Rochester learned of the sudden death of their friend Caro Lloyd Strobell, diminishing their constructed family. This death was another loss from among the older generation of women activists who had inspired and accompanied them, following those of Helena Stuart Dudley and Julia Lathrop. Hutchins wrote to Jessie Lloyd O'Connor immediately upon receiving a telegram with the news from Lloyd Goodrich, Caro Lloyd Strobell's nephew and Jessie's cousin. "We shall miss her very sadly," Hutchins said, "and personally I know I have lost one of my dearest friends. She was also one of our ablest research workers," she went on, "always discriminating and careful. Only last week she sent us another batch of material. She kept steadily at work on it all summer." Hutchins let O'Connor know that there would be articles in the *Daily Worker*. (All items were undoubtedly written largely, or at the very least prompted, by Hutchins and Rochester.) But would O'Connor and others in the family be willing to allow a special meeting of remembrance later in the fall in New York?[38] Just as she worked to make women and their accomplishments visible in the movement, Hutchins also made sure that they were recognized and remembered in times of distress.

Some members of the older generation remained—and remained active. In November 1940, when Mother Bloor's autobiography was published by International Publishers, Rochester wrote to her expressing her pleasure with the book; Bloor responded, saying, "Your beautiful letter . . . was so good that I have put it away, not only the letter itself, but the spirit of understanding in the letter, I shall treasure in my heart." She had just returned from a book tour in New York and explained to Rochester how she was using the book: "as a springboard to make others understand the wonderful history of our movement. The real joy it is to be a C. I know," she said, "you feel that always, but in our Book meetings so far, we find that the outsiders are brought *inside*, and seem to understand better than ever before, what we are trying to do." Wordlessly acknowledging Rochester's partnership with Hutchins, she added her love to Hutchins in the final paragraph and in closing.[39]

Hutchins's mother, writing a month later to thank Hutchins for remembering to send flowers on the fiftieth anniversary of the deaths of her sisters, added her love to Rochester, too, although in a postscript. When Hutchins went to Boston in late February to celebrate her mother's birthday, Rochester, mourning the temporary absence, sent her a letter, knitting together as usual their love and their work. "Precious Grace," she wrote, "The time is approaching when you will *not* be coming up the stairs with your cheerful voice and your loving greeting." She confided that she had bought an upholstery needle and would be repairing the ripped chairs in the living room, a proletarian skill she certainly didn't learn at her mother's knee. By this simple act, however, she cemented yet again her relationship with Hutchins. "Very best love to you that I know how to give," she offered in closing.[40]

Hutchins narrated the larger expression of this spirit of women's self-sufficiency in her April 1, 1941, article in *China Today*, "China's Women in the Struggle." In the zones of the Fourth and Eighth Route Armies, "young China," Hutchins explained, "women as well as men, are thinking in terms of democratic government, of equality of opportunity and a higher standard of living for all. To train girls as leaders in this long struggle for a better way of life, the Yenan government has established the Nu Tsz Ta Hsueh or Women's University, where 400 students live in loess caves and work their way through college." The students rose early to work in the fields before their classes, raising the food for their vegetarian diet. They wore cotton clothes and army caps over short hair. "They don't have to use cosmetics to be good-looking," she said pointedly. She then contrasted the lives of these women with the "artificial existence" of others, women of the bourgeoisie who prize silk clothing and makeup above all else, having forgotten "China's struggle for freedom." Carrying within her a thirteen-year-old's horror at the oppression of Chinese girls, Hutchins said that although bound feet were no longer considered acceptable in urban centers, in the outlying areas, "middle-aged and older Chinese women still hobble on those half-feet, 'lily feet' that cost so many tears." She went on to compare the women of the liberated Yenan region with Japanese women, who were still enduring arranged marriages regardless of their level of education.[41] Although Hutchins was depicting progressive Chinese women, astute readers would have realized that her comments should be read globally, and certainly readers ought to think twice before passing judgment on women who chose not to conform to bourgeois standards of behavior and appearance.

As Hutchins and Rochester sought to draw women together across the globe to promote equality, in the United States their efforts did not go unnoticed. On April 1, 1941, J. Edgar Hoover wrote a memo to Mr. L. M. C. Smith, chief of the Special Defense Unit, to accompany a dossier on Rochester he was sending. His recommendation was that she "be considered for custodial detention in the event of a national emergency."[42] Six days later, a similar memo was placed in Hutchins's file. By the end of April, agents had determined that Hutchins owned, or co-owned, the building at 799 Broadway (80 East 11th) that housed the LRA and a host of other left-wing organizations.

Although they took measures to screen others from scrutiny, Rochester and Hutchins sturdily refused to curtail their own activities. Rochester had signed the Call for the Fourth American Writers Congress, held at the Hotel Commodore in New York City June 5–8, 1941. She and Hutchins attended the congress, joining three thousand other participants who listened as Richard Wright eloquently listed the reasons that African Americans might be less than keen on American entry into the war.[43] They also heard Dashiell Hammett announce, prophetically, the US government's campaign against civil liberties.

Clearly, this was a difficult time for those who were seeking to intervene rhetorically. On May 10, the Germans had launched their most devastating air raid on London, killing three thousand people. By this measure, they sought to camouflage their plans to invade the Soviet Union in disregard of the 1939 Nazi-Soviet pact. Most Writers Congress participants, however, like Wright, were firmly antiwar, seeing the escalating conflict as a battle for land and resources between capitalist powers, like World War I.[44] But two weeks after the congress, on June 22, 1941, Germany invaded the Soviet Union, and that changed everything.

During this time of crisis—as she had at other times—Hutchins continued to do the kinship work of the party, offering services that functioned as social glue, speaking at memorials and caring for survivors, offering advice and comfort to those who were questioning party involvement of spouses, offering assistance to those suffering illnesses.[45] She did not draw lines around party membership, though; rather, she extended her care to all who were actively working for social justice. One of those about whom Hutchins worried was her long-time friend Winifred Chappell. Commonwealth College, where Chappell was dean of the faculty during 1939–1940, had closed in 1940, a victim of harassment by a local Arkansas justice of the peace.[46] Chappell joined the People's Institute for Applied Religion, an organization founded by Rev. Claude Williams, with whom she had worked at Commonwealth, but she lacked an adequate system of support. Still, she wanted to work for the People's Institute, even if it meant yet more privation than that to which she had been accustomed. At some point during 1940–1941, Hutchins offered to subsidize her work. The agreement between the two of them was that, in addition to her work with People's Institute, Chappell would research and speak out publicly on conditions in the South. In return, Hutchins would provide between $400 and $500 per year,[47] another means—following the gifts and loans to Devere Allen, Grace Lumpkin, and Esther Shemitz; the underwriting of *The World Tomorrow*, the LRA, and the *Daily Worker*; and the ownership of buildings housing the *Daily Worker* and the Worker's Bookshop—by which Hutchins and Rochester demonstrated the materialist foundation of their rhetorical principles.

Hutchins and Rochester's resources, however, were no match for those of the FBI. Although neither Rochester nor Hutchins seems to have been aware of the specific circumstances, Dashiell Hammett's predictions of a US government campaign against civil liberties were coming true for them in especially intrusive ways.[48] On November 1, 1941, the New York branch of the FBI ordered a thirty-day "mail cover" for Hutchins, asking that the post office trace the names and addresses of her correspondents from the outsides of envelopes. Winifred Chappell undoubtedly was snagged during this time—although the FBI had been keeping track of her at least since 1919.[49]

Slightly over a month later, the Japanese navy and air force attacked Pearl Harbor in Hawaii as well as sites in the Philippines, Guam, and Wake Island, despite the fact that the United States and Japan had not been officially in conflict. By December 8, however, that situation had changed, as Congress declared war on Japan or "on the fascist imperialist government of Japan," as Hutchins clarified in her pamphlet *Japan Wars on the U.S.A.*, published a few days later. She was, of course, making a crucial distinction between the people of Japan and the government, a government whose war plans she had documented as early as 1932 in a book review and 1935 in her pamphlet *Japan's Drive for Conquest*. "Forces endeavoring to enslave the world thus moved toward this hemisphere," she charged. Because Japan, Germany, and Italy had signed the Tripartite Pact, Italy and

Germany declared war on the United States on December 11, 1941. Congress replied on the same day with a declaration of war against Germany and Italy.[50] Reluctantly, Hutchins and Rochester surrendered their pacifism and supported the US entry into the war. And, with US involvement in the war, Hutchins returned to her keen antifascist research and arguments for the first time in several years.

What exactly did Japanese imperialism want? Hutchins asked in her pamphlet. In short, raw materials—primarily oil. In the past, the United States and the Dutch East Indies (now Indonesia) had supplied approximately 75 percent of Japan's oil; however, since early 1941, no oil had been shipped, meaning that Japan was relying on reserves. Thus, "she wants to take by force of arms the oil of the Dutch East Indies," oil that had been developed by a combination of American and British oil companies, including Standard Oil and Royal Dutch Shell. Moreover, US companies had been supplying 91 percent of Japan's iron and steel scrap prior to 1941, when shipments decreased to a fraction of that amount. Other war-based industries suffered similarly.[51]

Hutchins did not produce a simple Allied war argument but offered instead a feminist analysis of Japanese internal propaganda. She quoted from a 1934 Japanese pamphlet issued by the Japanese Ministry of War and adopted as policy by the Japanese parliament: "War is the 'father of creative work, the mother of culture, the vital energy and driving force of the life of the state.'" Without saying as much, she suggested that a government intent on deceiving its own people by emptying out the language of family relationships and replacing it with warmongering deserved the full measure of US retaliation.

Rochester, too, appealed to the American farm population for support in the war effort, providing a 30-page pamphlet, *Farmers in Nazi Germany*, published by Farm Research, Inc.[52] Like Hutchins, she made a clear distinction between the current government of Germany and the German people, especially the farmers. The party's rhetorical tasks, never easy, had been exponentially compounded by the Nazi-Soviet pact. The current position now left the party open to superficial analyses of "flip-flopping." Rochester argued that "this world war means much more than revenge for the sinking of American ships and the Japanese attack on Pearl Harbor. It is determining the conditions of life for all of us in the future. . . . Farmers, no less than others, would be slaves to the Leader's fiendish will if fascism should prevail." She went on to explain the organization of fascism around the needs of big capital, describing first conditions for workers in Germany and then conditions for farmers. She recounted the Reichstag fire, saying that Hitler and "his pal Hermann Goering fixed up a plot to burn down the Parliament Building in Berlin and throw the blame upon the Communists. Their frame-up was very crude," and although the Communists were exonerated, Hitler nonetheless used the event as an excuse to outlaw the Communist Party. This, she said, was the first move against the workers. The second move came two months later, as all trade unions were dissolved. As a sop to the people, the Nazis limited the legal dividend rate; the limitation, however, did nothing to prevent increasing profits, especially to armaments manufacturers. "The inner circles of capitalist-Nazi rulers merely worked out new devices for channeling greater returns than ever before into their own pockets."[53]

German farmers were now required to sell all their grain to the National Food Corporation, Rochester told readers; if they needed any for livestock feed, they had to buy it back at a higher price. They were also required to buy expensive agricultural chemicals from the chemical trusts. And now, at the time of writing, Hitler had drafted all the young men, leaving the farms without sufficient labor. These measures had led, Rochester said, to further impoverishment of the farmers. In those countries conquered so far, people were starving, as the Nazis took their crops for war purposes. In the Soviet Union, however, people had destroyed their crops rather than let them fall into Nazi hands. Americans must "hold our country to a course of liberty and expanding democracy," Rochester contended. Certainly America was not perfect: we had "Hearst and Ford and Colonel McCormick of the *Chicago Tribune* who encourage fascism at home."[54] Yet we had a strong tradition of freedoms, she insisted, that would support us as we both defended our nation and demolished the fascist military machine.

Hutchins and Rochester's support for the international war effort did nothing to stop the covert war against them at home, and the freedoms Rochester was celebrating were not as strong as she would have liked. The results of the FBI-initiated mail cover on Hutchins showed that most of her correspondence came from her brother Henry in New Haven, Connecticut. The agents apparently didn't know that Henry was her brother, so they asked the New Haven field office to "conduct a discreet neighborhood investigation relative to the associations and activities of this individual." They planned to snoop around in Hutchins and Rochester's neighborhood as well, researching the ownership of their apartment, among other things. It took until April 1942 for the FBI to determine that Henry Hutchins "bears a good reputation," by which they apparently meant that he was not connected with the CPUSA.[55]

During that time, agents probably noticed that Henry and his new wife Alice had had a baby, Mary Louise, and that Hutchins and Rochester called them and sent flowers after receiving a special delivery letter announcing the 7 lb. 10 oz. news. Hutchins traveled to Boston to see the new baby—Henry's first child at age fifty-three—in late January, undeterred by the slushy streets and carrying a baby blanket as a gift. While there, she had the good sense to compliment Alice on her arrangement of the apartment, a comment which pleased Alice and helped to ease a relationship made difficult by Alice Hutchins's class anxieties.[56] Having married into a Boston Brahmin family, Alice Hutchins struggled with her own feelings of inferiority, and she could not begin to understand a sister-in-law who had deliberately cast off much of her privilege and aligned herself with the working class. Alice Hutchins's anxieties would only be exacerbated ten years later when Hutchins refused to be intimidated by Congressional committees and Department of Justice functionaries.

At this point, however, few people were aware of what was unfolding in the offices of the FBI. On February 23, 1942, Rochester was placed in Internal Security Group A: "Individuals believed to be the most dangerous and who in all probability should be interned in event of War." Given that the United States was already at war, "War" suggests advance planning for conflict with the Soviet Union. Whittaker Chambers, who by now was making himself useful by naming certain carefully selected names, informed the FBI that "there were certain persons in the CP who supplied members with money. Grace Hutchins was mentioned as such a financial agent." (Thus he described the loans made to Esther and himself.) He said that he had been told "that Grace Hutchins was the chief financial transactor for the Communist Party."[57] He may have been referring to the fact that she served as treasurer of the party's campaign committee during the latter 1930s or that she had been treasurer of the New York state section of the party, both matters of public knowledge. Chambers, however, in what would become his trademark hyperbolic manner, spun an ordinary fact into self-serving high drama. This statement to the FBI marked Chambers's first sortie in a skirmish with Hutchins that would develop into a prolonged and public battle, with implications extending far beyond the two of them. And just as Grace Hutchins and Eleanor Stevenson had been the ones sent to retrieve Chambers, Chambers's choice of Hutchins to name at this point could not have been accidental.

However, Hutchins knew nothing of Chambers's stories at this point. And by now, there was plenty of anti-Axis propaganda available and little need for them to contribute more, so Rochester and Hutchins turned back to challenging both poverty and racism at home, reminding readers that wartime patriotism should not paper over the serious ongoing structural problems in the United States. In the February 17 issue of *New Masses*, Hutchins continued her practice of extending and promoting the work of other progressive women, reviewing Grace Abbott's writings from the late 1930s, which had been edited by her sister Edith Abbott into a collection entitled *From Relief to Social Security*. She cited Grace Abbott's 1939 statement that " 'Relief has at all times been necessary, and the sharp curtailments of WPA have always meant sudden and unexpected increases in the relief load. . . . These relief crises have left their physical marks on the very bones of the children.' " Even now in 1942, Hutchins commented, five million people were jobless and layoffs continued, with defense employment unable to absorb the numbers laid off in other industries. She then pointed to the logic of Grace Abbott's call for the extension of Social Security to a much greater segment of the population than called for in the original legislation. In the current system, both agreed, relief would always be necessary.[58]

Rochester, too, focused on the problem of irregular employment and the gaps in social services, especially for migrant laborers, in her review of Carey McWilliams's *Ill Fares the Land*. Migrant laborers, she emphasized, did not qualify for Social Security. In all but four states they had no access to workmen's compensation, and they were excluded from coverage under the Fair Labor Standards Act. As a result of constant moving, they were ineligible for any forms of relief. It was critical, she said, that they organize for survival.[59]

Organizing was far from easy, though. Mother Bloor wrote to Rochester describing a two-day visit from an organizer for the National Farmer's Union, a Dr. M. Dickinson. She had showed him Rochester's new book, *Why Farmers Are Poor*, she said, "When, Lo! and Behold he grabbed "Rulers of America" and became utterly fascinated with it." Dickinson, however, was a "real Southerner." When he picked up Bloor's autobiography, he commented that he agreed with her "on political and economic equality for the negroes" but could not "believe in Social Equality." She said to him, "In other words you wouldn't want to sit down to the table with colored folks." " 'That's just it,' he answered." She despaired, she said, of ever reaching "the masses of men and women who still live, move, and have their being in darkest ignorance of what *real freedom*, real democracy actually means." Choosing Paul's admonition to the Athenians about the ubiquitous nature of God and against the worship of human-constructed altars to articulate her despair over the possibility of reaching people grounded in racism, Bloor suggested that racism is more than idolatrous; that it imbues humans with a negative, "darkened" source of life and spirit. How, then, can one intervene at the point of struggle? Where, in fact, is the point of struggle? Still, she did not give in to this despair, saying that she was so happy to see new faces all the time, giving her the assurance of "ultimate victory." Indeed, she said, she was even feeling closer now to Rochester and to Hutchins and other comrades. "Your understanding means so much to me these days," she said, and closed: "with love always, Mother."[60]

Hutchins responded again by strengthening social ties, arranging a birthday celebration for Mother Bloor, who was turning eighty that year. Hutchins, Elizabeth Gurley Flynn, Josephine Truslow Adams, and Audley Moore[61] sent out messages to selected comrades, inviting them to send greetings to Mother Bloor on her eightieth birthday and to Anita Whitney on her seventy-fifth. "In the stern and grim realities of our lives today," they said, "there are but few occasions for rejoicing." In fact, there had been few opportunities to open the discourse to women lately, with men marching off to war. But the two birthdays were such occasions, because the "lives [of Bloor and Whitney] emphasize the progressive role of women in all the past struggles for human rights," Hutchins insisted. "They are a glorious example to all younger women today. . . . To annihilate the barbaric Nazi concepts of women, to help free our sisters who are suffering under their cruel enforcement in the conquered countries, we must emulate the unconquerable spirit of just such great fighters as these."[62]

Hutchins's own birthday—her fifty-seventh—was celebrated quietly by her family and friends, the "stern and grim realities" preventing anything more elaborate. Her mother sent a check, saying that she wished she could have bought her a gift, but that gasoline rationing prevented any trips other than those made to meet the trains of arriving visitors. "Here is a check for a bit of cheer," she said, "in these sad days with best wishes for a happy day and a happier year than seems possible now. . . . At any rate, it goes with a great deal of love." She added that she hoped that Grace would take at least half a day off on her birthday.[63]

This loving exchange with her mother was one of Hutchins's last; three weeks later, Hutchins rushed to Boston after learning that her mother had fallen and was being cared

Figure 11.2. Anna Rochester in the 1940s

for in Phillips House, a medical facility. She planned to stay for two days, returning on Sunday in order to return to work on Monday: an issue of *Railroad Notes* was due out the following month.

Soon realizing the seriousness of the situation, Rochester wrote to Hutchins, offering to come to Boston to be with her. Whether Hutchins wanted to spare Rochester the stress of traveling to Boston or whether she actually felt that her mother would recover is unclear. The following day, after a worried telephone call, Hutchins wrote, reassuring Rochester of her continuing love: "No, dearest Anna," she wrote, "I do not for a moment regret my independent life. Mother came to understand it and herself thought it was better all 'round. Even the relatives and friends understand it now and think it quite natural in my case that I do not live in Boston." Then, in a world at war and facing her mother's imminent death, Hutchins added a line placing her partnership with Rochester at the center of life, a clear challenge to forces that sought to characterize same-sex partnerships as nonprocreative and therefore antilife: "Of course nothing in the world would make me change or regret our precious partnership—life itself to me. Your own loving Grace."[64]

Susan Hutchins died on September 20, 1942. She had been an active participant in Boston society—a member of the Society of Colonial Dames and the Chilton Club

Figure 11.3. Grace Hutchins in the 1940s

(Boston's most exclusive women's club)—and had served on the boards of directors of the Baldwinsville Hospital and the Home for Aged Women. Services were held at Trinity Episcopal Church, Copley Square, on the afternoon of September 22, with interment in the family plot at Mt. Auburn Cemetery, next to her husband, son, and two daughters. Of her family of origin, Hutchins was left with only her brother Henry, apart from an aunt in Boston and an uncle, from whom she was estranged, in New Mexico.

Hutchins's life with Anna Rochester continued to be her foundation, as she wrote in a message accompanying a gift three months later: "For my beloved Anna at this Christmas time with a love that deepens through the years, from Grace." Although she remained in touch with her brother throughout her life and enjoyed visits from her nieces, Hutchins had formed a closer family by this time with Rochester, Lucie Myer, Bob Dunn and his wife and son, Mother Bloor, and other comrades, a constructed family organized around work, usually writing and publishing, aiming to benefit others beyond themselves.

During this time, Anna Rochester made several more efforts to provide farmers with her economic analyses, none notably successful. Although she could occupy Marxist-Leninist discourse with ease, making these concepts available to farmers was another matter. Her first attempt after *Why Farmers Are Poor* was an explanation of Lenin's agricultural commentaries, *Lenin on the Agrarian Question*. Here, she argued forcefully that Lenin viewed the study of economics not as an end in itself but as way to develop useful action. Marx's intent in writing *Capital* was to explain the economic laws driving society; Lenin extended this analysis to agriculture. What this meant in Russia and in Europe generally, she said, was that Marxists and reformist Socialists differed in their analyses of the role of the peasants in bringing about a socialist revolution. Reformist Socialists did not "recognize the essentially capitalist nature of small-scale agriculture producing for the market." They dreamed of a romantic return to the soil, "oblivious to the economic forces which operate to undermine it and which make possible and necessary the struggle for a more productive, more civilized form of agriculture."[65]

After recapping Lenin's analysis of the effects on agriculture of the movement from feudalism to capitalism, Rochester offered a brief analysis of conditions for farmers in the United States, comparing them with agricultural development in the Soviet Union. "Our economic history and our own farm traditions still color the prevailing approach to the problem of mass poverty on the land," she said. "They make it peculiarly difficult for Americans to abandon the dream that by regulating some abuse, eliminating some obvious injustice, providing some federal aid, we can restore the 'good old days' of our forefathers' farms."[66] It was especially important to recall, she insisted, that there never was an agrarian "golden age" in the United States, although the class lines had been less rigidly drawn in the early days of the country.

What was important now [in 1942], she insisted, was an

> understanding between the organised wage workers and the two mass groups of working farmers—the middle-income commercial producers and the very poor. . . . Without this the United States cannot achieve the national unity which is essential for victory over fascism. And as the war effort develops into a genuine people's war in defense of democratic rights it will bring new changes, both social and political, which may even affect basic economic relationships.[67]

This optimism was lost on reviewers such as 1914 alumna Elizabeth Reynolds Hapgood, who wrote for the *Bryn Mawr Alumnae Bulletin* expressing polite puzzlement over Rochester's elision of the fate of the kulaks.[68] What she wanted, she said, was an explanation. Having heard in detail from the capitalist press that the kulaks were massacred and that millions had starved to death, she wanted to hear about more than "the 'historic resolution of the Central Committee . . . on January 5th, 1930, that the policy of *restricting* the kulaks . . . should now give place to a determined policy of *eliminating* the kulaks as a class.'" She continued: "Miss Rochester speaks of the removal of 'kulaks from European Russia and the Ukraine to the rich Siberian frontier land,' implying generous treatment of them, whereas most of the outside world is under the impression that these removals resulted directly or indirectly in the loss of several million lives."[69]

Hapgood's critique represents one of the most significant rhetorical problems that Rochester and Hutchins—and their comrades—were facing. What was the truth? What did happen? And why? More important, what did events in the Soviet Union have to do with American workers? The capitalist media were clearly lying about American workers' struggles, so were they likewise distorting the truth about the Soviet Union? How could another analysis be presented by those who had some media resources but nothing to compare with the scale of Hearst and others? Was readership to be restricted to a small circle of the already convinced?

Responses to the book called for a reappraisal of Rochester's efforts. A California comrade named Grace wrote to thank and praise Rochester for *Lenin on the Agrarian Question*, adding:

> I am sorry that we have been unable to use your pamphlet [probably *Farmers in Nazi Germany*] in the quantities which we anticipated. It is, I am afraid, too presumptuous of a political understanding on the part of California farmers which they do not have.
>
> The word "Communism" to them is still enough of a barrier to prejudice an entire treatise. They are fed daily with prejudice and misstatements of fact and cannot be extricated from such a morass by material of this kind. For those already "in the know" the facts and conclusions are of course irrefutable.[70]

Louis Budenz, with whom Rochester had worked as a member of the LID, was one who was ostensibly "in the know," and his review of *Lenin on the Agrarian Question* in the *Daily Worker* was less a review than a summary, reiterating the need for farmers and workers to join together to defeat Nazism.[71] Although Rochester wrote to him thanking him for the review, he responded saying that he had feared that the review was inadequate and promising that the book would be revisited in the pages of the *Daily Worker* and that union leaders would be encouraged to read it in order to hasten collaboration between organized labor and farmers. Such a return visit, however, never took place, and Louis Budenz would prove to be seriously unreliable in the future.

Lem Harris enthused over the book in the pages of *New Masses*, calling it "brilliant," and "a book for everyone." "All people," he said, "who are deeply concerned over the future of American democracy will want to read and re-read this book, not only in these wartime years, but in the years to come."[72] But few heard Harris's call.

These discouraging responses to *Lenin on the Agrarian Question* pushed Rochester to write material that was more suited to the audience she wished to reach. Her next pamphlet, *Farmers and the War*, did not mention the word "Communism," focusing instead on antifascism. Using the technique that Hutchins had perfected in her missionary days, Rochester opened the pamphlet with a little story, telling of Peter, a farmer's son, who had joined the Navy. Peter's father, "chugging back to the farm in his old car, was proud that Peter was starting off for active duty at sea. He himself had dashed off to fight for democracy in 1917, and he still believed that there are peoples' wars which must be fought to the end, even though the First World War had turned out differently."[73] Farm families such as Peter's, Rochester argued, were critical to the war effort, because they raised the food that supported those who made the munitions as well as those who fought at the front. Not only that, but the "United States is the greatest reservoir of agricultural production remaining within [the] reach" of English and Soviet allies.[74]

What American farmers needed to do, Rochester insisted, returning to the old rhetorical model that called for a plan of action concluding any article or pamphlet, was to develop a sense of common responsibility. Because many farm laborers had been conscripted, large farms were having difficulty finding enough workers—and they sought to hire small farmers away from their farms, causing the small farmer's acreage to lie fallow. This profit-seeking practice on the part of the large farms, Rochester argued, was unpatriotic; they should instead seek the help of the Department of Agriculture and the War Manpower Commission in Washington and allow small farmers to continue to farm: all farms should be productive. Now would be an especially good time to get over racism, she added to her largely Euro-American audience (probably having in mind Mother Bloor's conversation with Dr. Dickinson), as there were thousands of unemployed African Americans in the South, and Northern farms were desperate for help. Women, too, should be hired for farming jobs: "If they can be shipyard welders, and machinists, and operators of a turret lathe, surely they can be trained to master the work of the hired man!"[75] What's more, seasonal laborers hired from Mexico should be paid at least the government-prescribed minimum of thirty cents per hour. The distribution and pricing of food, she acknowledged, had not been perfect. Supporting the Tolan-Pepper bill calling for centralized planning of production and manpower would go a long way toward fixing these problems, she said.

The pamphlet was a creditable effort, but Rochester's skills were still better suited to audiences of middle-class liberals with some policy-making power. In the January 12, 1943, issue of *New Masses*, Rochester published "The Farmer Wants a Plan," an article that did not hesitate to mention the CPUSA by name: "Earl Browder, in his brilliant and constructive analysis of war production problems, at the recent National Conference of the Communist Party, suggested a further development of farm labor measures carried out successfully on a small scale by the FSA [Farm Security Administration]. The government might set up an organization of labor service through voluntary labor battalions for seasonal farm work."[76] Here Rochester unleashed her trademark irony against profit takers: "Large Arizona cotton-growers won their niche in the Hall of Infamy by letting long-staple cotton—badly needed for war textiles—rot in the fields rather than pay a thirty cents an hour minimum promised" in an agreement with Mexico.[77] Rochester herself, it should be noted, along with Lem Harris and Bob Digby, a scholarly man who worked at Farm Research in Washington, had helped produce Earl Browder's report.[78]

As Rochester struggled to influence farmers and worked with a committee of men to advise the head of the CPUSA, Hutchins continued working ceaselessly to promote women, advertising their accomplishments and advocating their inclusion. Much of Hutchins's organizational work now was with the International Workers' Order (IWO), a fraternal insurance organization that started in 1930 as a spinoff of the Workmen's Circle. In 1943, Hutchins joined the IWO. On March 5, 1943, she was quoted in a *Daily Worker* article saying, "I heartily endorse the IWO's present plan of making the month of March IWO Women's Month to enroll many new American women into this great Order."[79] With her membership, she was issued a term life insurance policy, on which she listed Rochester as beneficiary, calling her "friend dependent."[80]

In tandem with advocacy for inclusion, Hutchins also persisted in challenging the standard heterosexual romance narratives that were filling the presses during the war years, reviewing Susan B. Anthony II's book *Out of the Kitchen—Into the War*. "Women are the margin for victory," Hutchins argued, citing Anthony, as well as "'the margin for the economic life of the peace.'" Yet men, she pointed out, often have difficulty accepting women in the workplace. Hutchins began the review, as usual, with an anecdote:

> In a large war plant, Mary Brown operates a crane—a highly skilled job. One of the five million women entering industry since 1940, she has been subject to taunts and ridicule from some of the men. One in particular—call him Joe Smith—made a kissing noise whenever she was around. Joe was in the yard one day, scoffing while Mary swung the giant crane. With one sweep of the great crane arm she scooped him up and held him aloft. When she finally put him down Joe had evidently learned respect for at least one woman's abilities. He has stopped scoffing.[81]

Such individual actions might be effective, but for lasting change, said Anthony, great-niece of the well-known suffragist leader, women need to be included in the unions.

While drawing attention to Anthony's book and emphasizing the importance of mass action, Hutchins took the opportunity to append a none-too-subtle critique of traditional heterosexual power arrangements and the culture of romance that supported those arrangements. The mininarrative began with Joe's power-driven "kissing noises," meant to reduce Mary Brown to the status of sexual object, and ended with Mary Brown "sweeping him off his feet," as it were, rendering Joe powerless and revealing the inequality built into stories of "romance."

Apart from the review of Anthony's book and a review of Dr. Alice Hamilton's autobiography for *New Masses*, Hutchins wrote little during this time, devoting herself to Rochester, keeping the LRA funded, and providing some of the emotional work that held the party together. "Your little 'flower' note touched my heart," Mother Bloor wrote to Hutchins in early 1943. "You are so *human*, so understanding." Later that year, Hutchins wrote a letter to the *Daily Worker* informing readers that the grandson of Ferdinanda Reed, co-owner of the paper, had been killed in the defense of Leningrad.[82] And a month after that, when Jacob Golos, a representative of Amtorg, the Russian trade organization, died suddenly, Hutchins was called upon as a representative of the IWO to take care of the arrangements, much to the annoyance of Elizabeth Bentley, Golos's lover.[83] (Some time later, Bentley, bereft of Golos, discovered that the men at the FBI would pay a lot of attention—and money—to her if she would talk to them about her experiences. This partnership resulted in a book that helped to fuel the anticommunist hysteria of the late 1940s and 1950s.[84])

Still attempting to find an intellectually respectful means of reaching farmers, Rochester was, by this time, finishing her next project: a history of the Populist movement in the United States. Subtitled "The Rise, Growth, and Decline of the People's Party—A Social and Economic Interpretation," the small book aimed to show how the Populist movement arose and "why it failed to achieve economic and political freedom for people."[85] This book was not intended to be a scholarly treatise but rather an organizing tool, an inexpensive and accessible way of reminding small farmers of their history and their linkages with the labor movement. Not only did Rochester address these groups, she was careful to include both women and African Americans in her focus, noting the ways in which members of these groups had participated or had been excluded. "The struggle which culminated in the People's Party [in 1892] was primarily a defensive movement of farmers and other small business interests against the relentless advance of finance capital," she argued.[86] The basis of Populism was, in short, the mortgage.

The Populist Movement in the United States was Rochester's first attempt to write a popular history, and, like her other recent work, it met with mixed reviews. E. L. Bogart in the *American Economic Review* could not have been less happy with the book, taking Rochester to task for, among many faults, relying almost exclusively on secondary sources,[87] but a writer for the *Springfield Republican* was enthusiastic, referring to Rochester as an "authority on America's agrarian life" and indicating that she "has presented the essential facts and has done an excellent job of interpreting them in the light of American political and economic life and developing tradition."[88]

Judy Peterson, writing in *Science and Society*, pointed to the book as "the first to attempt to relate specifically the problems of the People's Party of the nineties to the present fight against fascism."[89] However, she found Rochester's analysis underdeveloped on the point of "the relationship of the developing working class to agrarian radicalism in the nineties."[90] She also disapproved of Rochester's condemnation of Vice President Henry Wallace, seeing him as an important progressive figure and arguing that "the utilization of our productive capacities in the years to come will not be achieved by advocating the nationalization of banks and industries, whatever the virtues of such nationalization might be. It will rather be achieved by the harmonious cooperation of the American worker and farmer and industrialist within the framework of the two-party system and capitalism, in close collaboration with the other capitalist democracies of the world and their great socialist ally."[91]

Rochester herself had acknowledged that she did not see the American people embracing socialism any time soon, but she apparently had not anticipated the rightward direction that would be taken by the CPUSA in late 1943, a new alignment alluded to in Peterson's reference to "the harmonious cooperation of the American worker and farmer and industrialist." Although Rochester did adapt quickly to the new war-driven policies, the countermove that followed would serve to disrupt her carefully established and pioneering position within the party leadership.

Chapter Twelve

Love and Loyalty

The basic principle of this country as embodied in the Bill of Rights of the U.S. Constitution was violated during 1947–1948 as never before in the past 150 years of its history.

—Grace Hutchins (Labor Research Association, *Labor Fact Book 9*, 71)

Anna Rochester and Grace Hutchins had committed themselves to intervening rhetorically at the point of struggle, but as the war progressed and capitalist and socialist countries allied themselves against fascism, locating the point of struggle for workers in the United States became increasingly difficult. In June 1943, as a means of promoting good will and cooperation among the antifascist countries, the Communist International dissolved itself. The Comintern's move encouraged Hutchins and Rochester to revisit old friendships, reweaving webs of love and loyalty; it did not, however, dissuade the FBI from burrowing into the lives of Americans, often disrupting such connections.

The Red Army had been fighting the Nazi army on Soviet soil while the United States and Britain postponed an invasion of France. In December 1943, Roosevelt, Churchill, and Stalin met in Teheran, Iran, and agreed upon a date for the invasion, opening a second front. The CPUSA, under the leadership of Earl Browder, interpreted this move as an indicator that in the postwar years capitalism and socialism would coexist peacefully and that labor and finance capital would work together productively in the United States. This sunny set of assumptions led the National Committee of the Communist Party to propose re-forming in January 1944 as an educational organization, the Communist Political Association, rather than as a political party, a move that was confirmed at the party's convention during May 20–22, 1944.

Responses to Hutchins and Rochester's overtures of renewed friendship never failed to allude to differences yet often acknowledged the shared identities that transcended these differences. In mid-February 1944, Rochester and Hutchins even went up to Boston to visit Hutchins's old friend Lucy Sturgis. Writing to Hutchins after the visit, Sturgis said: "Even if I did not admire [Anna Rochester] for her own sake,—brains, zeal, convictions, loyalty,—etc. I would always be grateful to her for making your life so full of satisfaction and worth-while activity."[1] This was a generous statement coming from a woman who had confessed her love to Hutchins thirty years earlier, saying, "If you were a man, I would marry you tomorrow!"[2]

Pleased with a Christmas card from Rochester and Hutchins, Vida Scudder wrote back: "Always I have gone on," she said provocatively, "thinking of myself as your comrade although no longer your Companion." After testing the waters with several challenging political statements, she retreated, saying: "You'll like to know about our private life. It is serene." Returning to their common political interests, Scudder confessed that she persisted, "however Stalin decrees, in singing the Internationale in my heart. But I suspect," she said "that only Christians have a right to sing it." Then, seeming to catch herself, she added: "Oh, I shouldn't have written you that!" She was "keen," she said, "to see Anna's book [on populism]." And she closed, reminding Rochester and Hutchins that "we both love you dearly."[3]

Scudder was not the only one eager to convert Rochester and Hutchins to a different political orientation at this moment. Molly Dewson wrote to Rochester in early February 1944, telling her that "the Porter-Dewsons are reading your book aloud,"[4] a quiet acknowledgment of their partnership grounded in political work. "Now Anna that you are to choose between the Dem. and Rep. Parties, I expect we are to become fellow workers. Does this mean I can look for a small contribution to the Women's Division [of the Democratic Party] some day?" Dewson also expressed approval of Earl Browder's change in direction, telling Rochester:

> Maybe people cannot be trained sufficiently to make a democratic government the best kind. I do not know but temperamentally I am against goose stepping. If the people prefer some more socialistic government I am all for having the majority have their chance to experiment. That is the reason why I am so glad to hear Browder say that is what he wants. It shows real belief in communism when its leader is willing to get it by education and not by the force of a minority.[5]

Although Dewson revealed, in her line about the "force of a minority," a fundamental misunderstanding about the aims of the CPUSA, she also clarified the questions that the party's shift in direction was raising. To what degree should the party modify its program in order to appeal to people who are "train[ed] to individualistic thought and action,"—Dewson's conception of the foundation of democracy? Yet, like Scudder, Dewson closed fondly: "My love to both you girls."[6] Polly Porter, Molly Dewson, Lucy Sturgis, Vida Scudder, and Florence Converse all belonged to the circle within which Rochester and Hutchins had met each other and which had nurtured their love and their partnership and had given them the courage to spend their lives trying to create more space in the world for women.

The FBI, however, did not change course. Both Hutchins and Rochester had for several years been on the FBI's "most dangerous" list, those scheduled to be detained should the United States go to war against the Soviet Union. In July 1943, the attorney general decided that the classification system was not useful; this did not mean that surveillance ended, however. Instead, the "most dangerous" were placed on a "key figure" list. The FBI took note of the fact that Rochester and Hutchins attended the 26th Anniversary Dinner of the National Council of American Soviet Friendship, held at the Hotel Commodore in New York City on February 22, 1944. Later that spring, on April 3, an informant reported on a conversation Alexander Trachtenberg had with him and Hutchins, discussing what should be done about an article that had appeared in the *New York Times* the previous day.[7] Agents were eager to intervene in the already less-than-free exchange of ideas.

The FBI, too, subscribed to a material rhetoric. Seeking to quash ideas by throttling the funding behind them, the FBI paid particular attention to gifts and to questions of ownership of property used by CPUSA (now CPA)-related publications. Because she now had more access to wealth (as she was now receiving a larger portion of the trust fund income after her mother's death), Hutchins began giving greater sums to *New Masses* and the *Daily Worker*. In October 1944, she donated $100 to the People's Radio Foundation to help cover the costs of radio broadcasts. All donations were duly noted by the FBI.[8]

The increasing tensions may have caused Hutchins and Rochester to lose a friend as well. Hutchins had not been especially active in the ILD for some years, having turned over the work to newer recruits. Still, when Anna Damon, longtime secretary of the ILD, died on May 18, 1944, Rochester and Hutchins lost an important comrade. They both wrote tributes to her work, Hutchins commenting on her "tireless energy and unusual ability" and Rochester focusing on her personal integrity as someone who was "a staunch and able defender of those who are persecuted for resisting injustice." Damon's work, Rochester said, was "a great contribution to the cause of true democracy."[9] Evidence suggests that Damon's death was due to suicide,[10] but the source of her distress can only be a matter of speculation.

For now, Anna Rochester wholeheartedly followed the party's adjustments, beginning work on a small book, to be called *Capitalism and Progress*, that would explain the Marxist-Leninist understanding of the historical development of capitalism to people such as Dewson. She was most eager to clarify for a broad readership the party's understanding of its role in revolutionary change. As she insisted to Algernon Black of the Ethical Culture Society: "We do not aim at minority manipulation of a deluded mass. No political group—and I say this advisedly—is more frank in its statement of purposes and more honest in its efforts at organization and education."[11] The new book would not be available immediately, however, and Rochester knew that the world faced a critical moment.

The pervasive world crisis seeped into the otherwise edenic Back Log Camp as well. Writing to Alexander Trachtenberg during their annual vacation in 1944, Rochester observed that the Cadburys were "snowed under with folks much closer to the real problems of the world."[12] She and Hutchins were having a "grand time" nonetheless, she assured him. That year, Rochester had written Hutchins one of her trademark poems for her birthday, expressing her love and devotion:

August 19

Warm heart, clear brain,
Straight back, no pain.
Friend to many, loved by all,
Spring of youth,
Tho nearly sixty, heeds the call
Of truth
And struggle.
Dear Grace,
Beloved Grace.

On the reverse side, she addressed the poem: "for 'Papa's' HAPPY BIRTHDAY."[13] Apparently they found it amusing to trade gender classifications back and forth, another instance of their commitment to fluidity rather than static identities.

Usually, for the outside world, Rochester occupied traditionally male discursive space, maintaining close contact with the party leadership. Perhaps in return for his consultation on the manuscript of *Capitalism and Progress*, Rochester reviewed Earl Browder's *Teheran: Our Path in War and Peace*, in which he set out his rationale for the conversion of the CPUSA into the Communist Political Association. The review was published in the September 1944 issue of *Soviet Russia Today*, an English-language magazine edited by Jessica Smith. Rochester began the review with what at first appears to be a statement of fact:

> *Teheran* definitely ended the division of the anti-Hitler camp into two sections. It expressed the conviction of the three leading world powers that their inner differences offer no obstacle to their collaboration. It recorded the joint determination of President Roosevelt, Premier Stalin and Prime Minister Churchill to continue and strengthen this collaboration in the future.[14]

Rochester continued, however, by indicating that this was the "viewpoint" upon which Browder based his "valuable analysis of the present world situation and the perspectives for the post-war period."[15] Although her tone in the review was generally laudatory, Rochester was careful not to declare herself decisively in favor of Browder's analysis. Instead, she assured readers that "*Teheran* is no magic formula. It opens the door to closer peaceful cooperation between capitalist powers and the Soviet Union. But the road they must follow is still uncharted."[16] Although Rochester and Hutchins were generally in agreement with Earl Browder's position and were friendly with Browder and his wife, Irene, Rochester undoubtedly realized that this statement on Browder's part was a serious departure from the Leninist analysis upon which the CPUSA had been constructed.

Certainly the activity of the FBI during that time did not suggest a government that was preparing to embrace the Soviet Union as a peacetime partner. Agents attended the Madison Square Garden Rally of the National Council of American-Soviet Friendship on November 16, 1944, and noted furtively that Hutchins was there with Rochester.[17]

Hutchins and Rochester either didn't notice or ignored the FBI agents, concentrating instead on their big news of March 1945—the publication of Rochester's book-length attempt to explain the possibilities for socialist progress within a capitalist framework, *Capitalism and Progress*. With this volume, Rochester cemented a line of argument she had only suggested in her review of Earl Browder's *Teheran* six months earlier. Capitalism, Rochester argued, grew unplanned out of earlier, simpler forms of economic life, and, despite internal contradictions, it had been a force for progress. Nonetheless, it was important to understand the nature of class relations and of the contradictions inherent in capitalism. And it was critically important that Americans retain their hold on democratic government. That said, this book, Rochester announced, "considers the possibilities of further progress under capitalism along the path opened up by the agreement of the leading democratic nations at Teheran."[18]

Capitalism, Rochester said, assumed that laborers were free men; in this way, the exploitation of workers was hidden behind a veil of freedom. However, she said, "repeatedly, in the development of American capitalism, it has appeared that the capitalist wealth comes to its fullest flower only when the roots of a fortune are manured with corruption, crooked dealings, and special privilege."[19]

Nonetheless, with a victory over fascism resulting from collaboration between the democratic capitalist and socialist powers, Rochester insisted that there was now the possibility of relatively stable progress even within the capitalist framework. In a moment of prescience, Rochester acknowledged the possibility of reactionaries rushing in with business as usual, seeking profits by "impoverishing the people and stifling" democracy. They would, she acknowledged, "drive us into a profound and unnecessary crisis."[20]

Following the book's publication, heralds of reaction arrived soon enough. T. J. Kreps, writing for the *Annals of the American Academy*, dismissed the book because it was not documented in a scholarly manner.[21] The Springfield *Republican* sniffed: "If you can believe all . . . that is contained in this little book, your background is very different from the reviewer's."[22] Only the *New Masses* reviewer, Ralph Bowman, praised the book in print, yet he, too, was not especially fulsome, commenting that "this little book covers an enormous range of problems, far too many for adequate treatment. Nevertheless," he said, "it serves as a valuable introduction to Marxist political economy. The carefully selected list of sources and references serves as a guide for further study of the subject here so ably condensed and summarized."[23]

Rochester's comrades and friends were more enthusiastic about her work, although in at least one case the comments drew her back into an old life and old struggles. Rochester had sent a copy to Vida Scudder and Florence Converse, inscribing an accompanying card: "To the friends who gave me such a push on the downward (!) path some forty years ago." On April 2, 1945, Vida Scudder wrote back:

Anna Very Dear—

It is a keen pleasure to this old lady, that you cared to send her and Florence this book, all about the roots of economic fact and theory to which your "downward" quest has led you. For haven't I always known that your downward journey was forced on you by your quest for Reality? And I have grieved more than you know that it took you away from the sound of my voice and that you didn't try to talk to me any longer. I can listen, even if I can't follow.

She continued, saying that the book had helped her understand some of the puzzling aspects of current Communist policy, although she still found, she said pointedly, Earl Browder's "pleasant attitude toward the Manufacturers Assn. hard to take seriously."[24]

Rochester, too, was trying to grapple with the new postwar situation and had moved on to another, more arcane, project by this time: reading and preparing to review volume 23 of the *Collected Works of V. I. Lenin*. In the finished review, which appeared in *New Masses* on May 22, 1945, Rochester described Lenin's commentary on the difficult period following the revolution, then shifted direction abruptly, saying, "Today we face a wholly new world situation of peaceful collaboration between a democratic socialist power and democratic capitalist countries, which even Lenin's superb understanding could not foresee." She ended with a rather ineffective insistence that despite this new situation, there is much to be learned from reading Lenin.[25]

But the situation had already changed by the time the review hit the newsstands. Jacques Duclos, secretary of the Communist Party of France, had published an article in the *Cahiers du Communisme* the previous month severely criticizing the policies of Earl Browder and "his followers." Duclos was reacting to an article in the Communist journal *Nouvelle France* that had praised these policies, calling for a similar dissolution of the Communist Party of France. Arguing that Browder's interpretation of the international situation was a serious error, an unwarranted revision of Marx, Duclos called the dissolution of the CPUSA unjustifiable.[26] This criticism, coming from the leader of one of the strongest parties in the world, served to galvanize Browder's critics—foremost among whom was William Z. Foster. Two days later, on May 24, the translated text of Duclos's article was published in the *Daily Worker*, opening the debate to everyone.

Rochester wrote to Browder, calling her May 25 letter "my considered reaction to the Duclos bombshell." Duclos, she insisted, "betrays colossal ignorance of the relation between Communists and the rest of the population in this country, both numerically and psychologically." He failed to "grapple with our basic problem: How can a small minority function best in building toward socialism in this country, where for historical reasons even the majority of the working class has been hostile to socialism and filled with unreasoning prejudice against the Reds?" She hoped, she said, that an open discussion of the article would soon be undertaken, so as to educate both members and nonmembers of the CPA. And in a postscript written the next day, Rochester added: "Since drafting this letter yesterday, we have had the privilege of hearing your masterly and uncompromising contribution to the debate—forum—last evening. Would that the audience had been ten times as large."[27]

Rochester followed this letter with another, this time addressed to the *Sunday Worker*. In it, she responded to the June 2 resolution of the National Board of the CPA, the gist of which was that American capital was swiftly making alliances with European capitalists such as the du Ponts. "The economic and social roots of fascism in Europe have not yet been fully destroyed. This is so," board members argued, "because the extremely powerful reactionary forces in the United States and England, which are centered in the trusts and cartels, are striving to reconstruct liberated Europe on a reactionary basis." Earl Browder's policies were perceived as appeasement of these forces, and, the board insisted, "The camp of reaction must not be appeased—it must be isolated and routed."[28] All members of the board except Earl Browder had voted in favor of the resolution, although one member had abstained at first, later changing his vote.

Yet Rochester persisted in supporting Earl Browder's position, arguing that the work of Communists must be, at this historical juncture, primarily educational. She pointed out that the board's statement actually made that point as well. Duclos, on the other hand, made much of the transition from political party to political association—a nonissue, she insisted. She did not understand, she said, why Earl Browder had voted against the resolution, but she ventured to guess that he might be disagreeing with the board's "self-contradictory acceptance of the Duclos article."[29] Hutchins, disinclined to participate in theoretical debates dominated by men, remained quiet during this period.

Seventeen days later, in a sharp reversal, Rochester wrote a terse letter to the *Daily Worker*, saying:

> Since writing my first letter (*DW*, 6-10-45) in the current discussion, I have realized that the points at issue within our leadership are more basic than at first appeared. We who have not heard the inner discussions do not yet know all the points that have been brought forward in criticism of our wartime policy.
>
> But we know enough to see that the program of the National Board's Resolution on **The Present Situation and the Tasks Ahead** is successfully focussed on immediate goals and actions. It is also tied in directly with the basic class conflicts of capitalism which we were, in practice, ignoring.
>
> I wish now to record my support of the National Committee's position as stated in **The Daily Worker** of June 22d.[30] (boldface type in the original)

By the following February, Earl Browder had been expelled from the CPUSA. "The mistake" the party made, according to *New Masses*, was in its appraisal of the Teheran Conference, drawing "the erroneous conclusion that . . . capitalism as a system had entered into long-term cooperation with socialism as a system. . . . The proponents of this theory . . . forgot that Roosevelt's and Churchill's signatures on the Teheran accord could not dissolve the dynamics of the class relations in the monopoly capitalist countries for which they spoke."[31] Browder had not been able to let go of his blueprint for American Communists, and others realized that they had "converted a tactic, growing out of a given set of historical circumstances, into a universal principle."[32]

As a supporter and friend of Browder, with her generally positive review of his book, her own book reiterating his analyses and her public letter of support for him, Rochester must have felt deeply unnerved by the criticism. For all her research and writing explaining Lenin and challenging the likes of John D. Rockefeller and J. P. Morgan, she had been excluded from discussions charting the course of the party. Indeed, these discussions and the resulting changes challenged the movement's coherence. If even Rochester felt that there were points raised in conversations to which she had not been privy, then members living and working at greater distances had to have felt even more alienated. Rebuilding became the primary goal. In a speech to the District convention in Philadelphia, Ella Reeve Bloor emphasized the importance of solidarity within the party, attempting to quell the factionalism that threatened to develop upon the ouster of Earl Browder, who had led the party through the Depression. What set the CPUSA apart from others, she said, was discipline. Once a decision was made, after extended discussions, members were bound to abide by that decision.[33] This time Anna Rochester and Grace Hutchins did not leave the organization that seemed to leave them behind when it made a sharp turn in policy.

The organization that had dissolved itself into the Communist Political Association in June 1943 reorganized itself again as a political party, the Communist Party, USA, during the July 26–28, 1945, convention in New York. Abiding by the party's decisions, Rochester and Hutchins simply continued their work, the ongoing activities of organizing and educating. Still owners of the *Daily Worker*, both Hutchins and Rochester were members of the Committee to Sponsor the *Daily Worker* and *The Worker* 1945 Fund Campaign, joining fifty-one others, including committee chair Rockwell Kent, Dr. Harry F. Ward, Meridel LeSueur, Theodore Dreiser, Albert Maltz, Ruth McKenney, Rev. Wm. Howard Melish, Hon. A. Clayton Powell, Jr., and Dr. Dirk J. Struik. In spite of the recent turmoil, "This is not an ordinary newspaper," the committee's announcement read. "And we are not ordinary readers. We demand of a newspaper the utmost in honesty, in clarity, in vision. We insist on fundamental discussion of vital questions. We call for non-partisanship, and permit only the bias that stems from complete identification with the interests of the nation."[34]

Reentered as second class matter Oct. 22, 1947, at the post office at New York, N. Y., under the Act of March 3, 1879

Vol. XXVI, No. 192   New York, Tuesday, September 27, 1949
(16 Pages) Price 5 Cents

Figure 12.1. *Daily Worker* masthead

Rochester also approved the reissuing of *Rulers of America*, and, still reaching out, she and Hutchins sent copies to friends, including Molly Dewson and Polly Porter. Dewson wrote back, thanking them and telling them how impressed she and Polly were with the book and all their many achievements. They liked the way Rochester wrote but, Dewson said, they could not take the *Daily Worker*. It seemed so propagandistic, she said, that she tended to assume that what was said was untrue. "Now I guess you girls will want to send me to a Buchenwald," she confessed, "but I can't lie to my friends."[35] Dewson's reference to Rochester and Hutchins as "you girls" was a tacit acknowledgment of their status as independent from men yet partnered with each other. When she suggested that they might want to consign her to Buchenwald (a fresh horror in 1945) for failure to grasp the *Daily Worker*'s rhetoric, she reinscribed the old elision of same-sex affiliations and fascism, calling into question the entire liberatory trajectory of their work. Yet her appreciation for Rochester's classic Marxist-Leninist analysis of finance capital suggests that the problem was primarily a rhetorical one. If Dewson, of all people, was eliding the Communist and fascist programs based on the discourse of the *Daily Worker*, their rhetorical challenges were steep indeed.

Despite their status as owners of the *Daily Worker*, there wasn't much Rochester and Hutchins could do to make the newspaper appeal to Molly Dewson. Rochester did hasten to shift the argument in *Capitalism and Progress* to reflect the recent change in circumstances. Where *Capitalism and Progress* underscored the struggle between fascism and democracy, *The Nature of Capitalism* emphasized the importance of free organization and discussion toward the building of socialism. She admitted, for example, that "failure to distinguish correctly between the nature of capitalist democracy and the more developed character of socialist democracy leads to perilous misunderstandings among those who are opposed to fascism."[36] The political conversation with the Porter-Dewsons seems to have ended here, although the friendship itself did not dim.

During this time, Rochester's old friend Rebecca James, wife of the Reverend Fleming James, was carrying on a more or less successful conversation with Rochester through letters. In November 1946, she wrote saying that she was trying to counteract Reinhold Niebuhr's enormously influential anticommunist diatribes in her discussions with students at Sewanee Theological Seminary in Tennessee. Bill Spofford tried to answer Niebuhr, she said, but "he did not give any very convincing arguments." Did she not "believe in the Venture of Socialism in the U.S.S.R."? Rochester had asked her. Yes, she answered, "though not in all it is doing." She recognized, of course, that the Soviet Union was "surrounded by hostile forces" and thus must "take certain stands. But if only the nations could give it the benefit of the doubt." Despite the seeming hopelessness of the situation, she did "feel more hopeful," she said, and realized how important it was to give those with whom she worked "things to think about in contradistinction to what the newspapers are printing and the tools of Capitalism are telling their audiences."[37]

It was just such thinking as this that the FBI hoped to quash. In November 1946, the Washington bureau of the FBI informed the New York bureau that "the Bureau desires that your office prepare a report in summary form in this case setting forth by witnesses only such information of a legally admissible character as will tend to prove, directly or circumstantially, membership in or affiliation with the Communist Party, and knowledge of the revolutionary aims and purposes of that organization."[38] The Department of Justice was preparing its case to make CPUSA membership illegal—and specifically to charge Hutchins with membership.[39]

Neither Rochester nor Hutchins seems to have been aware of the gathering storm. As John Abt, American Communist lawyer, wrote in his autobiography, "I was completely unprepared for the terror that was to face the labor movement and, most particularly, the Communist party in the coming years. I can't speak for others," he said, "but I know of no one who was any more clairvoyant than I was on this score."[40]

Perhaps absorption in the daily skirmishes kept people from realizing the larger changes taking place. Rochester herself was involved in a legal battle against monopolizing forces—particularly the interpretation of language that either allowed or prevented the construction of American capitalism. From her parents, she had inherited stock in at least one telegraph company. This company, along with two others, had been absorbed by Western Union, but in such a way that the companies remained in existence and Western Union paid them for the use of their lines. As a stockholder, she received part of the income from the leasing of these lines. The smaller companies required Western Union to pay not only the leasing fees but also the federal income taxes on the income from these fees. Western Union filed suit against the companies in New York state court to challenge that requirement.

Rochester's friend and lawyer Alice Dillingham joined several other lawyers, including Arthur Garfield Hays,[41] in representing the defendants. The case was construed as a landlord and tenant issue. Beginning in the 1870s, Western Union had leased lines from the three companies for a period of years, for a fee of 4 or 5 percent of each company's capital stock. Western Union owned a majority of the shares of the stock in these companies; Rochester served as one of the representatives of the minority stockholders.

On September 9, 1946, the New York Supreme Court ruled against Western Union, declaring that it was liable for all federal income taxes on the income from fees to the telegraph companies. The telegraph companies had, in fact, no other income than the fees from leasing their lines.[42] Thus, if they were required to pay income tax on those fees, payments to minority stockholders would necessarily be reduced. The following year, Western Union appealed the decision to the Appellate Division of the Supreme Court of New York; the decision was upheld.[43] Western Union then moved to appeal to the Court of Appeals[44]; that motion was granted, and on November 20, 1947, the decisions were reversed.

The Western Union decision signaled openly to Rochester and Hutchins the reluctance of the courts to challenge the trend toward monopoly in American capitalism. And by now they must have begun to sense that the creeping fascism in the country during this time was more than simply a reluctance on the part of the courts to challenge the corporations. On March 21, 1947, Truman signed Executive Order 9835, establishing federal loyalty review boards. These boards, according to Albert Fried, "more than anything else launched McCarthyism on its inexorable course."[45] Meanwhile, the newly elected Republican Congress was intent on interrupting the labor-protection activities of the National Labor Relations Board. Two months later, on May 19, 1947, Rochester wrote to President Truman asking him to veto the "anti-union, anti-labor bill which enemies of the people have passed in Congress by a shocking majority."[46] Truman did, in fact, veto the Taft-Hartley Act, which

> abolishes the closed shop, establishes a 60-day "cooling-off" period before strikes can be declared, outlaws mass picketing, authorizes employer interference to prevent the unionization of their plants, condemns secondary boycotts, re-establishes the use of injunctions in labor disputes, enables unions to be sued for "unfair labor practices," denies the unions the right to use their funds for political purposes, grants decisive powers to the National Labor Relations Board, and compels union officials to sign affidavits to the effect that they are not Communists.[47]

However, Truman failed to ensure that the Democratic members of Congress would support him, with the result that Congress overrode the veto, thus writing the act into law in June 1947. Almost simultaneously, Rochester suffered a heart attack. Her friend Bob Minor, no doubt informed by Hutchins, wrote a note to people at party headquarters advising them of her illness and suggesting that she would like flowers and visitors at Woman's Hospital.[48]

After her release from the hospital, Rochester spent the summer recuperating at the cottage in Croton-on-Hudson, continuing, when she could, her research into the structures of capitalism. But the reign of terror had begun in earnest. In addition to caring for Rochester and managing the day-to-day operations of the LRA, Hutchins was raising bail money for the victims of the House Un-American Activities Committee's persecutions. Under the leadership of J. Parnell Thomas, congressman from New Jersey, and John E. Rankin, congressman from Mississippi, HUAC had summoned members of the Joint Anti-Fascist Refugee Committee to appear and to name contributors and Spanish Republicans who had been aided by the committee. Organized by New York surgeon Dr. Edward Barsky, the JAFRC supported the Spanish Republicans who could not openly return to Spain under the Franco military dictatorship. The JAFRC invited British Labour Party leader Harold Laski to speak to a meeting in Madison Square Garden in 1946. After Laski criticized the Vatican's role in the conflict, the local representatives of the Catholic Church pressured the House Un-American Activities Committee to investigate the JAFRC.[49] When board members refused to name the local contributors or the Spanish Republicans, many of whom were by this time back in Spain working in the antifascist underground, eleven members of the board of directors of the JAFRC were convicted on June 27, 1947 of contempt of Congress. Among the convicted were writer Howard Fast; several faculty members of local universities; Charlotte Todes Stern, former LRA staff member; and Hutchins and Rochester's friend Helen Bryan, executive secretary of the organization.

By now the point of struggle was becoming clearer. Seeing the material ground on which authorities were challenging progressive forces, Hutchins continued to intervene in the way to which she was accustomed: she expanded her fundraising efforts. "These are difficult times!" Hutchins wrote to Jessie Lloyd O'Connor on November 3, 1947. "More arrests are expected and it is urgent to have a large bail fund ready so that those taken up need not languish but can be bailed out promptly and thus have everyone's morale sustained."[50] Another of the earliest targets of HUAC was Hollywood, an attempt to shut off the flow of progressive ideas into film, perhaps the single most broadly distributed medium in American culture. HUAC's interrogations of nine Hollywood screenwriters (and one director) had begun on October 18, 1947. The ten refused to answer questions about the Screen Writers Guild and about their personal political beliefs, earning themselves citations for contempt of HUAC. A bail fund was established through the Civil Rights Congress, a new organization formed in 1946 from the merger of the ILD with the National Negro Congress and the National Federation for Constitutional Liberties. The bail fund trustees, Hutchins told Jessie O'Connor, included Dashiell Hammett, Bob Dunn, and George Marshall, all of whom "pledge[d] their personal integrity that this is for bail only and will be returned if not used." The situation was so dire, she said, that she herself had taken $1000 from her savings and "bought a bond of the transferable negotiable, coupon-bearing kind, and turned it in." She personally, she said, did not have access to large amounts of capital. Her father had left his money in trust for her, giving her only an income for life. "Can you, will you, send $1000 to Bob for this purpose?" she asked Jessie O'Connor.[51]

The post–World War II era in the United States was becoming a very expensive free speech battle, a fact that led to increasing surveillance of Rochester and Hutchins, as they had spent most of their lives working to build, both materially and discursively, the progressive press in the United States. On December 18, 1947, the FBI decided to keep Hutchins on the Security Index, because of her "writing and long position in the Party."[52] Rochester's status as a Security Index subject was reaffirmed on January 20, 1948—because she was a "Communist writer."[53]

On January 22, 1948, the head of the FBI's Domestic Intelligence Division, D. Milton Ladd, wrote a memo to J. Edgar Hoover outlining a plan to set up a "judicial precedent" establishing that "the Communist Party as an organization is illegal. . . . Once this precedent is set," he said, "then individual members and close adherents or sympathizers can be readily dealt with as substantive violators."[54] A week later, on February 5, 1948, Hoover forwarded to Attorney General Tom Clark a ten-volume brief "to establish the illegal status of the Communist Party of the United States of America."[55]

Potentially a "substantive violator," Hutchins continued her campaign to engineer space for women, promoting women's organizations and writing a short manuscript for the *Congress of American Women Bulletin* explaining the centrality of labor to the origins of International Women's Day, an attempt to dissolve the rigid class barriers that a decade before had undermined the Women's Charter movement.[56] A group with ties to the Women's International Democratic Federation, an organization made up of delegates from forty-one nations, representing 80 million women, the Congress of American Women (CAW) had been established in New York City on International Women's Day—March 8, 1946. Betty Millard, Hutchins and Rochester's close friend, was among the early CAW activists, along with Mary Van Kleeck and Susan B. Anthony II. The CAW aimed to promote political action to defend the rights and welfare of women and children, to fight against fascism, and to promote international peace. In the process of doing so, during its brief four-year life, the CAW encouraged the activities of many women—including Gerda Lerner and Eleanor Flexner—whose work has been more directly tied to the modern feminist movement. Both Lerner and Flexner took strong leadership roles in the CAW.[57]

Before her involvement with the CAW, Betty Millard was working with Joe North editing *New Masses*—yet her name did not appear on the masthead. In a signature move to ensure that the work of women—especially that of "independent" women—was not taken for granted, Hutchins took on one of the party's preeminent writers again. One day, while she was having lunch with Elizabeth Gurley Flynn, she commented that it was disgraceful that Millard's name should be left off the masthead, thus enlisting Flynn in the fight. The two then marched into the offices of *New Masses*, collared Joe North, and accused him of male chauvinism for his oversight. North approached Millard later, saying that he had been reprimanded for failing to credit her. She responded in typical fashion for the times, saying that of course she didn't mind. Yet upon thinking it over, she realized that Hutchins and Flynn were indeed correct, and that acquiescing in one's own oppression would not contribute to any form of liberation. She proceeded to write a three-part series of articles for *New Masses* on how women collude in their own subjugation; the series was later collected into a pamphlet entitled *Woman against Myth*. Not meant to be a compendium of "all the economic, legal and political barriers against women," the pamphlet instead sought to answer "such questions as: How does a woman in such a society feel about herself as a woman? She is a majority of the electorate; does the fact that she hasn't yet achieved equality mean that she doesn't really want it after all? Is it true or is it a myth that 'women like to be dominated'?"[58]

Figure 12.2. Elizabeth Gurley Flynn, ca. 1940s

Betty Millard's answer to that question began by rehearsing some of the same ideas that Hutchins had presented in her 1923 *World Tomorrow* article "Our Inferiority Complex": "It is hardly remarkable that the great majority of women are from earliest childhood convinced—if only subconsciously—of their inferiority to men." This condition, she maintained, is evident in laws, customs, language, and religion. She continued, echoing Hutchins's arguments in *Women Who Work*: "But by themselves they couldn't do the job. Day-to-day attacks in books, films, radio shows, and magazine articles are called for, since women are more and more coming awake, discovering that their problems are tied up with the great over-all struggle for democracy." During the war, Millard said, women were treated with editorials praising their work and "magazine articles praising their new-found mechanical abilities." Yet in 1948, "we read about the 'foolishness' of women, their 'immaturity.'"[59] Identifying the same specious authority that Vida Scudder had named in 1937, Millard said: "The difference is that the authority quoted is no longer God but Freud. Today women are attacked by Ferdinand Lundberg and Dr. Marynia Farnham in *Modern Woman—The Lost Sex* not for attempting to subvert God's will but for unconsciously seeking to deprive the male of his power, to castrate him." Explaining the differences between Soviet and American attitudes toward women, Millard said:

After a hundred years of the modern struggle for woman's equality Soviet women are urged in their magazines to educate themselves and grow, to fulfill their pro-duction quotas and thus add to the happiness and well-being of the nation; while judging from the number of square feet given over to the subject in every issue of the *Ladies Home Journal*, the highest ideal of American womanhood is smooth, velvety, kissable hands.[60]

Millard herself, however, failed to identify one significant element in her analysis. "It goes without saying," she declared, "that all normal women, including Soviet women, want to be as attractive as possible and also to achieve a happy marriage."[61] Engels's writing on the family provided no comfortable way to talk about gender and sexuality. Edward Carpenter's paeans to same-sex love were framed by an outdated socialism, and few young people were reading Carpenter at that point anyway. Freud offered a discourse on homosexuality, but within a system that pathologized lesbianism. Popular culture furnished metaphors of vampirism for lesbians—images of blood or knives attended any mention of attraction between women.

Still, relationships such as those between Rochester and Hutchins, Ruth Erickson and Eleanor Stevenson, Molly Dewson and Polly Porter flourished, having been planted in more fertile pre-Freudian soil celebrating love and intellect. Private languages contin-ued, but public languages did not begin to describe their experiences. Thus, Hutchins's effort to encourage freedom for women, while producing a strong indictment of ideologies of women's inferiority, unwittingly underscored heteronormativity and led to unfortunate ellipses, in writing by Millard and others, of partnerships such as that between herself and Rochester. This failure to articulate more openly the gender fluidity and openness to same-sex desire that characterized the lives of many of the women in Hutchins and Roch-ester's circle would prove to be a serious mistake. Although Hutchins, in particular, aimed to strengthen women's identification with the labor movement and, likewise, strengthen labor's identification with women, creating an unassailable mass base, the gap left open by the lack of any reasonable discourse of same-sex desire proved to be an ideal source of division ready-made for exploitation by conservative forces anxious to undo the legislation and movements that gained strength during the 1930s.

Although Rochester, too, systematically neglected to challenge openly the negative public depictions of same-sex love—apart from her own uncamouflaged presence with Grace Hutchins—she was clearly aware of—and addressed openly—other linguistic distor-tions. On March 10, 1948, in a moment of remarkable prescience, she wrote to the editor of the *Daily Worker* suggesting that the paper start printing definitions of key terms. "This seems to me," she said, "to be a basic responsibility of our press, no less important than all the valuable news about this country which is concealed in the commercial press."[62] Perhaps this was a good idea—but it was much too little and much too late; the proverbial horse had already been stolen.

Sure enough, less than a month later, another of the heralds of the reaction-to-come announced itself in Rochester, New York, when a mob, some members of which were wear-ing the insignia of the Catholic War Veterans and the Veterans of Foreign Wars, attacked a CPUSA meeting and burned a number of books, including *The Nature of Capitalism*.[63]

Within four months, the *Daily Worker* was warning readers that "a frame-up is on the way."[64] Hoover and others in the FBI, the Justice Department, and Congress were determined to establish their "judicial precedent" outlawing the CPUSA. The arrests came on July 20, 1948, as a result of grand jury indictments that had been in preparation for more than a month. Using provisions of the Smith Act,[65] the Department of Justice charged members

of the National Board—many of them good friends of Rochester and Hutchins—with conspiracy to organize the Communist Party of the United States of America, an organization
that allegedly taught and advocated the overthrow of the US government by force and
violence and whose constitution was based upon principles of Marxism-Leninism. Board
members were also charged with conspiracy to publish and circulate printed material advocating the principles of Marxism-Leninism and to conduct schools and classes for the study
of the principles of Marxism-Leninism, in which, it was claimed, the duty and necessity of
overthrowing the US government by force and violence was taught and advocated. Feminist,
antiracist, and anticlassist ideas were arrested along with the people who articulated them.

Anna Rochester and Grace Hutchins continued to express the essence of their
partnership in their work, leaving Betty Millard to hide herself and others in prose that
simultaneously reinscribed and undermined heteronormativity for women ("It goes without saying that. . . ."). However, in Los Angeles during that summer of 1948, CPUSA
organizer Harry Hay heard that men were being fired from State Department positions
for having "slept with someone named Andrew."[66] Hay decided that it was time to fight
back—and fighting back meant organizing. In August, Hay started very quietly signing
up members for what would become, in November 1950, the country's first gay rights
organization, the Mattachine Society. Hay, however, was organizing men. And although
women's issues came to be included, rather secondarily, in a later offshoot of the Mattachine Society (ONE, Inc.) and an organization for women, the Daughters of Bilitis,
formed in California some years later, at that moment, in New York in 1948, Hutchins
and Rochester's attention was focused on the arrests of CPUSA leaders and the damage
rippling out from the anticommunist campaigns.

On December 15, 1948, the persecution mania suddenly became very personal for
Grace Hutchins. Of course, she was aware that her friend Esther Shemitz's husband, Whittaker Chambers, had accused the president of the Carnegie Endowment for Peace, Alger
Hiss, of having been a member of the CPUSA while he worked at the State Department a
decade earlier. When Hiss sued Chambers for libel, Chambers produced State Department
documents, claiming they had come from Hiss. Both the House Un-American Activities
Committee and a federal grand jury investigated Alger Hiss. Just as the grand jury was
deciding to charge Hiss with two counts of perjury, Whittaker Chambers told a group of
voracious reporters in a courtroom corridor[67] that Hutchins had visited his brother-in-law,
Reuben Shemitz, a lawyer at 276 Fifth Avenue in New York "while he and his wife were
taking turns at guarding and sleeping. . . . Under instructions, he charged, she told Shemitz
that if the latter would disclose Chambers' whereabouts and surrender him to the party,
the Commies in turn would guarantee the safety of Mrs. Chambers and the two Chambers
youngsters, a boy and a girl." Reached at her desk at the LRA, Hutchins said: "It must
be that he is losing his mind. . . . It's a most ridiculous thing. I categorically deny it. I
haven't seen Mr. Chambers for at least 11 years, or perhaps 12 or 13."[68]

The hallway narrative marked Chambers's first sortie in an extended scapegoating
struggle with Hutchins over the politics of sexuality, a struggle characterized by linguistic
maneuvers that eluded most readers. The obvious interpretation of Chambers's story was
the linkage between the CPUSA (represented by Hutchins) and death. However, for those
in the know, Chambers was deploying the "lesbian = death" trope borrowed from D. H.
Lawrence and, by means of this trope, reducing Hutchins and Rochester's partnership to
sex, erasing their years of social justice work.[69] It appears likely that Hutchins failed to
understand the full import of the way Chambers framed his tale. Indeed, Si Gerson later
remarked about Hutchins's encounters with Chambers, "She was an innocent maid," sug-

gesting by his choice of terms that she remained unaware of Chambers's sexual innuendos.[70] Had she correctly interpreted all of his connotations, she undoubtedly would not have said what she did to later interviewers.

Perhaps not coincidentally, on the same day, Elizabeth Bentley told the *New York World-Telegram* that Hutchins had been sent by Lem Harris to make arrangements through the International Workers Order after the death of Jacob Golos in 1943. "Grace Hutchins, named by Whittaker Chambers as the Communist emissary who made an implied threat against his life, has been for many years one of a small group of Communist big wheels assigned to handle special, delicate jobs on which only the most trusted party members could be utilized," trumpeted the *World-Telegram*.[71] Thus the press reshaped Hutchins's kinship work into a nefarious authority-driven conspiracy.

The *Daily Worker* did its best to stem the verbal attacks, reverting to the largely ineffective debunking methods of the mid-1930s. The December 15, 1948, issue featured pictures of Hutchins and Marion Bachrach, public relations director of the CPUSA and sister of attorney John Abt, under large black headlines: "2 Women Debunk Pumpkin Spy Tales." According to *Daily Worker* journalist Louise Mitchell, Hutchins said that she had gone to Reuben Shemitz's office in 1937, not 1938, to find out what had happened to her old friend Esther Shemitz. "She was told by [Reuben] Shemitz that the Chambers 'don't want to be found,' said Miss Hutchins."[72]

This version of the story was also not entirely accurate, however. Reuben Shemitz had kept the note that Hutchins left at his office, turning it over to the FBI at some point. The note, in Hutchins's handwriting, dated May 19, 1938, reads: "Dear Mr. Shemitz, There is a *very important* message for your sister: If she or her husband will call either Steve or me, we have some important news for them. Grace."[73] "Steve," of course, was Eleanor Stevenson, partner of Ruth Erickson. (It wouldn't be until some years later that Hutchins would acknowledge that she had, in fact, been sent to try to retrieve Chambers. She never did reveal publicly Stevenson's part in the event, nor did she ever mention who had sent her in the first place.[74])

The FBI went to work on the evidence, submitting the note to lab analysis on January 3 to determine whether the handwriting was indeed Hutchins's. (It was.) Two days later, J. Edgar Hoover wrote a long memo to agents asking for updates on all Security Index subjects—including Rochester and Hutchins and many of their friends. On January 19, 1949, the FBI interviewed Reuben Shemitz. The agent writing the report of this interview indicated that according to Shemitz, "at no time did Hutchins make any express threat or indicate that harm would come to Whittaker Chambers." He said, however, that although Hutchins had said that the safety of Esther and the children would be assured, she did not include Whittaker Chambers in this assurance. According to Shemitz, it could be inferred from this statement that Chambers, perhaps, was not safe.

The next day, the FBI paid a visit to Hutchins in her office at 80 East 11th. According to the report filed by the agents, she was "not a cooperative witness," although she did volunteer information about herself, saying that she was "a firm believer in the Constitution of the Communist Party," that she had been a member since 1927, and that she had run for office on the CPUSA ticket in 1936. When asked about the reason for her visit to Shemitz's office, Hutchins substituted the story about Chambers's teeth, telling the agents that in 1934 or 1935 Chambers had asked her for a loan, claiming that he wanted to have his teeth fixed. In 1937, she said, she needed the money—which he had not repaid—and so she visited the office of Reuben Shemitz to ask where Chambers could be found. Hutchins did not know at the time of this interview that the FBI had her note to Shemitz dated May 19, 1938; the agents indicated that "she was startled on learning that such a note was in existence, although newspaper accounts made previous reference to one such written note." Still, she denied having been sent by anyone in the CPUSA to locate Chambers, and she denied that anyone by the name of Steve or Miss Stevens was involved in the incident. In a desperate attempt to create division herself between Chambers and the FBI, Hutchins also apparently told the agents about the rumors of Chambers's sexual behavior and the fact that he had been hospitalized for mental illness.[75]

On January 27, 1949, Hutchins offered this same information to Horace Schmahl, a representative of the Hiss defense team, saying that "it was 'common knowledge that Chambers had been a sex pervert when he was employed at the *Daily Worker*.'"[76] Schmahl then shared the information with Chambers. Although Sam Tanenhaus claims that Schmahl later switched sides, Stephen W. Salant argues persuasively that Schmahl was employed by Army Intelligence and was acting as a double agent.[77] Hutchins's attempt to undermine Chambers's credibility by referencing his sexuality, linking it to his mental health, was quite possibly the worst rhetorical decision she ever made, not only for herself but for the movement to which she had devoted herself.

About the same time, someone in party headquarters apparently asked Hutchins how she was faring with all the negative publicity. She responded with a memo, saying: "My personal difficulties have not really amounted to much. I have had no bad repercussions (as yet!) from the absurd and outrageous statement by Whittaker Chambers." She went on to explain her connection with Esther, dating from the *World Tomorrow*, and her agreement to serve as witness to the Chambers's wedding. Esther's friends, she said, "had already known at that time that he was *not* an honest or decent sort of man. All that Drew Pearson said of him over the radio, national hook-up, on December 19th, was really true. He (Chambers) was, probably still is, a homosexual pervert, a psychopathic case, who was in an asylum for mental cases for quite a period of time."[78]

There were few mentions of sexuality in public presentations of the case. Privately, however, sexuality seems to have been the engine driving many of the conversations, with the major players trading insults, each trying to defame the other, to suggest motives of tainted or questionable morals or, at the least, disease.[79] A sturdy sexological framework for these conversations was already in place, having been more deeply politicized at the time of the Reichstag fire and the subsequent "Night of the Long Knives"—the murders of Ernest Rohm and other members of the Brownshirts—and reinforced over the years by medical and juridical language.[80] Hutchins, it would seem, was engaging in what Kenneth Burke would call "faulty means-selecting."

Kenneth Burke explained the twin phenomena of blame and identity-based scapegoating in *Permanence and Change*, expanding his explanation ten years later in A *Grammar of Motives*. In his first explanation, Burke pointed as an example to a tendency among some Southern whites to blame African Americans for their economic distress rather than looking to the economic structure for the source of their misery. This, Burke argued, is not scapegoating, because there is "no evidence of an evasive process here distinguishable in its mental functioning from some non-scapegoat or realistic way of response."[81] Rather, it is a case of "faulty means-selecting." Thus, although Chambers was clearly not guilt free in the situation, his sexuality should not have been an issue, and there were much larger forces at work toward which Hutchins ought to have directed her animus. Had Hutchins been trying to off-load her own guilt or shame onto Chambers, as J. Edgar Hoover apparently did in his campaigns against homosexuals, then we could have said she was scapegoating him. But this was not the case. This distinction would become important later in Chambers's public response.

There were very few counterdiscourses available—Edward Carpenter had been long forgotten except for loving spaces made on private bookshelves. "We were under deep cover," Betty Millard said of her own and others' experiences at the time.[82] Deep cover or not, stories of Chambers's liaisons with men abound, each bringing with it a slightly different attitude. What Hutchins and Rochester would have found reprehensible was the fact that Chambers was sexually involved with *anyone* else after his marriage to Esther Shemitz—plus the fact that his relations with men did not constitute partnerships but rather anonymous encounters, not always welcomed by the other party.[83,84,85]

At the same time, right-wing writers and politicians were attempting to pin the homosexual label on Communists. Ralph de Toledano wrote to Chambers on January 22, 1949, saying: "Is this information of any value? Ralph de Sola called me last night and told me that he met Alger Hiss in 1937. It was at the [Maryland] home of two Communist women [celebrating their 'wedding anniversary']."[86] Chambers probably did not find this disclosure useful. On February 15, 1949, prompted by the revelations of Hutchins and others, Chambers acknowledged to FBI agents years of anonymous same-sex activity. With this, the FBI gained more control over Chambers.[87]

Although she did support her husband, Esther Shemitz Chambers did not participate in the insult flinging, perhaps because she recalled the loans, gifts, and years of mentoring and protection that Hutchins and Rochester had provided her. Interviewed by the FBI on February 10, 1949, she told agents about *Jesus Christ and the World Today*, mentioned Hutchins's missionary service, and described Community House to the agents, right down to the chapel. She thought they were Episcopalians, she said. Esther Chambers restricted her comments to factual statements predating 1927, which, in this case, was probably as generous as she could afford to be. She made no reference to the illustrations for *Labor and Silk* nor to the job Rochester arranged for her at Amtorg.[88]

Grace Lumpkin, however, now working part time at Calvary Episcopal church in New York City, was considerably more aggressive, telling the agent that Rochester and Hutchins were close friends and that both had been—and in her opinion still were, at the time of the interview—members of the CPUSA. A member of the Hiss defense team had interviewed her, she said, and had claimed that Hutchins denied membership in the CPUSA. (Was this Horace Schmahl again, sowing discord?) But Hutchins "was lying," Lumpkin declared, because she had seen Hutchins's party membership card. Perhaps the animosity between Grace Hutchins and Grace Lumpkin had been established sometime earlier.[89] Grace Hutchins told an interviewer later that "she understood—though of course she does not *know*—that 'Grace Lumpkin used to pray with him [Whittaker Chambers]—they used to get down on their knees, Buchmanite fashion, and she used to urge him to tell "all the truth."' "[90] (Any alignment Lumpkin made with the Buchman movement would have been sufficient to cause a rift with Hutchins.) What is significant about Grace Lumpkin's report is that she refers to Rochester and Hutchins simply as "close friends," not making any suggestive comments that would lead an investigator to question the nature of Hutchins and Rochester's relationship. Perhaps she felt that to say otherwise would reflect on her.

Understandings and attitudes about same-sex love had undergone a serious mutation since Edward Carpenter's celebratory lines were written. Although Communists and other progressives understood how capitalists used race and gender to their benefit, creating divisions and pitting people against each other, they were less able, Grace Hutchins's implicit efforts notwithstanding, to distinguish the same dynamics with regard to same-sex partnerships, their vision muddied by moral judgments and echoes of past alignments. It was not sufficiently clear to most people, apparently including Hutchins herself at this point, that the creation of identities based on sexuality used the same mechanism of division and petrifying of categories. The early twentieth-century cultures celebrating women's love and work had now largely vanished, remaining alive only within small groups of friends.

Chapter Thirteen

Cold War at Home

Then shall the King say unto them on his right hand, Come, ye blessed of my Father, inherit the kingdom prepared for you from the foundation of the world: For I was an hungred, and ye gave me meat: I was thirsty, and ye gave me drink: I was a stranger, and ye took me in: Naked, and ye clothed me; I was sick, and ye visited me: I was in prison, and ye came unto me.

Then shall the righteous answer him, saying, Lord, when saw we thee an hungred, and fed thee? Or thirsty, and gave thee drink? When saw we thee a stranger and took thee in? or naked, and clothed thee? Or when saw we thee sick, or in prison, and came unto thee?

And the King shall answer and say unto them, Verily I say unto you, Inasmuch as ye have done it unto one of the least of these my brethren, ye have done it unto me.

—Matthew 25: 34–40

Rochester and Hutchins—and their friends—were aging. There were signs all around them of the passage of time. Word came that Winifred Chappell had fallen and broken her hip, effectively ending her active work. And Sally Cleghorn's handwriting had become visibly unsteady. Still, Cleghorn could see the larger forces at work, quoting Christina Rossetti to Rochester, Hutchins, and Lucie Myer: "Oh, dear friends!" Cleghorn wrote on New Year's Day of 1949, "how can governments drag us into war, while individually we are all so eager for 'Mercy, Pity, Love and Peace'?"[1] Rochester and Hutchins would have added codicils about free speech to Cleghorn's plea. Their remaining years were spent struggling to hold back the postwar forces of reaction determined to occupy or annihilate the discursive space they had created. The mass arrests and foreclosing of progressive ideas had begun.

Rochester never completely recovered from the heart attack she suffered in the summer of 1947. Nonetheless, she persevered in writing her last book, *American Capitalism 1607–1800*, although the process exhausted her—and worried Hutchins: "Anna darling," she wrote, finally, "What troubles me so deeply is that your eyes, your whole face, and your carriage speak of a *tiredness* that might easily result in more difficulty." Following some suggestions for rest, she closed, offering the most important part of the message: "With *all* my love, Grace."[2]

American Capitalism, published in 1949, was Rochester's way of addressing the need to return to the party's Marxist roots of economic analysis but in the context of American history. Communism, as far as Rochester and Hutchins were concerned, was still twentieth-century Americanism.[3] The book, divided into two parts—pre-Revolution and post-Revolution—demonstrated the viability of Marxist analysis in explaining American history and in illuminating the decline of capitalism.

Rochester located the inception of American history in European imperialism of the sixteenth century. Mercantilism in general led to the prospering of the nation, as the colonies grew more self-sufficient and began producing a surplus for export. English control was the other primary shaping factor in the colonies' economic development. Struggles against English repression often took the form of incipient local democracies—people's councils and colonial legislatures. A "common interest in greater business freedom was perhaps the most important root of a new national consciousness," Rochester argued.[4]

In the post-Revolution period, she maintained, three problems emerged that required joint action of the states: need for a uniform, stable currency; desire on the part of merchants to forestall defaults on debt; and desire on the part of frontier settlers and land speculators for a national policy regarding land and Indian relations. In 1787, the Constitutional Convention convened, with merchants, landowners, and lawyers represented and workingmen and poor farmers left out. Small farmers, in fact, opposed ratification of the Constitution because it protected the rights of property above the rights of man. Rochester noted that Thomas Jefferson and James Madison supported widespread calls for coverage of human rights, which finally passed and became effective in December 1791. Then she said pointedly, "[The amendments] guaranteed freedom of speech, freedom of the press, the right to petition, freedom of assembly, religious liberty, the right to trial by jury, and other rights—rights that are being abrogated and have to be fought for all over again after 158 years."[5]

In the remainder of the book, Rochester traced the linkages between the government and the wealthy, pinpointing the development of corporations and the increasing disparity between rich and poor. Only Marxism, Rochester concluded, adequately accounted for these developments. "No mechanistic theory of economic determinism could explain the clash of forces that brought about social and cultural changes in our history."[6]

Yet forces within the government, most especially the Department of Justice and the House Un-American Activities Committee, were intent upon erasing Marxism—and attendant liberatory movements that grew from Marxist roots—as an explanatory method in the United States. Much of Hutchins and Rochester's time during 1949 was given over to fighting these efforts on behalf of others, although (especially after Hutchins's run-in with Whittaker Chambers) they knew that they themselves were being watched and talked about. They could not know, however, what sorts of stories were being manufactured, nor did they realize all the means by which that information was being collected. On May 16, for instance, former CPUSA activist Paul Crouch testified before the Senate Sub-Committee on Immigration and Naturalization of the Committee on the Judiciary, submitting a list that included Hutchins as one of the most important national and district leaders of the CPUSA.[7] Still, as Hutchins said about her experience with Chambers, they were feeling few repercussions from their surveillance, especially as they compared themselves with their friends facing jail terms.

Seeking to ease that disparity, Hutchins poured herself into fund-raising efforts, continuing to work with Bob Dunn to raise bail money for those who had been arrested. The Bail Fund of the Civil Rights Congress had been formally established, creating a more certain vehicle by which to collect and promptly apply funds to gain prisoners' release. Citing the eighth amendment to the U. S. Constitution, "Excessive bail shall not be required," the fund's trustees sought to raise $1 million.[8] The material rhetoric to which

Hutchins and Rochester subscribed had taken a significant turn. Although the ILD had raised funds for the defense of labor prisoners during the 1920s and 1930s, now the entire party was in a defensive position.

On October 14, 1949, the eleven members of the national board of the CPUSA were convicted of conspiracy to violate the Smith Act, which prohibited the teaching or advocacy of the use of force or violence to overthrow the US government.[9] Their old comrade Louis Budenz had been the government's handsomely compensated prime witness, arguing that CPUSA literature, which forswore acts of violence, was written in a secret code, "Aesopian language," known only to the initiated.[10] Budenz thus undermined the very means—writing—by which Hutchins and Rochester were trying to change economic and social conditions for countless people, women chief among them. Typically, however, Rochester and Hutchins did not think of themselves. Two days later, Rochester wrote to Jack Stachel: "Those of us who are as yet free to work and play think a great deal about you front-rank fighters who are bearing high witness to the cause we all try to serve. We are all proud of you and will try to do our part to prevent the further spread of fascism in this country. We salute you!"[11] The following day, Hutchins wrote to John Williamson. Both Rochester and Hutchins made it a practice to write frequently to those in prison, also remembering them regularly on important holidays. (And the FBI remembered to collect and file their messages.)

Even though such letters and fundraising were taking increasing amounts of Hutchins and Rochester's time and emotional resources, their network of friends remained a source of warmth and pleasure. In February, Mother Bloor wrote to Hutchins, saying: "Your card came to me last eve and is sending me on my way rejoicing. I wrote to a comrade who calls me 'Mother' 'I'm thinking of writing a book called "My Glorious Children."' Won't *that* be some book? Think of it, you and Anna and Bob D. and thousands of 'Glorious' ones you know *will be there*."[12]

But while Mother Bloor was drawing in the younger people around her—"thousands" of them—with familial warmth, Rochester's old mentor Vida Scudder was reading ancient mystics. Still, she wrote to Rochester and Hutchins on the last day of 1949, also seeking in them a source of community. "The greeting from you," she said, "shed a ray of light into the somber future of the waiting year. I cannot feel that our ancient fellowship is broken." She added: "I'm sure you think of me as an old Has-Been—and indeed I take comfort in my freedom now from any responsibility to *do* anything." She had escaped, she said, from the Christmas rush by immersing herself in the "Mystics dear to my youth: the Gita and the Vedas, underlying and preceding all Christian records of reality." Of course, she insisted, Marxian dialectic helped her to contemplate the new atomic bomb. And "I'm sure you know that I am with you in relieved satisfaction over the spread of Communism, and I hope you dissociate it as completely as I do from the policies of Stalin." Closing, Scudder signed herself: "Your Companion in Time and Beyond."[13] Scudder, however, could still be counted on to sign petitions, maintaining the records of which helped to keep several FBI agents and office personnel on the federal payroll.

Two weeks after Senator Joseph McCarthy gave his speech in Wheeling, West Virginia, in which he claimed to have in his possession a list of 205 card-carrying Communist State Department employees, Sally Cleghorn, too, sent Hutchins a reminder of the strength of their long friendship and her carefully considered grasp of the national temperament: "I feel the persecution of the Salem witches has never really been renounced: it only moved hither & yon to other victims individual and collective." Upon moving to Philadelphia and joining the Quaker movement, Cleghorn had become closely acquainted with Margaret

Reeve Cary, Hutchins's old college friend. Cary had asked Cleghorn how Rochester and Hutchins felt about the trial of Alger Hiss; Cleghorn replied that she couldn't say, but that she herself "felt it was a miserable piece of persecution." Margaret Cary, she reported to Hutchins, "seemed to feel about the same."[14]

Seeking to challenge this paralyzing misery, Rochester's friends within the party—undoubtedly prompted by Hutchins—made it a point to celebrate her seventieth birthday in March 1950. Many greetings came from publishers, telling her of their appreciation for her work and tacitly challenging the forces colonizing their words. "Dear Comrade Anna," wrote Milton Howard of the *Daily Worker* on March 30, "Congratulations on your 70th birthday. Your diligence and scientific work in behalf of human freedom have always inspired us."[15] Alexander Trachtenberg sent Rochester a letter tracing the books of hers that he had published, saying that she had "been a most cooperative author" and hoping that she counted him "among your friends."[16] The LRA, too, had celebrated with a small party, presenting her with a book. Despite the paeans, Rochester knew that she did not have the energy of years past; she wrote to Bob Dunn on April 3, announcing her intention to enter semiretirement. She was available, she said, for "very part-time editorial work."[17]

Unbeknownst to Hutchins and Rochester, on July 27, 1950, Louis Budenz named Hutchins to the FBI as a "concealed" Communist. Budenz pointed to Hutchins among others, straining to argue that although there was little public doubt that Hutchins was a CPUSA member (given her publications and her campaigns for office on the CPUSA ticket), "many people will not believe that she is a Communist [because of her class background] and consequently we have to regard her as concealed."[18] The FBI was not notably impressed with Budenz's "revelations," but that did not stop the government from paying Budenz more than $70,000 for his services as an informer.[19] The witch hunts were beginning a materially produced crescendo that would not peak for several years.

Just as President Truman was ordering American troops to invade Korea, Hutchins was invited to speak before her Bryn Mawr class at its forty-third reunion, honoring Alice Hawkins, who was retiring that year. Friends dating from Hutchins's putative upper class origins found no problems with her very unconcealed CPUSA membership and labor activism. She offered her Bryn Mawr classmates what she often gave friends in CPUSA circles—a moment of social cohesiveness and the opportunity to appreciate each other. Hawkins wrote to Hutchins after the event, thanking her for the tribute: "I shall always treasure your words and shall often re-read them especially when I am depressed and feeling a rather useless member of society."[20] Cornelia Meigs, "Tink" to her friends, also retired that year from her position as English professor at Bryn Mawr. She wrote to Hutchins, telling her, "I feel as close and at home and as happy in your company as I ever did," adding that Hutchins's "speech about Alice at the dinner was by all odds the best moment of Reunion."[21]

Nonetheless, Hutchins, normally ebullient, was being circumspect. Hutchins and Rochester still devoted themselves wholly to labor and feminism, but the cultural insistence upon rigid sexual identities, some acceptable and some abject, had been encroaching on their rhetoric of the whole person. Lacking any clear linguistic platform from which to argue about the taxonomies now in place, Hutchins had not fought the most recent upsurge in repression—a call by Nebraska Senator Kenneth Wherry to remove homosexuals from government employment.[22] And when she wrote to the *Turtle Progress Reporter* that year, she said: "With two friends I share an apartment in Greenwich Village in a cooperative where Anna Rochester (B. M. 1903) and I have lived 26 years," a chaste and considered statement compared to her jubilant 1932 announcement that she and Rochester had just celebrated the tenth anniversary of their partnership. Only those with long memories would be able to read through the words to find Hutchins's partnership with Rochester.[23]

Although Rochester's pace, at age 70, had slowed, Hutchins, at 65, seemed to accelerate, as she cared for Rochester at home, kept the LRA going, and shouldered more and more responsibilities for her friends who had been arrested or threatened with deportation. She was not alone in her anguish, though. On July 21, Jessie Lloyd O'Connor wrote to Hutchins, saying: "With so many people going to jail for being decent, it is time we reacted as energetically as possible." She enclosed a check, telling Hutchins that it was made out to her so that she could use it for whatever she deemed necessary—with no need even to report back about its disposition. "With all the outrageous thought-control bills and asinine red-baiting going on, the tiresome big-lies and half lies and half truths, I am willing to give a lift to the underdogs of the moment, even though I know," she added, "they are far from perfect themselves. It is one way to express my contempt for the unctuous self-deceit of the top-dogs and their arrogant attempt to lead the American people to the slaughter." She went on, warming to the subject: "How can they call it patriotism, to pledge the land of liberty to the support of every tyrant who calls himself anti-Communist? Can't they even imagine how they are making our kind-hearted people hated? What a rotten shame!" O'Connor did not leave CPUSA purists untouched, though, saying: "As for the bottom dogs, in their purity of theory I guess they will go on insulting the character of people who have honest disagreements with them (a heck of a way to get popular, says I). But at least they do raise a holler about various injustices—and how can we make America ever finer and better if we don't even hear about what goes wrong?"[24]

Hutchins wrote back, thanking her for her "fine letter and the very generous check." Disregarding O'Connor's assertion that she needn't provide an accounting of the money, Hutchins told her that she had sent the money to the Civil Rights Congress, to be used for overhead expenses to free other donations to be used for bail—"needed in every direction these days!" The Civil Rights Congress, she told O'Connor, was "the one most responsible for winning the stay of execution in the cases of Willie McGee and the Martinsville Seven. And it has provided the bail in most of the defense cases."[25]

Seeking to relieve the increasingly grim mood as repressive law after repressive law was passed and friend after friend was arrested, Hutchins joined with William Patterson to chair a "testimonial" at Webster Hall for Elizabeth Gurley Flynn in celebration of her birthday.[26] Perhaps not coincidentally, the FBI chose the same day, August 11, 1950, to arrest Ethel Rosenberg on charges of conspiring to transmit atomic secrets to the Soviet Union; she was accused of recruiting her brother, David Greenglass, to gather information for Dr. Klaus Fuchs and Harry Gold. And four days later, Louis Budenz, still trying to make good on his claim of two hundred "concealed Communists," gave the FBI Rochester's name. As the FBI had been collecting information on her for almost ten years, the revelation certainly came as no surprise. Still, it was duly noted in her file.

Morton Sobell was arrested just as Hutchins and Rochester were leaving for Back Log Camp in August 1950. Now, the gracious and lively mix of political opinions and affiliations at the camp, first compromised by fascism, was beginning to yield to the polarizing effects of the government inquisition. In June 1950, three ex-FBI agents published *Red Channels*, a wide-ranging, gossip-driven listing of people primarily involved in various types of cultural work who were alleged to have Communist ties. The book served as a blacklist. Government employees such as Olga Halsey, fearing the taint of association, told Henry and Lydia Cadbury that they could no longer attend the camp if Rochester and Hutchins were there, never mind that Henry Cadbury himself had accepted the Nobel

Peace Prize in 1947 on behalf of the Quakers. As Thomas Shipley Brown put it: "federal employees . . . were terrified that suspicion and keel-hauling might come upon them
because they had attended the same Camp with Anna Rochester and Grace Hutchins,
and who knows what dark and dirty conspiracies were shaped behind the woodpiles?"[27]
Although Rochester and Hutchins never returned after the summer of 1950, this fear of
contamination initiated the decline of the camp, which was forced to close some years
later, one of many unremarked victims of the witch hunts.

Shortly after Hutchins and Rochester's return from camp, on September 15, 1950,
Attorney General Howard McGrath extended his list of subversive organizations, adding
three labor schools, two of which had already closed; fourteen national subdivisions of the
International Workers Order, of which Hutchins was a member; and, just for good measure,
the Associated Klans of America. Less than a week later, on September 20, 1950, Congress passed the Internal Security Act (McCarran Act). President Truman vetoed the act,
saying that it would "make a mockery of the Bill of Rights," but both houses of Congress
overrode his veto, by a wide margin. The Bill of Rights was duly mocked.[28]

The Senate Internal Security Subcommittee, chaired by Patrick McCarran, had been
hard at work—making more work for Hutchins and others, too. Hutchins's friend Rose Nelson Lightcap, with whom she had worked on the International Workers Order, had already
been arrested by the Immigration and Naturalization Service; Hutchins volunteered to serve
as secretary for Lightcap's defense committee. "Strongly protest your hold Rose Nelson
Lightcap," Hutchins telegraphed to the Commissioner of Immigration and Naturalization.
"Request decent, human treatment for this woman who has committed no crime."[29] Less
than a month later, the FBI noted, Hutchins also signed a protest against the detention
of Miriam Stevenson, drawn by her feminist instincts to the case. Stevenson was a single
mother in Los Angeles who had survived two marriages to alcoholic and abusive husbands.[30]

In addition to intervening on behalf of women, Hutchins was producing the monthly
issues of *Railroad Notes*, working on another volume of the *Labor Fact Book*, and shepherd-
ing *Monopoly Today* into print. *Monopoly Today*, published in November 1950, was a brief
update of Anna Rochester's *Rulers of America*. One of the most significant sections of the
book at the time was section three, which documented the increasing influence of "big
business in mass communication." Citing, among others, Robert M. Hutchins, chancellor
of the University of Chicago and chairman of the 1947 Commission on Freedom of the
Press, the book documented the grip of finance capital on the US media. "'The agencies of
mass communication are big business and their owners are big businessmen,'" said Robert
Hutchins (not a close relation to Grace Hutchins). Noting especially the new medium,
television, the book showed how the major financial interest groups owned and controlled
the vast majority of stations, patents, and station interconnections, thus guaranteeing that
any messages transmitted would be acceptable to those groups. In one especially egregious
act of censorship noted in section three, Charles R. Denny, former chairman of the Federal Communications Commission, who had then moved into the position of executive
vice-president and director of the National Broadcasting Co. (NBC), a subsidiary of RCA,
announced that NBC's invitation to Paul Robeson to appear on a symposium program
had been rescinded.[31]

It is doubtful that anyone involved in the capitalist publishing world felt particularly
worried by the challenges contained in this small volume, but attacks on progressive publications continued nonetheless. *Colliers* magazine published a story by Frederick Woltman in
the October 21, 1950, issue, cunningly titled "Pravda, U.S.A.," which purported to claim
that the *Daily Worker* was "Stalin's American mouthpiece." Artwork accompanying the

article featured a larger-than-life Stalin holding a tightrope, across which teetered John Gates, *Daily Worker* editor. Beneath him lay crumpled bodies, apparently those of dismissed former editors who did not "toe the line." Woltman began by describing federal appeals court judges reading *Daily Worker* clippings and agreeing to uphold the convictions of the party leaders. He quoted Judge Irving Saypol: "'A reading of the *Daily Worker* since the invasion of Korea justifies the conclusion that, with the welfare and security of the United States and its armed forces at stake, appellants' loyalty to the communist forces in Korea and throughout the world is undivided and unquestioned.'" Woltman then proceeded to blame the newspaper for every historical shift in party analysis, capitalizing on seeming inconsistencies. The article had its effect: three months later, the New York newsstands banned sales of the paper, and circulation fell.[32] Among other revelations, Woltman had described the ownership of the *Daily Worker*, characterizing it as a "dummy corporation to end all dummy corporations." He named one of the owners: "Miss Grace Hutchins, an elderly, white-haired, efficient-looking party functionary, writer and researcher, who ran for New York State comptroller on the Communist ticket in 1936 and lives in Greenwich Village."[33]

Undeterred by such cheap shots, Hutchins wrote a review of *Monopoly Today* for *Railroad Notes*; then she moved on to other more pressing publication tasks, most especially the production of *Labor Fact Book 10*. Still, despite the overwhelming work of publication, Hutchins found time to do the small—and sometimes not so small—tasks that kept the organization functioning, focusing her efforts on the unsung work of women. In February 1951, she sent an obituary for Maud Malone to the *Daily Worker*.[34] Malone was an early suffrage activist, "commander of the Flying Squad of Street Suffragettes,"[35] and a librarian who had organized the first union of library employees, in New York City; from 1946 to 1951 she served as librarian for the *Daily Worker*.[36] Born in 1877, she had organized the Harlem Equal Rights League. During the suffrage campaign, she broke with the Progressive Woman's Union over the question of class, insisting that the movement worry less about what its proponents wore on marches and at demonstrations and more about including everyone, regardless of class—or race or religion.[37] Malone had made it a practice to attend the campaign speaking engagements of presidential candidates, interrupting them at key moments—such as during Theodore Roosevelt's extended disquisition on sewing machine tariffs—to ask, "What about votes for women, Colonel?"[38] By paying for the publication of Malone's obituary, Hutchins continued her efforts to reshape Marxist-Leninist discourse, ensuring that Malone's name and work were written into history.

In early March 1951, Hutchins was called to Quakertown, Pennsylvania, to care for Mother Bloor, eighty-eight years old, who had returned from a lengthy speaking and organizing trip with a serious case of pneumonia. A teletype from the local FBI, referring to Hutchins as an "old-time functionary," told headquarters that Hutchins had been sent because the party feared what Mother Bloor would say in her irrational state, a minor instance of FBI colonizing Communist speech with conspiracies.[39] Although Hutchins did tend to her, it was less because of a fear of what she would say than a desire to care for and protect her. Mother Bloor recovered for a time, writing to Lem Harris and saying, "My Dear Lem, You almost lost your Mother." Her trip to Ohio, although exhausting, had not been fruitless, she said. "There were some good results for Defense, but bad for me. I overworked and came home on a stretcher. Fortunately, I got home." She was delirious, she said, "and told all and sundry that I had been hounded by K.K.K. on my way home in Ohio. I still see them in my dreams." Hutchins had come immediately, she told him. "She is a Major General of a nurse, and she organized *everything*."[40]

Somehow, Hutchins also found a few spare moments during that difficult time to write a letter to the *Daily Worker* on International Women's Day, asking that readers recognize the work of Helen Bryan, who had served for ten years as the chair of the Joint Anti-Fascist Refugee Committee.[41] Daughter of a Presbyterian minister, she had just been released from Alderson women's prison in West Virginia, where she had spent three months for her refusal to release the names of refugees or contributors to House Un-American Activities Committee inquisitors. Like Hutchins and Rochester, Helen Bryan's emotional commitments were to women. Hutchins used the channels of publication available to celebrate Bryan's bravery, along with the courage of Maud Malone, Betty Millard, and others like them.[42]

Despite the fact that speech was becoming more and more circumscribed, Hutchins worked hard to keep the lines of publication, such as they were, open, knowing it was all she had. She owned stock in the Freedom of the Press Foundation (the *Daily Worker* publisher) and the People's Radio Foundation. And she managed to coax another volume of the *Labor Fact Book* into print. This volume described the economic state of the union, showing the ways in which both age and race were implicated in the range of incomes, and Hutchins made sure that a section was devoted to the special situations of women workers, emphasizing the failure of bills in Congress that would have guaranteed equal pay for equal work.[43]

In the meantime, the House Un-American Activities Committee was busy supporting Whittaker Chambers's ongoing efforts to sabotage Hutchins. They had called Oliver Edmund Clubb to testify in March 1951 about his visit to the office of *New Masses* in 1932, during which time he met Whittaker Chambers and, as Chambers told it, carried a letter that he was to transmit to Grace Hutchins.[44] Clubb denied ever having seen Hutchins before the previous month, on February 27, when he visited her in New York City in an attempt to determine whether he had ever met her before. He said he could not even recall having visited the office of *New Masses* in 1932, though he did visit New York City that year while in the United States on leave.[45] In June 1951, HUAC called in former *New Masses* editor Walt Carmon to ask him about the same events.[46] And as government committees harassed current and former editors of left-wing publications, mass media publishers kept whipping up public fears with articles about spies.

The July 1951 issue of *McCall's* featured an excerpt of Elizabeth Bentley's soon-to-be-released book and a photograph of her standing in front of Hutchins and Rochester's apartment building, with the caption, "Miss Bentley had friends in these Greenwich Village apartments, housed Communist visitors there."[47] Hutchins did not allow the intimidation to slow her efforts; indeed, she responded to every call for assistance, sponsoring the National Women's Appeal for the Rights of Foreign Born Americans in April 1951 and, the next month, signing an open letter generated by the American Committee for the Protection of the Foreign Born (ACPFB) protesting deportations.

When called to Washington, DC, herself to testify before the House Un-American Activities Committee, Hutchins did not flinch. The committee wanted to know about her history, particularly regarding Oliver Edmund Clubb. The hearing, on June 21, 1951, was held in executive session, as the committee members no doubt realized that Hutchins was not going to give them anything (if, indeed, she even had anything to give), and they would not have wanted her "unfriendly" response to be publicized.[48] Predictably, Hutchins "refused to affirm or deny Communist Party membership," a euphemism for the fact that she claimed immunity from self-incrimination under the Fifth Amendment.[49]

The precedent-setting first convictions of CPUSA leaders under the Smith Act, plus the passage of the McCarran Act, created conditions that allowed for increasing persecution. The "second string" of twenty-one CPUSA leaders was arrested while Hutchins was away in Washington testifying. Among those arrested were Hutchins and Rochester's friends Elizabeth Gurley Flynn and Alexander Trachtenberg. Five days later, on June 25, the New York Supreme Court ordered the closure of the 162,000-member progressive insurance company International Workers Order, claiming that it was "Communist-dominated."[50]

As it became increasingly clear that the US government was attempting to arrest all leaders of the CPUSA, the decision was made that four of the eleven "first string" leaders, convicted of conspiracy to advocate the overthrow of the US government by force and violence, would go into hiding rather than present themselves for incarceration. The eight remaining leaders would serve their sentences. The four who fled were Gus Hall, Henry Winston, Robert Thompson, and Gilbert Green.

Because bail for the four had been provided by the Bail Fund of the Civil Rights Congress, this decision had the unfortunate effect of giving the government a reason to pursue—and abolish—the Bail Fund. On July 3, 1951, Judge Sylvester Ryan of New York declared the bail posted by the fund unacceptable. He ordered the trustees of the fund to name those who had posted the money. The trustees refused, claiming Fifth Amendment immunity, and were given sentences ranging from three to six months for contempt of court.[51] Because bail posted by the fund had been declared invalid, those who had been arrested under the Smith and McCarran acts and released on Bail Fund securities on July 13 were forced to return to jail on July 17 until other means of raising bail could be devised. On July 26, another twelve party activists were arrested across the country; the arrests continued through the summer.

In practice, what the prohibition of the Bail Fund meant was that there could be no more anonymous support for those arrested. Bail had to be posted by individuals, whose names would thereupon be made public. This new situation had profound implications for Hutchins's efforts to create a collective material rhetoric. Among other things, it effectively divided the membership into those who could afford to be known and those who couldn't so afford, recreating typical American pressures of shame and humiliation around ownership or lack thereof. Those who could afford to be known were under pressure to step up, yet at the same time they risked alienation from the collective by acknowledging their comfortable position. Others were embarrassed by their inability to provide help when it was needed.

In the midst of the arrests and indictments, on July 21, Hutchins and Rochester's long-time friend Winifred Chappell died in Chicago at age 72.[52] And on August 10, 1951, Mother Bloor died. "Mother Bloor will be missed more than words can say," Rochester wrote via telegram from Croton-on-Hudson. "Who else has given so many people the warm personal interest that encourages each one of us to do the best we can?" The funeral service was a massive outpouring of love and strength. More than seven thousand people filed past "as she lay in state for four hours amid a mountain of floral wreaths surrounding the mahogany coffin."[53] At the service held at St. Nicholas Arena in New York, Paul Robeson said: "Mother would tell us tonight we've got to fight for peace. Her forebears helped free my people. Her sons and millions of America's sons will carry on until this is truly the land of the free and the home of the brave."[54] Tributes arrived from people across the country and throughout the world.[55]

It took Rochester some time to recover enough from this loss to write to Devere Allen acknowledging his semiannual check.[56] Finally, on September 23, she wrote, telling him that "Grace's pace is faster than mine," and asking for news from him.[57] He responded in November with one of his trademark detailed communications, telling Rochester that "we do, through Worldover Press, reach a really astonishing series of papers, over 550 of them, and most of them reprint our stuff generously. I think you would like much of this outreach, for we do push very hard on inter-racialism, and we have at least been socking the McCarthys and other witch-hunters. And asking for a less bellicose foreign policy."[58]

Several days later, Rochester responded, saying, "Since receiving your interesting letter the other day, we have had a bright idea." The idea, she said, was that he should stop making payments to her now, having probably sent by this time the equivalent of the original cost of the land. "This is not a gift. Just a straight business proposition," she added, echoing her words to Sally Cleghorn at Community House some thirty years earlier. Rochester included many items from the LRA, hoping that Allen would use them in his publications that were reaching into those 550 newspapers.[59] No doubt Rochester realized that the CPUSA press was in danger of annihilation. John Gates, *Daily Worker* editor, had surrendered on July 2, 1951, and had begun to serve his five-year term. Of the four who fled, Gus Hall was arrested in Mexico City on October 8.[60] Supporting Devere Allen would be one way to continue the spread of progressive ideas.

Government efforts to crush the left, although damaging and deeply painful, were not entirely successful. On the same day that Gus Hall was arrested in Mexico City, former members of the American Civil Liberties Union announced the formation of a new organization, the Emergency Civil Liberties Committee. Headed by Columbia University professor Corliss Lamont, this group, in contrast to the ACLU, would include CPUSA members.[61] Lamont would learn much later—along with the rest of the country—that during this time some ACLU officers had been quietly funneling information to and from the FBI.[62] Whether Rochester and Hutchins knew of or suspected this consummate betrayal on the part of their former friends is unclear. However, Rochester did join the new organization at its inception.

Yet for all the terrifying events compounding on a nearly daily basis, Hutchins and Rochester were never too busy or too worried to pay attention to children or to remember friends. For years, they had made valentines, often strings of dancing girls cut out of red paper, for their neighbor, Ruth Stiles Gannett, as she grew up.[63] In 1951, during the Christmas holidays, Hutchins's nieces came for their first overnight visit. Mary-Louise Henson remembered the delight of visiting Aunt Grace and Aunt Anna: "Grace would pick us up at Grand Central in a taxi," she said, "which we thought was divine because they were those big Checker cabs, and she knew exactly how to open those doors out and put down the little seats and put us in the seats, and then she'd sit back, and she'd ask us about what we wanted to do." Of course, they wanted to go to Schrafft's. Then, after lunch, Hutchins would take them to children's theater at Greenwich House. At home, Lucie Myer would play the piano and sing. "We just had a marvelous time with them," Mary-Louise Henson recalled. "They were always reading us stories and telling jokes and being absolutely wonderful. . . . They weren't, you know, silly. They were intelligent, but they respected us, [and] didn't go over our heads."[64]

Fortunately, the FBI did not choose this moment to show up at Hutchins and Rochester's door. When an agent did present himself on January 30, 1952—in error, as it turned out—Rochester made no secret of her affiliation. She told him forthrightly that she was still active in the CPUSA, paying dues and attending meetings, and that she would continue to do so even if the party were forced to go underground. She favored a revolution in the United States, she said—although she neglected, wisely, to define the term "revolution."[65]

Although Hutchins, too, "favored a revolution," she had her hands full trying to forestall the US drift toward fascism. On January 18, 1952, the trustees of the Bail Fund of the Civil Rights Congress resigned their positions and nominated Hutchins as a single trustee to oversee the liquidation of the fund, under pressure from the State Banking Department. Mary Metlay Kaufman, lawyer for the fund, pointed out that the fund was, indeed, solvent, as the $100,000 deficit had been covered by lenders who waived and subordinated their claims in the amount of $125,000.[66] This solvency apparently made no difference to the State of New York, officials of which were anxious to put the fund out of business and to gain access to the names of those involved. Hutchins accepted the position of liquidating trustee, marking the beginning of a nine-year process during which she sought to return the money to donors and protect their names from FBI scrutiny.

Hutchins's efforts were fruitless; by April 16 the State Banking Department had turned the Bail Fund's records over to the New York State Office of the Attorney General, with liquidation to be conducted by a receiver to be named by the governor. On April 28, 1952, the State of New York filed suit against the former trustees, plus Hutchins, charging them with electing Hutchins to office illegally and, more importantly, violating the state banking code. This move greatly increased the likelihood that names of contributors would be published—and those contributors would run the risk of blacklisting—despite the fact that the original trustees had served time in prison rather than release the names and had only turned the records over to the State Banking Department after having received promises that all names would be kept strictly confidential. On top of this, contributors stood to lose a significant amount of their money, as a court fight plus a state-run liquidation would be very costly, in contrast to a privately run liquidation.[67]

In May 1952, what Bail Fund trustees had tried so hard to prevent finally happened: New York State Attorney General Nathaniel I. Goldstein announced that he had turned over the list of Bail Fund contributors to the FBI. Hutchins responded immediately, "I am outraged and horrified. . . . In doing this, the New York State Attorney General has violated the confidential status of the fund records and exposed to possible persecution and harassment innocent people who did no more than exercise their constitutional rights in defense of a paramount constitutional right—the right to bail."[68]

While she worked to protect others, Hutchins never once mentioned her own ongoing horror: Whittaker Chambers's very public—and very negative—characterization of her in the *Saturday Evening Post*. On February 9, 1952, Whittaker Chambers's book manuscript began to appear in weekly installments entitled "I Was the Witness"; the *Post* had paid Chambers $75,000 for the privilege of publishing his memoir of life as an agent in an alleged Communist underground. And as if these installments weren't bad enough, it turned out that they were only a truncated version of a much lengthier book, *Witness*, which appeared on May 21, 1952, published by Random House and designated the June Book-of-the-Month Club selection.

Repeating D. H. Lawrence's "lesbian = death" trope that he had used to attack Hutchins in December of 1948,[69] Chambers devoted several pages in *Witness* specifically to what we would now call homophobic and misogynist accusations of Hutchins—all expressed in life-and-death language with biblical overtones. In one instance, he claimed that Hutchins had paid a visit to Esther Shemitz, his fiancée, to deliver a message from the party that she was to end her relationship with him: "I was never quite sure how official Miss Hutchins' mission was, and how much was self-imposed. For I sensed, behind the political ban another force, serpentine and cold, that deeply hated life."[70,71]

Certainly this negative characterization was Chambers's way of paying Hutchins back for her revelations about him to the FBI. Having already established, in 1948, a link between the CPUSA and homosexuality via the persons of Hutchins and Rochester, Chambers took this opportunity to expand his scapegoating efforts, publicly offloading charges of sexual deviance onto Hutchins and Rochester while proclaiming in heroic detail his devotion to his wife and family. Chambers undoubtedly had other motives as well. As the trial of Julius and Ethel Rosenberg progressed, he most likely was attempting to secure protection for himself and his wife by mounting the best possible offense, appearing to reveal every secret and then some, while portraying his wife, who had worked for Amtorg, as an innocent child. What's more, a close reading of Chambers's book reveals an elaborate scheme to ensure the inviolability of his narrative: he constructed *Witness* as a snare that would force any persons foolish enough to challenge the content or the framing devices to reveal compromising details about their own knowledge.

How exactly did Chambers do this? Although the Department of Justice used Louis Budenz's claim that the CPUSA had written its constitution and organizing pamphlets in "Aesopian language" to convict party leaders, planting the term in the public lexicon, most readers took *Witness* at face value, despite several statements in the book that should have put alert readers on their guard. Like Budenz, Chambers claimed that "double-talking" and "reading between the lines" were Communist literary techniques; then he announced that he was using "those arts which Communism had taught me,"[72] a clear reference to Budenz's allegations, which by then were sealed into cases approved by the Supreme Court. Chambers also said more specifically that "the habit of my mind is ironic."[73] Irony requires a knowing reader, because it functions by emphasizing what is *not* meant and de-emphasizing what *is* meant. Reading *Witness*, we can see Chambers's "ironic habit of mind" at work, as he foregrounds tales of communist espionage while framing and shaping them in subterranean gay cultural allusions invisible except to those who were already familiar with them.

To facilitate and embellish his ironic method, Chambers engaged in hyperbole, anchoring his narrative in minor and obvious facts, then inflating and distorting the story with wild exaggerations and outright duplicity. For example, he told readers (for no apparent reason) that Hutchins and Rochester named their summer cottage "The Little Acorn."[74] This, in fact, was close to true. Readers were meant to assume that if this insignificant detail was correct, then so were all the other claims.

Chambers's "death threat" story about Hutchins formed one of the foundations of *Witness* and served as one part of the trap built into the narrative. Chambers expanded upon the account he had given reporters of Hutchins in 1948, declaring that the message left in his brother-in-law's office in May 1938 "said something very close to this: 'Tell Esther's husband to contact Steve at once. Very urgent.' Esther is my wife. Steve is Alexander Stevens, alias J. Peters, the head of the underground section of the American Communist Party."[75] Chambers was baiting Hutchins, who had taken Eleanor Stevenson, known as "Steve," with her. He was daring her to correct the error of "Steve's" identity—and in the process, to reveal both herself and her partner, Anna Rochester, as well as Eleanor Stevenson and Ruth Erickson. Wisely, Hutchins refused to take the bait. Although she did expose some elements of Chambers's method, there is no evidence to suggest that either she or Rochester knew enough to grasp the entirety of Chambers's hoax. So we can assume that the trap Chambers set was perhaps a bit too sophisticated.

What do we see when reading it now, some sixty years later? We should begin by acknowledging that "Aesopian language," far from being "Communist code," was a term coined by nineteenth-century Russian writers to refer to the common literary methods (metaphor, satire, irony, hyperbole, paraphrasis, ellipsis, metonomy, allegory—just about any literary device) they used to avoid the czar's censors. According to literary critic Lev Loseff, Aesopian language uses a system of screens and markers in order to convey a message to readers who are "in the know." Screens mask or point away from the meaning; markers guide the reader toward the meaning.[76] Reading *Witness* as an Aesopian document, we plow through eight hundred pages of verbal screens about communism and the evils thereof, as well as paeans to Chambers's perfect marriage. The screens include lengthy declarations of love and devotion to his wife and children, long disquisitions on morality and the nature of good and evil, frequent asides about the importance of God, and numerous cloak-and-dagger stories of Communist espionage. Within all this, the markers of a same-sex subculture can be difficult to locate, but they are there, appearing on nearly every page.

One set of markers consists of language that is common now but that was a subcultural code at the time: the word "gay," and a variant, "gayety"—always spelled with a y rather than an i—pop up all through the book. In fact, Chambers locates the microfilm lab where purloined documents allegedly were copied for transmission where else but on Gay Street in Greenwich Village. Most significantly, at one point Chambers tells a story of meeting with his Russian contact and the man's wife who, he claims, can only articulate one English phrase, which is "It's a gay farce." Chambers repeats the phrase twice, and he insists that she repeated it three or four times during their meeting. Because there is no other reason for him to tell this story, it can be read as a message to the reader: *Witness*, in all its sexual innuendo and melodramatic hyperbole, is a gay farce.

In addition to these linguistic markers and many others like them, there are several more sets, all farcical allusions to other fictions. Chambers drew the framework of *Witness* from several sources. Hutchins herself noticed Chambers's penchant for using plots of published stories, pointing out that he had alleged Juliet Stuart Poyntz's death by retelling an Edgar Allen Poe story.[77] Moreover, Chambers quoted liberally from Shakespeare, Rimbaud, and the Bible and alluded without attribution to a wide range of Russian and German novels and to popular American films of the time.[78] The unnamed sources included passages from Paul's "Letter to the Romans," in which he enjoins against homosexuality, and, most significantly, *The Scorpion*, a lesbian novel that Chambers translated from German to English in 1932, as well as the sequel to that novel, *The Outcast*, translated a year later by Guy Endore, another left-wing writer.[79] The plot of *Witness* bears a more than coincidental resemblance to the plot of the lesbian novels, if one substitutes Communism for the love interest in *The Scorpion*. The plots both include (1) rebellion against bourgeois convention that leads the main character into illicit activities; (2) initiation into an underground antibourgeois culture—in Chambers's case, he claims the CPUSA underground, and in the case of *The Scorpion*, the Weimar-era Berlin gay and lesbian scene; (3) flight and fear of pursuit; (4) rejection of the underground cultures in favor of a devotion to God and cultivation of the individual soul; and (5) relocation to a new home in the country, working the land.

There are strong thematic similarities as well: all three books swing hyperbolically between celebrations of life and death, with suicide a major focus in each.[80] Within the first nineteen pages of *Witness*, Chambers placed no fewer than ten key elements from *The Scorpion* and *The Outcast*, including the word "outcast," applied to himself. There are references to suicide, a revolver, loneliness, death, children, blood, the soul, the importance of God, and pleasure in work on the land. More parallels abound, which we do not have the space to enumerate here.

So, not only was *Witness* an exercise in scapegoating, it was scapegoating taken to a new level, a sophisticated, campy trap set for Grace Hutchins in particular (and any other CPUSA members or friends who might have had sufficient knowledge to understand the allusions). An extended midcentury gay cryptogram, *Witness* could only be decoded by those with intimate knowledge of same-sex texts and cultural references to an underground culture that developed in the shadow of the sexological establishment.[81]

Hutchins and Rochester's partnership, founded in an earlier era, had continued largely unmodified over time. Although Chambers made every attempt to force them into an abject identity, they resisted, largely because they were simply unfamiliar with the subcultural markers. In 1952, few had this knowledge, and, most important, fewer still could risk making such a public decoding. In order to challenge the narrative of *Witness*, a reader would have had to reveal the extent of his or her own knowledge, in today's language, "outing" themselves and thus completing Chambers's scapegoating scheme.

What's more, if anyone at the time had adequate literary and cultural knowledge to understand what Chambers had written—and the fortitude to reveal that knowledge—they had little access to publication in order to produce a counternarrative, with the result that that piece of American history now is largely history-according-to-Chambers. Hutchins tried every avenue to which she had access in order to counteract Chambers's story. She found, of course, that most previously open avenues were closed to her. Writing to Random House, Hutchins said: "On page 60 of his book *Witness*, published by you, Whittaker Chambers says that I threatened his life with the statement that unless he showed up by 'such and such a day' he would be killed! This is absolutely false, without the slightest basis in fact." She goes on to provide her own bona fides, listing her years in China and her work with St. Faith's, as well as her twenty-five years with the LRA. "It is shocking," she said, "to thousands of persons in this country that such a reputable publisher as Random House should issue such a scurrilous book."[82]

Random House editor Bennett Cerf, who had sponsored publishing parties for International Publishers during the 1930s, now disregarded her entreaties.[83] The book was, after all, number one on the *New York Times* best-seller list for the entire summer of 1952. Hutchins nonetheless sent copies of her letter to Random House to newspapers and to many of her friends and acquaintances; some friends even wrote to request a copy. Few newspapers published the letter, the notable exceptions being the *Daily Worker* and the *Daily Compass*, a progressive newspaper that was forced out of business shortly thereafter. Hutchins did receive assurances from most of her friends that they were not taking Chambers seriously, although most were either puzzled or angry, and none seemed to have any idea what the book was really about. A representative of her father's law firm in Boston, Charles Cheney, wrote back, saying: "None of us have read the Chambers book—or had any desire to—and consequently were unaware of his comments about you. Certainly, as you so well put it, nobody who knows you could possibly believe such a cock-and-bull story."[84]

Cheney and other members of the firm reassured Hutchins of their continuing love, as did many others who wrote to her. Dorothy Canfield Fisher wrote to Rochester asking to see a copy of the letter Hutchins had written to Random House: "In my opinion, she is quite accurate in saying that the book is fiction rather than autobiography."[85] Margaret Reeve Cary wrote immediately, telling Hutchins, "What the liar says about Mysticism, and what the Critics have SWALLOWED whole about Mysticism, whose hem they have never touched, makes me sickest of all. The very idea of that liar being a Quaker makes me sick at my stomach. He does not know one thing about the Society of Friends and how I would love to quiz him."[86]

Hutchins must have been feeling especially hurt by Esther Chambers's failure to rein in or, at the very least, contradict her husband.[87] Margaret Cary tried to explain what she believed was Esther's position: "I think our precious Esther would WANT to understand

and sympathize with our point of view, but dearest, hers has been too sheltered a life, too conventional a life, for her to understand REALLY. Her mind has never been clear anyway." Cary assured Hutchins that she, at least, would never abandon her: "You and Anna both know, without my repeating it, that always and forever and with whatever personal sacrifice I would defend you both at the Bar, that I would go to any length to give you perfect character references."[88]

Letters followed, from Hutchins's college classmate, Alice Hawkins, as well as several other classmates; from former Community House resident Helen Hendricks; from their former Companion Margaret Shearman; from Alice Hamilton; and from Devere Allen, responding to Hutchins's critique of his review of *Witness* for *The Churchman*. Hutchins had taken him to task for claiming that Chambers was "sincerely devout" and had characterized *Witness* as a work of fiction.

Allen refused to apologize for the review, but he did acknowledge that he had written it from a part of the *Saturday Evening Post* version of the book, as he did not have access to the complete Random House publication—and did not realize that Hutchins had been personally attacked. "The whole book was a florid, mean, distasteful job," he finally conceded, also deploring the fact that Chambers was calling himself a Quaker.

The book review editors to whom Hutchins wrote professed less outrage. They either declined completely to publish her letter—for a variety of reasons—or said that they might publish a part of it. Lewis Gannett, reviewer for the *New York Herald Tribune*, insisted that most of his correspondents had castigated him for publishing a *negative* review of the book. He suggested that "some day, if you ever write it, I'd be interested to read your story of your own relations with Whittaker Chambers."[89]

Hutchins undoubtedly knew that writing her story of her "own relations with Whittaker Chambers" would only reinforce the popular image of a battle between individuals and would do nothing to change minds, not to mention the fact that she had no interest in feeding the profit machinery that had produced the situation. Chambers's book would be the last move in this high-stakes game, leaving him, in the popular imagination, appearing to be a most devout heterosexual family man—and fueling decades of anticommunist hysteria.

Meanwhile, Hutchins had more than enough to do supporting the larger movement through this most difficult time. As more and more people were arrested, the need for a legal defense fund had become critical. Organizers established the Citizens Emergency Defense conference, to which Hutchins contributed. She herself continued to serve as trustee of the Bail Fund of the Civil Rights Congress, her time consumed with work that had nothing to do with providing bail for those who needed it and everything to do with trying to protect the funds—and the names—of those who had already contributed. On July 21, 1952, she was replaced as liquidating trustee by Frederick Greenman, a lawyer of the government's choosing. Working with her own team of lawyers, Hutchins continued trying to return the money to those who had loaned it.

This year, instead of time with others in community at Adelynrood or Back Log Camp, Rochester, Hutchins, and Lucie Myer spent their self-allowed two-week vacation on Cape Ann, a Massachusetts tourist destination. Then, as soon as they returned from their somewhat lonely vacation, Hutchins frantically tried to raise enough funds to maintain the LRA for another year. Writing to Jessie O'Connor, she lamented the loss of a contribution the LRA had been counting on—in the amount of $1500. To make up the loss, she was asking fifteen contributors to provide another $100 each. Would Jessie agree to be among the fifteen?[90] O'Connor did not hesitate, sending the contribution by return mail. "Let us hope there will be a turning of the tide soon," she wrote, "so that causes can stand or fall on their rational merits and not on the basis of shouting and persecution."[91] Louise Berman, too, responded quickly to Hutchins's appeal ("Of course you can count on me") and sent along with it a message of appreciation: "Let me take this opportunity to tell you how much I have admired your courage and gallantry during these difficult days. I think you have been really magnificent."[92]

Perhaps it was messages such as these that kept Hutchins going during the dark times of the 1950s. In addition to all her fund-raising work, she still sought to intervene at the point of struggle, somehow finding the time to rewrite *Women Who Work*, her 1934 signature effort. As she had before, Hutchins focused her feminism on women of the working class. But this time, although conditions remained difficult, Hutchins had more to report—more women working outside the home, more women in unions, and more women who were agitating for the freedom that would come with equal pay, racial equality, and peace. Even better, there were activist women whom she could name, passing the responsibility for the liberation of women to a younger generation.

More than 30 percent of women were employed in the work force in March 1952, Hutchins noted, far more than the 20 percent she had documented in 1930. In this edition of the book, she emphasized the "double burden" faced by mothers who worked outside the home, challenging the prevailing ideology that insisted upon mothers staying home with their children without regard for the circumstances in which many working class mothers found themselves. The first half of the book described and explained those circumstances, covering farm and migrant work, unequal pay for women, the lack of medical care, speed-ups on the job, and the inadequacy of the social security system for which she had worked so hard twenty years earlier.

Hutchins devoted the second half of the book to answering the question: why do women organize? Unions, she pointed out, had much to offer women workers, garnering higher wages and, thus, higher pensions for them. Older women and African American women especially had much to gain from unionizing, she argued. She also emphasized the benefits to all concerned when African American and white workers collaborated on projects of mutual interest, citing the integration of Stuyvesant Town, a New York City housing project, by the concerted actions of a mixed-race housing organization against the efforts of the owner, Metropolitan Life Insurance Company.

She closed the book with a short narrative describing the work of American Women for Peace, the organization established in August 1950 that had taken the place of the Congress of American Women when that organization was dissolved in January 1950 so that leaders would not be forced to register under the Foreign Agents Registration Act.[93] Hutchins pointed to the collective efforts of women, such as the women's peace delegation, which was composed of some one thousand women, "both negro and white, from 40 states and 80 organizations," yet she did not stop at women's efforts for peace. Citing the miners' strikes in New Mexico, she emphasized women's picketing as central to the workers' victories: "As fast as the sheriffs arrested the women [at the Empire Zinc Company] other women and children came down the hill from the mining camp to take their places. . . . Tear-gas bombs were thrown at the picket lines, but when the gas cleared away, the women were still there."[94] She also underscored the work of the Sojourners for Truth and Justice as "a leading association of forward-looking women," quoting their mission statement, which read in part: "We shall not be trampled upon any longer. We shall resist all attempts to muffle our voices or shorten our strides toward freedom."[95] And she cited again the work of individual women, including actress "Miss Beulah Richardson

[who] first read her dramatic poem, 'A Negro Woman Speaks of White Womanhood, of White Supremacy, of Peace,' at the conference of the American Women for Peace."[96] Finally, she showcased her friend Betty Millard, whose new pamphlet, *Women on Guard*, documented her "two years abroad as a member of the secretariat of the Women's International Democratic Federation." *Women on Guard*, Hutchins said, provided evidence that 602,570,000 people worldwide had signed petitions requesting peace talks between the major powers.[97]

Despite these efforts, peace talks had yet to occur, and peace at home was equally elusive. Government efforts to harass Communists—indeed, any progressives—continued to flourish. Having emptied and refilled CPUSA language to their own liking, prosecutors now sought to shut down all possible Marxist publication venues. When her publisher and friend Alexander Trachtenberg was arrested, Rochester fought back. Trachtenberg, more than anyone else, had been responsible for creating a space in which she could speak. Rochester helped to organize a committee of support, whose members included her old friends Vida Scudder, Scott Nearing, and Harry F. Ward, as well as W. E. B. DuBois, Michael Gold, Rockwell Kent, John Howard Lawson, Albert Maltz, Louise Pettibone Smith, and Paul Robeson, among others. Writing in the *Daily Worker*, Rochester tried to remind readers of what they seemed to have forgotten—"the great struggles for liberty which brought many of the earliest settlers to these shores." Trachtenberg, she pointed out, was among those who had escaped tyranny and come to the United States, leaving Czarist Russia as a young man and studying at both Trinity College and Yale before establishing International Publishers. "He has devoted his life," she said, "to the publication of books on labor and economic problems. The Marxist classics he has issued are in most of the libraries of this country."[98]

On June 12, 1952, Rochester organized a meeting of Trachtenberg's supporters. A small booklet containing speeches from the meeting included Rochester's expression of outrage: "To anyone brought up with respect for the Bill of Rights and for the freest possible discussion of the world in which we live, it seems almost unbelievable that Alexander Trachtenberg, as publisher of economic and historical books, should be indicted for making available in this country books which are seriously critical of the capitalist economy."[99]

By this time, it had been two years since *Collier's* had published its red-baiting article on the *Daily Worker*, naming Hutchins as an owner. Hutchins and Rochester had been stockholders in the corporation publishing the *Daily Worker* since the early 1940s. Hutchins became a director in August 1951. In late 1952, during a time of financial constriction, the publishers arranged a dinner to honor the stockholders, who were loyally supporting the paper during these difficult times. Just exactly how difficult, they probably did not know. On October 8, 1952, J. Edgar Hoover sent a memo to the New York FBI office requesting information about the *Daily Worker* "in connection with some writing being done at the Bureau." He had several questions. Could the office supply information about the mechanics of editing the *Daily Worker*?

> Who are the really important individuals determining the policy and preparation of the *Daily Worker* at this time? Do you have any knowledge of jealousy, envy, the clash of personalities in the staff of the *Daily Worker*? Do you have any examples of the lack of independent thought and individual initiative and creativeness prevailing among its staff members? Do you have any other examples which touch upon matters of human interest or personality items which would be interesting to the man on the street?[100]

Hoover was discreet about his publication plans, but the use of government resources to undermine the *Daily Worker* could not be more clear.

Likewise, government agents continued to keep the Bail Fund tangled in red tape. In November 1952, Hutchins wrote to Frederick Greenman, the liquidating trustee of the Bail Fund, worrying about the long delay in the return of the funds, saying: "I am deeply troubled at the increasing number of persons, holding certificates in the Bail Fund, who come in to ask me *when* they can get back their money. . . . They are workers in no position to borrow from the bank, or from friends, to meet their immediate needs."[101] Greenman's reply was cordially, almost cheerfully, dismissive: there was no delay, he said, and no date could be forecast for the return of the loans.[102]

The losses continued to climb. In late November, Hutchins and Rochester's friend Robert Minor died. Rochester had felt particularly close to Minor because they both had sacrificed careers as artists—he as a cartoonist and she as a pianist—to devote themselves to a working class revolution. They had been neighbors: Bob Minor and his wife, Lydia Gibson, had a summer cottage on Mt. Airy Road near Hutchins and Rochester and Bob and Slava Dunn in Croton-on-Hudson. But more than that, Minor respected Rochester and did not allow gender prejudice to interfere with their work toward common goals. Writing for the *Daily Worker*, Rochester said: "A great fighter has gone—one of the rare artists whose art was a weapon and a comrade who inspired others to action."[103] She also served as a member of the honor guard at Bob Minor's funeral service. Not only was Rochester a good friend to Bob Minor, but many of his other friends were in prison and unable to attend his service.

During the rest of the month of December, Rochester and Hutchins spent much of their time writing letters to and for these imprisoned comrades, especially to Elizabeth Gurley Flynn, who had been sentenced to thirty days for contempt of court. Rochester mounted a public campaign to free Flynn and to prevent her conviction and further imprisonment, drawing this time on old friends from past activist women's communities. Collaborating with Flynn's friend Alice Hamilton, Harvard professor emerita and expert on occupational diseases, with whom she had become acquainted during her years at the US Children's Bureau, Rochester wrote a fund-raising letter to be sent to selected individuals while Hamilton wrote a letter to the editors of the *New York Times*. In her November 22 letter to the *Times*, published on December 3, 1952, Hamilton emphasized Flynn's refusal to name names, saying, "I know, of course, that Miss Flynn is not the first to go to jail rather than turn informer. Her fate moves me especially because I have known her for many years and have followed her career with admiration for her selfless idealism. This last action of hers is further proof of her essential nobility."[104] Rochester enclosed a copy of Hamilton's letter with her own, in which she pointed out that "Miss Flynn was jailed because she showed her contempt for those who sell immunity to paid informers in return for perjured testimony to convict honest men and women or hound them out of gainful employment."[105]

Rochester asked recipients to adopt Hamilton's statement as their own and send a contribution to help in Flynn's defense. More than sixty people responded, sending amounts ranging from $1 to $100 and subscribing to Hamilton's statement. Hamilton wrote saying that she herself had had twenty-five responses, only four of which were negative. But Albert Einstein, she said, had written her a "favorable" letter. "It is a strange and terrible change that has come over our country," Hamilton despaired, "much worse and much deeper than that in the days of Mitchell Palmer." Recalling Rochester's work as a "young radical" in the US Children's Bureau, she commented, "It is good that [Julia Lathrop] did not live to see this day."[106]

As Rochester was organizing a support network, Hutchins wrote to Flynn in prison. Upon her release, after seven weeks, Flynn wrote back, thanking Hutchins: "I was really glad to get out—seven weeks is enough in such a place of tragedy where one's inability to do anything about it at all in any personal way, at least, is frustrating."[107] On January 31, 1953, Flynn, Alexander Trachtenberg, and fifteen others were convicted and sentenced to three years in prison plus a $6,000 fine.

Despite their work together on the committee supporting Alexander Trachtenberg, Rochester and Vida Scudder had done little more than exchange Christmas greetings for some time. In September 1952, when she was 90 years old, Scudder wrote a letter to Rochester apparently attempting to make a final acknowledgment of their importance to each other, saying: "Can you remember this old 'Has Been' comrade? She often thinks of you wistfully."[108] Scudder had recently run across *Jesus Christ and the World Today* on her bookshelf and confessed that she had completely forgotten it. She reread it, she said, "with sad respect: it expressed completely the attitude of decades ago, when you and I shared the social awakening in the Christian Church. . . . How obsolete and inadequate in some ways it seems today!" She went on to remind Rochester how "grieved" she had been when Rochester "found more sympathy and recognition of values in others, especially Mrs. [Mary Emily] Bruce." "But we both followed Guidance," she insisted, "and as you repudiated the Christian faith and joined Communist activities, I, led in a contrary direction, felt more sympathetic fellowship with you than you know." She enclosed a copy of her final work, *My Quest for Reality*, a small book that she had had privately printed for friends.

Vida Scudder sought out Rochester for another reason, she said: the references to Rochester in Whittaker Chambers's "melodramatic book, *Witness*"—and many more references to Hutchins, she said pointedly. Revealing her characteristic ambivalence—and an astonishing gullibility for a former English professor—Scudder said, "I found the book very exciting and illuminating, in its revelation of invasions of our political and social life by revolutionary, definitely organized, Marxist Communism, which was drawing to itself so many choice spirits among the cultured intelligenzia. I confess that I felt a little sad, as I compared your courage with my sheltered academic security." She wasn't all *that* comfortable, though, she hastened to add, having recently received a letter advising her to " 'go to Russia where you belong! you God-damned Communist.' " Although she would send two more messages to Hutchins and Rochester before her death, this letter, along with her book, was clearly a final attempt to repair broken connections, to whatever degree was possible, and to acknowledge a continuity of spirit: "I want you both to know with what respect and affection I have always regarded you, in spite of our sharp divergence." And she signed herself, "Your ancient fellow-traveller, Vida D. Scudder." A postcard followed a few days later, thanking Hutchins for sending a copy of her statement to Random House. "I do regret the contemptuous distaste with wh. Wh. Chambers—a man professedly returned to the Christian Church—inspires in me."[109]

Rochester must have realized that if she herself was slowing, there was surely little time left for the person who had drawn her into the community that had made the love and work in her life possible. She wrote a warm letter to Vida Scudder, dissolving much of the tension of the past twenty years. In her last communication with Rochester and Hutchins, Vida Scudder wrote to Hutchins, thanking her for sending her a copy of *Women Who Work*. "Dear, dear Grace," Scudder wrote, "one of the most satisfying events of my increasingly decrepit old age is the renewal of loving relations with you and Anna. Such a lovely greeting came from her! And now here is your impressive and valuable little book."[110] Acknowledging Hutchins's work, she went on: "What fine and wide-spread work it represents! I congratulate you most respectfully." However, being Vida Scudder, she couldn't let it go at that. She had finally read the book, she said. It had had to wait, though, until she completed a "little review for the *New York Call*. You know that I'm still a member of the Socialist party. I think I voted six times for Norman Thomas as president, and I still feel that Socialism as an economic plan is the most penetrating, elastic, and comprehensive formula for our needed revolution that I know."

If only they could talk! Scudder declared, warming to her subject. "I have to school myself now to pure passivity of both mind and body. But I won't say that I should ignore the most dynamic power, I think, that we have, of co-operation with a stern and loving God: that is, the power of intercessory prayer." If only Hutchins and Rochester would return to the old Church League for Industrial Democracy, now re-named the Episcopal League for Social Action, ELSA. The current secretary of that organization agreed with her, she said, that it was through the Christian Church that the "new social order" surely would come. "Dear Grace," she mourned, recapitulating the language Hutchins had noted fifteen years prior, "I'm very wistful about the withdrawal from that Church, and from the S.C.H.C., of you and Anna." No longer trusting herself to write, she closed this final letter, saying, "I am sure that we still aim at the same goal even if we follow different paths thither. And we move more closely together than we know. Your wistful old fellow-traveller, Vida D. Scudder."

Rochester and Hutchins did not seek out the ELSA. Instead, they spent their time writing to their friends in prison.[111]

Chapter Fourteen

"Purpose: Keep the Group Going"

Are the powers that be in the United States feeling so uncertain of the future that they can tolerate no analysis of the source of their wealth, no honest study of classes in the capitalist world? They have forgotten the great struggles for liberty which brought many of the earliest settlers to these shores. To them our Bill of Rights seems to have become a dead letter.

—Anna Rochester ("Can Capitalism Take Criticism?" in *Publisher on Trial*, 47)

Isn't it about time that a halt is called on the use of paid informers by our government to put behind bars people whose main "crime" was that they disagreed with war in Korea, A-Bombs and H-Bombs as a solution to our relations with the rest of the world?

—Andy Harris (secretary of the San Francisco Chapter, Civil Rights Congress, letter to the editor, *San Francisco Chronicle*, April 27, 1955)

During the latter years of Rochester' and Hutchins's lives, as their own energy and health began to fail, they struggled against forces determined to ensure that the institutions of free speech and publication that they had helped to build would fail as well. Within a polarized postwar American society, Rochester and Hutchins worked to maintain space for voices challenging capitalism, racism, and sexism. The battle became primarily a financial one, as they re-experienced the lesson they had learned at *The World Tomorrow* in 1926: "free speech" is often an oxymoron in a capitalist society. Of their own partnership, however, Rochester and Hutchins said little, choosing instead to slide beneath the social radar and focus their rhetorical gifts outwards, crafting an inclusive space wherein others might flourish. This public quietude did not mean that the partnership starved. If anything, their devotion to each other increased, as first Rochester and then Hutchins suffered debilities eliciting the other's care. Despite these debilities, neither Hutchins nor Rochester abandoned her work. Even as late as January 1, 1962, Hutchins wrote to herself in her personal notebook—"Purpose: keep the group going."[1]

The "second string" trial ended on January 21, 1953, with convictions for all defendants, including Alexander Trachtenberg and Elizabeth Gurley Flynn. Both Hutchins and Rochester sent letters to Trachtenberg in prison the next day. "Dear Trachty," Rochester wrote, "I often wonder what Thomas Jefferson would have said about the present-day political cases! And we don't *have* to wonder about the popular judgment at the next turn of a century—But meantime it is no fun to be an historic figure—And your friends don't forget you," she reminded him.[2]

Friends had not forgotten Trachtenberg—or the hundreds of others across the country facing trials. Yet the efforts to provide support were taxing the collective emotional and financial resources. After the convictions of the "second string," Hutchins worked to raise money to post bail for the second-string prisoners, to free them while their case was on appeal. In mid-February 1953, Hutchins posted $15,000 of the $25,000 bail required for Alexander Trachtenberg, plus $10,000 in cash and $10,000 in US Treasury bonds for Elisabeth Gurley Flynn. Stanley Blumenthal borrowed $5,000 from Hutchins to post bail for Albert Lannon, another of the "second string."[3] This use of her share of the income from the family trust caused problems with Grace Hutchins's brother, Henry, and especially with his wife, Alice, who may have seen Grace Hutchins's withdrawal of money from interest-bearing accounts as the quintessential American heresy.

In fact, much of what Grace Hutchins did was a mystery and an irritation to Alice Hutchins, who found Hutchins and Rochester's appearances a particular affront. The two women rarely wore jewelry—certainly never earrings—nor did they use makeup. Their clothes were plain, usually black, after the manner of Vida Scudder, although they did bow to the summer heat and invest in a few seersucker dresses. "Why can't they at least do something with their hair?" Alice Hutchins fretted, referring to the short, serviceable cuts that bespoke a lack of interest in hair fashion and its associated costs in time and money. She was losing patience with this annoying part of her husband's family and finally decreed that Grace Hutchins was not welcome in the Hutchins home. For a number of years after that, Grace Hutchins would travel to Boston to meet her brother Henry in the train station, where they would converse.[4]

Nonetheless, if Alice Hutchins banished her, Grace Hutchins still had the family of choice that she and Rochester had created. To assuage the pain of rejection and betrayal by family and friends, Hutchins and Rochester nurtured old friendships, deepening connections. They had become especially close to Ruth Erickson and Eleanor Stevenson, sharing with Erickson and Stevenson an unspoken acknowledgement of their devoted partnerships, occasionally a source of "insider" amusement, such as the time nine men showed up to install a furnace in the Stevenson/Erickson house. "We never had such a party of men before," Erickson wrote.[5]

Most important, Rochester and Hutchins never allowed themselves to take each other for granted. Rochester expressed her love for Hutchins that February in a Valentine's Day poem:

> I know a gal—the grandest pal
> That ever walked this earth.
> She keeps such a pace (and her name is Grace)
> That her energy keeps down her girth.
> It's always of others—like sisters and brothers—
> She thinks as the hours go by.
> Folks like her a lot, but I know that we're not
> As thoughtful and warm and devoted
> As such a grand gal sure deserves.
> But we all do our best (though we don't pass that test)
> And we love that grand gal
> (And forever we shall)
> Without the slightest least bit of reserves.[6]

Certainly it was of others, "like sisters and brothers," that Grace Hutchins usually thought. She continued to beseech her friends and acquaintances to act on behalf of those facing prison or deportation, always thanking those who did. Not everyone whom Hutchins contacted responded generously. In desperation, she even wrote to their old friend Roger Baldwin, with whom their friendship had lapsed over the question of Elizabeth Gurley Flynn's membership in the ACLU Board of Directors back in 1940. Would the ACLU request commutations of the Smith Act convictions? Baldwin declined, claiming that they must "wait a little time, even in a case like Elizabeth Flynn's where age and health can be urged. Governments don't admit error," he argued, "by acting so soon after commitment, especially when public prejudice is still so unreasoning." After a few months, he said, the ACLU might consider stepping in; she should consider inquiring then. Thus, he declined even to bring the question up himself in a few months, asking Hutchins "or others" to take full responsibility for the situation.[7]

More responsibility was not what Hutchins needed or wanted just then. In addition to all her efforts on behalf of prisoners and those threatened with prison, Hutchins should have been promoting her revised edition of *Women Who Work*, which International Publishers had brought out in an affordable paperback edition. This time, however, little attention was paid to the book outside of publications such as *The Worker*, *Masses and Mainstream*, *The Fur and Leather Worker*, and *Federated Press*.

If most reviewers feared association with a book written by Grace Hutchins and published by Alexander Trachtenberg, those who had no such fears did offer serious commentary. Jean Josephs, writing in *The Worker*, introduced her review with the story of a woman imprisoned and threatened with deportation, praising her husband who was now undertaking both his nine-to-five job and the housekeeping and child care. "Almost 50 percent of all working mothers," Josephs pointed out, "are temporarily or permanently without husbands. . . . As I write this, a procession of these women goes before my eyes. They are smiling a little at this story of the remarkable father because these are their lives and their burdens day in day out, year in year out, and no one has stopped to call them remarkable."[8]

Elizabeth M. Bacon, writing in *Masses and Mainstream*, summed up the book: "In short, the book demolishes male supremacy. More than that, it puts the fight against male supremacy high on the agenda for all who are concerned with the struggle for democracy, peace, and socialism." Bacon's critique, however, spoke to the very difficult rhetorical situation of 1953. Hutchins examined women's organizations of the Left, but "what of church auxiliaries, women's clubs, professional associations and the like?" Bacon asked. "It would be useful to know something of the programs of the less progressive organizations and the degree of their influence among women generally."[9] Clearly, the Left could no longer talk to itself and expect anyone else to listen—apart from the FBI. The extreme polarization of American society meant that Hutchins's insights languished unconsidered until twenty years later, when they were rediscovered by a subsequent generation of women—and even then rarely with Hutchins's name attached.

Some old friends wrote to Hutchins, congratulating her on the publication of *Women Who Work*. Polly Porter commented playfully: "Never again, even if I were in New York, would I dare just casually call you up and say, 'Let's Anna and you and I meet for lunch at Wanamakers.' Your book has overawed me—you know so much, you are a really learned woman!" She then redrew a familiar picture for Hutchins—of two women, partners, in a scene of domestic harmony, focusing their attention outward into the world, in this case by means of Hutchins's book: "I read it aloud to M. W. D. in the evenings as we sat before the living room fire, she mending the family clothes."[10]

Wanamaker's, the Greenwich Village department store, proved to be Rochester's undoing: she fell on the store's steps in March 1953, breaking her leg. While maintaining the LRA, arguing for the return of money loaned to the Bail Fund, writing to friends in prison, and publicizing her book, Hutchins took care of Rochester, now even more disabled. During Rochester's hospitalization, Hutchins read aloud to her from E. B. White's recently published meditation on love, writing, and social interdependence, *Charlotte's Web*, drawing her own picture of love for Rochester: "Wilbur never forgot Charlotte. . . . She was in a class by herself. It is not often that someone comes along who is a true friend and a good writer. Charlotte was both."[11] Despite a dearth of language with which to express love within a same-sex partnership in midcentury America, Hutchins and Rochester drew creatively upon available sources to strengthen and maintain their feelings for each other.

Increasingly frail, Rochester did less research-based writing, restricting herself to signing petitions, translating materials for the LRA and the Farm Commission, and sending financial contributions to keep various organizations and publications functioning. Despite Rochester's infirmities, the Immigration and Naturalization Service (INS), the FBI, and the Senate Permanent Subcommittee on Investigations of the Committee on Government Operations continued their enthusiastic pursuit of her. The INS asked the FBI to find out whether either Hutchins or Rochester could be deported; they intended, they said, to deport or denaturalize anyone ever mentioned by either Elizabeth Bentley or Whittaker Chambers.[12] No, the FBI replied, not bothering to add that, if it mattered, both Rochester's and Hutchins's families probably predated those of most people working for either the FBI or the INS.

In June, the Senate Permanent Subcommittee on Investigations of the Committee on Government Operations finally landed on a pretext to subpoena Rochester. The committee wanted her to testify regarding books she had authored that were included in the State Department's overseas libraries and information centers.[13] She pled ill health and managed to evade the committee's bellicose questioning. Even after she had professed her inability to travel to Washington, DC, the committee apparently considered relocating the hearings to New York for her benefit.[14] Hutchins later told Jessie O'Connor that "Anna Rochester was also summoned . . . , but was not well enough to go, so Cohn finally stopped harassing her (at least for the present)."[15] The last point, in parentheses, was an afterthought on Hutchins's part, as she undoubtedly realized that she could not hope to think that Roy Cohn had been permanently discouraged from harassing Rochester.

Despite the easy formula of American Communists as loyal to the USSR rather than to the United States, there is no evidence that Stalin's death in March 1953 had any significant effect on either Rochester or Hutchins. They looked to the Soviet Union as a source of information about worker governance and a more equitable system for women. This information did not always reach them, as the federal government imposed its own version of a material rhetoric. On May 26, 1953, the New York City postmaster gave the FBI a list of mailings received from the USSR. Hutchins was supposed to have received the first issue of *Soviet Woman*. The solicitor general in Washington instructed the US Post Office in methods of dealing with these allegedly incendiary materials, so she probably never saw the magazine.[16] If Hutchins would not cooperate with HUAC, and Joseph McCarthy and Roy Cohn could not browbeat Rochester, the Post Office could at least impound some of their mail as the FBI continued to monitor their trash and telephone.

Despite all evidence from mail, trash, and telephone to the contrary, for some reason, in late 1953, agents in the New York FBI office thought that perhaps Hutchins had had enough aggravation and might like to switch sides, serving as an FBI informant. "The above subject has been selected for interview under the Security Informant Program of the NYO," wrote an agent in a letter to J. Edgar Hoover, requesting permission to waylay Hutchins during her walk to or from work. Agents watched her long enough to establish her routine, then, on October 15, approached her as she was walking home. She retorted that she had "nothing whatsoever to discuss with the FBI."[17] This lack of sociability on Hutchins's part ensured that she would continue to be included in the Security Index, a listing of those whose activities were closely monitored and who would be apprehended should hostilities break out between the United States and the Soviet Union.

As it harassed writers and closed down sources of information, the FBI also was collaborating with presses such as Devin-Adair to ensure that anticommunist materials reached wide audiences. Hutchins's name came up again in late 1953, as the FBI checked the manuscript of what would become Elizabeth Bentley's book *Out of Bondage* against the statement that she had made in FBI offices, to ensure a consistent story. Bentley had not been a close friend, but Hutchins and Rochester had not expected the sort of outright profiteering that she, Budenz, and Chambers were engaged in.

The LRA, meanwhile, struggled for the cash to stay afloat. Hutchins wrote to supporters, pointing out that, unlike membership organizations, the LRA had to rely on the generosity of a few contributors, in addition to the income from services provided to labor unions. Writing her annual request letter to longtime contributor Jessie O'Connor, Hutchins expressed her admiration for "Harvey and you, too, for the courage he shows in challenging the would-be American Hitler."[18] (Harvey O'Connor had invoked the First Amendment rather than the Fifth Amendment when subpoenaed to appear before the Senate Permanent Subcommittee.) When Jessie O'Connor sent the money, Hutchins wrote back, thanking her, and mentioned Harvey's courage again: "Please tell Harvey we are really very proud to know him. His stand takes more guts than the 5th Amendment which I invoked when I went before the Un-American Committee. His courage gives more of it to others."[19]

Certainly more courage would be needed. Six months later, on August 24, 1954, President Eisenhower signed the Communist Control Act, a bill outlawing the CPUSA. In addition to withdrawing the "'rights privileges * * * [and] immunities attendant upon legal bodies,' previously granted to the CP * * * and subsidiaries," the act "prohibit[ed] members of Communist organizations from serving in certain representative capacities," such as positions in labor unions.[20] This was yet another piece of legislation designed to increase fear both within and outside the party. Other bills signed by Eisenhower at the same time included one granting immunity from prosecution to those willing to testify against other party members.

This exceptionally cold climate grew a bit colder, especially for Anna Rochester, on October 9, 1954, when Vida Scudder died in her home in Wellesley. It had been fifty years since Vida Scudder and Florence Converse had challenged Rochester to consider in greater depth the theology to which she ascribed, showing her a committed partnership between women grounded in work toward a future free from oppression. The FBI had faithfully charted all the petitions Scudder had signed and had paid close attention when Louis Budenz, seeking to serve up the two hundred "concealed Communists" he had promised, proffered Scudder, claiming that he "was advised in the early 1940's that Miss

Scudder had agreed to come under Communist discipline, this advice being given me by **** and later by both **** and ****. She is now eighty-nine years of age and has been much influenced by former students of hers who are Communists."[21] Clearly, Budenz was not well acquainted with Vida Scudder—or perhaps he assumed that the FBI wouldn't know any better.

At almost the same time, the 185,000-member International Workers Order was liquidated, after a protracted legal battle with the State of New York. Unable to prosecute the order on the basis of finances (the order was in sound financial health), the State of New York had chosen to prefer a charge of subversion, based on the IWO's appearance on the attorney general's November 1947 list of subversive organizations. By tracing the publications and personnel of the IWO, an official of the New York State Department of Insurance argued that the IWO's activities violated its charter, which put it in violation of insurance law. After almost four years of legal struggles, the IWO was forced to disband most of its operations.[22] Hutchins, however, continued her policy with a private company, still listing Rochester as "friend dependent."

To counter the well-publicized subpoenas, dissolutions, arrests, convictions, and imprisonments, party activists were anxious to remind the membership and the rest of the world that the work of the party was continuing. Victor Perlo praised the LRA in an article published on November 28, 1954, in the *Daily Worker*. Robert W. Dunn, Grace Hutchins, and Anna Rochester, he said, "have been the sparkplugs of Labor Research Association since its organization in 1927. Its purpose was, and is, to 'conduct investigations and studies of social, economic and political questions in the interest of the labor movement, and to publish its findings in articles, leaflets, pamphlets and books.'"

Perlo did not fail to point out that Alexander Trachtenberg had been one of the "founding fathers," as well. Trachtenberg, he noted, "had organized years before the first labor research institute in this country, the research department of the then-Socialist Rand School of Social Science, and he had in earlier years headed the research division of the International Ladies Garment Workers of America." All of LRA's major publications had been published, he said, by International Publishers.[23]

At that point, however, International Publishers was continuing to suffer from the imprisonment of its founder and editor, Alexander Trachtenberg. While he was out on bail, Trachtenberg worked to keep the press alive, arranging to publish a book of excerpts from forthcoming works. *Looking Forward* appeared in late 1954, celebrating the thirtieth anniversary of the publishing house. Trachtenberg signed a copy of the book for Rochester, prompting her to reply, telling him how pleased she was to have the book with his personal inscription. "It has meant a great deal to have the opportunity to study and write for the great cause," she wrote. "And your guidance has been invaluable. Why do I put this in the past tense?" she mused aloud on paper, "I still count on chores of research and translation (wonderful work for advancing years!) And for you I wish many more years of work and service. Here's to the common cause—."[24]

The common cause continued to suffer from the repeated blows delivered by the courts. Elizabeth Gurley Flynn's appeals ran out, and she was incarcerated in Alderson Women's Prison in West Virginia, where she remained until May 25, 1957.[25] On March 2, 1955, six of the party's leaders, including Jacob Stachel and John Williamson, were released from federal penitentiaries only to be immediately rearrested for "knowingly being members of a party dedicated to violent overthrow of the government." Hutchins provided bail money for both Stachel and Williamson, telling a reporter who had the temerity to question her motives that "she was 70 years old and 'an old American who believes in the right of everyone to bail.' " The reporter informed readers of the *New York Times* that she was a "tall, straightbacked woman wearing a black cloth coat with beaver-fur collar and sleeve cuffs." He also generously provided the readership with her home address.[26]

Despite these activities, some parts of the engine of persecution were beginning to break down. The New York State Banking Department finally had returned loans made to the Bail Fund, at a rate of fifty cents on the dollar; checks for another 20 percent were sent in mid-1955. The remainder went to pay the costs of liquidation, plus various fines.[27] The televised Army-McCarthy hearings had pretty well destroyed Joseph McCarthy himself. He, however, was only the most visible front person for the system. In late January 1955, one of the paid informers, Harvey Matusow, decided that he could no longer perjure himself for a living; he was deposed in a Texas district court, recanting his testimony in several cases, including that of Alexander Trachtenberg, who had by this time spent three months in prison, after his conviction. Both Trachtenberg and George Charney won the opportunity to be retried as a result of Matusow's change of heart. Again, Hutchins posted the bail money for Trachtenberg and Charney. (They were convicted again the following year, but those convictions were set aside on appeal, ending Trachtenberg's singling out as an individual, although not the harassment of the party or the press.)

Those who remained free were celebrated. As part of a series, "Women Who Made America," Julia Martin, whose story Hutchins had told two decades earlier, celebrated Rochester's seventy-fifth birthday in the *Sunday Worker* of March 27, 1955. Just as Victor Perlo had placed Rochester's *Rulers of America* at the center of the LRA's work, Julia Martin placed Rochester at the center of early twentieth-century radicalism: "Those were the days when Socialist Gene Debs and others were challenging the growing power of such giant trusts as Standard Oil, U.S. Steel and the railroad system." And, for the first time, Martin revealed publicly the sacrifice that Rochester had made: "After studying music in Europe she decided in 1911 to give up a promising career as a pianist in order to work full-time in the field of labor and economic conditions." When Martin interviewed her, Rochester paid "tribute to those with whom she has worked, especially to Robert W. Dunn" and Alexander Trachtenberg,[28] seeming to suggest that the solitary life of a concert pianist could never have offered the comradeship that progressive political work provided.

The comradeship was shattered for many, however, in early 1956, when Khrushchev gave what came to be known as his "secret speech" to the Central Committee of the Communist Party of the Soviet Union, detailing Stalin's departure from the conventions established by Lenin:

> Stalin acted not through persuasion, explanation, and patient cooperation with people, but by imposing his concepts and demanding absolute submission to his opinion. Whoever opposed this concept or tried to prove his viewpoint, and the correctness of his position was doomed to removal from the leading collective and to subsequent moral and physical annihilation. This was especially true during the period following the 17th party congress [early 1934], when many prominent party leaders and rank-and-file party workers, honest and dedicated to the cause of communism, fell victim to Stalin's despotism.[29]

The speech wasn't secret for long. It found its way to the *New York Times*, which published a brief report on March 15 and a more complete version on June 5, 1956. The *Daily Worker* soon followed suit. How Rochester and Hutchins reacted at this moment is unclear. It is likely that they, like Milton Howard, editor of *Masses and Mainstream* (and

Khrushchev himself), saw beyond the specifics of Stalinist misrule. Bolshevism was never meant to be a model for everyone everywhere to replicate, Howard argued.

> What is immortal in scientific Socialism is its historical-materialist method, its confirmed estimate of the relations between the private owners of the industries and their hired workers, . . . of the social necessity for replacing the private ownership (and hence private governmental domination) of the industries with a new basis—social ownership and hence a new social system, a greater democracy, abolition of poverty and insecurity, with the new class guiding the nation's political life.[30]

Hutchins and Rochester may also have found some basis of agreement with Anna Louise Strong, who argued that the historical context of the late 1930s—the rise of fascism and the war in Spain—was as much to blame as Stalin himself. The events of the late 1930s in the USSR were, in short, "the Russian phase of a worldwide sickness," in the words of W. E. B. Dubois. In any event, Hutchins and Rochester did not leave the party, as did many during that time.

Shrinking numbers notwithstanding, the FBI was not scaling back its efforts to scrutinize the Left. Agents had decided during the summer of 1955 that Hutchins should be retained on the Security Index, but that her file need not be tabbed for "Detcom"—the detention camp program that had been developed to incarcerate Communists. On February 21, 1956, an agent followed her and noted in her file that she looked very much like the description of her that was on file. Agents continued to rifle through Hutchins and Rochester's trash, discovering postcards sent by Erickson and Stevenson when they went on vacation and receipts from donations that Hutchins and Rochester made to such causes as the *Daily Worker* and the American Committee for the Protection of the Foreign Born. They also discovered that Rochester's annual income from stock dividends, in 1956, was $4,475; her holdings amounted to $81,738 in 1957. By contrast, Hutchins's annual income from her share of her father's estate, at least in 1951, was closer to $25,000 annually.[31]

In addition to giving 10 percent annually to the LRA, Hutchins used some of this income to purchase shares in International Publishers. Already a longtime stockholder with Rochester and four others in Publishers New Press, Inc. (publishers of the *Daily Worker*), Hutchins would be called upon to offer more financial support specifically to the Party during the coming year. The arrests and deportations had declined—most who could be arrested or deported under current legal conditions already had been—but the economic bullying was increasing, as the government sought to drain away funds that would otherwise have gone to publishing, labor organizing, and civil rights struggles. Hutchins and Rochester's rhetorical strategies became increasingly material, as they wrote less and underwrote more.

On March 27, 1956, agents of the IRS made a levy of the property and effects of the CPUSA by virtue of a jeopardy assessment executed pursuant to a lien based on a claim of unpaid income taxes. IRS agents took over the CPUSA office and ejected party staff members. At almost the same time, the offices of the *Daily Worker* were occupied for the same reason. Political parties were exempt from taxes, although apparently there was nothing in the tax code specifying which groups were legally able to claim this exemption. The Republican and Democratic parties, the *Daily Worker* noted wryly, had not been visited by similar gangs of raiders.

Eugene Dennis, national secretary of the CPUSA, contended that the raid was an "'assault on the rights of free speech and assembly guaranteed in the Bill of Rights. For if the *Daily Worker* and Communists can be padlocked today, then trade unions, liberals, Negro organizations and others can be padlocked tomorrow. That," he said, "is the bitter lesson of history." Despite the attack, *Daily Worker* writers found moments of humor in the event. A small safe, they said, had been broken open to reveal a 1942 issue of *New Masses* as well as mastheads for the *Daily Worker* and the Michigan *Worker*. Another two-ton safe yielded rolls of microfilm—copies of the *Daily Worker* from 1924 to January 1956—to the efforts of six Treasury officers. "Four money-boxes were found," the *Daily Worker* reported, "in or near the small safe, and were broken open by the six T-men, led by Irving Fink, after lengthy labors with a sledge hammer." The money boxes, including one which contained 48 pennies, produced a total of about $11.[32]

A day later, party activists, including John T. McManus, editor of the *National Guardian*; Howard Fast; Angus Cameron; Helen Alfred; Dr. W. E. B. DuBois; Dr. Doxey Wilkerson; and Robert Dunn formed the Emergency Committee for a Free Press. Doxey Wilkerson was named president and Bob Dunn treasurer. Hutchins agreed to serve as secretary. The organization not only publicized the seizure of the offices but sought to raise funds to fight the IRS and to support the ongoing publication of the newspaper.[33] Arguably, the seizure of the offices had less to do with specific financial matters than with a desire on the part of the government to close the tap of information that the *Daily Worker* provided, although government operatives also wanted access to the addressograph, with its list of subscribers.

The *Daily Worker* staff quickly sent out a fact sheet answering questions about the situation. The *Daily Worker* had, indeed, filed income tax returns. Had the paper paid taxes? No. The paper operated at a deficit, and "the income tax laws are applicable only to profits." The IRS, however, claimed that the paper owed $46,000—arguing that gifts to the paper were taxable. "The Revenue Service demanded to know the names of every donor, every person who loaned money to us, and every person who voluntarily distributed our paper."[34] The $46,000 was, of course, an arbitrary figure designed to extract names. To circumvent the IRS claims to property, those involved purchased the office furnishings—the newspaper's only real assets. Hutchins, represented in the transaction by Lement Harris, purchased the party's office furniture in New York, California, Eastern Pennsylvania, Delaware, and New Jersey. Max Gordon, editor of the *Daily Worker*, bought the assets of the newspaper. This move allowed the party and the paper to reclaim their offices. It did not, however, remove the threat of the jeopardy assessment.[35]

By April 8, 1956, the *Daily Worker* and the CPUSA were back in their respective offices. "Freedom of Press Wins—We're Back" proclaimed the headline on the front page of the *The Sunday Worker*. The paper had put up a bond in the amount of $3000, pending determination of the IRS claim. However, when the party and the paper sought an injunction, Judge Levet denied it, saying, among other things, "The physical property of the plaintiff, although sold to one Grace Hutchins, is still being used by the Party in its office."[36]

On top of the assessment, the paper had lost about $10,000 in the seizure of its bank account, loss of income, and repairs needed to restore offices to their former order. (See above re: sledgehammers.) "Returning staff members found the offices a shambles. Desks had been rifled and papers were scattered about. One large trash can had been smashed, with the bottom knocked out in an apparent imbecilic search for a false bottom. Many items were missing . . . [and] the major damage was in the mailing room, where plates had been damaged, mishandled and bent" to the point that repairs were going to cost in excess of $1000. Material taken in the raid included a new set of screwdrivers, pencils, prestamped envelopes, and rolls of cellophane tape. CPUSA headquarters sustained similar damage, although here missing items included four copies of the New York State Party budget, fund drive information, and a "to do" file purloined from a worker's desk.[37] The budget found its way into Grace Hutchins's FBI file (100-13470, Section 3), apparently a gift from the IRS to the FBI.

Hutchins's efforts to "keep the group going" during this time must have been extraordinary. The FBI reported in May 1956 that Rochester was "becoming senile." She "is not physically alert and is a person to whom responsibility cannot be trusted due to faulty memory."[38] Agents had learned from their trash inspections that Hutchins was leaving notes for Rochester to remind her about what she should be doing, when to take medicine and what quantity, what was for lunch and where it was located in the refrigerator, or when to be ready to go to various events they were planning to attend.[39]

Rochester was 78 years old. She used a hearing aid, and her left shoulder was permanently hunched. She wore a large man's watch, presumably for ease of reading.[40] The heart attacks of the previous few years had taken their toll. She was apt to write several letters instead of just one, forgetting that she had already written to a given correspondent. On days when evening events were to make for late nights, Hutchins reminded Rochester to take a nap in the afternoon so as to be prepared.[41] Nonetheless, Rochester continued to work, producing translations from French or German for the LRA.

In addition to Rochester's needs, Hutchins herself was beginning to suffer from age-related physical problems, developing cataracts that were compromising her vision. In October 1956, she wrote to a physician, asking about the possibility of having the lens in her left eye removed. Cataract surgery at that time was difficult and required a lengthy recovery. There was no guarantee of success, and Hutchins was told that she could be left blind in that eye.[42] The next month—in preparation, perhaps—she made out her will, leaving 130 shares of stock (her entire holdings) in International Publishers to Alexander Trachtenberg as well as $17,000 in Treasury bonds, apparently his bail money. Similarly, she provided $5,000 in Treasury bonds for Jack Stachel.[43]

Somehow this intimation of mortality did not discourage the FBI, whose agents decided in February 1957 that they needed to have a photograph of Hutchins. It was noted that she left for work at nine a.m. and took the crosstown bus from Hudson and W. 10th (presumably after leaving off Rochester at the branch library there). Accordingly, the photo was taken four days later, on February 5. Not completely satisfied with this record of the nation's subversives, the FBI attended the National Convention of the Communist Party held in New York February 9–12 at the Chateau Gardens, 105 Houston, where, aided by an informant, they photographed both Rochester and Hutchins again.

The convention was a much smaller affair than in years past, the 38-year-old party having been battered by events of the past ten years. Indeed, there was a sizable lobby, including John Gates, *Daily Worker* editor, who advocated reorganizing the party again as a "political action association."[44] Eugene Dennis delivered a speech designed to reconcile opposing forces and provide a foundation upon which to rebuild the movement.[45] Most important, he said, the party must actively work for "enforcement of desegregation everywhere; reduction of the arms budget; cutting of taxes on low income groups; introduction of the 30-hour week; extension of social security; repeal of all legislation which violates the Bill of Rights; banning all H-bomb tests and atomic weapons; the calling of a new Summit Conference."[46]

Dennis maintained that the most important job of the convention was to define *how* the party would carry out its work. "To bring to the millions, already concerned about the future, greater consciousness of why and how its shape will be determined by concerted popular mass action to curb and eventually break the power of the monopolies—this is labor's and our greatest challenge," he argued. Of paramount importance in this effort, Dennis said, were the *Daily Worker, Sunday Worker,* and *Political Affairs* (a magazine).

Hutchins and Rochester approved of the speech, calling it "well-balanced and constructive."[47] Following the convention, they both increased their donations to favored organizations, most notably the publications Dennis had mentioned. Hutchins sent $100 each to the *Daily Worker* and the American Committee for the Protection of the Foreign Born in late March. Rochester followed with $50 to the *Daily Worker,* saying, "Most important contribution—Will try to repeat before many weeks go by."[48] Dennis had called for patience and forbearance, asking that members mend ties broken during the previous ten years: "Let us be slow to condemn the temporarily disoriented, and ever ready to help those who wish to find their way back eventually, or who presently may engage us in friendly discussion or join in united-front activity on certain specific issues."[49]

When called upon to address the fiftieth anniversary gathering of her Bryn Mawr classmates shortly thereafter, Hutchins drew some of her inspiration from Dennis, building bridges and drawing her colleagues together. She took her title, "What's Past Is Prologue"— a quotation from "The Tempest"—from the inscription over the door of the National Archives in Washington, DC, offering a taxi driver's interpretation of the inscription: "You ain't seen nothing yet!" (while noting that Adlai Stevenson had actually said it first).[50] Some in her audience undoubtedly realized that she had seen the inscription when she had had to travel to Washington, DC, to testify before HUAC. But she didn't say that.

In her usual manner of foregrounding the work of others, Hutchins highlighted Cornelia Meigs's recent history of Bryn Mawr, saying "She writes of the past with an eye to the future as well." And she recalled for her audience the messages of other colleagues and previous gatherings. Apart from her book, Hutchins had had few opportunities during the past decade to continue her efforts to script new lines for women. So, using the multivalent word "independent," evoking economic and intellectual independence and thus the possibility of same-sex love, she brought back for them the teachings of Carey Thomas, reminding them that "Bryn Mawr under Miss Thomas did encourage us to think independently, didn't it? to be open-minded about new ideas and changes when the time for them came." This event was about nothing if not time, so Hutchins framed their collective past in such a way that they were predisposed to accept the new ideas she would present.

In this way, Hutchins drew her friends into her personal and political framework, linking them with both the past and the future and forewarning any who might be inclined to judge her from the newspaper accounts of her activities. She cited three developments that they had experienced in the past fifty years, choosing carefully those from which they had benefited: the enactment of woman suffrage, the instituting of Social Security, and the establishment of the United Nations, our great hope for the future, she said. Hutchins ended her brief talk with the words of the United Nations hymn, calling it "a Prologue in itself": "As surely as the sun meets the morning/And rivers go down to the sea,/A new day for mankind is dawning./Our children shall live—proud and free." To close, she said, echoing Eugene Dennis's speech three months earlier: "And we may add: In the singing tomorrows of a world *at peace.*" Peace, Hutchins knew, was a necessary precondition for all freedoms—intellectual, economic, and personal.

Hutchins's friends and colleagues of fifty years loved the speech and appreciated her, as well. Her old buddy Ellen Thayer, serving as toastmistress at the reunion dinner, wrote to Hutchins afterward, regretting that they had not had time for a "tête-à-tête," but telling

her "Your speech was so good—and you gave it so well."[51] Margaret Cary, evidently reply-
ing to Hutchins's question about how the speech had been received, reassured her: "As
for the Reunion speech,—I thought it exactly right. Rich in ideas beautifully expressed
and high and satisfying in ideals. You looked so stunning, too, and I am sure everyone felt
as I did that the speech was worthy of our hopes for you fifty some years ago, and that
is saying much, dear Grace."[52] Another friend, now living in a convent, told Hutchins:
"You certainly were most distinguished looking and had such a beautiful expression—full
of love and sympathy. What a full life you have lived."[53]

A full life certainly—yet by no means a life that was over, despite the reunion's sense
of finality. Still, Hutchins was not immune to the assaults of age. By late October 1957,
she could no longer ignore the cataract in her right eye. She checked into the hospital to
have the lens removed, precipitating a heartfelt wail from Rochester. "You don't know how
different this spot feels when you are away," Rochester wrote. Soon, however, Rochester's
missive turned to work, the substance of their lives: "Edith is at work on dinner—and I
have a mess of clippings to sort and file—so I guess I'd better stop this—short as the note
is." She closed, telling Hutchins: "Edith is here at the moment and we all three send lots
of love. (Mine is extra special.) Anna."[54]

By the late 1950s, not only were Hutchins and Rochester suffering debilities, but
many of their friends had died or been deported. The *Daily Worker* had become the
weekly *Worker*, and the LRA was having trouble raising enough money to continue its
work. What's more, other institutions that Rochester and Hutchins had helped to build
were crumbling, including their own home. When a vacancy occurred at some point during the early 1950s in their Socialist-organized co-op apartment community, the secretary
of a nearby Methodist church applied to move in. Because her church shared its space
with a synagogue—an unusually liberal gesture at the time—the secretary was admitted
to the co-op. As was the practice for new members, she joined the board of directors.
And, being a woman, she was appointed secretary. As secretary, she was in charge of
interviewing prospective new members. Over time, Methodists applied to move in—and
came to populate the board.

The board's population was not a problem until early 1959, when co-op member and
radical journalist Alex Crosby sought permission for Alger Hiss to sublet Leo Huberman's
unit for the summer.[55] The Methodist-packed board was horrified. A meeting of the membership was called, during which the shocked Methodists protested that they simply could
not live in such close proximity to a Communist. (Never mind the considerable doubt
about Hiss's alleged CPUSA membership.) But they already did, other members pointed
out. Consider Anna Rochester and Grace Hutchins. "What!?" the Methodists exclaimed,
"those nice old ladies?" "Of course. They've been very political for years." "Oh, well," said
the Methodists. "We just thought it was their favorite charity."[56]

What the Methodists did not discern was that Hutchins's financial moves were
calculated to create specific rhetorical openings and that her efforts went far beyond the
merely financial to spur women's struggles for independence. At the end of the summer,
she reviewed Eleanor Flexner's *Century of Struggle* for *The Sunday Worker*. A CPUSA member since 1936, Eleanor Flexner had been an active member of the League of American
Writers and the CAW[57]; she was also the cousin of Hortense Flexner, one of Hutchins's
friends from Bryn Mawr days. Flexner shared her life with Helen Terry, a faculty member at Smith College; she was one of a cohort of younger "independent women" whom
Hutchins sought to encourage and celebrate. "The long-awaited story of women's efforts

to gain their political rights in this country has now appeared," Hutchins announced. "Of special interest to those involved in present-day struggles are the chapters on early steps toward equal education and on the part women have played in the organized labor movement." Without mentioning the likely importance of her own work to Flexner's, Hutchins noted that Flexner ended the book calling for action: " 'Perhaps in learning more of the long journey these, and hundreds more, made into our present time, we can face our own future with more courage and wisdom, and greater hope.' " With greater prescience than she realized, Hutchins pointed to *Century of Struggle* as a volume that "will stand for years to come as the first full, well-rounded story of the woman's suffrage movement and its dauntless leaders."[58]

Sarah N. Cleghorn's death on April 4, 1959, must have come as a serious shock to Rochester—and a reminder of her own mortality. Rochester and Cleghorn had been friends for almost sixty years; indeed, with the exception of Alice Dillingham, Cleghorn was Rochester's oldest friend. Likewise, fewer people were available to celebrate Rochester's eightieth than had been present to acknowledge her seventieth birthday ten years earlier, but Alexander Trachtenberg did send a heartfelt letter, recollecting that he had known her more than half her life, beginning in the Rand School days—"a decade before you and Grace came to see me at International Publishers to discuss the work both of you were considering after the return from abroad." He reminded her—and all those who would read the letter in the future—that it had been he who had "recommended the L.R.A. where Bob was already laying the foundation of a very useful and authoritative labor research organization to serve the needs of the labor movement. The three of you became the main support as writers, editors, and advisors to other researchers who joined you in the very important work." He then listed all her books and pamphlets published by International Publishers, noting that she had the largest number of titles of any of International Publishers' authors. Her book *Lenin on the Agrarian Question*, Trachtenberg said, had recently been sent to an exhibition in Moscow celebrating Lenin's ninetieth birthday. "I salute you, Anna, on your 80th birthday as an old friend, coworker and devoted comrade and wish you many more years of health and ability to contribute in the field in which you are tops." After this long document, clearly intended for a wider audience than just Rochester, Trachtenberg added a personal postscript: "I wish I could write you a little poem as you used to send me on my birthdays."[59]

Trachtenberg's letter was a spot of warmth in an otherwise cold climate. The McCarran and Smith Acts—combined with other economic and political forces—had had a profoundly chilling effect upon the CPUSA and upon progressives in general. Fewer people were willing to speak out, and even fewer were available to do the work. Hutchins was one of only three directors of Publishers New Press, publishers of *The Worker*; another of the three was Rochester. As of March 26, 1962, Hutchins was treasurer of International Publishers.[60] Hutchins also continued to provide financial support, primarily to publications. During the previous year, she had invested another $5000 in International Publishers, sent in two separate payments; with this purchase, she owned 130 shares of preferred stock and Alexander Trachtenberg owned 880.4 shares of preferred stock and 750 shares of common stock.[61] The two were apparently the only stockholders in the corporation.

At age 76, Hutchins still had her fearless passion for justice, but her health was absorbing more of her time. Sometime during early 1962—before Medicare became available—Hutchins had another cataract operation; this time, she contracted a staphylococcus infection that bothered her for months afterward. Still, when writing to Ruth Erickson and Eleanor Stevenson, who had expressed concern about her, Hutchins responded with humor and optimism, saying,

> The bug I got (stapholoccocus [sic]) has evidently been making a world tour! Mary Van Kleeck went to Switzerland last December for the same kind of cataract operation I had. As a result of the same kind of bug she was in the hospital for <u>17 weeks</u> and is only now able to come home! So I was relatively lucky as I have one very good eye.[62]

Hutchins did not return to work full-time until the fall of 1962. When she did return, it was to become fully immersed in gathering, writing, and editing materials for *Labor Fact Book 16*.

In her last major publication, expanding material from *Labor Fact Book 16*, Hutchins published a five-part series in *The Worker* examining American struggles for civil liberties and women's rights since 1919. Intended to celebrate *The Worker's* fortieth anniversary, the articles drew from the LRA's *Daily Worker* files, illustrating the newspaper's coverage of major civil rights battles. They documented significant events in Hutchins's life, as well, and served to chart the focus of her attention over the years. Beginning with Sacco and Vanzetti and ending with Henry Winston, Hutchins traced the party's efforts to win civil rights victories within a court system often biased against workers and especially against workers who aligned themselves with radical political and labor organizations. Still, although she offered fine vignettes of historic cases, quoting *Daily Worker* articles written at the time, she provided little analysis to explain the cases.[63]

Writing about the history of working women's struggles for equality and independence, Hutchins offered a more nuanced analysis. She established suffrage as the starting point for women's battles, then outlined the fights for improved working conditions and for increased union representation. Quoting the *Daily Worker*, she documented women's activities in labor actions and foregrounded the work of leaders such as Frances Perkins, Ann Burlak, Florence Kelley, Mother Jones, Mother Bloor, Dr. Mary McLeod Bethune, Anita Whitney, Helen Keller, and Rosa Parks. Throughout the two installments of the article on women's rights, Hutchins wove the evidence that women had been seeking equal pay for the past forty years and still, in 1963, had not achieved this basic right.[64]

After the first part was published, Elizabeth Rogers wrote to Hutchins from New Orleans, congratulating her on the series. She had just finished reading the first installment, she said. "It will be a welcome pamphlet much needed. You are brave to go on with the work in spite of sorrow of which my sister Anne wrote me." Rogers's metonymic use of "sorrow" to describe Rochester's continued decline offered Hutchins some understanding that she had not been willing to ask for herself. Hutchins had, for some time, been doing all of Rochester's correspondence, always being careful to make it appear perfectly reasonable that Rochester would not be writing herself. Even to close friends, she minimized the severity of Rochester's condition. In a letter to Ruth Erickson and Eleanor Stevenson dated July 17, 1964, she wrote: "Anna is 84 and in good health, though forgetting a little more than before."[65]

Despite Rochester's obvious infirmities, the FBI maintained her on the Reserve Index, a lesser form of the Security Index. The reason for her inclusion was the fact that she continued to make donations to groups alleged to be related to the CPUSA, such as the American Committee for Protection of Foreign Born, to which she donated $25 per year. Hutchins, on the other hand, was still, at age 79, on the main Security Index.

In addition to her work for the LRA, one of Hutchins's more subversive activities during this time was agreeing to serve as secretary of the memorial committee for Elizabeth Gurley Flynn, who had died in Moscow on September 5, 1964, of " 'acute gastroenterocolitis . . . aggravated by a thromboembolus blood clot in the lung artery.' "[66] One day after Flynn's death, Hutchins was contacted and asked to be secretary of the committee; she was also asked to think of people outside the CPUSA who should be asked to participate on the committee. Flynn would have been pleased with Hutchins's choices: Harvey O'Connor, Louise Pettibone Smith, Dorothy Day, and Dr. Willard Uphaus all delivered eulogies.

The following year, Rochester was still listed on the Reserve Index, although by this time she was having difficulty even recognizing friends. In late April 1965, the House Committee on Un-American Activities compiled a list of names for possible subpoena; both Hutchins and Rochester were on the list. Hutchins continued to be listed on the main Security Index; agents noted on August 18, 1965, that she was sent a floral tribute by Gus Hall and Associates, with the message: "Happy 80th Birthday, Best wishes for years of health and happiness."[67] Although she undoubtedly appreciated the gesture and the wishes for her happiness, Hutchins was now experiencing losses of such magnitude that happy moments were rare. In June 1965, Lucie Myer died. She had been Hutchins's friend since 1917. By this time, Rochester's mental capacities were so compromised that it is unlikely that she was able to comprehend the loss or offer the sympathy that Hutchins needed.

The FBI continued undeterred. They followed Hutchins again to determine her daily routine, noting that she left the apartment at 9:13 a.m. in order to catch the crosstown bus at Christopher Street. Then she got off the bus at 8th and Broadway and walked to 80 East 11th. On December 28, 1965, she was photographed with a concealed camera during this journey. Agents observed that she was wearing glasses with small gold frames, although she still didn't see well, and that she wore a brown hat, coat, and shoes and usually carried a zippered brown briefcase. She walked quickly for her age, they remarked.[68] Hutchins, too, realized that her energy was unusual, commenting to Stevenson and Erickson in December 1965 that "I don't seem to feel my 80 years (!) as I should."[69]

Hutchins's steps slowed the next year, when Rochester went into the New York Infirmary with bronchopneumonia in early May. She died a week later, on May 11, 1966, ending a partnership of 45 years. Hutchins was never the same.

The *New York Times* published an obituary, listing Rochester's works and summarizing her 1936 argument: "In Miss Rochester's view, a number of very large industrial enterprises, with interlocking connections and interests, were the economic, political and social sovereigns of the United States." The *Times* also observed that "although Miss Rochester dealt largely with statistics, she commanded a brisk style and an ability to popularize complex material—a circumstance frequently commented on in reviews that challenged the point of view of her books." At the end, the *Times* erased Hutchins, saying: "Miss Rochester leaves no immediate survivors."[70]

The Worker picked up this obituary, condensing it and concluding also: "There are no close survivors."[71] It was not until May 24 that James S. Allen (Sol Auerbach) published a detailed account of Rochester's life, suggesting, without naming precisely, the significance of Hutchins in her life. Allen pointed to Rochester's "original contributions of lasting importance to the social sciences" and described her role in founding the LRA with "Alexander Trachtenberg, whom she knew from Rand School days; Robert W. Dunn who still serves today as Secretary of the LRA, and Grace Hutchins, her life-long friend and co-worker." After naming Hutchins, Allen observed, in place of the obligatory list of children, that the LRA had "helped raise an entire generation of researchers, economists and writers for the labor movement."[72]

An informal memorial gathering was held at Hutchins and Rochester's apartment, from two until four o'clock in the afternoon on a date shortly after Rochester's death. All in attendance recognized and understood Hutchins and Rochester's partnership, and although some spoke of Rochester, most were there to offer their support to Hutchins. Unlike those who maintained an exclusively heterosexual appearance, Anna Rochester was not accorded a public memorial. The housekeeper hovered, offering tea and cookies. Yet even in her grief, Hutchins was, according to Tamiment librarian Dorothy Wick, a formidable presence. When Wick spoke to her optimistically about the Vietnam war protests, Hutchins dismissed the demonstrations as trivial in comparison with the larger struggle for socialism. Although her companion had died, Hutchins maintained her belief in a higher purpose; she, too, would die, but the larger struggle for socialism would go on.[73]

When Rochester's estate was finally settled, the value was placed at $266,977.11. After taxes and small bequests to relatives, approximately $200,000 was left to Hutchins, Bob Dunn, and Betty Millard. They, in turn, donated $10,000 to the CPUSA. The remainder probably went to the LRA, although *The Worker*, International Publishers, and other organizations that Rochester had supported over the years may have benefited as well. It was common practice for those with substantial estates to leave the money to trusted individuals, who would then pass it on to the organizations that the donor had privately named. This avoided any publicity that might encourage challenges to the will. Or, as the FBI put it: "The possibility exists that the residual beneficiaries, all of whom have substantial subversive backgrounds, voluntarily agreed or entered into an agreement whereby in consideration for their bequests they agreed to donate $10,000 to the CPUSA."[74]

Letters poured in to Hutchins and to the LRA from friends and comrades, remembering Rochester's contributions, her sense of humor, and her dedication. Jurgen Kuczynski, East German economist and historian, wrote: "The news about Anna Rochester was a real shock. Was anything published about her death? How well I remember her, though it is 28 years since I saw her, and how highly I estimate her work!"[75] Victor and Ellen Perlo wrote to Hutchins, saying: "We were most distressed to read about Anna and want you to know of our great sympathy. The world has lost one of its great women; the forces for progress, one of its staunch leaders."[76] Corliss Lamont wrote a similar comment to Bob Dunn: "Sorry to see in the *Times* the other day that Anna Rochester had died. She was one of the most effective and stalwart individuals in the Old Left, which I personally prefer to the New Left." Hutchins later provided the underlining.

Most of those who wrote understood Hutchins and Rochester's devotion to each other as well as the work that their devotion made possible. Leo Huberman, editor of *Monthly Review*, wrote to Hutchins: "The contribution made by Anna Rochester was of such importance that even the *New York Times*, in its obituary notice, treated it with great respect. The good people of the United States share your grief." Jack Woods, perhaps more than almost anyone, seemed to understand the significance of Hutchins and Rochester's partnership: "Dear Grace," he wrote the day after Rochester died,

> Emotions and memories must be filling you at this time. The end of a beautiful and fruitful partnership is an occasion for recalling your wonderful life with Anna—personal and creative. It is good to have maintained integrity in this turbulent century. We can regret that Anna did not live to see victories nearer home than

those we have witnessed. Perhaps for us there is hope and the promise for real advance in the current ferment in spite of the odds against us.

My sympathy for your great loss, my admiration for your mutual accomplishments, my belief, my conviction (?) that good memories of your good lives together will sustain you now.[77]

Indeed, it was these memories that sustained Hutchins for the next three years. Although she herself was failing, in a last act of devotion before her own death, she wordlessly bought a $1,000 lifetime subscription to *The Worker,* the medium through which she and Rochester had channeled their passion, on what would have been Rochester's eighty-ninth birthday in March 1969.

Epilogue

Oh mommy how sad—can we help Grace?

> —Janet Kleinbord (to Nancy Wertheimer Kleinbord,
> on being told of Anna Rochester's death in 1966)

History will record her great contributions to the cause of peace and justice.

> —Carl and Anne Braden (to Bob Dunn,
> after Grace Hutchins's death in 1969)

"Dear dear Grace," wrote Eleanor Stevenson and Ruth Erickson, upon learning of Rochester's death, "We were shocked and saddened when we read in *The Worker* today that our dear Anna left us on Wednesday. In a sense we two felt we had 'lost' her when she no longer remembered us—but the loss to you must be great, and we are deeply concerned about *you*—Do let us know how *you* are, and when you can make plans, tell us what you will do?"[1]

The final three years of Hutchins's life were very difficult, although few people realized just how difficult they were. Her childhood friend Polly Porter was one of the few to whom Hutchins confessed her despair. "Oh, Grace, my dear," Porter wrote in early October, "Indeed I do know how profoundly you must miss Anna. A loss that can never be made up."[2]

The losses only compounded, as Alexander Trachtenberg died seven months after Rochester. Hutchins, along with several hundred others, attended the memorial service on December 22, 1966, at Riverside Plaza. She listened as Philip Foner reminded the gathering that Trachtenberg was "second only to John Reed in explaining to the American people, in meeting after meeting, the meaning of the struggle in Russia." Trachtenberg had, in fact, foretold the revolution in September 1917, Jessica Smith added.

One of Trachtenberg's skills, which he shared with Hutchins, was the ability to maintain friendships across party lines. A. J. Muste, Roger Baldwin, and Norman Thomas all sent messages, Thomas emphasizing that his "'friendship with Alexander Trachtenberg . . . began with our common interest in socialism [and] survived the split on important matters in which each held his own views. . . . Alexander Trachtenberg,'" he said, "'had convictions and lived up to them.'"[3]

Hutchins's work was not on stage. She overcame her own despair temporarily to help Rosalind Trachtenberg cope with the loss of her husband, making a list of those writing about Trachty. A few weeks later, she signed on as a sponsor for the International Women's Day celebration and attended the event, which featured two women "recently returned from Hanoi." Yet despite Hutchins's years of emphasizing women as workers and activists in their own right, the International Women's Day organizers persisted in identifying women only in their relation to men, telling attendees that the speakers' message "will stir the mothers, sisters, wives, and sweethearts of the men being sacrificed in Vietnam."[4]

Then, two days after the first anniversary of Rochester's death, Hutchins was hospitalized in critical condition with a pulmonary embolism. She never recovered her health after this episode, although she lived for another two years. Her vision was poor, limiting her reading, and her memory was impaired, so Bob Dunn answered letters sent to her, much as she had answered letters for Rochester, although he himself had lost his wife, Slava, recently. Hutchins's correspondents included her friends from childhood, college, and Community House as well as comrades from the past few decades. Ellen Thayer, Polly Porter, and Mae Kennard wrote and visited when they could. Polly Porter sent a precious gift—photographs of Hutchins and her family that she had torn from the Porter-Dewson albums.[5] Ruth Erickson and Eleanor Stevenson sent a copy of Ruth's self-published book of poetry, *Sonnets to a House and Garden*.[6] The FBI, too, wanted to stay in touch, so agents fabricated a reason to call the LRA, where they were told that Hutchins was in ill health. She was 82 years old, but she was nevertheless retained on the Security Index as a threat to the national safety.

Although Hutchins wanted to return to her work at the LRA office, she had developed chronic arteriosclerosis by this time and could not leave the apartment. There was no elevator, and she could not manage the flights of stairs. She did what she could via the telephone and postal service, mailing out (or most likely having someone else post) a letter advocating readers to use the "chain letter" method, sending on an antiwar message to ten others. Bob Dunn wrote to a friend who had inquired after Hutchins that she "is quite clear on past events and would doubtless be glad to talk over old times with you."[7]

One of Hutchins's last correspondents was Ann Mundelein, her old Community House and SCHC companion, who wrote in July 1968 from Sioux Falls, South Dakota, where she was still working for the Episcopal Church. Mundelein had continued to write to Hutchins, despite not receiving any replies for the previous three years. Bob Dunn answered her letter, letting her know that Rochester had passed away in 1966—and telling her that Hutchins could neither write nor read any more. "Write her again when you can," he urged.[8]

Hutchins died a year later, on July 15, 1969.[9] Her sister-in-law had come down from New Haven to be with her, more out of duty than love, as she had never understood the meaning of Hutchins's life.[10] Someone called the FBI at 11:40 that evening to report Hutchins's death, telling the FBI what they undoubtedly already knew, that Hutchins had been a co-owner and publisher of the *Daily World*.[11]

The *New York Times* listed many of Hutchins's accomplishments but could not resist digging up the old news that she had "figured in Congressional testimony of Whittaker Chambers, a self-labeled Communist courier, in 1948," adding that "Mr. Chambers swore that Miss Hutchins, a witness at his wedding in 1931, approached him seven years later with a demand to 'surrender' to the party."[12]

Hutchins left an estate worth between $25,000 and $50,000. After bequeathing some jewelry to her nieces and nephew, she left the property at Croton-on-Hudson to Bob Dunn and the remaining assets to Dunn and another person, probably Betty Millard. This last bequest was made "unconditionally and without reservations of any kind, but in confident knowledge that the proceeds therein will be used . . . to support such organizations and causes to which I was devoted in my lifetime," a final rhetorical gesture.[13] Most likely, the money went to support the Labor Research Association, which continues its work, using updated media, to this day.

In her personal notebook, Hutchins wrote that "if it seems appropriate at the time, I would suggest a very simple funeral service, perhaps at the Community Church Chapel of Peace." She recommended that Rev. William Howard Melish, an Episcopal clergyman who had been relieved of his working class parish due to his progressive views, officiate, and that two or three others, such as Lement Harris, be asked to offer brief statements about the ideas and interests that had motivated her "in recent years." "Mr. Melish," she added, "might close with a brief prayer."[14] If such a memorial was ever held, no record remains in either Hutchins's papers or the Labor Research Association papers.

Rochester had been buried in the family plot in Englewood, New Jersey, her name chiseled on the headstone as a sort of afterthought beneath the names of her parents. Hutchins was buried in the Hutchins section of Mt. Auburn Cemetery in Cambridge, Massachusetts, a small headstone identifying her only as the daughter of Edward Hutchins. Hutchins and Rochester's partnership is memorialized only in the letters and papers that Bob Dunn carefully preserved and placed in the archives at the University of Oregon.[15]

Letters poured in to the office of the LRA from comrades offering Bob Dunn condolences. Miriam Friedlander of the Citizens Committee for Constitutional Liberty sent her sympathy and recalled how much the committee had appreciated Hutchins's "sponsorship, encouragement and practical help."[16] Philip Bart wrote of his "feeling of profound loss. . . . She was a noble woman in the finest humanist sense," he said. "She left the comforts of a middle class family and associated herself with the struggles of the working class. She was a part of that grand army which is in the forefront of the struggle for socialism."[17] Carl and Anne Braden of the Southern Conference Educational Fund wrote: "History will record her great contributions to the cause of peace and justice."[18] And Clara Colon suggested that someone should write Hutchins's life. "Because she was self-effacing," she said, "not many people know the details of her useful, principled and generous deeds."[19]

Although she might have appeared "self-effacing," Hutchins spent her life resisting the very forces that sought to efface her and others like her. Yet although Hutchins and Rochester lived and worked together openly, using all of their rhetorical and financial resources to resist repression, their partnership remained invisible to many of those raised on the meager mid-century diet of social possibilities. Bettina Aptheker recalls growing up knowing of Rochester and Hutchins, reading their work and meeting them occasionally at the offices of New Century Publishers. "Of course I had no idea that Anna Rochester and Grace Hutchins were lovers," she said, "not a clue." Years later, after she had found her own partnership with Kate, Bettina learned the truth. "My father very casually said, 'You know, by the way, Anna Rochester and Grace Hutchins were . . . ' [I think he said, 'partners' or 'a couple'; he would never use the word *lovers* . . .]. I said: 'Really?' He said: 'Oh, yes. Everybody knew that. It was an open secret in the Party and inner circles.' It would have been very important to me," she said, "had I known that, but nobody told me."[20]

Like many women of their generation, Hutchins and Rochester failed to negotiate the shifting discourses of same-sex desire without stumbling, leaving younger women to find their way in silence and setting off a coded attack that has hampered progressive forces for years. Yet behind their quiet exterior, Anna Rochester and Grace Hutchins spent their lives trying to disrupt the systems that held the silence and codes in place, fusing feminism and Marxism-Leninism to create new discourses and then funding the presses that published the writing that ensued. Later generations would appropriate these discourses of racial, gender, and economic equality to build yet newer freedoms.

Notes

Notes to Introduction

1. Russell, "Life's Illusions," 152.
2. See Sahli, "Smashing," 17–27. See also, for example, Ware, *Partner and I*. For an extended discussion of female partnerships, see Freedman, "'The Burning of Letters Continues,'" 192–200, and Franzen, *Spinsters and Lesbians*. See especially much of the work of Lillian Faderman.
3. Franzen, *Spinsters and Lesbians*, 108.
4. Ibid., 119.
5. Franzen, *Spinsters and Lesbians*. Several of the women Franzen studied were friends of Hutchins and Rochester.
6. "A new type of evangelism which would result in a person's giving his whole self to the whole community." Minutes of the Fellowship Council, 9–13 February 1923, Fellowship of Reconciliation Papers, Swarthmore College Peace Collection, Swarthmore College, Swarthmore, PA.
7. Carpenter elaborated these arguments in *England's Ideal* and in *Civilization*.
8. Carpenter, *The Intermediate Sex*, 108–9. The term "Uranians" never caught on beyond a limited circle.
9. See Converse, *Diana Victrix* and Scudder, *A Listener in Babel*.
10. James E. Porter's clear definition continues to serve: "A discourse community shares assumptions about what objects are appropriate for examination and discussion, what operating functions are performed on these objects, what constitutes 'evidence' and 'validity,' and what formal conventions are followed." Porter, "Intertextuality and the Discourse Community" 34–47. Marilyn M. Cooper extends the concept to argue for a dialectical view of discourse communities in "The Ecology of Writing."
11. Burke emphasized the foundational qualities of language, whereas, as Marxist-Leninists, Rochester and Hutchins recognized the importance of material conditions in shaping consciousness (or, in Burke's terminology, motives).
12. Kenneth Burke, *Permanence and Change*, liv. Readers of *Permanence and Change* in the later editions should understand that Burke deleted many of his references to capitalism and communism, feeling that postwar readers would not understand the spirit in which he was writing. These passages have been recuperated by Edward Schiappa and Mary F. Keehner in "The 'Lost' Passages of *Permanence and Change*," 191–8.
13. Burke, *Permanence and Change*, 14.
14. Burke, *Attitudes toward History*, 263–4.
15. Burke, *Permanence and Change*, 169.
16. Burke, *Attitudes toward History*, 308.
17. Burke, *Permanence and Change*, 142.
18. Selzer, "Habeas Corpus," 8.
19. Ibid., 10.
20. Ibid.
21. Ibid.
22. McComiskey, review of *Rhetorical Bodies*, 703.
23. Cloud, "Change Happens," 55.
24. Ibid., 57.

25. Ibid., 63.

26. Ibid., 62.

27. Franzen, *Spinsters and Lesbians*, 130.

28. Ibid., 119.

29. Hennessy, *Profit and Pleasure*, 101.

30. John D'Emilio also sees capitalism as a significant element in the formation of gay and lesbian identities. However, he argues that capitalism's wage labor system has allowed greater movement and flexibility among workers who then have formed communities based upon same-sex desires. See D'Emilio, "Capitalism and Gay Identity."

31. Smith-Rosenberg, *Disorderly Conduct*, 278.

32. Terry, *An American Obsession*, 51.

33. Faderman, *Odd Girls and Twilight Lovers*, 35.

34. Wallace, "Edith Ellis," 196.

35. Wallace, "Case of Edith Ellis," 30.

36. See Terry, *An American Obsession*, for a detailed discussion of the scientific preoccupation with same-sex relationships from the late nineteenth through the twentieth century.

37. See Faderman, "Nineteenth-Century Boston Marriage," for a discussion of the complexities that may have characterized partnerships such as that between Hutchins and Rochester. I am not suggesting that their partnership was necessarily asexual; I am saying that we cannot know, nor is it any of our business, and that therefore the defining quality should be the degree of emotional intensity and commitment, which is indisputable. Elizabeth Lapovsky Kennedy argues that "the framework of analysis developed by feminist scholarship on the New Woman" has led to an erasure of many lesbians from the turn-of-the-century era, creating categories, especially those that replicate traditional gender characteristics, that "camouflage some lesbians." Kennedy, "'But We Would Never Talk about It,'" 17. See also Cook, "Female Support Networks and Political Activism," 43–61, for a clear argument against taxonomies based exclusively upon sexual activity. See, too, Raitt, "Sex, Love, and the Homosexual Body." Raitt traces the erasure of love as a defining quality in same-sex desire from Carpenter and Ellis to Freud.

38. Franzen, *Spinsters and Lesbians*, 173–4.

39. Vida Scudder, journal, January 11, 1935, Vida D. Scudder Papers, book 4, series 1, box 1, folder 6, V. Scudder Papers, Sophia Smith Collection, Smith College, Northampton, MA. In Scudder's published autobiography, the line has been modified but not eliminated. She says: "Freud is of course largely responsible; and he has much to answer for"; Scudder, *On Journey*, 211.

40. Cloud, "First Lady's Privates," 43n46. Cloud also points out that men had more access to language than women during this era.

41. Franzen, *Spinsters and Lesbians*, 123.

42. In fact, the party, caught in antifascist efforts, took theoretical shortcuts, accepting linkages made by some between homosexuality and fascism. See Oosterhuis, "The Dubious Magic of Male Beauty," 181–206.

43. Hutchins and Rochester were not alone in leaving an archive that leans heavily to the public sphere. See Franzen, *Spinsters and Lesbians*, 122. Drawing a simple line between public and private, however, can be misleading. As Jeff Weintraub maintains in saying "The public/private distinction, in short, is not unitary, but protean," the referent of each term changes depending upon the ideological bent of the person using it. Weintraub, "The Theory and Politics of the Public/Private Distinction," 2. Feminist arguments, Weintraub points out, have called attention to the public, or collective, importance of what has heretofore been labeled private. Hutchins herself insisted upon feminist visibility in every organization she joined, raising questions concerning gender in ostensibly public spaces of work and political organizing but also writing about issues of housework, birth control, and sexual harassment in the workplace.

44. Hay to author, August 18, 1996, letter. Harry Hay served as educational director at both the section and county levels of the CPUSA in New York and Los Angeles between 1938 and 1951. In 1951, he organized the Mattachine Society, usually identified as the first gay rights organization in the United States. See Timmons, *The Trouble with Harry Hay*. See also Hay, *Radically Gay*.

45. Annette Rubinstein, interview with the author, New York City, May 29, 1999.

46. Lement Harris, interview with the author, Norwalk, CT, June 4, 1999. "Their own attitude about life" was a euphemistic way of acknowledging Hutchins and Rochester's partnership.

47. Simon Gerson, telephone interview with the author, New York City, July 6, 1998.

48. Sophie Gerson, telephone interview with the author, New York City, July 6, 1998.

49. In 1933, after the acquittal of Communists in Germany for setting the fire that burned the Reichstag, the USSR outlawed male homosexuality. Lesbians were not mentioned. Although the CPUSA had different cultural politics than did other Communist parties, changes in the USSR reflective of larger international shifts in attitude could not help but influence opinion in the United States. See Feinberg, "Can a Homosexual Be a Member?"

50. Rubinstein, interview.

51. Chambers's book is still in print and continues to buoy the efforts of conservative political figures. Ronald Reagan posthumously awarded Chambers the Presidential Medal of Freedom in 1984. "America's highest civilian honor, the Medal of Freedom is awarded to individuals who make an especially meritorious contribution to the security or national interests of the United States, world peace, cultural or other significant public or private endeavors." See Clines, "White House Freedom Medal Set for Whittaker Chambers," A21. On July 9, 2001, the George W. Bush administration held a 140-guest celebration of Chambers's hundredth birthday. William F. Buckley addressed the group, but the press was excluded. See Buckley, "Witness and Friends."

52. Sidney Blumenthal commented in a review of Sam Tanenhaus's biography of Whittaker Chambers that "Chambers described Communism in phrases commonly used to describe homosexuality." See Blumenthal, "The Cold War and the Closet," 117.

53. For details on the influence of former CPUSA activists on early second wave feminism, see Weigand, *Red Feminism.*

54. Freedman, "Partners for Life," 13.

55. Although Ellen Kay Trimberger has argued for a significant shift in consciousness and approach—especially regarding personal lives—between women active in the Old Left and those active in New Left circles, I see a dialectical relationship between the two, with Old Left activists such as Hutchins and Rochester opening territory for later women to explore and develop. Peggy Dennis, in response to Trimberger, has argued that historians must account for the circumstances in which women have lived and engaged in political work. See Trimberger, "Women in the Old and New Left," and Dennis, "A Response."

Notes to Chapter One

1. For more on the Society of the Companions of the Holy Cross, see Gillespie, "The Companions of the Holy Cross," 55–69. In the same volume, see Schmitt, "'Sacrificial Adventure,'" 180–92. See also Chrisman, "*To Bind Together.*"

2. Report of Special Agent [redacted], May 10, 1943, Internal Security-C, Custodial Detention, Federal Bureau of Investigation, file 100-12805, Anna Rochester, section 1; The SCHC was organized in 1886 by Emily Malbone Morgan at the request of her friend Adelyn Howard. Ill with a degenerative disease, Adelyn was housebound and missed the fellowship of her church more than anything. When Morgan asked what she wanted, she replied that she wanted a "spiritual companionship." Chrisman, "*To Bind Together*" 2. Morgan admits that she knew little about religious societies: "My leading characteristic at the time was undeviating and hilarious high spirits. But dear Adelyn wanted such a society, and I loved Adelyn." Morgan, *Letters to Her Companions* 23. Emily Morgan described her vision of Adelynrood as it was being constructed: "Two years before [Adelyn] died, I used to fling my imagination into talking of 'Adelyn House' to make her forget her pain. A house, not lacking in simplicity, but with the walls covered with the pictured thoughts of many ages and peoples; with hospitable chairs, plenty of books and a real fireside. I want to have it full of soft, sunshiny colors, and filled with little memorials of love, so that we shall feel her spirit with us, past all of time or change." Morgan, *Memories,* 2.

3. Emily Malbone Morgan, *Memories*, 8, Archives of the Society of the Companions of the Holy Cross, Adelynrood, South Byfield, MA.

4. *Manual of the Society of the Companions of the Holy Cross*, 1909, Archives of the Society of the Companions of the Holy Cross.

5. Morgan, *Memories*, 12.

6. For more on Mary Simkhovitch, see Donovan, "Creating a Neighborhood," 165–79.

7. See Donovan, *A Different Call.*

8. For many years, Scudder served as Companion-in-Charge of Probationers for the SCHC. Membership in the organization is restricted to those sponsored by two other members; prospective members must spend a year as probationers, studying the principles upon which the organization is founded.

9. Carpenter had served for a time as curate under Christian Socialist F. D. Maurice until, unable to shake a "feeling of falsity," he left the position, choosing instead to "throw in [his] lot with the mass-people and manual workers" and engaging in farm labor and writing. Carpenter, *My Days and Dreams*, 58. Frederick Denison Maurice (1805–1872) was the first (in recent Anglican history) to announce that the Kingdom of God was not an ethereal notion to be aimed for but never reached but was rather a reality to be established here on earth. Earthly suffering was not necessary and, in fact, must be abolished, according to Maurice. Orens, "Politics and the Kingdom: The Legacy of the Anglican Left," 63–84. Maurice was a strong influence on Phillips Brooks, rector of Trinity Church, Boston, who convinced Vida Scudder's mother to convert from Congregationalism to Anglicanism. Scudder credits Maurice with having made it possible for her to remain a Christian within the "realities of modern civilization." See Markwell, *The Anglican Left*, for a detailed discussion of the theological backgrounds of Scudder's thinking.

10. Carpenter, *England's Ideal*, 87.

11. Ibid., 86.

12. Mary Simkhovitch was the exception; the wife of Vladimir Simkhovitch, Columbia University professor of economic history, she spent her life building Greenwich House.

13. Tom Mooney was a California labor activist who was convicted after a bomb went off in 1916 during a Preparedness Day Parade in San Francisco, killing 10 people. No evidence connected him with the crime, and he was several blocks away when it took place. He served twenty-three years in prison and died within three years after his release in 1939, his health broken.

14. Shaw, "Closed Towns," 59.

15. Converse, *Long Will*, 37.

16. Carpenter, *Towards Democracy*, 49.

17. Ibid., 33.

18. Ibid., 67.

19. Converse, *Diana Victrix*. Scudder told her own history in her 1937 autobiography, *On Journey*. There, she related that heterosexual courtship had held no attraction for her: "Some fairly good verses addressed to me were murmured in my ear at those times. But while mildly flattered, I was rather bored" (74). Instead, she had found a heartfelt connection with Clara French, a college friend with whom she traveled to Oxford. When Clara French suddenly died in 1888, Scudder said, "the door to what people call passion swung to in my heart. That door had previously been open, and open to a stormy land. My years have been passed," she said, "in calmer air" (113).

20. Martha Boonin-Vail suggests that this novel should be termed "antiautobiographical" because the events depicted therein differ from those of Scudder's life. Boonin-Vail, "New Wine in Old Bottles," 148n39. I see her point, but I think the fact that the book covers issues with which Scudder struggled—despite the fact that she may have made different choices than did the novel's protagonist—earns the novel its designation as autobiographical. Scudder herself referred to it in *On Journey* as "semi-fiction, semi-autobiography" (181).

21. In the *Phaedrus*, Socrates attempts to demonstrate the nature of love to his student Phaedrus by giving a speech that contrasts with two others—each displaying a certain cynicism about love. (The love in question, it should be noted, is between older and younger men.) Socrates' second speech describes the soul as a charioteer in the heavens driving a chariot with two horses,

one docile and obedient and the other unruly, pulling constantly earthward trying to satisfy baser instincts. The job of the charioteer is to control the unruly horse and thereby achieve the higher reaches of heaven.

22. Not insignificantly, the novel is subtitled *Being a Series of Imaginary Conversations Held at the Close of the Last Century and Reported by Vida D. Scudder*. The conversations differ from the Platonic dialogues in that there is no definitive Socratic figure, but the novel is constructed, nonetheless, as a series of dialogues, as Scudder herself pointed out in *On Journey* (181). The conversations usually involve more than two people, however, and the setting is for the most part within a city, not outside the walls under a plane tree.

23. Drawing her language from Plato and Carpenter, Scudder spoke throughout her life of her "Quest for Reality," titling her last book *My Quest for Reality*.

24. Carpenter, *The Intermediate Sex*, 114.

25. Ibid., 26.

26. Ibid., 116

27. Morgan, *Letters to Her Companions*, 53.

28. See Dutton and Braceland, *Aelred of Rievaulx*.

29. See, for example, Schwarz, *The Radical Feminists of Heterodoxy*.

30. Minutes of the New York Chapter, November 26, 1920, Archives of the Society of the Companions of the Holy Cross.

31. The year 1919 can be read as a turning point in the social approbation of women's partnerships. Lillian Faderman points to that date as the last year in which a popular magazine published a story featuring one woman's love for another. See Faderman, *Odd Girls*, 307.

32. Intercession Letter, January 1919, Archives of the Society of the Companions of the Holy Cross. The phrase "loving kindness" was a favorite of Rochester's friend Sarah N. Cleghorn.

33. Twenty-Third Annual Conference, 1919, report, 54–5, Archives of the Society of the Companions of the Holy Cross.

34. Statement of Principles of the Church League for Industrial Democracy, ca. 1927, Organizations and Institutions Files, Church League for Social and Industrial Democracy, box 2, Archives of the Episcopal Church, USA, Episcopal Theological Seminary of the Southwest, Austin, TX.

35. Darling, *New Wine*, 107.

36. Donovan, *A Different Call*, 162–3.

37. Scudder, *Socialism and Character*, 240.

38. Ibid., 249.

Notes to Chapter Two

1. The city of Rochester was founded by Colonel Nathaniel Rochester, the grandson of Nicholas Rochester, who arrived in 1689 and who Anna Rochester believed was an indentured servant. Nicholas Rochester, however, apparently was not an indentured servant. See N. Rochester, *Early History*. Although the family promoted the idea that Colonel Rochester came to believe in the immorality of slavery and freed his slaves, recently published evidence suggests otherwise. See Nolte et al., "'We Called Her Anna,'" 1–26.

2. Reid, *The Telegraph in America and Morse Memorial*, 688.

3. Valentine, *Manual of the Corporation of the City of New York*, 271.

4. L. Rochester, "AR Annals," 1880–1919, Anna Rochester Papers, Ax 624, series 1, box 1, folder 3, 19–20, Special Collections and University Archives, University of Oregon Libraries, Eugene.

5. Ibid., 20.

6. Ibid., 21.

7. Ibid., 22.

8. Ibid., 24.

9. Ibid., 33.

10. Ibid., 34.

11. Ibid., 38.

12. Ibid., 42.

13. Ibid., 45.

14. Ibid., 59.

15. Ibid., 69.

16. Ibid., 71.

17. Ibid., 71. Although as a young woman Anna Rochester was well on her way to a career as a musician, she gave it up to spend her life working for social justice, playing only for friends and later for Grace Hutchins's young nieces.

18. Ibid., 76.

19. Ibid., 78.

20. Ibid., 79.

21. Ibid., 80.

22. Ibid., 81

23. Ibid., 85

24. Anna Rochester to Mother, May 7, 1899, letter in L. Rochester, "AR Annals," Anna Rochester Papers, series 1, box 1, folder 3.

25. L. Rochester, "AR Annals," 86.

26. A. Rochester, "The Religious Experience," 47.

27. L. Rochester, "AR Annals," 107.

28. Ibid., 107.

29. Ibid., 108.

30. Steinfels, "On the Stump," B5.

31. Rauschenbusch, *Christianity and the Social Crisis*, xiii.

32. Ibid., 5.

33. Ibid., 7.

34. Ibid., 49.

35. Ibid., 91.

36. Ibid., 67.

37. Ibid., 102.

38. Ibid., 254.

39. Ibid., 197.

40. Ibid., 272.

41. Ibid., 420.

42. Emily Malbone Morgan, annual letter, 1908, Archives of the Society of the Companions of the Holy Cross.

43. L. Rochester, "AR Annals," 110.

44. Intercession Paper, June 1909, Archives of the Society of the Companions of the Holy Cross.

45. The work of the conference was not finished, as participants went on to publish the papers of Harriette Keyser and Anna Whitcomb as a small pamphlet under the title of "Modern Christianity and Social Justice." Harriette Keyser, lifelong companion of Margaret Lawrance, was the first secretary of the Church Association for the Assistance of Industrial Labor (CAIL), itself the first church society for the protection of workers, founded by Father James Huntington and eight other clergymen during the 1890s.

46. Horton, "Science and Theology," 95.

47. Branscomb, "Interpretation of the Bible," 171.

48. Modernism was not without its opponents. Those opponents, often calling themselves Fundamentalists, claimed the infallibility of the Bible and argued for its literal interpretation. In 1909, oil millionaire Lyman Stewart and his brother Milton provided $300,000 to publish a twelve-volume set entitled *The Fundamentals* and to send copies for free to missionaries, students of theology, and members of the clergy. Stump, *Boundaries of Faith*, 25. In 2011 dollars, $300,000 would be close to $7.4 million.

49. Probably William Edward Pattison French, a popular writer of the period.

50. French, "It Seems Odd," 3–4.

51. A. Rochester, letter to the editor, *The Call*.

52. Vida D. Scudder to My Dearest Anna, December 20, 1910, Anna Rochester Papers, series 2, box 2, folder 66.

53. Secretary's Report, 1911, Archives of the Society of the Companions of the Holy Cross.

54. Ibid.

55. L. Rochester, "AR Annals," 115.

56. Intercession Paper, October 1911, Archives of the Society of the Companions of the Holy Cross.

57. "Statement by Anna Rochester," September 18, 1917, Anna Rochester Papers, series 1, box 1, folder 5.

58. For more on the National Child Labor Committee, see Trattner, *Crusade for the Children*.

59. Secretary's Report, 1912, 3, Archives of the Society of the Companions of the Holy Cross.

60. A. Rochester to Flynn, February 15, 1926, copy courtesy of Rosalyn Baxandall.

61. A. Rochester, "The Battle Lines of Child Labor Legislation," 86.

62. Ibid., 87.

63. A. Rochester, letter to the editor, *Life*.

64. L. Rochester, "AR Annals," 117.

65. Anna Rochester and Grace Hutchins, "Tell Us about Russia," Berlin, June 11, 1927, Grace Hutchins Papers, Ax 625, series 4, box 7, folder 8, Special Collections and University Archives, University of Oregon Libraries, Eugene. "Tell Us about Russia" gives Sukloff's name as Schkolnik. She used both names.

66. Robert Frost referred to the women as "Vermont's 'three verities': Dorothy Canfield (Fisher), 'wise and a novelist'; Zephine Humphrey (Fahnestock), 'mystic and an essayist'; and Sarah Cleghorn, 'saintly and a poet.'" Federal Writers Project, *Vermont*, 73.

67. Anna Rochester, untitled manuscript labeled "Dorset summer probably 1913," Anna Rochester Papers, series 3, box 4, folder 6.

68. A. Rochester, "The Eight-Hour Day for Children," 42.

69. Roger Baldwin went on to become a key figure in the American Civil Liberties Foundation; Anna Rochester served as a member of the ACLU board of directors during the late 1920s.

70. Anna Rochester, "Plan Magna Charta," *The Commonwealth*, June 12, 1915, Anna Rochester Papers, clipping, series 3, box 4, folder 2.

71. Lillian Wald to Jane Addams, Apr. 3, 1914, quoted in Kriste Lindenmeyer, "A *Right to Childhood*," 53.

72. Edith Klein, later Edith McGrath, worked for Louise and Anna Rochester for many years and remained a close family friend throughout Anna Rochester's life.

73. Approximately $32,700 in 2011 dollars.

74. L. Rochester, "AR Annals," 120.

75. Addams, *My Friend*, 49.

76. Ibid., 88.

77. Ibid., 143.

78. Edith Abbott to Julia Lathrop, quoted in Addams, *My Friend, Julia Lathrop*, 161.

79. Addams, *My Friend, Julia Lathrop*, 53.

80. Ibid., 173.

81. Lindenmeyer, "A *Right to Childhood*," 149.

82. US Department of Labor, Children's Bureau, *Facilities for Children's Play*, 7–8.

83. "The golf links lie so near the mill/That almost every day/The laboring children can look out/And see the men at play." The poem, describing an actual situation Cleghorn observed, has been widely available for years but apparently was first published in Franklin Pierce Adams's column in the *New-York Tribune* on January 23, 1915. See Cleghorn, *Threescore*, 139–40.

84. I use the terms that the Department of Labor employed in 1917.

85. US Department of Labor, Children's Bureau, *Facilities for Children's Play*, 14.

86. Secretary's Report, 1916, 19, Archives of the Society of the Companions of the Holy Cross.

87. The single tax was first advocated by Henry George, who argued that economic policies had moral consequences, not simply economic consequences. Working people had little access to land, as rents were prohibitive. Thus, he advocated a single tax on land, with no tax on wages or interest. Land, he said, belonged to the Creator; we use it temporarily. Not only that, he argued: taxes on wages and interest are destructive, whereas a tax on land is not.

88. Secretary's Report, 1916, 20, Archives of the Society of the Companions of the Holy Cross.

89. Ibid., 27.

90. A. Rochester, "Child Labor in Warring Countries," *Child Labor Bulletin*, February, 1918, 232.

91. Ibid.

92. Ibid., 240.

93. Intercession Paper, April 1918, Archives of the Society of the Companions of the Holy Cross.

94. Intercession Paper, May 1918, Archives of the Society of the Companions of the Holy Cross.

95. Federal Bureau of Investigation, report referencing November 18, 1942, report of special agent (redacted), May 10, 1943, Anna Rochester file 100-12805, section 1.

96. News Leaflet, April 1919, 11, Archives of the Society of the Companions of the Holy Cross.

97. Abbott, "Letter of Transmittal," 17.

98. Federal Bureau of Investigation, summary of personnel file of Children's Bureau, Department of Labor, November 18, 1942, Anna Rochester File 100-12805, section 1.

99. Secretary's Report, 1919, 35, Archives of the Society of the Companions of the Holy Cross.

Notes to Chapter Three

1. Durrell, "Memoirs of Deceased Members," 185.

2. U.S. Senate Committee on the Judiciary, *Nomination of Louis D. Brandeis*, 611–24.

3. Mary Louise Henson, interview with the author, Laguna Niguel, CA, November 9, 1996.

4. Grace Hutchins, "Letters of Travels," September 11, 1898, to March 28, 1899, Grace Hutchins Papers, unpublished bound ms., 4–5, series 4, box 7, folder 1.

5. Ibid., 9.

6. Ibid., 12.

7. Ibid., 13.

8. Ibid., 21.

9. Ibid., 22.

10. Ibid., 23.

11. Ibid., 51.

12. Ibid., 63.

13. Ibid., 64.

14. Ibid., 67.

15. Ibid., 68.

16. Ibid., 72.

17. Pluvvers, also known as plovers, probably the American Golden Plover. Once widespread, they are now scarce and declining; hunting plovers was banned in 1918.

18. Grace Hutchins, letter of application for service in the mission field, January 23, 1912, Domestic and Foreign Missionary Society Missionary Files, box 50, UP 194, Archives of the Episcopal Church, USA.

19. Field hockey had arrived in America in 1901 when it was demonstrated at the Harvard Summer School by an Englishwoman, Constance M. K. Applebee. See Cottrell, "Women's Minds, Women's Bodies."

20. Basketball—or, as it was spelled at the time, basket-ball—was also a relatively new sport, having been invented in 1891 at the YMCA Training School in Springfield, Massachusetts. See Lee, *Memories of a Bloomer Girl*, quoted in Kenney, "The Realm of Sports," 133. Bryn Mawr had a history of support for women's athletics, having been the site of the first Women's Athletic Association, also in 1891. See Noonkester, "The American Sportswoman," 190. Basketball was largely a women's sport for a number of years, played in intramural events on college campuses. The rules were modified to fit what administrators saw as the circumstances on each campus, so there was little use in trying to form intermural leagues. Bryn Mawr, for instance, played outside instead of in a gymnasium; used "men's rules," which allowed players to grab the ball from an opponent; and did not impose zones on the court. Instead, players ran the full length. See Kenney, "The Realm of Sports," 109.

21. For details of Hutchins's college athletic activities, see Bryn Mawr student publication *Tipyn o'Bob*, 1904–1905 and 1905–1906.

22. Hutchins, letter of application.

23. Ibid.

24. Ibid.

25. Parker, *Kingdom of Character*.

26. Corbett, "Permanent Factors," 344–5.

27. Devins, "The Kind of Articles," 591–5.

28. Gailor, "Christianity," 83.

29. Saunders, "The Missionary Possibilities," 75–7.

30. Eddy, *Pathfinders of the World Missionary Crusade*, 3.

31. Grace Hutchins, application form, 1906, Student Volunteer Movement for Foreign Missions, Student Volunteer Movement Archives, RG 42, Special Collections, Yale Divinity School Library, New Haven, CT.

32. Hutchins, letter of application.

33. Ibid. See also Hutchins, application form, 1909, Student Volunteer Movement for Foreign Missions, Student Volunteer Movement Archives.

34. Grace Lindley, recommendation form, August 22, 1910, Domestic and Foreign Missionary Society Missionary Files, box 50, UP 194, Archives of the Episcopal Church, USA.

35. Sturgis and Hutchins, *Pickaninnies' Progress*.

36. Lucy C. Sturgis, recommendation form, August 25, 1910, Domestic and Foreign Missionary Society Missionary Files, box 50, UP 194, Archives of the Episcopal Church, USA.

37. Grace Hutchins, "Personal Questions," Domestic and Foreign Missionary Society Missionary Files, box 50, UP 194, Archives of the Episcopal Church, USA.

38. Grace Hutchins to John Wood, September 18, 1910, Domestic and Foreign Missionary Society Missionary Files, box 50, UP 194, Archives of the Episcopal Church, USA.

39. Rev. Alexander Mann to John Wood, August 21, 1910, Domestic and Foreign Missionary Society Missionary Files, box 50, UP 194, Archives of the Episcopal Church, USA.

40. Ibid.

41. William Lawrence to John Wood, August 26, 1910, Domestic and Foreign Missionary Society Missionary Files, box 50, UP 194, Archives of the Episcopal Church, USA.

42. Cottrell, "The Sargent School," 32.

43. "Militants Should Exercise," *New York Times*, quoted in Cottrell, "Women's Minds, Women's Bodies," 145.

44. Sargent, "Physical Development of Women," 181, quoted in Cottrell, "Women's Minds, Women's Bodies," 148.

45. Roots, "Report of the Bishop," 70.

46. "Light-Bearers in Dark Places," *Spirit of Missions*, 919.

47. Bates, "The Theology of American Missionaries in China, 136.

48. Phillips, "The Student Volunteer Movement," 101.

49. Parker, *The Kingdom of Character*, 61.

50. Hunter, *The Gospel of Gentility*, 41.

51. See Cook, "Female Support Networks," 43–61.

52. Now called United Thank Offering. The Woman's Auxiliary supported the (male-controlled) Board of Missions but established the United Offering in 1889 in order to provide funds for specific projects, often those that would directly benefit women and children. See Donovan, *A Different Call*, 76–80, for a detailed account of the establishment of the United Offering.

53. Hutchins, "Outside the Little East Gate," 563.

54. He was traveling to the General Convention.

55. Bishop Logan Roots to Grace Hutchins, September 22, 1913, Grace Hutchins Papers, series 2, box 4, folder 75.

56. Ibid.

57. Hutchins, "St. Hilda's Outside the Wall," 564.

58. "Jane" [Lucy Sturgis] to Dear old Grace, August 14, [1914], Grace Hutchins Papers, series 2, box 4, folder 65.

59. Although the monarchical "movement" was cancelled on March 22, 1916, the resentment had grown to such a degree that Yuan Shih-kai could no longer govern effectively. A new president, Li Yuan-hung, took over in May.

60. Lean, "Frank Buchman." Buchman's own sexual identity remains a point of controversy, with a number of commentators suggesting that his obsession with homosexuality was an elaborate defense. See, for example, Driberg, *The Mystery of Moral Re-Armament*.

61. Bishop Lloyd to Grace Hutchins, September 9, 1916, RG 64, Domestic and Foreign Missionary Society China Records, 1834–1954, box 134, Archives of the Episcopal Church, USA.

62. See the photograph captioned "Women Who Are Carrying Religion to the Heathen," *St. Louis Star* (October 13, 1916), clipping, series 1, box 1, folder 6, Grace Hutchins Papers.

63. Grace Hutchins, "A Day at the Woman's Department," in *Our Plan for the Church General Hospital, Wuchang*, 14, RG 64, Domestic and Foreign Missionary Society China Records, 1834–1954, box 134, Archives of the Episcopal Church, USA.

64. Grace Hutchins to Janet Waring, February 10, 1917, RG 64, Domestic and Foreign Missionary Society China Records, 1834–1954, box 134, Archives of the Episcopal Church, USA.

65. Grace Hutchins to Janet Waring, February 24, 1917, RG 64, Domestic and Foreign Missionary Society China Records, 1834–1954, box 134, Archives of the Episcopal Church, USA.

66. Grace Hutchins to John Wood, April 4, 1917, RG 64, Domestic and Foreign Missionary Society China Records, 1834–1954, box 72, Archives of the Episcopal Church, USA.

67. Grace Hutchins to John Wood, April 23, 1917, RG 64, Domestic and Foreign Missionary Society China Records, 1834–1954, box 72, Archives of the Episcopal Church, USA.

68. Grace Hutchins, China notes, Grace Hutchins Papers, series 4, box 7, folder 3.

69. Outline of the courses offered at St. Faith's, 1917–1919, New York Training School for Deaconesses Papers, TSD22-File#30, Archives of the Episcopal Diocese of New York.

70. Ibid.

71. Grace Hutchins, Statement of Responsibilities, New York Training School for Deaconesses Papers, TSD20-File#5, Archives of the Episcopal Diocese of New York.

72. Faculty Minutes, New York Training School for Deaconesses Papers, TSD20-File#5, Archives of the Episcopal Diocese of New York.

73. G. Hutchins, "Greetings on Our Twenty-Fifth Anniversary," 21.

74. Faculty Minutes, New York Training School for Deaconesses Papers, TSD20-File#5, Archives of the Episcopal Diocese of New York.

75. Ibid.

76. Coe, *A Social Theory of Religious Education*, vii.

77. Grace Hutchins to Jane Gillespie and Romola Dahlgren, second Sunday after Trinity, New York Training School for Deaconesses Papers, TSD22-File#34, Archives of the Episcopal Diocese of New York.

78. Student Government Body, Minutes of Meetings of Student Government Body, December 3, 1919, New York Training School for Deaconesses Papers, TSD20-File#6, Archives of the Episcopal Diocese of New York.

79. *Alumnae Bulletin*, June 1920, New York Training School for Deaconesses Papers, TSD17-File#9, Archives of the Episcopal Diocese of New York. Grace Hutchins was replaced by Dr. Fleming James, formerly a missionary in China and then serving as rector of St. Paul's in Englewood, New Jersey, Anna Rochester's church. Dr. James was the brother of Dr. Mary James, Grace Hutchins's former Bryn Mawr classmate and a physician at the Church General Hospital in Wuchang.

80. Hutchins served as a member of the Episcopal Church's Department of Religious Education Commission on the Vocational and Recruiting of Young People during 1921. See *The Living Church Annual*.

81. Minutes of the New York Chapter, October 29, 1919, Archives of the Society of the Companions of the Holy Cross.

82. Minutes of the New York Chapter, January 11, 1920, Archives of the Society of the Companions of the Holy Cross.

Notes to Chapter Four

1. "Definite Beginning," in "Community House '352' 1921–1924 and 'Little Acorn' 1932," Anna Rochester Papers, series 4, box 9, folder 2.

2. For a detailed explanation of Simpson's ideas, see Simpson, "What Can the Individual Do?" 106–8.

3. *Twenty-Fourth Annual Conference*, August 28, 1920, report, 52, Archives of the Society of the Companions of the Holy Cross.

4. Ibid., 54–5.

5. "Concerning Books and the Conference," 1920, Archives of the Society of the Companions of the Holy Cross.

6. *Twenty-Fourth Annual Conference*, 57–8, Archives of the Society of the Companions of the Holy Cross.

7. The case study method aims to increase understanding by means of direct personal encounter and experience with an entity, possibly an individual person but more likely a group, institution, population, or other collectivity. For a clear exposition of the case study method, see Stake, "The Case Study Method," 5–8.

8. Hutchins completed one year or perhaps less; her life shifted dramatically with the establishment of the collective household in February 1921.

9. An address made famous by its owner ca. 1969–1973, Bob Dylan. The apartment block was later known as the Macdougal-Sullivan Gardens. Purchased and renovated in 1920 by William Sloane Coffin, New York businessman and heir to the W. J. Sloane Furniture Company, the building's apartments all opened onto a community garden space. Coffin had been disturbed by the flight of middle-class professionals from the inner city and by the deterioration of the housing stock. He bought the block in order to provide homes for "writers, businessmen, artists, actors, and musicians," intending to sell the newly refurbished old houses to their occupants at attractive rates. See Drayton, "Secret Gardens," 108–11.

10. Hutchins, *Women Who Work*, 1932, 20.

11. A small chapel.

12. "The House," in "Community House '352' 1921–1924 and 'Little Acorn' 1932," Anna Rochester Papers, series 4, box 9, folder 2.

13. Vida D. Scudder to Ellen Gates Starr, February 10, 1921, Ellen Gates Starr Papers, series 2, box 10, folder 11, Sophia Smith Collection, Smith College, Northampton, MA.

14. I am grateful to Jocelyn Cohen for this translation. The term contains a greater sense of commitment than does *housemate* in English; perhaps *house comrade* is closer to the meaning of the term.

15. Helen Hendricks to Tung-wu-li's, March 23, 1921, Anna Rochester Papers, series 4, box 9, folder 4.

16. The phrase is attributed to economist Adam Smith. Obviously I am not using it in the benevolent sense he intended.

17. Socialist Party records dating prior to the 1920s are, for this reason, thin, although they may exist in detail somewhere in the Justice Department.

18. Morgan, *Letters to Her Companions*, 200.

19. Morgan, *Letters to Her Companions*, 204.

20. Minutes of the Council, April 9, 1921, Fellowship of Reconciliation Papers, series A, subseries A-2, box 1.

21. *News Leaflet*, April 1920, Archives of the Society of the Companions of the Holy Cross.

22. Roberts, *The Untried Door*, 59.

23. For a detailed account of the contemporary published discussions of love and desire between women, see Faderman, *Odd Girls*.

24. Hutchins and Rochester, *Jesus Christ and the World Today*; see especially 145–9.

25. Hutchins and Rochester, *Jesus Christ and the World Today*, 30.

26. Ibid., 48.

27. Ibid., 71.

28. Ibid., 95.

29. Ibid., 98. They would learn in the years to come that their assumption that this would be a nonviolent scenario was naïve, given the military and police support for corporate ownership, one hundred thousand men notwithstanding.

30. Founder of Mt. Holyoke Female Seminary for Women (now Mt. Holyoke College). The success of this school opened the doors of higher education to women in the United States.

31. Hutchins and Rochester, *Jesus Christ and the World Today*, 30.

32. Ibid., 128.

33. Ibid., 138.

34. Ibid., 140.

35. The Church Service League was a federation of Episcopal Church–affiliated women's organizations. In 1921, Hutchins, along with Mary Simkhovitch, was a delegate-at-large, and Hutchins's friend Lucy Sturgis was treasurer. See *The Living Church Annual*, 180.

36. Anna Rochester to Lucie Myer, August 15, 1921, Anna Rochester Papers, series 2, box 3, folder 5.

37. "In the Name of the Father," probably 1921, Anna Rochester Papers, series 6, box 12, folder 2. The SCHC at the time included few, if any, members who were not Caucasian.

38. See Cleghorn, *Threescore*, for a more complete discussion of the change at Brookwood.

39. Cleghorn, *Threescore*, 250.

40. "Day Full of Joy in the Community," December 1921, Anna Rochester Papers, series 4, box 9, folder 5.

41. This idea pervades Carpenter's work. See especially *Civilisation* 1–62. For an explication of the work of Edward Carpenter, see Lewis, *Edward Carpenter*.

42. Rochester had become well known in Christian radical circles and, with her background at the Children's Bureau, was a logical choice to take over an editing position from Norman Thomas. She had just completed a two-part article for *The World Tomorrow* entitled "Immigration and Internationalism," which presented a historical overview of immigration in the United Stated and argued forcefully against the many (still familiar) claims of those advocating restrictive immigration policies.

43. Cleghorn, *Threescore*, 248.

44. The fellowship had been organized in the United States on November 11 and 12 of 1915 with sixty-eight members, as a mirror organization to the original in England. Rochester had joined by October 1916 and Hutchins by April 1918, both perhaps persuaded by Margaret Shearman, Helena

Stuart Dudley, or Mary Simkhovitch, all of whom were among the original sixty-eight. One of the earliest statements of principle of the organization declared: "That Love, as revealed and interpreted in the life and death of Jesus Christ, involves more than we have yet seen, that it is the only power by which evil can be overcome and the only sufficient basis of human society." The Council of the Fellowship included, among others, Jane Addams, Helena Stuart Dudley, Rufus Jones, A. J. Muste, Richard Roberts, J. Nevin Sayre, Margaret Shearman, Scott Nearing, and Norman Thomas. The organization emphasized the idea that Christianity was to be considered a way of life for the present, not an ideal for the future. Members were committed to following the way of Jesus as it applied to social problems and were intent upon persuading others of the importance of the Christian gospel. They were not, as a group, aiming to carry out specific reforms, but they did commit themselves to working independently to put into practice the fellowship's principles.

45. A. Rochester, "A Scientist Dissects War," 28–9.

46. A. Rochester, "New York, 1922," 36.

47. Sally Cleghorn to Grace and Anna, Anna Rochester Papers, series 4, box 9, folder 4.

48. Cleghorn, *Threescore*, 155–6.

49. A. Rochester, "Interpreting the Labor Movement," 57.

50. Hutchins, "For Group Discussion," 59–60.

51. Vida D. Scudder to Dearest Ellen, February 28, 1922, Ellen Gates Starr Papers, series 2, box 10, folder 11.

52. Rev. Hogue interpreted their criticisms personally, which they had not intended, and a few months he later resigned his position. See Grace Hutchins to William Spofford, May 4, 1922, William Spofford Papers, AR1993.018, box 2, Archives of the Episcopal Church, USA. Upon learning of the resignation, Rochester returned to the league, agreeing to join the twenty-member executive committee, and, hoping to bring Christian progressives together, she proposed that a CLID member should become an associate editor of *The World Tomorrow*. Hutchins agreed to serve as a member of the nominating committee, which was charged with the task of finding someone to serve as general secretary. See F. D. Barnett, "Triennial Meeting of the League," document accompanying letter to the membership, Organizations and Institutions Files, Church League for Social and Industrial Democracy, box 2, Archives of the Episcopal Church, USA. Hutchins undoubtedly was a strong advocate for offering the position to Rev. William Spofford, a field secretary for the league in the Midwest. This solution was accepted by the membership, and Bill Spofford served as head of the organization for the next twenty-five years. He attracted other key Episcopal activists to the league, including Mary Van Kleeck, who served as vice president, and the Reverends Fleming James and J. Howard Melish, who were both on the administrative committee. Spofford was able to retain Rochester and Hutchins only as friends, however, as they had begun to realize the futility of their attempts to move the institutional church into greater action and were devoting more of their time to the FOR and the LID, organizations not affiliated with a particular denomination or even with any religious institution.

53. Minutes of the Executive Committee of the Fellowship of Reconciliation, March 21, 1922, Fellowship of Reconciliation Papers, series A, subseries A-2, box 1.

54. Anna Rochester to The Community, March 21, 1922, Anna Rochester Papers, series 4, box 9, folder 4. The parody is a happy one but is nonetheless a portent of her developing unease with a theological solution to economic problems. Rochester even included a note saying that "the text at this point is obscure"—a sly reference to the instability of biblical interpretations of ancient scripts.

55. Minutes of the Executive Committee of the Fellowship of Reconciliation, April 27, 1922, Fellowship of Reconciliation Papers, series A, subseries A-2, box 1.

56. A. Rochester, "What Property Does," 105–6.

57. Vida Scudder to Anna Rochester, August 1922, Grace Hutchins Papers, series 3, box 6, folder 1.

58. Ibid.

59. Ibid. Dr. Julia M. Dutton was a homeopath practicing in the Boston area.

60. Scudder, "What Is Luxury?" 164.

61. Ibid., 164.

62. A. Rochester, "What Eleven Families Spend," 172.

63. Ibid., 172. Nearly three-quarters of the bituminous coal miners in the country struck in April 1922, protesting a move on the part of operators to reduce their wages below the 1920 level. In 1931, Rochester published a book on workers in the coal mines entitled *Labor and Coal*. See Chapter Eight for more on *Labor and Coal*.

64. A. Rochester, "What Eleven Families Spend," 172.

65. Devere Allen to John Nevin Sayre, August 23, 1922, Devere Allen Papers, series C-4, box 2.

66. A. Rochester, "In Quest of an Answer," 25.

67. A. Rochester, "Next Steps," 58.

68. Minutes of the Council of the Fellowship of Reconciliation, February 9–13, 1923, Fellowship of Reconciliation Papers, series A, subseries A-2, box 1.

Notes to Chapter Five

1. Sally Cleghorn to Grace Hutchins, April 15, 1923, Anna Rochester Papers, series 3, box 9, folder 4.

2. Ibid.

3. Ibid.

4. After leaving *The World Tomorrow* a year and a half later, Alice Beal Parsons wrote a book-length feminist argument for professional equality for women, followed by numerous short stories and several novels.

5. Anna Rochester to Alice Parsons, May 26, 1923, Devere Allen Papers, series C-4, box 2.

6. Saltmarsh, "The Terrible Freedom," 377.

7. Nearing, "What Can the Radical Do?" quoted in Saltmarsh, *Scott Nearing*, 185.

8. A. Rochester. "The Future in the Present," 203–5.

9. Anna Rochester to Folks at Home, July 21, 1923, Anna Rochester Papers, series 2, box 3, folder 3.

10. Anna to Lucie, June 26, 1923, Anna Rochester Papers, series 2, box 3, folder 1.

11. Ibid.

12. Ibid.

13. See Nexo, *Ditte: Towards the Stars*, 61. "'I'll tell you what—you ought to get hold of Pelle,' said Ditte with conviction. 'He would put matters straight for you.' Karl laughed. 'Oh yes, he has the gift of the gab,' he said, slightly ironically, 'but there's not much powder left in him—however great he may have been once. He's burned out, you see? And he doesn't want to have anything to do with the new ideas. He's planting cabbage at the Bispebjaerg Settlement, and believes the world is going to be saved by co-operative societies and small-holdings. Every man his own cabbage, is his watchword!'"

14. Anna Rochester to Folks at Home.

15. This comment is an interesting one, given that *Ditte* seems to contain an autobiographical element. At one point, Ditte finds work—and is happy, for once—in the home of Mr. and Mrs. Vang, thinly disguised representations of Nexo and his wife. She leaves, at the gentle behest of Mrs. Vang, after having an affair (if that's the appropriate word, given the power imbalance) with Mr. Vang. Later, Ditte, near death from impoverishment and overwork, accosts Mr. Vang, accusing him of being cold and uncaring. One wonders the degree to which guilt motivated the writing of *Ditte* and what part that guilt played in Nexo's understanding of the limitations of reformism.

16. Anna Rochester to Folks at Home.

17. "Violence or Solidarity?" *The New York Communist*, quoted in Saltmarsh, "The Terrible Freedom," 402.

18. Rochester and Hutchins were not yet convinced of the viability of a dictatorship of the proletariat. This would change over the course of the next few years.

19. Anna Rochester to Folks at Home.

20. Hutchins, "The Joy of Being a Missionary."

21. Stachura, *The German Youth Movement*, 107. The Youth Movement had developed in the late nineteenth century as a reaction to the stiff and authoritarian culture of the Kaiser Wilhelm regime—in much the same way that hippie culture developed in response to 1950s America. Beginning as a single organization, the Wandervogel, the movement championed activities such as hiking, camping, and folksinging. Within a few years, chapters had arisen across most of Germany. At first a single-sex male organization, some chapters of the Wandervogel were strongly homoerotic in nature, although by 1911 most chapters had agreed to admit girls. Other similar organizations arose, and they merged into a loose confederation in 1913 called Free German Youth. The war changed the essentially romantic nature of what had become a large movement, and it splintered into separate groups with varying purposes, some religious, some neoconservative, and some progressive. Because there were so many organizations that considered themselves the German Youth Movement, it is difficult to determine exactly which one sponsored the conference that Hutchins and Rochester attended.

22. Ibid., 108.

23. Kurt Klaeber [Held] was the author of several children's books. He is best known for *The Outsiders of Uskoken Castle*, a story of orphan children in a Yugoslavian fishing village who live on their own in an abandoned castle, seeing themselves as the reincarnation of famous fighters for justice, the Uskoken. They support themselves by gifts from some poor villagers and thefts from wealthy ones. The story, based on true events witnessed by Kurt Held, ends with a childless fisherman teaching them to fish—and to resist the corporatization of the fishing industry in the village.

24. Estelle Freedman has argued that the demise of women-only spaces in the 1920s led to a period of retrenchment and loss of momentum for the feminist movement. The experience of Hutchins and Rochester suggests that not only were cross-class women-only spaces difficult, if not impossible, to maintain economically, but other, more established all-women's institutions were, in response to larger cultural trends, losing their radical edge as well. See Freedman, "Separatism as Strategy," 21–35.

25. Ward had been hired at Union Theological Seminary at the behest of his friend George Coe, with whom Hutchins had studied in 1919. Like Coe, Ward believed in an activist theology, feeling "that the economic order was an unethical and mechanized structure that was creating individuals who could only be released from being culture bound by participating in social reconstruction." Link, *Labor-Religion Prophet*, 231. Ward argued that "'God is doing. . . . He is in and of the social process. He is found in change itself.'" Both Ward and Coe used a "religious scientific method" consisting of fact-finding, hypothesizing, and action, interpreted as "God functioning and creating." Ward typically urged students to ask three questions in any given situation: "What are the facts? . . . What do they mean? . . . What should be done?" (233). In addition to his position on the faculty of Union Theological Seminary, Ward was a contributing editor of *The World Tomorrow* and served in two other positions aimed at implementing his activist theology: for many years he was head of both the newly organized American Civil Liberties Union and the Methodist Federation for Social Service.

26. Minutes of the Executive Committee of the Fellowship of Reconciliation, September 28, 1923, Fellowship of Reconciliation Papers, series A, subseries A-2, box 1.

27. Committee on FOR Statement, November 1923, Fellowship of Reconciliation Papers, series A, subseries A-1, box 1.

28. Ibid.

29. For more on the separate institutions within which women like Grace Hutchins flourished during the early part of the century, see Freedman, "Separatism as Strategy," 21–35.

30. Hutchins. "Our Inferiority Complex," 362.

31. A. Rochester, "Work of the Fellowship," February 1923, Fellowship of Reconciliation Papers, series A, subseries A-1, box 1.

32. Nearing had completed his book, *The American Empire*, in 1921. He followed that with *The Next Step: A Plan for Economic World Federation* and was working, in 1924, with Joseph Freeman, on *Dollar Diplomacy: A Study in American Imperialism*.

33. For a detailed account of Scott Nearing's intellectual and political development during this period, see Saltmarsh, *Scott Nearing*.

34. John Nevin Sayre to Devere Allen, May 20, 1924, Devere Allen Papers, series C-4, box 2.

35. Anna Rochester to Devere Allen, May 9, 1924, Devere Allen Papers, series C-4, box 2.

36. Ibid.

37. John Nevin Sayre to Devere Allen, May 20, 1924, Devere Allen Papers, series C-4, box 2.

38. Grace Hutchins to John Nevin Sayre, June 19, 1924, Devere Allen Papers, series C-4, box 1.

39. Hutchins, "A Week," 221.

40. Dunn, "Democracy and the Russian Revolution," 175–6.

41. A. Rochester, "The Pacifist's 'Preparedness,'" 214.

42. Ibid., 215.

43. Ibid.

44. Consisting of seven buildings, each with five apartments, numbered 62, 64, 66, and 68 Barrow Street and 85, 87, and 89 Bedford Street in Greenwich Village, the co-op was established by Socialists in 1924. Beginning in the nineteenth century, Socialists and Populists across the country had developed laws that allowed the growth of co-operative business ventures, such as farmers' marketing co-operatives approved by the Capper-Volstead Act—an amendment of the Sherman antitrust laws—in 1922. Although these laws had not been intended to apply to housing, Socialists, concerned about the escalating rental market, saw in them a way to circumvent the rental system. See the Consumers' Co-Operative Housing Association papers, in possession of the secretary of the Consumers' Co-Operative Housing Association, New York.

45. I am grateful to Andy Marber, co-op secretary, for sharing information with me.

46. Betty Millard used the term "cell-like" to describe the bedrooms in the apartment at 85 Bedford Street in a conversation with the author in New York City on May 28, 1999.

47. The Social Justice Conference was secondary to the annual Companion Conference but offered Companions the opportunity to focus exclusively on issues of political and economic importance.

48. A historian, first at Columbia University and then at the New School for Social Research, who argued that history should be a record of human activities rather than an accounting of political events.

49. "Report of Conference Held at Adelynrood in Aug. by Committee on Social Justice," 1924, 7–8, Archives of the Society of the Companions of the Holy Cross.

50. Hutchins, Labor and Silk, 148; Feldman, "Grace Hutchins Tells," 12.

51. Ibid.

52. Hutchins, Labor and Silk, 148.

53. Ibid., 149–50.

54. Grace Hutchins to Devere Allen, November 24, 1924, Devere Allen Papers, series C-4, box 2.

55. A close corporation is a business with a limited number of shareholders, often operating in a more informal manner than a standard corporation.

56. Grace Hutchins to Devere Allen, December 25, 1924, Devere Allen Papers, series C-4, box 2.

57. "To All Friends of The World Tomorrow," May 15, 1926, Devere Allen Papers, series C-4, box 2.

58. A. Rochester, "Need We Fear Class Consciousness?" 6.

59. A. Rochester, "The Religious Experience of a Christian Radical," 48.

60. Ibid., 50.

61. Baldwin, "A Puritan Revolutionist," 270. "Coupon-clipping" at that time referred to the means by which investors received the income from bonds.

62. A. Rochester, "The Religious Experience," 47.

63. Anna Rochester to Devere and Marie, May 1, 1925, Devere Allen Papers, series C-4, box 2.

64. Grace Hutchins to Devere Allen, May 25, 1925, Devere Allen Papers, series C-4, box 2.

65. T. S. Brown to author, June 20, 1998.

66. I am especially grateful to Warder Cadbury, son of Henry J. Cadbury and Lydia Cadbury, for a tour of Back Log Camp on July 2, 1998, and for supplying me with many details of camp life. Lydia Cadbury was a daughter of Thomas Kite Brown.

67. Garland had inherited money from his father, a Wall Street broker; among those active in directing the fund were Roger Baldwin, Scott Nearing, Robert Morss Lovett, James Weldon Johnson, and Norman Thomas. The money helped to support the NAACP, to buy a radio station to broadcast labor news, and to establish Vanguard Press, a socialist publishing house.

68. A. Rochester, "Sowing the Wind," 330.

69. Grace Hutchins to John Sayre, May 20, 1926, Devere Allen Papers, series C-4, box 2. "Mrs. Elmhirst" most likely was Dorothy Payne Whitney Elmhirst, an exceptionally wealthy American philanthropist who, with her second husband, Leonard K. Elmhirst, established Dartington Hall in the late 1920s, an elaborate educational experiment in Devon, England. See "Dartington—The Story so Far."

70. Minutes of the Council of the Fellowship of Reconciliation, November 2–3, 1925, Fellowship of Reconciliation Papers, series A, subseries A-2, box 1.

71. Minutes of the Council of the Fellowship of Reconciliation, December 28, 1925, Fellowship of Reconciliation Papers, series A, subseries A-2, box 1.

72. Minutes of the Executive Committee of the Fellowship of Reconciliation, December 17, 1925, Fellowship of Reconciliation Papers, series A, subseries A-2, box 1.

73. Edward Hutchins to Grace, December 31, 1925, Grace Hutchins Papers, series 2, box 4, folder 18.

74. Grace Hutchins to Devere Allen, March 3, 1926, Devere Allen Papers, series C-4, box 2. Hutchins's choice of Merrill Root was a singularly bad one, if his later publications are any indication of his lack of judgment during the 1920s. During the 1950s, he published two rabidly right-wing books denouncing "Communist professors" and decrying the influence of Communists on the writing of American history textbooks.

75. "To All Friends of *The World Tomorrow*."

76. John Nevin Sayre to Editorial Board and Directors of *The World Tomorrow*, April 5, 1926, Devere Allen Papers, series C-4, box 2.

77. Kirby Page to Dear Friend, April 17, 1926, Devere Allen Papers, series C-4, box 2.

78. Grace Hutchins to Devere Allen, May 20, 1926, Devere Allen Papers, series C-4, box 2.

79. Grace Lindley to Grace Hutchins, May 29, 1926, RG 64, Domestic and Foreign Missionary Society China Records 1934–1954, box 72, Archives of the Episcopal Church, USA.

80. Minutes of the Board of Directors of the L.I.D., June 2, 1926, Tamiment 049, League for Industrial Democracy Records, series 1, box 28, folder 15, Tamiment Library, Elmer Holmes Bobst Library, New York University.

81. Minutes of the Fellowship Council, June 5, 1926, Fellowship of Reconciliation Papers, series A, subseries A-2, box 1.

82. Cable from Bishop Roots to Grace Hutchins, June 14, 1926, RG 64, Domestic and Foreign Missionary Society China Records 1934–1954, box 72, Archives of the Episcopal Church, USA.

83. A. Rochester, letter to the editor, *The Nation*, 59.

Notes to Chapter Six

1. V.D.S. [Vida Scudder] to Dearest Anna—and Grace, August 12, 1926, Anna Rochester Papers, series 2, box 2, folder 68.

2. Grace Hutchins and Anna Rochester to Friends, August 27, 1926, Grace Hutchins Papers, series 4, box 7, folder 11.

3. Ibid. Rochester uses the term "fancy dress," a now-archaic term for a costume.

4. A. Rochester, " 'Dangerous Thoughts' in Japan," unpublished manuscript, Grace Hutchins Papers, series 4, box 7, folder 10.

5. A. Rochester, "Japanese Labor News," 59.

6. Ibid.

7. A bacterial infection.

8. Hutchins, "Kagawa as Labor Leader," 1328–9.

9. Founded by William B. Pettus, the Language School was later named the College of Chinese Studies. After the Japanese invasion of China, the school moved to the University of California, Berkeley, where it remains.

10. In March 1926, sixteen thousand woolen mill workers, mostly immigrant women, went out on strike against wage cuts. Their peaceful march through the streets of Passaic, New Jersey was attacked by the police, and they were tear-gassed. The events were captured on film by news reporters and published widely. This reporting helped to bring the strike to a reasonably successful close.

11. Abbey, "Treaty Ports and Extraterritoriality."

12. The Nationalist (Kuomintang) Party was founded by Sun Yat-Sen in 1911 and, until his death in 1925, included Chinese Communists within the larger program; it also accepted aid and advice from the USSR. In 1927, after having used the Communists in his campaign to overthrow the northern warlords, General Chiang Kai-shek expelled the Communists, initiating a long struggle for control of the country.

13. A. Rochester to Dear Friends, October 10, 1926, Grace Hutchins Papers, series 4, box 7, folder 10.

14. Sheean, *Personal History*, 270.

15. Grace Hutchins, Notes on China, Grace Hutchins Papers, series 4, box 7, folder 4.

16. Anna Rochester to friends, Peking, October 10, 1926, Anna Rochester Papers.

17. Hutchins, Notes on China.

18. Ibid. The "May 30th incident" informed many of Hutchins and Rochester's conversations in China. During May 1925, the Second All-China Labor Congress was held in Canton, attracting some 514,000 workers from across China. The Japanese responded by demanding that the Chinese discontinue the textile union. (Most textile factories were owned by the Japanese.) Then a Japanese factory guard killed Communist trade-union activist Ku Cheng-hung and wounded other workers. When students and sympathizers tried to raise funds for the injured workers, they were imprisoned. Representatives of the "International Settlement," an organization representing the imperialist powers in Shanghai and chaired by Stirling Fessenden, an American, called for censorship of the press. On May 30, the Settlement police, under the command of "British Inspector Everson fired into a demonstration of 10,000 students and others who were demanding the release of the arrested men and the cessation of foreign interference in Chinese politics." A superficial inquiry exonerated Everson—and "the people throughout China rose in fury." Epstein, *From Opium War to Liberation*, 36–7. In particular, Grover Clark told Rochester and Hutchins that the report of the May 30th investigation was suppressed because it was a criticism of McEwen, the alcoholic chief of police, who was away drinking during the events. The British wanted to get themselves whitewashed, and the Americans lent themselves to the next investigation, which they should not have done. Strikes and boycotts of British and Japanese goods were organized; French and British troops fired on demonstrators, illustrating again the need to remove foreign powers from Chinese soil, and for sixteen months there ensued a general strike in the British colony of Hong Kong, which was just in the process of ending as Hutchins and Rochester were arriving.

19. Grace Hutchins, "Grey Terror in Peking," Grace Hutchins Papers, series 4, box 7, folder 10. This article may or may not have been published.

20. Hutchins, Notes on China.

21. Nancy Lee Swann, 1881–1966, is considered by some to have been the first female academician in the West focusing on Chinese studies.

22. Hutchins, Notes on China.

23. Ibid.

24. Ibid.

25. An American Observer in China, "An Attempt," 197.

26. Wood, "Missionaries All Safe," 669.

27. Wood, "Dr. Wood Summarizes Situation," 69.

28. Littell, "Writing from Outside," 17.

29. Hutchins, Notes on China.

30. Ibid. Phoebe Hoh's analysis was gentle compared with that of James H. Dolsen, who wrote in 1926 that missionaries functioned to prepare the way for capitalist development. See Dolsen, *The Awakening of China*, 240.

31. Sheean, *Personal History*, 238.

32. Hutchins, "Seeing Red in Canton," 776.

33. Ibid., 776.

34. A. Rochester, "Shanghai Workers Swear by Unions," 7.

35. Anna Rochester to friends, Baguio, Philippine Islands, December 9, 1926, Grace Hutchins Papers, series 4, box 7, folder 10. As Rochester predicted, the Kuomintang split the next year, with Chiang Kai-shek massacring Communists in Shanghai in April 1927 and overturning the left-leaning Hankow government in November 1927, replacing it with a government purged of Communist influence.

36. Ibid.

37. Ibid.

38. Bulosan, *America Is in the Heart*, 66–7.

39. Rochester to friends, Baguio, Philippine Islands.

40. Anna Rochester to friends, Singapore, December 29, 1926, Grace Hutchins Papers, series 4, box 7, folder 10.

41. Ibid. For information on the Laubach literacy method, see "The Laubach Literacy International instructional program," http://www.sil.org/lingualinks/literacy/implementaliteracyprogram/TheLaubachLiteracyInternationa.htm. Accessed October 18, 2012.

42. A. Rochester, "Notes from the Philippines," 133.

43. A. Rochester, "Filipino Cigarmakers Get Strike Compromise," 6.

44. Rochester to friends, Singapore.

45. Ibid.

46. Anna Rochester to friends, *President Garfield*, Indian Ocean, February 5, 1927, Grace Hutchins Papers, series 4, box 7, folder 10.

47. A tonga is a simple two-wheeled cart widely used at the time in India, especially by the British; a phaeton is a more elegant four-wheeled form of transport.

48. Anna Rochester to friends, *President Garfield*.

49. Hutchins, "Gandhi in the Villages," 203.

50. Ibid.

51. Rochester to friends, *President Garfield*.

52. Hutchins, "Gandhi in the Villages," 203.

53. Rochester to friends, *President Garfield*.

54. Ibid.

55. Report of the Labor Research Department, Tamiment 007, Rand School of Social Science Records, film R-7124, reel 49, frame 13:F:1:1, Tamiment Library, Elmer Holmes Bobst Library, New York University.

56. The Permanent Mandates Commission was a League of Nations body charged with overseeing the territories that had been transferred from the control of one country to another after World War I.

57. An agency of the League of Nations, established in 1919 to ensure reasonable labor standards for workers across the world.

58. Dr. Adelaide Brown cofounded Planned Parenthood with Dr. Florence Holsclaw and Margaret Sanger.

59. For more on Miriam Van Waters—who in the 1950s became a member of the Society of the Companions of the Holy Cross—see Freedman, *Maternal Justice*.

60. This turned out not to be the case. Thurman went on to work as an editor at two publishing houses. See Henderson, "Portrait of Wallace Thurman."

61. Thurman was arrested when, needing money, he accepted a proposition in a New York restroom. A minister paid his bail. Chauncey, *Gay New York*, 265. The minister, who then requested favors for his silence on the matter, was apparently engaged by a friend of Thurman, who borrowed the money to pay the fine. Thurman later narrated this event in a letter to his friend William Rapp. Ganter, "Decadence, Sexuality," 86.

62. Was Thurman, for instance, trying to grow his nest egg with a house party? Or was he simply entertaining friends? Evidence suggests that he did pay back the loan, although it took him four years. Johnson and Johnson, "Forgotten Pages," 368.

63. For more on Wallace Thurman, see Garber, "T'ain't Nobody's Bizness," 7–16.

64. Anna Rochester to Dear Friends, Berlin, April 3, 1927, Grace Hutchins Papers, series 4, box 7, folder 10.

65. Ibid.

66. Hutchins, "German Police Arm," 7.

67. The Berliner *Tageblatt* was a liberal German newspaper.

68. Rochester to Dear Friends, Berlin.

69. Ibid.

70. Ibid. This literary method of conveying ideas would prove a source of difficulty to them several decades later.

71. Anna Rochester to Friends, Moscow, May 2, 1927, Grace Hutchins Papers, series 4, box 7, folder 10.

72. Ibid.

73. See Nearing, *Education in Soviet Russia*.

74. Rochester and Hutchins, "Tell Us about Russia."

75. Ward, *The New Social Order*, 384.

76. Either Harriet G. Eddy or her sister. Harriet G. Eddy established California's county library system and then traveled to the USSR at the invitation of Anatol Lunacharsky to set up a modern library system there. She was in the Soviet Union from April to August of 1927. For more on Harriet G. Eddy, see Richardson, "Harriet G. Eddy," 2–13.

77. Rochester and Hutchins, "Tell Us about Russia."

78. Rochester to friends, Moscow.

79. Rochester and Hutchins, "Tell Us about Russia."

80. Olgin, "Comrade Lunacharsky," 24.

81. Ibid.

82. Upon their return, the American Trade Union Delegation, which included James Maurer as chairman, John Brophy, Stuart Chase, Jerome Davis, Paul H. Douglas, and R. G. Tugwell, among many others, published the widely circulated *Russia after Ten Years: Report of the American Trade Union Delegation to the Soviet Union*, one of the early publications of International Publishers, founded by Trachtenberg.

83. Rochester and Hutchins, "Tell Us about Russia."

84. Ibid.

85. The shorter workday for office workers was not because of any sense of hazard on the job; rather, it was due to historical precedents. For a detailed outline of working conditions in the Soviet Union in 1927, see American Trade Union Delegation, *Russia after Ten Years*.

86. Rochester and Hutchins, "Tell Us about Russia."

87. Hutchins, "Labor Likes Its Lot," 7.

88. Harold Ware was the son of Ella Reeve Bloor (known to most as "Mother Bloor"). He was a largely self-taught agricultural specialist who, in the early 1920s, persuaded the nascent Soviet government to let him bring modern farming equipment to Russia for a demonstration project. The project was such a success that he was invited to continue the work on a larger scale. For nine years, he organized Americans to contribute time and machinery to the new Soviet farming endeavors.

Returning to the United States in 1931, he worked to organize American farmers, establishing Farm Research, Inc. in Washington, DC and founding a newspaper, *The Farmers National Weekly*. Ware died in an automobile accident in Pennsylvania on August 13, 1935. See Harris, *Harold M. Ware*.

89. Jessica Smith was the daughter of an artist father and pianist mother, neither of whom were politically active. She was raised in Stuyvesant Square in New York City. Although not a Quaker herself, she was educated in Quaker schools, and in 1922 she went to Russia to do famine relief work with the American Friends Service Committee. It was here that she met and fell in love with Hal Ware. They were married by Norman Thomas during a return visit to the United States. When she and Ware returned to the United States permanently in 1931, she helped to organize the Friends of the Soviet Union (FSU), a group organized to work for American recognition of the USSR. She worked for several years in the Soviet Information Bureau in Washington, and when recognition finally came, she set up an information department for the new Soviet embassy. After Ware's death in 1935, Smith moved to New York to take over editorship of the FSU-sponsored magazine *Soviet Russia Today*. While in New York, she met and married John Abt, a lawyer with the New Deal and later, during the 1950s, chief counsel for the CPUSA. For more on Jessica Smith, see Abt with Myerson, *Advocate and Activist*.

90. Rochester and Hutchins, "Tell Us about Russia."

91. Ibid.

92. Ibid.

93. Ibid.

94. Rochester, "Japanese Labor News." 6.

95. Rochester and Hutchins, "Tell Us about Russia."

96. Gladkov, *Cement*, 308.

97. Anna Rochester to Sally, Berlin, June 13, 1927, Sarah N. Cleghorn Papers, box 2, folder 11, University of Vermont Library, Burlington.

98. Ibid.

99. *The Hammer*, "Transoceanic Guests in Rostov," May 22, 1927, trans. Sonja Franeta, Grace Hutchins Papers, series 4, box 7, folder 9.

100. Ibid.

Notes to Chapter Seven

1. Rochester to Sally, Berlin.

2. Ward, *The New Social Order*, 384.

3. Grace Hutchins to Mother, July 11, 1927, Grace Hutchins Papers, series 2, box 4, folder 66.

4. Grace Hutchins to My Dearest, July 1927, Grace Hutchins Papers, series 2, box 4, folder 69.

5. Grace Hutchins to Beloved, July 1927, Grace Hutchins Papers, series 2, box 4, folder 69.

6. Grace Hutchins to Devere Allen, July 26, 1927, Devere Allen Papers, series C-4, box 2; Grace Hutchins to Sayre, July 27, 1927, Devere Allen Papers, series C-4, box 2.

7. Caiola to Burritt, February 17, 1927, Community Service Society Records, series 2, box 44, folder 289, Rare Book and Manuscript Library, Columbia University in the City of New York.

8. Sayre to Grace Hutchins, August 2, 1927, Devere Allen Papers, series C-4, box 2.

9. Nevin to Devere, New York, August 2, 1927, Devere Allen Papers, series C-4, box 2. Several years later, when he wrote a brief history of the Fellowship of Reconciliation in the United States, Sayre occluded Rochester's and Hutchins's contributions almost completely. See Sayre, *The Story of the Fellowship of Reconciliation*.

10. By 1929, Scudder had become disillusioned with the USSR. Writing in the *New Leader*, she said "Russia proves that socialism and liberty are not synonymous." Scudder, "Problems of Socialism," 132. In 1934, she too was using the word *antiChrist*, although with more ambivalence. In an article entitled "The Christian Attitude toward Private Property" for *New Tracts for New Times*, she argued for a Christian challenge to the property-rights system, saying: "But it would be a disconcerting and embarrassing situation were we to behold Christianity lined up in defense of the privileged classes, as

they chant defiantly, 'May I not do what I like with my own?' while the forces of Anti-Christ—or shall we say of dialectical materialism—were beheld sustaining the claims of the disinherited and the poor." Scudder, "The Christian Attitude toward Private Property," 178.

11. Vida D. Scudder to Anna Rochester, July 31, 1927, Anna Rochester Papers, series 2, box 2, folder 68.

12. Scudder, *Brother John*, 252.

13. See Augustine, *De Doctrina Christiana*, book 4.

14. Angelo Sacco and Bartolomeo Vanzetti, both Italian immigrants, had been charged with holding up a factory paymaster and his guard in South Braintree, Massachusetts on April 15, 1920. Most accounts attribute the failure to consider all evidence to official anxiety over the anarchist organizing activities of the two; their guilt has long been in serious question.

15. Correlation Summary, December 29, 1955, 7, Federal Bureau of Investigation, file 100-13470, Grace Hutchins, section 3.

16. See "Arrests Check Picketing," 1, 2, and "Boston Situation is Tense," 1, 3, both in the *New York Times*.

17. The ILD provided legal and financial help to those arrested or injured in labor actions.

18. Bloor, *We Are Many*, 209. Twenty-five dollars in 1927 would be more than $325 in 2012 dollars.

19. Mother to My dear daughter [Grace Hutchins], August 16, 1927, Grace Hutchins Papers, series 2, box 4, folder 20.

20. Harold [Hurd] to My dear Sister [Susan Hutchins], August 20, 1927, Grace Hutchins Papers, series 2, box 4, folder 16.

21. Grace Hutchins to My dear Father and Mother, August 21, 1927, Grace Hutchins Papers, series 2, box 4, folder 70. This copy of the letter is written in the hand of Susan Hutchins.

22. Grace Hutchins and Anna Rochester, telegram to Citizens National Committee, August 23, 1927, Francis Russell Papers, series 3, folder 3.144, Robert D. Farber University Archives and Special Collections Department, Brandeis University, Waltham, MA.

23. Nearing, "Confession and Avoidance," 26.

24. Norman Thomas to Anna Rochester, October 11, 1927, Tamiment 129, League for Industrial Democracy Records, Labor Research Association Records, series 1, box 13, folder 3, Tamiment Library, Elmer Holmes Bobst Library, New York University. Responded to by Anna Rochester on October 15, 1927.

25. Walker, *In Defense of American Liberties*, 11. See also Federal Bureau of Investigation, American Civil Liberties Union files, part 14, http://nara-wayback001.us.archive.org/peth04/20041016005102/http://foia.fbi.gov/foiaindex/aclu.htm. Accessed October 18, 2012.

26. Walker, *In Defense of American Liberties*, 55.

27. Anna Rochester to Kirby and Devere, November 18, 1926, Anna Rochester Papers, series 2, box 3, folder 7.

28. Anna Rochester to Devere, November 18, 1927, Anna Rochester Papers, series 2, box 3, folder 8.

29. Anna Rochester to Nevin, November 18, 1927, Anna Rochester Papers, series 2, box 3, folder 9.

30. Trachtenberg, a Russian émigré born in Odessa in 1884, had considerable experience in pacifist and socialist activities, having engaged in peace propaganda on the front lines during the Russo-Japanese war and fled Russia after having been arrested and imprisoned for involvement in the failed 1905 revolution. Arriving penniless in the United States at age 22, he managed to gain admission to Trinity College and then Yale, studying economics. During this time, he helped to found the Socialist newspaper *New York Call* and served on its board of directors. At Yale, he wrote his PhD dissertation on "The History of Legislation for the Protection of Coal Miners in Pennsylvania." Also at Yale, he organized a chapter of the Intercollegiate Socialist Society in 1914, calling it the "Yale Society for the Study of Socialism" to appeal to Yale students. After leaving Yale in 1915, he began working for the Rand School of Social Science, where he initiated the publication of the annual *American*

Labor Year Book; he also went to work as an economist for the International Ladies Garment Workers Union. In 1921, he resigned from the Socialist Party and joined the incipient United Communist Party (the CPUSA). Four years later, he founded International Publishers, an independent publishing house that sought to provide class-conscious information for workers. See "Alexander Trachtenberg Dies," *New York Times,* 33, and "Trachtenberg, Marxist Leader, Dies at 82," *The Worker,* 5.

31. "Proposal for a Permanent Organization to be known as American Committee for Labor Service," 1926, 3, Labor Research Association Records, series 8, box 15, folder 14, Tamiment 129, Labor Research Association Records, Tamiment Library, Elmer Holmes Bobst Library, New York University. The LRA bought the equipment, files, and library of the Workers Health Bureau, an organization founded in the early 1920s to address job-related health issues, then in the process of dissolving, and continued some of the bureau's work. Some, but not all, of the funding for LRA activities was provided by the American Fund for Public Service (Garland Fund). Other funds came from sympathetic individuals and from organizations seeking information.

32. Early drafts of "Into the Underground," Elinor Ferry Papers, box 16, file 9, Harvard Law School Library, Harvard University, Cambridge, MA. The source of that "concern" is discussed in Chapter 8.

33. Summary of interview of Jay Lovestone by William Tompkins, assistant attorney general, November 28, 1956, Federal Bureau of Investigation, file 100-13470, Grace Hutchins, section 3. This file cites minutes of the party's Political Committee meeting of November 2, 1927, and also documents an interview in 1941 with Solon De Leon in which he was asked about the founding of the LRA. He said that "about 1930 he with Anna Rochester (CP member, NYC) and Grace Hutchins founded the LRA to carry on labor research getting information together for the workers and trade unions." He "also stated that the founding of the LRA was not a CP assignment and he did not consult the Party regarding it." Correlation Summary, December 29, 1955, 10.

34. Dunn. "The Job of Labor Research," 23.

35. A. Rochester, "Wages and Prosperity," 12–4.

36. Grace Hutchins to Beloved Partner, Hospital, February 7, 1928, Grace Hutchins Papers, series 2, box 4, folder 77.

37. Ibid.

38. O'Connor, O'Connor, and Bowler, *Harvey and Jessie,* 123.

39. Harvey O'Connor, a thirty-year-old working class man, had just returned from a visit to the Soviet Union with an unofficial labor delegation. While there, he had visited many of the same sites that Rochester and Hutchins had seen just a few months earlier, and he had delivered a eulogy at the funeral for their friend Rayna Prohme in Moscow, who had died from encephalitis. Although O'Connor was not a member of the CPUSA, he was committed to labor organizing, and he admired and worked closely with Communist organizers.

40. Hutchins, "New Bedford Fights for Union," 144–5.

41. Hutchins, "Flowers and Song Pep Spinners," 2; the same article, with some excisions, appears in *Labor Defender,* July 1928, 144.

42. Grace Hutchins to Most Precious Anna, September 10, 1928, Grace Hutchins Papers, series 2, box 4, folder 77.

43. Grace Hutchins, "Women of Leisure Oppose Protective Laws," *Federated Press Sheet* 4, October 23, 1928, Grace Hutchins Papers, series 3, box 5, folder 7.

44. The first was Theresa Wolfson, who wrote *The Woman Worker and the Labor Unions* (1926).

45. Pseudonym of S. A. Dridzo.

46. Hutchins, *Labor and Silk,* 97.

47. Eleanor Lansing Dulles, review of *Labor and Silk* by Grace Hutchins, *Bryn Mawr Bulletin,* June 1929, 16–7, clipping, Grace Hutchins Papers.

48. Muste, "Organizing the Textile Workers," review of *Labor and Silk,* July 6, 1929, clipping, Grace Hutchins Papers.

49. Lumpkin, "War and Underwear," 6, 5; Lloyd, "FP Writer Portrays Hell," 5. Jessie Lloyd, twenty-four years old at the time, recently returned from Russia herself and working as a reporter

for the Federated Press, was the granddaughter of Henry Demarest Lloyd, author in 1894 of *Wealth Against Commonwealth*, an exposé of corruption and monopolistic motives in the Standard Oil Company, and the daughter of Lola Maverick Lloyd, a founder of the Women's International League of Peace and Freedom and a designee on the DAR's 1927 list of "Doubtful Speakers." Jessie Lloyd was also the niece of Caro Lloyd Strobell, with whom Rochester had worked in the League for Industrial Democracy. The family was very wealthy, and Jessie Lloyd had inherited part of the *Chicago Tribune* fortune as well as income from Texas land on her mother's side. She placed this wealth—as well as her own writing ability—at the service of the Federated Press, the LRA, and other progressive organizations.

50. Nearing, "Slaves of the Machine," 18–9.

51. A. Rochester, "The Coal Miners and Injunctions," 48.

52. Hutchins, "Textile Union Born in Strike," 2.

53. Weisbord, *A Radical Life*, 182; the book as a whole offers a detailed account of the strike and its aftermath.

54. Hutchins, "Mill Owners on Defensive," 8.

55. Known as the "Red Flame," Ann Burlak (later Timpson), 1911–2002, was a fiery textile workers organizer and CP activist.

56. Tribute from Judge Almy (class of 1872) and note from Grace Hutchins, ca. July 1929, Grace Hutchins Papers, series 1, box 2, folder 1.

57. Simmons, "Companionate Marriage," 54. See also Faderman, "Love Between Women."

58. Henry Hutchins to Grace Hutchins, June 26, 1929, Grace Hutchins Papers, series 1, box 1, folder 12.

59. Kurt Klaeber to Grace, July 31, 1929, Grace Hutchins Papers, series 1, box 1, folder 12. I am grateful to the late Professor Robert Coleman-Senghor of Sonoma State University for translating Klaeber's letter from the original German.

60. "Cheer New York Delegates for Unity Congress," *Daily Worker*, 1.

61. The average age of delegates to the TUEL was 32. Foster, *History of the Communist Party*, 257.

62. It is unclear which measure of wealth was used by the TUEL. In 2010 (the latest date for which figures are available), 1 percent of Americans owned 42.1 percent of the financial wealth; the bottom 80 percent owned 4.7 percent. Of total net worth, 1 percent of Americans owned 35.4 percent, 19 percent owned 53.5 percent, and 80 percent owned the remaining 11.1 percent. See Domhoff, "Power in America."

63. Foster, *History of the Communist Party*, 257.

64. "Militant Program for Class War," *Daily Worker*.

65. Having studied at the London School of Economics after graduation from Wellesley and developed expertise on social insurance in England and Germany, Halsey returned to the United States and began working for the American Association for Labor Legislation in Washington, DC, writing all of that organization's materials on health insurance. During the late 1920s and early 1930s, she worked for the International Labor Office. Having attended Wellesley, she knew Florence Converse and Vida Scudder. She may also have become acquainted with Juliet Stuart Poyntz at the London School of Economics.

66. Anna Rochester to Grace Hutchins, Back Log Camp, August 30, 1929, Grace Hutchins Papers, series 2, box 4, folder 40.

67. A. Rochester, "Pennsy Drops 61,500 Miners," 5.

68. "Bar from Jury All Who Read," *Daily Worker*, 2.

69. "Resolution on the 'Daily Worker,'" *Daily Worker*, 4.

70. Trachtenberg, "The Recruiting Drive," 4.

71. Ibid.

72. Stachel, "The Coming Seventh Year," 4.

73. Lenin, "Lenin on Working Class Literature," 7.

74. Elinor Ferry, "Marriage," unpublished chapter, Tamiment 116, box 5, Elinor Ferry Papers, Tamiment Library and Robert F. Wagner Labor Archives.

75. Society of the Companions of the Holy Cross, Intercession Paper, November 1929, 13, Archives of the Society of the Companions of the Holy Cross.

76. Anna Rochester to Alexander Trachtenberg, November 21, 1934, Trachtenberg Papers, Mss. 117, box 1, file 1, State Historical Society of Wisconsin, Madison.

77. A. Rochester, "A Favorable Interpretation," 80–1.

78. Ibid., 87.

Notes to Chapter Eight

1. Carl R. Burgchardt has pointed out the rhetorical errors made by Communists during the Third Period (the era roughly from 1929–1934). Although I find Burgchardt's criticisms largely valid, I believe that he has suggested a stronger link between rhetorical errors and the CPUSA's alleged failure to thrive than I think is warranted. In the first place, the party had more influence than Burgchardt has allowed, and second, its failures stemmed from a wider array of causes than rhetorical missteps. See Burgchardt, "Two Faces of American Communism."

2. The Comintern met from July 17 to September 1, 1928.

3. Foster, *History of the Communist Party*, 266.

4. Ibid., 266. As the international party consolidated its efforts, individual differences became unbridgeable in some circumstances. Trotsky was expelled in October 1928. The American party expelled a group of members headed by Jay Lovestone the following June.

5. The ILD was a cross-party membership organization set up to defend workers persecuted for their activism. The ILD offered support to families as well, recognizing that all would suffer if an income source were cut off.

6. Poyntz was a Communist activist who had been going back and forth between New York and Gastonia providing aid for the imprisoned National Textile Workers Union organizers after the shooting of police chief Aderholt. Hutchins had originally met Juliet Poyntz in 1927, possibly in the Sacco-Vanzetti Defense Committee, and had assisted her in establishing an account at the Corn Exchange Bank in Manhattan.

7. Hutchins, "Women Workers Hail the I.L.D.," 6.

8. Hutchins, "Negro Women Workers," 76.

9. Hutchins, "Schrafft Profits on Unemployed Workers," 6.

10. Although her report, titled "Hint Capitalist Interest in Church Crusade Against Soviet," was given a byline of simply "Federated Press," a line at the foot of the page indicates that it was "Prepared for Federated Press by Labor Research Assn.," and the accompanying initials are hers.

11. Grace Hutchins, "Hint Capitalist Interest in Church Crusade Against Soviet," *Federated Press Central Bureau Sheet 2*, no. 0304, March 4, 1930, Labor Research Association Records, box 6, folder 6.

12. Society of the Companions of the Holy Cross, Intercession Paper, April 1930, 16, Archives of the Society of the Companions of the Holy Cross.

13. Correlation Summary, December 29, 1955, 19. The Workers School, located in Manhattan, offered courses such as "History of the American Working Class" and "Fundamentals of Communism." Course materials included publications produced by the Labor Research Association. The school was established to continue the tradition of worker education offered by the Rand School, which had declined along with the Socialist Party. See Gettleman, "The New York Workers School," 261–80.

14. Hutchins herself was surety for Joseph Harrison, an organizer from Passaic, NJ, and one of the four who were convicted of murder in Aderholt's death, in what Vera Buch Weisbord, one of the original defendants, called a "trial by prejudice." The four had each been sentenced to seventeen to twenty years in the state prison in Raleigh, NC, with ten-year concurrent sentences for assault. For a clear account of the events surrounding the shooting of Aderholt and the prejudicial nature of the trial, see Weisbord, *A Radical Life*.

15. Anna Rochester to Grace Hutchins, probably late 1929, Grace Hutchins Papers, series 2, box 4, folder 37.

16. Drew had been sentenced to thirty days for the crime of biting a policeman on the knuckle while he was dragging her off the speakers' stand at a meeting to organize workers in the needle trades.

17. Grace Hutchins, "Organizer in Jail Tells of Jobless Fellow Prisoners," *Federated Press Eastern Bureau Sheet* 3, December 30, 1930, Labor Research Association Records, box 6, folder 6.

18. Rochester's book describes the increasing concentration and financialization of capital; that is, the tendency of capital to become a commodity used to create more capital rather than to produce goods and services.

19. Anna Rochester and Harvey O'Connor, "38 Giant Concerns Total over a Billion Dollars Dividends," *Federated Press Central Weekly Letter*, 1930, Labor Research Association Records, box 6, folder 6.

20. Anna Rochester et al., "Rockefeller Dominates World's Largest Bank," *Federated Press Central Weekly Letter*, sheet 2, March 21, 1930, Labor Research Association Records, box 6, folder 6.

21. Earl Browder, "Report of the Political Committee to the 12th Central Committee Plenum, CPUSA," November. 22, 1930, 11, Tamiment 132, CPUSA Records, box 221, folder 17, Tamiment Library, Elmer Holmes Bobst Library, New York University.

22. Hutchins, "Speedup Cuts Office Jobs," 5.

23. Hutchins, "Westinghouse Cuts Wages," 5.

24. Hutchins, "Negro Organizers Expect Lynchings," 2.

25. Browder, "Next Tasks of the Communist Party," 972.

26. A Rochester, *Labor and Coal*, 8.

27. Ibid., 46–53.

28. Ibid., 31.

29. Ibid., 158.

30. Review of *Labor and Coal*, *Christian Century*, quoted in *Book Review Digest* 27, 907.

31. Grace Hutchins to Paul Hutchinson, February 3, 1931, Labor Research Association Papers, Tamiment 116, box 6, folder 23, Tamiment Library and Robert F. Wagner Labor Archives.

32. Paul Hutchinson to Grace Hutchins, February 6, 1931, Labor Research Association Papers, Tamiment 116, box 6, folder 23, Tamiment Library and Robert F. Wagner Labor Archives.

33. Ward, "The Coal Situation," 6. In January 1930, *The Communist* published the text of the Political Committee's report; Harry F. Ward quite likely read it.

34. Julia Lathrop to Anna Rochester, January 15, 1931, Anna Rochester Papers, series 3, box 6, folder 4.

35. Julia Lathrop to Anna Rochester, May 28, 1931, Anna Rochester Papers, series 2, box 2, folder 32.

36. Helena Dudley to My dear Anna, January 11, 1931, Anna Rochester Papers, series 3, box 6, folder 4.

37. Lathrop to Rochester, May 28, 1931.

38. Rochester to Hutchins, probably late 1929.

39. Anna Rochester to Grace Hutchins, "Just before lights out," probably ca. early 1930s, Grace Hutchins Papers, series 2, box 4, folder 47.

40. Anna Rochester to Grace Hutchins, December 17, ca. 1931, Grace Hutchins Papers, series 2, box 4, folder 36. I am indebted to Sonja Franetta for her translation of this phrase.

41. Elinor Ferry, "Notes, Literary Left, 30s," ca. 1950s, Elinor Ferry Papers, box 17, file 20, Harvard Law School Library.

42. "Marriage (finished)," probably ca. 1950s–early 1960s, Elinor Ferry Papers, box 16, file 7, Harvard Law School Library.

43. Notes from interview with A. B. Magil, probably ca. early 1950s, Elinor Ferry Papers, box 17, file 19, Harvard Law School Library.

44. For more on the ideological changes regarding sexuality during the late 1920s, see Faderman, "Love Between Women."

45. Elinor Ferry, "Marriage," probably ca. 1950s–early 1960s, unpublished chapter, Tamiment 116, box 5, Elinor Ferry Papers, Tamiment Library.

46. Although Rochester spent most of her time in the safe confines of the New York Public Library, she placed herself in some danger at conventions, such as the big national conference of coal miners in Pittsburgh on July 15 and 16, 1931. She had written again on the murderous policies of the mining companies, who were in league with state and federal government officials, saying,

> This Pennsylvania apparatus of White Terror has been perfected in recent years. It includes judges and local governments; state police, sheriffs and sheriffs' deputies, and private armies of gunmen; it uses yellow-dog contracts, evictions, blacklists, sheriffs' proclamations, injunctions, ordinances, criminal sedition laws, frameups, clubbing, shooting and murder. It reaches up into the president's cabinet, where Andrew Mellon talks of "good will" when he travels abroad, while the Mellon family coal companies carry on war against their workers in Pennsylvania. It holds in reserve the state militia and the United States army. . . . The new sharpness of the struggle in Pennsylvania reflects the depth of the crisis which has sharpened the class line-up in every capitalist country.

See A. Rochester, "Cossacks to Kill," 128.

47. Anna Rochester to Grace Hutchins, August 3, 1931, Grace Hutchins Papers, series 2, box 4, folder 36.

48. T. S. Brown to author, June 20, 1998, letter.

49. Hutchins, "The Greatest Disaster in History," 5, 14. Estimates suggest that 145,000 people died in the flooding.

50. Phillip Bonosky, personal conversation, New York City, July 6, 1998.

51. Labor Research Association, foreword to *Labor Fact Book*, 9.

52. Ibid., 10.

53. A. Rochester, review of *The Challenge of Russia*, 18–19.

54. Ibid.

55. A. Rochester, review of *New Russia's Primer*, 16–7.

56. Ilin, *New Russia's Primer*, 150–1.

57. Hutchins, "Away with that Little Penitentiary!" 55.

58. "Resolution on the Work," *New Masses*, 20–1.

59. The report from the Kharkov Conference asked writers "to struggle against the petit-bourgeois tendencies in our work." It also addressed two other points: to fight against fascism, and "to struggle for the development and strengthening of the revolutionary labor movement." See "Kharkov Conference," *New Masses*.

60. "Resolution on the Work," *New Masses*, 20–1.

61. "The RILU on *Labor Unity*," *Labor Unity*, 26–8.

62. Gold, "Toward an American Revolutionary Culture," 12.

63. Hutchins, *Women Who Work*, 1932, 4.

64. Ibid., 7.

65. Ibid., 31.

66. Burke, *Attitudes toward History*, 256.

67. A. Rochester, *Profit and Wages*.

68. A. Rochester, *Wall Street*, 3.

69. Ibid., 11.

70. Burke, *Attitudes toward History*, 93. *Attitudes toward History* was published in 1937. Burke provided a more detailed critique of debunking in "The Virtues and Limitations of Debunking." The chapter was first published in *Southern Review* in the spring of 1938.

71. Burke, *Attitudes toward History*, 92.

72. Ann George and Jack Selzer, *Kenneth Burke in the 1930s*, 154.

73. Ibid., 93.

74. A. Rochester, "Those Liberals!" 16.

75. Burke, *Attitudes toward History* (see "Perspective by Incongruity," part 3, chapter 2, 308–14).

76. Hutchins, "Far Away and Long Ago," 26.

77. Foster, *History of the Communist Party*, 291.

78. Correlation Summary, December 29, 1955, 17.

79. Foster, *History of the Communist Party*, 291.

80. Ibid., 282–3.

81. Grace Hutchins, *Turtle Progress-Dispatch*, 1931, Grace Hutchins Papers, series 1, box 1, folder 7.

82. Tamagne, *A History of Homosexuality*, vol. 2, 112. See Tamagne for a detailed account of the events surrounding the politicization of sexuality in Germany during the interwar period.

83. Ibid., 116.

84. Ibid.

85. Ibid., 117.

86. Ibid., 119.

87. Ignaz Wrobel (alias Kurt Tucholsky), *Die Weltbuhne*, no. 17, April 26, 1932, cited by Tamagne, *A History of Homosexuality*, vol. 2, 114.

88. Klaus Mann, *Le Tournant* (Paris: Solin, [1949] 1984), 162, quoted in Tamagne, *A History of Homosexuality*, vol. 2, 118. For a more thorough examination of "masculinism" in pre-war Germany, see Hewitt, *Political Inversions*.

89. Tamagne, *A History of Homosexuality*, vol. 2, 113.

90. *The Masses* was a radical journal published between 1911 and 1917, known for its cover art; cartoons by artists such as Art Young, Stuart Davis, and Robert Minor; and coverage (by John Reed, Mary Heaton Vorse, Max Eastman, and others) of major labor and political events, including the war in Mexico, the Lawrence textile strike, and the Bolshevik revolution. *The Liberator* and then *New Masses* succeeded *The Masses*, which succumbed to government attacks following its declaration of opposition to the United States's entry into World War I. ·

91. Northshield, *History of Croton-on-Hudson*, 151ff.

92. Henry Hutchins to Grace Hutchins, July 14, 1932, Grace Hutchins Papers, series 2, box 4, folder 19.

93. *Preussiche Pressidienst*, quoted in World Committee for the Victims of German Fascism, *Brown Book of the Hitler Terror*, 57.

94. World Committee for the Victims of German Fascism, *Brown Book*, 55.

95. Ibid., 57.

96. Ibid., 62.

97. Ibid., 165–9.

98. World Committee for the Victims of German Fascism, *The Reichstag Fire Trial*, 162.

99. Ibid.

100. Andrew Hewitt argues that the authors of the *Brown Book* "avoided examining the political appeal of fascism to the proletariat by insisting on van der Lubbe's homosexual lack of class consciousness." Hewitt, *Political Inversions*, 82. They "saw in the homosexual an anarchic petit bourgeois individual *inevitably* alienated from class interests and aligned him with the interests of reaction" (emphasis mine), 88.

101. See both Tamagne, *A History of Homosexuality*, vols. 1 and 2, and Hewitt, *Political Inversions*, for a more detailed explanation of Bluher's arguments and influence.

102. World Committee for the Victims of German Fascism, *The Reichstag Fire Trial*, 161.

103. Ibid., 161.

104. M. Sereisky, "Gomoseksualizm," *Bolshaya Sovetskaya Entsiklopediya* (Moscow: Columns, 1930), 17:593–596, quoted in Kon, "Russia," 223.

105. Sereisky, quoted in Kon, 224. In her excellent series for *Workers World* tracing the history of gay and lesbian sexualities in the Soviet Union, Leslie Feinberg notes changes in discussions among Soviet scientists during the late 1920s, citing arguments between those favoring "nature" and those favoring "nurture," a "faultline" that allowed the later imposition of the repressive Article 121. According to Feinberg, "On Sept. 15, 1933—shortly after German-Soviet relations were severed by

the rise of Hitler to power—G.G. Iagoda, deputy chief of the Soviet political police, proposed the stricture against male homosexuality." See Feinberg, "Can a Homosexual Be a Member?"

106. For an extended discussion of the recriminalization of sodomy in the USSR, see Healey, *Homosexual Desire*, especially Chapter 7. Healey provides details about the German Communist Party's attempts to overturn Paragraph 175, the section of the German legal code criminalizing sex between men.

107. Quoted in Tamagne, *A History of Homosexuality*, 2:104.

108. Feinberg points out: "At no point was lesbianism raised. Masculine lesbians in the ranks and leadership of the military were seen as strong and loyal. Feminine male homosexuals were viewed as weak and untrustworthy." Feinberg also documents a challenge to the new Soviet policy sent to Stalin by British Communist Harry Whyte, then living in Moscow and writing for the *Moscow Daily News*. Whyte's challenge was rebuffed in an essay by Maxim Gorky, "Proletarian Humanism," published on May 23, 1934 in both *Pravda* and *Izvestia*. See also Hewitt, *Political Inversions*.

Notes to Chapter Nine

1. Pen and Hammer, formed in the early 1930s and headquartered at 114 West 21st Street in Manhattan, had chapters in large cities such as Philadelphia, Chicago, Pittsburgh, Detroit, Los Angeles, and Louisville. The January 26, 1933, issue of the *Pen and Hammer Bulletin* called for "a lucid writer with a dialectical (racy) style . . . to put a finished L. R. A. pamphlet into shape." *Pen and Hammer Bulletin*, January 26, 1933, 2.

2. Millard, interview.

3. Grace Hutchins to Anna Rochester, April 18, ca. early 1930s, Grace Hutchins Papers, series 2, box 4, folder 77.

4. Perchik, "Bolshevik Agitation," 37.

5. Ibid., 38.

6. Browder, "'Fewer High-Falutin' Phrases,'" 21.

7. Editorial Committee, "*The Working Woman.*"

8. Hutchins, "Julia Martin," 9. Julia Martin was a party activist; how close the story hews to actual events is unclear.

9. A. Rochester, "The Morgan Empire," 3.

10. A. Rochester, "Morgan, Wage Cutter," 4.

11. Ibid.

12. A. Rochester, "Morgan: A World Money Power," 4.

13. A. Rochester, *Your Dollar under Roosevelt*, 11.

14. Ibid.

15. Ibid., 16.

16. Ibid., 22.

17. Rochester published her only article for *Labor Unity*, the organ of the Trade Union Unity League, in January 1934, explaining the poor contract for bituminous coal miners that had been negotiated by the United Mine Workers and the equally miserable contract being offered by mine owners to anthracite workers. As she pointed out, however, this latter contract was at least being contested by rank-and-file anthracite miners, both employed and unemployed, through the United Anthracite Miners and Unemployed Leagues and Unemployed Councils.

18. A. Rochester, "The Banking Crisis," 344.

19. Miriam to Grace Hutchins, April 24, 1933 (internal evidence suggests that the date should be 1934), Grace Hutchins Papers, series 3, box 6, folder 3.

20. Elinor Ferry, "Chapter III, Marriage," probably 1950s–early 1960s, unpublished manuscript, Tamiment 116, Elinor Ferry Papers, box 5.

21. Hutchins, "Preparing Women for War," 4.

22. Van Kleeck's partner was Mary Fledderus, a Dutch personnel reformer whom she invited to come to the United States in 1927 and with whom she worked in the International Industrial Relations Institute.

23. David Saposs to Robert Dunn, Brookwood, Katonah, NY, January 10, 1934, Grace Hutchins Papers, series 3, box 6, folder 3.

24. Mary van Kleeck to Grace Hutchins, January 28, 1934, Grace Hutchins Papers, series 3, box 6, folder 3.

25. Hutchins, *Women Who Work*, 1934, 9.

26. Ibid., 16.

27. Ibid., 23.

28. Ibid., 8.

29. Ibid., 9.

30. Ibid., 209.

31. Ibid., 225.

32. Ibid., 256.

33. Ibid., 256–7.

34. Dorothy Wolff Douglas, a Bryn Mawr graduate with a PhD from Columbia, had divorced her husband, Paul Douglas, in 1930 and established a partnership with Katharine DuPre Lumpkin, sister of Hutchins and Rochester's friend Grace Lumpkin.

35. Molly Dewson to Grace Hutchins, April 28, 1934, Grace Hutchins Papers, series 3, box 6, folder 3.

36. Olga Halsey to Anna Rochester and Grace Hutchins, May 20, 1934, Grace Hutchins Papers, series 3, box 6, folder 3.

37. "Women and Work," *New York Times*, BR12.

38. Lucy Parsons to Comrade Grace Hutchins, May 10, 1934, Grace Hutchins Papers, series 3, box 6, folder 3.

39. Small, "A Complete Study," 7.

40. Lumpkin, "Emancipation and Exploitation," 26–7.

41. Fairchild, review of *Women Who Work*, 272.

42. Marshall, "Policy of Employers to Hire Men Handicaps Women," *New York Evening Journal*, March 17, 1934, n.p., clipping, Grace Hutchins Papers, series 3, box 6, folder 12.

43. Hutchins, "In Re Review of Women Who Work," June 20, 1934, Grace Hutchins Papers, series 3, box 6, folder 7.

44. Gold, "Change the World!" 5.

45. Ibid.

46. See Zetkin, *Reminiscences of Lenin*.

47. Hutchins, "Feminists and the Left Wing," 15.

48. Ibid.

49. See John Chabot Smith, typewritten notes from interview with Elinor Ferry, August 30, between 1972 and 1975, Alger Hiss Defense Files, Special Collections, Harvard Law School Library, Harvard University, Cambridge, MA.

50. Putatively exact accounts of antifascist work among Communists during the 1930s, such as those of Elizabeth Bentley, suffer from serious inconsistencies, as well as from word choices that encourage readers to infer malice and intrigue where none may have existed. Whittaker Chambers's story of having been recruited for "underground" work by Max Bedacht, for example, has been discredited by Bedacht himself. See Bedacht, unpublished autobiography, Max Bedacht Papers, Tamiment 072, Tamiment Library, Elmer Holmes Bobst Library, New York University. These stories make it difficult to determine exact events and activities. Nonetheless, given the antifascist struggles of the time and her frequent travels abroad, it is not unlikely that Poyntz would have tried to participate in this way.

51. See Federal Bureau of Investigation, file #100-206603, Juliet Stuart Poyntz. Poyntz was working on an analysis of the European political situation.

52. How Chambers used the money is unclear. He did not have his teeth fixed. Moreover, Sam Krieger had offered to take him to a dentist who would do the work for free, so his story about the teeth to Grace Hutchins was a fabrication.

53. Hutchins, "Statement by Author of *Women Who Work* (International Publishers)," Grace Hutchins Papers, series 1, box 1, folder 5.

54. A. Rochester, "Private Insurance Racket," 2. Ecker's salary would have been more than $2.5 million in 2011 dollars.

55. F. Brown, "Check-Up on Organization," 5.

56. F. Brown, "Campaign against Hearst," 2.

57. Hutchins, "Who Makes the Guns?," 16.

58. Grace Hutchins, "On the Picket Line," ms., Grace Hutchins Papers, series 3, box 5, folder 7.

59. Father Charles E. Coughlin, also known as "The Radio Priest," broadcast sermons on Sunday afternoons during most of the 1930s. He railed against Wall Street but blamed Jews for the economic depression. Although he supported Franklin D. Roosevelt in the beginning, he later referred to Roosevelt's administration as a "communist conspiracy."

60. In his efforts to create a comprehensive theory of motives, Kenneth Burke offered the "representative anecdote," requiring, for its efficacy, both adequate scope and necessary reduction. Burke had global intentions for the concept, wanting to articulate the means by which humans organize consciousness, but he did not publish his work on the comprehensive theory until 1945. The representative anecdote nonetheless serves to describe the means by which writers such as Hutchins were seeking to create identification with and persuade audiences. Burke, *Grammar of Motives*, 59ff.

61. Hutchins, "What Every Working Woman Wants," 5.

62. The bonus referred to was the sum promised by the federal government to World War I soldiers, payable upon demand. When large numbers of veterans asked for their bonuses in the early 1930s, the government declined to pay them, prompting the Bonus March of 1932.

63. Jackson, "Labor Must 'Take It on Chin,'" 5.

64. Hutchins, "Notes from Abroad," 11. Thirty-three years old at the time of her death, Glatzer was a former member of the Free Socialist Youth and then the Communist Youth before joining the antifascist resistance. See "Helene Glatzer."

65. The title of the book most likely originated with a *New York Times* journalist who asked former ambassador to Germany James W. Gerard in 1930 to give him the names of "'the rulers of America.'" See Gerard, *My First Eighty-Three Years*, 320. Gerard responded with a list of 59 names. Bob Dunn wrote an article citing Gerard for the October 1930 issue of *Labor Defender*; his article is entitled "Today's Rulers of America." In it, he noted that newspapers and politicians hastened to claim that Gerard was wrong, "that these men—most of them bankers, manufacturers, capitalists—were not the power behind the throne in American life." But workers, he said, knew from their experience that Gerard was right. He went on to name John D. Rockefeller; Fred J. Fisher of General Motors; Frederick K. Weyerhauser; W. W. Atterbury, head of the Pennsylvania Railroad; Andrew W. Mellon; Myron C. Taylor; and James A. Farrell, head of the United States Steel Corporation, describing their antilabor practices and explaining the role of the ILD in countering those practices. "Examine the list of the political prisoners now in the dungeons of this country," he said. "Look over the list of the cases now being handled by the International Labor Defense. Behind practically all of them will be found one of the fifty-nine rulers or a company in which they are a director" (199).

66. Phillip Bonosky, personal conversation.

67. A. Rochester, review of *The Challenge of Russia*, 18–19.

68. See Lenin, *Essential Works of Lenin*.

69. A. Rochester, *Rulers of America*, 9.

70. Ibid., 135–6.

71. Ibid., 135.

72. Ibid., 136.

73. Ibid.

74. Francis Brown, "Looking at Industrial Leaders," BR6.

75. "Revolutionary Research," *New Masses*, 10.

77. Chappell, "Industrial Czars," 18.

76. Anna Rochester, text of talk given at publication dinner, March 1936, Anna Rochester Papers, series 3, box 6, folder 7.

78. Vida Scudder to Anna Rochester, April 11, 1936, Anna Rochester Papers, series 3, box 6, folder 7.

Notes to Chapter Ten

1. The event was held at the Hotel Lismore on West 73rd Street in Manhattan on January 24, 1936.

2. Program for Mother Bloor's 45th Anniversary Banquet, January 24, 1936, Ella Reeve Bloor Papers, box 1, folder 1, Sophia Smith Collection, Smith College, Northampton, MA. Ann Burlak (May 24, 1911–July 9, 2002) was active as a union organizer and CPUSA organizer throughout her life.

3. Grace Hutchins to Sally Cleghorn, April 1, 1936, Sarah N. Cleghorn Papers, box 3, folder 2. Despite her earlier article articulating her solution to feelings of inferiority after having moved out of same-sex organizations (see Chapter 5), Hutchins's struggle apparently did not end. Robert Shaffer documents sexist attitudes within the CPUSA during the 1930–1940 period, although, unlike Hutchins, who argued that women themselves must act to change their situations, Schaeffer seems to charge the men of the party with the entire responsibility. See Shaffer, "Women and the Communist Party."

4. Anna Rochester to Sally Cleghorn, April 5, 1936, Sarah N. Cleghorn Papers, box 3, folder 2.

5. *The World Tomorrow* had printed a letter from Floyd in December 1923 responding to a letter from Rochester and Hutchins expressing distress at his phrase "offensively religious." In the 1923 letter, he explained this usage, saying that "to be offensively religious is to preach the doctrines embodied in the creeds, the antiquated jumbles of theology derived from false premises. . . . It is offensive when it appropriates to itself morality while departing from ethical standards whenever deemed expedient and attempts to justify wrong action by quoting from so-called holy writ." Floyd, " 'Offensively Religious,' " 380.

6. Anna Rochester to William Floyd, June 22, 1936, Anna Rochester Papers, series 3, box 6, folder 7.

7. Healey, *Homosexual Desire*, 195.

8. Ibid., 196.

9. "Foster to Head Communist Election," *Daily Worker*, 1.

10. Alice Hawkins, class notes, 1907, 32.

11. "Grace Hutchins," *Turtle Progress Dispatch*, 1936, Grace Hutchins Papers, series 1, box 1, folder 7.

12. Streat, "Grace Hutchins," 7.

13. Harris, interview. Lement Harris, the son of John Harris, a founder of Texaco as well as of Harris, Winthrop & Co., a Wall Street brokerage, had also tried and discarded the Episcopal Church as an organized way to address "the maldistribution of wealth." Like Hutchins and Rochester, he discovered the Quakers and spent three years working on a Quaker-run dairy farm in New Hope, PA, after college. A trip to the Soviet Union in June 1929 led him to Harold Ware, the son of Mother Bloor, who was engaged in modernizing Soviet agriculture. Upon returning from the Soviet Union, Harris spent the rest of his life working to organize American farmers. See Harris, *My Tale of Two Worlds*, 1986.

14. A. Rochester, "The Middle Class Today," 31–2.

15. Ibid., 32.

16. Hutchins, "Professionals Speak," 671–2.

17. A. Rochester, "Finance Capital and Fascist Trends," 524.

18. Ibid., 524.

19. Ibid., 531.

20. Ibid., 534–5.

21. Ibid., 536.

22. This paper apparently has not survived, or perhaps it was simply a reiteration of Rochester's *New Masses* article.

23. Vida Scudder to Anna Rochester, Wellesley, August 16, 1936, Anna Rochester Papers, series 2, box 2, folder 70.

24. Vida Scudder to Virginia Huntington, Shelburne, September 23, probably 1936, Vida Scudder Papers, Archives of the Society of the Companions of the Holy Cross.

25. In June 1938, the National Committee and Earl Browder published *A Message to Catholics*, a one-cent pamphlet advocating that Americans build a united front like that developed in France between Catholics and Communists. See Browder, *A Message to Catholics*.

26. William Spofford to Mary van Kleeck, August 20, 1936, Mary van Kleeck Papers, Sophia Smith Collection, Smith College, Northampton, MA, series 2, box 29, folder 11.

27. Hutchins, *The Truth about the Liberty League*.

28. See Morris, "Pink Herring."

29. Theoharis and Cox, *The Boss*, 150.

30. Hutchins, "The Black Night," 14, 25.

31. Correlation Summary, August 31, 1954, 22, Federal Bureau of Investigation, file 100-13470, Grace Hutchins, section 3.

32. "Control Tasks," *Party Organizer*, 5.

33. F. Brown, "The Party Building," 15.

34. A. Rochester, "Greetings on Our Twenty-Fifth Anniversary," 21. Rochester's greeting followed the text of Ernest Hemingway's telegram apologizing for not sending a promised story; he was, he said, working nonstop on a novel.

35. Hutchins, "Greetings on Our Twenty-Fifth Anniversary," 21.

36. Hutchins, "1001 Laws," 21.

37. Johnson was still an active sculptor at the time of Hutchins's writing, although she never received the attention her work deserved. For a photo of the sculpture, go to http://www.aoc.gov/cc/art/rotunda/suffrage.cfm (accessed August 15, 2012).

38. Hutchins, "A Socialist Reads Lenin," 25.

39. Ibid.

40. Ibid., 25–6.

41. Scudder, *On Journey*, 300.

42. Vida Scudder to Virginia Huntington, Wellesley, fourth Sunday in Advent, Vida Scudder Papers, Archives of the Society of the Companions of the Holy Cross.

43. The title of Scudder's article is reminiscent of—and perhaps a parody of—Elbert Hubbard's *Little Journeys* series, published by the Roycrofters in East Aurora, New York (e.g., "Little Journeys to the Homes of Great Business Men: Andrew Carnegie"); the Roycrofters published handcrafted books after the manner of William Morris.

44. Scudder, "A Little Tour," 77.

45. Quoted in Maglin, "Vida to Florence," 17.

46. Vida Scudder, Journal, Book IV, January 11, 1935, Vida Scudder Papers, series 1, box 1, folder 6, Sophia Smith Collection. In Scudder's published autobiography, the line was modified, but not eliminated. She said: "Freud is of course largely responsible; and he has much to answer for." Scudder, *On Journey*, 211.

47. Devere Allen to Anna Rochester, February 12, 1937, Devere Allen Papers, series C-4, box 18. The committee, chaired by John Dewey and referred to as the Dewey commission, cleared Trotsky of all charges leveled against him during the Moscow trial.

48. Labor Research Association, *Arsenal of Facts*, 110. Rochester was one of the primary authors behind the *Arsenal of Facts* (published by the Labor Research Association in 1938).

49. Ibid., 111.

50. General Francisco Franco, with the support of some members of the Spanish military as well as the Catholic hierarchy, had invaded Spain from Morocco on July 18, 1936, in an attempt to overthrow the elected Republican Popular Front government, which included a parliament with

fourteen Communists, ninety-eight Socialists, sixty-five centrists, 135 right-wing conservatives, and ten Basque separatists. Within one week, the insurgents controlled one-third of Spain. Italy and Germany, which had been helping to plan the uprising, sold trucks, planes, and armaments on credit to the insurgents, to be paid for after they were in control of the government. The United States, Great Britain, and France professed neutrality and prevented the sale of weapons or other supplies to the Republicans; they did not prevent Texaco, however, from selling fuel to the fascists. The Soviet Union was the only country willing to support the Republicans. Under the auspices of the Comintern, volunteers from around the world came to fight in Spain on the Republican side; the first ninety-six Americans had left to fight in Spain in December 1936. Ultimately, some three thousand Americans fought in Spain, fifteen hundred of whom did not return home.

51. Morehead and Parlatore, "Around Town," 13.

52. This early Equal Rights Amendment read as follows:

Section 1. Equality of rights under the law shall not be denied or abridged by the United States or by any state on account of sex.

Section 2. The Congress shall have the power to enforce, by appropriate legislation, the provisions of this article.

Section 3. This amendment shall take effect two years after the date of ratification.

53. The Equal Rights Amendment would have prohibited legislation designed to protect women from working conditions that could threaten their health. This question of protective legislation for women can still provoke impassioned debates. In general, however, working class women had more to lose by the abolition of protective legislation.

54. Grace Hutchins to Margaret Cowl, "Women's Charter," June 3, 1937, Labor Research Association Records, box 4, folder 15.

55. Hutchins, "Children under Capitalism," 25–6.

56. Eleanor Stevenson to Ted and Glad, May 8, 1925, Ruth Erickson Papers, box 1, folder 3, Special Collections and University Archives, University of Oregon Libraries, Eugene. Sadie Krieger reported (2002) that on a trip to the Soviet Union in the 1960s, Eleanor, still not conventionally feminine in appearance, was the object of comments by other comrades, particularly the men, on the tour.

57. Freedman, "'Uncontrolled Desires,'" 205.

58. New York Herald Tribune, September 26, 1937, quoted in Frosch and Bromberg, "The Sex Offender," quoted in Freedman, "'Uncontrolled Desires,'" 206.

59. Freedman, "'Uncontrolled Desires,'" 283, 292.

60. Brush, "Are Sex Crimes Due to Sex?" 15–6.

61. Browder, A Message to Catholics, 9.

62. Ferry, "Jan. to Jun., 1938," Elinor Ferry Papers, Tamiment 116, box 5.

63. Report, See Reference 100-51757-10, September 7, 1944, Alger Hiss Defense Files.

Notes to Chapter Eleven

1. Marjorie White to Winifred Chappell, March 23, 1938, Winifred Chappell Papers, M86-280, Letters to W.C. from Marjorie White, State Historical Society of Wisconsin, Madison.

2. "A Statement by American Progressives," New Masses, 4.

3. Hutchins, "No Quiet on the Labor Front," 26–7.

4. A state-sanctioned night of destruction and looting of synagogues, homes, and places of business in Germany owned by Jews. Ninety-one people were killed, and twenty-six thousand Jewish men were arrested and transported to concentration camps.

5. Hutchins, "It Comes on Cat's Feet," 7.

6. Ibid.

7. Ibid., 8.

8. Ibid., 9.

9. What did Hutchins make of Bishop Roots's simultaneous friendship with Chou En-Lai and enthusiastic support for Frank Buchman and the Moral Re-Armament campaign? Undoubtedly she was disappointed in the latter. See Auden and Isherwood, *Journey to a War*, especially 52, an account of Auden and Isherwood's visit with Bishop Roots in China shortly before he returned to the United States. Hutchins and Rochester's friend Agnes Smedley was staying with Roots and his daughter at the time, an arrangement that Auden and Isherwood report was referred to as the "Moscow-Heaven axis."

10. Hutchins, "It Comes on Cat's Feet," 7.

11. Thurman Arnold, Margaret Culkin Banning, Van Wyck Brooks, Henry Pratt Fairchild, Langston Hughes, George S. Kaufman, Ruth McKenney, and Donald Ogden Stewart (president of the league). See League of American Writers, *We Hold These Truths*.

12. League of American Writers, *We Hold These Truths*, 81–3.

13. Hutchins, review of *All in the Day's Work*.

14. Anna Rochester, Back Log Camp, August 19, 1939, G. Hutchins Papers, series 2, box 4, folder 52.

15. US House Special Committee to Investigate Un-American Activities, *Investigation of Un-American Propaganda*, 4918–9.

16. Anna Rochester to Lydia Cadbury, October 12, 1939, Anna Rochester Papers, series 2, box 3, folder 10.

17. Grace Hutchins to Editors, *The Nation*, October 15, 1939, Grace Hutchins Papers, series 3, box 5, folder 7.

18. Anna Rochester to Precious Grace, November 13, 1939, Grace Hutchins Papers, series 2, box 4, folder 49.

19. Ibid.

20. Ella Reeve Bloor to Anne [sic], March 26, 1940, Anna Rochester Papers, series 2, box 2, folder 5.

21. Lamont, introduction to *The Trial of Elizabeth Gurley Flynn*, 21.

22. Milner, *Education of an American Liberal*, 275.

23. "Gurley Flynn Charges Accusers," *Daily Worker*, 1, 4.

24. Ibid., 4.

25. Elizabeth Gurley Flynn, press release, May 13, 1940, Anna Rochester Papers, series 2, box 2, folder 22.

26. Roger Baldwin to Anna Rochester, May 17, 1940, Anna Rochester Papers, series 2, box 2, folder 87.

27. Grace Hutchins to Roger Baldwin, May 18, 1940, Anna Rochester Papers, series 2, box 2, folder 12.

28. American Civil Liberties Union, *Crisis in the Civil Liberties Union*, 3.

29. Stephen Peabody, "Rochester Papers, Please Copy!" clipping, Anna Rochester Papers, series 1, box 2, folder 8.

30. A. Rochester, *Why Farmers Are Poor*, 19.

31. Cutler, review of *Why Farmers Are Poor*, 453–5.

32. Schultz, review of *Why Farmers Are Poor*, 294.

33. Vance, review of *Why Farmers Are Poor*, 857.

34. Alexander Trachtenberg to Anna Rochester, June 13, 1940, Anna Rochester Papers, series 2, box 2, folder 82. In fact, Rochester's books on agriculture were widely used in party schools and organizing in rural areas. Lement Harris commented: "Several times I participated in Party Schools held in rural Minnesota in which we used this material, especially the capitalist trend in agriculture as in industry for units to grow larger and fewer and fewer." Letter to the author, September 11, 1999.

35. A. Rochester, "'Mothers of the South,'" sections 2, 4.

36. A. Rochester, "Soil, Coal, and Oil," 25–6.

37. Hutchins, "A Labor Press Guide," 27.

38. Grace Hutchins to Jessie Lloyd O'Connor, September 17, 1940, Jessie Lloyd O'Connor Papers, series 2, box 50, folder 10, Sophia Smith Collection, Smith College, Northampton, MA.

39. Ella Reeve (Mother) Bloor to Anna Rochester, November 26, 1940, Anna Rochester Papers, series 2, box 2, folder 6.

40. Anna Rochester to Precious Grace, February 27, 1941, Grace Hutchins Papers, series 2, box 4, folder 43.

41. Hutchins, "China's Women in the Struggle," 15–6.

42. J. Edgar Hoover to Mr. L. M. C. Smith, memo, April 1, 1941, Federal Bureau of Investigation, file 100-12805, Anna Rochester, section 1.

43. Richard Wright, address to the Fourth American Writers Congress, quoted in Folsom, *Days of Anger*, 198.

44. For information on the League of American Writers, see Folsom, *Days of Anger*.

45. On kinship work, see Di Leonardo, "The Female World," 440–53.

46. The college was fined $2,500 by Justice of the Peace Clem Brown for "displaying an illegal emblem and failing to display an American flag." The "emblem" in question was apparently a hammer and sickle embedded in the cornerstone of one of the college buildings. See Knepper, "'At Grips With Life,'" 36–67.

47. Winifred Chappell to Grace Hutchins, June 13, 1941, Grace Hutchins Papers, series 2, box 4, folder 5.

48. Although they may not have known exactly what was happening to themselves, they would have understood that the FBI was increasing surveillance. On January 11, 1940, Congressman Vito Marcantonio responded to J. Edgar Hoover's testimony announcing that since 1939 the bureau had been compiling index cards with information on them about individuals who might prove to be subversive. His speech was reprinted in *Equal Justice*, the periodical of the ILD. See Marcantonio, "Terror by Index Cards," 2.

49. Federal Bureau of Investigation, Re: Winifred L. Chappell, memorandum, file 100-6372-6, Winifred Chappell. I am indebted to Rev. Jeanne Knepper for sharing her research materials on Chappell with me.

50. Hutchins, *Japan Wars on the U.S.A.*, 3–5.

51. Ibid., 9–11.

52. Farm Research, Inc. was founded in 1931 by Lement Harris and Harold Ware to offer farmers services similar to those the Labor Research Association offered to workers and unions. See Dyson, "Radical Farm Organizations," 111–20.

53. A. Rochester, *Farmers in Nazi Germany*, 9.

54. Ibid., 29.

55. Henry Hutchins to Grace Hutchins, February 8, 1942, Grace Hutchins Papers, series 2, box 4, folder 19.

56. Federal Bureau of Investigation, File 100-13740, Grace Hutchins, FBI Report, February 2, 1942; FBI Report April 27, 1942.

57. Federal Bureau of Investigation, "On May 13, 1942, Confidential Informant T-4 [Whittaker Chambers] was interviewed," September 7, 1944, file 100-13740, Grace Hutchins. Excerpt located in Alger Hiss Defense Files.

58. Hutchins, "Good and Welfare," 26

59. A. Rochester, "Migratory Workers," 25–6.

60. Mother [Ella Reeve Bloor] to Anne [Anna Rochester], April 20, probably 1942, Anna Rochester Papers, series 2, box 2, folder 2.

61. Audley Moore rose from a childhood of extreme privation in Louisiana to become one of Harlem's most well-known and well-loved leaders. An early follower of Marcus Garvey, she was a member of the CPUSA during the 1930s and 1940s, leaving in 1950 to focus on the African nation-

alist movement. Not enough has been written about Audley Moore, who was given the title Queen Mother by the Ashanti people in Ghana during the 1960s. See Pace, "Queen Mother Moore," B15.

62. Josephine Truslow Adams, Grace Hutchins, Elizabeth Gurley Flynn, and Audley Moore (on Grace Hutchins's letterhead) to Miss van Kleeck, June 19, 1942, Mary van Kleeck Papers, series 5, box 68, folder 13.

63. Mother to Grace, Grace Hutchins Papers, series 2, box 4, folder 20.

64. Grace Hutchins to dearest Anna, September 14, 1942, Grace Hutchins Papers, series 2, box 4, folder 73.

65. A. Rochester, *Lenin on the Agrarian Question*, 174.

66. Ibid., 199.

67. Ibid., 209.

68. The kulaks were the "upper class" of peasants, those who had benefited from an earlier policy allowing the development of large farms. Their relative wealth led to generally conservative political views and a resistance to collectivization.

69. Hapgood, review of *Lenin on the American Question*, 16.

70. Grace (no last name provided) to Anna Rochester, August 25, 1942, Anna Rochester Papers, series 3, box 6, folder 5.

71. Budenz, "From the Plough," 6.

72. Harris, "City and Country," 25–6.

73. A. Rochester, *Farmers and the War*, 3.

74. Ibid., 6.

75. Ibid., 22.

76. A. Rochester, "The Farmer Wants a Plan," 21.

77. Ibid., 22.

78. Lement Harris, Bob Digby, and Anna Rochester to Earl Browder, memo, December 7, 1942, Anna Rochester Papers, series 3, box 4, folder 11.

79. "Fraternally Yours," *Daily Worker*, 8.

80. Untitled form with details gleaned by FBI from International Workers Order files, July 7, 1958, Federal Bureau of Investigation, file 100-13470, Grace Hutchins, section 4.

81. Hutchins, "Women in Overalls," 26.

82. Hutchins, letter to the editor, *Daily Worker*, October 14, 1943. Reed's grandson had grown up in the Soviet Union. Reed's son, a Marine captain, had died the year before in the Pacific.

83. "Funeral of Red Spy," *New York World-Telegram*, 11.

84. See Chapters 12, 13, and 14 for more on Bentley.

85. A. Rochester, foreword to *The Populist Movement*, 6.

86. Ibid., 9.

87. Bogart, review of *The Populist Movement*, 365.

88. S. L. Jackson, review of *The Populist Movement*, *Springfield Republican*, 10.

89. Peterson, review of *The Populist Movement*, 267–8.

90. Ibid., 268.

91. Ibid., 270–1.

Notes to Chapter Twelve

1. Lucy Sturgis to Grace Hutchins, February 17, 1944, Grace Hutchins Papers, series 2, box 4, folder 65.

2. See Chapter 3.

3. Vida Scudder to "Dear and Cherished Ones" (Anna Rochester and Grace Hutchins), December 31, 1943, Anna Rochester Papers, series 2, box 2, folder 69.

4. Polly Porter and Molly Dewson referred to themselves as the "Porter-Dewsons."

5. Quoted in Anna Rochester to Alter Brody, December 12, 1943, Anna Rochester Papers, series 2, box 3, folder 4.

6. Molly Dewson to Anna Rochester, February 7, 1944, Anna Rochester Papers, series 3, box 6, folder 6.

7. Report of special agent (redacted), September 19, 1945, Federal Bureau of Investigation, file 100-51757, Grace Hutchins, section 1. The article in question may have been Will Lissner's "Communist Dogmas Basically Revised," published in the *New York Times* on April 2, 1944.

8. Correlation Summary, December 29, 1955, 65.

9. International Labor Defense, *Equal Justice and Democracy*, 30.

10. "BUREAU URGENT," New York May 18, 1944, Federal Bureau of Investigation, file 100-9260, Anna Rochester, section 1.

11. Anna Rochester to Algernon Black, March 22, 1944, A. Rochester Papers, series 2, box 3, folder 21.

12. Anna Rochester to Trachty (Alexander Trachtenberg), August 30, 1944, Federal Bureau of Investigation, file 100-9260, Anna Rochester, section 1.

13. "Aug. 19," Grace Hutchins Papers, series 2, box 4, folder 52.

14. A. Rochester, "Teheran," 28.

15. Ibid.

16. Ibid., 29.

17. Report of special agent (redacted), September 19, 1945, 2.

18. A. Rochester, *Capitalism and Progress*, 8.

19. Ibid., 61.

20. Ibid, 104.

21. Kreps, review of *Capitalism and Progress*, 186.

22. Gamble, review of *Capitalism and Progress*, 6, quoted in *Book Review Digest*, 1945, 601.

23. Bowman, *Capitalism in America*, 25.

24. Vida Scudder to Anna Rochester, April 2, 1945, Anna Rochester Papers, series 2, box 2, folder 7.

25. A. Rochester, "Lenin in 1918," 24–5.

26. Foster, *History of the Communist Party*, 434.

27. Anna Rochester to Earl Browder, May 25, 1945, Earl Browder Papers, Special Collections Research Center, Syracuse University Library, Syracuse, NY.

28. "The Present Situation," *Sunday Worker Magazine*, 6.

29. A. Rochester, letter to the editor, *Sunday Worker Magazine*, June 10, 1945.

30. A. Rochester, letter to the editor, *Daily Worker*, June 27, 1945.

31. "NM Evaluates Its Course," *New Masses*, 17.

32. Ibid., 18.

33. Quoted in FBI file 61-80, 1946, Ella Reeve Bloor, Ella Reeve Bloor Papers, series 1, box 2, folder 8.

34. "To Our Fellow Readers," *Daily Worker*, 8.

35. Molly Dewson to Grace Hutchins and Anna Rochester, May 3, 1946, Anna Rochester Papers, series 3, box 6, folder 7.

36. A. Rochester, *The Nature of Capitalism*, 84.

37. Rebecca James to Anna Rochester, November 15, 1946, Anna Rochester Papers, series 2, box 2, folder 19. Dr. Fleming James, Rebecca James's husband, was dean of the seminary from 1940 to 1946. A noted Old Testament scholar, he served as executive secretary of the Old Testament committee of the Revised Standard Edition of the Bible. His sister, Mary James, was a friend of Hutchins who served as a physician at the Church General Hospital in Wuchang, China, for which Hutchins had raised funds during 1916–1917.

38. Director, Federal Bureau of Investigation, to SAC (special agent in charge), New York City, November 26, 1946, FBI file 100-13470, Grace Hutchins, section 1.

39. For a clear and detailed analysis of the Cold War era in the United States, see Schrecker, *Many Are the Crimes*.

40. Abt with Myerson, *Advocate and Activist*, 133.

41. Arthur Garfield Hays worked on the Scopes trial, the trials of Sacco and Vanzetti, the Scottsboro case, and the Reichstag fire trial, representing Georgi Dimitrov.

42. Western Union Telegraph Company v. Pacific and Atlantic Telegraph Company et al., 65 N.Y.S. 2d 349, 189 Misc. 7 (September 9, 1946), LEXIS 2820–22.

43. *Id.* at LEXIS 4010.

44. *Id.* at LEXIS 4388 (Anna Rochester, intervener, defendant, July 3, 1947).

45. Fried, *McCarthyism*, 28.

46. Anna Rochester to My dear Mr. President [Harry S. Truman], May 19, 1947, Anna Rochester Papers, series 2, box 3, folder 26.

47. Foster, *History of the Communist Party*, 488.

48. Bob Minor to [redacted], June 3, 1947, Federal Bureau of Investigation, file 100-9260, Anna Rochester, section 1.

49. The Vatican had recognized Franco on August 28, 1937, nineteen months before the Republicans finally surrendered.

50. Grace Hutchins to Jessie Lloyd O'Connor, Nov. 3, 1947, Jessie Lloyd O'Connor Papers, series 2, box 50, folder 10.

51. Ibid.

52. Federal Bureau of Investigation, Re: Name and Alias Grace Hutchins Security Matter—C, memo, December 18, 1947, file 100-13470, Grace Hutchins, section 1.

53. Federal Bureau of Investigation, Re: Name and Alias Anna Rochester Security Matter—C, memo, January 20, 1948, file 100-9260, Anna Rochester, section 1.

54. Quoted in Steinberg, *The Great "Red Menace,"* 97.

55. Ibid., 99.

56. Grace Hutchins, "International Women's Day," January 27, 1948, manuscript, Labor Research Association Records, box 4, folder 15.

57. Labor Research Association, *Labor Fact Book 8*, 82. See Weigand, *Red Feminism*, and Rosenberg, *Changing the Subject*, 200–1.

58. Millard, *Woman against Myth*, 6.

59. Ibid., 11.

60. Ibid., 21.

61. Ibid. Millard's construction "it goes without saying" gives the game away, although few in her audience probably read the erasure in the sentence, including Millard herself. Asked about this statement years later, Millard indicated that just as women had been convinced of their inferiority by a "barrage of propaganda," she, too, at the time, had been unable to see beyond the conventional gender pairing implied by marriage, despite her friendship with Rochester and Hutchins and her own relationships with women. For a more detailed explanation of her attitudes toward homophobia, see Springer and Millard, "Why Aren't You Angrier About Homophobia?" 130–7.

62. A. Rochester, letter to the editor, *Daily Worker*, March 10, 1948.

63. "Rochester Notables Scorn Mob Attack," *Daily Worker*, 6.

64. Quoted in Steinberg, *The Great "Red Menace,"* 117.

65. Alien Registration Act of 1940, 18 USC § 2385 (1940). Section 10, as revised in 1948, reads:

It shall be unlawful for any person—

to knowingly or willfully advocate, abet, advise, or teach the duty, necessity, desirability, or propriety of overthrowing or destroying any government in the United States by force or violence, or by the assassination of any officer of any such government;

with the intent to cause the overthrow or destruction of any government in the United States, to print, publish, edit, issue, circulate, sell, distribute, or publicly display any written or printed matter advocating, advising, or teaching the duty, necessity, desirability, or propriety of overthrowing or destroying any government in the United States by force or violence;

to organize or help to organize any society, group, or assembly of persons who teach, advocate, or encourage the overthrow or destruction of any government in the United States by force or violence; or to be or become a member of, or affiliated with, any such society, group, or assembly of persons, knowing the purposes thereof.

For the purposes of this section, the term "government in the United States" means the Government of the United States, the government of any State, Territory, or possession of the United States, the government of the District of Columbia, or the government of any political subdivision of any of them.

Quoted in Marion, *The Communist Trial*, 191–2.

66. Hay, *Radically Gay*, 61. Hay's efforts were prescient, as the persecutions of gay men and lesbians would increase during the 1950s. For an account of this era, see D. Johnson, *The Lavender Scare*.

67. Chambers claimed that he was diverting the attention of reporters so that his wife could leave the courthouse quietly after testifying to the grand jury. For a detailed timeline and analysis of the crusade against Alger Hiss, see The Alger Hiss Story, http://homepages.nyu.edu/~th15/home.html.

68. Abrams and Lee, "Bryn Mawr Grad," C8.

69. The most famous lines are in Chapter 12 of *The Rainbow*. See Lawrence, *The Rainbow*. For an analysis, see Edwards, "At the End of *The Rainbow*." Vito Russo documents the film version of this trope, which became especially pronounced around 1950. See Russo, *The Celluloid Closet*, 99ff.

70. Simon Gerson, interview.

71. "Funeral of Red Spy," *New York World Telegram*, 11.

72. Mitchell, "2 Women Debunk," 1.

73. Grace Hutchins to Mr. (Reuben) Shemitz, May 19, 1938, Federal Bureau of Investigation, file [document unnumbered], Grace Hutchins, Alger Hiss Defense Files.

74. The correspondence between Hutchins/Rochester and Stevenson/Erickson, carefully retained and annotated by Erickson and Stevenson, displays a significant gap from 1947 to 1954, suggesting that references to the events of that era may have been consciously discarded.

75. "RE: GRACE HUTCHINS, REUBEN SHEMITZ," report of interview of Grace Hutchins by Special Agents Francis J. Gallant and Robert F. X. O'Keefe, January 20, 1949, Alger Hiss Defense Files.

76. Weinstein, *Perjury*, 381.

77. Tanenhaus, *Whittaker Chambers*, 342. See Salant, "Successful Strategic Deception."

78. Grace Hutchins, "Not For Publication," January 1949, Grace Hutchins Papers, series 5, box 8, folder 12.

79. In a 1997 review written for the *New Yorker* of *Whittaker Chambers* by Sam Tanenhaus, Sidney Blumenthal points out Tanenhaus's failure to take into account Chambers's homosexuality. Blumenthal argues that "[a] key to the story is that Whittaker Chambers lived in a time when it was easier to confess to being a spy than to confess to being a homosexual." He points out that Chambers's later book *Witness* describes communism in phrases used at the time to discuss homosexuality. See Blumenthal, "The Cold War," 112–5.

80. See Terry, *An American Obsession*.

81. Burke, *Permanence and Change*, 15.

82. Betty Millard, interview with the author, New York, May 28, 1998.

83. Leon Herald, for instance, provided a notarized statement to Elinor Ferry in November 1952 describing an event that had taken place some twenty years earlier: at the July 1932 national convention of the John Reed Clubs in Chicago, he had given Chambers a place to stay in his rooming house. Herald awoke in the middle of the night to find that Chambers had made his way to his room and was in his bed with his (Herald's) penis in his mouth. Herald kicked Chambers in

the face to force him to leave and later, still upset, could not remember whether he had returned to the convention the following days. Notarized document, November 26, 1952, Elinor Ferry Papers, box 4, file 6, Harvard Law School Library.

84. Walt Carmon, who had worked with Chambers, apparently told an interviewer that "it was known that Chambers was a homosexual." Excerpts from interview with Walt Carmon, September 29, probably early 1950s, Elinor Ferry Papers, box 17, file 19, Harvard Law School Library.

85. Maus V. Darling, however, a dentist who worked with Chambers as a writer for *Time* magazine during the 1940s, cautioned Ferry: "Do watch out on homosexual angle—don't even like idea of using word. I do say Chambers had unhealthy power over two, maybe three men. Don't know where it came from." Note from Maus, ca. 1949–1952, Elinor Ferry Papers, box 1, file 4, Harvard Law School Library.

86. de Toledano, *Notes from the Underground*, 3.

87. For an account of the development of the FBI's concerns with sexuality, see Morris, "Pink Herring," 228–44.

88. Federal Bureau of Investigation, report, 11, February 24, 1950, file 100-13470, Grace Hutchins, section 1.

89. Ibid.

90. Memo, October 20, 1952, Alger Hiss Defense Files.

Notes to Chapter Thirteen

1. Sally Cleghorn to Anna, Grace & Lucie, Anna Rochester Papers, series 2, box 2, folder 11.

2. Grace Hutchins to Anna Rochester, November 3, 1948, Grace Hutchins Papers, series 2, box 4, folder 76.

3. They would not, however, have classified themselves as adherents to "American exceptionalism"—a so-called "right-wing deviation" that claimed the United States differed from other countries to the extent that it did not follow the same economic patterns.

4. A. Rochester, *American Capitalism*, 70.

5. Ibid., 86.

6. Ibid., 112.

7. Correlation Summary, December 29, 1955, 83.

8. Frederick V. Field to "Dear Friend," September 29, 1949, Jessie Lloyd O'Connor Papers, series 4, box 111, folder 3. The Civil Rights Congress was the successor organization to the ILD. Trustees included Frederick V. Field, Dashiell Hammett, Robert W. Dunn, Abner Green, and Dr. W. Alphaeus Hunton.

9. See J. M. Allen, " 'That Accursed Aesopian Language,' " 109–34.

10. Aesopian language is the name nineteenth-century Russian writers gave to standard literary tropes used in czarist Russia to avoid censorship.

11. Anna Rochester to Comrade Stachel, October 16, 1949, Federal Bureau of Investigation, file 100-9260, Anna Rochester, section 1.

12. Mother (Ella Reeve) Bloor to Grace Hutchins, February 25, 1949, Grace Hutchins Papers, series 2, box 4, folder 3.

13. Vida Scudder to Anna Rochester and Grace Hutchins, December 31, 1949, Anna Rochester Papers, series 2, box 2, folder 71.

14. Sally Cleghorn to Grace Hutchins, February 22, 1950, Grace Hutchins Papers, series 2, box 4, folder 6.

15. Milton Howard to Anna Rochester, March 30, 1950, Anna Rochester Papers, series 2, box 2, folder 78.

16. Alexander Trachtenberg to Anna Rochester, March 29, 1950, Anna Rochester Papers, series 2, box 2, folder 82.

17. Anna Rochester to Bob Dunn, April 3, 1950, Anna Rochester Papers, series 2, box 3, folder 32.

18. Louis Budenz, "Grace Hutchins," written statement, Federal Bureau of Investigation, file 100-13470, Grace Hutchins, section 1.

19. In 1953, Budenz admitted that he had received $70,000 for his testimony and other activities as an excommunist. See Packer, *Ex-Communist Witnesses*, 124. (In 2011 dollars, Budenz's compensation would amount to well over half a million dollars.)

20. Alice Hawkins to Grace Hutchins, July 2, 1950, Grace Hutchins Papers, series 2, box 4, folder 14.

21. "Tink" (Cornelia Meigs) to Grace Hutchins, July 8, 1950, Grace Hutchins Papers, series 2, box 4, folder 65.

22. See Miller, *Out of the Past*, 258ff.

23. Ambivalence often characterized women who shared their lives with other women, as they struggled to align their own emotions with heteronormative ideologies. Margaret Rose Gladney has provided a glimpse of these mixed feelings in a narrative of her discovery of letters between Lillian Smith and Paula Snelling and her subsequent interview with Snelling on the subject of the partnership. See Gladney, "Personalizing the Political," 93–104.

24. Jessie Lloyd O'Connor to Grace Hutchins, July 21, 1950, Jessie Lloyd O'Connor Papers, series 2, box 50, folder 10.

25. Grace Hutchins to Jessie Lloyd O'Connor, July 27, 1950, Jessie Lloyd O'Connor Papers, series 2, box 50, folder 10. The stays of execution did not last. Willie McGee, an African American truck driver, was executed in Laurel, MS, on May 8, 1951, for allegedly raping a white woman, despite evidence that the two had been intimate for four years. The Martinsville Seven were seven African American men who were executed in February 1951 for having raped a white woman in Martinsville, VA. The latter case was notable for the poor defense mounted by their attorneys and for the fact that, in contrast, no white man had ever been executed for rape in Virginia.

26. Elizabeth Gurley Flynn Testimonial, August 11, 1950, program, Tamiment 118, Elizabeth Gurley Flynn Papers, film R-7263, reel 10, 22:17, Tamiment Library, Elmer Holmes Bobst Library, New York University.

27. T. S. Brown to author, June 20, 1998.

28. The Internal Security Act provided that a five-person board be appointed to administer all aspects of the act. This panel came to be called the Subversive Activities Control Board. The act also required that all Communists register with the Justice Department. Moreover, all so-called front organizations and their officers were required to register. The act directed that arrangements be made for the internment of any potential saboteurs or spies, in case of war or increased hostilities. Communist organizations were required to report all financial activities; they were also required to label their publications. Needless to say, Communists were to be prevented from holding government jobs or working in defense plants (however they were defined), and the passports of all Communists were to be withdrawn. So-called subversive aliens were to be deported, and the statute of limitations on espionage, previously set at three years, was extended to ten years. See Legislative Reference Service of the US Library of Congress, *World Communist Movement*, vol. 2, 465. This extension would allow the prosecution of anyone who had assisted the Soviet Union during the war, when the United States and USSR ostensibly were allies.

29. "Start Drive to Halt Raids on Non-Citizens," *Daily Worker*, October 29, 1950, 2, Federal Bureau of Investigation, file 100-13470, Grace Hutchins, section 3.

30. American Committee for the Protection of the Foreign Born, "Women Protest Justice Dept's Month-Long Detention of Mother Without Bail," December 29, 1955, file summary, December 11, 1950, news release summary, Federal Bureau of Investigation, file 100-13470, Grace Hutchins, section 3.

31. Labor Research Association, *Monopoly Today*, 100.

32. Legislative Reference Service of the US Library of Congress, *World Communist Movement*, vol. 3, 492.

33. Woltman, "Pravda, USA," 81. The FBI was already paying close attention to Communists' devotion to the *Daily Worker*. On the occasion of the newspaper's twenty-fifth anniversary, tributes

from around the world were published. Agents placed an alert in Hutchins's file, pointing to the statement written by the New York State Committee, CPUSA:

> We Communists of New York hail the 25th anniversary of our fighting newspaper, the *Daily Worker*. We express our great love for it today, for we know it belongs to us, to all people who want peace to triumph, prosperity to reign, and democracy to be the law of our land. We live in the largest city of the world, the place of the nation's most powerful newspapers. We know what vast havoc the billionaire-press in our city has wrought. And we know what a tragedy it would be if New York did not have a daily newspaper for all working people, for Labor, for the Negroes, the Jews, the Puerto Ricans, all the minorities in our metropolis. On this 25th anniversary, we pledge unstinting effort to build the *Daily Worker* into the foremost organ of New York. It merits that place because of its peerless crusade for the Common Man of our city. And we pledge it shall have it."

"World Communists Greet 'Worker' on 25th Anniversary," *Sunday Worker*, 4.

34. Note, February 7, 1951, Federal Bureau of Investigation, file 100-13470, in Grace Hutchins, section 1. The source of the note is unclear, but given that the FBI was monitoring the trash of the *Daily Worker*, it seems likely that it was picked up there.

35. "The Suffrage Quest," *New York Times*, 16.

36. Flynn, *I Speak My Own Piece*, 46.

37. "Miss Malone Quits the Suffragettes," *New York Times*, 4.

38. "Maud Malone Stops Roosevelt," *New York Times*, 1.

39. Federal Bureau of Investigation, file PH 61-80, Ella Reeve Bloor, teletype, March 5, 1951, Ella Reeve Bloor Papers, series 1, box 2, folder 8.

40. Mother (Ella Reeve) Bloor to Lement Harris, May 2, probably 1951, Ella Reeve Bloor Papers, series 2, box 7, folder 38.

41. Hutchins, letter to the editor, *Daily Worker*, March 9, 1951.

42. See Freedman, "'The Burning of Letters Continues,'" 181–200.

43. Labor Research Association, *Labor Fact Book 10*, 59–62.

44. It seems likely that this story was part of Chambers's campaign to pay Hutchins back for her comments about him to the FBI.

45. O. Edmund Clubb, testimony before HCUA, summary, August 20, 1951, Federal Bureau of Investigation, file 100-13740, Grace Hutchins, section 3.

46. Federal Bureau of Investigation, file 100-13740, section 3, Grace Hutchins, summary of Walt Carmon's testimony before HCUA, June 15, 1951.

47. Bentley, "How I Was Used," 30.

48. Federal Bureau of Investigation, File 100-13740, section 3, Grace Hutchins, summary of Grace Hutchins's testimony before HCUA, June 21, 1951.

49. *CIS U. S. Serial Set*, CIS-NO: 82 HUna-T.26.

50. For the complete story of the legal events surrounding the dissolution of the International Workers Order, see Sabin, *Red Scare in Court*.

51. Labor Research Association, *Labor Fact Book 11*, 62–3; see also Horne, *Communist Front?* 240–5.

52. SAC, Chicago, to Director SAC, January 9, 1952, office memorandum, Federal Bureau of Investigation, file 100-6372-1, Winifred Chappell. Chappell's death suggested to agents that they should cancel her security index card. Chappell escaped notice longer than Hutchins and Rochester, but during the late 1940s, the FBI received letters from American "patriots" drawing attention to articles she had written twenty years earlier, alleging that they were treasonous. In 1950, an agent had paid a visit to her "under suitable pretext" at her rooms at the Methodist Deaconesses' Home in Chicago, where he learned that she was affiliated with the Peoples' Institute for Applied Religion, whose aim was to "demonstrate a way of reaching the multitude on their level with a democratic message designed to counteract fascist and reactionary forces in the United States," and had worked

in the past for the Methodist Federation for Social Service. See Report, Winifred Leola Chappell, March 1, 1950, Federal Bureau of Investigation, file 100-6372-1, Winifred Chappell. I am grateful to Rev. Jeanne Knepper for sharing with me her extensive research on Chappell.

53. "People Everywhere," *Daily Worker*, 3.

54. Jones, "Mother Bloor, Great American," 1, 6.

55. "People Everywhere," *Daily Worker*, 3.

56. Allen had been making semiannual, interest-only payments on the land where he and his family lived in Wilton, CT.

57. Anna Rochester to Devere Allen, September 23, 1951, Devere Allen Papers, series C-4, box 70.

58. Devere Allen to Anna Rochester, November 25, 1951, Anna Rochester Papers, series 2, box 2, folder 1.

59. Anna Rochester to Devere Allen, December 6, 1951, Anna Rochester Papers, series 2, box 3, folder 33. Allen died three and a half years later, at the age of sixty-four.

60. Robert Thompson had settled into a small town near Sonora in the California Sierras, his cover not blown until August 1953 when, apparently, he made the tactical error of asking for sour cream in the rural grocery store. Gilbert Green voluntarily surrendered on February 27, 1956, establishing a precedent of decent treatment for Henry Winston, who was African American and who surrendered shortly thereafter.

61. "150 Notables Form Emergency Civil Rights Committee," *Daily Worker*, 1. Headed by acting chairman Professor Paul Lehman of Princeton Theological Seminary, the organization stated that its purposes were "to help mobilize public opinion, nationally and regionally, in support of traditional American guarantees of civil liberties and to render such aid as it can to victims of current abridgement of these liberties in politics, education, and the professions. . . . The committee does not aim to compete with existing civil liberties organizations, but hopes to be able to move with dispatch in situations where these organizations are unable or unwilling to act." Rochester and Hutchins's old friend Florence Converse was among the original members.

62. Lamont, *Yes to Life*, 140–1.

63. Ruth Kahn [Ruth Stiles Gannett], interview with the author, June 19, 1998.

64. Henson, interview.

65. Memo, January 30, 1952, Federal Bureau of Investigation, file 100-9260, Anna Rochester, section 1.

66. Bail Fund of the Civil Rights Congress of New York, minutes, January 18, 1952, Labor Research Association Records, series 6, box 6, folder 38.

67. "Assail Move to Blacklist," *Daily Worker*, 3.

68. "Grace Hutchins Hits," *Daily Worker*, July 1, 1952, 6.

69. See Chapter 12. Kenneth Burke argues that "the soundest reward for service (in either practical activities or art) is an improvement in one's human relations." He goes on to describe efforts such as that of Chambers, saying that the writer "has settled a score—and, strengthened by the insignia of success, may even make terms as a victor, and be welcomed home. Yet, has he not merely attained individual salvation at the expense of the collectivity? For has his work not contributed more to the *blunting* of human relationships than to their *refinement?*" (*Attitudes toward History*, 316–7).

70. Chambers, *Witness*, 267.

71. In a 1952 interview with a member of the Alger Hiss defense team, Hutchins was asked whether "she told Esther she disapproved of him as a partner for her. She said, 'Why, of course not. Why should I? It is all complete rubbish.'" Memo, October 20, 1952, Alger Hiss Defense Files. If Hutchins did visit Esther Shemitz, she may have tried to counsel her against a hasty marriage, reminding her of the importance of her work and possibly alluding to Chambers's less-than-stellar sexual reputation. "Her friends had already known at that time that he was not an honest or decent sort of man," Hutchins said in January 1949. "Not For Publication," Grace Hutchins Papers, series 5, box 8, file 12. Elinor Ferry later explained in more detail what Hutchins was referring to in her

coded manner, saying that Chambers would disappear for days at a time from his post at the *Daily Worker*, leading his friends to engage in "ribald talk about which sex was being favored." "Marriage," Elinor Ferry Papers, box 16, file 7, Harvard Law School Library. Hutchins's 1952 comment suggests that, if such a premarital conversation did take place, either the conversation was framed differently or perhaps Hutchins was trying to protect someone by obscuring the event. At this remove, we can only speculate on the motives behind Hutchins's responses.

72. Chambers, *Witness*, 753, 401.

73. Ibid., 350.

74. Ibid., 241 n.

75. Ibid., 48.

76. Loseff, Lev. *On the Beneficence of Censorship*.

77. Hutchins was especially concerned that Poyntz not be assumed dead. In a conversation with Elinor Ferry, Hutchins said that she had had a letter from friends in 1943 stating that Poyntz was married and living happily in the Soviet Union. See Memo, 1951 or 1952 [sic], Alger Hiss Defense Files. It is doubtful that Hutchins was sufficiently gullible to believe this story, but she had none to replace it. For statement on Edgar Allen Poe, see Memo, May 21, 1957, William A. Reuben Papers, box 8, Grace Hutchins folder, Labadie Collection, University of Michigan, Ann Arbor.

78. Others, too, have noted Chambers's allusions and borrowings. Dr. Carl Binger argued that Chambers had drawn material from *Class Reunion* by Franz Werfel, a novel that Chambers had translated in 1928. Chambers tried to discount this charge in *Witness*. See Chambers, *Witness*, 261. See also Worth, *Whittaker Chambers*. Worth argued that Chambers had structured his narrative following the plots of novels by Dostoevsky. Other allusions, among many, include Gogol's *The Overcoat* (see *Witness*, 752) and the 1949 film *Beyond the Forest*.

79. Or at least Endore's name appears, in slightly altered form, as translator.

80. Weirauch, *The Scorpion* and *The Outcast*.

81. See Chapter 12, note 79.

82. Grace Hutchins to "Gentlemen," letter, May 29, 1952, Grace Hutchins Papers, series 5, box 8, folder 11.

83. Garlin, "Publisher on Trial," 18.

84. Charles Cheney to Grace Hutchins, June 1952, Grace Hutchins Papers, series 5, box 8, folder 11.

85. Dorothy Canfield Fisher to Anna Rochester, June 9, 1952, Grace Hutchins Papers, series 5, box 8, folder 11.

86. Margaret Reeve Cary to Grace Hutchins, June 12, 1952, Grace Hutchins Papers, series 5, box 8, folder 11.

87. In addition to publishing negative portrayals of Hutchins and Rochester, who had befriended and aided Esther Chambers, Whittaker Chambers characterized his wife as "a child," not "a revolutionist." *Witness*, 744. Esther Chambers had worked for Amtorg, which the FBI considered a front for Soviet spying, and had been arrested during the Passaic strike. At the time of Chambers's writing, Ethel Rosenberg was being prosecuted for far less. Thus, by infantilizing Esther, Chambers was probably attempting to protect her (and himself). Nonetheless, Hutchins was probably incensed that Esther would have allowed this view of herself to be published.

88. Margaret Reeve Cary to Grace Hutchins, June 12, 1952, Grace Hutchins Papers, series 5, box 8, folder 11.

89. Lewis Gannett to Grace Hutchins, June 3, 1952, Grace Hutchins Papers, series 5, box 8, folder 11.

90. Grace Hutchins to Jessie Lloyd O'Connor, September 7, 1952, Jessie Lloyd O'Connor Papers, series 2, box 50, folder 10.

91. Jessie Lloyd O'Connor to Grace Hutchins, September 9, 1952, Jessie Lloyd O'Connor Papers, series 2, box 50, folder 10.

92. Louise Berman to Grace Hutchins, September 9, 1952, Grace Hutchins Papers, series 2, box 4, folder 1.

93. Weigand, *Red Feminism*, 63–4.

94. Hutchins, *Women Who Work*, 1952, 75.

95. Ibid., 62–3.

96. Ibid., 83.

97. Ibid., 85.

98. A. Rochester, "Do Capitalists Fear," 7.

99. A. Rochester, "Can Capitalism Take Criticism?"

100. Director, FBI, to SAC, New York, October 8, 1952, Federal Bureau of Investigation, file 61-4478-514, *Daily Worker*.

101. Grace Hutchins to Frederick Greenman, November 12, 1952, Robert W. Dunn Papers, Bail Fund Liquidation Correspondence.

102. Frederick Greenman to Grace Hutchins, November 13, 1952, Robert W. Dunn Papers, Bail Fund Liquidation Correspondence.

103. Hall, "Robert Minor's Fellow Workers," 7.

104. Hamilton, letter to the editor.

105. Anna Rochester to "Dear Friend," December 16, 1952, Anna Rochester Papers, series 2, box 2, folder 27.

106. Alice Hamilton to Miss (Anna) Rochester, January 14, 1953, Anna Rochester Papers, series 2, box 2, folder 27.

107. Elizabeth Flynn to Grace Hutchins, February 15, 1953, Grace Hutchins Papers, series 2, box 4, folder 11. This seven-week stint would not, of course, be Flynn's last in prison.

108. Vida Scudder to Anna Rochester, September 17, 1952, Anna Rochester Papers, series 2, box 2, folder 73.

109. V.D.S. (Vida Scudder) to Grace Hutchins, September 23, 1952, Anna Rochester Papers, series 2, box 2, folder 72.

110. Vida Scudder to Grace Hutchins, January 8 1953, Grace Hutchins Papers, series 3, box 6, folder 3.

111. On January 26, 1953, Rochester joined Hutchins, Sarah N. Cleghorn, Vida Scudder, Louise Pettibone Smith, Meridel LeSueur, and a host of others in signing an appeal to the White House for amnesty for eleven leaders. See "150 Women Sign Plea for Amnesty for '11,'" *Daily Worker*, 3.

Notes to Chapter Fourteen

1. G. Hutchins, Personal Notebook, 1 Jan. 1962, Series 1, Box 1, Folder 4, G. Hutchins Papers.

2. A. Rochester to Trachty [Alexander Trachtenberg] 22 Jan. 1953, in A. Rochester FBI file 100-9260, Section 1.

3. Correlation Summary, December 29, 1955, 108–9.

4. Henson, interview. It is possible that Alice Hutchins feared that her husband would lose his job at Yale if his relationship to Grace Hutchins were known. During this time, professors at schools ranging from Brooklyn College to Harvard were being dismissed for simple refusal to sign a loyalty oath or to name names for government committees.

5. RE (Ruth Erickson) to Grace Hutchins and Anna Rochester, November 22, 1960, Ruth Erickson Papers, box 2, folder 10.

6. "A Valentine in 1953," Grace Hutchins Papers, series 2, box 4, folder 52.

7. Roger Baldwin to Miss (Grace) Hutchins, February 24, probably 1953, Mary Metlay Kaufman Papers, series 3, box 9, folder 7, Sophia Smith Collection, Smith College, Northampton, MA. Corliss Lamont argues that because Roger Baldwin as head of the ACLU allowed the exclusion of Elizabeth Gurley Flynn in 1940, he bears much responsibility for the McCarthy-era persecutions. See Lamont, *Yes to Life*.

8. Josephs, "Double Burden," 12.

9. Bacon, "America's Working Women."

10. Polly Porter to Grace Hutchins, Castine, Maine, March 4, 1953, Grace Hutchins Papers, series 3, box 6, folder 3.

11. White, *Charlotte's Web*, 184.

12. Raymond F. Farrell to J. Edgar Hoover, Subject: Grace Hutchins, May 20, 1953, Federal Bureau of Investigation, file 100-51757, Grace Hutchins, section 1; Director, FBI to Commissioner, Immigration and Naturalization Service, RE: Anna Rochester, May 8, 1953, Federal Bureau of Investigation, file 100-12805, Anna Rochester, section 1.

13. "M'Carthy Calls 23 for Book Inquiry," *New York Times*, 33.

14. *Committee on Government Operations: Hearings, Part 7, Before the Permanent Subcomm. on Investigations*, 83rd Cong. 439 (1953), 439.

15. Grace Hutchins to Jessie Lloyd O'Connor, September 11, 1953, Jessie Lloyd O'Connor Papers, series 2, box 50, folder 10.

16. Correlation Summary, December 29, 1955, 110–1.

17. SAC, New York to Director, FBI, re Grace Hutchins, SM-C, September 18, 1953, Federal Bureau of Investigation, file 100-13470, Grace Hutchins, section 2.

18. Grace Hutchins to Jessie Lloyd O'Connor, January 26, 1954, Jessie Lloyd O'Connor Papers, series 2, box 50, folder 10.

19. Grace Hutchins to Jessie Lloyd O'Connor, March 3, 1954, Jessie Lloyd O'Connor Papers, series 2, box 50, folder 10.

20. Legislative Reference Service of the Library of Congress, *World Communist Movement*, vol. 4, 858–9.

21. SAC, New York to Director, FBI, Re: Vida Scudder (DR) Security Matter–C, August 21, 1950, Federal Bureau of Investigation, file 100-0027156, Vida Scudder.

22. For more on the IWO and the state's case against the organization, see Sabin, *Red Scare in Court*.

23. Perlo, "LRA—That Stands for Facts," 9.

24. Anna Rochester to Trachty (Alexander Trachtenberg), December 4, 1954, Alexander Trachtenberg Papers, MSS 117, box 3, file 6.

25. See Flynn, *The Alderson Story*.

26. Gruson, "Six Red Leaders," 1, 10.

27. The liquidating trustee was not discharged from his position until September 19, 1960.

28. Martin, "Greetings to Anna Rochester," 12.

29. Khrushchev, "The Secret Speech."

30. Howard, "Letter to a Friend," 6.

31. SA [redacted] to SAC, New York, re: G. Hutchins, SM-C, memo, May 16, 1956, Federal Bureau of Investigation, file 100-13470, Grace Hutchins, section 3. In 2011 dollars, Hutchins's annual income would be slightly over $200,000. SA [redacted] to SAC, New York, office memorandum, May 31, 1957, Federal Bureau of Investigation, file 100-9260, Anna Rochester, Section 2; Page of calculations in Grace Hutchins's handwriting, FBI, file 100-9260-1A, Anna Rochester, section 1. Rochester's holdings in 2011 dollars would be more than $650,000; her income on that amount would be a little more than $36,000 per year.

32. Rodney, "Freedom of Press Wins," 1, 13.

33. Committee for a Free Press, "Resolution of Unincorporated Association," April 3, 1956, Tamiment 129, Labor Research Association Records, box 4, folder 2.

34. *Daily Worker*, Fact Sheet: Seizure of the *Daily Worker* by the Internal Revenue Service, ca. April 1956, Labor Research Association Records, box 4, folder 2.

35. Rodney, "Freedom of Press Wins," 1, 13.

36. The Communist Party, U.S.A., v. Donald C. Moysey, District Director of Internal Revenue for the District of Lower Manhattan, New York, 141 F. Supp. 332; 1956 U.S. Dist. LEXIS 3282 (U.S. Dist. Ct South. Dist. N.Y. May 23, 1956).

37. Rodney, "Freedom of Press Wins," 1, 13.

38. SA [redacted] to SAC, New York, office memorandum, May 28, 1956, Federal Bureau of Investigation, file 100-9260, Anna Rochester, section 2.

39. Ibid.

40. SAC, New York, request for photograph, May 17, 1957, Federal Bureau of Investigation, file 100-9260, Anna Rochester, section 3.

41. Federal Bureau of Investigation file 100-9260, section 3, Anna Rochester, office memorandum, subject Anna Rochester, May 28, 1956.

42. SA [redacted] to SAC New York, office memorandum paraphrasing rough draft of letter retrieved from trash at 85 Bedford St., November 8, 1956, Federal Bureau of Investigation, file 100-13470, Grace Hutchins, section 3.

43. SAC, New York to Director, FBI, memo, June 19, 1958, Federal Bureau of Investigation, file 100-13470, Grace Hutchins, section 5.

44. Dennis, "Keynote Address," 3–14. The speech was a condensed version of Dennis's report to the National Committee, which had been published by New Century Publishers in 1956 as *The Communists Take a New Look*. On the idea of a political association, see Charney, *A Long Journey*, 284ff.

45. Dennis, "Keynote Address," 7.

46. Ibid., 9.

47. Grace Hutchins and Anna Rochester to Peggy Dennis, ca. 1961, Eugene and Peggy Dennis Papers, MSS 607, box 6, file 4, State Historical Society of Wisconsin, Madison.

48. "Most important contribution," note, April 16, probably 1957, Federal Bureau of Investigation, file 100-9260, Anna Rochester, section 3.

49. Dennis, "Keynote Address," 13.

50. Grace Hutchins, "'What's Past Is Prologue,'" Grace Hutchins Papers, series 3, box 5, folder 7.

51. E. T. (Ellen Thayer) to Grace Hutchins, South Norwalk, CT, June 1957, Grace Hutchins Papers, series 2, box 4, folder 2.

52. Margaret Reeve Cary to Grace Hutchins, Philadelphia, June 1957, Grace Hutchins Papers, series 2, box 4, folder 4.

53. Deborah (no last name provided) to Grace Hutchins, Jamestown, RI, July 31, 1957, Grace Hutchins Papers, series 2, box 4, folder 65.

54. Anna Rochester to Precious Grace, October 28, 1957, Grace Hutchins Papers, series 2, box 4, folder 46.

55. Leo Huberman was cofounder of *Monthly Review*.

56. Mary Hansen, telephone interview with author, May 17, 1998.

57. For more on Flexner, see DuBois, "Eleanor Flexner," 81–90.

58. Hutchins, "The Struggle for Women's Political Rights in America," 20. *Century of Struggle* has been a standard textbook in women's history classes since the early 1970s.

59. Trachty (Alexander Trachtenberg) to Dearest Anna (Anna Rochester), April 18, 1960, Anna Rochester Papers, series 2, box 2, folder 29.

60. Supplemental Correlation Summary, G. Hutchins, June 17, 1963, 20, Federal Bureau of Investigation, file 100-51757, Grace Hutchins, section 2. It is hard to say how long Hutchins may have held this position. The papers of International Publishers were sent to the Soviet Union for safekeeping during the late 1950s.

61. Grace Hutchins to International Publishers, June 10, 1960; Grace Hutchins to Alexander Trachtenberg, June 27, 1960; SA [redacted] to SAC, New York, memo, October 31, 1962, all in Federal Bureau of Investigation, file 100-13470, Grace Hutchins, section 6.

62. Grace Hutchins to Dear Girls (Ruth Erickson and Eleanor Stevenson), May 1, 1962, Ruth Erickson Papers, box 2, folder 10.

63. Hutchins, "Four Decades of Struggle for Civil Liberties," 4; Hutchins, "Civil Liberties Struggles," 4; Hutchins, "The Smith Act," 4.

64. Hutchins, "Four Decades of Struggle for Women's Rights," 4, and "Four Decades of Struggle for Women's Rights, Part 2," 4.

65. Grace Hutchins to Ruth Erickson and Eleanor Stevenson, July 17, 1964, Ruth Erickson Papers, box 2, folder 10.

66. Camp, *Iron in Her Soul*, 321.

67. SA [redacted] to SAC, New York, US government memo, subject: Grace Hutchins, August 26, 1965, Federal Bureau of Investigation, file 100-13470, Grace Hutchins, Section 6.

68. SA [redacted] to SAC, New York, memo, Subject: Grace Hutchins, December 29, 1965, 2, Federal Bureau of Investigation, file 100-13470, Grace Hutchins, Section 6.

69. Grace Hutchins and Anna Rochester to Eleanor Stevenson and Ruth Erickson, December 1, 1965, Ruth Erickson Papers, box 2, folder 10.

70. "Anna Rochester," *New York Times*, 45.

71. *The Worker*, "Anna Rochester Dies at 86," 11.

72. J. S. Allen (Sol Auerbach), "Anna Rochester," 5.

73. Dorothy Wick, interview with author, New York City, April 20, 1998.

74. SA [redacted] to SAC, memo, March 26, 1970, 3, Federal Bureau of Investigation, file 100-13470, Grace Hutchins, section 6; SA [redacted] to SAC, US government memo, subject: CP-USA Funds, August 11, 1966, 3, FBI, file 100-9260, Anna Rochester, section 4.

75. Jurgen Kuczynski to unknown addressee, July 11, 1966, Anna Rochester Papers, series 1, box 1, folder 7.

76. Victor and Ellen Perlo to Grace Hutchins, May 14, 1966, Anna Rochester Papers, series 1, box 1, folder 7.

77. Jack Woods to Grace Hutchins, May 12, 1966, Anna Rochester Papers, series 1, box 1, folder 7.

Notes to Epilogue

1. Eleanor Stevenson and Ruth Erickson to Grace Hutchins, May 1966, Anna Rochester Papers, series 1, box 1, folder 7.

2. M. G. P. (Polly Porter) to Grace Hutchins, October 2, 1966, Anna Rochester Papers, series 1, box 1, folder 7.

3. "Hundreds at Trachtenberg Rites," *The Worker*, 10.

4. Ad Hoc Women's Committee, invitation to celebrate International Women's Day 1967, Grace Hutchins Papers, series 1, box 1, folder 3.

5. These albums have been microfilmed; the microfilms are archived at the Schesinger Library at Radcliffe College, Cambridge, MA.

6. See Erickson, *Sonnets to a House*. The first page of the book reads: "Sonnets To A House and Garden/by Ruth C. Erickson, a Gardener/To E. S., another Gardener." In 1967, Ruth Erickson could not name Eleanor Stevenson, even in a self-published book meant only for friends.

7. Bob Dunn to Bliss, March 15, 1968, Grace Hutchins Papers, series 2, box 4, folder 79.

8. Bob Dunn to Ann Mundelein, July 26, 1968, Grace Hutchins Papers, series 1, box 1, folder 10.

9. Several days earlier, as Grace Hutchins was slipping from this world to the next, night-time fires lit her neighborhood, trash cans ignited by organized Stonewall protestors. See Marotta, "What Made Stonewall Different?" 33–5.

10. Henson, interview.

11. Federal Bureau of Investigation, File 100-13470, section 6, Grace Hutchins, memo, Subject: Grace Hutchins, July 16, 1969.

12. "Grace Hutchins, Labor Economist," *New York Times*, 45.

13. SA [redacted] to SAC, memo, subject: CP, USA Funds, March 26, 1970, 3, Federal Bureau of Investigation, file 100-13470, Grace Hutchins, section 6.

14. "Memorial Service and Burial," Labor Research Association Records, series 8, box 15, folder 11.

15. The Special Collections at the University of Oregon was chosen most likely because the library actively sought collections of papers to support the university's Labor Studies program.

16. Miriam Friedlander, for the Citizens Committee for Constitutional Liberty, to Bob Dunn, New York, July 1969, Grace Hutchins Papers, series 1, box 1, folder 10.

17. Philip Bart to Bob Dunn, July 16, 1969, Grace Hutchins Papers, series 1, box 1, folder 10.

18. Carl and Anne Braden to Dear Friends, July 17, 1969, Grace Hutchins Papers, series 1, box 1, folder 10.

19. Clara Colon to Bob Dunn, July 27, 1969, Grace Hutchins Papers, series 1, box 1, folder 10. Clara Colon succeeded Grace in offering a feminist analysis within the CPUSA. See, for example, Colon, "An Outline on the Fight." In March 1970, Colon produced *Enter Fighting: Today's Woman*, published by New Outlook Publishers.

20. Bettina Aptheker, conversation with author, Santa Rosa, CA, November 12, 2001.

Bibliography

Abbey, Philip R. "Treaty Ports and Extraterritoriality in 1920s China." China the Beautiful. Last modified April 9, 2005. http://www.chinapage.com/transportation/port/treatport1.html.

Abrams, Norma, and Henry Lee. "Bryn Mawr Grad, 63, Accused by Chambers." *Daily News*, December 15, 1948, C3.

Abt, John, with Michael Myerson. *Advocate and Activist: Memoirs of an American Communist Lawyer.* Urbana: University of Illinois Press, 1993.

Addams, Jane. *My Friend, Julia Lathrop.* New York: Macmillan, 1935.

The Alger Hiss Story: Search for the Truth. Last modified July 19, 2010. http://homepages.nyu.edu/~th15/home.html.

Allen, Devere. Papers. Swarthmore College Peace Collection, Swarthmore College, Swarthmore, PA.

Allen, James S. [Sol Auerbach]. "Anna Rochester—Marxist Scholar." *The Worker*, May 24, 1966.

Allen, Julia M. "'That Accursed Aesopian Language': Prosecutorial Framing of Linguistic Evidence in *U.S. v. Foster*, 1949." *Rhetoric and Public Affairs* 2, no. 4 (2001): 109–34.

American Civil Liberties Union. *Crisis in the Civil Liberties Union: A Statement Including the Basic Documents Concerned, Giving the Minority Position in the Current Controversy in the A.C.L.U.* New York: American Civil Liberties Union, 1940.

An American Observer in China. "An Attempt to Analyze the Situation in China." *Spirit of Missions*, March 1926, 197–200.

American Trade Union Delegation. *Russia after Ten Years: Report of the American Trade Union Delegation to the Soviet Union.* New York: International Publishers, 1927.

The Archives of the Episcopal Church, USA. Episcopal Theological Seminary of the Southwest, Austin, TX.

The Archives of the Society of the Companions of the Holy Cross. Adelynrood, South Byfield, MA.

Augustine. *On Christian Doctrine.* Translated by D. W. Robertson, Jr. New York: Library of Liberal Arts Press, 1958.

Auden, W. H., and Christopher Isherwood. *Journey to a War.* New York: Random House, 1939.

Bacon, Elizabeth M. "America's Working Women," review of *Women Who Work*, by Grace Hutchins. *Masses & Mainstream*, March 1953, 63–4.

Baldwin, Roger. "A Puritan Revolutionist." In *Adventurous Americans*, edited by Devere Allen, 263–76. New York: Farrar and Rinehart, 1932.

Bates, M. Searle. "The Theology of American Missionaries in China, 1900–1950." In *The Missionary Enterprise in China and America*, edited by John K. Fairbank, 135–58. Cambridge, MA: Harvard University Press, 1974.

Bedacht, Max. Unpublished autobiography. Max Bedacht Papers. Tamiment Library. Elmer Holmes Bobst Library. New York University.

Bentley, Elizabeth. "How I Was Used by the Red Spy Ring." *McCall's*, July 1951, 120–25, 127.

Bloor, Ella Reeve. Papers. Sophia Smith Collection. Smith College, Northampton, MA.

———. *We Are Many.* New York: International Publishers, 1940.

Blumenthal, Sidney. "The Cold War and the Closet." *The New Yorker*, March 17, 1997, 117.

Bogart, E. L. Review of *The Populist Movement in the United States*, by Anna Rochester. *American Economic Review*, June 1944, 363–65.

Book Review Digest. "Rochester, Anna. *Capitalism and Progress*." 41 (1945): 601.

———. "Rochester, Anna. *Labor and Coal* (Labor and ind. ser.)." 27 (1932): 907.

————. "Rochester, Anna. *Populist Movement in the United States.*" 40 (1944), 644.

Boonin-Vail, Martha. "New Wine in Old Bottles: Anglo-Catholicism in the United States, 1840–1919." PhD diss., Yale University, 1993.

Bowman, Ralph. "Capitalism in America," review of *Capitalism and Progress,* by Anna Rochester. *New Masses,* May 8, 1945, 24–5.

Branscomb, B. Harvie. "The Study and Interpretation of the Bible." In *The Church Through Half a Century: Essays in Honor of William Adams Brown,* edited by Samuel McCrea Cavert and Henry Pitney Van Dusen, 165–82. New York: Charles Scribner's Sons, 1936.

Browder, Earl. "'Fewer High-Falutin' Phrases, More Simple Every-Day Deeds.'" *The Communist,* January 1931, 7–31.

————. "Next Tasks of the Communist Party of the USA." *The Communist,* November–December, 1930, 972–8.

————. *A Message to Catholics.* New York: Workers Library Publishers, 1938.

————. Papers. Special Collections Research Center, Syracuse University Library, Syracuse, NY.

Brown, F. "The Campaign against Hearst and the Dickstein Committee." *Party Organizer,* February 1935, 1–4.

————. "Check-Up on Organization (Excerpts from Report to Plenum)." *Party Organizer,* March 1935, 3–17.

————. "The Party Building and Daily Worker Drives." *Party Organizer,* March–April 1937, 13–19.

Brown, Francis. "Looking at Industrial Leaders from the Left and Right." *New York Times,* June 21, 1936, BR6.

Brush, Michael. "Are Sex Crimes Due to Sex?" *New Masses,* October 26, 1937, 15–6.

Buckley, William F. "Witness and Friends: Remembering Whittaker Chambers on the Centennial of His Birth." *National Review,* August 6, 2001. http://old.nationalreview.com/flashback/2001200511220837.asp.

Budenz, Louis. "From the Plough to the Tractor: Anna Rochester's New Book on Lenin." *Daily Worker,* August 23, 1942.

Bulosan, Carlos. *America Is in the Heart.* Seattle: University of Washington Press, 1973.

Burgchardt, Carl R. "Two Faces of American Communism: Pamphlet Rhetoric of the Third Period and the Popular Front." In *Readings on the Rhetoric of Social Protest,* edited by Charles E. Morris III and Stephen H. Browne, 235–52. State College, PA: Strata Publishing, 2001.

Burke, Kenneth. *Attitudes toward History.* 3rd ed. Berkeley: University of California Press, 1984.

————. *Grammar of Motives.* Berkeley: University of California Press, 1969.

————. *Permanence and Change.* 3rd ed. Berkeley: University of California Press, 1984.

————. "The Virtues and Limitations of Debunking." In *The Philosophy of Literary Form.* 3rd ed., 168–90. Berkeley: University of California Press, 1973.

Camp, Helen C. *Iron in Her Soul: Elizabeth Gurley Flynn and the American Left.* Pullman, WA: Washington State University Press, 1995.

Carpenter, Edward. *Civilization: Its Cause and Cure.* New York: Charles Scribner's Sons, 1921.

————. *England's Ideal and Other Papers on Social Subjects.* London: Swan Sonnenschein, Lowrey & Company, 1887.

————. *The Intermediate Sex: A Study of Some Transitional Types of Men and Women.* London: George Allen & Company, 1912.

————. *My Days and Dreams.* 3rd ed. London: George Allen and Unwin, 1918.

————. *Towards Democracy: Complete Edition of Four Parts.* 5th ed. With a foreword by Gilbert Beith. London: George Allen & Unwin, 1949. First published 1883 by S. Sonnenschein & Co. Citations refer to the Allen & Unwin edition.

Chambers, Whittaker. *Witness.* Washington, DC: Regnery, 1980. First published in 1952 by Random House.

Chappell, Winifred. "Industrial Czars," review of *Rulers of America,* by Anna Rochester. *The Fight Against War and Fascism,* May 1936, 18.

————. Papers. State Historical Society of Wisconsin, Madison.

Charney, George. *A Long Journey*. Chicago: Quadrangle, 1969.

Chauncey, George. *Gay New York*. New York: Basic Books, 1994.

Chrisman, Miriam U. "*To Bind Together*." South Byfield, MA: Society of the Companions of the Holy Cross, n.d.

Christian Century. Unsigned review of *Labor and Coal*, by Anna Rochester. 48 (January 28, 1931): 141.

CIS U. S. Serial Set. House Unpublished Hearings Collection, June 21, 1951, CIS-NO: 82 HUna-T.26.

Cleghorn, Sarah N. Papers. University of Vermont Library, Burlington.

———. *Threescore*. New York: Harrison Smith & Robert Haas, 1936.

Clines, Francis X. "White House Freedom Medal Set for Whittaker Chambers." *New York Times*, February 22, 1984, A21.

Cloud, Dana. "Change Happens: Materialist Dialectics and Communication Studies." In *Marxism and Communication Studies: The Point Is to Change It*, edited by Lee Artz, Steve Macele, and Dana L. Cloud, 53–70. New York: Peter Lang, 2006.

———. "The First Lady's Privates: Queering Eleanor Roosevelt for Public Address Studies." In *Queering Public Address*, edited by Charles E. Morris III, 23–44. Columbia, SC: University of South Carolina Press, 2007.

Coe, George Albert. *A Social Theory of Religious Education*. New York: Charles Scribner's Sons, 1917.

Colón, Clara. *An Outline on the Fight for Women's Freedom*. New York: National Education Department, US Communist Party, 1969.

Community Service Society. Records. Rare Book and Manuscript Library, Columbia University in the City of New York.

Consumers' Co-Operative Housing Association. Papers. In possession of the secretary of the Consumers' Co-Operative Housing Association, New York.

Converse, Florence. *Diana Victrix*. Boston: Houghton, Mifflin and Company, 1897.

———. *Long Will*. New York: E. P. Dutton & Company, 1939.

Cooper, Marilyn M. "The Ecology of Writing." *College English* 48, no. 4 (1986): 364–75.

Cook, Blanche Wiesen. "Female Support Networks and Political Activism: Lillian Wald, Crystal Eastman, Emma Goldman." *Chrysalis* 3 (1977): 43–61.

Corbett, Hunter. "Permanent Factors which Make China a Most Inviting Field." In *Students and the Modern Missionary Crusade*, 342–47. New York: Student Volunteer Movement for Foreign Missions, 1906.

Cottrell, Debbie Mauldin. "The Sargent School for Physical Education." *Journal of Physical Education, Recreation and Dance*, March 1994, 32–7.

Cottrell, Debora Lynn. "Women's Minds, Women's Bodies: The Influence of the Sargent School for Physical Education." PhD diss., University of Texas at Austin, 1993.

Cutler, Addison T. Review of *Why Farmers Are Poor: The Agricultural Crisis in the United States*, by Anna Rochester. *Science and Society*, Fall 1940, 453–5.

Daily Worker. "Assail Move to Blacklist Bail Fund Contributors." April 16, 1952.

———. "Bar from Jury All Who Read." August 29, 1929.

———. "Cheer New York Delegates for Unity Congress." August 30, 1929.

———. "Foster to Head Communist Election Campaign Committee: 14 Radio Broadcasts Planned." July 18, 1936.

———. "Fraternally Yours." International Workers Order Column, March 5, 1943.

———. "Grace Hutchins Hits Illegal Use of Bail List," July 1, 1952, 6.

———. "Gurley Flynn Charges Accusers with Scuttling ACLU Civil Rights Program as 'Trial' Begins." May 8, 1940.

———. "Militant Program for Class War on All Fronts Offered for Adoption at Cleveland." August 29, 1929.

———. "150 Notables Form Emergency Civil Rights Committee." October 8, 1951.

———. "150 Women Sign Plea for Amnesty for 11.'" January 27, 1953.

———. "Over 100 Delegates Are Arrested after Miners Drive Back Army of 200 Gangsters and Detectives." September 10, 1928.

————. "People Everywhere Mourn Mother Bloor." August 17, 1951.

————. "Resolution on the 'Daily Worker.'" December 10, 1929.

————. "Rochester Notables Scorn Mob Attack on CP Meeting." April 16, 1948.

————. "To Our Fellow Readers." June 24, 1945.

Darling, Pamela W. *New Wine: The Story of Women Transforming Leadership and Power in the Episcopal Church.* Cambridge, MA: Cowley Publications, 1994.

Dartington—The Story so Far. Dartington. Last modified July 2012. http://www.dartington.org/about-the-trust/the-story-so-far.

D'Emilio, John. "Capitalism and Gay Identity." In *Making Trouble*, 3–17. New York: Routledge, 1992.

Dennis, Eugene. "Keynote Address." *Political Affairs*, March 1957, 3–14.

————, and Peggy Dennis. Papers. State Historical Society of Wisconsin, Madison.

Dennis, Peggy. "A Response." *Feminist Studies* 5, no. 3 (1979): 451–61.

de Toledano, Ralph, ed. *Notes from the Underground: The Whittaker Chambers—Ralph de Toledano Letters: 1949–1960.* New York: Regnery, 1997.

Devins, John Bancroft. "The Kind of Articles Calculated to Do the Most Good in Educating and Inspiring the Church." In *Students and the Modern Missionary Crusade*, 591–5. New York: Student Volunteer Movement for Foreign Missions, 1906.

Di Leonardo, Micaela. "The Female World of Cards and Holidays: Women, Families, and the Work of Kinship." *Signs: Journal of Women in Culture and Society* 12, no. 3 (1987): 440–53.

Dolsen, James H. *The Awakening of China.* Chicago: Daily Worker Publishing Company, 1926.

Domhoff, G. William. "Power in America: Wealth, Income, and Power." Who Rules America? University of California, Santa Cruz. Last modified October 2012. http://sociology.ucsc.edu/whorulesamerica/power/wealth.html.

Donovan, Mary Sudman. *A Different Call: Women's Ministries in the Episcopal Church 1950–1920.* Wilton, CT: Morehouse-Barlow, 1986.

————. "Creating a Neighborhood: The Social Service Networks of Mary Kingsbury Simkhovitch." In *Deeper Joy*, edited by Fredrica Harris Thompsett and Sheryl Kujawa-Holbrook, 165–79. New York: Church Publishing, 2005.

Drayton, William. "Secret Gardens." *The Atlantic*, June 2000, 108–11.

Driberg, Tom. *The Mystery of Moral Re-armament.* New York: Knopf, 1965.

DuBois, Ellen. "Eleanor Flexner and the History of American Feminism." *Gender & History* 3, no. 1 (1991): 81–90.

Dunn, Robert W. "Democracy and the Russian Revolution." *World Tomorrow*, June 1924, 175–6.

————. "The Job of Labor Research." *New Masses*, August 1931, 23.

————. Papers. Special Collections and University Archives, University of Oregon Libraries, Eugene.

————. "Today's Rulers of America." *Labor Defender*, October 1930, 199.

Durrell, Harold Clarke. "Memoirs of Deceased Members of the New England Historic Genealogical Society: Mrs. Edward Webster Hutchins (Susan Barnes Hurd)." *New England Historical and Genealogical Society Register* 97 (April 1943): 184–5.

Dutton, Marsha L., ed. Lawrence C. Braceland, trans. *Aelred of Rievaulx: Spiritual Friendship.* Cistercian Studies Series. Collegeville, MN: Order of St. Benedict, 2010.

Dyson, Lowell K. "Radical Farm Organizations and Periodicals in America, 1920–1960, *Agricultural History*, April 1971, 111–20.

Eddy, Sherwood. *Pathfinders of the World Missionary Crusade.* New York: Abingdon-Cokesbury Press, 1945.

Editorial Committee. "*The Working Woman*: Changes to a Magazine." *The Working Woman*, March 1933.

Edwards, Justin D. "At the End of *The Rainbow*: Reading Lesbian Identities in D. H. Lawrence's Fiction." *International Fiction Review* 27, nos. 1 and 2 (2000). http://journals.hil.unb.ca/index.php/IFR/article/view/7659/8716.

Epstein, Israel. *From Opium War to Liberation.* 2nd ed. Peking: New World Press, 1964.

Erickson, Ruth. Papers. Special Collections and University Archives, University of Oregon Libraries, Eugene.

———. *Sonnets to a House and Garden*. New Milford, CT: Litch-Fair, Marsh & Loewe, 1968.

Faderman, Lillian. "Love Between Women in 1928: Why Progressivism Is Not Always Progress." In *Historical, Literary, and Erotic Aspects of Lesbianism*, edited by Monika Kehoe, 23–42. New York: Harrington Park Press, 1986

———. "Nineteenth-Century Boston Marriage as a Possible Lesson for Today." In *Boston Marriages*, edited by Esther D. Rothblum and Kathleen A. Brehony, 29–42. Amherst: University of Massachussetts Press, 1993.

———. *Odd Girls and Twilight Lovers*. New York: Penguin, 1991.

Fairchild, Mildred. Review of *Women Who Work*, by Grace Hutchins. *Annals of the American Academy of Political and Social Science* 175 (September 1934): 271–2.

Federal Bureau of Investigation. File 61-4478-514. *Daily Worker*.

———. File 100-0027156. Vida Dutton Scudder.

———. File 100-12805. Anna Rochester.

———. File 100-13470. Grace Hutchins.

———. File 100-206603. Juliet Stuart Poyntz.

———. File 100-51757. Grace Hutchins.

———. File 100-6372-1. Winifred Chappell.

———. File 100-9260. Anna Rochester.

Federal Writers Project. *Vermont: A Guide to the Green Mountain State*. Boston: Houghton Mifflin, 1937.

Feinberg, Leslie. "Can a Homosexual Be a Member of the Communist Party?" *Workers World*, October 7, 2004. http://www.workers.org/ww/2004/lgbtseries1007.php.

Feldman, Betty. "Grace Hutchins Tells About 'Women Who Work.'" *The Worker*, March 1, 1953, 12.

Fellowship of Reconciliation. Papers. Swarthmore College Peace Collection. Swarthmore College, Swarthmore, PA.

Ferry, Elinor. Papers. Tamiment Library. Elmer Holmes Bobst Library. New York University.

———. Papers. Special Collections, Harvard Law School Library, Harvard University, Cambridge, MA.

Floyd, William. "'Offensively Religious.'" *The World Tomorrow*, December 1923, 380.

Flynn, Elizabeth Gurley. *The Alderson Story: My Life as a Political Prisoner*. New York: International Publishers, 1963.

———. *I Speak My Own Piece*. New York: Masses & Mainstream, 1955.

———. Papers. Tamiment Library. Elmer Holmes Bobst Library. New York University.

Folsom, Franklin. *Days of Anger, Days of Hope*. Boulder: University Press of Colorado, 1994.

Foster, William Z. *History of the Communist Party of the United States*. New York: International Publishers, 1952.

Franzen, Trisha. *Spinsters and Lesbians: Independent Womanhood in the United States*. New York: New York University Press, 1996.

Freedman, Estelle. "'The Burning of Letters Continues': Elusive Identities and the Historical Construction of Sexuality." *Journal of Women's History* 9, no. 4 (1998): 181–200.

———. "Partners for Life." *The Women's Review of Books* 5, no. 5 (1988): 13.

———. *Maternal Justice: Miriam Van Waters and the Female Reform Tradition*. Chicago: University of Chicago Press, 1996.

———. "Separatism as Strategy: Female Institution Building and American Feminism, 1870–1930." In *Feminism, Sexuality, & Politics: Essays by Estelle B. Freedman*, 21–35. Chapel Hill: University of North Carolina Press, 2006.

———. "'Uncontrolled Desires': The Response to the Sexual Psychopath, 1920–1960." *The Journal of American History* 74, no. 1 (1987): 83–106.

French, W.E.P. "It Seems Odd: A State Church in Disguise." *The New York Call*, December 6, 1910.

Fried, Albert. *McCarthyism: The Great American Red Scare*. Oxford: Oxford University Press, 1997.

Frosch, Jack, and Bromberg, Walter. "The Sex Offender: A Psychiatric Study." *American Journal of Orthopsychiatry* 9 (October 1939), 761–7.

Gailor, Thomas F. "Christianity: The Only Absolute Religion." In *Students and the Modern Missionary Crusade*, 81–5. New York: Student Volunteer Movement for Foreign Missions, 1906.

Gamble, P. L. Review of *Capitalism and Progress*, by Anna Rochester. *Springfield Republican*, June 20, 1945, 6.

Ganter, Granville. "Decadence, Sexuality, and the Bohemian Vision of Wallace Thurman." *MELUS* 28 (Summer 2003): 83–104.

Garber, Eric. "T'ain't Nobody's Bizness: Homosexuality in 1920s Harlem." In *Black Men, White Men*, edited by Michael J. Smith, 7–16. New York: Harrington, 1999.

Garlin, Sender. "Publisher on Trial: The Lifework of Alexander Trachtenberg." *Masses & Mainstream*, October 1952, 17–27.

George, Ann, and Jack Selzer. *Kenneth Burke in the 1930s*. Columbia: University of South Carolina Press, 2007.

Gerard, James W. *My First Eighty-Three Years in America*. New York: Doubleday and Company, 1951.

Gettleman, Marvin E. "The New York Workers School, 1923–1944." In *New Studies in the Politics and Culture of U.S. Communism*, edited by Michael E. Brown, Randy Martin, Frank Rosengarten, and George Snedeker, 261–80. New York: Monthly Review Press, 1993.

Gillespie, Joanna. "The Companions of the Holy Cross: A Vocation to Prayer Companionship." In *Deeper Joy*, edited by Fredrica Harris Thompsett and Sheryl Kujawa-Holbrook, 55–69. New York: Church Publishing, 2005.

Gladkov, Fyodor Vasilievich. *Cement*. Translated by A. S. Arthur and C. Ashleigh. New York: Frederick Ungar, 1966.

Gladney, Margaret Rose. "Personalizing the Political, Politicizing the Personal: Reflections on Editing the Letters of Lillian Smith." In *Carryin' On in the Lesbian and Gay South*, edited by John Howard, 93–104. New York: New York University Press, 1997.

Gold, Michael. "Change the World!" *Daily Worker*, February 12, 1934.

———. "Toward an American Revolutionary Culture." *New Masses*, July 1931, 12–3.

Gorky, Maxim. "Proletarian Humanism." *Pravda* and *Izvestia*, May 23, 1934.

Gruson, Sidney. "Six Red Leaders End Prison Terms." *New York Times*, March 2, 1955.

Hall, Robert. "Robert Minor's Fellow Workers Pay Tribute to a Fearless Fighter for Peace, Socialism." *Daily Worker*, December 1, 1952.

Hamilton, Alice. letter to the editor. *New York Times*, December 3, 1952.

Hapgood, Elizabeth Reynolds. Review of *Lenin on the American Question*, by Anna Rochester. *Bryn Mawr Alumnae Bulletin*, March 1943, 16.

Harris, Lement. "City and Country," review of *Lenin on the Agrarian Question*, by Anna Rochester. *New Masses*, October 27, 1942, 25–6.

———. *Harold M. Ware (1890–1935): Agricultural Pioneer, U.S.A. and U.S.S.R.* Occasional Paper No. 30. New York: American Institute for Marxist Studies, 1978.

———. *My Tale of Two Worlds*. New York: International Publishers, 1986.

Hawkins, Alice. Class Notes. 1907. *Bryn Mawr Alumnae Bulletin*, March 1938, 32.

Hay, Harry. *Radically Gay: Gay Liberation in the Words of Its Founder*. Boston: Beacon Press, 1996.

Healey, Dan. *Homosexual Desire in Revolutionary Russia: The Regulation of Sexual and Gender Dissent*. Chicago: University of Chicago Press, 2001.

Held, Kurt. *The Outsiders of Uskoken Castle*. Garden City, NJ: Doubleday, 1967.

"Helene Glatzer." Frauenwiki-Dresden. Last modified March 5, 2009. http://www.frauenwiki-dresden. de/index.php/Helene_Glatzer.

Henderson, Mae G. "Portrait of Wallace Thurman." In *The Harlem Renaissance 1920–1940*. vol. 5. *Remembering the Harlem Renaissance*, edited by Cary D. Wintz, 289–312. New York: Garland, 1996.

Hennessy, Rosemary. *Profit and Pleasure: Sexual Identities in Late Capitalism*. New York: Routledge, 2000.

Hewitt, Andrew. *Political Inversions: Homosexuality, Fascism, and the Modernist Imaginary*. Palo Alto, CA: Stanford University Press, 1996.

Hiss, Alger. Defense files. Special Collections, Harvard Law School Library, Harvard University, Cambridge, MA.

Horne, Gerald. *Communist Front? The Civil Rights Congress, 1946–1956*. Rutherford, NJ: Fairleigh Dickinson University Press, 1988.

Horton, Walter Marshall. "Science and Theology." In *The Church Through Half a Century: Essays in Honor of William Adams Brown*, edited by Samuel McCrea Cavert and Henry Pitney Van Dusen, 93–109. New York: Charles Scribner's Sons, 1936.

Howard, Milton. "Letter to a Friend." *Masses and Mainstream*, August 1956, 1–11.

Hunter, Jane. *The Gospel of Gentility*. New Haven: Yale University Press, 1984.

Hutchins, Grace. "Away with that Little Penitentiary!" *Labor Defender*, March 1932, 55.

———. "The Black Night." *The Fight Against War and Fascism*, September 1936, 14, 25.

———. "Children under Capitalism," review of *Child Workers in America*, by Katharine DuPre Lumpkin and Dorothy Wolff Douglas. *New Masses*, June 29, 1937, 25–6.

———. "China's Women in the Struggle." *China Today*, April 1941, 15–6.

———. "Civil Liberties Struggles in the McCarthy Era." *The Worker*, February 25, 1964, 4, 6.

———. "Far Away and Long Ago," review of *Only Yesterday*, by Frederick Lewis Allen. *New Masses*, April 1932, 26.

———. "Feminists and the Left Wing." *New Masses*, November 20, 1934, 14.

———. "Flowers and Song Pep Spinners." *Federated Press Labor Letter*, June 14, 1928, 2.

———. "For Group Discussion." *The World Tomorrow*, February 1922, 59–60.

———. "Four Decades of Struggle for Civil Liberties." *The Worker*, February 18, 1964, 4, 7.

———. "Four Decades of Struggle for Women's Rights." *The Worker*, March 17, 1964, 4–5.

———. "Four Decades of Struggle for Women's Rights, Part 2." *The Worker*, March 24, 1964, 4.

———. "Gandhi in the Villages." *The World Tomorrow*, May 1927, 202–4.

———. "German Police Arm as Women Workers March with Red Bandannas." *Federated Press Labor Letter*, April 6, 1927, 7.

———. "Good and Welfare," review of *From Relief to Social Security*, by Grace Abbott. *New Masses*, February 17, 1942, 26.

———. "The Greatest Disaster in History." *Solidarity*, October 1931, 5, 14.

———. "Greetings on Our Twenty-Fifth Anniversary." *New Masses*, December 29, 1936, 21.

———. "Hint Capitalist Interest in Church Crusade Against Soviet." Federated Press Central Bureau, March 4, 1930, sheet 2.

———. "It Comes on Cat's Feet." *New Masses*, December 13, 1938, 7–9.

———. *Japan Wars on the U.S.A.* New York: International Publishers, 1941.

———. "The Joy of Being a Missionary." *North American Students and World Advance*, edited by Burton St. John, 275–7, 599. New York: Student Volunteer Movement, 1920.

———. "Julia Martin: A Story." *Working Woman*, March 1933, 9.

———. "Kagawa as Labor Leader." *Christian Century*, October 1926, 1328–9.

———. *Labor and Silk*. New York: International Publishers, 1929.

———. "Labor Likes Its Lot in Soviet Russia." *Federated Press Labor Letter*, June 22, 1927, 7.

———. "A Labor Press Guide," review of *The American Labor Press: An Annotated Directory*, by American Council on Public Affairs. *New Masses*, October 22, 1940, 27.

———. letter to the editor. *Daily Worker*, October 14, 1943.

———. letter to the editor. *Daily Worker*, March 9, 1951.

———. "Mill Owners on Defensive." *Federated Press Labor's News*, April 27, 1929, 8.

———. "Negro Organizers Expect Lynchings." *Federated Press Labor's News*, November 15, 1930, 2.

———. "Negro Women Workers Fight Against Conditions of Slavery." *The Working Woman*, February 1930, 6.

———. "New Bedford Fights for Union." *Labor Defender*, July 1928, 144–5.

———. "No Quiet on the Labor Front," review of *Labor's New Millions*, by Mary Heaton Vorse. *New Masses*, June 7, 1938, 26–7.

———. "Notes From Abroad." *Working Woman*, September 1935, 10–11.

———. "1001 Laws Discriminate Against Women." *The Woman Today*, April 1937, 20–1.

———."Organizer in Jail Tells of Jobless Fellow Prisoners." Federated Press Eastern Bureau, December 30, 1930, sheet 3.

———. "Our Inferiority Complex." *The World Tomorrow*, December 1923, 362–3.

———. "Outside the Little East Gate." *Spirit of Missions*, July 1913, 562–4.

———. Papers. Special Collections and University Archives, Ax 625. University of Oregon Librar-
    ies, Eugene.

———. "Preparing Women for War." *Working Woman*, July 1933, 4.

———. "Professionals Speak," review of *Creative America: Its Resources for Social Security*, by Mary
    Van Kleeck. *The Communist*, July 1936, 671–2.

———. "Prophets and the People." *The World Tomorrow*, June 1924, 182–3.

———. Review of *All In The Day's Work*, by Ida Tarbell. *Book Union Bulletin*, May 1939.

———. "St. Hilda's Outside the Wall." *Spirit of Missions*, September 1914, 687–90.

———. "Schrafft Profits on Unemployed Workers." *Labor Unity*, February 8, 1930, 6.

———. "Seeing Red in Canton." *Survey*, March 15, 1927, 775–6.

———. "The Smith Act Attack on Civil Liberties." *The Worker*, March 3, 1964, 4.

———. "A Socialist Reads Lenin," review of *On Journey*, by Vida Dutton Scudder. *New Masses*,
    May 11, 1937, 25–6.

———. "Speedup Cuts Office Jobs." *Federated Press Labor's News*, May 10, 1930, 5.

———. "The Struggle for Women's Political Rights in America." review of *Century of Struggle*, by
    Eleanor Flexner. *Sunday Worker*, September 20, 1959, 10.

———. "Textile Union Born in Strike." *Federated Press Labor's News*, March 21, 1929, 2.

———. *The Truth about the Liberty League*. New York: International Pamphlets, 1936.

———. Review of *A Week*, by Iury Libedinsky. *The World Tomorrow*, July 1924, 221.

———. "Westinghouse Cuts Wages." *Federated Press Labor's News*, October 11, 1930, 5.

———. *What Every Working Woman Wants*. New York: Workers Library Publishers, 1935.

———. "Who Makes the Guns?" *The Fight Against War and Fascism*, June 1934, 16.

———. "Women in Overalls," review of *Out of the Kitchen—Into the War*, by Susan B. Anthony II.
    New Masses, December 14, 1943, 26.

———. *Women Who Work*. New York: International Pamphlets, 1932.

———. *Women Who Work*. New York: International Publishers, 1934.

———. *Women Who Work*. Rev. ed. New York: International Publishers, 1952.

———. "Women Workers Hail the I.L.D." *Daily Worker*, June 28, 1930, 6.

——— and Anna Rochester. *Jesus Christ and the World Today*. New York: George H. Doran, 1922.

Ilin, M. *New Russia's Primer*. New York: Harcourt, Brace and Company, 1931.

International Labor Defense. *Equal Justice and Democracy in the Service of Victory: Continuing the
    Work of Anna Damon*. New York: International Labor Defense, 1944.

Jackson, Roger. "Labor Must 'Take It on Chin,' Says (Happy Warrior) Sullivan." *Daily Worker*,
    September 20, 1935.

Jackson, S. L. Review of *The Populist Movement*, by Anna Rochester. *Springfield Republican*, March
    3, 1944, 10.

Johnson, Abby, Ann Arthur, and Ronald M. Johnson. "Forgotten Pages: Black Literary Magazines
    in the 1920s." *Journal of American Studies* 8 (December 1974): 363–82.

Johnson, David K. *The Lavender Scare: The Cold War Persecution of Gays and Lesbians in the Federal
    Government*. Chicago: University of Chicago Press, 2004.

Jones, John Hudson. "Mother Bloor, Great American, Laid to Rest." *Daily Worker*, August 16, 1951.

Josephs, Jean. "Double Burden." *The Worker*, February 14, 1954.

Kaufman, Mary Metlay. Papers. Sophia Smith Collection, Smith College, Northampton, MA.

Kennedy, Elizabeth Lapovsky. "'But We Would Never Talk about It': The Structures of Lesbian
    Discretion in South Dakota, 1928–1933." In *Inventing Lesbian Cultures in America*, edited by
    Ellen Lewin, 15–39. Boston: Beacon Press, 1996.

Kenney, Karen. "The Realm of Sports and the Athletic Woman 1850–1900." In *Her Story in Sport:
    A Historical Anthology of Women in Sports*, edited by Reet Howell, 107–40. West Point, NY:
    Leisure Press, 1982.

Khrushchev, Nikita S. "The Secret Speech—On the Cult of Personality, 1956." 84th Cong. 2nd
    sess. 9389–403 (June 4, 1956). Modern History Sourcebook. http://www.fordham.edu/halsall/
    mod/1956khrushchev-secret1.html.

Knepper, Jeanne, "'At Grips with Life': The Life of Winifred L. Chappell, 1879–1951." In *Journey toward Justice*, edited by Jan Kindwoman and Ron Ozier, 36–67. Staten Island, NY: Methodist Federation for Social Action, 1988.

Kon, Igor. "Russia." In *Sociolegal Control of Homosexuality: A Multi-Nation Comparison*, edited by Donald J. West and Richard Green, 221–42. New York: Plenum Press, 1997.

Kreps, T. J. Review of *Capitalism and Progress*, by Anna Rochester. *Annals of the American Academy*, 241 (Spring 1945): 186.

Labor Research Association. *Arsenal of Facts*. New York: International Publishers, 1938.

———. foreword to *Labor Fact Book*. New York: International Publishers, 1931, 9–10.

———. *Labor Fact Book 8*. New York: International Publishers, 1949.

———. *Labor Fact Book 10*. New York: International Publishers, 1951.

———. *Labor Fact Book 11*. New York: International Publishers, 1953.

———. *Monopoly Today*. New York: International Publishers, 1950.

———. Records. Tamiment Library. Elmer Holmes Bobst Library. New York University.

Labor Unity. "The RILU on *Labor Unity*." September 1932, 26–8.

Lamont, Corliss, ed. introduction to *The Trial of Elizabeth Gurley Flynn*. New York: Horizon Press, 1968.

———. *Yes to Life*. New York: Horizon Press, 1981.

Lawrence, D. H. *The Rainbow*. New York: B. W. Huebsch, 1915.

League for Industrial Democracy. Records. Tamiment Library. Elmer Holmes Bobst Library. New York University.

League of American Writers. *We Hold These Truths*. New York: League of American Writers, 1939.

Lean, Garth. *Frank Buchman: A Life*. London: Constable & Co., 1985. www.frankbuchman.info/.

Lee, Mabel. *Memories of a Bloomer Girl*. Reston, VA: American Alliance for Health, Physical Education, Recreation and Dance, 1977.

Legislative Reference Service of the US Library of Congress. *World Communist Movement: Selective Chronology 1818–1957*. vol. 2. *1946–1950*. Washington, DC: US Government Printing Office, 1963.

———. *World Communist Movement: Selective Chronology 1818–1957*. vol. 3. *1951–1953*. Washington, DC: US Government Printing Office, 1963.

———. *World Communist Movement: Selective Chronology 1818–1957*. vol. 4. *1954–1955*. Washington, DC: US Government Printing Office, 1965.

Lenin, V. I. *Essential Works of Lenin*. Edited by Henry M. Christman. New York: Dover Publications, 1987.

———. "Lenin on Working Class Literature." Translated by Anna Rochester. *New Masses*, October 1929, 7.

Lewis, Edward. *Edward Carpenter: An Exposition and an Appreciation*. 2nd ed. London: Methuen, 1915.

Lindenmeyer, Kriste. *"A Right to Childhood": The U.S. Children's Bureau and Child Welfare, 1912–1946*. Urbana: University of Illinois Press, 1997.

Link, Eugene P. *Labor-Religion Prophet: The Times and Life of Harry F. Ward*. Boulder, CO: Westview Press, 1984.

Littell, Edward H. "Writing from Outside Nanchang, Kiangsi, China, 28 September 1926." *The Newsletter*, District of Hankow, Special War Issue, October 1926, 16–8.

The Living Church Annual. Milwaukee, WI: Morehouse Publishing, 1920.

Lloyd, Jessie. "FP Writer Portrays Hell in America's Silk Mills." *Labor's News*, January 4, 1930, 5.

Loseff, Lev. *On the Beneficence of Censorship: Aesopian Language in Modern Russian Literature*. Arbeiten und Texte zur Slavistik. Munich: Verlag Otto Sagner in Kommission, 1989.

Lumpkin, Grace. "Emancipation and Exploitation." *New Masses*, May 15, 1934, 26–7.

———. "War and Underwear," review of *Labor and Silk*, by Grace Hutchins. *The Office Worker*, May 1929, 5, 6.

Maglin, Nan Bauer. "Vida to Florence: 'Comrade and Companion.'" *Frontiers: A Journal of Women Studies* 3 (Autumn, 1979): 13–20.

Marcantonio, Vito. "Terror by Index Cards." *Equal Justice*, February 1940, 2.

Marion, George. *The Communist Trial: An American Crossroads.* 2nd ed. New York: Fairplay Publishers, 1950.

Markwell, Bernard Kent. *The Anglican Left.* Brooklyn, NY: Carlson Publishing, 1991.

Marotta, Toby. "What Made Stonewall Different?" *Gay and Lesbian Review,* March–April 2006, 33–5.

Margaret Mooers Marshall. "Policy of Employers to Hire Men Handicaps Women." *New York Evening Journal,* March 17, 1934.

Martin, Julia. "Greetings to Anna Rochester." *The Worker,* March 27, 1955.

McComiskey, Bruce. Review of *Rhetorical Bodies. Journal of Advanced Composition* 20, no. 3 (2000): 699–703.

Millard, Betty. *Woman against Myth.* New York: International Publishers, 1948.

Miller, Neil. *Out of the Past.* New York: Vintage, 1995.

Milner, Lucile. *Education of an American Liberal.* New York: Horizon Press, 1954.

Mitchell, Louise. "2 Women Debunk Pumpkin Spy Tales." *Daily Worker,* December 15, 1948, 1.

Morehead, Eleanor, and James Parlatore. "Around Town." *PM,* December 26, 1944.

Morgan, Emily Malbone. *Adelyn's Story.* Privately printed, 1915.

———. *Letters to Her Companions.* South Byfield, MA: Society of the Companions of the Holy Cross, 1944.

———. *Memories: Passages from Annual Letters to the Society of the Companions of the Holy Cross, 1884–1915.* Privately printed. New York: Longmans, Green and Co., 1917.

Morris, Charles E. III. "Pink Herring & The Fourth Persona: J. Edgar Hoover's Sex Crime Panic." *Quarterly Journal of Speech* 88, no. 2 (May 2002): 228–44.

Nearing, Scott. "Confession and Avoidance," review of *New Tactics in Social Conflicts,* by Harry W. Laidler and Norman Thomas. *New Masses,* February 1927, 26.

———. *Education in Soviet Russia.* New York: International Publishers, 1926.

———. "Slaves of the Machine," review of *Labor and Silk,* by Grace Hutchins, and *Labor and Automobiles,* by Robert W. Dunn. *New Masses,* June 1929, 18–9.

———. "What Can the Radical Do?" *Call Magazine,* February 4, 1923, 5.

New Masses. "Greetings on Our Twenty-Fifth Anniversary." December 1, 1936, 21.

———. "Kharkov Conference of Revolutionary Writers." February 1931, 6–7.

———. "NM Evaluates Its Course." June 26, 1945, 17.

———. "Resolution on the Work of *New Masses* for 1931." September 1932, 20–1.

———. "Revolutionary Research." March 17, 1936, 10.

———. "A Statement by American Progressives on the Moscow Trials." May 3, 1938, 19.

The New York Communist. "Violence or Solidarity?" June 14, 1919, 7.

New York Herald Tribune Books. "Industry and Women," review of *Women Who Work,* by Grace Hutchins. June 17, 1934, 7.

New York Times. "Alexander Trachtenberg Dies: Top Publisher of Marxist Books." December 17, 1966.

———. "Anna Rochester, an Economist, 86: Author of Books on History of American Business Dies." May 12, 1966.

———. "Arrests Check Picketing: New York Writers Are in Group of 39 Jailed at Boston." August 11, 1927, 1, 2.

———. "Boston Situation Is Tense: Agitation on Eve of Date of Execution Brings Many Arrests." August 10, 1927, 1, 3.

———. "Grace Hutchins, Labor Economist." July 16, 1969.

———. "M'Carthy Calls 23 for Book Inquiry." June 28, 1953.

———. "Maud Malone Stops Roosevelt." March 26, 1912.

———. "Militants Should Exercise instead of Throwing Bombs." August 13, 1924.

———. "Miss Malone Quits the Suffragettes." March 27, 1908.

———. "The Suffrage Quest a Wild Goose Chase." December 13, 1909.

———. "Women and Work." June 17, 1934.

New York Training School for Deaconesses. Papers. Archives of the Episcopal Diocese of New York, New York.

New York World-Telegram. "Funeral of Red Spy Run by Grace Hutchins." December 15, 1948, 11.

Nexo, Martin Andersen. *Ditte: Towards the Stars.* New York: Henry Holt and Company, 1922.

Nolte, Marilyn S., Victoria Sandwick Schmitt, and Christine L. Ridarsky. "'We Called Her Anna': Nathaniel Rochester and Slavery in the Genesee Country." *Rochester History* 71, no. 1 (2009): 1–26.

Noonkester, Barbara. "The American Sportswoman from 1900–1920." In *Her Story in Sport: A Historical Anthology of Women in Sports,* edited by Reet Howell, 107–40. West Point, NY: Leisure Press, 1982.

Northshield, Jane. *History of Croton-on-Hudson, New York.* Croton-on-Hudson, NY: The Croton-on-Hudson Historical Society and The Croton-on-Hudson Bicentennial Celebration Committee, 1976.

O'Connor, Jessie Lloyd. Papers. Sophia Smith Collection. Smith College, Northampton, MA.

———, Harvey O'Connor, and Susan M. Bowler. *Harvey and Jessie: A Couple of Radicals.* Philadelphia: Temple University Press, 1988.

Olgin, Moissaye J. "Comrade Lunacharsky: A Brief Appreciation." *New Masses,* January 9 1934, 24.

Oosterhuis, Harry. "The Dubious Magic of Male Beauty: Politics and Homoeroticism in the Works of Thomas and Klaus Mann." In *Queering the Canon: Defying Sights in German Literature and Culture,* edited by Christoph Lorey and John L. Plews, 181–206. Columbia, SC: Camden House, 1998.

Orens, John Richard. "Politics and the Kingdom: The Legacy of the Anglican Left." In *The Anglican Moral Choice,* edited by Paul Elmen, 63–84. Anglican Studies Series. Harrisburg, PA: Morehouse Publishing, 1983.

Pace, Erik. "Queen Mother Moore, 98, Harlem Rights Leader, Dies." *New York Times,* May 7, 1997, B15.

Packer, Herbert L. *Ex-communist Witnesses: Four Studies in Fact Finding.* Stanford, CA: Stanford University Press, 1962.

Parker, Michael. *The Kingdom of Character: The Student Volunteer Movement for Foreign Missions (1886–1926).* Lanham, MD: American Society of Missiology and University Press of America, 1998.

Party Organizer. "Control Tasks on Building the Party and the Circulation of Our Press." March–April 1937, 1–9.

Pen and Hammer Bulletin. January 26, 1933.

Perchik, Lev. "Bolshevik Agitation among the Masses." Abridged. *Party Organizer,* November–December 1932, 37–9.

Perlo, Victor. "LRA—That Stands for Facts that Aid Labor." *Daily Worker,* November 28, 1954.

Peterson, Judy. Review of *The Populist Movement in the United States,* by Anna Rochester. *Science and Society* 8 (Summer 1944), 267–71.

Phillips, Clifton J. "The Student Volunteer Movement and Its Role in China Missions, 1886–1920." In *The Missionary Enterprise in China and America,* edited by John K. Fairbank, 91–131. Cambridge, MA: Harvard University Press, 1974.

Porter, James E. "Intertextuality and the Discourse Community." *Rhetoric Review* 5, no. 1 (1986): 34–47.

Raitt, Suzanne. "Sex, Love, and the Homosexual Body." In *Sexology in Culture,* edited by Lucy Bland and Laura Doan, 150–164. Chicago: University of Chicago Press, 1998.

Rand School of Social Science. Records, microfilm edition. Tamiment Library. Elmer Holmes Bobst Library. New York University.

Rauschenbusch, Walter. *Christianity and the Social Crisis.* New York: Macmillan, 1907.

Reid, James D. *The Telegraph in America and Morse Memorial.* New York: Polhemus, 1882. http://archive.org/details/telegraphinameri00reid

Reuben, William A. Papers. Labadie Collection. University of Michigan, Ann Arbor.

Richardson, John V., Jr., "Harriet G. Eddy (1876–1966): California's First County Library Organizer and Her Influence on USSR Libraries." *California State Library Foundation Bulletin* 94 (2009), 2–13.

Roberts, Richard. *The Untried Door.* New York: The Woman's Press, 1921.

Rochester, Anna. *American Capitalism 1607-1800.* New York: International Publishers, 1949.

———. "The Banking Crisis in the U.S." *The Communist,* April 1933, 337–51.

———. "The Battle Lines of Child Labor Legislation." *Survey*, April 19, 1913, 86–8.

———. "Can Capitalism Take Criticism?" In *Publisher on Trial: The Case of Alexander Trachtenberg: A Symposium*, by the Committee to Defend Alexander Trachtenberg. New York: The Committee, 1952.

———. *Capitalism and Progress*. New York: International Publishers, 1945.

———. "Child Labor in Warring Countries: Address Delivered at Meeting of Massachusetts Child Labor Committee, Boston, January 21, 1918." *The Child Labor Bulletin*, February 1918, 230–40.

———. "The Coal Miners and Injunctions." *Labor Defender*, March 1929, 48.

———. "Cossacks to Kill." *Labor Defender*, July 1931, 128.

———. "Do Capitalists Fear Analysis of Their Origins?" *Daily Worker*, June 11, 1952, 7.

———. "The Eight-Hour Day for Children." *The Child Labor Bulletin*, February 1914, 40–53.

———. "The Farmer Wants a Plan." *New Masses*, January 12, 1943, 21–2.

———. *Farmers and the War*. New York: Workers Library, 1943.

———. *Farmers in Nazi Germany*. New York: Farm Research, Inc., 1942.

———. "A Favorable Interpretation of Communism." In *A New Economic Order*, edited by Kirby Page, 67–88. New York: Harcourt, Brace and Co., 1930.

———. "Filipino Cigarmakers Get Strike Compromise." *Federated Press Labor Letter*, February 9, 1927, 6.

———. "Finance Capital and Fascist Trends in the United States." *The Communist*, June 1936, 523–36.

———. "The Future in the Present." *The World Tomorrow*, July 1923, 203–5.

———. "Greetings on Our Twenty-Fifth Anniversary," *New Masses*, December 1, 1936, 21.

———. "Immigration and Internationalism. Part 1." *The World Tomorrow*, November 1921, 336–9.

———. "Immigration and Internationalism. Part 2." *The World Tomorrow*, December 1921, 375–8.

———. *Infant Mortality: Results of a Field Study in Baltimore, MD Based on Births in One Year*. Washington, DC: US Government Printing Office, 1923.

———. "In Quest of an Answer," review of *The Jew and American Ideals*, by John Spargo. *The World Tomorrow*, January 1923, 25–6.

———. "Interpreting the Labor Movement," review of *Labor's Challenge to the Social Order*, by John Graham Brooks. *The World Tomorrow*, February 1922, 57.

———. "Japanese Labor News." *Federated Press Labor Letter*, November 17, 1926, 6.

———. *Labor and Coal*. New York: International Publishers, 1931.

———. "Lenin in 1918," review of *Collected Works of V. I. Lenin*, vol. 23. *New Masses*, May 22, 1945, 24–5.

———. *Lenin on the Agrarian Question*. New York: International Publishers, 1942.

———. letter to the editor. *The Call*, December 9, 1910.

———. letter to the editor. *Daily Worker*, March 10, 1948.

———. letter to the editor. *Daily Worker*, June 27, 1945.

———. letter to the editor. *Life*, June 5, 1913.

———. letter to the editor. *The Nation*, July 21, 1926, 59.

———. letter to the editor. *Sunday Worker Magazine*, June 10, 1945.

———. "The Middle Class Today and Tomorrow: The Old World of Capitalism." *New Masses*, April 7, 1936, 31–2.

———. "Migratory Workers," review of *Ill Fares the Land*, by Carey McWilliams. *New Masses*, April 21, 1942, 25–6.

———. "Morgan: A World Money Power." *Daily Worker*, May 30, 1933, 4.

———. "The Morgan Empire." *Daily Worker*, May 27, 1933, 3.

———. "Morgan, Wage Cutter and Slave Driver: One Aspect the Senate Won't Investigate." *Daily Worker*, May 29, 1933, 4.

———. "'Mothers of the South' Is Portrait of Poverty," review of *Mothers of the South: Portraiture of the White Tenant Farm Woman*, by Margaret Jarman Hagood. *Sunday Worker*, August 18, 1940.

———. *The Nature of Capitalism*. New York: International Publishers, 1946. Revision of *Capitalism and Progress*, 1945.

———. "Need We Fear Class-Consciousness?" *The World Tomorrow*, January 1925, 5–6.

———. "New York, 1922." *The World Tomorrow*, February 1922, 36.

———. "Next Steps," review of *The Next Step*, by Scott Nearing. *The World Tomorrow*, February 1923, 58.

———. "Notes from the Philippines." *The World Tomorrow*, March 1927, 132–3.

———. "The Pacificist's 'Preparedness': How Can We Work for Non-violent Revolutionary Change?" *The World Tomorrow*, July 1924, 213–5.

———. Papers. Special Collections and University Archives, Ax 624. University of Oregon Libraries, Eugene.

———. "Pennsy Drops 61,500 Miners." *Federated Press Labor's News*, September 14, 1929, 5.

———. *The Populist Movement in the United States*. New York: International Publishers, 1943.

———. "Private Insurance Racket Preys on Workers." *Daily Worker*, November 8, 1934, 2.

———. *Profit and Wages*. New York: International Pamphlets, 1932.

———. "The Religious Experience of a Christian Radical." *Religious Education*, February 1925, 46–50.

———. Review of *The Challenge of Russia*, by Sherwood Eddy, *The Russian Experiment*, by Arthur Feiler, *The Economic Life of Soviet Russia*, by Calvin B. Hoover, *The Red Trade Menace*, by H.R. Knickerbocker, and *These Russians*, by William C. White. *New Masses*, April 1931, 18.

———. Review of *New Russia's Primer: The Story of the Five-Year Plan*, by M. Ilin. *New Masses*, June 1931, 16–7.

———. *Rulers of America*. New York: International Publishers, 1936.

———. "A Scientist Dissects War," review of *The Biology of War*, by G. F. Nicolai. *The World Tomorrow*, January 1922, 28–9.

———. "Shanghai Workers Swear by Unions." *Federated Press Labor Letter*, December 29, 1926, 7.

———. "Soil, Coal, and Oil," review of "My Country, 'Tis of Thee" by Lucy Sprague Mitchell, Eleanor Bowman, and Mary Phelps. *New Masses*, December 10, 1940, 25–6.

———. "Sowing the Wind." *The World Tomorrow*, November 1925, 330–2.

———. statement. In *We Hold These Truths. . . . Statements on Anti-Semitism by 54 Leading American Writers, Statesmen, Educators, Clergymen and Trade-Unionists*. League of American Writers. New York: League of American Writers, 1939.

———. "Teheran," review of *Teheran: Our Path in War and Peace*, by Earl Browder. *Soviet Russia Today*, September, 1944, 28–9.

———. "Those Liberals!" Review of *Strike Injunctions in the New South*, by Duane McCracken. *New Masses*, March 1932, 26.

———. "Wages and Prosperity." *Labor Age*, February 1928, 12–4.

———. *Wall Street*. New York: International Pamphlets, 1932.

———. "What Eleven Families Spend: The Cost of Comfort that Is Not Luxury." *The World Tomorrow*, June 1922, 169–72.

———. "What Property Does to the Individual." *The World Tomorrow*, April 1922, 105–6.

———. *Why Farmers Are Poor*. New York: International Publishers, 1940.

———. *Your Dollar under Roosevelt*. New York: Workers Library, 1933.

Rochester, Anna, Grace Hutchins, and Harvey O'Connor. "Rockefeller Dominates World's Largest Bank." *Federated Press Central Weekly Letter*, March 21, 1930, sheet 2.

Rochester, Anna, and Harvey O'Connor. "38 Giant Concerns Total over a Billion Dollars Dividends." *Federated Press Central Weekly Letter*, 1930, sheet 2.

Rochester, Nathaniel. *Early History of the Rochester Family in America*. Buffalo, NY: Matthews, Northrup & Co., 1882. http://international.loc.gov/master/gdc/scdser01/200401/books_on_film_project/BOF001/20060329012ea.pdf.

Rodney, Lester. "Freedom of Press Wins—We're Back." *The Worker*, Sunday, April 8, 1956.

Roots, Logan. "Report of the Bishop of the Missionary District of Hankow, 1911–1912." In *The Annual Report of the Board of Missions of the Protestant Episcopal Church in the United States of America, Board of Missions, Foreign Section*. Protestant Episcopal Church in the United States of America, 1911–1912.

Rosenberg, Rosalind. *Changing the Subject: How the Women of Columbia Shaped the Way We Think about Sex and Politics*. New York: Columbia University Press, 2004.

Russell, Francis, Papers. Robert D. Farber University Archives and Special Collections Department. Brandeis University, Waltham, MA.

Russell, Penny. "Life's Illusions: The 'Art' of Critical Biography." *Journal of Women's History* 21, no. 4 (2009): 152–6. *eLibrary*. Accessed October 17, 2011. http://elibrary.bigchalk.com.

Russo, Vito. *The Celluloid Closet: Homosexuality in the Movies*. Rev. ed. New York: Harper & Row, 1987.

Sabin, Arthur J. *Red Scare in Court: New York versus the International Workers Order*. Philadelphia: University of Pennsylvania Press, 1993.

Sahli, Nancy. "Smashing: Women's Relationships before the Fall." *Chrysalis* 8 (Summer 1979): 17–27.

Salant, Stephen W. "Successful Strategic Deception: A Case Study." MLibrary Digital Collections, University of Michigan, 2010. http://quod.lib.umich.edu/h/hiss/.

Saltmarsh, John A. *Scott Nearing: An Intellectual Biography*. Philadelphia: Temple University Press, 1991.

———. "The Terrible Freedom: An Intellectual Biography of Scott Nearing." PhD diss., Boston University, 1989.

Sargent, Dudley Allen. "The Physical Development of Women." *Scribner's*, February 1889, 172–84.

Saunders, Una. "The Missionary Possibilities of the Women Students of the World." In *Students and the Modern Missionary Crusade: Addresses Delivered before the Fifth International Convention of the Student Volunteer Movement for Foreign Missions, Nashville, Tennessee, February 28–March 4, 1906*, 75–8. New York: Student Volunteer Movement for Foreign Missions, 1906.

Sayre, John Nevin. *The Story of The Fellowship of Reconciliation, 1915–1935*. New York: The Fellowship of Reconciliation, 1935.

Schiappa, Edward, and Mary F. Keehner. "The 'Lost' Passages of *Permanence and Change*." *Communication Studies* 42, no. 3 (Fall 1991): 191–8.

Schmitt, Jacqueline. "'Sacrificial Adventure': Episcopal Women of the Progressive Era." In *Deeper Joy*, edited by Fredrica Harris Thompsett and Sheryl Kujawa-Holbrook, 180–92. New York: Church Publishing, 2005.

Schrecker, Ellen. *Many Are the Crimes: McCarthyism in America*. Boston: Little, Brown, 1998.

Schultz, T. W. Review of *Why Farmers Are Poor: The Agricultural Crisis in the United States*, by Anna Rochester. *The Journal of Political Economy* 49, no. 2 (1941): 293–94.

Schwarz, Judith. *The Radical Feminists of Heterodoxy: Greenwich Village, 1912–1940*. Rev. ed. Norwich, VT: New Victoria Publishers, 1986.

Scudder, Vida D. *Brother John*. New York: Little, Brown, 1927.

———. "The Christian Attitude toward Private Property." In *New Tracts for New Times*. Wilton, CT: Morehouse-Gorham, 1934. Reprinted in *The Privilege of Age*, 175. New York: E. P. Dutton, 1939.

———. *A Listener in Babel: Being a Series of Imaginary Conversations Held at the Close of the Last Century and Reported by Vida D. Scudder*. New York: Houghton, Mifflin and Company, 1903.

———. "A Little Tour in the Mind of Lenin." *Christian Century* 54 (March 24, 1937): 379–82. Reprinted in *The Privilege of Age*, 66. New York: E. P. Dutton, 1939.

———. *My Quest for Reality*. Wellesley, MA: Vida Dutton Scudder, 1952.

———. *On Journey*. New York: E. P. Dutton and Company, 1937.

———. Papers. Archives of the Society of the Companions of the Holy Cross. Adelynrood, South Byfield, MA.

———. Papers. Sophia Smith Collection. Smith College, Northampton, MA.

———. "Problems of Socialism: From a College Window." *New Leader* 3 (January 29, 1927). Reprinted in *The Privilege of Age*, 132. New York: E. P. Dutton, 1939.

———. *Socialism and Character*. New York: Houghton Mifflin Company, 1912.

———. "What Is Luxury?" *The World Tomorrow*, June 1922, 163–64.

Selzer, Jack. "Habeas Corpus: An Introduction." In *Rhetorical Bodies*, edited by Jack Selzer and Sharon Crowley, 3–15. Madison: University of Wisconsin Press, 1999.

Shaffer, Robert. "Women and the Communist Party, USA, 1930–1940." *Socialist Review* 45 (1975): 73–118.

Shaw, S. Adele. "Closed Towns." *The Survey*, November 8, 1919, 58–64, 87–9, 92–3.

Sheean, Vincent. *Personal History*. Garden City, NJ: Doubleday, Doran, 1938.

Simmons, Christina. "Companionate Marriage and the Lesbian Threat." *Frontiers*, Autumn 1979, 54.

Simpson, William. "What Can the Individual Do?" *The World Tomorrow*, April 1922, 106–8.

Small, Sasha. "A Complete Study of Working Women in the United States." *Daily Worker*, April 7, 1934.

Smith-Rosenberg, Carroll. *Disorderly Conduct: Visions of Gender in Victorian America*. New York: Knopf, 1985.

Society of the Companions of the Holy Cross. *A Church Year-Book of Social Justice: Advent 1919–Advent 1920*. New York: E. P. Dutton, 1919.

———. Papers. Archives of the Society of the Companions of the Holy Cross. Adelynrood, South Byfield, MA.

Spirit of Missions. "Light-Bearers in Dark Places." December 1912, 919.

Spofford, William. Papers. Archives of the Episcopal Church USA, AR1993.018. Episcopal Theological Seminary of the Southwest, Austin, TX.

Springer, Lisa, and Betty Millard. "Why Aren't You Angrier about Homophobia?" In *Letters of Intent*, edited by Meg Daly and Anna Bondoc, 130–7. New York: The Free Press, 1999.

Stachel, Jack. "The Coming Seventh Year of *Daily Worker*." *Daily Worker*, January 10, 1930, 4.

Stachura, Peter D. *The German Youth Movement 1900–1945: An Interpretative and Documentary History*. New York: St. Martin's Press, 1981.

Stake, Robert E. "The Case Study Method in Social Inquiry." *Educational Researcher*, February 1978, 5–8. http://education.illinois.edu/CIRCE/Publications/1978_Stake.pdf.

Starr, Ellen Gates. Papers. Sophia Smith Collection, Smith College, Northampton, MA.

Steinberg, Peter L. *The Great "Red Menace": United States Prosecution of American Communists, 1947–1952*. Westport, CT: Greenwood Press, 1984.

Steinfels, Peter. "On the Stump, in the Rights Arena, Echoes of a Religious Thinker's Vision Live on." *New York Times*, August 7, 2004, B5.

Streat, Sidney. "Grace Hutchins—Revolutionary." *Daily Worker*, September 16, 1936.

Student Volunteer Movement Archives. Special Collections, RG 42. Yale Divinity School Library, New Haven, CT.

Stump, Roger W. *Boundaries of Faith: Geographical Perspectives on Religious Fundamentalism*. Lanham, MD: Rowman & Littlefield Publishers, 2000.

Sturgis, Lucy C., and Grace Hutchins. *Pickaninnies' Progress*. Hartford, CT: Church Missions Publishing Company, 1910.

Sunday Worker. "World Communists Greet 'Worker' on 25th Anniversary." January 23, 1949, sec. 1, 4.

Sunday Worker Magazine. "The Present Situation and Next Tasks: Resolution of the National Board, CPA, adopted on June 2, 1945." June 10, 1945.

Tamagne, Florence. *A History of Homosexuality in Europe: Berlin, London, Paris, 1919–1939*. 2 vols. New York: Algora Publishing, 2004.

Tanenhaus, Sam. *Whittaker Chambers: A Biography*. New York: Random House, 1997.

Terry, Jennifer. *An American Obsession: Science, Medicine, and Homosexuality in Modern Society*. Chicago: University of Chicago Press, 1999.

Theoharis, Athan, and John Stuart Cox. *The Boss: J. Edgar Hoover and the Great American Inquisition*. Philadelphia: Temple University Press, 1988.

Timmons, Stuart. *The Trouble with Harry Hay*. Boston: Alyson, 1990.

Tipyn o'Bob. Bryn Mawr, PA: Bryn Mawr College, 1904–1905.

———. Bryn Mawr, PA: Bryn Mawr College, 1906–1906.

Trachtenberg, Alexander. "The Recruiting Drive and Literature Distribution." *Daily Worker*, January 1, 1930, 4.

———. Papers. State Historical Society of Wisconsin, Madison.

Trattner, Walter I. *Crusade for the Children: A History of the National Child Labor Committee and Child Labor Reform in America*. Chicago: Quadrangle Books, 1970.

Trimberger, Ellen Kay. "Women in the Old and New Left: The Evolution of a Politics of Personal Life." *Feminist Studies* 5, no. 3 (1979): 431–50.

US Communist Party Records. Tamiment Library. Elmer Holmes Bobst Library. New York University.

US Department of Labor. Children's Bureau. *Facilities for Children's Play in the District of Columbia.* Washington, DC: US Government Printing Office, 1917.

US House of Representatives Special Committee to Investigate Un-American Activities. *Investigation of Un-American Propaganda Activities in the United States.* Washington, DC: US Government Printing Office, 1939.

US Senate Committee on Government Operations. Hearings. *State Department Information Program— Information Centers, Part 7, Before the Permanent Subcomm. on Investigations.* 83rd Cong., 439, 1953.

US Senate Committee on the Judiciary. *Nomination of Louis D. Brandeis.* Washington, DC: US Government Printing Office, 1916.

Valentine, David T. *Manual of the Corporation of the City of New York.* New York: New York Common Council, 1863. http://books.google.com/books/about/Manual_of_the_corporation_of_the_city_of.html?id=vH04AAAAMAAJ.

Vance, Rupert B. Review of *Why Farmers Are Poor: The Agricultural Crisis in the United States,* by Anna Rochester. *The American Economic Review* 30, no. 4 (1940): 856–8.

van Kleeck, Mary. Papers. Sophia Smith Collection, Smith College, Northampton, MA.

Walker, Samuel. *In Defense of American Liberties: A History of the ACLU.* New York: Oxford University Press, 1990.

Wallace, Jo-Ann. "The Case of Edith Ellis." In *Modernist Sexualities,* edited by Hugh Stevens and Caroline Howlett, 13–40. Manchester: Manchester University Press, 2000.

———. "Edith Ellis, Sapphic Idealism, and *The Lover's Calendar* (1912)." In *Sapphic Modernities: Sexuality, Women and National Culture,* edited by Laura Doan and Jane Garrity, 183–99. New York: Palgrave Macmillan, 2006.

Ward, Harry F. "The Coal Situation." Review of *Labor and Coal,* by Anna Rochester. *The World Tomorrow,* May 1931, 6.

———. *The New Social Order.* New York: Macmillan, 1920.

Ware, Susan. *Partner and I: The Life of Molly Dewson, New Deal Politician.* New Haven, CT: Yale University Press, 1987.

Warner Michael. introduction to *Fear of a Queer Planet.* Minneapolis: University of Minnesota Press, 1993.

Weigand, Kate. *Red Feminism.* Baltimore, MD: Johns Hopkins, 2001.

Weinstein, Allen. *Perjury: The Hiss-Chambers Case.* New York: Random House, 1997.

Weintraub, Jeff. "The Theory and Politics of the Public/Private Distinction." In *Public and Private in Thought and Practice: Perspectives on a Grand Dichotomy,* edited by Jeff Weintraub and Krishan Kumar, 1–23. Chicago: University of Chicago Press, 1997. http://jeffweintraub.blogspot.com/1997/03/publicprivate-limitations-of-grand.html.

Weirauch, Anna Elisabet. *The Scorpion.* Translated by Whittaker Chambers. New York: Greenberg, 1932.

———. *The Outcast.* Translated by S. Guyendore. New York: Greenberg, 1933.

Weisbord, Vera Buch. *A Radical Life.* Bloomington: Indiana University Press, 1977.

Western Union Telegraph Company v. Pacific and Atlantic Telegraph Company et al., 65 N.Y.S. 2d 349, 189 Misc. 7 (September 9, 1946).

White, E. B. *Charlotte's Web.* New York: Harper, 1952.

Woltman, Frederick. "Pravda, USA." *Colliers,* October 21, 1950, 15–7, 80–4.

Wood, John W. "Dr. Wood Summarizes Situation in China." *Spirit of Missions,* January 1927, 69–70.

———. "Missionaries All Safe after the Siege of Wuchang." *Spirit of Missions,* November 1926, 669–70.

The Worker. "Anna Rochester Dies at 86." May 15, 1966.

———. "Hundreds at Trachtenberg Rites." January 1, 1967.

———. "Trachtenberg, Marxist Leader, Dies at 82." December 20, 1966.

World Committee for the Victims of German Fascism. *Brown Book of the Hitler Terror and the Burning of the Reichstag*. London: Victor Gollancz, 1933.

———. *The Reichstag Fire Trial: The Second Brown Book of the Hitler Terror*. New York: Howard Fertig, 1969. First published 1934 by John Lane The Bodley Head.

Worth, E. J. *Whittaker Chambers: The Secret Confession*. London: Mazzard, 1993.

Zetkin, Clara. *Reminiscences of Lenin*. London: Modern Books Limited, 1929.

Index